ALTERNATIVE INVESTMENTS

ALTERNATIVE INVESTMENTS

WILEY

Cover image: © bgblue/Getty Images
Cover design: Wiley

Published by John Wiley & Sons, Inc., Hoboken, New Jersey.
Published simultaneously in Canada.

For general information on our other products and services or for technical support, please contact our Customer
Care Department within the United States at (800) 762-2974, outside the United States at (317) 572-3993 or
fax (317) 572-4002.

Wiley publishes in a variety of print and electronic formats and by print-on-demand. Some material included with
standard print versions of this book may not be included in e-books or in print-on-demand. If this book refers to
media such as a CD or DVD that is not included in the version you purchased, you may download this material
at http://booksupport.wiley.com. For more information about Wiley products, visit www.wiley.com.

Library of Congress Cataloging-in-Publication Data

Names: Pinto, Jerald E., author. | Pirie, Wendy L., author.
Title: Derivatives / Jerald E. Pinto, CFA, Wendy L. Pirie, CFA.
Description: Hoboken, New Jersey : John Wiley & Sons, Inc., [2017] | Series:
   CFA Institute investment series | Includes index. |
Identifiers: ISBN 9781119850618 (pdf) | ISBN 9781119850625 (epub) | ISBN 9781119850601
   (cloth)
Subjects: LCSH: Derivative securities.
Classification: LCC HG6024.A3 (ebook) | LCC HG6024.A3 P535 2017 (print) | DDC
   332.64/57—dc23

Printed in the United States of America

SKY08A48180-628E-4AD3-8835-D74AACAF4A55_102921

CONTENTS

CHAPTER 3
Real Estate Investments   145

CHAPTER 4
Private Equity Investments   **239**

CHAPTER 5
Introduction to Commodities and Commodity Derivatives — 279

CHAPTER 6
Hedge Fund Strategies   331

CHAPTER 7

Capital Market Expectations: Forecasting Asset Class Returns 415

CHAPTER 8
Asset Allocation to Alternative Investments   **475**

CHAPTER 9
Integrated Cases in Risk Management: Institutional   563

FOREWORD

Since the breakthrough introduction of the Black–Scholes–Merton options pricing model in 1973, the field of financial derivatives has evolved into an extensive and highly scientific body of theoretical knowledge alongside a vast and vibrant market where economic producers, investors, finance professionals, and government regulators all interact to seek financial gains, manage risk, or promote price discovery. It is hard to imagine how even the most thoughtful and diligent practitioners can come to terms with such a broad and complex topic—until they read this book.

CFA Institute has compiled into a single book those parts of its curriculum that address this critically important topic. And it is apparent from reading this book that CFA Institute attracted preeminent scholars to develop its derivatives curriculum.

This book has several important virtues:

1. It is detailed, comprehensive, and exceptionally accessible.
2. It is efficiently organized in its coverage of topics.
3. It makes effective use of visualization with diagrams of transactions and strategy payoffs.
4. It includes numerous practice problems along with well-explained solutions.
5. And finally, unlike many academic textbooks, its focus is more practical than theoretical, although it does provide more-than-adequate treatment of the relevant theory.

The book begins by addressing the basics of derivatives, including definitions of the various types of derivatives and descriptions of the markets in which they trade.

It goes on to address the purpose of derivatives and the benefits they impart to society, including risk transfer, price discovery, and operational efficiency. It also discusses how derivatives can be misused to enable excessive speculation and how derivatives could contribute to the destabilization of financial markets.

The book provides comprehensive treatment of pricing and valuation with discussions of the law of one price, risk neutrality, the Black–Scholes–Merton options pricing model, and the binomial model. It also covers the pricing of futures and forward contracts as well as swaps.

The book then shifts to applications of derivatives. It discusses how derivatives can be used to create synthetic cash and equity positions along with several other positions. It relies heavily on numerical examples to illustrate these equivalencies.

It offers a comprehensive treatment of risk management with discussions of market risk, credit risk, liquidity risk, operational risk, and model risk, among others. It describes how to measure risk and, more importantly, how to manage it with the application of forward and futures contracts, swaps, and options.

This summary of topics is intended to provide a flavor of the book's contents. The contents of this book are far broader and deeper than I describe in this foreword.

Those who practice finance, as well as those who teach it, in my view, owe a huge debt of gratitude to CFA Institute—first, for assembling this extraordinary body of knowledge in its curriculum and, second, for organizing this knowledge with such cohesion and clarity. Anyone who wishes to acquire a solid knowledge of derivatives or to refresh and expand what they have learned about derivatives previously should certainly read this book.

Mark Kritzman

PREFACE

We are pleased to bring you *Alternatives, 1st Edition.* The content was developed in partnership by a team of distinguished academics and practitioners, chosen for their acknowledged expertise in the field, and guided by CFA Institute. It is written specifically with the investment practitioner in mind and is replete with examples and practice problems that reinforce the learning outcomes and demonstrate real-world applicability.

The CFA Program Curriculum, from which the content of this book was drawn, is subjected to a rigorous review process to assure that it is:

- Faithful to the findings of our ongoing industry practice analysis
- Valuable to members, employers, and investors
- Globally relevant
- Generalist (as opposed to specialist) in nature
- Replete with sufficient examples and practice opportunities
- Pedagogically sound

The accompanying workbook is a useful reference that provides Learning Outcome Statements, which describe exactly what readers will learn and be able to demonstrate after mastering the accompanying material. Additionally, the workbook has summary overviews and practice problems for each chapter.

We are confident that you will find this and other books in the CFA Institute Investment Series helpful in your efforts to grow your investment knowledge, whether you are a relatively new entrant or an experienced veteran striving to keep up to date in the ever-changing market environment. CFA Institute, as a long-term committed participant in the investment profession and a not-for-profit global membership association, is pleased to provide you with this opportunity.

THE CFA® PROGRAM

If the subject matter of this book interests you and you are not already a CFA charterholder, we hope you will consider registering for the CFA Program and starting progress toward earning the Chartered Financial Analyst designation. The CFA designation is a globally recognized standard of excellence for measuring the competence and integrity of investment professionals. To earn the CFA charter, candidates must successfully complete the CFA Program, a global graduate-level self-study program that combines a broad curriculum with professional conduct requirements as preparation for a career as an investment professional.

Anchored in a practice-based curriculum, the CFA Program Body of Knowledge reflects the knowledge, skills, and abilities identified by professionals as essential to the investment decision-making process. This body of knowledge maintains its relevance through a regular, extensive survey of practicing CFA charterholders across the globe. The curriculum covers 10 general topic areas, ranging from equity and fixed-income analysis to portfolio management to corporate finance—all with a heavy emphasis on the application of ethics in professional practice. Known for its rigor and breadth, the CFA Program curriculum highlights principles common to every market so that professionals who earn the CFA designation have a thoroughly global investment perspective and a profound understanding of the global marketplace.

CFA INSTITUTE

CFA Institute is the premier association for investment professionals around the world, with over 170,000 members more than 160 countries. Since 1963 the organization has developed and administered the renowned Chartered Financial AnalystÒ Program. With a rich history of leading the investment profession, CFA Institute has set the highest standards in ethics, education, and professional excellence within the global investment community, and is the foremost authority on investment profession conduct and practice.

Each book in the CFA Institute Investment Series is geared toward industry practitioners along with graduate-level finance students and covers the most important topics in the industry. The authors of these cutting-edge books are themselves industry professionals and academics and bring their wealth of knowledge and expertise to this series.

ACKNOWLEDGMENTS

Special thanks to all the reviewers, advisors, and question writers who helped to ensure high practical relevance, technical correctness, and understandability of the material presented here

We would like to thank the many others who played a role in the conception and production of this book: the Curriculum and Learning Experience team at CFA Institute with special thanks to the curriculum directors, past and present, who worked with the authors and reviewers to produce the chapters in this book, the Practice Analysis team at CFA Institute, and the Publishing and Technology team for bringing this book to production.

ABOUT THE CFA INSTITUTE INVESTMENT SERIES

CFA Institute is pleased to provide you with the CFA Institute Investment Series, which covers major areas in the field of investments. We provide this best-in-class series for the same reason we have been chartering investment professionals for more than 50 years: to lead the investment profession globally by setting the highest standards of ethics, education, and professional excellence.

The books in the CFA Institute Investment Series contain practical, globally relevant material. They are intended both for those contemplating entry into the extremely competitive field of investment management as well as for those seeking a means of keeping their knowledge fresh and up to date. This series was designed to be user friendly and highly relevant.

We hope you find this series helpful in your efforts to grow your investment knowledge, whether you are a relatively new entrant or an experienced veteran ethically bound to keep up to date in the ever-changing market environment. As a long-term, committed participant in the investment profession and a not-for-profit global membership association, CFA Institute is pleased to provide you with this opportunity.

THE TEXTS

Corporate Finance: A Practical Approach is a solid foundation for those looking to achieve lasting business growth. In today's competitive business environment, companies must find innovative ways to enable rapid and sustainable growth. This text equips readers with the foundational knowledge and tools for making smart business decisions and formulating strategies to maximize company value. It covers everything from managing relationships between stakeholders to evaluating merger and acquisition bids, as well as the companies behind them. Through extensive use of real-world examples, readers will gain critical perspective into interpreting corporate financial data, evaluating projects, and allocating funds in ways that increase corporate value. Readers will gain insights into the tools and strategies used in modern corporate financial management.

Fixed Income Analysis has been at the forefront of new concepts in recent years, and this particular text offers some of the most recent material for the seasoned professional who is not a fixed-income specialist. The application of option and derivative technology to the once staid province of fixed income has helped contribute to an explosion of thought in this area. Professionals have been challenged to stay up to speed with credit derivatives, swaptions, collateralized mortgage securities, mortgage-backed securities, and other vehicles, and this explosion of products has strained the world's financial markets and tested central banks to provide sufficient oversight. Armed with a thorough grasp of the new exposures, the professional investor is much better able to anticipate and understand the challenges our central bankers and markets face.

International Financial Statement Analysis is designed to address the ever-increasing need for investment professionals and students to think about financial statement analysis from a global perspective. The text is a practically oriented introduction to financial statement analysis that is distinguished by its combination of a true international orientation, a structured presentation style, and abundant illustrations and tools covering concepts as they are introduced in the text. The authors cover this discipline comprehensively and with an eye to ensuring the reader's success at all levels in the complex world of financial statement analysis.

Investments: Principles of Portfolio and Equity Analysis provides an accessible yet rigorous introduction to portfolio and equity analysis. Portfolio planning and portfolio management are presented within a context of up-to-date, global coverage of security markets, trading, and market-related concepts and products. The essentials of equity analysis and valuation are explained in detail and profusely illustrated. The book includes coverage of practitioner-important but often neglected topics, such as industry analysis. Throughout, the focus is on the practical application of key concepts with examples drawn from both emerging and developed markets. Each chapter affords the reader many opportunities to self-check his or her understanding of topics.

One of the most prominent texts over the years in the investment management industry has been Maginn and Tuttle's *Managing Investment Portfolios: A Dynamic Process.* The third edition updates key concepts from the 1990 second edition. Some of the more experienced members of our community own the prior two editions and will add the third edition to their libraries. Not only does this seminal work take the concepts from the other readings and put them in a portfolio context, but it also updates the concepts of alternative investments, performance presentation standards, portfolio execution, and, very importantly, individual investor portfolio management. Focusing attention away from institutional portfolios and toward the individual investor makes this edition an important and timely work.

Quantitative Investment Analysis focuses on some key tools that are needed by today's professional investor. In addition to classic time value of money, discounted cash flow applications, and probability material, there are two aspects that can be of value over traditional thinking. The first involves the chapters dealing with correlation and regression that ultimately figure into the formation of hypotheses for purposes of testing. This gets to a critical skill that challenges many professionals: the ability to distinguish useful information from the overwhelming quantity of available data. Second, the final chapter of *Quantitative Investment Analysis* covers portfolio concepts and takes the reader beyond the traditional capital asset pricing model (CAPM) type of tools and into the more practical world of multifactor models and arbitrage pricing theory.

The New Wealth Management: The Financial Advisor's Guide to Managing and Investing Client Assets is an updated version of Harold Evensky's mainstay reference guide for wealth managers. Harold Evensky, Stephen Horan, and Thomas Robinson have updated the core text of the 1997 first edition and added an abundance of new material to fully reflect today's investment challenges. The text provides authoritative coverage across the full spectrum of wealth management and serves as a comprehensive guide for financial advisors. The book expertly blends investment theory and real-world applications and is written in the same thorough but highly accessible style as the first edition. The first involves the chapters dealing with correlation and regression that ultimately figure into the formation of hypotheses for purposes of testing. This gets to a critical skill that challenges many professionals: the ability to distinguish useful information from the overwhelming quantity of available data. Second, the final chapter of Quantitative Investment Analysis covers portfolio concepts and takes the reader beyond the traditional capital asset pricing model (CAPM) type of tools and into the more practical world of multifactor models and arbitrage pricing theory.

All books in the CFA Institute Investment Series are available through all major book-sellers. And, all titles are available on the Wiley Custom Select platform at http://customselect .wiley.com/ where individual chapters for all the books may be mixed and matched to create custom textbooks for the classroom.

ALTERNATIVES

CHAPTER 1

INTRODUCTION TO CORPORATE GOVERNANCE AND OTHER ESG CONSIDERATIONS

Assem Safieddine, PhD, Young Lee, CFA, Donna F. Anderson, CFA, Deborah S. Kidd, CFA, and Hardik Sanjay Shah, CFA

LEARNING OUTCOMES

The candidate should be able to:

- describe corporate governance;
- describe a company's stakeholder groups, and compare interests of stakeholder groups;
- describe principal–agent and other relationships in corporate governance and the conflicts that may arise in these relationships;
- describe stakeholder management;
- describe mechanisms to manage stakeholder relationships and mitigate associated risks;
- describe functions and responsibilities of a company's board of directors and its committees;
- describe market and non-market factors that can affect stakeholder relationships and corporate governance;
- identify potential risks of poor corporate governance and stakeholder management, and identify benefits from effective corporate governance and stakeholder management;
- describe factors relevant to the analysis of corporate governance and stakeholder management;
- describe environmental and social considerations in investment analysis;
- describe how environmental, social, and governance factors may be used in investment analysis.

1. INTRODUCTION AND OVERVIEW OF CORPORATE GOVERNANCE

Weak corporate governance is a common thread found in many company failures. Lack of proper oversight by the board of directors, inadequate protection for minority shareholders, and incentives at companies that promote excessive risk taking are just a few of the examples that can be problematic for a company. Poor corporate governance practices resulted in several high-profile accounting scandals and corporate bankruptcies over the past several decades and have been cited as significantly contributing to the 2008–2009 global financial crisis.

In response to these failures, regulations have been introduced to promote stronger governance practices to protect financial markets and investors. Academics, policy makers, and other groups have published numerous works discussing the benefits of good corporate governance and identifying core corporate governance principles believed to be essential to ensuring continuous, well-functioning capital markets and the stability of the financial system.

The investment community has also demonstrated a greater appreciation for the importance of good corporate governance. The assessment of a company's corporate governance structure and controls, including consideration of conflicts of interest and transparency of operations, has been an essential factor in investment analysis. More data availability and demands for better governance have increased the weight of corporate governance in the investment decision-making process. In addition, investors have become more attentive to environmental and social issues related to a company's operations. Collectively, these concepts often are referred to as environmental, social, and governance (**ESG**).

Section 1 of this chapter provides an overview of corporate governance, including its underlying principles and theories. Section 2 discusses the various stakeholders of a company and conflicts of interest that exist among stakeholder groups. Section 3 describes the principal–agent and other relationships in corporate governance and the conflicts that may arise in these relationships. Section 4 describes stakeholder management, reflecting how companies manage their relationships with stakeholders. Section 5 focuses on mechanisms to manage stakeholder relationships and mitigate associated risks. Section 6 focuses on the role of the board of directors and its committees as overseers of the company. Section 7 explores certain key factors that affect stakeholder relationships and corporate governance. Section 8 highlights the risks and benefits that underlie a corporate governance structure. Section 9 synthesizes corporate governance concepts that should be considered by investment professionals. Finally, Section 10 discusses the growing use of environmental, social, and governance factors in investment analysis and portfolio construction processes.

1.1. Corporate Governance Overview

Corporate governance can be defined as "the system of internal controls and procedures by which individual companies are managed. It provides a framework that defines the rights, roles, and responsibilities of various groups within an organization. At its core, corporate governance is the arrangement of checks, balances, and incentives a company needs in order to minimize and manage the conflicting interests between insiders and external shareowners."[1]

---

[1] CFA Institute Centre for Financial Market Integrity, *The Corporate Governance of Listed Companies: A Manual for Investors*, 2nd ed. (Charlottesville, VA: CFA Institute, 2009).

Corporate governance practices differ among countries and jurisdictions, and even within countries different corporate governance systems may co-exist. The corporate governance systems adopted in most of the world typically reflect the influences of either *shareholder theory* or *stakeholder theory* to a varying extent, as well as historical, cultural, legal, political, and other influences specific to a region.

Shareholder theory takes the view that the most important responsibility of a company's managers is to maximize shareholder returns. Stakeholder theory broadens a company's focus beyond the interests of only its shareholders to its customers, suppliers, employees, and others who have an interest in the company. The approach to corporate governance in a given country typically places greater emphasis on one of the two theories but can also exhibit a combination of the two. Notwithstanding the system of corporate governance used, nearly all companies depend on contributions from a number of stakeholders for their long-term success. The company's strategy is set by the board of directors, which also oversees management. In turn, the company's strategy is executed by its managers; financial capital to fund the company's activities and operations is supplied by shareholders, creditors, and suppliers; human capital is provided by employees; and demand for goods and services comes from customers. Other stakeholders include governments and regulators, which seek to protect the interests and well-being of their citizens. Certain external forces, such as the legal environment and competition, affect the way a company operates and the relationships among its stakeholders.

Two reports issued during the 1990s, the Cadbury Report and the Principles of Corporate Governance, were particularly influential in shaping the global corporate governance landscape. In 1991, the Committee on the Financial Aspects of Corporate Governance was established in the United Kingdom by the Financial Reporting Council, the London Stock Exchange, and the accountancy profession to examine corporate governance. In the following year, the report of the committee—commonly referred to as the Cadbury Report, after its chairperson— defined corporate governance simply as "the system by which companies are directed and controlled." The report focused on the responsibilities of a company's board of directors, shareholders, and auditors, with shareholders implicitly identified as the primary stakeholders. In 1999, the Organisation for Economic Co-Operation and Development (OECD) produced the *Principles of Corporate Governance*, which expanded the scope of corporate governance to consider the interests of other stakeholders—notably, employees, creditors, and suppliers. According to the OECD, "Corporate governance includes a set of relationships between a company's management, its board, its shareholders, and other stakeholders." The *Principles of Corporate Governance*, which has been revised numerous times since its initial publication, also discusses potential positive outcomes of good corporate governance practices (including financial market stability and economic growth) and includes standards and guidelines designed to evaluate and improve the corporate governance framework throughout the world.

There is evidence that some movement toward global convergence of corporate governance systems is underway. One trend is the increased acceptance and adoption of corporate governance regulations with similar principles from one jurisdiction to another. For example, several countries implemented regulations similar to those of the US Sarbanes–Oxley Act of 2002 (SOX) in response to corporate and accounting scandals of the early 2000s. Although these regulations are not identical, they share the same objective of improving internal controls and restoring investor confidence in financial disclosures. Another trend is initiatives by international agencies to build greater consensus on important corporate governance principles. The *Principles of Corporate Governance*, for example, has been ratified by more than 30 member countries, representing a broad range of corporate governance models. The *Principles of Corporate Governance* do not mandate, or even promote, the adoption of a single corporate governance regime; rather, the principles were designed to serve as a framework that can be adopted by any number of corporate governance systems.

EXAMPLE 1   Corporate Governance Overview

Which statement regarding corporate governance is *most* accurate?

A. Most countries have similar corporate governance regulations.
B. A single definition of corporate governance is widely accepted in practice.
C. Both shareholder theory and stakeholder theory consider the needs of a company's shareholders.

Solution: C is correct. Both shareholder and stakeholder theories consider the needs of shareholders, with the latter extending to a broader group of stakeholders. A is incorrect because corporate governance regulations differ across countries, although there is a trend toward convergence. B is incorrect because a universally accepted definition of corporate governance remains elusive.

---

2. STAKEHOLDER GROUPS

A corporate governance system is likely to be influenced by several stakeholder groups. These groups do not necessarily share similar goals or needs; in fact, the interests of any one group may conflict with the interests of another group. The varying influences of these groups are important considerations for investment professionals when analyzing a corporate governance system. This section provides an overview of a corporation's primary stakeholder groups, followed by a discussion of principal–agent considerations and the conflicts that may arise among the groups.

2.1. Stakeholder Groups

The primary stakeholder groups of a corporation consist of shareholders, creditors, managers (or executives), other employees, the board of directors, customers, suppliers, affected individuals and community groups, and governments/regulators. The interests of each of these groups are discussed in the following sections.

2.1.1. Shareholders

Shareholders own shares of stock in a corporation and are entitled to certain rights, such as the right to receive dividends and to vote on certain corporate issues.[2] In terms of capital structure, shareholders are the most junior class of capital providers; in case of a company bankruptcy,

---

[2]The Modern Corporation, "Statement on Company Law." https://themoderncorporation.wordpress.com/company-law-memo/.

shareholders receive proceeds only after all creditors' claims are paid. Shareholder interests are, therefore, typically focused on growth in corporate profitability that maximizes the value of a company's equity.

As a company grows in size and its operations and structure become more complex, most individual shareholders have limited or no involvement in the company's activities. Shareholders maintain control over the company through their power to elect the board of directors and vote for specified resolutions. The board of directors is expected to represent shareholders—protecting their interests, appointing senior management, providing strategic direction, and monitoring company and management performance. In publicly traded companies that have dispersed ownership, the voting power in general meetings is distributed among a large number of shareholders. But in some companies, a particular shareholder or block of shareholders may hold a percentage of shares that gives them sufficient voting power to control the election of the board of directors and to influence the approval or blockage of a company resolution; these shareholders are known as **controlling shareholders**. In contrast, non-controlling shareholders (**minority shareholders**) hold a much smaller proportion of a company's outstanding shares, resulting in a more limited ability to exercise control in voting activities.

2.1.2. Creditors
Creditors, most commonly bondholders and banks, are a company's lenders and the providers of debt financing. Creditors do not hold voting power (unlike common shareholders) and typically have limited influence over a company's operations. Creditors may protect themselves and exert some control over a company by using covenants, which restrict activities of the borrower. In return for capital provided, creditors expect to receive interest and principal payments. These payments are pre-determined from the terms of a debt contract and are typically not contingent on the company's performance. Creditors usually do not participate in a company's superior performance beyond receiving promised interest and principal payments. The company's ability to generate cash flows, mainly through its operations, is the primary source of payments for creditors. Consequently, creditors generally prefer stability in company operations and performance, which contrasts with the interests of shareholders, who generally are inclined to tolerate higher risks in return for higher return potential from strong company performance.

2.1.3. Managers and Employees
Senior executives and other high-level managers are normally compensated through salary, bonuses, equity-based remuneration (or compensation),[3] and certain perquisites. As a result, managers may be motivated to maximize the value of their total remuneration while also protecting their employment positions. Lower-level employees typically seek fair remuneration, good working conditions, access to promotions, career development opportunities, training and development, job security, and a safe and healthy work environment. Overall, remuneration packages that are designed to prevent employees from chasing short-term profits are likely to be most effective and aligned with long-term shareholder interests.

As with shareholders and creditors, managers and employees have a significant interest in the company's viability. Managers and employees tend to benefit if the company performs well

---

[3]The terms "remuneration" and "compensation" are typically interchangeable, with compensation generally used in North America and remuneration generally used outside North America. In this chapter, unless specifically identified with North America, we primarily use "remuneration."

and are among the most adversely affected stakeholders if a company's financial position weakens. Despite some similarities, the interests of managers and employees and other stakeholders can conflict. For example, a company may be presented with a takeover offer that is attractive to shareholders but would jeopardize the interests of managers in preserving their employment at the company.

2.1.4. Board of Directors

A company's board of directors is elected by shareholders to protect shareholders' interests, provide strategic direction, and monitor company and management performance. A board is typically structured as either *one-tier* or *two-tier*.

A one-tier structure consists of a single board of directors, composed of executive and non-executive directors. Executive (sometimes called "internal") directors are employees, typically senior managers, of the company. Non-executive (sometimes called "external") directors are not employees of the company. Countries in which one-tier boards are common include the United States, the United Kingdom, and India. A two-tier structure consists of two separate boards: (1) a *supervisory board*, which is primarily composed of non-executive directors, and (2) a *management (executive) board*, which is composed of executive directors. The supervisory board oversees the management board. Two-tier boards are common in such countries as Germany, the Netherlands, Finland, and China.

In this chapter, unless specified otherwise, the term "board" refers to the single board of directors in a one-tier structure and the supervisory board in a two-tier structure. Directors, both internal and external, are typically experienced individuals who are focused on fulfilling their responsibilities toward shareholders and the company while maintaining a good reputation in the business community. Directors are also typically concerned with their exposure to liability for breach of duty. Directors can mitigate this exposure, *inter alia*, by exercising appropriate levels of control over the company's operations and its management or by obtaining independent access to company documentation. A company's board of directors is discussed in more detail in Section 6 of this chapter.

2.1.5. Customers

Customers expect a company's products or services to satisfy their needs and provide appropriate benefits given the price paid, as well as to meet applicable standards of safety. Depending on the type of product or service and the duration of their relationship with the company, customers may desire ongoing support, product guarantees, and after-sale service. Companies are concerned with customer satisfaction given its potential correlation with sales revenue and profit. They are also increasingly concerned about brand boycotts due to adverse environmental and social impacts and controversies caused by their products and services. Compared with other stakeholder groups, customers tend to be less concerned with, and affected by, a company's financial performance. However, customers, particularly those who are dependent on the goods or services provided by the company, typically have an interest in a company's stability.

2.1.6. Suppliers

A company's suppliers have a primary interest in being paid as contracted or agreed on, and in a timely manner, for products or services delivered to the company. Suppliers often seek to build long-term relationships with companies for the benefit of both parties and aim for these relationships to be fair and transparent. Suppliers, like creditors, are concerned with a company's ability to generate sufficient cash flows to meet its financial obligations.

2.1.7. Governments/Regulators

Governments and regulators seek to protect the interests of the general public and ensure the well-being of their nations' economies. Because corporations have a significant effect on a nation's economic output, capital flows, employment, and social welfare, among other factors, regulators have an interest in ensuring that corporations behave in a manner that is consistent with applicable laws. Moreover, as the collector of tax revenues from companies and their employees, a government can also be considered one of the company's major stakeholders.

Stakeholders in Non-profit Organizations

The stakeholders of a non-profit organization tend to differ from those of for-profit companies. Non-profit organizations do not have shareholders. Their stakeholders most commonly include board directors or trustees, employees, regulators, society, patrons of the organization, donors, and volunteers. The stakeholders of non-profit organizations are generally focused on ensuring that the organization is serving the intended cause and that donated funds are used as promised.

EXAMPLE 2   Stakeholder Groups

Which stakeholders would *most likely* realize the greatest benefit from a significant increase in the market value of the company?

A. Creditors
B. Customers
C. Shareholders

Solution: C is correct. Shareholders own shares of stock in the company, and their wealth is directly related to the market value of the company. A is incorrect because creditors are usually not entitled to any additional cash flows (beyond interest and debt repayment) if the company's value increases. B is incorrect because customers may have an interest in the company's stability and long-term viability, but they do not benefit directly from an increase in a company's value.

---

3. PRINCIPAL–AGENT AND OTHER RELATIONSHIPS IN CORPORATE GOVERNANCE

A **principal–agent relationship** (also known as an agency relationship) is created when a principal hires an agent to perform a particular task or service. The principal–agent relationship involves obligations, trust, and expectations of loyalty; the agent is expected to act in the best interests of the principal. In a company, agency theory stipulates that principal–agent relationships often lead to conflicts—for example, when managers do not act in the best interests of shareholders.[4] Examples of principal–agent relationships and potential conflicts between the principal and agent are discussed in the following sections. Other conflicts among stakeholder groups not involving principal–agent relationships are also discussed.

3.1. Shareholder and Manager/Director Relationships

In shareholder-owned companies, shareholders typically grant directors and managers the responsibility to make most corporate decisions. According to traditional shareholder theory (discussed earlier), the central duty of directors and managers is to act in the best interests of shareholders. In certain circumstances, however, managers may seek to maximize their personal benefits (e.g., remuneration and perquisites) to the detriment of shareholders' interests.

Shareholder interests can also diverge from those of managers and directors with respect to risk tolerance. In some cases, shareholders with diversified investment portfolios may have a relatively high risk tolerance because the risk undertaken by a specific company can be diversified across the shareholders' investments. Managers and directors, however, are typically more risk averse in their corporate decision making so they can better protect their employment status. Such behavior may differ from the company's value creation objective. In addition, compared with shareholders, managers typically have greater access to information about the business and are more knowledgeable about its operations. Such information asymmetry (that is, unequal access to information) makes it easier for managers to make strategic decisions that are not necessarily in the best interest of shareholders and weakens the ability of shareholders to exercise control. Another conflict of interest might arise between shareholders and directors when the board is influenced by insiders. In this case, the ability of the board to properly perform its monitoring and control role may be hindered. Finally, a conflict between the two groups may occur if directors favor certain influential shareholders over other shareholders.

3.2. Controlling and Minority Shareholder Relationships

In companies in which a particular shareholder holds a controlling stake, conflicts of interest may arise among the controlling and minority shareholders. In such ownership structures, the opinions of minority shareholders are often outweighed or overshadowed by the influence of the controlling shareholders. Minority shareholders often have limited or no control over management and limited or no voice in director appointments or in major transactions that could have a direct effect on the value of their shares. For instance, in companies that adopt **straight voting** (that is, one vote for each share owned), controlling shareholders clearly wield the most influence in board of director elections, leaving minority shareholders with much less representation on the board.

The decisions made by controlling shareholders, or their board representatives, could also have an effect on corporate performance and, consequently, on minority shareholders' wealth. Takeover transactions are notable situations in which controlling shareholders

---

[4] Agency theory considers the problems that can arise in a business relationship when one person delegates decision-making authority to another. The traditional view in the investment community is that directors and managers are agents of shareholders. More recently, however, many legal experts have argued that in several countries, corporations are separate "legal persons"; thus, directors and managers are agents of the corporations rather than shareholders (or a subset of shareholders). See https://themoderncorporation .wordpress.com/company-law-memo.

typically have greater influence than do minority shareholders with regard to the consideration received and other deal terms. A historical example of note occurred in 2007 when Qtel, Qatar's largest telecommunications company, executed a deal with a consortium of the shareholders of Wataniya, Kuwait's telecommunications company, to acquire the consortium's shares in Wataniya (representing a 51% stake in the target). The consortium of Wataniya's shareholders sold their shares to Qtel at a premium of 48% on the stock price to the exclusion of minority shareholders.

Related-party transactions are another example for which controlling shareholders may place their interests ahead of minority shareholders' interests. Such a situation could occur when a controlling shareholder maintains a financial interest in a transaction between the company and a third party and that transaction conflicts with the company's best interests. Consider, for example, a controlling shareholder that arranges a deal between the company and a third-party supplier that is owned by the shareholder's spouse whereby the supplier provides the company with inventory at above-market prices. Such a transaction would benefit the controlling shareholder and the spouse's interests but could harm the profitability of the company and the interests of minority shareholders.

Lastly, an equity structure with multiple share classes in which one class is non-voting or has limited voting rights creates a divergence between the ownership and control rights of different classes of shareholders. Under a multiple-class structure (traditionally called a *dual-class structure* when there are two share classes), the company's founders, executives, and other key insiders control the company by virtue of ownership of a share class with superior voting powers. The multiple-class structure enables controlling shareholders to mitigate dilution of their voting power when new shares are issued. Examples of companies that have adopted multiple-class stock structures are Alibaba and Facebook (each with two share classes).

3.3. Manager and Board Relationships

Given that a board of directors typically relies on management to operate the company, the board's monitoring role can be compromised in the event of limited information provided to the board. This conflict is particularly pronounced for non-executive directors who are typically not involved in the day-to-day operations of a company.

3.4. Shareholder versus Creditor Interests

Shareholders typically seek growth in corporate profitability because of the residual nature of equity returns. However, the pre-determined returns of debt obligations normally prevent creditors from receiving any cash flows beyond principal and interest payments but do expose creditors to default risk in case of extremely poor corporate performance. From an investment perspective, shareholders would likely prefer riskier projects with a strong likelihood of higher return potential, whereas creditors would likely prefer stable performance and lower-risk activities. A divergence in risk tolerance regarding the company's investments thus exists between shareholders and creditors.

Creditors may also find their interests jeopardized when the company attempts to increase its borrowings to a level that would increase default risk. If the company's operations and investments fail to generate sufficient returns required to repay the increased interest and debt obligations, creditors will be increasingly exposed to default risk. The distribution of excessive dividends to shareholders might also conflict with creditors' interests if it impairs the company's ability to pay interest and principal.

3.5. Other Stakeholder Conflicts

In a corporation, interests can also conflict among other stakeholders. Some of these situations are as follows:

- *Conflict between customers and shareholders*: For example, a company decides to charge a high price for its products or reduces product safety features to reduce costs.
- *Conflict between customers and suppliers*: A company offers overly lenient credit terms to its customers, whereby the company's ability to repay suppliers on time may be affected.
- *Conflict between shareholders and governments or regulators*: Examples of such conflicts may include a company adopting accounting and reporting practices that reduce its tax burden, thus potentially benefiting shareholders, or a bank's shareholders preferring a lower equity capital base while regulators prefer a higher capital position. This last conflict is fairly common in the banking industry and has been increasingly in focus since the global financial crisis of 2008–2009.

EXAMPLE 3   Stakeholder Relationships

A controlling shareholder of XYZ Company owns 55% of XYZ's shares, and the remaining shares are spread among a large group of shareholders. In this situation, conflicts of interest are *most likely* to arise between:

A. shareholders and regulators.
B. the controlling shareholder and managers.
C. the controlling shareholder and minority shareholders.

Solution: C is correct. In this ownership structure, the controlling shareholder's power is likely more influential than that of minority shareholders. Thus, the controlling shareholder may be able to exploit its position to the detriment of the interests of the remaining shareholders. Choices A and B are incorrect because the ownership structure in and of itself is unlikely to create material conflicts between shareholders and regulators or shareholders and managers.

---

4. OVERVIEW AND MECHANISMS OF STAKEHOLDER MANAGEMENT

Because interests among stakeholder groups differ, companies often adopt mechanisms to more efficiently manage stakeholder relationships. **Stakeholder management** involves identifying, prioritizing, and understanding the interests of stakeholder groups, and, on that basis, managing the company's relationships with these groups.

4.1. Overview of Stakeholder Management

Effective communication and active engagement with the various stakeholders form the basis of stakeholder management. Although the practices underlying stakeholder management may vary, companies typically seek to balance the interests of their various stakeholders and thus limit the effect of conflicts.

To help balance these interests, corporate governance and stakeholder management frameworks reflect a legal, contractual, organizational, and governmental infrastructure that defines the rights, responsibilities, and powers of each group. The *legal infrastructure* defines the framework for rights established by law and the availability or ease of legal recourse for any violation of these rights. The *contractual infrastructure* is shaped by the contractual arrangements entered into by the company and its stakeholders that help define and secure the rights of both parties. The *organizational infrastructure* refers to internal systems, governance procedures, and practices adopted and controlled by the company in managing its stakeholder relationships. Lastly, the *governmental infrastructure* refers to regulations imposed on companies.

The corporate governance systems in such countries as France, Germany, and Japan focus on a broader range of stakeholders relative to the more shareholder-driven Anglo-American systems. Globally, there is a growing movement among regulators and practitioners to more effectively balance the interests of all stakeholders. For instance, the Companies Act 2006 in the United Kingdom introduced "enlightened shareholder value," which requires directors to consider the interests of all stakeholders—not just shareholders. Several regulators, such as those in the United Kingdom and Japan, have adopted stewardship codes that encourage more active engagement of institutional investors with companies.

EXAMPLE 4   Stakeholder Management

The component of stakeholder management in which a corporation has the *most* control is:

A. legal infrastructure.
B. contractual infrastructure.
C. governmental infrastructure.

Solution: B is correct. A corporation's contractual infrastructure refers to the contractual arrangements between the corporation and stakeholders. As such, the corporation has control over these arrangements. A is incorrect because the legal infrastructure is established by law, which is outside the corporation's own control. Similarly, C is incorrect because a corporation's governmental structure is largely imposed by regulators.

4.2. Mechanisms of Stakeholder Management

Stakeholder management and governance practices attempt to manage the interests of all stakeholders. As mentioned earlier, a prescribed or standard set of rights and practices does not exist across all companies, and the principles vary across countries and jurisdictions. Still, there are some common control elements and governance mechanisms among companies.

4.2.1. General Meetings

Corporate laws grant shareholders certain powers and controls. The participation of shareholders in general meetings, also known as general assemblies, and the exercise of their voting rights are among the most influential tools available. General meetings enable shareholders to participate in discussions and to vote on major corporate matters and transactions that are not delegated to the board of directors.

Companies are ordinarily required to hold an annual general meeting (AGM) within a certain period following the end of their fiscal year. The main purpose of those meetings is to present shareholders with the annual audited financial statements of the company, provide an overview of the company's performance and activities, and address shareholder questions. Shareholders also elect the directors at the AGM and, in some countries, may be required to approve the financial statements, discharge directors of their duties, appoint external auditors, or vote on the remuneration of the board and/or top management. Extraordinary general meetings can be called by the company or by shareholders throughout the year when significant resolutions requiring shareholder approval are proposed. These resolutions might relate to proposed material corporate changes, such as amendments to the company's bylaws or rights attached to a class of shares, mergers and acquisitions, or the sale of significant corporate assets or businesses.

All shareholders typically have the right to attend, speak at, and vote at general meetings. Regulations, particularly corporate laws, specify conditions for inviting shareholders to general meetings and circulating information to shareholders. These conditions vary across regulations but generally aim at ensuring the participation of a large number of shareholders in general meetings without imposing excessive restrictions on the ability of the company to hold a meeting. By engaging in general meetings, shareholders can exercise their voting rights on major corporate issues and better monitor the performance of the board and senior management. General meetings and the underlying voting procedures are among the most widely adopted practices by companies in mitigating agency problems and their associated risks.

Some resolutions, such as the approval of financial statements and the election of directors and auditors, are considered ordinary at general meetings because they require only a simple majority of votes to be passed. Decisions that are more material in nature may require a supermajority vote, such as two-thirds or 75% of votes, to be passed. Such special resolutions may include amendments to bylaws, voting on a merger or takeover transaction, or waiving preemptive rights. Depending on the ownership structure, supermajority requirements may make it harder for majority shareholders to influence corporate decisions at the expense of minority shareholders.

Proxy voting is a process that enables shareholders who are unable to attend a meeting to authorize another individual (for example, another shareholder or director) to vote on their behalf. Proxy voting is the most common form of investor participation in general meetings. Although most resolutions at most companies pass without controversy, sometimes minority shareholders attempt to strengthen their influence at companies via proxy voting. Several shareholders sometimes use this process to collectively vote their shares in favor of or in opposition to a certain resolution. **Cumulative voting** (as opposed to straight voting) enables shareholders to accumulate and vote all their shares for a single candidate in an election involving more than one director. This voting process raises the likelihood that minority shareholders are represented by at least one director on the board, but it may not be compatible with majority voting standards for director elections in which share ownership is widely dispersed. In terms of worldwide practice, the existence of cumulative voting varies; for example, it is mandated in Spain but not allowed in several countries, such as Germany, Japan, Singapore, and Turkey.

Minority shareholders are often granted rights to protect their interests in acquisitions. For example, companies in European Union member states are required to adopt sell-out rights. These rights allow minority shareholders who have voted against a merger offer to force a bidder with more than 90% of the target's voting rights to buy their shares at a fair price upon the deal's approval.

EXAMPLE 5   General Meetings

Which of the statements about extraordinary general meetings (EGMs) of shareholders is true?

A. The appointment of external auditors occurs during the EGM.
B. A corporation provides an overview of corporate performance at the EGM.
C. An amendment to a corporation's bylaws typically occurs during the EGM.

Solution: C is correct. An amendment to corporate bylaws would normally take place during an EGM, which covers significant changes to a company, such as bylaw amendments. A and B are incorrect because the appointment of external auditors and a corporate performance overview would typically take place during the AGM.

4.2.2. Board of Director Mechanisms

In companies with complex ownership structures and operations, it is impractical for shareholders to be involved in strategy formulation and day-to-day activities. Shareholders thus elect a board of directors to provide broad oversight of the company. Shareholders monitor the board's performance through exercise of voting power and participation in general meetings. The board, in turn, appoints the top management of the company. The board is accountable primarily to shareholders and is responsible for the proper governance of the company; in this regard, the board is the link between shareholders and managers. The board guides managers on the company's strategic direction, oversees and monitors management's actions in implementing the strategy, and evaluates and rewards or disciplines management performance. The board also supervises the company's audit, control, and risk management functions and ensures the adoption of proper governance systems and compliance with all applicable laws and regulations. In Section 6, we provide more detail regarding the functions and responsibilities of the board of directors and its committees.

4.2.3. The Audit Function

The audit function is an integral component of any governance structure. The function represents the systems, controls, and policies/procedures in place to examine the company's operations and financial records. Internal audits are conducted by an independent internal audit function or department. External auditors are independent from the company and conduct an annual audit of the company's financial records to provide reasonable and independent assurance of the accuracy of financial statements and their fair representation of the financial position of the company. External auditors are typically recommended by an audit committee (which we discuss later in the chapter) for appointment by shareholders or, in some jurisdictions, by the board. The board of directors is generally required to receive and review the financial statements and auditors' reports and confirm their accuracy before they are presented to shareholders for approval at the AGM. Senior management of publicly traded companies is also required to review and provide assurance of the effectiveness of the internal control systems to the board of directors or to shareholders. Overall, a company's audit function limits insiders' discretion with regard to the use of company resources and to its financial reporting. The audit function is also designed to mitigate incidents of fraud or misstatements of accounting and financial information.

4.2.4. Reporting and Transparency

Shareholders have access to a range of financial and non-financial information concerning the company, typically through annual reports, proxy statements, disclosures on the company's website, the investor relations department, and other means of communication (e.g., social media). This information may relate to the company's operations, its strategic direction or objectives, audited financial statements, governance structure, ownership structure, remuneration policies, related-party transactions, and risk factors. Such information is essential for shareholders to

- reduce the extent of information asymmetry between shareholders and managers;
- assess the performance of the company and of its directors and managers;
- make informed decisions in valuing the company and deciding to purchase, sell, or transfer shares; and
- vote on key corporate matters or changes.

4.2.5. Policies on Related-Party Transactions

The development and implementation of policies for related-party transactions and other conflicts of interest is an increasingly common practice among companies. These policies establish the procedures for mitigating, managing, and disclosing such cases. Typically, directors and managers are required to disclose any actual or potential, or direct or indirect, conflict of interest they have with the company, as well as any material interests in a transaction that may affect the company. Often, these policies require such transactions or matters to be voted on by the board (or shareholders) excluding the director (or shareholder) holding the interest. The adoption of these policies and procedures aims at ensuring that related-party transactions are handled fairly and that they do not advance the interests of the related party at the expense of the interests of the company or other shareholders.

4.2.6. Remuneration Policies

Executive remuneration plans have gained significant attention in the investment world, with a primary goal of aligning the interests of managers with those of shareholders. For this purpose, incentive plans increasingly include a variable component—typically profit sharing, stocks, or stock options—that is contingent on corporate or stock price performance. However, the granting of stock-based remuneration does not serve its purpose if managers can improve their personal gains at the expense of the company while limiting their exposure to weak stock performance. As a result, companies are increasingly designing incentive plans that discourage either "short-termism" or excessive risk taking by managers. Some incentive plans include granting shares, rather than options, to managers and restricting their vesting or sale for several years or until retirement. A long-term incentive plan delays the payment of remuneration, either partially or in total, until company strategic objectives (typically performance targets) are met.

Regulators across the world are also increasingly focused on remuneration policies. In some cases, regulators require companies to base remuneration specifically on long-term performance measures. A number of regulators are requiring companies, including many in the financial industry, to adopt clawback provisions. These provisions allow a company to recover previously paid remuneration if certain events, such as financial restatements, misconduct, breach of the law, or risk management deficiencies, are uncovered.

4.2.7. Say on Pay

Given the role of remuneration plans in aligning the interests of executives with those of shareholders, regulators and companies are increasingly seeking shareholder views on pay. The concept of **say on pay** enables shareholders to vote on executive remuneration matters. Say on pay was first introduced in the United Kingdom in the early 2000s. In an early example of shareholder rejection, in 2003 the shareholders of GlaxoSmithKline rejected the company's remuneration report because of opposition to the proposed executive pay. This was the first such rejection by the shareholders of a large UK-based company. Shortly thereafter, the practice of say on pay spread to other parts of the world and was implemented in the United States as part of the Dodd–Frank Act in 2011. In 2018, there were a number of instances in which shareholders voted against remuneration reports. In the United Kingdom, for example, Inmarsat plc's remuneration report was rejected by 58% of voters over concerns that executive compensation was not aligned with company performance. In the United States, 52% of Walt Disney Co.'s shareholders voted against what they believed was an excessive executive compensation package.

The scope and effect of say on pay varies across countries and companies. Some countries, such as Canada, have a non-mandatory and advisory (non-binding) say-on-pay system in which shareholders signal, rather than impose, their views on proposed remuneration. In other countries, such as the United States, France, and South Africa, say on pay is mandatory but non-binding. In these countries, the board is required to enable shareholders to vote on remuneration plans or packages, but the board does not have to abide by the result of the vote. Conversely, countries in which shareholder votes on say on pay are binding include the Netherlands, the United Kingdom, and China.

Say on pay has been subject to criticism because of the fact that shareholders often have limited involvement in a company's strategy and operations. These opponents argue that the board is better suited to determine remuneration matters. Conversely, by allowing shareholders to express their views on remuneration-related matters, companies can limit the discretion of directors and managers in granting themselves excessive or inadequate remuneration. This approach could thus reduce a critical agency conflict in stakeholder management by better aligning the interests of principals and agents.

5. MECHANISMS TO MITIGATE ASSOCIATED STAKEHOLDER RISKS

The rights of creditors are established by laws and according to contracts executed with the company. Laws vary by jurisdiction but commonly contain provisions to protect creditors' interests and provide legal recourse. One such provision is an **indenture**, which is a legal contract that describes the structure of a bond, the obligations of the issuer, and the rights of the bondholders. To limit creditors' risk during the term of a bond (or loan), debtholders may choose to impose **covenants** within indentures or contracts. Covenants are the terms and conditions of lending agreements, enabling creditors to specify the actions an issuer is obligated to perform or prohibited from performing. Affirmative covenants require bond issuers to perform certain actions, such as maintaining adequate levels of insurance. Restrictive covenants require bond issuers to not perform certain actions, such as allowing the liquidity level to fall below a minimum coverage ratio. **Collaterals** are another tool often used by creditors to guarantee repayment, representing assets or financial guarantees that are above and beyond an issuer's promise to repay its obligations.

To further protect their rights, creditors usually require the company to provide periodic information (including financial statements) to ensure that covenants are not violated and thus potential default risk is not increased. Because it is usually impractical and costly for individual bondholders to fully scrutinize a bond issue, companies often hire a financial institution to act as a trustee and monitor the issue on behalf of a class of bondholders. In some countries, credit committees, particularly for unsecured bondholders, are established once a company files for bankruptcy. Such committees are expected to represent bondholders throughout the bankruptcy proceedings and protect bondholder interests in any restructuring or liquidation.

5.1. Employee Laws and Contracts

Employee rights are primarily secured through labor laws, which define the standards for employees' rights and responsibilities and cover such matters as labor hours, pension and retirement plans, hiring and firing, and vacation and leave. In most countries, employees have the right to create unions. Unions seek to influence certain matters affecting employees. In the European Union, companies meeting specific size and geographic criteria are required to establish European Works Councils that are composed of employees who meet with management at least annually. Although not a common practice in the United States and many other parts of the world, employees are sometimes represented on the board of directors—or supervisory boards—of companies meeting certain size or ownership criteria (e.g., in Germany, Austria, and Luxembourg). In Japan, the employee model stresses reaching a consensus between management and employees in decision making.

At the individual level, employment contracts specify an employee's various rights and responsibilities. Employment contracts typically do not cover every situation between employees and employers, and thus there is some area of discretion in the employment relationship. Human resources policies also help companies manage their relationships with employees. Effective human resources policies seek to attract and recruit high-quality employees while providing remuneration, training/development, and career growth to improve employee retention. Some companies have employee stock ownership plans (ESOPs) to help retain and motivate employees. As part of an ESOP, a company establishes a fund consisting of cash and/or company shares. The shares, which have designated vesting periods, are granted to employees.

Codes of ethics and business conduct also serve an important role in the relationship between employees and the company. Such codes establish the company's values and the standards of ethical and legal behavior that employees must follow. Companies typically assign a compliance or corporate governance officer (or a board committee) to implement these codes, receive violation reports, and resolve ethical matters. In addition, whistleblower protection policies are another mechanism to ensure misconduct can be safely reported so as to mitigate associated stakeholder risks.

By managing its relationships with its employees, a company seeks to comply with employees' rights and mitigate legal or reputational risks in violation of these rights. Employee relationship management also helps ensure that employees are fulfilling their responsibilities toward the company and are qualified and motivated to act in the company's best interests.

5.2. Contractual Agreements with Customers and Suppliers

Both customers and suppliers enter into contractual agreements with a company that specify the products and services underlying the relationship, the prices or fees and the payment terms, the rights and responsibilities of each party, the after-sale relationship, and any guarantees. Contracts also specify actions to be taken and recourse available if either party breaches the terms of the contract.

5.3. Laws and Regulations

As part of their public service roles, governments and regulatory authorities develop laws that companies must follow and monitor companies' compliance with these laws. Such laws may address or protect the rights of a specific group, such as consumers or the environment. Some industries or sectors whose services, products, or operations are more likely to endanger the public or specific stakeholders' interests are usually subject to a more rigorous regulatory framework. Examples of these industries are banks, food manufacturers, and health care companies.

Many regulatory authorities have also adopted corporate governance codes that consist of guiding principles for publicly traded companies. Publicly traded companies, in turn, are generally required to annually publish corporate governance reports describing their governance structure and explain any deviations from guiding principles. Companies normally seek to adopt internal governance and compliance procedures and adhere to the relevant financial reporting and transparency requirements imposed by regulators.

EXAMPLE 6   Stakeholder Relationships

Which of the following is **not** typically used to protect creditors' rights?

A. Proxy voting
B. Collateral to secure debt obligations
C. The imposition of a covenant to limit a company's debt level

Solution: A is correct. Proxy voting is a practice adopted by shareholders, not creditors. B and C are incorrect because both collateral and covenants are used by creditors to help mitigate the default risk of a company.

6. COMPANY BOARDS AND COMMITTEES

As discussed earlier in the chapter, the board of directors is a central component of a company's governance structure. The board serves as the link between shareholders and managers and acts as the shareholders' monitoring tool within the company. As the relevance of corporate governance has grown within the investment field, the responsibilities of the board of directors have also increased in importance.

6.1. Composition of the Board of Directors

The structure and composition of a board of directors vary by company and geography. There is no single or optimal structure, and the number of directors may differ depending on the company size, structure, and complexity of operations. Most corporate governance codes require that the board include a diverse mix of expertise, backgrounds, and competencies. Such qualifications may include specialized knowledge of the company's industry as well as experience in certain functions, such as strategy, finance/audit, risk management, human resources, or legal. Moreover, many companies seek age, gender, and racial diversity in board composition.

Boards with one-tier structures comprise a mix of executive and non-executive directors. Executive (or internal) directors are employed by the company and are typically members of senior management. Non-executive (or external) directors provide objective decision making, monitoring, and performance assessment. Additionally, non-executive directors can serve an important role in challenging management and using past expertise in strategy and board issues. An *independent director* is a specific type of non-executive director that does not have a material relationship with the company with regard to employment, ownership, or remuneration.

In two-tier structures, the supervisory and management boards are independent from each other. Regulators generally prohibit members of the management board from serving on the supervisory board or limit the number of individuals serving on both boards. Employee representatives are typically elected by the company's employees and could make up half of the supervisory board in large companies.

In many countries, the chief executive officer (CEO) and chairperson roles are increasingly separated. In the United States, many companies have historically had "CEO duality," in which the CEO also serves as chairperson of the board. Nevertheless, the percentage of companies separating the two roles, particularly in the United States, has increased considerably since the global financial crisis of 2008–2009. The appointment of a lead independent director is an alternative that is sometimes practiced by boards of companies with CEO duality. The lead independent director generally has the authority to request and oversee meetings of all independent directors. Duality is not applicable in two-tier structures that prohibit the members of the management board from serving on the supervisory board. In these models, the chairperson of the supervisory board is typically external and the CEO usually chairs the management board.

Staggered Boards

The general practice for boards is that elections occur simultaneously and for specified terms (three years, for example). Some companies, however, have **staggered boards**, whereby directors are typically divided into three classes that are elected separately in consecutive years—that is, one class every year. Because shareholders would need several years to replace a full board, this election process limits their ability to effect a major change of control at the company. The positive aspect of a staggered board, though, is that it provides continuous implementation of strategy and oversight without constantly being reassessed by new board members thereby bringing short-termism into company strategy. This staggered board model was historically prevalent in the United States but has been generally replaced by regular board election terms. In contrast, the practice is common in Australia.

6.2. Functions and Responsibilities of the Board

As mentioned earlier, a company's board of directors is elected by shareholders to act on their behalf. In fulfilling their functions, directors have a responsibility to consider the interests of all stakeholders. The duties of directors are mandated by law in many countries but vary across jurisdictions. Two widely established elements of directors' responsibilities are the *duty of care* and the *duty of loyalty*. According to the OECD's *Principles of Corporate Governance*, duty of care "requires board members to act on a fully informed basis, in good faith, with due diligence and care." The OECD further notes that duty of loyalty "is the duty of the board member to act in the interest of the company and shareholders. The duty of loyalty should prevent individual board members from acting in their own interest, or the interest of another individual or group, at the expense of the company and all shareholders."

A board of directors does not typically engage in the company's day-to-day activities; rather, those activities are delegated to management. The board guides and approves the company's strategic direction, taking into consideration the company's risk profile. It delegates the implementation of the company's strategy to senior management, oversees the execution of the strategy, and establishes milestones to monitor the progress in reaching the objectives. The board also reviews corporate performance and determines relevant courses of action accordingly. In doing so, the board can monitor and evaluate management's performance and determine whether senior executive remuneration is aligned with the long-term interests of the company. The board is also responsible for selecting, appointing, and terminating the employment of senior managers (or the management board in case of a two-tier structure). One of the board's main responsibilities is to ensure leadership continuity through succession planning for the CEO and other key executives.

The board plays a central role in ensuring the effectiveness of the company's audit and control systems. It sets the overall structure of these systems and oversees their implementation, including oversight of the financial reporting practices and review of the financial statements for fairness and accuracy. The board also oversees reports by internal audit, the audit committee, and the external auditors and proposes and follows up on remedial actions. The board has the ultimate responsibility to ensure that the company adopts and implements proper corporate governance principles and complies with all applicable internal and external laws and regulations, including ethical standards.

In addition, the board typically ensures that the company has an appropriate enterprise risk management system in place, whereby risks are identified, mitigated, assessed, and managed appropriately. The board monitors the effectiveness of these systems through regular reviews and reports received from both management and the company's risk function. The board also has the responsibility to review any proposals for corporate transactions or changes, such as major capital acquisitions, divestures, mergers, and acquisitions, before they are referred to shareholders for approval, if applicable.

6.3. Board of Directors Committees

A company's board of directors typically establishes committees that focus on specific functions. Such committees, in turn, provide recommendations that are reported to the board on a regular basis. Despite the delegation of responsibilities to committees, the overall board remains ultimately responsible to shareholders and is not discharged of its liabilities to shareholders. Although board committees may vary by organization, some of the most common committees are discussed in the following sections.

6.3.1. Audit Committee

The audit committee is perhaps the most common board committee among companies worldwide. The audit committee plays a key role in overseeing the audit and control systems at the company and ensuring their effectiveness. In this regard, the committee monitors the financial reporting process, including the application of accounting policies; ensures the integrity of financial statements; supervises the internal audit function and ensures its independence and competence; and presents an annual audit plan to the board and monitors its implementation by the internal audit function. The audit committee is also responsible for recommending the appointment of an independent external auditor, periodically assessing the independence of the external auditor, and proposing the auditor's remuneration. Both internal and external auditors report their findings to the audit committee, which in turn proposes remedial action for highlighted issues or matters.

6.3.2. Governance Committee

The primary role of the governance (or corporate governance) committee is to ensure that the company adopts good corporate governance practices. In doing so, the committee develops and oversees the implementation of the corporate governance code, the charters of the board and its committees, and the company's code of ethics and conflict of interest policy. The governance committee reviews these policies on a regular basis to incorporate any regulatory requirements or relevant developments in the field. Most importantly, the committee monitors the implementation of the governance policies and standards as well as the compliance with applicable laws and regulations throughout the company. Remedial actions are recommended if any flaws or breaches of laws or regulations are identified. In some companies, the governance committee may be responsible for overseeing an annual evaluation of the board to ensure that its structure and activities are aligned with the governance principles.

6.3.3. Remuneration or Compensation Committee

The remuneration (or compensation) committee of the board specializes in remuneration matters. This committee develops and proposes remuneration policies for the directors and key executives and presents them for approval by the board or shareholders. The committee may also be involved in handling the contracts of managers and directors as well as in setting performance criteria and evaluating the performance of managers. The responsibilities of the remuneration committee may extend to establishing human resources policies for the company when remuneration matters are involved. In some companies, the remuneration committee also sets and oversees the implementation of employee benefit plans, including insurance, pension, severance benefits, and retirement plans (including monitoring the investment performance of benefit plan funds).

6.3.4. Nomination Committee

The nomination committee identifies candidates who are qualified to serve as directors and recommends their nomination for election by shareholders. The committee also establishes the nomination procedures and policies, including the criteria for board directors, the search process, and the identification of qualified candidates for director positions. Director independence, including what constitutes an independent director, is also a function of the nomination committee. Through these roles, the nomination committee can help ensure that the board's composition is well balanced and aligned with the company's governance principles.

6.3.5. Risk Committee

The risk committee assists the board in determining the risk policy, profile, and appetite of the company. Accordingly, the committee oversees establishing enterprise risk management plans and monitors their implementation. It also supervises the risk management functions in the company, receives regular reports, and reports on its findings and recommendations to the board.

6.3.6. Investment Committee

The investment committee of the board reviews material investment opportunities proposed by management and considers their viability for the company. Such opportunities may include large projects, acquisitions, and expansion plans, as well as divestures or major asset disposals. The committee often challenges, when necessary, management assumptions underlying investment prospects, monitors the performance of investments, and reports its findings to the board. The committee also is typically responsible for establishing and revising the investment strategy and policies of the company.

The specific board committees discussed in previous sections are the most commonly used, although the composition and number of committees may vary depending on the jurisdiction or on company-specific factors (e.g., company size, industry, complexity of operations, or regulatory requirements). An audit committee, for instance, is a regulatory requirement in a large number of jurisdictions. For banks and other financial institutions, a risk committee is strongly recommended by some regulators and required by others. In Brazil, the Central Bank of Brazil requires financial institutions to establish a remuneration committee at the board level. Some companies choose to combine two or more committees into one—for example, a nomination and remuneration (or compensation) committee or an audit and risk committee. Companies may also find it valuable to establish committees with other specializations, such as a compliance committee, an ethics committee, a human resources committee, or a health/environmental/safety committee.

The composition of a board committee is normally aligned with its scope of responsibilities. For instance, many regulators request that executive (internal) directors do not rule on matters underlying conflicts of interest or on matters requiring an unbiased judgment (such as audit, remuneration, or related-party transaction matters). As such, a large number of rules, including those adopted by the London Stock Exchange and the New York Stock Exchange, require that the audit and the compensation committees be composed of independent directors only. Countries with less-stringent regulations may require the audit committee to be composed of external (non-executive) directors, the majority of which should be independent (including the chairperson).

EXAMPLE 7 Responsibilities of Board Committees

A primary responsibility of a board's audit committee does **not** include the:

A. proper application of accounting policies.
B. adoption of proper corporate governance.
C. recommendation of remuneration for the external auditor(s).

Solution: B is correct. The adoption of proper corporate governance is the responsibility of a corporation's governance committee. Both A and C are incorrect because proper application of accounting policies and the remuneration of external auditors fall under the domain of the audit committee.

---

7. RELEVANT FACTORS IN ANALYZING CORPORATE GOVERNANCE AND STAKEHOLDER MANAGEMENT

This section explores ways in which certain factors, both market and non-market related, can affect stakeholder relationships and corporate governance. For this section, market factors include those that relate to capital markets, whereas non-market factors do not.

7.1. Market Factors

This section focuses on shareholder engagement, shareholder activism, and competitive forces, all of which are influential market factors for a company. Shareholder engagement involves a company's interactions with its shareholders to better understand how it manages its material risks and opportunities. Shareholder activism, on the other hand, involves more aggressive and sometimes public efforts by large shareholder(s) to create a significant change in a corporation's behavior. Meanwhile, competitive dynamics can help align managerial interests with those of its stakeholders.

7.1.1. Shareholder Engagement
The engagement of companies with shareholders—called **shareholder engagement**—has traditionally involved certain events, such as the annual shareholder meeting and analyst calls, the scope of which was limited to financial and strategic matters. There is a growing trend, however, for greater engagement between companies and their shareholders beyond these venues and topics. Companies have increasingly recognized the benefits that frequent, year-round engagement with shareholders can provide, such as building support against short-term activist investors, countering negative recommendations from proxy advisory firms, and receiving greater support for management's position.

7.1.2. Shareholder Activism
Shareholder activism refers to strategies used by shareholders to attempt to compel a company to act in a desired manner. Although shareholder activism can focus on a range of issues,

including those involving social or political considerations, the primary motivation of activist shareholders is to increase shareholder value. Activist shareholders often pressure management through such tactics as initiating proxy battles (fights), proposing shareholder resolutions, and publicly raising awareness on issues of contention.

Shareholder activists may pursue additional tactics, such as shareholder derivative lawsuits, which are legal proceedings initiated by one or more shareholders against board directors, management, and/or controlling shareholders of the company. The theory behind this type of lawsuit is that the plaintiff shareholder is deemed to be acting on behalf of the company in place of its directors and officers who have failed to adequately act for the benefit of the company and its shareholders. In many countries, however, the law restricts shareholders from pursuing legal action via the court system—in some cases, by imposing thresholds that enable only shareholders with interests above a minimum amount to pursue legal actions or by denying legal action altogether.

Hedge funds are among the most predominant shareholder activists. Compared with most traditional institutional investors, the fee structure of hedge funds often provides a significant stake in the financial success of any activist campaign. Furthermore, unlike regulated investment entities that are typically subject to restrictions on their investments (e.g., limitations on leverage or ownership of distressed or illiquid securities), hedge funds are loosely regulated and can thus pursue a greater range of activist opportunities.

7.1.3. Competition and Takeovers

Metrics that measure a company's success, such as market share or earnings growth, provide information that is useful for shareholders to judge the performance of a company's management team or board of directors and compare such performance with that of competitors. Senior managers risk their employment status in the event of underperformance, and directors, in turn, can be voted out by shareholders.

The traditional view of the market for corporate control (often known as the takeover market) is one in which shareholders of a company hire and fire management to achieve better resource utilization. Corporate takeovers can be pursued in several different ways. One mechanism is the **proxy contest** (or proxy fight). In a proxy contest, shareholders are persuaded to vote for a group seeking a controlling position on a company's board of directors. Managerial teams can also be displaced through a **tender offer**, which involves shareholders selling their interests directly to the group seeking to gain control. A contest for corporate control may attract arbitrageurs and takeover specialists, who facilitate transfers of control by accumulating long positions from existing shareholders in the target company and later selling the positions to the highest bidder. Finally, a **hostile takeover** is an attempt by one entity to acquire a company without the consent of the company's management.

Preservation of their employment status serves as an incentive for board members and managers to focus on shareholder wealth maximization. This threat of removal, however, can also have negative implications for a company's corporate governance practices if the company chooses to adopt anti-takeover measures, such as a staggered board or a shareholder rights plan (also known as a poison pill) to reduce the likelihood of an unwanted takeover. Staggering director elections can dilute the value of shareholder voting rights by extending the term that each director serves and eliminating the ability of shareholders to replace the entire board at any given election. Shareholder rights plans enable shareholders to buy additional shares at a discount if another shareholder purchases a certain percentage of the company's shares. These plans are designed to increase the cost to any bidder seeking to take over a company.

EXAMPLE 8   Shareholder Activism

Which of the following is true of shareholder activism?

A. Shareholder activists rarely include hedge funds.
B. Regulators play a prominent role in shareholder activism.
C. A primary goal of shareholder activism is to increase shareholder value.

Solution: C is correct. Although the subject of shareholder activism may involve social and political issues, activist shareholders' primary motivation is to increase shareholder value. A is incorrect because hedge funds commonly serve as shareholder activists. B is incorrect because regulators play a prominent role in standard setting, not shareholder activism.

7.2. Non-market Factors

This section focuses on certain non-market factors, such as a company's legal environment, the role of the media, and the corporate governance industry, that can have an effect on stakeholder relationships and corporate governance.

7.2.1. Legal Environment

The legal environment in which a company operates can significantly influence the rights and remedies of stakeholders. Countries that have a common law system (such as the United Kingdom, the United States, India, and Canada) are generally considered to offer superior protection of the interests of shareholders and creditors relative to those that have adopted a civil law system (such as France, Germany, Italy, and Japan). The key difference between the two systems lies in the ability of a judge to create laws. In civil law systems, laws are created primarily through statutes and codes enacted by the legislature. The role of judges is generally limited to rigidly applying the statutes and codes to the specific case brought before the court. In contrast, in common law systems, laws are created both from statutes enacted by the legislature and by judges through judicial opinions. In common law systems, shareholders and creditors have the ability to appeal to a judge to rule against management actions and decisions that are not expressly forbidden by statute or code, whereas in civil law systems, this option is generally not possible.

Regardless of a country's legal system, creditors are generally more successful in seeking remedies in court to enforce their rights than shareholders are because shareholder disputes often involve complex legal theories, such as whether a manager or director breached a duty owed to shareholders. In contrast, disputes involving creditors, such as whether the terms of an indenture or other debt contract have been breached, are more straightforward and therefore more easily determinable by a court.

7.2.2. The Media

The media can affect corporate governance and influence stakeholder relationships through its ability to spread information quickly and shape public opinion. As an example, negative media attention can adversely affect the reputation or public perception of a company or its managers and directors. Senior management's concern over reputational risk can thus reduce the cost of monitoring management activities by stakeholders. Media attention can motivate politicians and regulators to introduce corporate governance reforms or enforce laws that protect stakeholders and society at large. This influence was evident in the aftermath of the 2008–2009 global financial crisis, when significant media attention was a factor in the adoption of new laws and regulations designed to address perceived deficiencies in corporate governance.

Social media has become a powerful tool that stakeholders have increasingly used to protect their interests or enhance their influence on corporate matters. Prior to the advent of social media, companies typically had an advantage in distributing information because of their considerable resources as well as relationships with traditional media organizations. Through social media, stakeholders can instantly broadcast information with little cost or effort and are thus better able to compete with company management in influencing public sentiment.

7.2.3. The Corporate Governance Industry

An important catalyst for the rise of the corporate governance industry occurred in 2003, when the Securities and Exchange Commission (SEC) required US-registered mutual funds to disclose their proxy voting records annually. The same rule also required US mutual funds to adopt policies and procedures designed to reasonably ensure that proxies would be voted in the best interests of their clients. In the years following the SEC's 2003 mutual fund rule, institutional investors have, to varying degrees, committed additional resources to monitor and vote proxies for the large number of companies in which they invest.

With the increased importance and relevance of corporate governance among investors, the demand for external corporate governance services has grown considerably. In particular, some institutional investors have retained proxy voting firms to assist with corporate governance monitoring and proxy voting. In response to this demand, an industry that provides corporate governance services, including governance ratings and proxy advice, has developed. Because the corporate governance industry is relatively concentrated, these vendors have considerable influence in corporate governance practices, and in turn, corporations are generally compelled to pay attention to ratings and recommendations produced by the corporate governance industry.

8. RISKS AND BENEFITS OF CORPORATE GOVERNANCE AND STAKEHOLDER MANAGEMENT

As illustrated thus far, good corporate governance and stakeholder management can have a meaningfully positive effect on a company. A company will likely not meet the expectations of all stakeholders if one group is able to extract private benefits at the expense of another group. Depending on their nature and magnitude, unmanaged conflicts of interest and weak control over a company's operations may expose the company to various risks, such as legal, regulatory, reputational, or default risks. By adopting effective guidelines for managing the interests of stakeholder groups and instituting adequate levels of control, corporate governance can be reflected in better company relationships, superior levels of efficiency in operations, and improved financial performance.

8.1. Risks of Poor Governance and Stakeholder Management

Weaknesses in stakeholder management mechanisms or the adoption of poor governance structures can create various risks for a company and its stakeholders. A weak control environment can encourage misconduct and hinder the ability of the company to identify and manage risks.

8.1.1. Weak Control Systems

In a company with weak control systems or inefficient monitoring tools, such as poor audit procedures or insufficient scrutiny by the board, one stakeholder group may benefit at the expense of the company or other stakeholders. This could consequently have an adverse effect on the company's resources, performance, and value. The audit deficiencies at Enron, for instance, prevented the uncovering of the acts of fraud, erroneous accounting records, and other related issues that led to one of the largest corporate bankruptcies in US history.

8.1.2. Ineffective Decision Making

When the quality and quantity of information available to managers are superior to those available to the board or shareholders, in the absence of sufficient monitoring tools, managers have an opportunity to make decisions that benefit themselves relative to the company or shareholders. Without proper scrutiny, such practices might go unnoticed. Deficient decisions could include managing the company with a lower risk profile relative to shareholders' tolerance, thus avoiding investment opportunities that could create value for the company. Conversely, manager overconfidence may result in poor investment decisions without proper examination of their effect on the company or on shareholders' wealth.

Remuneration policies for management could also have significant implications for the company. Outsized remuneration packages for executives could have an adverse effect on shareholders' wealth, constitute a burden on corporate performance, and affect the interests of other stakeholders, such as employees, customers, or creditors. Remuneration policies that are not carefully designed may also encourage managers to seek immediate personal gains by taking excessive risks or focusing on creating short-term performance or stock price increases. Related-party transactions that underlie unfair terms for the company are another example of activities that are not aligned with the objective of value creation and that could be facilitated by a poor governance system.

8.1.3. Legal, Regulatory, and Reputational Risks

Compliance weaknesses in the implementation of regulatory requirements or lack of proper reporting practices may expose the company to legal, regulatory, or reputational risks. In such cases, the company may become subject to investigation by government or regulatory authorities for violation of applicable laws. A company could also be exposed to lawsuits filed by shareholders, employees, creditors, or other parties for breach of contractual agreements or company bylaws or for violation of stakeholders' legal rights. In today's markets, information flows rapidly. Improperly managed conflicts of interest or governance failures could bring reputational damage to the company, and its associated costs could be significant. Such risks are particularly acute for publicly listed companies subject to scrutiny by investors, analysts, and other market participants.

8.1.4. Default and Bankruptcy Risks

Poor corporate governance, including weak management of creditors' interests, can affect the company's financial position and may hinder its ability to honor its debt obligations. To the extent that the deterioration of corporate performance results in a debt default, the company may be exposed to bankruptcy risk if creditors choose to take legal action. The adverse consequences of corporate failures are not limited to the company's shareholders; they extend to other stakeholders, such as managers and employees and even society and the environment.

8.2. Benefits of Effective Governance and Stakeholder Management

The development of good governance practices can play a vital role in aligning the interests of managers and the board of directors with those of shareholders, while balancing the interests of the company's stakeholders. A good governance structure can be reflected in operational efficiency, improved control processes, better financial performance, and lower levels of risk.

8.2.1. Operational Efficiency

As part of a good governance structure, an organization clarifies the delegation of responsibilities and reporting lines across the company and ensures that all employees have a clear understanding of their respective duties. When balanced with adequate internal control mechanisms, the governance structure can ensure that corporate decisions and activities are properly monitored and controlled to mitigate risk and help improve the operational efficiency of the company.

8.2.2. Improved Control

Governance practices seek to institute more effective control exercised at all corporate levels, from shareholders to the board of directors and management. These practices can help identify and manage risk at early stages that can otherwise hinder corporate performance and/or damage reputation. Control can be enhanced by the proper functioning of a company's audit committee and the effectiveness of its audit systems. By adopting procedures for monitoring compliance with internal policies and external regulations and for reporting any violations, the company can better mitigate regulatory or legal risks and their associated costs. Additionally, the adoption of formal procedures with regard to conflicts of interest and related-party transactions allows the company to ensure fairness in its relationships with those parties.

8.2.3. Better Operating and Financial Performance

Good governance and stakeholder management can help a company improve its operating performance and reduce the costs associated with weak control systems. The costs of poor investments, legal proceedings against the company, and excessive perquisites are just a few examples that could be mitigated by well-functioning governance systems. Enhanced corporate governance could also allow the company to improve its decision-making process and respond faster to market factors. Proper remuneration policies are another governance tool that can motivate managers to make decisions with the objective of creating corporate value.

8.2.4. Lower Default Risk and Cost of Debt

Good corporate governance can lower business and investment risk. Governance arrangements that manage conflicts of interest with creditors, and that help protect creditor rights, can reduce a company's cost of debt and default risk. Default risk can also often be mitigated by proper functioning of audit systems, improved transparency (e.g., reporting of earnings), and the control of information asymmetries between the company and its capital providers.

With regard to credit risk, corporate governance mechanisms are increasingly relevant criteria among credit rating agencies when assessing a company's creditworthiness.

EXAMPLE 9   Benefits of Corporate Governance

Which of the following is **not** a benefit of an effective corporate governance structure?

A. Operating performance can be improved.
B. A corporation's cost of debt can be reduced.
C. Corporate decisions and activities require less control.

Solution: C is correct. A benefit of an effective corporate governance structure is to enable adequate scrutiny and control over operations. B is incorrect because an effective governance structure can reduce investors' perceived credit risk of a corporation, thus potentially lowering the corporation's cost of debt. A is incorrect because operating efficiency may indeed be a benefit of an effective corporate governance structure.

---

9. FACTORS RELEVANT TO CORPORATE GOVERNANCE AND STAKEHOLDER MANAGEMENT ANALYSIS

In the past, analysts may have considered corporate governance and stakeholder management issues to be only peripherally related to traditional fundamental analysis. Generally, these issues were seen as obscure and unlikely to be material drivers of performance. Following a number of governance failures since the early 2000s, the global financial crisis, and the rise of shareholder activism around the world, there is little doubt that governance and stakeholder issues have become increasingly important topics for analysts.

Some key questions that analysts may consider when assessing a company's corporate governance or stakeholder management system are as follows:

- What is the company's ownership and voting structure among shareholders?
- Who represents shareholders on this company's board?
- What are the main drivers of the management team's remuneration and incentive structure?
- Who are the significant investors in the company?
- How robust are the shareholder rights at the company, including relative to peers?
- How effectively is the company managing long-term risks, such as securing access to necessary resources, managing human capital, exhibiting integrity and leadership, and strengthening the long-term sustainability of the enterprise?

A qualitative analysis of these issues—typically provided by a company's proxy statements, annual reports, and sustainability reports, if available—can provide important insights about the quality of management and sources of potential risk.

9.1. Economic Ownership and Voting Control

Generally speaking, corporations with publicly traded equity have a voting structure that involves one vote for each share. That is, any shareholder's voting power is equal to the percentage of the company's outstanding shares owned by that shareholder. When there are exceptions to this norm and economic ownership becomes separated from control, investors can face significant potential risks.

In a small number of markets, dual-class structures are allowed under the local regulatory framework or exchange rules, which is the most common way that voting power is decoupled from ownership. In these cases, common shares may be divided into two classes, one of which has superior voting rights to the other. A common arrangement is when a share class (for example, Class A) carries one vote per share and is publicly traded, whereas another share class (for example, Class B) carries several votes per share and is held exclusively by company insiders or family members. This structure is used by Facebook, for example. In this way, the founders and/or insiders of a company may continue to control board elections, strategic decisions, and all other significant voting matters for a long period—even once their ownership level declines to less than 50% of the company's shares.

Another mechanism used to separate voting control from economic ownership is when one class of stock (held by insiders) elects a majority of the board; outside shareholders who hold a different share class would then be entitled to elect only a minority of the board. Technically, each share carries equal voting rights, but with this structure, the insiders retain substantial power over the affairs of the corporation because they control a majority of the board. Alibaba's partnership structure is one example of this type of control.

Proponents of dual-share systems, such as those just mentioned, argue that the systems promote company stability and enable management to make long-term strategic investments, insulated from the short-term pressures of outside investors. Critics of these structures believe they create conflicts of interest between the providers of capital and the management of the business.

It is virtually impossible for outside investors to dismantle dual-class structures because of the inherent design of their unequal voting rights. Therefore, these structures can remain in place even through generational changes within a founding family. Investors with long time horizons may want to consider the motivations of the controlling stockholders, generational dynamics, succession planning, and the relationship between the board and management. In addition, there may be potential valuation implications because dual-class companies tend to trade at a discount to their peers.

9.2. Board of Directors Representation

In most markets, investors have access to basic biographical information about the nonexecutive members of corporate boards. Analysts can assess the available information to determine whether the experience and skill sets on the board match the current and future needs of the company.

In particular, questions regarding directors' independence, tenure, experience, and diversity may bring useful investment insights. For example, if the board has multiple directors engaging in related-party transactions with the company, investors may have cause for concern about any conflicts of interest that arise. The issue of board tenure can also be a useful tool for investors. Directors with long periods of service to a company clearly offer valuable experience and expertise, but if the board composition is dominated by such long-tenured members, it may have a negative effect on the board's diversity and adaptability.

An example in which board composition had a significant effect on company performance occurred at a European pharmaceutical company. At one point in its history, the company had become overleveraged and faced significant financial distress. In response, non-executive directors with banking and turnaround experience were added to the board. With the help of these directors, the company recovered. Seven years later, the most promising product in the company's pharmaceutical portfolio began to cause serious side effects in its patient population. The situation required both a meaningful understanding of the medical issues involved and a rapid response from the company. However, the board was still composed of directors with financial expertise rather than medical training. The company struggled with its response to the crisis, and its stock price fell sharply. This situation was one in which the board's composition had been ideal for a certain point in the company's history, but ultimately the directors failed to refresh the board's membership as the needs of the business changed.

9.3. Remuneration and Company Performance

The availability and quality of information about executive remuneration plans varies widely across markets. In those markets where such disclosures are available, analysts can assess the elements of the remuneration program to determine whether they support or conflict with the key drivers of performance for the company.

Generally speaking, current executive remuneration programs consist of a base salary, a short-term bonus usually delivered in the form of cash, and a multi-year incentive plan delivered in one or more forms of equity (options, time-vested shares, and/or performance-vested shares). Often, these short-term and long-term plans are contingent on achieving financial or operational objectives, and often these objectives are disclosed. In these situations, an analyst can assess whether the primary drivers of the remuneration plan are the same factors that, in the analyst's view, drive overall company results.

Assessment of the suitability of a remuneration plan for a particular company is a subjective exercise and is highly dependent on industry and geographic norms. But there are some warning signs that may warrant particular scrutiny:

- **Plans offering little alignment with shareholders.** As an example, if a plan offers only cash-based payouts and no equity, there may be a misalignment of incentives between executives and investors unless management already owns a significant stake in the company.
- **Plans exhibiting little variation in results over multiple years.** If an award is described as performance-based but still pays in full every year regardless of the company's results, investors may have concerns about the rigor of the performance hurdles underlying the awards.
- **Plans with excessive payouts relative to comparable companies with comparable performance.** Investors may want to understand the cause of the anomaly and whether it is a temporary issue or a result of flawed remuneration plan design.
- **Plans that may have specific strategic implications.** As an example, some remuneration plans contain payouts tied to specific milestones, such as regulatory approval of a product, completion of an acquisition, or achievement of specific cost reductions. In addition, some companies offer particularly high post-employment pay arrangements tied to the sale of the company, whereas others offer no such arrangements. These factors are not necessarily negative features, but investors may want to understand whether the milestones driving the incentive plan align with the company's objectives.

- **Plans based on incentives from an earlier period in the company's life cycle.** A frequent example of such a plan relates to a company that has matured beyond its fast growth phase. The company's business may have matured, and competition may have limited the opportunity for market share gains. Investors may believe the company should become more focused on both returns and disciplined capital allocation. Even after the company communicates to the investor community a more returns-oriented strategy, the financial incentives in the remuneration plan may still be based purely on revenue growth. Investors may want to understand such potential misalignment of interests.

9.4. Investors in the Company

Examining the composition of investors in a company can be another source of useful insight for analysts. The behavior of these investors can result in both limitations and catalysts with regard to changes in the corporation. For example, cross-shareholdings are still prevalent in a number of markets. This situation occurs when a company, particularly a publicly listed one, holds a large, passive, minority stake in another company. Such holdings generally help to protect management from shareholder pressures because implicit in a cross-shareholding arrangement is the guarantee that the owner of the shares will support management on all voting issues. In effect, these shareholdings act as takeover defenses.

Similarly, the presence of a sizable affiliated stockholder (such as an individual, family trust, endowment, or private equity fund) can shield a company from the effects of voting by outside shareholders. As an example, a US consumer goods company has an affiliated charitable foundation that owns more than 20% of the outstanding shares. The company also has a provision in its corporate charter requiring that any changes to the charter must be approved by two-thirds of outstanding shares. As a result, it is virtually impossible for any measure to pass without the support of the foundation. The interests of the foundation thus conflict with the interests of the overall shareholder base. In effect, this single minority shareholder most likely holds the power to block the votes of the majority.

Analysts should note that market context is important in assessing the potential effects of affiliated stockholders. In certain countries, the presence of such shareholders is common, viewed by local market participants as a means of enhancing stability, strengthening the relationship between companies and their business partners, and fostering a long-term perspective by protecting the company against hostile takeover bids.

A final aspect of investor composition that has become increasingly relevant relates to activist shareholders, which we discussed earlier. The presence of activist shareholders can meaningfully and rapidly change the investment thesis for a company. Experienced activists, together with short-term-oriented investors who follow their activities, can create substantial turnover in a company's shareholder composition in a short amount of time. This is because an activist often serves as a catalyst for new strategic alternatives at a company and can attract new investors and/or arbitrageurs.

9.5. Strength of Shareholders' Rights

Within a framework of regional regulations and corporate governance codes, analysts may want to understand whether the shareholder rights of a particular company are strong, weak, or average compared with other companies. For example, if an analyst's viewpoint includes the possibility that a company will enter into a merger transaction in the future, he or she may want to understand whether there are significant structural obstacles to transactions that are embedded in the company's charter or bylaws. Similarly, if the thesis involves an outside catalyst, such as an activist shareholder who will introduce change at the company and improve performance, the analyst must take a position on whether shareholders are sufficiently empowered to advance such a change. If it is impossible for shareholders to remove directors from the board or to convene special stockholder meetings, it will be difficult for external initiatives to be successful.

In a number of developed markets, including the United Kingdom, the Netherlands, and Japan, regulatory agencies or stock exchanges have adopted governance codes, which are standards of governance reflecting local investors' expectations with regard to disclosure, board composition, shareholder rights, and other related issues. Often, these governance codes are implemented on a "comply or explain" basis, which indicates that standards are voluntary in nature. However, any deviation from the code must be explained by the company in a public disclosure. If a company has elected to deviate from the locally accepted governance practice, the analyst may want to understand the reasoning behind the decision.

9.6. Managing Long-Term Risks

Analysts may uncover useful insights regarding how a company manages various issues, such as long-term environmental risks, management of human capital, transparency, and treatment of investors and other stakeholders. Of particular note, the academic evidence linking these and other management quality issues to share price performance remains mixed, in part because indicators of management quality are often correlated with each other and, therefore, difficult to isolate. However, poor stakeholder relations and inadequate management of long-term risks have indeed had an enormous negative effect on share value in certain instances. Therefore, analysts may consider the assessment of such issues to be a useful component of their overall risk assessment of the company.

One way to evaluate management quality issues is to assess whether the company demonstrates a persistent pattern of wrongdoings, fines, regulatory penalties, investigations, and the like. A notable example is Toshiba Corp., beginning in 2015 when an investigation revealed that company managers had manufactured nearly $2 billion in profits since 2008. Poor internal controls allowed the fraudulent accounting to remain undetected for seven years. Over the next several years, Toshiba experienced the massive write-down of its Westinghouse Electric Co. unit, clashes with its auditors, negative equity, and legal disputes. Toshiba's dividend was withdrawn, Westinghouse filed for bankruptcy protection, and the company was forced to sell its profitable semiconductor unit along with other business units. Ultimately, the company's shares were moved to the second section of the Tokyo Stock Exchange, triggering forced sales from funds that track the first section (TOPIX) or the Nikkei 225 indexes. Even in the absence of circumstances as extreme as these, poor management of stakeholder interests can have a significant effect on company operations, reputation, and valuation.

9.7. Summary of Analyst Considerations

The analysis of corporate governance, stakeholder management, and other non-financial (often termed "extra-financial") considerations is inherently a subjective exercise. Governance practices that may raise the risk profile of one company may be perfectly acceptable in a different context, depending on geographic norms, mitigating circumstances, or the investor's risk tolerance and investment thesis. In this section, we have provided a basic framework for investors interested in uncovering incremental insights about a company by analyzing its governance standards, practices, and risks.

EXAMPLE 10   Analyst Considerations

1. Which of the following *best* describes dual-class share structures?
   A. Dual-class share structures can be easily changed over time.
   B. Company insiders can maintain significant power over the organization.
   C. Conflicts of interest between management and stakeholder groups are less likely than with single-share structures.
2. An investment analyst would likely be *most* concerned with an executive remuneration plan that:
   A. varies each year.
   B. is consistent with a company's competitors.
   C. is cash-based only, without an equity component.
3. Which of the following *best* describes activist shareholders? Activist shareholders:
   A. help stabilize a company's strategic direction.
   B. have little effect on the company's long-term investors.
   C. can alter the composition of a company's shareholder base.

Solution to 1: B is correct. Under dual-class share systems, company founders or insiders may control board elections, strategic decisions, and other significant voting matters. A is incorrect because dual-share systems are virtually impossible to dismantle once adopted. C is incorrect because conflicts of interest between management and stakeholders are more likely than with single-share structures because of the potential control element under dual systems.

Solution to 2: C is correct. If an executive remuneration plan offers cash only, the incentives between management and investors and other stakeholders may be misaligned. A is incorrect because a plan that varies over time would typically be of less concern to an analyst compared with one that did not change. B is incorrect because an analyst would likely be concerned if a company's executives were excessively compensated relative to competitors.

Solution to 3: C is correct. The presence of activist shareholders can create substantial turnover in the company's shareholder composition. A is incorrect because the presence of activist shareholders can materially change a company's strategic direction. B is incorrect because long-term investors in a company need to consider how activist shareholders affect the company.

10. ESG CONSIDERATIONS FOR INVESTORS AND ANALYSTS

10.1. Introduction to Environmental, Social, and Governance issues

The inclusion of governance factors in investment analysis has evolved considerably. Management and accountability structures are relatively transparent, and information regarding them is widely available. Also, the risks of poor corporate governance have long been understood by analysts and shareholders. In contrast, the practice of systematically considering environmental and social factors, which collectively with governance form the commonly used acronym ESG, has evolved more slowly. Issues driving the inclusion of environmental and social information in the investment process include scarcity of natural resources, physical impacts of climate change, global economic and demographic trends, diversity and inclusion, treatment of workers, and the rise of social media. A non-exhaustive list of ESG issues are shown in Exhibit 1 Typically, a smaller set of ESG factors are material for each company, influenced by the business segments it operates in as well as its geography of operation.

EXHIBIT 1   Example of ESG Factors

Environmental Issues	Social Issues	Governance Issues
• Climate change and carbon emissions	• Customer satisfaction & product responsibility	• Board composition (independence & diversity)
• Air and water pollution	• Data security and privacy	• Audit committee structure
• Biodiversity	• Gender and diversity	• Bribery and corruption
• Deforestation	• Occupational health & safety	• Executive compensation
• Energy efficiency	• Treatment of workers	• Shareholder rights
• Waste management	• Community relations & charitable activities	• Lobbying & political contributions
• Water scarcity	• Human rights	• Whistleblower schemes
	• Labor standards	

ESG factors were once regarded as intangible or qualitative information. Increased corporate disclosures and refinements in the identification and analysis of ESG factors have resulted in increasingly quantifiable and decision-useful information. Social issues, such as human capital management, are less quantifiable; however, they are not necessarily more difficult to integrate as qualitative factors into investment analysis. The process of reflecting quantitative ESG-related information and data—both quantitative and qualitative—in financial valuation continues to evolve.

10.2. ESG Investment Strategies

There is a lack of consensus on several ESG strategy-related terms used in the investment community. For the purposes of this chapter, we define ESG investment strategies as the following:

Responsible investing is the broadest (umbrella) term used to describe investment strategies that incorporate ESG factors into their approaches. Overall, responsible investing includes the following:

- ESG integration
- Socially responsible investing (SRI)
- Thematic investing
- Impact investing

Sustainable investing is a term used in a similar context to responsible investing, but its key focus is on factoring in sustainability issues while investing.

ESG integration generally refers to the careful consideration of *material* ESG factors in the investment analysis and portfolio construction processes. **ESG investing** is often used interchangeably with ESG integration. A material factor is one whose omission or misstatement could influence an investment decision and ultimately the product's investment objectives.

The materiality of ESG factors in investment analysis, particularly environmental and social factors, often differs meaningfully among sectors. An ESG factor is considered material when it has a potential to impact a company's ability to generate sustainable returns in the long term. For example, environmental factors, such as carbon emissions and water usage, will likely be material for utilities or mining companies yet are relatively inconsequential for financial institutions.

Socially responsible investing (SRI) is a related term that tends to have multiple meanings, creating confusion among investors. SRI has traditionally referred to the practice of excluding investments in companies or industries, such as controversial weapons or tobacco, that deviate from an investor's beliefs, either moral or faith based. The term has evolved to include investment objectives that promote positive environmental or social attributes, often by investing in companies with favorable environmental or social profiles.

Thematic investing refers to investment in themes or assets specifically related to ESG factors. This approach is often based on needs arising from economic or social trends.

Impact investing refers to investments made with the intention to generate positive, measurable social and environmental impact alongside a financial return.

Green Finance

Green finance is a responsible investing approach that utilizes financial instruments that support a green economy. According to the Organisation for Economic Co-operation and Development (OECD), green finance relates to "achieving economic growth while reducing pollution and greenhouse gas emissions, minimising waste and improving efficiency in the use of natural resources."[5] As with other previously mentioned ESG terms, there are several definitions for green finance in practice. The primary investment vehicles used in green finance are **green bonds**, in which issuers earmark the proceeds toward environmental-related projects. Green bond issuance has grown significantly. According to the Climate Bonds Initiative, total worldwide green bond issuance for 2019 totaled USD255 billion, compared to USD171.1 billion for 2018. The United States continues to be the largest green bond market in the world, with China being the second largest, accounting for about 12% of global green bond issuance in 2019. China's first green bond was issued in July 2015 as the country prioritized environmental projects to address air and water pollution issues resulting from its rapid growth. In addition to green bonds, **sustainability linked loans** (including **green loans**) are also gradually being employed across the globe. Sustainability linked loans are any types of loan instruments and/or contingent facilities (such as bonding lines, guarantee lines, or letters of credit) that incentivize the borrower's achievement of ambitious, predetermined sustainability performance objectives.

10.3. ESG Investment Approaches

ESG investment approaches range from *value*-based to *values*-based. The objective of a *value*-based approach is to mitigate risks and identify opportunities by analyzing and incorporating material ESG considerations in addition to traditional financial metrics. Conversely, the objective of a *values*-based approach is to express the moral or faith-based beliefs of an investor. Between the value-based and the values-based approaches lie a continuum of approaches that strives for value creation through values investing.

---

[5] Organisation for Economic Co-operation and Development, "Green Finance and Investment," OECD iLibrary. www.oecd-ilibrary.org/environment/green-finance-and-investment_24090344.

There is a lack of consensus in the investment community on terminology to classify specific ESG investment approaches. For the purposes of this chapter, we define six generic ESG investment approaches:

- Negative screening
- Positive screening
- ESG integration
- Thematic investing
- Engagement/active ownership
- Impact investing

Negative screening is the exclusion of certain sectors, companies, or practices from a fund or portfolio based on specific ESG criteria. Examples of a negative screen include excluding the fossil fuel extraction/production sector or excluding companies that deviate from globally accepted standards, in areas such as human rights or environmental management, from a portfolio. Many of these negative screens use a specific set of standards, such as the UN Global Compact's Ten Principles on human rights, labor, the environment, and corruption.

In contrast to negative screening, **positive screening** focuses on investments that manage their material ESG risks well relative to industry peers. Positive screening, typically implemented through an ESG ranking or scoring approach, is the inclusion of certain sectors, companies, or practices in a fund or portfolio based on specific ESG criteria. For example, positive screening may include seeking companies that promote employee rights, exhibit diversity in the workplace and in board rooms, or perform well in customer safety. While seeking to invest in sectors, companies, or projects that demonstrate best-in-class ESG performance relative to industry peers, this approach does not exclude any sectors. Instead, it focuses on finding the companies within each sector that perform best on the chosen criteria. This approach typically maintains sector weightings comparable to a relative benchmark index to avoid excessively overweighting or underweighting risk exposures.

ESG integration entails a systematic consideration of material ESG factors in asset allocation, security selection, and portfolio construction decisions for the purpose of achieving the product's stated investment objectives. There is an explicit inclusion of ESG factors into traditional financial analysis of individual stocks or bonds, such as inputs into cash flow forecasts, credit/default risk forecasts, and/or cost-of-capital estimates. The focus of ESG integration is to identify risks and opportunities arising from material ESG factors and to determine whether a company is properly managing these or not.

Thematic investing is investment in themes or assets specifically related to ESG factors, such as clean energy, green technology, sustainable agriculture, gender diversity, or affordable housing. This approach is often based on needs arising from economic or social trends. Two common investment themes focus on increased demand for energy and water, as well as the availability of alternative sources of each. Global economic development has raised the demand for energy at the same time as increased greenhouse gas emissions are widely believed to negatively affect the earth's climate. Similarly, rising global living standards and industrial needs have created a greater demand for water along with the need to prevent drought or increase access to clean drinking water in certain regions of the world. While these themes are based on trends related to environmental issues, social issues—such as access to affordable health care and nutrition, especially in the poorest countries in the world—are also of great interest to thematic investors.

Engagement/active ownership is the use of shareholder or bondholder power to influence corporate behavior through direct corporate engagement (i.e., communicating with senior management and/or boards of companies), filing or co-filing shareholder proposals, and proxy voting that is directed by ESG guidelines. Engagement/active ownership seeks to achieve targeted social or environmental objectives along with measurable financial returns. Engagement/active ownership can be executed through various asset classes and investment vehicles and often through direct transactions, such as venture capital investing. Collaborative engagement initiatives entail multiple investors collectively engaging with company management to influence positive action in managing their material ESG risks. Climate Action 100+, backed by more than 450 investors with over USD40 trillion in assets collectively under management (as of July 2020), is one such widely supported initiative that aims to influence the world's largest corporate greenhouse gas emitters to take necessary action on climate change. Other key ESG issues on which investors frequently engage are air pollution, plastic waste management, human and labor rights in the supply chain, and executive remuneration.

Impact investing is a relatively smaller segment of the broader sustainable and responsible investing market. Impact investments are investments made with the intention to generate positive, measurable social and environmental impact alongside a financial return.[6] An example would include investing in products or services that help achieve one (or more) of the 17 Sustainable Development Goals (SDGs) launched by the United Nations in 2015, such as "SDG 6: Clean Water and Sanitation—Ensure availability and sustainable management of water and sanitation for all" and "SDG 11: Sustainable Cities and Communities—Make cities and human settlements inclusive, safe, resilient and sustainable."

A summary of the six generic ESG Investment approaches and mapping to other classifications is shown in Exhibit 2.

EXHIBIT 2   ESG Investment Approaches

ESG Investment Approach	Description	Mapping to Other Classifications	
		Financial Analysts Journal	*Global Sustainable Investment Review*
Negative screening	Excluding companies or sectors based on business activities or environmental or social concerns	Negative screening	Negative/Exclusionary screening
			Norms-based screening
Positive screening	Including sectors or companies based on specific ESG criteria, typically ESG performance relative to industry peers	Positive screening Relative/Best-in-class screening	Positive/Best-in-class screening
ESG integration	Systematic consideration of material ESG factors in asset allocation, security selection, and portfolio construction decisions for the purpose of achieving or exceeding the product's stated investment objectives	Full integration Overlay/ Portfolio tilt Risk factor/Risk premium	ESG integration

---

[6]Global Impact Investing Network, "About Impact Investing." https://thegiin.org/impact-investing/.

EXHIBIT 2   Continued

Thematic investing	Investing in themes or assets related to ESG factors	Thematic investing	Sustainability-themed investing
Engagement/ Active ownership	Using shareholder power to influence corporate behavior to achieve targeted ESG objectives along with financial returns	Engagement/Active ownership	Corporate engagement/ Shareholder action
Impact investing	Investments made with the intention to generate positive, measurable social and environmental impact alongside a financial return	N/A	Impact/Community investing

Notes: For information on the *Financial Analysts Journal* column under "Mapping to Other Classifications," see www.tandfonline.com/doi/full/10.2469/faj.v74.n3.2. For the *Global Sustainable Investment Review* column, see http://www.gsi-alliance.org/wp-content/uploads/2019/06/GSIR_Review2018F.pdf.

10.4. Catalysts for Growth in ESG Investing

ESG considerations have become increasingly relevant for two key reasons. First, ESG issues are having more material financial impacts on a company's fair value. Many investors have suffered substantial losses due to mismanagement of ESG issues by corporations, which resulted in environmental disasters, social controversies, or governance deficiencies. Second, a greater number of younger investors are increasingly demanding that their inherited wealth or their pension contributions be managed using investment strategies that systematically consider material ESG risks as well as negative environmental and societal impacts of their portfolio investments.

Historically, environmental and social issues, such as climate change, air pollution, and societal impacts of a company's products and services, have been treated as negative externalities— ones whose costs are not borne by the concerned company. However, increased stakeholder awareness and strengthening regulations are internalizing environmental and societal costs onto the company's income statement either explicitly or implicitly by responsible investors.

At a *macro level*, such environmental risks as physical impacts of climate change—floods, droughts, wildfires, air pollution—are impacting our day-to-day lives both more frequently and on a larger scale than ever imagined. Wildfires in California, the Amazon forest, and Australia have caused loss of human life and billions of dollars in damages. Major cities, like Cape Town and Chennai, have had severe water shortages. The 2020 global slowdown due to Covid-19 demonstrated that such social factors as inequality, access to health care, and vulnerable labor can also have significant impacts on growth. While macro-level environmental and social risks have received widespread attention only since 2010, investors have been evaluating macro-level governance risks, such as quality of institutions and corruption, into their analysis since the 1990s.

At a *micro level*, there have been numerous examples of stakeholders penalizing companies that are unable to manage material ESG risks well. Facebook's Cambridge Analytica scandal, in which the personal data of over 80 million users were allegedly shared without consent and used in influencing voters, not only led to one of the largest US government fines in the technology sector (USD5 billion), but it also made a significant dent on user trust. Other examples of ESG risks materializing are shared later in this chapter. As prudent fiduciaries, investors are paying more attention to these factors while constructing portfolios and engaging with company management.

Another investor development that has supported ESG growth is the adoption of more sophisticated views about sustainable growth and its effect on investment performance. To this end, some large institutional asset owners embrace the concept of being "universal owners." **Universal owners** are long-term investors, such as pension funds, that have significant assets invested in globally diversified portfolios. Given their size and scope, the investment portfolios of universal owners are linked to economic growth and unavoidably exposed to costs resulting from external factors or externalities, such as environmental damages. Some universal owners strive to positively influence the way companies conduct business to minimize exposure to ESG-related costs because both their funds' long-term performance and the interests of their beneficiaries are at stake. Institutions that adhere to the universal owner philosophy believe that sustainable global economic growth is essential to successful investment performance.

10.5. ESG Market Overview

Reflecting the growth of ESG-related information in the marketplace, the amount of global assets under management (AUM) dedicated to the consideration of ESG factors in portfolio selection and management has increased substantially. According to the Global Sustainable Investment Alliance (GSIA), a collaboration of organizations dedicated to advancing sustainable investing in the financial markets, nearly USD31 trillion of AUM were dedicated toward sustainable investment mandates at the start of 2018, a 34% increase in two years. Europe (49%) and the United States (39%) accounted for the vast majority of these AUM. Determining the true size of the ESG investment universe is difficult, however, because managers and investors define and implement sustainable and ESG mandates in many different ways. There are often differences regarding which ESG factors should be considered—as well as how they are considered—in the investment analysis and portfolio construction processes.

The increased interest in sustainable investing has led to increased corporate disclosures of ESG issues, as well as a growing number of companies that collect and analyze ESG data. In addition to the GSIA, several organizations have been formed to monitor and advance the mission of sustainable investing. For example, the Global Reporting Initiative (GRI), a non-profit organization formed in 1997, produces a sustainability reporting framework that measures and reports sustainability-related issues and performance. In 2006, the United Nations and a consortium of institutional investors launched the Principles for Responsible Investment (PRI) Initiative to support investors committed to including ESG issues in their investment decision-making and ownership practices. In 2011, the non-profit Sustainability Accounting Standards Board (SASB) was formed to develop sustainability accounting standards for companies when disclosing material ESG information. To help educate investors, CFA Institute and PRI published "Guidance and Case Studies for ESG Integration: Equities and Fixed Income" in 2018. In addition to these key organizations, several others exist that promote the advancement of sustainable investing.

10.6. ESG Factors in Investment Analysis

Environmental factors that are generally considered material in investment analysis include natural resource management, pollution prevention, water conservation, energy efficiency and reduced emissions, the existence of carbon assets, and adherence to environmental safety and regulatory standards. A specific concern among investors of energy companies is the existence of "stranded assets," which are carbon-intensive assets at risk of no longer being economically viable because of changes in regulation or investor sentiment. Analysts may find it difficult to assess potentially significant financial risks of energy companies because of limited information on the existence of these companies' carbon assets, as well as the difficulty in determining political and regulatory risks. Material environmental effects can arise from strategic or operational decisions based on inadequate governance processes or errors in judgment. For example, oil spills, industrial waste contamination events, and local resource depletion can result from poor environmental standards, breaches in safety standards, or unsustainable business models. Such events can be costly in terms of regulatory fines, litigation, clean-up costs, reputational risk, and resource management.

Toxic Emissions and Waste as an Environmental Risk

Historically, environmental issues, such as toxic emissions and waste, have been treated as externalities and thus not fully provisioned for in a company's financial reporting. However, with growing awareness among all stakeholders, including the regulators, companies may now face financial liabilities associated with pollution, contamination, and the emission of toxic or carcinogenic substances and hence are required to manage these risks well. Gross mismanagement of these risks could not only lead to a permanent loss of a company's license to operate but also to other severe financial penalties.

In one notable example, the 2019 collapse of Dam I of the Córrego do Feijão Mine in Brumadinho, Brazil, resulted in the spillage of millions of tons of non-toxic mud. The plant and surrounding communities experienced the loss of 270 lives as well as the contamination of the nearby Paraopeba River. The mine was owned and operated by Vale, which has since been accused of hiding information about the dam's instability for many years to avoid hurting the company's reputation. Several employees from the company, including its ex-CEO, and its auditor, TÜV SÜD, were charged with murder and environmental crimes. Vale was also fined millions of dollars in addition to bearing clean-up costs.

Social factors considered in ESG implementation generally pertain to the management of the human capital of a business. These include human rights and welfare concerns in the workplace; data privacy and security; access to affordable health care products; and, in some cases, community impact. Staff turnover, worker training and safety, employee morale, ethics policies, employee diversity, and supply chain management can all affect a company's ability to sustain its competitive advantage. In addition, minimizing social risks can lower a company's costs (e.g., through higher employee productivity, lower employee turnover, and reduced litigation potential) and reduce its reputational risk.

Data Privacy and Security as a Social Risk

Data privacy and security focuses on how companies gather, use, and secure personally identifiable information and other meta-data collected from individuals. In some industries, such as internet software and services, this includes managing the risks associated with government requests that may result in violations of civil and political rights.

With the proliferation of the internet across the globe, more and more services are offered online. Consumers of such services are leaving a large digital footprint behind, often unknowingly. Some of this information may be personally identifiable in nature, leaving users vulnerable in case of theft or misuse. As per the "2019 Cost of a Data Breach Report" released by IBM and Ponemon Institute, the average cost of data breach is USD3.9 million, with cost per record lost being USD150.

Given the large amounts of sensitive data being managed by some of the largest internet and financial services companies today, mismanagement of data privacy and security risk can have materially damaging consequences both for a company's business model as well as financial performance. As an example, lax cybersecurity measures at Equifax, Inc., led to a data breach and the theft of identity and financial data belonging to more than 140 million US citizens in 2017. Equifax has since incurred hundreds of millions of dollars in expenses resulting from the breach and has faced numerous lawsuits and investigations.

As mentioned earlier, governance factors have long been recognized in investment analysis. Many performance indicators can help evaluate risks arising from governance issues, such as ownership structure, board independence and composition, and compensation. Although several governance factors may apply across industries and geographic regions, other factors are unique, such as systemic risk management for financial services companies. Wider adoption of responsible investing strategies enhances mainstream governance analysis via the addition of such factors as management oversight of environmental and social issues and tax transparency.

Corporate Governance: An All-Encompassing Risk

An example of investor loss related to corporate governance occurred in 2015 at German automaker Volkswagen. Volkswagen's "Dieselgate" scandal involved use of software to manipulate diesel vehicle emissions of more than 11 million cars globally. Specifically, many investors believed that inadequate governance oversight at Volkswagen permitted its diesel cars to pass emissions tests yet emit unlawful amounts of nitrogen oxide. Many investors attributed their losses to internal audit and compliance shortcomings as well as a lack of independence in Volkswagen's board of directors. The company has already incurred several billion dollars of civil and criminal penalties, and the scandal continues to pose significant legal and financial risks for the company.

One area of debate has been whether the consideration of ESG factors is consistent with fiduciary duty—particularly when overseeing and managing pension fund assets. (See Example 11.) Pension fund regulation regarding ESG considerations varies globally, however. PRI and the United Nations Environment Programme Finance Initiative (UNEP FI) promote the belief that ESG integration is a key part of investment analysis: "Investors that fail to incorporate ESG issues are failing their fiduciary duties and are increasingly likely to be subject to legal challenge."

EXAMPLE 11   ESG Investment Approach

The ESG investment approach that is *most* associated with excluding certain sectors or companies is:

A. thematic investing.
B. negative screening.
C. positive screening.

Solution: B is correct. Negative screening entails excluding certain companies or sectors, such as fossil fuel extraction, from a portfolio. A is incorrect because thematic investing typically focuses on investing in companies within a specific sector or following a specific theme, such as energy efficiency or climate change, as opposed to merely excluding a set of companies or industries from a portfolio. Likewise, C is incorrect because positive screening focuses on including companies that rank (or score) most favorably compared to their peers with regard to ESG factors.

SUMMARY

The investment community has increasingly recognized the importance of corporate governance as well as environmental and social considerations. Although practices concerning corporate governance (and ESG overall) will undoubtedly continue to evolve, investment analysts who have a good understanding of these concepts can better appreciate the implications of ESG considerations in investment decision making. The core concepts covered in this chapter are as follows:

- Corporate governance can be defined as a system of controls and procedures by which individual companies are managed.
- There are many systems of corporate governance, most reflecting the influences of either shareholder theory or stakeholder theory, or both. Current trends, however, point to increasing convergence.
- A corporation's governance system is influenced by several stakeholder groups, and the interests of the groups often diverge or conflict.
- The primary stakeholder groups of a corporation consist of shareholders, creditors, managers and employees, the board of directors, customers, suppliers, and government/regulators.
- A principal–agent relationship (or agency relationship) entails a principal hiring an agent to perform a particular task or service. In a corporate structure, such relationships often lead to conflicts among various stakeholders.
- Stakeholder management involves identifying, prioritizing, and understanding the interests of stakeholder groups and on that basis managing the company's relationships with stakeholders. The framework of corporate governance and stakeholder management reflects a legal, contractual, organizational, and governmental infrastructure.
- Mechanisms of stakeholder management may include general meetings, a board of directors, the audit function, company reporting and transparency, related-party transactions,

remuneration policies (including say on pay), and other mechanisms to manage the company's relationship with its creditors, employees, customers, suppliers, and regulators.

- A board of directors is the central pillar of the governance structure, serves as the link between shareholders and managers, and acts as the shareholders' internal monitoring tool within the company.
- The structure and composition of a board of directors vary across countries and companies. The number of directors may vary, and the board typically includes a mix of expertise levels, backgrounds, and competencies.
- Executive (internal) directors are employed by the company and are typically members of senior management. Non-executive (external) directors have limited involvement in daily operations but serve an important oversight role.
- Two primary duties of a board of directors are duty of care and duty of loyalty.
- A company's board of directors typically has several committees that are responsible for specific functions and report to the board. Although the types of committees may vary across organization, the most common are the audit committee, governance committee, remuneration (compensation) committee, nomination committee, risk committee, and investment committee.
- Stakeholder relationships and corporate governance are continually shaped and influenced by a variety of market and non-market factors.
- Shareholder engagement by a company can provide benefits that include building support against short-term activist investors, countering negative recommendations from proxy advisory firms, and receiving greater support for management's position.
- Shareholder activism encompasses a range of strategies that may be used by shareholders when seeking to compel a company to act in a desired manner.
- From a corporation's perspective, risks of poor governance include weak control systems; ineffective decision making; and legal, regulatory, reputational, and default risk. Benefits include better operational efficiency, control, and operating and financial performance, as well as lower default risk (or cost of debt).
- Key analyst considerations in corporate governance and stakeholder management include economic ownership and voting control, board of directors representation, remuneration and company performance, investor composition, strength of shareholders' rights, and the management of long-term risks.
- ESG investment approaches range from value-based to values-based. There are six broad ESG investment approaches: Negative screening, Positive screening, ESG integration, Thematic investing, Engagement/active ownership, and Impact investing.
- Historically, environmental and social issues, such as climate change, air pollution, and societal impacts of a company's products and services, have been treated as negative externalities. However, increased stakeholder awareness and strengthening regulations are internalizing environmental and societal costs onto the company's income statement by responsible investors.

PROBLEMS

1. Corporate governance:
   A. complies with a set of global standards.
   B. is independent of both shareholder theory and stakeholder theory.
   C. seeks to minimize and manage conflicting interests between insiders and external shareholders.

2. Which group of company stakeholders would be *least* affected if the firm's financial position weakens?
   A. Suppliers
   B. Customers
   C. Managers and employees

3. Which of the following represents a principal–agent conflict between shareholders and management?
   A. Risk tolerance
   B. Multiple share classes
   C. Accounting and reporting practices

4. Which of the following issues discussed at a shareholders' general meeting would *most likely* require only a simple majority vote for approval?
   A. Voting on a merger
   B. Election of directors
   C. Amendments to bylaws

5. Which of the following statements regarding stakeholder management is *most* accurate?
   A. Company management ensures compliance with all applicable laws and regulations.
   B. Directors are excluded from voting on transactions in which they hold material interest.
   C. The use of variable incentive plans in executive remuneration is decreasing.

6. Which of the following represents a responsibility of a company's board of directors?
   A. Implementation of strategy
   B. Enterprise risk management
   C. Considering the interests of shareholders only

7. Which of the following statements about non-market factors in corporate governance is *most* accurate?
   A. Stakeholders can spread information quickly and shape public opinion.
   B. A civil law system offers better protection of shareholder interests than does a common law system.
   C. Vendors providing corporate governance services have limited influence on corporate governance practices.

8. Which of the following statements regarding corporate shareholders is *most* accurate?
   A. Cross-shareholdings help promote corporate mergers.
   B. Dual-class structures are used to align economic ownership with control.
   C. Affiliated shareholders can protect a company against hostile takeover bids.

9. Which of the following statements about environmental, social, and governance (ESG) in investment analysis is correct?
   A. ESG factors are strictly intangible in nature.
   B. ESG terminology is easily distinguishable among investors.
   C. Environmental and social factors have been adopted in investment analysis more slowly than governance factors.

10. Which of the following statements regarding ESG investment approaches is *most accurate*?
    A. Negative screening is the most commonly applied method.
    B. Thematic investing considers multiple factors.
    C. Positive screening excludes industries with unfavorable ESG aspects.

CHAPTER 2

INTRODUCTION TO ALTERNATIVE INVESTMENTS

Steve Balaban, CFA, Steven G. Bloom, CFA, David Burkart, CFA,
Nasir Hasan, and Barclay T. Leib, CFE, CAIA

LEARNING OUTCOMES

The candidate should be able to:

- describe types and categories of alternative investments;
- describe characteristics of direct investment, co-investment, and fund investment methods for alternative investments;
- describe investment and compensation structures commonly used in alternative investments;
- explain investment characteristics of hedge funds;
- explain investment characteristics of private capital;
- explain investment characteristics of natural resources;
- explain investment characteristics of real estate;
- explain investment characteristics of infrastructure;
- describe issues in performance appraisal of alternative investments;
- calculate and interpret returns of alternative investments on both before-fee and after-fee bases.

1. INTRODUCTION

In this chapter, we explain what alternative investments are and why assets under management (AUM) in alternative investments have grown in recent decades. We also explain how alternative investments differ from traditional investments, and we examine their perceived investment merit. We conclude this chapter with a brief overview of the various categories of alternative investments; these categories will be explored further in later chapters.

"Alternative investments" is a label for a disparate group of investments that are distinguished from long-only, publicly traded investments in stocks, bonds, and cash (often referred to as traditional investments). The terms "traditional" and "alternative" should not imply that alternatives are necessarily uncommon or that they are relatively recent additions to the investment universe. Alternative investments include such assets as real estate and commodities, which are arguably two of the oldest types of investments.

Alternative investments also include non-traditional approaches to investing within special vehicles, such as private equity funds and hedge funds. These funds may give the manager flexibility to use derivatives and leverage, to make investments in illiquid assets, and to take short positions. The assets in which these vehicles invest can include traditional assets (stocks, bonds, and cash) as well as less traditional assets. Management of alternative investments is typically active. Alternative investments often have many of the following characteristics:

- Narrow specialization of the investment managers
- Relatively low correlation of returns with those of traditional investments
- Less regulation and less transparency than traditional investments
- Limited historical risk and return data
- Unique legal and tax considerations
- Higher fees, often including performance or incentive fees
- Concentrated portfolios
- Restrictions on redemptions (i.e., lockups and gates)

1.1. Why Investors Consider Alternative Investments

AUM in alternative investments have grown rapidly since the mid-1990s. This growth has largely occurred because of interest in these investments from institutions, such as endowments and pension funds, and from family offices seeking diversification and return opportunities. Alternative investments offer broader diversification (because of their lower correlation with traditional asset classes), opportunities for enhanced returns (by increasing the portfolio's risk–return profile), and potentially increased income through higher yields (particularly compared with traditional investments in low–interest rate periods).

The 2019 annual report for the Yale University endowment provides one institutional investor's reasoning behind the attractiveness of investing in alternatives:

> The heavy [75.2%] allocation to nontraditional asset classes stems from the diversifying power they provide to the portfolio as a whole. Alternative assets, by their very nature, tend to be less efficiently priced than traditional marketable securities, providing an opportunity to exploit market inefficiencies through active management. Today's portfolio has significantly higher expected returns and lower volatility than the 1989 portfolio.[1]

This quote neatly illustrates the expected characteristics of alternative investments: diversifying power (low correlations between returns), higher expected returns (positive absolute return), and illiquid and potentially less efficient markets. These links also highlight the

---

[1]Yale University, "Financial Report 2018–2019 Yale University" (2019, p. 18). https://your.yale.edu/sites/default/files/annual-report-2018-2019.pdf (accessed 27 April 2020).

importance of having the ability and willingness to take a long-term perspective. Allocating a portion of an endowment portfolio to alternative investments is not unique to Yale. INSEAD, as of April 2020, had allocated 33% of its endowment to private market strategies, including private equity, private debt, and real estate.[2] These examples are not meant to imply that every university endowment fund invests in alternative investments, but many do.

Family offices have also embraced alternative investments. According to the Global Family Office Report 2019 from UBS, over 40% of the average family office portfolio was invested in alternative assets.[3] According to Willis Towers Watson's "Global Pension Assets Study 2020," the typical pension plan had a 23% allocation to alternative investments at the end of 2019.[4]

Alternative investments are not free of risk, of course, and their returns may be correlated with those of other investments, especially in periods of financial crisis. Over a long historical period, the average correlation of returns from alternative investments with those of traditional investments may be low, but in any particular period, the correlation can differ from the average. During periods of economic crisis, correlations among many assets (both alternative and traditional) can increase dramatically.

EXAMPLE 1

True or false: Alternative investments focus solely on the private markets.

A. True
B. False

Solution: B is correct. Although many alternative investments are focused on private markets, there are alternative investments, such as hedge funds, that focus on the public markets.

1.2. Categories of Alternative Investments

Considering the variety of alternative investments, it is not surprising that no consensus exists on a definitive list. There is even considerable debate around categories versus sub-categories. The following list offers one approach to broad category definitions, and each category is described in detail later in this chapter.

- **Hedge funds.** Hedge funds are private investment vehicles that manage portfolios of securities and/or derivative positions using a variety of strategies. Although hedge funds may be invested entirely in traditional assets, these vehicles are considered alternative because

---

[2]INSEAD, "Finances and Endowment" (sec. 3), in "INSEAD Annual Report 2018/2019" (2019). https://annual-report.insead.edu/finances-and-endowment (accessed 27 April 2020).
[3] Campden Wealth Limited and UBS, "The Global Family Office Report 2019" (2019, p. 17). www.ubs .com/global/en/wealth-management/uhnw/global-family-office-report/global-family-office-report-2019.html.
[4]Thinking Ahead Institute, "Global Pension Assets Study 2020," Willis Towers Watson (2020).

of their private nature. Hedge funds typically have more leeway to pursue investments and strategies offering the potential for higher returns, whether absolute or compared with a specific market benchmark, but these strategies may increase the risk of investment loss. They may involve long and short positions and may be highly leveraged. Some aim to deliver investment performance that is independent of broader market performance.

- **Private capital**
  - **Private equity.** Investors participate in private equity through direct investments or indirectly through **private equity funds**. Private equity funds generally invest in companies, whether startups or established firms, that are not listed on a public exchange, or they invest in public companies with the intent to take them private. The majority of private equity activity involves leveraged buyouts of established profitable and cash-generating companies with solid customer bases, proven products, and high-quality management. **Venture capital funds**, a specialized form of private equity that typically involves investing in or providing financing to startup or early-stage companies with high growth potential, represent a small portion of the private equity market.
  - **Private debt.** Private debt largely encompasses debt provided to private entities. Forms of private debt include direct lending (private loans with no intermediary), mezzanine loans (private subordinated debt), venture debt (private loans to startup or early-stage companies that may have little or negative cash flow), and distressed debt (debt extended to companies that are distressed because of such issues as bankruptcy or other complications with meeting debt obligations).

EXAMPLE 2

Describe what the majority of private equity activity includes.

Solution: The majority of private equity activity involves leveraged buyouts of established profitable and cash-generating companies with solid customer bases, proven products, and high-quality management.

- **Real estate.** Real estate investments are made in buildings or land, either directly or indirectly. The growing popularity of securitizations broadened the definition of real estate investing. It now includes private commercial real estate equity (e.g., ownership of an office building), private commercial real estate debt (e.g., directly issued loans or mortgages on commercial property), public real estate equity (e.g., real estate investment trusts, or REITs), and public real estate debt (e.g., mortgage-backed securities).
- **Natural Resources**
  - **Commodities.** Commodity investments may take place in physical commodity products, such as grains, metals, and crude oil, either through owning cash instruments, using derivative products, or investing in businesses engaged in the production of physical commodities. The main vehicles investors use to gain exposure to commodities are commodity futures contracts and funds benchmarked to commodity indexes. Commodity indexes are typically based on various underlying commodity futures.

- **Agricultural land (or farmland).** Agricultural land is for the cultivation of livestock or plants, and agricultural land investing covers various strategies, including the purchase of farmland in order to lease it back to farmers or receive a stream of income from the growth, harvest, and sale of crops (e.g., corn, cotton, wheat) or livestock (e.g., cattle).
- **Timberland.** Investing in timberland generally involves investing capital in natural forests or managed tree plantations in order to earn a return when the trees are harvested. Timberland investors often rely on various drivers, such as biological growth, to increase the value of the trees so the wood can be sold at favorable prices in the future.
- **Infrastructure.** Infrastructure assets are capital-intensive, long-lived real assets, such as roads, dams, and schools, that are intended for public use and provide essential services. Infrastructure assets may be financed, owned, and operated by governments, but private sector investment is on the rise. An increasingly common approach to infrastructure investing is a **public–private partnership (PPP)** approach, in which governments and investors each have a stake. Infrastructure investments provide exposure to asset cash flows, but the asset itself is generally part of a long-term concession agreement, ultimately going back to the public authority. Investors may gain exposure to these assets directly or indirectly. Indirect investment vehicles include shares of companies, exchange-traded funds (ETFs), private equity funds, listed funds, and unlisted funds that invest in infrastructure.
- **Other.** Other alternative investments may include tangible assets, such as fine wine, art, antique furniture and automobiles, stamps, coins, and other collectibles, and intangible assets, such as patents and litigation actions.

2. INVESTMENT METHODS

This section introduces three methods of investing in alternative investments: direct investing, co-investing, and fund investing. Their advantages and disadvantages are examined, and a brief discussion of due diligence concludes the section.

2.1. Methods of Investing in Alternative Investments

In **fund investing**, the investor contributes capital to a fund, and the fund identifies, selects, and makes investments on the investor's behalf. For the fund's services, the investor is charged a fee based on the amount of the assets being managed, and a performance fee is applied if the fund manager delivers superior results. Fund investing can be viewed as an indirect method of investing in alternative assets. Fund investors have little or no leeway in the sense that their investment decisions are limited to either investing in the fund or not. Furthermore, fund investors are typically unable to affect the fund's underlying investments. Note that fund investing is available for all major alternative investment types, including hedge funds, private capital, real estate, infrastructure, and natural resources.

In **co-investing**, the investor invests in assets *indirectly* through the fund but also possesses rights (known as co-investment rights) to invest *directly* in the same assets. Through co-investing, an investor is able to make an investment *alongside* a fund when the fund identifies deals; the investor is not limited to participating in the deal solely by investing in the fund. Exhibit 1 illustrates the co-investing method: The investor invests in one deal (labeled

"Investment #3") indirectly via fund investing while investing an additional amount directly via a co-investment.

Direct investing occurs when an investor makes a direct investment in an asset (labeled "Investment A") without the use of an intermediary. In private equity, this may mean the investor purchases a direct stake in a private company without the use of a special vehicle, such as a fund. Direct investors have great flexibility and control when it comes to choosing their investments, selecting their preferred methods of financing, and planning their approach. The direct method of investing in alternative assets is typically reserved for larger and more sophisticated investors and usually applies to private equity and real estate. Sizable investors, such as major pensions and sovereign wealth funds, however, may also invest directly in infrastructure and natural resources.

Institutional investors typically begin investing in alternative investments via funds. Then, as they gain experience, they can begin to invest via co-investing and direct investing. The largest and most sophisticated direct investors (such as some sovereign wealth funds) compete with fund managers for access to the best investment opportunities.

EXHIBIT 1   Diagram of Co-investing in Alternative Assets

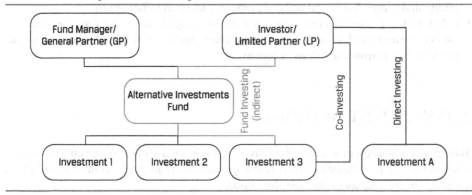

EXAMPLE 3

True or false: In co-investing, the investor is able to invest both directly and indirectly in the same assets.

A. True
B. False

Solution: A is correct. In co-investing, the investor is able to invest both directly and indirectly in the same assets.

2.2. Advantages and Disadvantages of Direct Investing, Co-investing, and Fund Investing

The direct investing, co-investing, and fund investing approaches naturally have distinct advantages and disadvantages.

2.2.1. Advantages of Fund Investing

The primary advantages of fund investing include the professional services offered by fund managers, a lower level of investor involvement (compared with the direct and co-investing methods), and access to alternative investments without the prerequisite of advanced expertise. Additionally, diversification benefits stem from the multiple investments found in a single investment vehicle overseen by a fund manager. (Consider instead the time and attention that would be required of a single investor to achieve similar diversification levels by directly investing in and managing multiple alternative assets.) Fund investing in alternative assets demands less participation from the investor than the direct and co-investing approaches, because it is up to the fund manager to identify, select, and manage the fund's investments. The investor may also heavily rely on the fund manager to carry out the due diligence that accompanies the investment process. Finally, specialist fund managers may expand the investment universe for an investor who lacks expertise for the sector in question.

2.2.2. Disadvantages of Fund Investing

Fund investing in alternative investments is costly because the investor is required to pay management fees and performance fees that are typically higher than fees for traditional asset classes. The higher fees can be attributed to the increased costs of: (1) running an alternative fund that may have a more complex strategy or require more skills and resources to source, (2) conducting due diligence, and (3) managing opportunities that have limited publicly available information. Alternative managers may also command higher fees if they face little competition. Despite the fact that a fund may provide due diligence expertise when it comes to choosing investments, an investor is still required to conduct thorough due diligence when selecting the right fund in the first place. Selecting the right fund itself is not an easy task because of asymmetry of information.

2.2.3. Advantages of Co-investing

Co-investors, who are essentially engaging in a hybrid of direct investing and fund investing, can learn from the fund's process and leverage the experience they gain to become better at direct investing. Many institutional investors begin with fund investing, because it provides instant diversification while requiring less costly minimum participation levels (lower minimums) and less due diligence. As investors' investment experience and investable assets grow, they may be granted "co-investment rights" with an investment in a fund, giving them a taste of direct investing. It works as follows: Alongside the fund's direct investment, investors co-invest an additional amount into that same investment often without paying management fees on the capital they used for the direct investment (a co-investment, in this case). Compared with fund investing, co-investing allows investors to be more actively involved with the management of their portfolio. Later, as their experience and capital increase, investors may prefer direct investing, bringing the expertise in-house and avoiding fund management fees.

2.2.4. Disadvantages of Co-investing

Co-investors have reduced control over the investment selection process (compared with direct investing) and may be subject to adverse selection bias, where the fund manager makes less attractive investment opportunities available to the co-investor while allocating its own capital to more appealing deals. Co-investing, furthermore, requires more active involvement from the investor, who must evaluate both investment opportunities and the fund manager, which demands more resources, concentration, and expertise. Moreover, co-investors usually have a limited amount of time to make the decision to invest or not. The co-investing approach can prove to be challenging for smaller firms with limited resources and due diligence experience.

2.2.5. Advantages of Direct Investing

When an investor chooses direct investing, she avoids paying ongoing management fees to an external manager because the investor conducts the investment process on her own, bypassing the use of a special vehicle, such as the fund. Direct investing allows the investor to build a portfolio of investments to her exact requirements. Direct investing provides the greatest amount of flexibility for the investor and grants the highest level of control over how the asset is managed. For example, an investor who directly purchases an ownership stake in a business typically has the ability to influence important matters, such as selecting the management team and controlling the strategic direction and investment decisions of the company.

2.2.6. Disadvantages of Direct Investing

Compared with fund investing and co-investing, direct investing demands more investment expertise and a higher level of financial sophistication. Such experience would otherwise be provided by a fund manager or investment firm during the complex investment and management process. Furthermore, concentration increases risk: The direct investor won't enjoy the ready diversification benefits of fund investing; it would require time and resources for an investor to mirror this advantage through direct investing. Plus, fund managers may enjoy reputational benefits that see them secure participation in attractive investments unavailable to certain direct investors operating on their own behalf.

Exhibit 2 provides a summary of the advantages and disadvantages of the three methods of investing in alternative investments.

EXHIBIT 2   Summary of Advantages and Disadvantages of Fund Investing, Co-investing, and Direct Investing

	Advantages	Disadvantages
Fund investing	• Fund managers offer investment services and expertise • Lower level of investor involvement compared with the direct and co-investing methods • Access to alternative investments without possessing a high degree of investment expertise • Potentially valuable diversification benefits • Lower minimum capital requirements	• Costly management and performance fees • Investor must conduct thorough due diligence when selecting the right fund because of the wide dispersion of fund manager returns

Co-investing	• Investors can learn from the fund's process to become better at direct investing • Reduced management fees • Allows more active management of the portfolio compared with fund investing and allows for a deeper relationship with the manager	• Reduced control over the investment selection process compared with direct investing • May be subject to adverse selection bias • Requires more active involvement compared with fund investing, which can be challenging if resources and due diligence experience are limited
Direct investing	• Avoids paying ongoing management fees to an external manager • Greatest amount of flexibility for the investor • Highest level of control over how the asset is managed	• Requires more investment expertise and a higher level of financial sophistication compared with fund investing and co-investing, resulting in higher internal investment costs • Less access to a fund's ready diversification benefits or the fund manager's sourcing network • Requires greater levels of due diligence because of the absence of a fund manager • Higher minimum capital requirements

EXAMPLE 4

Identify the advantages of direct investing for an investor.

Solution: An advantage of direct investing is that the investor can avoid paying ongoing management fees. In addition, a direct investor has great flexibility and control when it comes to choosing his investments, selecting his preferred methods of financing, and planning his approach.

EXAMPLE 5

In direct investing, an investor puts capital in an asset or business:

A. using a special purpose vehicle, such as a fund.
B. using a separate business entity, such as a joint venture.
C. without the use of an intermediary.

Solution: C is correct. Direct investing occurs when an investor makes a direct investment in an asset without the use of an intermediary.

2.3. Due Diligence for Fund Investing, Direct Investing, and Co-investing

One basic question an investor must consider when investing in alternative investments is whether to rely on the expertise of the fund manager or to undertake the investment selection process themselves via direct investing.

For direct investing, the investor has control over the choice of which company to invest in; however, the due diligence process of making an investment in a private company requires considerable expertise. In contrast, funds offer diversified portfolios, due diligence expertise, and the negotiation of favorable redemption terms, but these benefits come with additional fees. And although funds offer due diligence on the underlying investments, responsibility still falls to the investor for conducting due diligence when choosing among funds to invest in.

With co-investing, the investor is currently investing in a fund but is given an opportunity by the fund general partner (co-investment rights) to make an additional investment in a portfolio company (as shown in Exhibit 1). In this case, the investor will conduct direct due diligence on the portfolio company with the support of the general partner. A detailed discussion on due diligence is beyond the scope of this chapter (especially for direct investing). However, this section provides a brief overview of the due diligence process.

2.3.1. Due Diligence for Fund Investing

Manager selection is a critical factor in portfolio performance. A manager should have a verifiable track record and display a high level of expertise and experience with the asset type. The asset management team should be assigned an appropriate workload and provided sufficient resources. Moreover, it should be rewarded with an effective compensation package to ensure alignment of interest, continuity, motivation, and thoughtful oversight of assets.

Fraud, although infrequent, is always a possibility. The investor should be skeptical of unusually good and overly consistent reported performance. Third-party custody of assets and independent verification of results can help reduce the chance of an investor being defrauded. Diversification across managers is also wise. Finally, separate accounts make theft more difficult because the investor retains custody of the assets and sometimes can select the prime broker or other service providers, binding them to the client's interest.

For an investor considering a new investment, a proper due diligence process should be carried out to ensure that the targeted investment is in compliance with its prospectus and that it will meet her investment strategy, risk and return objectives, and restrictions. Existing investors should monitor results and fund holdings to determine whether a fund has performed in line with expectations and continues to comply with its prospectus.

Exhibit 3 lists key items that should be considered in a typical fund due diligence process.

EXHIBIT 3   A Typical Due Diligence Process

Organization	• Experience and quality of management team, compensation, and staffing • Analysis of prior and current funds • Track record/alignment of interests • Reputation and quality of third-party service providers (e.g., lawyers, auditors, prime brokers)

Portfolio management	• Investment process • Target markets/asset types/strategies • Sourcing of investments • Role of operating partners • Underwriting • Environmental and engineering review process • Integration of asset management/acquisitions/dispositions • Disposition process, including its initiation and execution
Operations and controls	• Reporting and accounting methodology • Audited financial statements and other internal controls • Valuations—frequency and approach(es) • Insurance and contingency plans
Risk management	• Fund policies and limits • Risk management policy • Portfolio risk and key risk factors • Leverage and currency—risks/constraints/hedging
Legal review	• Fund structure • Registrations • Existing/prior litigation
Fund terms	• Fees (management and performance) and expenses • Contractual terms • Investment period and fund term and extensions • Carried interest • Distributions • Conflicts • Limited partners' rights • "Key person" and/or other termination procedures

2.3.2. Due Diligence for Direct Investing

Due diligence for direct investing requires the investor to conduct a thorough investigation into the target asset or business, including but not limited to the quality of its management team, the quality of its customers, the competitive landscape, revenue generation, risks, and so on. When considering direct investments in private equity, the investor conducts reference checks and interviews to evaluate the quality of interactions between the business and each of its stakeholders (e.g., customers and suppliers). Due diligence for private debt investing could entail credit analysis of borrowers to assess their ability to service the regular interest and principal payments of debt, and background checks on the owners and management team would round out the effort. In direct real estate, the building's occupancy rate and the quality of its structure and tenants should be analyzed prior to investing. In infrastructure, an investor would perform an assessment of the quality of the assets held and operated (e.g., an airport) and their ability to generate future cash flows. In conducting due diligence, direct investors often supplement their due diligence with analysis prepared by external consultants.

2.3.3. Due Diligence for Co-investing

Given that direct investing is an element of co-investing, aspects of the due diligence process apply to both. In co-investing, investors often rely heavily on the due diligence conducted by the fund manager. Direct investing opportunities, however, are often sourced differently from co-investing opportunities, and so the level of independence sitting behind the due diligence can differ. Consider that direct investing opportunities are usually sourced by the direct investment team at a large pension or sovereign wealth fund, whereas co-investing opportunities are usually provided by the private equity, real estate, or infrastructure fund manager for the investor's consideration. Direct investing due diligence may be more independent than co-investing due diligence because the direct investing team is typically introduced to opportunities by third parties and they have more control over the due diligence process.

KNOWLEDGE CHECK 6

An investor with limited investment and due diligence experience will *most likely* invest in alternative assets using which method?

A. Fund investing
B. Co-investing
C. Direct investing

Solution: A is correct. An investor with limited investment and due diligence experience will likely choose fund investing to benefit from the expertise that a fund manager would provide.

---

3. INVESTMENT AND COMPENSATION STRUCTURES

This section explores the investment partnership and compensation structures used in alternative investments. We examine the contractual provisions typically included in partnership agreements and why they exist to protect investors. An overview of the most common investment clauses is provided.

3.1. Partnership Structures

In the world of alternative investments, partnership structures are common. In limited partnerships, the fund manager is the **general partner (GP)** and investors are the **limited partners** (LPs). LPs, who are generally accredited investors (owing to legal restrictions on the fund), are expected to understand and be able to assume the risks associated with the investments, which are less regulated than offerings to the general public. The GP runs the business and theoretically bears unlimited liability for anything that goes wrong. The GP may also run multiple funds at a time.

Limited partners are outside investors who own a fractional interest in the partnership based on the amount of their initial investment and the terms set out in the partnership documentation. LPs commit to future investments, and the upfront cash outflow can be a small portion of their total commitment to the fund. Funds set up as limited partnerships typically have a limit on the number of LPs allowed to invest in the fund. LPs play passive roles and are not involved with the management of the fund (although co-investment rights allow for the LPs to make additional direct investments in the portfolio companies); the operations and decisions of the fund are controlled solely by the GP. Exhibit 4 illustrates the limited partnership structure for a hypothetical $500 million investment fund.

EXHIBIT 4   Example of a Limited Partnership Structure

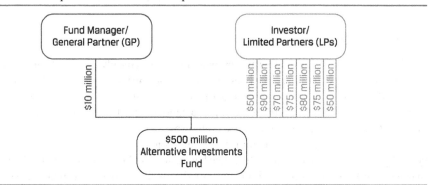

The partnership between the GP and LPs is governed by a **limited partnership agreement (LPA)**, a legal document that outlines the rules of the partnership and establishes the framework that ultimately guides the fund's operations throughout its life. LPAs vary in length and complexity and may be dense with provisions and clauses, some of which are discussed later in this section. In addition to LPAs, **side letters** may also be negotiated. Side letters are side agreements created between the GP and a certain number of LPs that exist *outside* the LPA. Some examples of clauses or details that may be included in a side letter include the following:

- Potential additional reporting due to an LP's unique circumstances, such as regulatory or tax requirements
- First right of refusal and other similar clauses to outline potential treatment (regarding fees, co-investment rights, secondary sales, and, potentially, other matters) in comparison to other LPs
- Notice requirements in the event of litigation, insolvency, and related matters
- Most-favored-nation clauses, such as agreeing that if similar LPs pay lower fees, they will be offered to the LP

Certain structures are commonly adopted for specific alternative investments. For example, infrastructure investors frequently enter into public–private partnerships, which are agreements between the public sector and the private sector to finance, build, and operate public infrastructure, such as hospitals and toll roads. In real estate fund investing, investors may be classified as unitholders, and joint ventures are a partnership structure common in real estate direct investing.

EXAMPLE 7

Fill in the blank: Investments in limited partnerships are _____ regulated than offerings to the general public.

Solution: Investments in limited partnerships are **less** regulated than offerings to the general public.

3.2. Compensation Structures

Funds are generally structured with a **management fee** typically ranging from 1% to 2% of assets under management (e.g., for hedge funds) or **committed capital** (e.g., for private equity funds), which is how much money in total that LPs have committed to the fund's future invest-ments. On top of the management fee, a **performance fee** (also referred to as an *incentive fee* or *carried interest*) is applied based on excess returns.

Private equity funds raise committed capital and draw down on those commitments, generally over three to five years, when they have a specific investment to make. Note that the management fee is typically based on committed capital, *not* invested capital; the committed-capital basis for management fees is an important distinction from hedge funds, whose man-agement fees are based on AUM. Having committed capital as the basis for management fee calculations reduces the incentive for GPs to deploy the committed capital as quickly as possible to grow their fee base. This allows the GPs to be selective about deploying capital into investment opportunities.

The partnership agreement usually specifies that the performance fee is earned only after the fund achieves a return known as a **hurdle rate**. The hurdle rate is a *minimum* rate of return, typically 8%, that the GP must exceed in order to earn the performance fee. GPs typically receive 20% of the total profit of the private equity fund net of any *hard hurdle rate*, in which case the GP earns fees on annual returns in excess of the hurdle rate, or net of the *soft hurdle rate*, in which case the fee is calculated on the entire annual gross return as long as the set hurdle is exceeded. Hurdle rates are less common for hedge funds but do appear from time to time.

Performance fees are designed to reward GPs for enhanced performance and to motivate investment professionals to work hard and stay involved for years to come. Exhibit 5 illus-trates a simple example of how performance fees are calculated using a typical "2 and 20" compensation structure, where management fees are calculated on 2% of AUM or commit-ted capital and performance fees are calculated on 20% of profits. An investment that was purchased in Year 1 for $10 million and sold in Year 4 for $20 million represents a return of 26% on an internal rate of return (IRR) basis. The LPs receive 80% of profits (80% × $10 million profit = $8 million), and the GP receives 20% of profits (20% × $10 million profit = $2 million). Note that this example assumes the hurdle rate has been exceeded and a catch-up clause exists in the partnership agreement; these concepts will be discussed in the next section.

In addition to both management and performance fees charged to investors, leveraged buyout firms in private equity may charge consulting fees and monitoring fees to the underlying companies.

EXHIBIT 5   Simple Performance Fee Calculation

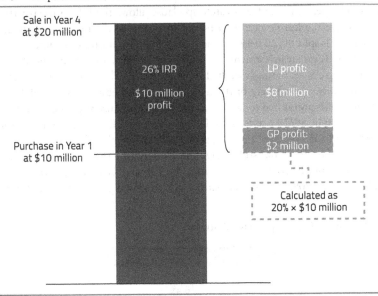

As for hedge fund managers, they generally accrue an incentive fee on their quarterly performance, but they typically crystalize (realize) their incentive fee once annually. If they make money in the first quarter but then lose the same amount in the second, the investor recoups the Q1 incentive fee and pays only at the end of the year an incentive fee based on total annual returns net of management fees and other expenses.

EXAMPLE 8

Fill in the blank: A _____ fee is typically added to a management fee for a fund governed by a limited partnership agreement.

Solution: A <u>performance (incentive or carried interest)</u> fee is typically added to a management fee for a fund governed by a limited partnership agreement.

3.3. Common Investment Clauses, Provisions, and Contingencies

For most alternative investment funds, particularly hedge funds and private equity funds, the GP does not earn a performance fee until the LPs have received their initial investment *and* the total return generated on the investment has exceeded a specified hurdle rate. In our example, the LPs receive 80% of the total profit of the fund plus the amount of their initial investment.

A **catch-up clause** may be included in the partnership agreement. Essentially, for a GP who earns a 20% performance fee, a catch-up clause allows the GP to receive 100% of the distributions above the hurdle rate *until* he receives 20% of the profits generated, and then every excess dollar is split 80/20 between the LPs and GP. To illustrate, assume that the GP has earned an 18% IRR on an investment, the hurdle rate is 8%, and the partnership agreement includes a catch-up clause. In this case, the LPs would receive the entirety of the first 8% profit, the GP would receive the entirety of the next 2% profit—because 2% out of 10% amounts to 20% of the profits accounted for so far, as the catch-up clause stipulates—and the remaining 8% would be split 80/20 between the LPs and the GP. Effectively, the LPs earned 14.4% (18% × 80%) and the GP earned 3.6% (18% × 20%). Imagine the same scenario, absent a catch-up clause: The LPs would still receive the entirety of the first 8% profit; however, the remaining 10% would be split 80/20 between the LPs and GP, reducing the GP's return to 2.0% [(18% − 8%) × 20%]. These calculations are presented graphically in Exhibit 6.

EXHIBIT 6   Simple Catch-Up Clause Illustration

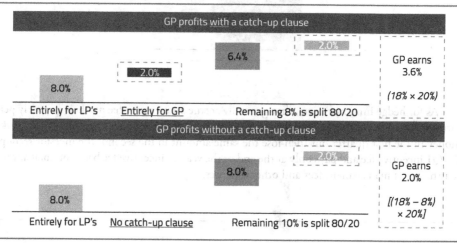

In hedge funds, fee calculations also take into account a **high-water mark**, which reflects the highest value used to calculate an incentive fee. A high-water mark is the *highest* value of the fund investment ever achieved at a performance fee crystallization date, net of fees, by the individual LP. A high-water mark clause states that a hedge fund manager must recuperate declines in value from the high-water mark before performance fees can be charged on newly generated profits. The use of high-water marks protects clients from paying twice for the same performance.

With all alternative investments, investor high-water marks generally carry over into new calendar years, although with hedge funds, an investor will no longer be able to claw back any incentive fees paid for a given calendar year if portfolio losses are subsequently incurred in a later calendar year. Given the generally more illiquid and longer-term nature of their holdings, private equity and real estate investments are more likely to contain clawback clauses for the entire life of the portfolio.

Given that different clients invest at different times, it is possible that not all clients will be at their respective high-water marks at the same time; a client who invests on a dip will enjoy the fund's recovery and pay an incentive fee, whereas a client who invested at the top will need to earn back what was lost before being obliged to pay the incentive fee.

Needless to say, individual capital account fund accounting can become quite complicated when tracking such investment timing differences. Even careful administrators make accounting mistakes when handling high-water mark and incentive fee issues. The astute alternative asset investor will always double-check the incentive fee calculations provided to them. Best-practice accounting for hedge funds is far more complex than the simple issuance of shares (carried at a single net asset value, or NAV), which is more common in the mutual fund industry.

EXAMPLE 9

The minimum rate of return that a GP must exceed in order to earn an incentive or performance fee is called the:

A. high-water mark.
B. hurdle rate.
C. performance threshold.

Solution: B is correct. A high-water mark is the highest value used to calculate an incentive fee. "Performance threshold" is not a term that is generally used in the industry.

In alternative investments, a **waterfall** represents the distribution method that defines the order in which allocations are made to LPs and GPs. GPs usually receive a disproportionately larger share of the total profits relative to their initial investment, which incentivizes them to maximize profitability. There are two types of waterfalls: *deal-by-deal* (or *American*) waterfalls and *whole-of-fund* (or *European*) waterfalls. Deal-by-deal waterfalls are more advantageous to the GP because performance fees are collected on a per-deal basis, allowing the GP to get paid before LPs receive both their initial investment *and* their preferred rate of return (i.e., the hurdle rate) on the entire fund. In whole-of-fund waterfalls, all distributions go to the LPs as deals are exited and the GP does not participate in any profits until the LPs receive their initial investment and the hurdle rate has been met. In contrast to deal-by-deal waterfalls, whole-of-fund waterfalls occur at the aggregate fund level (i.e., after *all* investments have been exited) and are more advantageous to the LPs. Exhibits 7 and 8 illustrate deal-by-deal waterfalls and whole-of-fund waterfalls, respectively.

EXHIBIT 7   Deal-by-Deal (American) Waterfall Example

Investment No.	Year Invested	Year Sold	Amount ($mm) Invested	Amount ($mm) Sold	Profit $mm	Profit %	GP at 20%
1	1	4	$10	$20	$10	26.0%	$2
2	2	5	$20	$35	$15	20.5%	$3
3	2	7	$40	$80	$40	14.9%	$8
4	3	7	$20	$20	-	-	-
5	3	8	$35	$25	($10)	neg	($2)
6	4	9	$25	$20	($5)	neg	($1)
7	5	9	$30	-	($30)	neg	($6)
8	5	10	$20	-	($20)	neg	($4)
Total	1	10	$200	$200	-	-	-

EXHIBIT 8   Whole-of-Fund (European) Waterfall Example

Investment No.	Year		Amount ($mm)		Profit		
	Invested	Sold	Invested	Sold	$mm	%	GP at 20%
1	1	4	$10	$20	$10	26.0%	-
2	2	5	$20	$35	$15	20.5%	-
3	2	7	$40	$80	$40	14.9%	-
4	3	7	$20	$20	-	-	-
5	3	8	$35	$25	($10)	neg	-
6	4	9	$25	$20	($5)	neg	-
7	5	9	$30	-	($30)	neg	-
8	5	10	$20	-	($20)	neg	-
Total	1	10	$200	$200	-	-	-

A **clawback** provision reflects the right of LPs to reclaim part of the GP's performance fee. Along either waterfall path, if a GP ever accrues (or actually pays itself) an incentive fee on gains that are not yet fully realized and then subsequently gives back these gains, an investor is typically able to claw back prior incentive fee accruals and payments. Clawback provisions are usually activated when a GP exits successful deals early on but incurs losses on deals later in the fund's life.

4. HEDGE FUNDS

4.1. Characteristics of Hedge Funds

In 1949, Alfred Winslow Jones, a sociologist investigating fundamental and technical research in order to forecast the stock market for *Fortune* magazine, set up an investment fund with himself as GP. The fund followed three tenets: (1) Always maintain short positions, (2) always use leverage, and (3) charge only an incentive fee of 20% of profits with no fixed fees. Jones called his portfolio a "hedged" fund (eventually shortened to "hedge" fund) because his short positions offset his long positions in the stock market. Theoretically, the overall portfolio was hedged against major market moves.

Although Jones's original three tenets still have some relevance to today's hedge fund industry, not all hedge funds restrict themselves to equities. Many trade sovereign and corporate debt, commodities, futures contracts, options, and other derivatives. Even real estate investments are found in hedge fund structures. Nor do all hedge funds maintain short positions or use leverage. Instead, many simply exploit niche areas of expertise in a sophisticated manner; hedging and leverage may or may not be part of it.

Fee structures have evolved to include management fees in addition to Jones's incentive fee. The performance fees we discussed previously may vary from his simple 20% while including hurdle rates and other mechanisms.

Investors in modern hedge funds are subject to extended holding periods (known as **lockup periods**) and subsequent **notice periods** before an investment redemption is possible. Such mandatory periods combine with a lighter regulatory compliance burden (in certain areas) than mutual funds face, for instance, allowing hedge funds more flexibility. Most hedge funds do not need to guarantee liquidity on one day's redemption notice as the large majority of mutual funds do. Instead, they may avail themselves of less liquid and unnoticed opportunities, the true valuation of which may at times be opaque.

Hedge funds are generally deemed riskier from an oversight (fraud risk) point of view, but some hedge funds take less absolute market risk in their portfolio construction than registered products available to retail investors might take. The distinction between regulatory risk and illiquidity risk when compared with true market risk is often confused.

Hedge Funds and Mutual Funds

Overall, the term "hedge fund" today can be seen more as a reference to a certain vehicle type—a private limited partnership or offshore fund open only to high-net-worth and institutional investors from a regulatory perspective—that may contain different types of investments and where incentive fees are allowed to be charged. This situation remains quite distinct from the mutual fund world, where incentive fees are typically not allowed and investment and liquidity restrictions are more tightly defined. Although in recent years, there has been some "blurring of the lines" with the introduction of so-called liquid alternative mutual funds and what are known as UCIT funds in Europe (many of which offer more hedged styles and approaches than traditional daily-liquidity products), such offerings are not to be confused with true limited-access and limited-liquidity hedge funds.

A contemporary hedge fund generally has the following characteristics:

- It is a creatively managed portfolio of investments involved in one or more asset classes (equities, credit, fixed income, commodities, futures, foreign exchange, and sometimes even hard assets, such as real estate), sometimes trading in different geographic regions, that is often leveraged, generally takes both long and short positions (when possible), and quite often uses derivatives to express a view or establish a hedge.
- Its goal is to generate high returns, either in an absolute sense or on a risk-adjusted basis relative to its portfolio-level volatility. It may be hard to gauge a hedge fund's performance relative to a traditional index benchmark (after all, low correlation with traditional asset investing is frequently a selling point), and it generally enjoys light investment restrictions that are detailed in each hedge fund's private placement offering memorandum.
- It is set up as a private investment partnership or offshore fund that under certain legal restrictions (which vary by jurisdiction) make the offering open to a limited number of investors willing and able to make a substantive initial investment.

As noted previously, restrictions on **redemptions** are typically imposed. Investors may be required to keep their money in the hedge fund for a minimum period (referred to as a lockup period) before they are allowed to make withdrawals or redeem shares. Investors may be required to give notice of their intent to redeem; the notice period is typically 30–90 days. To redeem shares, investors may be charged a fee, typically payable to the fund itself (rather than the manager) so as not to disadvantage remaining investors in the fund, particularly in circumstances where the redemption takes place during the lockup period.

This characteristic is called a *soft lockup*, and it offers a path (albeit an expensive one) to redeem early. Again, such restrictions allow hedge fund managers more flexibility in portfolio construction, giving them leeway to invest in situations in which time may be needed to generate an expected return and that, therefore, are not typically suitable for a mutual fund that offers daily liquidity.

Funds of hedge funds are funds that hold a portfolio of hedge funds. They create a diversified portfolio of hedge funds and invite participation from smaller investors or those who do not have the resources, time, or expertise to choose among hedge fund managers. Also, the managers of funds of hedge funds (commonly shortened to "funds of funds") are required to have some expertise in conducting due diligence on hedge funds and may be able to negotiate better redemption or fee terms than individual investors can. Funds of funds may diversify across fund strategies, investment regions, and management styles.

Funds of funds may charge an additional 1% management fee and an additional 10% incentive fee (1 and 10) on top of the fees charged by the underlying hedge funds held in the fund of funds. At both the hedge fund level and the fund-of-funds level, the incentive fee is typically calculated on profits net of management fees.

Fee structures are important to scrutinize here. Fee layering can sorely reduce the initial gross return of an investment in a hedge fund or fund of funds for the end investor. Each hedge fund into which a fund of funds invests is structured to receive a management fee plus an incentive fee. The result may be that the investor is paying fees more than once for the management of the same assets. Finally, liquidity can be of additional concern for investors in funds of funds in times of crisis, when fund redemptions can hurt performance.

EXAMPLE 10

Fill in the blank: The goal of hedge fund redemption restrictions is typically to _____ manager flexibility.

Solution: The goal of hedge fund redemption restrictions is typically to <u>increase</u> hedge fund manager flexibility.

EXAMPLE 11

Define funds of hedge funds, and identify their primary purpose.

Solution: Funds of hedge funds are funds that hold a portfolio of hedge funds. Their primary purpose is to add value in manager selection and due diligence and create a diversified portfolio of hedge funds accessible to smaller investors.

Few investors were worried about high fees as hedge funds were achieving average net-of-fee returns of 10%–20% in the 1990s and early 2000s, but as returns migrated toward 6%–9% and the drag on returns from fee structures became much more relevant on a percentage basis, institutional investors challenged these high fees. In late 2013, the largest pension plan in the United States, CalPERS, announced it would curtail its hedge fund allocations partly for this reason.

According to Eurekahedge, by 2018 the average hedge fund fee level had compressed to 1.3% in management fees and 15.5% in incentive fees—considerably less than the 2 and 20 structure envisions but still quite high relative to traditional mutual funds. Fund-of-funds fee levels similarly have compressed; funds of funds can be found charging, for example, either a 1% flat management fee or a 50 bp management fee and only a 5% incentive fee.

Realization of the value-destruction potential of fee layers conspired with increasingly compressed hedge fund returns (for a variety of reasons) to leave funds of funds far less popular in 2020 than they were between 2000 and 2005. Still, a fund of funds may offer compensating advantages, such as access for smaller investors, diversified hedge fund portfolios, better redemption terms, and due diligence expertise.

The overall popularity of hedge funds is illustrated by AUM and net asset flows. Hedge Fund Research, Inc. (HFR, or HFRI in named indexes), reported that AUM grew from approximately $39 billion in 1990 to $491 billion in 2000 and to $3.32 trillion as of December 2019—a clear decade-spanning boom in investment, even if growth has slowed somewhat in the last five years.

Exhibit 9 compares the returns, risk, and performance measures for the HFRI Fund of Funds Composite Index, the MSCI ACWI Index, and the Bloomberg Barclays Global Aggregate Index. The HFRI Fund of Funds Composite Index is an equally weighted performance index of funds of hedge funds included in the HFR Database. Hedge fund indexes suffer from issues related to self-reporting and **survivorship bias**. Survivorship bias relates to the inclusion of only current investment funds in a database. As such, the returns of funds that are no longer available in the marketplace (have been liquidated) are

EXHIBIT 9   Historical Risk–Return Characteristics of Hedge Funds and Other Investments, 1990–2014

	FoF	Global Stocks	Global Bonds
Annualized return	7.2%	6.9%	6.3%
Annualized volatility	6.0%	16.5%	5.8%
Sharpe ratio	0.63	0.21	0.49
Sortino ratio	0.74	0.43	1.09
Percentage of positive months	69.3%	61.3%	62.7%
Best month	6.8%	11.9%	6.2%
Worst month	–7.5%	–19.8%	–3.8%
Worst drawdown	–22.2%	–54.6%	–10.1%
FoF correlation (avg. monthly)		0.56%	0.07%

Sources: Fund-of-funds (FoF) data are from the HFRI Fund of Funds Composite Index; global stock data are from the MSCI ACWI Index; global bond data are from the Bloomberg Barclays Global Aggregate Index.

excluded from the database. However, the HFRI Fund of Funds Composite Index reflects the actual performance of portfolios of hedge funds. The measures shown here may reflect a lower reported return because of the added layer of fees, but they likely represent a fairer, more conservative, and more accurate estimate of average hedge fund performance than HFR's composite index of individual funds. The returns are likely just mildly biased toward equity long–short funds since these are always a substantial portion of funds of funds' allocation mix.

As shown in Exhibit 9, over the 25-year period between 1990 and 2014, hedge funds enjoyed higher returns than either stocks or bonds and a standard deviation almost identical to that of bonds. On the basis of the Sortino ratio, hedge funds do not appear as attractive as bonds if returns are adjusted for downside deviation, as reflected in the relative Sortino measures shown in Exhibit 9. The worst **drawdown**, or period of largest cumulative negative returns for hedge funds and global equities, began in 2007 (when each peaked) and ended in 2009.

Notwithstanding this period of stress, when accounting for hedge fund returns' modest overall correlation with global stock returns (0.56) and negligible correlation with global bond returns (0.07) over this 25-year period, hedge funds have certainly offered added value to institutional investors as a portfolio diversification agent.

Notably, as shown in Exhibit 10, for the subsequent five-year period between 2015 and 2019, the absolute return of funds of funds relative in particular to global equities has declined, while their performance correlation with equity markets actually increased. This trend has made hedge fund allocations arguably less useful and also somewhat less popular. But some allocators have continued to find value to maintain or actually increase their allocation to a mix of hedge funds as a bond market substitute in their overall portfolio building.

EXHIBIT 10   Historical Risk-Return Characteristics of Hedge Funds and Other Investments, 2015–2019

	FoF	Global Stocks	Global Bonds
Annualized return	2.48%	10.41%	2.42%
Annualized volatility	1.08%	11.42%	1.33%
FoF Correlation (avg. monthly)		0.86%	0.03%

Sources: Fund-of-funds (FoF) data are from the HFRI Fund of Funds Composite Index; global stock data are from the MSCI ACWI Index; global bond data are from the Bloomberg Barclays Global Aggregate Index (USD Unhedged). The risk-free rate used in the Sharpe ratio calculation is from the average of one-month T-bill rates over the period.

4.2. Hedge Fund Strategies

Hedge funds are typically classified by strategy, although categorizations vary. Many classifying organizations focus on the most common strategies, but others classify on the basis of different criteria, such as the underlying assets in which the funds are invested. Classifications change over time as new strategies, often based on new products and market opportunities, are introduced. Classifying hedge funds is important so that investors can review aggregate performance data, select strategies with which to build a portfolio of funds, and select or construct appropriate performance benchmarks. HFR classifies hedge funds under four broad strategy categories: event-driven, relative value, macro, and equity hedge. As of March 2019, hedge fund assets stood at approximately $3.18 trillion. Exhibit 11 shows the approximate percentage of hedge fund AUM by strategy, according to HFR, for 1990, 2010, and 2019. Based on this AUM measure, event-driven and relative value strategies have grown in popularity during the last 30 years, while macro and equity hedge funds have declined.

EXHIBIT 11   Percentage of AUM by Strategy

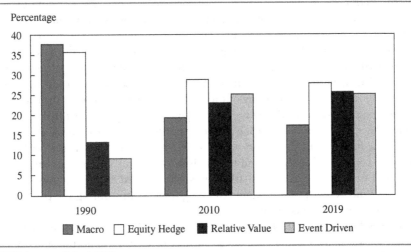

Source: HFR data, as of March 2019.

4.2.1. Equity Hedge Strategies

Equity hedge strategies can be thought of as the original hedge fund category. They are focused on public equity markets and take long and short positions in equity and equity derivative securities. Most equity hedge strategies use a bottom-up security-specific approach—company-level analysis, followed by overall industry analysis, followed by overall market analysis—with relatively balanced long and short exposures. A top-down approach, in contrast, entails global macro analysis, followed by sector/regional analysis, followed by individual company analysis or any market-timing approach. Some strategies use individual equities only, whereas others use index ETF securities for portfolio-balancing purposes. Examples of equity hedge strategies include the following:

- **Market neutral.** These strategies use quantitative (technical) and fundamental analysis to identify under- and overvalued equity securities. The hedge fund takes long positions in securities it has identified as undervalued and short positions in securities it has identified as overvalued. The hedge fund tries to maintain a net position that is neutral with respect to market risk and other risk factors (size, industry, momentum, value, etc.). Ideally, the portfolio has an overall beta of approximately zero. The intent is to profit from the movements of individual securities while remaining largely indifferent to market risk. To achieve a meaningful return, market-neutral portfolios may require the application of leverage. They are generally stable, low-return portfolios but are exposed to occasional spurts of volatility, at which point sudden leverage reduction may be required.

- **Fundamental Long–Short (L/S) growth.** These strategies use fundamental analysis to identify companies expected to exhibit high growth and capital appreciation. The hedge fund takes long positions in these companies while shorting companies with business models that are being disintermediated or are under downward pressure—where continued revenue growth is deemed unlikely. Long–short growth managers tend to end up long-biased overall.
- **Fundamental value.** These strategies use fundamental analysis to identify companies that are deemed undervalued and unloved for any number of corporate-performance or sector-driven reasons, but the manager identifies a path to corporate rejuvenation. The hedge fund takes long positions in these companies and sometimes hedges the portfolio by shorting index ETFs or more growth-oriented companies deemed overvalued. Such managers also tend to be long biased and have a positive factor bias to value as well as to small-cap factors since many underappreciated value situations tend to reside in the small-cap sector.
- **Short biased.** These strategies use quantitative (technical) and fundamental analysis to focus the bulk of their portfolio on shorting overvalued equity securities (against limited long-side exposures or none at all). Many of these funds are more forensic in their fundamental analysis, and some turn activist by trying to expose previously unrecognized accounting or business flaws, thereby also improving their own portfolio's chance for profits. The degree to which these funds adjust their short exposure over time varies by manager. Such managers tend to be contrarian by nature, and the funds can be useful additions to larger portfolios in terms of weathering periods of market stress. Short-biased managers, however, have had a difficult time overall posting meaningful long-term returns during the past 30 years of generally positive market conditions.
- **Sector specific.** These strategies exploit manager expertise in a particular sector and use quantitative (technical) and fundamental analysis to identify opportunities. Technology, biotech/life sciences, and financial services are common areas of focus. Given our era of increased democratization in the dissemination of news, added sector-specialist expertise may be a prerequisite for truly differentiated security selection. The more complex a sector (as in biotechnology, with its binary outcomes on drug trials) or the more opaqueness in accounting practices (as with financial or insurance stocks), the more value sector-specific managers bring.

4.2.2. Event-Driven Strategies

Event-driven strategies seek to profit from defined catalyst events, typically those that involve changes in corporate structure, such as an acquisition or restructuring. This strategy is considered to be underpinned by bottom-up security-specific analysis, as opposed to top-down analysis. Investments may include long and short positions in common and preferred stocks, debt securities, and options. Further subdivisions of this category by HFR include the following:

- **Merger arbitrage.** Generally, these strategies involve going long (buying) the stock of the company being acquired at a discount to its announced takeover price and going short (selling) the stock of the acquiring company when the merger or acquisition is announced. The manager may expect to profit once the initial deal spread narrows to the closing value of the transaction after it is fully consummated. The spread exists because there is always some uncertainty over whether the deal will actually close in the face of legal and regulatory hurdles. Equally, a sudden change in market conditions could damage the perceived attractiveness of the merger to the acquirer, who could step away. Shorting the acquirer is also a way to express the risk that the acquirer has overpaid for the acquisition or will suffer from an increased debt load following the merger. The primary risk in merger arbitrage is that the announced merger or acquisition fails to take place and the deal spread re-widens to pre-merger levels before the hedge fund manager is able to unwind its position. Since the expected risk and return on a merger arbitrage strategy typically starts off being quite modest, managers regularly use leverage to amplify merger spreads into financially worth-while total return targets. Unfortunately, this application of leverage also increases the mag-nitude of losses should real-world circumstances move against the manager's bet.

- **Distressed/restructuring.** These strategies focus on the securities of companies that are either in bankruptcy or perceived to be near bankruptcy. One strategy sees hedge funds simply purchasing fixed-income securities that are trading at a significant discount to par but are still senior enough to be deemed "money good" (backed by enough corporate assets to be fully repayable at par or at least at a significant premium to the available bond purchase price) in a bankruptcy situation. Alternatively, a hedge fund may purchase the so-called fulcrum debt instrument that is expected to convert into new equity in the case of a restruc-turing or bankruptcy.
- **Special situations.** These strategies focus on opportunities to get involved in the equity of companies that are engaged in restructuring activities other than mergers, acquisitions, or bankruptcy. These activities include security issuance or repurchase, special capital distribu-tions, rescue finance, and asset sales/spin-offs.
- **Activist.** The term "activist" is short for "activist shareholder." Here, managers secure suf-ficient equity holdings to allow them to influence a company's policies or direction. The hedge fund manager thus tries to create his or her own catalyst, influencing the investment's ultimate destiny by creating a desired corporate outcome. For example, the activist hedge fund may advocate for divestitures, restructuring, capital distributions to shareholders, or changes in management and company strategy that will affect their equity holdings. Such hedge funds are distinct from private equity because they operate primarily in the public equity market.

These event-driven strategies tend to be long biased. Although merger arbitrage is the least long biased among them, the strategy still tends to suffer when market conditions weaken because the risk that mergers will fail increases.

4.2.3. Relative Value Strategies

Relative value funds seek to profit from a pricing discrepancy, an unusual short-term relation-ship, between related securities. The expectation is that the pricing discrepancy will be resolved over time. Examples of relative value strategies include the following:

- **Convertible bond arbitrage.** This conceptually market-neutral investment strategy seeks to exploit a perceived mispricing between a convertible bond and its component parts— namely, the underlying bond and the embedded stock option—relative to the pricing of a reference equity into which the bond may someday convert. The strategy typically involves buying convertible debt securities and simultaneously selling a certain amount of the same issuer's common stock. Residual bankruptcy risks can be further hedged using equity put options or credit default swap derivative hedges on the credit of the issuer.
- **Fixed income (general).** These strategies focus on the relative value within the fixed-income markets, with an emphasis on sovereign debt and, at times, the relative pricing of investment-grade corporate debt. Strategies may incorporate long–short trades between two

different issuers, between corporate and government issuers, between different parts of the same issuer's capital structure, or between different parts of an issuer's yield curve. Currency dynamics and government yield-curve considerations may also come into play.

- **Fixed income (asset backed, mortgage backed, and high yield).** These strategies focus on the relative value of a variety of higher-yielding securities, including asset-backed securities (ABS), mortgage-backed securities (MBS), and high-yield loans and bonds. The hedge fund seeks both to earn an attractive highly secured coupon and to take advantage of relative security mispricings. At times, some of these securities may be further parsed into structured note products with unique return attributes relative to interest rate movements and general credit spread changes. Opaque **mark-to-market** pricing and illiquidity issues are significant considerations. "Mark-to-market" refers to the current expected fair market value for which a given security would likely be available for purchase or sale if traded in current market conditions, but in the case of structured products, absent hard broker/dealer quotes, this is often a "mark-to-model" type of calculation that is less reliable than an actual bid–offer spread seen between active market participants.

- **Volatility.** These strategies typically use options to go long or short market volatility, either in a specific asset class or across asset classes. For example, a short-volatility strategy involves selling options to earn the premiums and benefit from calm markets but can experience significant losses during unexpected periods of market stress. A long-volatility strategy tends to suffer the cost of small premiums in anticipation of larger market moves where positions may benefit from both directionality and the ability to rebalance option-based exposure through a variety of methods.

- **Multi-strategy.** These strategies trade relative value within and across asset classes or instruments. Rather than focusing on one type of trade (e.g., convertible arbitrage), a single basis for a trade (e.g., volatility), or a particular asset class (e.g., fixed income), this strategy instead looks for investment opportunities wherever they might exist, often with different pods of managers executing their own unique market approaches. The goal of a multi-strategy manager is to initially deploy (and later redeploy) capital efficiently and quickly across a variety of strategy areas as market conditions change.

4.2.4. Macro and CTA Strategies

Macro hedge funds emphasize a top-down approach to identify economic trends. Trades are made on the basis of expected movements in economic variables. Generally, these funds trade opportunistically in fixed-income, equity, currency, and commodity markets. Macro hedge funds use long and short positions to profit from a view on the overall direction of the market as it is influenced by major economic trends and events. Macro managers were generally very successful during the 1980s and 1990s, but return profiles have weakened over the past two decades as markets have arguably become more closely managed by central bankers. Because macro managers generally enjoy periods of higher volatility compared with lower volatility, the active moves by national authorities, such as central banks, to smooth out economic shocks likely shrink managers' investment sphere.

Managed futures funds are actively managed funds making diversified directional investments primarily in the futures markets on the basis of a variety of technical and fundamental strategies. Managed futures funds are also known as commodity trading advisers (CTAs) because they historically focused on commodity futures. However, CTAs may include investments in a variety of futures, including commodities, equities, fixed income, and foreign exchange. CTAs generally use models that measure trends and momentum over different time horizons. Investing in CTAs can be useful for portfolio diversification, particularly in times of strong trending market conditions and especially during periods of acute market stress when other fundamental strategies may be expected to perform poorly. However, mean-reverting markets, which may cause false momentum breakout signals, can lead to uncomfortable and occasionally extended drawdown periods before strong trends emerge for the CTA. To the extent that many CTAs have migrated to trade more and more financial products (such as stock index futures and bond futures), the reliability of CTA diversification benefits has diminished.

4.3. Hedge Funds and Diversification Benefits

Hedge funds were generally a niche business throughout much of the 1980s and 1990s, supported mostly by high-net-worth investors. Traditional long–short equity managers shared the spotlight with successful macro-oriented managers, bringing to mind George Soros's Quantum Fund or Julian Robertson's Tiger Management, which took advantage of global currency, equity, and interest rate imbalances between countries.

But when hedge funds generally performed well during the dot-com bubble unwinding of 2000–2002—particularly compared with traditional long-only investment products— endowments, foundations, and pensions started to allocate more money to them. Initially investing in funds of funds, after the 2008 period of market stress, they increasingly made direct allocations. They did so in spite of the high fees charged by hedge funds, and this trend stemmed from an overall effort to achieve better diversification and risk mitigation. This latter era of hedge funds can be characterized by a search for absolute and uncorrelated risk-adjusted returns rather than for outsized upside performance. The institutionalization of the hedge fund industry changed its very nature: Most hedge funds failed to keep pace with the positive equity and bond market advances of 2009–2019, but they maintained a place in institutional asset allocations because of their risk-diversification properties.

5. PRIVATE CAPITAL

5.1. Overview of Private Capital

Private capital is the broad term for funding provided to companies that is not sourced from the public markets, such as proceeds raised from the sale of equities, bonds, and other securities on exchanges, nor from traditional institutional providers, such as a government or bank. When capital is raised from sources other than public markets and traditional institutions and it is provided in the form of an equity investment, it is called private equity. If similarly sourced capital is instead extended to companies through a loan or other form of debt, it is referred to as private debt. Private capital looks at the entire capital structure, comprising private equity and private debt.

The private capital space largely consists of private investment funds and entities that invest in the equity or debt securities of companies, real estate, or other assets that are privately held. Many private investment firms have private equity and private debt arms; however, these teams typically refrain from investing in the same assets or businesses to avoid overexposure to a single investment and to avoid the conflict of interest that arises from sitting on both sides of the creditors' table. Private investment firms are typically referred to as "private equity firms" even when they have private debt arms. Although private equity is the largest component of private capital, using "private equity" as a generic term could be less accurate and possibly misleading because other forms of private alternative finance have grown considerably in size and popularity.

5.2. Description: Private Equity

Private equity refers to investment in privately owned companies or in public companies with the intent to take them private. As business conditions and the availability of financing change, the focus of private equity firms may change. A firm may manage many private equity funds, each composed of several investments, and the company the firm invests in is often called a **portfolio company** because it will become part of a private equity fund portfolio. According to one possible categorization, we can name leveraged buyouts, venture capital, and growth capital as the primary private equity strategies.

Private equity activity has grown over time, but it is cyclical. Exhibit 12 shows the portion of committed capital that has not yet been called; the industry term for it is "dry powder." Note that detailed information on private equity activity is not always readily available.

EXHIBIT 12   Global Private Equity: Uncalled Capital by Fund Type (US$ trillions)

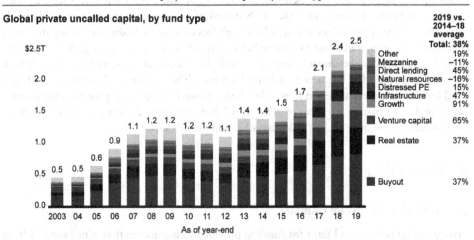

Buyout ($B) 183 176 256 379 447 493 491 440 410 378 469 485 521 563 665 796 832

Notes: Other includes fund-of-funds, secondaries and coinvestments; buyout includes balanced and buyout funds; discrepancies in bar heights displaying the same value are due to rounding

Source: Bain & Company, "Global Private Equity Report 2020" (2020).

5.2.1. Leveraged Buyouts

Leveraged buyouts (LBOs) or highly leveraged transactions arise when private equity firms establish buyout funds (or LBO funds) to acquire public companies or established private companies, with a significant percentage of the purchase price financed through debt. The target company's assets typically serve as collateral for the debt, and the target company's cash flows are expected to be sufficient to service the debt. The debt becomes part of the target company's capital structure if the buyout goes through. After the buyout, the target company becomes or remains a privately owned company. LBOs are sometimes referred to as "going-private" transactions because after the acquisition of a publicly traded company, the target company's equity is substantially no longer publicly traded. (When the target company is private, it is not a going-private transaction.) The LBO may also be of a specific type. In **management buyouts** (MBOs), the current management team is involved in the acquisition, and in **management buy-ins** (MBIs), the current management team is being replaced and the acquiring team will be involved in managing the company. LBO managers seek to add value by improving company operations, boosting revenue, and ultimately increasing profits and cash flows. Cash-flow growth, in order of contribution, comes from organic revenue growth, cost reductions and restructuring, acquisitions, and then all other sources. The financial returns in this category, however, depend to a large extent on the use of leverage. If debt financing is unavailable or costly, LBOs are less likely to take place.

5.2.2. Venture Capital

Venture capital (VC) entails investing in or providing financing to private companies with high growth potential. Typically these are start-ups or young companies, but venture capital can be provided at a variety of stages, ranging from the inception of an idea for a company to the point when the company is about to launch an IPO (initial public offering) or be acquired. The investment return required varies on the basis of the company's stage of development. Investors in early-stage companies will demand higher expected returns relative to later-stage investors because the earlier the stage of development, the higher the risk.

Venture capitalists, like all private equity managers, are not passive investors. They are actively involved with the companies in which they invest.

VC funds typically invest in companies and receive an equity interest but may also provide financing in the form of debt (commonly, convertible debt).

Formative-stage financing is for a company that is still in the process of being formed. Its steps are as follows:

A. *Pre-seed capital*, or *angel investing*, is capital provided at the idea stage. Funds may be used to transform the idea into a business plan and to assess market potential. The amount of financing at this stage is typically small and provided by individuals, often friends and family, rather than by VC funds.

B. *Seed-stage financing*, or *seed capital*, generally supports product development and marketing efforts, including market research. This is the first stage at which VC funds usually invest.

C. *Early-stage financing* (early-stage VC), or *start-up stage financing*, is provided to companies that are moving toward operation but have not yet started commercial production or sales, both of which early-stage financing may be injected to initiate.

Later-stage financing (expansion VC) is provided after commercial production and sales have begun but before an IPO takes place. Funds may be used to support initial growth, a major expansion (such as a physical plant upgrade), product improvements, or a major marketing campaign.

Mezzanine-stage financing (mezzanine venture capital) prepares a company to go public. It represents the bridge financing needed to fund a private firm until it can complete an IPO or be sold. The term mezzanine-stage financing is used because this financing is provided at the stage between being a private company and being a public company. The focus is on when the financing occurs rather than the financing mechanism itself.

Formative-stage financing is generally carried out by providing ordinary or convertible preferred share sales to the investor or investors, likely the VC fund, while management retains control of the company. Later-stage financing generally involves management selling control of the company to the VC investor; financing is provided through equity and debt, although the fund may also use convertible bonds or convertible preferred shares. The VC fund offers debt financing not for reasons of income generation but, rather, for reasons of recovery and the control of assets in a bankruptcy situation. Simply put, debt financing affords the VC fund more protection than equity does.

To make an investment, a venture capitalist needs to be convinced that the portfolio company's management team is competent and is armed with a solid business plan and strong prospects for growth. Because these investments are not made in mature businesses with years of operational and financial performance history, estimating company valuations on the basis of future prospects is highly uncertain. Accurate estimation is more difficult than in LBO investing, which targets mature, underperforming public companies. Certainty around valuation increases as the portfolio company matures and moves into later-stage financing, but even then, there remains more certainty around LBO investments. Exhibit 13 take us through the growth stages of a company and the types of financing it may receive at each stage.

EXHIBIT 13   The Private Equity Stage Continuum

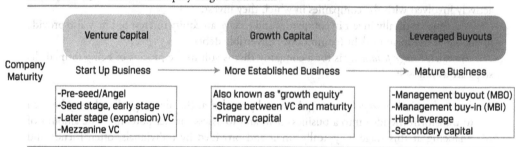

Source: Private Equity Primer, "What Is Private Equity" (12 February 2016). www.pe-primer.com/dealsherpapress/2016/2/12/bbcati52gcwdzrl34pts0x2tl783do (accessed June 18, 2020).

5.2.3. Other Private Equity Strategies

Among several other specialties, some private equity firms specialize in *growth capital*, also known as growth equity or minority equity investing. Growth capital generally refers to minority equity investments, whereby the firm takes a less-than-controlling interest in more mature companies that are looking for capital to expand or restructure operations, enter new markets, or finance major acquisitions. Many times, minority equity investing is initiated and sought by the management of the investee company, which is interested in realizing earnings from selling a portion of its shares before the company can go public but still seeks to retain control and participation in the success of the company. Although this scenario occurs most commonly with private companies, publicly quoted companies can seek private equity capital through PIPEs (private investments in public equities). Other private equity strategies secure returns by investing in companies in specific industries.

EXAMPLE 12

Identify two of the four stages of the private equity continuum and the company growth stage each finances.

Solution: The stages of the entire PE continuum and their associated growth stage financing are as follows:

1. Venture capital focuses on start-up and seed-stage businesses.
2. Growth equity focuses on more established businesses.
3. Recapitalizations focus on more mature businesses, either healthy or distressed.
4. Buyouts/LBOs focuses on mature businesses.

5.2.4. Exit Strategies

Private equity firms seek to improve new or underperforming businesses and then exit them at higher valuations, buying and holding companies for an average of five years. The time to exit, however, can range from less than six months to more than 10 years. Before deciding on an exit strategy, private equity managers take into account the dynamics of the industry in which the portfolio company competes, the overall economic cycle, interest rates, and company performance. Managers pursue the following common exit strategies:

- **Trade sale.** This refers to the sale of a company to a strategic buyer, such as a competitor. A trade sale can be conducted by auction or by private negotiation. Benefits include: (a) an immediate cash exit for the private equity fund, (b) the potential willingness of strategic buyers to pay more because they anticipate synergies with their own business, (c) fast and simple execution, (d) lower transaction costs than for an IPO, and (e) lower levels of disclosure and higher confidentiality than for an IPO because private equity firms generally deal with only one other party. Disadvantages of trade sales include: (a) possible opposition by management (management may wish to avoid being purchased by a competitor for job security reasons), (b) lower attractiveness to employees of the portfolio company than for an IPO (an IPO allows for the monetizing of shares), (c) a limited universe of potential trade buyers, and (d) a potentially lower price for the sale than would be achieved from an IPO.
- **IPO.** In an initial public offering, the portfolio company sells its shares, including some or all of those held by the private equity firm, to public investors. Advantages of an IPO exit include (a) the potential for the highest price, (b) management approval (because management will be retained), (c) publicity for the private equity firm, and (d) future upside potential (because the private equity firm may choose to remain a large shareholder). Disadvantages of an IPO exit include (a) the high transaction costs paid to investment banks and lawyers, (b) long lead times, (c) the risk of stock market volatility (including short-term focus of some investors), (d) onerous disclosure requirements, (e) a potential lockup period (which requires the private equity firm to retain an equity position for a specified period after the IPO), and (f) the fact that IPOs are usually appropriate only for larger companies with attractive growth profiles.

- **Recapitalization.** Recapitalization in the context of private equity describes the steps a firm takes to increase or introduce leverage to its portfolio company and pay itself a dividend out of the new capital structure. A recapitalization is not a true exit strategy, because the private equity firm typically maintains control; however, it does allow the private equity investor to extract money from the company to pay its investors and improve IRR. A recapitalization may be a prelude to a later exit. However, LP investors should be aware that a recapitalization can be used as a method for the GP to manipulate fund IRRs.
- **Secondary sales.** This approach represents a sale of the company to another private equity firm or another group of investors. With the growth of "dry powder" (Exhibit 12), we have seen an increase in the proportion of secondary sales exits.
- **Write-off/liquidation.** A write-off occurs when a transaction has not gone well. The private equity firm revises the value of its investment downward or liquidates the portfolio company before moving on to other projects.

The foregoing exit strategies may be pursued individually or in concert or may be used for a partial exit strategy. For example, private equity funds may sell a portion of a portfolio company to a competitor via a trade sale and then complete a secondary sale to another private equity firm for the remaining portion. Company shares may also be distributed to fund investors, although such a move is unusual.

5.3. Description: Private Debt

Private debt primarily refers to the various forms of debt provided by investors to private entities. In the past decade, the expansion of the private debt market has been largely driven by private lending funds filling the gap between borrowing demand and reduced lending supply from traditional lenders in the face of tightened regulations following the 2008 financial crisis. We can organize the primary methods of private debt investing into four categories: direct lending, mezzanine loans, venture debt, and distressed debt. The broad array of debt strategies offers not only diversification benefits but also exposure to other investment spheres, such as real estate and infrastructure.

5.3.1. Direct Lending

Private debt investors get involved in direct lending by providing capital directly to borrowers and subsequently receiving interest, the original principal, and possibly other payments in exchange for their investment. As with typical bank loans, payments are usually received on a fixed schedule, and the loan itself typically is senior and secured and has covenants in place to protect the lender/investor. The loan is provided by a small number of investors to private and sometimes public entities, and it differs from traditional debt instruments, such as bonds, that are issued to many participants and can be publicly traded in the market.

Direct lending primarily involves private debt firms (or private equity firms with private debt arms) establishing funds with money raised from investors looking for higher-yielding debt. Fund managers will then seek opportunities to deploy that capital, such as providing a loan to a mid-market corporation or extending debt to another private equity fund that is seeking financing for acquisitions. In general, private debt funds provide debt, at higher interest rates, to entities that require capital but lack favorable alternatives to traditional bank lenders, who themselves may be uninterested or unable to provide debt to these borrowers. As in private equity, private debt fund managers conduct thorough due diligence before selecting the fund's investments.

In direct lending, many firms may also provide debt in the form of a *leveraged loan*, which is a loan that is itself levered. In other words, private debt firms that invest in leveraged loans will borrow money to finance the debt that the firm then extends to another borrower. By using leverage, a private debt firm can enhance the return on its loan portfolio.

5.3.2. Mezzanine Debt

In private debt, mezzanine debt refers to private credit that is subordinated to senior secured debt but is senior to equity in the borrower's capital structure. Mezzanine debt makes a pool of additional capital available to borrowers beyond senior secured debt, and it is often used to finance LBOs, recapitalizations, corporate acquisitions, and similar transactions. Because of its typically junior ranking and the fact that it is usually unsecured, mezzanine debt is riskier than senior secured debt; to compensate investors for this heightened risk profile, investors commonly demand higher interest rates and may require options for equity participation. Mezzanine debt often comes with additional features, such as warrants or conversion rights, which provide equity participation to lenders/investors, meaning they have the option of converting their debt into equity or purchasing the equity of the underlying borrower under certain circumstances.

5.3.3. Venture Debt

Venture debt is private debt funding provided to start-up or early-stage companies with venture capital backing that may be generating little or negative cash flow. Entrepreneurs may seek venture debt, which often takes the form of a line of credit or term loan, as a way to obtain additional financing without further diluting shareholder ownership in their business. Venture debt can complement existing equity financing, allowing shareholders to maintain ownership and control over the company for a longer period of time. Similar to mezzanine debt, venture debt may carry additional features that compensate the investor/lender for the increased risk of default or for the fact that start-up and early-stage companies often lack substantial assets that can be pledged as collateral for the debt. One such feature could grant the lender rights to purchase equity in the borrowing company under certain circumstances.

5.3.4. Distressed Debt

Involvement in distressed debt typically entails buying the debt of mature companies with financial difficulty. These companies may be in bankruptcy proceedings, have defaulted on debt, or seem likely to default on debt. Some investors identify companies with a temporary cash-flow problem but a good business plan that will help the company survive and, in the end, flourish. These investors buy the company's debt in expectation of both the company and its debt increasing in value. Turnaround investors buy debt and plan to be more active in the management and direction of the company. They seek distressed companies to restructure and revive.

5.3.5. Other Private Debt Strategies

Private debt firms may have specialties other than the aforementioned strategies, one of which is investing in or issuing collateralized loan obligations (CLOs), which are leveraged structured vehicles that are collateralized by a portfolio of loans covering a diverse range of tranches, issuers, and industries. A CLO manager extends several loans to corporations—usually to firms involved in LBOs, corporate acquisitions, or similar transactions—pools these loans together, and then divides that pool into various tranches of debt and equity that differ in seniority and security. The CLO manager then sells each tranche to different investors according to their risk profile; the most senior portion of the CLO will be the least risky, and the most junior portion of the CLO (i.e., equity) will be the riskiest.

Another type of debt that could be directly extended to borrowers is **unitranche debt**. Unitranche debt consists of a hybrid or blended loan structure that combines different tranches of secured and unsecured debt into a single loan with a single, blended interest rate. Since unitranche debt is a blend of secured and unsecured debt, the interest rate on this type of loan will generally fall in between the interest rates often demanded on secured and unsecured debt, and the unitranche loan itself will usually be structured between senior and subordinated debt in terms of priority ranking.

Some private debt firms invest in real estate debt or infrastructure debt. *Real estate debt* refers to loans and other forms of debt provided for real estate financing, where a specified real estate asset or property serves as collateral. *Infrastructure debt* encompasses the many forms of debt used to finance the construction, operation, and maintenance of infrastructure assets.

Private debt firms may also provide *specialty loans*, where debt is extended to niche borrowers in specific situations. For example, litigation finance is the practice of a specialist funding company providing debt to clients, usually plaintiffs in litigation, for their legal fees and expenses in exchange for a portion of any case winnings.

EXAMPLE 13

Which of the following is not considered a strategy in private debt investing?

A. Direct lending
B. Recapitalization
C. Mezzanine debt

Solution: B is correct. Recapitalization is when a private equity firm increases leverage or introduces it to the company and pays itself a dividend.

EXAMPLE 14

Which of the following forms of debt are likely to have additional features, such as warrants or conversion rights?

A. Mezzanine debt
B. Venture debt
C. Both A and B

Solution: C is correct. Both mezzanine and venture debt are likely to have additional features, such as warrants and conversion rights, to compensate debt holders for increased risk, including the risk of default.

5.4. Risk/Return of Private Equity

The higher-return opportunities that private equity funds may provide relative to traditional investments are a function of their ability to invest in private companies, their influence on portfolio companies' management and operations, and their use of leverage. Investing in private equity, including venture capital, is riskier than investing in common stocks. Investors require a higher return for accepting higher risk, including illiquidity and leverage risks.

Exhibit 14 shows the mean annual returns for the Cambridge Associates US Private Equity index, the NASDAQ index, and the S&P 500 Index for a variety of periods ending 31 December 2019. Because private equity returns are based on IRR, however, it is difficult to identify reliable benchmarks for comparing returns to investments. Some investors may use the public market equivalent (PME) to match the timing of cash flows with the public market. Other investors may use an index of publicly traded private equity firms as a benchmark for private equity returns.

EXHIBIT 14   Comparison of Mean Annual Returns for US Private Equity and US Stocks

Index	1 Year	5 Years	10 Years	20 Years	25 Years
US private equity	13.95	12.00	14.35	11.08	13.24
NASDAQ	35.23	13.63	14.74	4.03	10.43
S&P 500	31.49	11.70	13.56	6.06	10.22

Source: US Private Equity index and selected benchmark statistics, 31 December 2019, Cambridge Associates.

Published private equity indexes may be an unreliable measure of performance. Measuring historical private equity performance is challenging; as with hedge funds, private equity return indexes rely on self-reporting and are subject to survivorship, backfill, and other biases, which typically lead to an overstatement of returns. Moreover, prior to 2009, in the absence of a liquidity event, private equity firms did not necessarily mark their investments to market. This failure to mark to market leads to an understatement of measures of volatility and correlations with other investments. Thus, data adjustments are required to more reliably measure the benefits of private equity investing. Investors should require a higher return for accepting a higher risk, including illiquidity and leverage risks.

5.5. Risk/Return of Private Debt

Private debt investments may provide higher-yielding opportunities to fixed-income investors seeking increased returns relative to traditional bonds. Private debt funds may generate higher returns by taking opportunistic positions based on market inefficiencies. Indeed, private lending funds stepped into the financing gap left by traditional lenders following the 2008 financial crisis. Investors in private debt could realize higher returns from the illiquidity premium, which is the excess return investors require to compensate for lack of liquidity, and may benefit from increased diversification in their portfolios.

The potential for higher returns is connected to higher levels of risk. Private debt investments vary in risk and return, with senior private debt providing a steadier yield and moderate risk and mezzanine private debt carrying higher growth potential, equity upside and higher risk. As a whole, however, investing in private debt is riskier than investing in traditional bonds. Investors should be aware of these risks, which include illiquidity and heightened default risk when loans are extended to riskier entities or borrowers in riskier situations.

Exhibit 15 shows annualized returns and standard deviations for private debt funds (2004–2016). Based on these figures, private debt funds appear to offer an attractive risk–return trade-off.

EXHIBIT 15   Historical Annualized Returns and Standard Deviation of Returns for Private Debt Funds, 2004–2016

Private Debt Fund	Annualized Return	Standard Deviation
Mezzanine	7.4%	2.5%
Distressed	7.9%	6.7%
Direct lending only:		
All direct lending	9.2%	2.0%
Direct lending	11.1%	3.4%
(excl. mezzanine)		

Source: S. Munday, W. Hu, T. True, and J. Zhang, "Performance of Private Credit Funds: A First Look," Institute for Private Capital (7 May 2018, pp. 32–3).

Although there is no widely used benchmark for private debt, various indexes may serve investors' purposes as long as they understand the pros and cons of each index. The ICE Bank of America Merrill Lynch Global High Yield Index (HYI) tracks publicly traded, non-investment-grade corporate bonds of large, international corporations; the S&P/LSTA U.S. Leveraged Loan Index (LLI) covers syndicated and over-the-counter traded, non-investment-grade loans for large US corporations; the S&P Net Total Return BDC Index tracks publicly traded business-development companies (BDCs); and the Cliffwater Direct Lending Index (CDLI) is based on quarterly SEC filings covering more than 60 private and public BDCs.

Investments in private equity and private debt vary in terms of risk and return because of various factors, including but not limited to ranking in an entity's capital structure. Exhibit 16 contains a graph that plots private equity and private debt categories by their risk and return levels. (Mirroring the risk–return pathway for traditional equity and debt investing, Exhibit 16 plots private equity and private debt using categories that are broadly similar to how we have defined them. Note the trade-off as investors select between junior and senior debt and between equity and debt.)

EXHIBIT 16   Private Capital Risk and Return Levels by Category

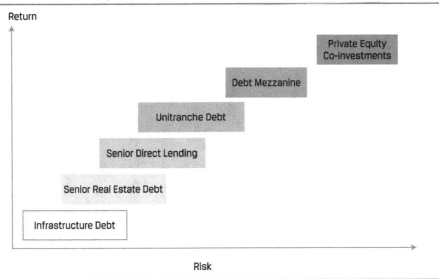

Source: Based on graph from Leon Sinclair, "The Rise of Private Debt," IHS Markit (7 August 2017).

EXAMPLE 15

Fill in the blank by choosing from among the following options:
_____ is the type of private debt expected to have the greatest excess return potential.

A. Unitranche
B. Mezzanine
C. Infrastructure

Solution: B is correct. As a junior form of subordinated debt, mezzanine private debt private debt offers higher growth potential, equity upside, and higher risk, with the comparatively highest returns. Infrastructure debt is senior and poses the lowest risk. Unitranche debt is less risky than subordinated debt but riskier than infrastructure debt and is a blend of secured and unsecured debt; its interest rate generally falls in between the interest rates often demanded on secured and unsecured debt, and the loan itself is usually structured between senior and subordinated debt.

5.6. Diversification Benefits of Investing in Private Capital

Investments in private capital funds can add a moderate diversification benefit to a portfolio of publicly traded stocks and bonds, with correlations with public market indexes varying from 0.47 to 0.75, as shown in Exhibit 17. And if investors identify skillful fund managers, they may benefit from excess returns given the additional leverage, market, and liquidity risks.

EXHIBIT 17   Private Capital's Average Correlations with Public Market Indexes, 2013–2018

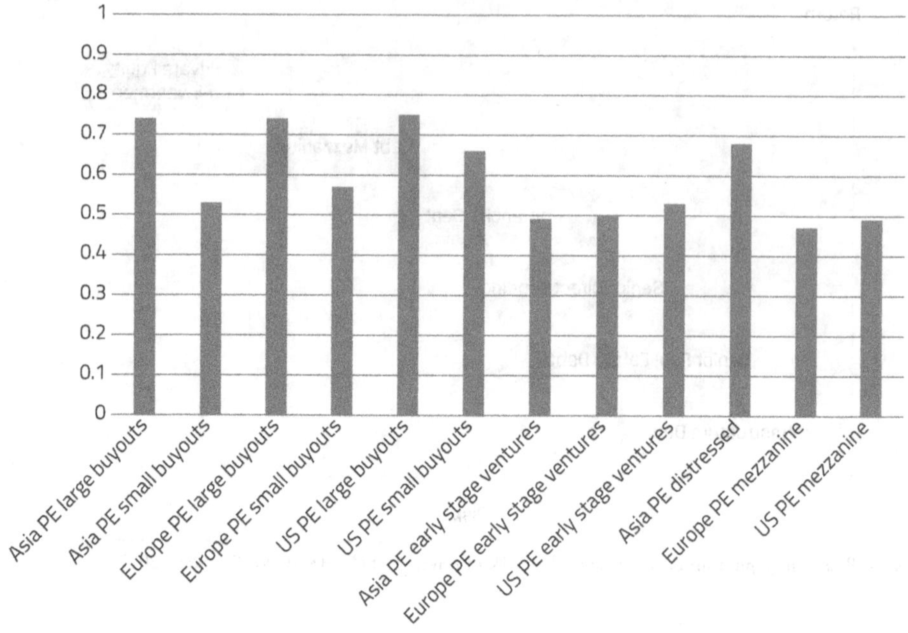

Source: MSCI. www.msci.com/www/blog-posts/did-private-capital-deliver-/01697376382 (accessed 20 July 2020).

Private equity investments may offer vintage diversification because capital is not deployed at a single point in time but invested over several years. Private debt investments, which offer more options than bonds and public forms of traditional fixed income, can also serve diversification efforts. Ultimately, investors should prudently avoid concentration risk, aiming to diversify across different managers, industries, and geographies.

6. NATURAL RESOURCES

6.1. Overview of Natural Resources

We can define natural resources as a unique asset category comprising commodities and raw land used for farming and timber. Some investors also include real estate assets and infrastructure in this category to form a "real assets" asset class, which can include inflation-protected securities and miscellaneous investments designed to protect against an increase in consumer prices. Others include timberland and farmland in their real estate portfolios. Regardless, the particular investment characteristics of natural resources, the specialized knowledge that their investors require, and their inclusion in more portfolios today than a decade ago call for a separate examination of the sector.

Commodities are broadly familiar to both professional investors and the general public. Crude oil, soybeans, copper, and gold are all commodities. Commodities are considered either hard (those that are mined, such as copper, or extracted, such as oil) or soft (those that are grown over a period of time, such as livestock, grains, and cash crops, such as coffee).

Timberland investment involves ownership of raw land and the harvesting of its trees for lumber, thus generating an income stream and the potential for capital gain; it has formed part of large institutional portfolios for decades. Farmland as an investment is a more recent phenomenon, with only a few dedicated funds involved. With population growth, weather, and water management becoming more topical, however, investors may turn to these sustainable land assets to address such concerns in their portfolio.

An examination of natural resources investment requires an important clarification up front: The aspects discussed here are associated with investing in the physical land and products that come from that land—petroleum, metals, grains—not from the companies that produce those products. Until about 20 years ago, the only commonly available investment vehicles related to this asset class were, indeed, financial instruments, such as stocks and bonds. Nowadays, the wide variety of direct investments via ETFs, limited partnerships, REITS, swaps, and futures opens the door for almost everyone to invest in these assets directly.

This section covers both commodities and land (farmland and timberland) in each subsection, leaving the broader real estate category for the next section.

6.2. Characteristics of Natural Resources

Here, we offer an overview and describe properties that separate these investments from the more commonly known asset classes addressed earlier in this chapter.

6.2.1. Commodities

Commodities are physical products that can be standardized on quality, location, and delivery for the purpose of investing. Returns on commodity investments are primarily based on changes in price rather than on income from interest, dividends, or rent. In fact, holding commodities (i.e., the physical products) incurs transportation and storage costs. Therefore, trading in physical commodities is primarily limited to a smaller group of entities that are part of the physical supply chain. Most commodity investors do not trade actual physical commodities but, rather, trade commodity derivatives. The underlying asset of the commodity derivative may be a single commodity or an index of commodities.

Because the prices of commodity derivatives are, to a significant extent, a function of the underlying commodity prices, it is important to understand the physical supply chain and general supply–demand dynamics. In fact, the price volatility associated with commodity derivative indexes is highly correlated with the underlying physical goods. This fact should make intuitive sense because the supply chain participants use futures to hedge their forward purchases and sales of the physical commodities. Imagine how uncertain food prices would be if a soybean farmer could not hedge his crop risk. Investors, sometimes referred to as speculators, trade commodity derivatives in search of profit based largely on changes or expected changes in the price of the underlying commodities. Such non-hedging investors include retail and institutional investors, hedge funds, proprietary desks within financial institutions, and trading desks operating in the physical supply chain. (Yes, commodity producers and consumers both hedge *and* speculate on commodity prices.)

Commodity sectors include precious and base (i.e., industrial) metals, energy products, and agricultural products. Exhibit 18 offers examples of each type. The relative importance, amount, and price of individual commodities evolve with society's preferences and needs. For example, the increasing industrialization of China, India, and other emerging markets has driven strong global demand for commodities. Developing markets need increasing amounts of oil, steel, and other materials to support manufacturing, infrastructure development, and the consumption demands of their populations. Emerging technologies, such as advanced cell phones and electric vehicles, create demand for new materials and destroy demand for old resources. The supply and demand for specific commodities evolves over time.

EXHIBIT 18   Examples of Commodities

Sector	Sample Commodities
Energy	Oil, natural gas, electricity, coal
Base metals	Copper, aluminum, zinc, lead, tin, nickel
Precious metals	Gold, silver, platinum
Agriculture	Grains, livestock, coffee
Other	Carbon credits, freight, forest products

Commodities may be further classified on the basis of physical location and grade or quality, for example. There are many grades and delivery locations for crude oil, and there are many grades and delivery locations for wheat. Commodity derivative contracts, therefore, specify quantity, quality, maturity date, and delivery location.

EXAMPLE 16

Which of the following can be considered as an investment in the commodities asset class?

A. A set of rare antique coins, some of which are made of silver and gold
B. A lease on an oil tanker shipping oil between Saudi Arabia and China
C. Ownership of a battery factory that uses industrial metals
D. A metric tonne of coffee packed in jute bags in a warehouse in Brazil

Solution: D is correct, assuming the investor owns the commodity directly, not via a derivatives contract. A describes an investment in collectables (whose value has more to do with the rarity of the collectible rather than the actual value of the silver or gold). B describes a financial contract—effectively, a lease or bond. C is also a financial contract that pays on the use of commodities but depends on many other factors (technology, marketing, rent, and employees) for returns.

In order to be transparent, investable, and replicable, commodity indexes typically use the price of the futures contracts rather than the prices of the underlying commodities. As a result, the performance of a commodity index can differ from the performance of the physical commodities. Different commodity indexes are composed of different commodities and weight their component commodities differently. Thus, exposures to specific commodities and commodity sectors vary. However, the low correlation between commodities and other asset

classes (e.g., stocks and bonds) means that an investor can achieve improved portfolio diversification regardless of the index she chooses.

Futures are the basis for the vast majority of commodity investment, and each contract is
for the future delivery or receipt of a set amount of the commodity in question—for example,
1,000 barrels of oil or 10 metric tonnes of cocoa. This means that the price can be formalized
in the following form:

$$\text{Futures price} \approx \text{Spot price}(1 + r) + \text{Storage costs} - \text{Convenience yield,}$$

where r is the period's short-term risk-free interest rate. The collateral posted for the contract
should also be included if a total return calculation is required. The storage and interest costs
together are sometimes referred to as the "cost of carry" or the "carry." We recognize that the
buyer of the futures contract has no immediate access to the commodity and, therefore, cannot
benefit from it, and so the futures price is adjusted for the loss of convenience, a value that
varies. For example, the convenience yield from possessing heating oil in in Finland during the
winter is higher than the convenience yield from possessing heating oil in Finland during the
summer.

Futures prices may be higher or lower than spot prices depending on the convenience
yield. When futures prices are higher than the spot price, the commodity forward curve is
upward sloping, and the prices are referred to as being in **contango**. Contango generally occurs
when there is little or no convenience yield. When futures prices are lower than the spot price,
the commodity forward curve is downward sloping, and the prices are referred to as being
in **backwardation**. Backwardation occurs when the convenience yield is high. As a rule of
thumb, a contango scenario generally lowers the return of the long-only investor, and a backwardation scenario enhances it.

The pricing of derivatives and the theories of commodity pricing are covered in other
readings in the CFA Program curriculum.

6.2.2. Timberland and Farmland

Real estate property ownership is represented by a title and may reflect access to air rights,
mineral rights, and surface rights in addition to building and land-use rights. For the purposes
of this section, we are discussing land owned or leased for the benefit of the returns it generates
from crops and timber. Given that these resources consume carbon as part of the plant life
cycle, their value comes not just from the harvest but also from the offset to human activity.
Water rights are also part of the direct and implied value of these properties; conservation
easements may create value by supporting traditions and nature conservation. As interest in
investments that adhere to environmental, social, and governance (ESG) considerations grows,
arable land may fit the criteria.

Sustained interest in these investments stems from their global nature (everyone eats,
everyone requires shelter), the income generated from selling crops, inflation protection from
holding land, and the degree of insulation they offer from financial market volatility. US farmland, for example, enjoyed positive returns during the two periods after World War II when
US GDP declined significantly (1973–1975 and 2007–2009) and during the three periods
after World War I (1915–1920, 1940–1951, and 1967–1981) when the United States experienced higher-than-normal inflation. Timberland has been part of institutional and ultra-high-
net-worth portfolios for decades, typically trading in larger units of land. Farmland can be
found in much smaller sizes—perhaps tens of or a few hundred acres. Many farms are still

family owned, as is 98% of US farmland. One of the main challenges of these investments cited by industry participants is their long market cycle, particularly in new-growth forest and crops that are picked, such as fruit.

Timberland offers an income stream based on the sale of trees, wood, and other timber products and has been not highly correlated with other asset classes. Timberland can be thought of as both a factory and a warehouse. Timber (trees) can be grown and easily stored by simply not harvesting them. This characteristic offers the flexibility of harvesting more trees when timber prices are up and delaying harvests when prices are down. The three primary return drivers are biological growth, changes in spot prices and futures prices of lumber (cut wood), and changes in the price of the underlying land.

Farmland is often perceived to provide a hedge against inflation. Similar to timberland, the returns include an income component related to harvest quantities and agricultural commodity prices. Farmland consists mainly of row crops that are planted and harvested (i.e., more than one round of planting and harvesting can occur in a year depending on the crop and the climate) and permanent crops that grow on trees (e.g., nuts) or vines (e.g., grapes). Unlike timberland, farm products must be harvested when ripe, so there is little flexibility in production. Therefore, commodity futures contracts can be combined with farmland holdings to generate an overall hedged return. Recall that a farm is inherently "long" the crop and, therefore, will sell futures that require delivery at the time of the harvest. Farmland may also be used as pastureland for livestock. Similar to timberland, farmland has three primary return drivers: harvest quantities, commodity prices (e.g., the price of corn), and land price changes.

EXAMPLE 17

Alexandra is considering buying a tract of farmland for long-term capital appreciation and current income. Which of the following factors play a role in evaluating the attractiveness of the investment?

A. The land's rights to preferential water access
B. The land's proximity to a large, privately held nature reserve
C. The land's soil chemical composition allowing the growth of a variety of crops
D. All of the above

Solution: The answer is D. A is important to ensure that crops can be grown with a reasonable chance of success. B allows for the land to be rented to the stewards of the nature reserve and to lay fallow instead of growing food for human consumption. Nature preserve foundations are interested in the land around them because: (1) runoff and pesticide use affect the plants and animals in the preserve, (2) migration of animals in the preserve may incur onto the farmland, and (3) foundations often look to add to their holdings, allowing for a future sale of the land. C allows for the possibility of being able to react to market preferences and more stable productivity and thus more reliable income.

EXAMPLE 18

Large institutional investors consider timberland an investment because:

A. The small parcel sizes permit fine tuning of their holdings across geography and wood types.
B. The optionality around harvesting gives investors the choice between cutting trees for lumber and current income or letting them grow another year for future gain.
C. The short return history allows for many alpha opportunities by knowledgeable active managers.
D. Clear-cutting trees and destroying nature is appreciated by ESG investors, which are becoming a larger portion of the investment universe.

Solution: B is the correct answer. A is incorrect because the parcel sizes are generally large, especially compared with farmland. C is incorrect because the return history is relatively long, not short. D states the opposite reason why ESG investors may be interested in timberland investments—for the opportunity to create "conservation zones."

6.3. Risk/Return of Natural Resources

Although we present commodities, farmland, and timberland in the same section, they do have different return drivers and cycles. Commodities are priced on a second-by-second basis on public exchanges, whereas land generally has an infrequent pricing mechanism and may include estimates as opposed to actual transactions. Keeping these market structure differences in mind will help investors consider their relative benefits and challenges.

6.3.1. Risk/Return: Commodities

The arguments for investing in commodities include the potential for returns, portfolio diversification, and inflation protection. Investors may choose commodities if they believe prices will increase in the short or intermediate term. Since commodity prices directly feed into inflation index level calculations, commodities serve as a real hedge against inflation risk even when they yield little or no real return. Commodity futures contracts may offer investors a liquidity premium or other trading opportunities, creating the prospect for a real return greater than zero. Note that commodity investments, especially when combined with leverage, exhibit high volatility (see Exhibit 19), which has led to many well-publicized losses among commodity players.

EXHIBIT 19   Historical Returns of Commodities, 1990–Q1 2020 (quarterly data)

	Global Stocks	Global Bonds	Commodities
Annualized return	4.8%	5.3%	−1.7%
Annualized standard deviation	16.2%	6.0%	23.8%
Worst calendar year	−43.5%	−5.2%	−46.5%
	(2008)	(1999)	(2008)
Best calendar year	31.6%	19.7%	49.7%
	(2003)	(1995)	(2000)

Sources: Global stocks = MSCI ACWI; global bonds = Bloomberg Barclays Global Aggregate Index; commodities = S&P GSCI Total Return.

Before investors dismiss commodities as a source for returns, let us examine the period before the 2008–2009 global financial crisis (GFC). If we look at the world economy before central banks began injecting trillions of dollars, euros, yuan, yen, and so on, in liquidity and capital market purchases, we can see that commodities held their own in terms of returns. (See Exhibit 20.) In fact, commodities well outperformed global stocks. Therefore, asset allocators need to ask whether conditions or sentiment can return to the pre-GFC situation when inflation was a factor and government bonds yielded mid to high single digits.

EXHIBIT 20   Historical Returns of Commodities, 1990–Q4 2007 (quarterly data)

	Global Stocks	Global Bonds	Commodities
Annualized return	5.2%	7.0%	6.8%
Annualized standard deviation	17.0%	6.3%	18.3%
Worst calendar year	−20.5%	−5.2%	−35.7%
	(2002)	(1999)	(1998)
Best calendar year	31.6%	19.7%	49.7%
	(2003)	(1995)	(2000)

Sources: Global stocks = MSCI ACWI; global bonds = Bloomberg Barclays Global Aggregate Index; commodities = S&P GSCI Total Return.

Commodity spot prices are a function of supply and demand, the costs of production and storage, the value to users, and global economic conditions. Supplies of physical commodities are determined by production and inventory levels and secondarily by the actions of non-hedging investors. Demand for commodities is determined by the needs of end users and secondarily by the actions of non-hedging investors. Investor actions can both dampen and stimulate commodity price movements, at least in the short term.

Producers cannot alter commodity supply levels quickly because extended lead times are often needed to affect production levels. For example, agricultural output may be altered by planting more crops and changing farming techniques, but at least one growing cycle is required before there is an effect. And for agricultural products, at least one factor that is outside the producer's control—the weather—will significantly affect output. Building the necessary infrastructure for increased oil and mining production may take many years. It is a matter not just of developing the mine itself but also of the necessary transportation and smelting components. For commodities, suppliers' inability to quickly respond to changes in demand levels may result in supply levels that are too low in times of economic growth and too high when the economy slows. And despite advancing technology, the cost of new supply may grow over time. For example, new energy and mineral exploration is frequently more expensive because the easy discoveries tend to be exploited first. If fixed production costs are high, producers are unlikely to produce more than what is needed to meet anticipated demand, and they are unlikely to maintain more than modest levels of inventory, leading to the risk of shortages and price spikes.

Overall demand levels are influenced by global manufacturing dynamics and economic growth. Manufacturing needs can change in a period of months as orders and inventories vary. Investors seek to anticipate these changes by watching inventories closely and monitoring economic conditions, including those relating to government policy and growth forecasts. When demand levels and investors' orders to buy and sell during a given period change quickly, the resulting mismatch of supply and demand may lead to price volatility.

6.3.2. Risk/Return: Timberland and Farmland

Turning to land, Exhibit 21 provides a comparison of returns on US timber and farmland. The National Council of Real Estate Investment Fiduciaries (NCREIF) constructs a variety of appraisal-based indexes for property, timber, and farmland. Over the 1990–Q1 2020 period, farmland had the highest annualized return and timber had the highest standard deviation.

EXHIBIT 21   Historical Returns of US Real Estate Indexes, 1990–Q1 2020, Quarterly Data

	NCREIF Data	
	Timber	Farmland
Annualized return	9.1%	11.0%
Annualized standard deviation	7.0%	5.9%
Worst calendar year	−5.2%	2.0%
	(2001)	(2001)
Best calendar year	37.3%	33.9%
	(1992)	(2005)

Although the data in Exhibit 21 make farmland appear to be a very attractive investment, they do not tell the whole story. Liquidity is very low and the risk of negative cash flow high because fixed costs are relatively high (remember that the land must be cared for and crops need fertilizer, seed, and so on) and revenue is highly variable based on the weather. The risks of timber and farmland are similar to those of other real estate investments in raw land, but we highlight weather as a unique and more exogenous risk for these assets compared to traditional commercial and residential real estate properties. Drought and flooding can dramatically decrease the harvest yields for crops and thus the income stream expected by investors. The second primary risk is the international competitive landscape. Although real estate is often considered a local investment, productive land generates commodities that are globally traded and consumed. For example, there have been interruptions in world trade, and growing agricultural competition has resulted in declining grain prices. Therefore, looking ahead, these returns seem unlikely to be repeated in the next 30 years. Timber and farmland investments should consider the international context as a major risk factor.

EXAMPLE 19

Describe a risk of farmland that distinguishes it from real estate investment in raw land.

Solution: There are two significant risks differentiating farmland from raw land investment:

1. Weather is a more unique and exogenous risk for farmland, with drought or flooding dramatically decreasing many crop yields and thus the expected income stream.
2. Productive land generates globally traded and consumed commodities. This international competitive landscape can result in interruptions in world trade, growing foreign agricultural competition, and resulting declines in crop prices.

6.4. Diversification Benefits of Natural Resources

Although they often entail higher transaction costs and higher informational hurdles, alternative assets generally offer diversification as a major benefit. Where that diversification comes from needs to be understood in order for managers to better set investor expectations.

6.4.1. Diversification Benefits: Commodities

Commodity investing may be attractive to investors not only for the potential profits but also because of the following perceptions: (1) Commodities are effective hedges against inflation, which is to say that commodity prices have historically been positively correlated with inflation, because they are an input to prices, and (2) commodities are effective for portfolio diversification, which is to say that commodity returns have historically had a low correlation with other investment returns. Institutional investors, particularly endowments, foundations, and increasingly corporate and public pension funds and sovereign wealth funds, are allocating more of their portfolios to commodities and commodity derivatives.

The portfolio diversification argument is based on the observation that commodities historically have behaved differently from stocks and bonds during the business cycle. Exhibit 22 shows the quarterly correlation between selected commodity, global equity, and global bond indexes. In the period from 1990 through Q1 2020, commodities exhibited a low correlation with traditional assets; the correlations of commodities with global stocks and global bonds were 0.37 and 0.05, respectively. The correlations of stocks, bonds, and commodities are expected to be positive because each of the assets has some exposure to the global business cycle. Note that the selected commodity index, the S&P GSCI (Goldman Sachs Commodity Index), is heavily weighted toward the energy sector and that each underlying commodity may exhibit unique behavior.

EXHIBIT 22   Historical Commodity Return Correlations, 1990–Q1 2020 (quarterly data)

	Global Stocks	Global Bonds	Commodities	US CPI
Global stocks	1	0.09	0.37	0.21
Global bonds		1	0.05	−0.03
Commodities			1	0.64

Sources: Global stocks = MSCI ACWI; global bonds = Bloomberg Barclays Global Aggregate Index; commodities = S&P GSCI Total Return.

The argument for commodities as a hedge against inflation is related to the fact that some commodity prices are a component of inflation calculations. Commodities, especially energy and food, affect consumers' cost of living. The positive correlation between quarterly commodity price changes and quarterly changes in the US CPI of 0.64 supports this assertion. In contrast, the quarterly return correlations between the US CPI and global stocks and global bonds are close to zero. The volatility of commodity prices, especially energy and food, is much higher than that of reported consumer inflation. Note that consumer inflation is computed from many products used by consumers, including housing, that change more slowly than commodity prices, and inflation calculations use statistical smoothing techniques and behavioral assumptions. However, even in the recent period of low inflation (or even negative inflation in many countries), investing in commodities outperformed global stocks and bonds on average during the same calendar year if inflation was relatively high (i.e., US CPI greater than 2%; see Exhibit 23).

EXHIBIT 23   Historical Asset Class Returns When US CPI Was >2% versus <2%, 1990–2019 (quarterly data)

	Global Stocks	Global Bonds	Commodities
Higher inflation	+10.9%	+7.1%	+15.6%
Lower inflation	+0.3%	+2.7%	−20.0%

Sources: Global stocks = MSCI ACWI; global bonds = Bloomberg Barclays Global Aggregate Index; commodities = S&P GSCI Total Return.

In addition, Exhibit 23 affirms the sensitivity of commodities to inflation as measured by its relatively high correlation.

Note that changes in commodity prices will coincidentally affect inflation because those changes are included in inflation measures. However, in looking at the weight of food and energy in inflation calculations, they are a relatively small portion. A review of the US CPI calculations indicates an approximate 13% weight of the commodity price impacts. Furthermore, this number is overstated because these price changes as measured by CPI include all the other costs to consumers, such as gasoline taxes, supermarket rent and labor costs, and brand marketing. Therefore, even though there is a direct impact from changes in commodity costs on consumer inflation, it is marginal for the purposes of this discussion.

Exhibit 24 outlines a number of common assets in various regimes of inflation with certain sector callouts that highlight their impact. One example is that mining equities have performed notably better than overall equities in periods of high inflation because of the operational leverage inherent in mining businesses (high fixed costs, low operating costs). This example again highlights the diversification opportunities that can exist between commodities and traditional asset classes.

EXHIBIT 24

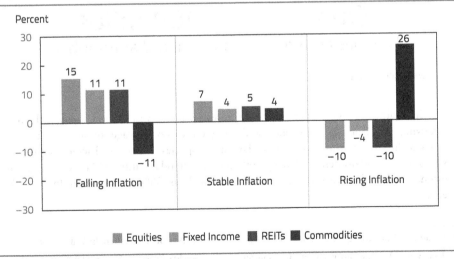

Source: Wellington Management Company LLP

6.4.2. Diversification Benefits: Timberland and Farmland

Investors look at diversification in many forms; the numbers tell part of the story, but there are qualitative considerations as well. For example, investors can adhere to ESG principles of responsible and sustainable investing by including timberland and farmland in their portfolios. The Campbell Global case study provides a discussion of timberland assets and how investing in timberland can help mitigate climate change.

Timberland Case Study: Campbell Global

Investing Responsibly in Timberland Assets: A Climate-Conscious Case Study

Campbell Global (CG) is a global investment manager focused on forest and natural resources investments. Based in Portland, Oregon, with offices in 14 US states and New Zealand, the firm has nearly four decades of experience in sustainable value creation. CG is committed to managing its forests in a manner that promotes the best long-term interests of its clients, while also striving to address economic and ESG considerations.

FIGURE 1

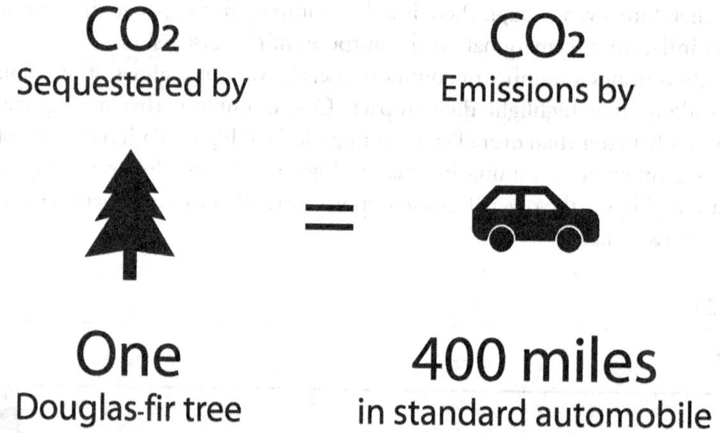

CO_2
Sequestered by

=

CO_2
Emissions by

One
Douglas-fir tree

400 miles
in standard automobile

Source: Campbell Global, LLC

In addition to their economic value, forests serve as vast carbon sinks, with trees removing CO_2 from the atmosphere and using it as carbon storage. In one year, a single Douglas fir tree, a common commercial timber species in the US Pacific Northwest, stores the CO_2 equivalent of driving 400 miles in a standard automobile.[5] Globally, it is estimated that the Earth's forests absorb as much as 30% of human-induced CO_2 emissions.[6]

---

[5] Estimated carbon storage of a 20-inch Douglas fir using the National Tree Benefit Calculator.

[6] Y. Pan et al., "A Large and Persistent Carbon Sink in the World's Forests," *Science* (19 August 2011): 988–93.

Sustainably harvested wood products and materials also store atmospheric CO_2 long after they have been removed from a forest, with one cubic meter of wood capable of storing nearly a metric ton of CO_2[7]. In addition to carbon sequestration, forests also provide other benefits, such as clean water and wildlife habitat, recreational opportunities, and a source of living-wage jobs in rural communities. These attributes positively align with the UN's Sustainable Development Goals and contribute to advancing the UN's mission for a sustainable future for all. In light of these considerations, there is increasing awareness that well-managed forests are a critical component of any global climate change strategy.

CG uses scenario analyses to identify climate-related risks beginning at a broad country-level scale, narrowing down to a specific property, and then testing the impact of various risks to site suitability now and into the future. Factors analyzed to gauge climate risks include precipitation patterns, temperature fluctuations, the severity of weather events, the presence of pests or disease, and the annual average growth rates for commercial tree species. While many climate-related risks in forestry are mitigated through active management, during this iterative process CG analyzes both the potential positive and negative impacts associated with these risks to assess potential changes in net asset value. The following table illustrates climate risks evaluated, their impact on the forest, and our ability to mitigate the risks.

Climate Risk	Implication	CG Mitigants
Change in temperature	Increased fire danger	Property-specific fire plans; re-evaluate target regions/country for investment
Change in precipitation patterns	Changes in tree species range; increased drought and related fire risk	Vegetation suitability modeling and genetic tree improvement; re-evaluate target regions/country for investment
Frequency of extreme weather events	Loss of standing timber from wind events	Re-evaluate target regions; property-specific response plans; geographically diverse portfolio construction
Presence of pests or disease	Early onset and increased frequency of individual tree mortality	Immediate treatment, which may include removal of effected trees to prevent further spread of pests or disease in the forest
Change in growth	Increased or decreased growth rates	Effects will vary by region, may influence planting stock decisions; re-evaluate forest growth model assumptions

---

[7]Oregon Forest Resources Institute, "Forest to Frame" (2017).

Specific examples of how CG identifies opportunities and challenges in its investment process related to climate change include the following:

- Identifying afforestation opportunities that mitigate climate change by sequestering CO_2 emissions from the atmosphere in trees and soil, while offering many important co-benefits for communities, biodiversity, and soil and water quality.
- Protecting existing carbon stocks by minimizing impacts to carbon stored on the forest floor through tailored forest management practices.
- Enhancing forest carbon sequestration by replanting areas as soon as possible so the new forest will quickly begin removing CO_2 from the atmosphere.

The ability to quantify, evaluate, and report the year-over-year changes in the carbon footprint of a forest has the potential to influence the impacts an organization has on the environment, leading to increased transparency and more-informed business decisions. Incorporating climate change factors in its investment process not only mitigates climate-related risks; it also promotes and enhances the natural solutions forests provide. Understanding and measuring the comprehensive carbon stores of forests may lead to business decisions that improve carbon sequestration, a critical factor in addressing climate change.

Exhibit 25 shows the quarterly correlation between timber, farmland, and selected global equity and global bond indexes. In the 30-year period from 1990 through 2020, timber and farmland exhibited low correlation with traditional assets; the correlation of timber with global stocks and global bonds was 0.04 and 0.07, while the correlation of farmland with global stocks and global bonds was 0.15 and −0.04, respectively.

EXHIBIT 25   Historical Commodity Return Correlations, 1990–Q1 2020

NCREIF Data	Timber	Farmland
Global stocks	0.04	0.15
Global bonds	0.07	−0.04

Sources: Global stocks = MSCI ACWI; global bonds = Bloomberg Barclays Global Aggregate Index. Quarterly basis.

The United States has experienced three periods of elevated inflation as measured by the US Consumer Price Index since the early 1900s: 1915–1920, 1940–1951, and 1967–1981. In all three periods, farmland provided investors with meaningful inflation protection: +9.9% annualized farmland compound return versus +13.5% annualized inflation, +7.9% versus +5.9%, and +12.0% versus +7.6%, respectively.

Real estate return data pitfalls will be discussed in more detail in the next section, but note the inherent smoothing in quarterly versus monthly or daily data and the relative infrequency of transactions that make return projections problematic. After all, can one reliably or consistently compare a plot of prime farmland with a more marginal neighbor? How about the price of one piece of land that has generous water rights with another that is water restricted? As is the case with other alternative benchmarks (e.g., hedge fund indexes), productive land indexes may offer a good overall understanding but limited specific value.

EXAMPLE 20

Is the following statement true or false?

For the most appropriate instrument to invest in natural resources today, retail investors should focus on the stocks and bonds of companies producing in this sector.

A. True
B. False

Solution: B is correct; the statement is false. Up to about 20 years ago, the only commonly available investment vehicles related to this asset class were indeed financial instruments (stocks and bonds). Rather than investing in the physical land and the products that come from it, investors concentrated on the companies that produced natural resources. Nowadays, however, the wide variety of direct investments via ETFs, limited partnerships, REITS, swaps, and futures opens the door for almost everyone to participate in these assets directly.

6.5. Instruments

To achieve the exposures they are after, investors require suitable instruments. Fortunately, there are many publicly traded and indexed choices, and there is still room for specialized value-added alternative mangers.

6.5.1. Instruments: Commodities

The majority of commodity investing is implemented through derivatives, and commodity futures are a popular choice. Physical commodities often generate unwelcome price opacity, tax obligations, and costs arising from storage, brokerage, and transportation, all of which may increase the attractiveness of standardized futures traded on transparent exchanges. Commodity derivatives include futures, forwards, options, and swaps. These contracts may be traded on exchanges or over the counter (OTC).

Futures contracts are obligations to buy or sell a specific amount of a given commodity at a fixed price, location, and date in the future. Futures contracts are exchange traded, are marked to market daily, and may or may not be settled with the delivery or receipt of the physical commodity at the end of the contract. This delivery obligation became dramatically important during the global financial crisis in 2008 and in the 2020 COVID-19 pandemic as demand collapsed, oil producers could not find buyers for their petroleum, and global storage filled suddenly. Even commodity-related ETFs were affected, forcing some to close and impose large losses on their investors. For futures contracts, counterparty risk is managed by the exchange and clearing broker. Commodity exposure can be achieved through means other than direct investment in commodities or commodity derivatives, including the following:

- Exchange-traded products (ETPs, either funds or notes) may be suitable for investors who are restricted to equity shares or are seeking the simplicity of trading through a standard brokerage account. ETPs may invest in commodities or commodity futures. For example, the SPDR Gold Shares exchange-traded fund attempts to track the price of physical gold by holding bullion in vaults. It owned just under $49 billion in gold bullion as of March 2020. ETPs may use leverage and may be long or short (also known as "inverse"). Similar to mutual funds or unit trusts, ETPs charge fees that are included in their expense ratios.

- Commodity exposure can also be obtained by investing in managed futures, also known as CTAs. However, in order to obtain pure commodity exposure, one would need to choose to invest in a managed futures fund focused solely on commodities because modern CTAs often invest in a variety of futures, including commodities, equities, fixed income, and foreign exchange. Such a fund might concentrate on a specific commodity, such as grains or livestock, or it may be broadly diversified to cover all commodities. Commodity-focused managed futures funds are unique (versus global macro) because there is a constant price tension between suppliers and consumers: High prices cripple demand (and thus lead to lower prices), and low prices shut in supply (and thus raise prices). This situation creates a unique balance that is not present in traditional asset classes, such as stocks and bonds.
- Funds that specialize in specific commodity sectors exist. For example, private energy partnerships, similar to private equity funds, are a popular way for institutions to gain exposure to the energy sector. Management fees can range from 1% to 3% of committed capital, with a lockup period of 10 years and extensions of 1- and 2-year periods. Publicly available energy mutual funds and unit trusts typically focus on the oil and gas sector and often act as fixed-income investments, paying out dividends from rents or capital gains. They may focus on upstream (drilling), midstream (refineries), or downstream (chemicals). Management fees for these funds are in line with those of other public equity managers and range from 0.4% to 1%.

6.5.2. Instruments: Timberland and Farmland

The primary investment vehicles for timber and farmland are investment funds, whether offered on the public markets, such as real estate investment trusts (REITs) in the United States, or administered privately through limited partnerships. Larger investors can consider direct investments if there are particular assets that have appeal. For example, Middle Eastern sovereign wealth funds have made investments in farmland in Africa and Southeast Asia. Owning physical farmland opens the door to a wider variety of foodstuffs: spices, nuts, fruits and vegetables—a much broader array than the corn, soy, and wheat offered by futures investment. However, there is limited price transparency or information to guide investment decisions without the assistance of sector specialists. The illiquidity of direct farm and timberland investments is also limiting.

7. REAL ESTATE

7.1. Overview of the Real Estate Market

Individuals and institutions buy real property for their own use, as an investment, or both. The residential, or housing, market is made up of individual single-family detached homes and multi-family attached units, which share at least one wall with another unit (e.g., condominiums, townhouses), owned by the resident. Commercial real estate includes primarily office buildings, retail shopping centers, and warehouses. In contrast to the owner-occupied market, rental properties are leased to tenants. A lease is a contract that conveys the use of the property from the owner (the landlord or *lessor*) to the tenant (*lessee*) for a predetermined period in exchange for compensation (rent). When residential real estate, be it single or multi-unit, is owned with the intention to let, lease, or rent the property in order to generate income, it is classified as commercial (i.e., income-producing) real estate.

Real estate investing is typically thought of as either direct or indirect ownership (equity investing) in real estate property, such as land and buildings. However, it also includes lending (debt investing) against real estate property. Loans secured by real estate are called mortgages. Investors can access real estate debt by lending, buying mortgages, or purchasing mortgage-backed securities with the property ultimately serving as collateral. The key reasons for investing in real estate include the following potential benefits:

- Competitive long-term total returns driven by both income generation and capital appreciation
- Multiple-year leases with fixed rents for some property types potentially providing stable income over many economic cycles
- Historically low correlations with other asset classes
- Inflation hedge if leases provide regular contractual rent step-ups or can be frequently marked to market

A title or deed represents real estate property ownership and covers building and land-use rights along with air, mineral, and surface rights. Titles can be purchased, leased, sold, mortgaged, or transferred together or separately, in whole or in part. Title searches are a crucial part of buyer and lender due diligence, ensuring the seller/borrower owns the property without any liens or other claims against the asset, such as from other owners, lenders, or investors or from the government for unpaid taxes.

Residential real estate is by far the largest sector of the real estate market by value and size. Savills World Research estimated in July 2018 that residential real estate accounted for more than 75% of global real estate values. Although the average value of a home is less than the average value of an office building, the aggregate space required to house people is much larger than the space required to accommodate office use and retail shopping. Homeownership rates are at least 80% in many of the largest countries by population, including China, India, Mexico, Japan, and Russia, and are high in other large countries, such as Brazil, at more than 74%, and the United States, with at least 64% homeownership. Germany is a notable exception, at approximately 52%, according to OECD.org.

The size of the professionally managed, institutional-quality global real estate market increased to US$9.6 trillion at the end of 2019, as shown in Exhibit 26, from US$6.8 trillion in 2013, representing a compound average annual growth rate of 5.8%. It should come as no surprise that the largest and most developed countries have the highest-valued real estate markets. Institutional-quality real estate generally consists of high-quality properties owned by institutional investors and high-net-worth individuals. It is typically of higher value than most individuals can afford. Smaller and out-of-date properties typically do not qualify as institutional quality.

EXHIBIT 26   Size of Professionally Managed Global Real Estate Market, 2018 (US$ billions)

Country or Region	Size	% of Total
United States	3,418.1	35.8%
Japan	881.4	9.2%
United Kingdom	745.5	7.8%
China	592.2	6.2%
Germany	580.1	6.1%
France	441.2	4.6%
Hong Kong SAR	378.3	4.0%
Canada	361.0	3.8%
Australia	306.8	3.2%
Rest of world	1,848.4	19.3%
Total	9,553.0	100%

Source: MSCI Real Estate.

Real estate is different from other asset classes: the large capital investment required; the illiquidity; the fact that no two properties are identical in terms of location, tenant credit mix, lease term, age, and market demographics; and the necessarily fixed location of the asset. All these have important investment implications.

Furthermore, price discovery in the private market is opaque, historical prices may not reflect market conditions, transaction costs are high, and transaction activity may be limited in certain markets. It may be difficult for small investors to establish a diversified portfolio of wholly owned properties. Private market indexes are not investable, and property typically requires professional operational management.

Numerous other considerations will give investors pause before investing independently. Involvement in unfamiliar real estate markets calls for specialized knowledge of country, regional, and local market dynamics and the practices, regulations, and taxation that apply. Government regulations dictate what can be built or modified, with further complications coming from each locality's zoning and permit approval process, rules around ownership transfer, and possible rent controls. Local supply and demand dynamics may override wider market trends, complicating analysis. Many countries have limits on foreign investors with respect to property type and location, and they may require higher withholding taxes on foreign-owned property.

EXAMPLE 21

True or false: The largest sector of the real estate market by value and size is commercial real estate.

A. True
B. False

Solution: B is correct; the statement is false. Residential real estate is by far the largest sector of the real estate market by value and size. The residential debt market greatly exceeds commercial property debt because of the larger total value of residential properties combined with property owners' greater ability to use leverage—up to 80% of the property's value or more in some cases. In addition, home mortgages are subsidized in some markets, including government guarantees.

7.2. Characteristics: Forms of Real Estate Ownership

Real estate investing takes a variety of forms best illustrated with the four-quadrant model that arranges the quadrants by type of capital (debt or equity) and source of capital (private or public markets). Investors can choose to own all or part of a property's equity, either unlevered (100% equity) or with a levered approach that relies on debt as well as equity to finance the purchase. Alternatively, investors can gain exposure to real estate through debt ownership, either as a lender/originator or as a purchaser of debt instruments.

Banks and insurance companies are among the largest originators/owners of mortgage debt. The residential debt market greatly exceeds commercial property debt because the total value of residential properties is larger and property owners have a greater ability to use leverage— securing loans for up to 80% of the property's value or more in some cases. In addition, home mortgages are subsidized in some markets and enjoy government guarantees.

Exhibit 27 presents examples of the basic forms of real estate in each of the quadrants: public or private structures, debt or equity ownership.

EXHIBIT 27   Basic Forms of Real Estate Investments and Examples

	Debt	Equity
Private	• Mortgages • Construction lending • Mezzanine debt	• Direct ownership of real estate: ownership through sole ownership, joint ventures, separate accounts, or real estate limited partnerships • Indirect ownership via real estate funds • Private REITs
Public	• MBS (residential and commercial) • Collateralized mortgage obligations • Mortgage REITs • ETFs that own securitized mortgage debt	• Shares in real estate operating and development corporations • Listed REIT shares • Mutual funds • Index funds • ETFs

Within the basic forms, there can be many variations.

7.2.1. Direct Real Estate Investing

Direct private investing involves purchasing a property and originating debt for one's own account. Ownership can be free and clear, whereby the title to the property is transferred to the owner(s) unencumbered by any financing liens, such as from outstanding mortgages. Owners can also borrow from mortgage lenders to fund the equity acquisition. Debt investors can also use leverage. Initial purchase costs associated with direct ownership may include legal expenses, survey costs, engineering/environmental studies, and valuation (appraisal) fees. In addition, ongoing maintenance and refurbishment charges are also incurred. Additional debt closing costs are incurred when owners take out loans to fund their investments.

There are several benefits to owning real estate directly. One is control. Only the owner decides when to buy or sell, when and how much to spend on capital projects (subject to lease terms and regulatory requirements), whom to select as tenants based on credit quality preference and tenant mix, and what types of lease terms to offer. Another benefit relates to taxes. Property investors in the largest countries as ranked by the size of the institutional-quality real estate market can use non-cash property depreciation expenses and interest expense, with some limitations, to reduce taxable income and lower their income tax bills. In fact, real estate investors in a country that permits accelerated depreciation and interest expense deductions can reduce taxable income below zero in the early years of asset ownership, and losses can be carried forward to offset future income. Thus, a property investment can be cash-flow positive while generating accounting losses and deferring tax payments. If the tax losses do not reverse during the life of the asset, depreciation-recapture taxes can be triggered when the property is sold.

Major disadvantages to investing directly include the extensive time required to manage the property, the importance of local real estate market expertise to success, and the large capital requirements. Smaller investors bear additional risks from portfolio concentration.

The owner may choose to handle all aspects of investing in and operating the property, including property selection, asset management, property management, leasing, and administration. To address the complexity of owning and managing commercial real estate, investors hire advisers to perform any number of functions, including identifying investments, negotiating terms, performing due diligence, conducting operations, asset management, and eventual disposal. Asset management focuses on maximizing property returns by deciding when and how much to invest in the property and when to sell the property.

Many investors prefer to hire advisers or managers to manage the investors' direct real estate investment in what is called a *separate account*, which contains only the single investor's equity or perhaps a nominal stake from the adviser to help align interests. A separate account allows the investor to control the timing and value of acquisitions and dispositions and perhaps to make operating decisions as well. There is no commingling of capital with other investors.

Sometimes investors will form joint ventures with other investors to access real estate. Joint ventures are especially common when one party can contribute something of value that the other lacks, such as land, capital, development expertise, debt due diligence, or entrepreneurial talent. Joint ventures can be structured as general partnerships or, more commonly, as limited liability companies.

Numerous parties can pool their resources to acquire property, to develop or redevelop assets, or to lend capital. The equity stakes that investors contribute to pooled investment vehicles vary on the basis of their contribution of real assets, capital, entrepreneurial talent, and services. When structured as a limited partnership, there must by a general partner to manage the partnership and accept unlimited liability.

7.2.2. Indirect Real Estate Investing

Indirect investing provides access to the underlying real estate assets through a variety of pooled investment vehicles, which can be public or private, such as limited partnerships, mutual funds, corporate shares, REITs, and ETFs. Equity REITs own real estate equity, mortgage REITs own real estate mortgages and MBS, and hybrid REITs own both. Institutional investors and some high-net-worth investors can invest in MBS. Intermediaries facilitate the raising and pooling of capital and creating investable structures.

7.2.3. Mortgages

Mortgages represent passive investments in which the lender expects to receive a predefined stream of payments throughout the finite life of the mortgage. Mortgages may require full amortization or partial amortization with balloon payments due at maturity or may be interest only (IO). Borrowers can often choose among fixed-rate, floating-rate, and adjustable-rate options. Some of the floating- and variable-rate mortgages may have limitations, or caps, on how much the rate can change over a given period. For example, a borrower could apply for a mortgage that carries a fixed rate for five years, after which the rate resets to a predetermined spread over the lender's benchmark rate, with any rate change limited to 200 bps during the first year of the reset. Residential mortgages in developed markets usually have 15-, 25-, or 30-year maturities. Commercial property loans may be similarly long for long-term property owners. Other owners will take out 5-, 7-, or 10-year loans to correspond with the owners' anticipated holding period. Selling the property before the mortgage is due may result in prepayment penalties for the commercial borrower. If the borrower defaults on the loan, the lender may seek to take possession of the property. Investments may take place in the form of "whole" loans based on specific properties, typically by way of direct investment through private markets, or through participation in a pool of mortgage loans, typically by way of indirect investment in real estate through publicly traded securities, such as MBS.

REITs and partnerships carry fees and administrative overhead for managing the assets embedded in their valuations. Fee structures for private REITs can be similar to those for private equity funds, with investment management fees based on either committed capital or invested capital. These fees typically range from 1% to 2% of capital per annum. Funds also charge performance-based fees.

7.2.4. Private Fund Investing Styles

Capital committed to or invested by *real estate private equity funds* exceeded $900 billion in mid-2018. Most real estate private equity funds are structured as *infinite-life open-end funds*, which, like mutual funds, allow investors to contribute or redeem capital throughout the life of the fund. Investor subscriptions and redemptions are commonly accepted by the GP on a quarterly basis and are subject to the manager's ability to acquire or sell real estate or match investor redemption requests with pending investor subscriptions. Open-end funds generally offer exposure to *core* real estate, which is characterized by well-leased, high-quality institutional real estate in the best markets. Investors expect core real estate to deliver stable returns, primarily from income. Returns are typically driven by real estate beta, although managers can add value through better market selection, property management, and execution.

In addition to investing in core real estate, *core-plus* strategies will also accept slightly higher risks derived from *non-core* markets and sectors or properties with slightly more leasing risk. Non-core properties include large sectors with different risk profiles, such as hotels and nursing homes. Assets in secondary and tertiary markets and such niches as student housing, self-storage, and data centers are also considered non-core.

Investors seeking higher returns may also accept development, redevelopment, repositioning, and leasing risk. *Finite-life closed-end* funds are more commonly used for alpha- and beta-generating value-add and opportunistic investment styles. *Value-add* investments may require modest redevelopment or upgrades, the leasing of vacant space, or repositioning the underlying properties to earn a higher return than core properties. *Opportunistic* investing accepts the much higher risks of development, major redevelopment, repurposing of assets, taking on large vacancies, and speculating on significant improvement in market conditions. Closed-end fund managers will sell assets to realize the value created by management and lock in the investment's IRR. There are exceptions to the fund style/life/structure relationships—that is, core/infinite life/open end or opportunistic/finite life/closed end. On occasion, you will see core, closed-end, finite-life funds or open-end, infinite-life, value-add funds.

7.2.5. REITs

Real estate investment trusts are the preferred investment vehicles for owning income-producing real estate of both private and public investors. The main appeal of the REIT structure is the elimination of double corporate taxation: Corporations pay taxes on income, and then the dividend distributions of after-tax earnings are subsequently taxed at the shareholder's personal tax rate. REITs can avoid corporate income taxation by distributing dividends equal to 90%–100% of their taxable net rental income.

In the United States, taxable real estate corporations can elect REIT status by meeting a number of important criteria. Among the many rules, the company must invest at least 75% of its assets in real estate, cash, or US Treasuries and derive at least 75% of its income from rents on real property or real estate mortgages.

REIT and REIT-like structures in most countries are similar to those in the United States. Whereas REITs are a popular vehicle in the United States, other countries have structures separate from corporations for REITs that still permit dividend deductibility from the entities' income taxes. Primary differences relate to whether REITs can be internally managed, operated, and advised or are required to hire external managers and advisers, how much income the REIT must distribute (90%–100% is the standard), and whether the REIT is a corporation as in the United States or an independent structure. REITs that are self-managed and self-administered typically benefit from a better alignment of interests between management and shareholders than externally advised or managed companies.

Companies that have other sources of non-qualifying income or wish to retain earnings to reinvest in the business will choose an operating company structure. Note that the income taxes due for companies that can deduct depreciation and interest expense from operating income in calculating pretax income may not be high enough to accept the restrictions that come with REIT and REIT-like structures.

Publicly traded REITs address many of the disadvantages related to private real estate investing. Listed REITs provide investors with much greater liquidity, lower trading costs, and better transparency. Management is employed internally by the REIT in most countries rather than brought in as a separate organization on contract, which results in better alignment of interests with investors. Importantly, when an investor wants to modify its real estate holdings, the investor need only buy or sell REIT shares on listed markets instead of buying or selling real estate directly. The REIT is not forced to sell the company's underlying real estate the way open-end funds are when there are mass redemptions.

EXAMPLE 22

Fill in the blank: Compared with private real estate investing, publicly traded real estate investment trusts provide much greater _____, lower _____, and better _____.

   Choices of words: transparency, liquidity, trading costs, variety, happiness

Solution: Compared with private real estate investing, publicly traded real estate investment trusts provide much greater <u>liquidity</u>, lower <u>trading costs</u>, and better <u>transparency</u>.

7.3. Characteristics: Real Estate Investment Categories

The majority of real estate property may be classified as either commercial or residential. In this chapter, residential properties are defined narrowly to include only owner-occupied, single residences (often referred to as single-family residential property). Residential properties owned with the intention to let, lease, or rent them are classified as commercial. Commercial properties also include office, retail, industrial and warehouse, and hospitality (e.g., hotel and motel) properties. Commercial properties may also have mixed uses. Commercial properties generate returns from income (e.g., rent) and capital appreciation. Several factors will affect opportunities for capital appreciation, including development strategies, market conditions, and property-specific features.

7.3.1. Residential Property

For many individuals and families, real estate investment takes the form of direct equity investment (i.e., ownership) in a residence with the intent to occupy it. In other words, a home is purchased. Given the price of homes, most purchasers cannot pay 100% cash up front and must borrow funds to make the purchase. Most lenders require an equity contribution of at least 10%–20% of the property purchase price in countries with well-developed mortgage markets. Any appreciation (depreciation) in the value of the home increases (decreases) the owner's equity in the home and is magnified by mortgage leverage. In countries without well-developed mortgage markets, homebuyers must save for a much longer period and may have to ask family for assistance in order to raise enough money to buy a home.

   Home loans may be held on the originator's balance sheet or securitized and offered to the financial markets. Securitization provides indirect debt investment opportunities in residential property to other investors via securitized debt products, such as residential mortgage-backed securities (RMBS).

7.3.2. Commercial Real Estate

Commercial property has traditionally been considered an appropriate direct investment, whether through equity or debt, for institutional funds and high-net-worth individuals with long time horizons and limited liquidity needs. This perception was primarily the result of the complexity, size, and relative illiquidity of the investments. Direct equity investing (i.e., ownership) is further complicated because commercial property requires active day-to-day management. The success of the equity investment is a function of a variety of factors, including how well the property is managed, general economic and specific real estate market conditions, and the extent and terms of any debt financing.

In order to provide direct debt financing, the lender (investor) will conduct financial analysis to determine the borrower's creditworthiness, to ensure the property can generate sufficient cash flow to service the debt, to estimate the property's value, and to evaluate economic conditions. The estimate of the property value is critical because the size of the loan relative to the property value, the loan-to-value ratio, determines the amount of risk held by the lender versus the borrower (equityholder). The borrower's equity in the property is an indicator of commitment to the success of the project, and it provides the lender with a cushion because the property is generally the sole collateral for the loan.

7.3.3. REIT Investing

As of 2019, REITs were listed on stock exchanges in 39 countries, and their combined market capitalization exceeded $1.6 trillion.[8] The risk and return characteristics of REITs depend on the type of investment they make. Mortgage REITs, which invest primarily in mortgages, are similar to fixed-income investments. Equity REITs, which invest primarily in commercial or residential properties and use leverage, are similar to direct equity investments in leveraged real estate.

The business strategy for equity REITs is simple: Maximize property occupancy rates and rents in order to maximize income and dividends. Equity REITs, like other public companies, must report earnings per share based on net income as defined by generally accepted accounting principles (GAAP) or International Financial Reporting Standards (IFRS). Many report non-traditional measures, such as net asset value or variations of gross cash flow, to better estimate a company's dividend-paying ability, because non-cash depreciation expenses can be high for asset-intensive businesses.

7.3.4. Mortgage-Backed Securities

MBS structuring is based on the asset-backed securitization model of transforming illiquid assets (mortgages) into liquid securities and transferring risk from asset owners (banks, finance companies) to investors. An MBS issuer/originator forms a special purpose vehicle (SPV) to buy mortgages from lenders and other mortgage owners and use them to create a diversified mortgage pool. The MBS issuer assigns the incoming stream of mortgage interest income and principal payments to individual security tranches, which will be sold to investors. Each tranche is assigned a priority distribution ranking.

Exhibit 28 illustrates the basic process for creating commercial mortgage-backed securities (CMBS). On the right-hand side of the exhibit, the ranking of losses indicates the priority of claims against the real estate property. Risk-averse investors, primarily insurance companies, prefer the lowest-risk tranches, which are the first to receive interest and principal. Investors who choose the senior notes with the highest credit rating expect to earn a low return consistent with the senior tranche's low risk profile. Investors seeking the highest returns, which carry the highest risk, will invest in the lowest-rated, most junior securities, which are the last to receive interest and principal distributions. If mortgage defaults and losses are high, the lowest-ranked tranches bear the cost of the shortfall. The most junior tranche is referred to as the first-loss tranche.

---

[8] Nareit, "Global Real Estate Investment," Investing in REITs webpage. www.reit.com/investing/global-real-estate-investment (accessed 12 August 2019).

EXHIBIT 28   CMBS Security Structure

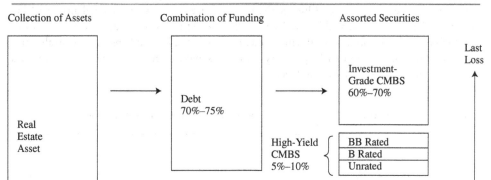

MBS may be issued privately or publicly, and the securities are typically offered in $1,000 increments in the United States. MBS valuations are influenced by the underlying borrowers' behavior. When interest rates decline, fixed-income security prices usually rise, but borrowers are also likely to refinance their loans at a faster pace than before, resulting in the faster amortization of each MBS tranche, which leaves MBS investors to reinvest their principal at the lower rates. Conversely, when rates rise, not only do fixed-income instrument prices decline, but also property owner prepayments can also slow, lengthening the duration of most MBS tranches and contributing to further price weakness. These unusual traits are well understood by investors. MBS are often included in broad fixed-income indexes and in indexes that are used to indicate the performance of real estate investments.

7.4. Risk and Return Characteristics

7.4.1. Real Estate Indexes
There are a variety of indexes globally that are designed to measure total and component real estate returns for listed securities and non-listed investment vehicles. Listed REIT indexes are straightforward in that, like other listed equity indexes, security pricing is reported by the major exchanges. Total returns are calculated assuming dividends are reinvested in the index. Importantly, listed REIT indexes are investable when their constituent stocks are freely traded. The more frequently the shares trade, the more reliable the index. Indexes containing small-cap, closely held, and low-float real estate stocks may not be as representative of investor returns, and REIT indexes in general are not necessarily representative of the entire real estate universe because of different geographic concentrations, property types (residential, commercial, etc.), and the asset quality of the publicly traded REIT company portfolios. The National Association of Real Estate Investment Trusts (Nareit) in the United States, the European Public Real Estate Association (EPRA), and the Asian Public Real Estate Association (APREA) publish listed real estate company indexes for their respective regions and contribute to global indexes. Most of the leading for-profit index providers also offer a variety of REIT and real estate indexes.

As shown in Exhibit 29, REITs are the predominant structure among listed real estate companies in the United States. Outside the United States, there is an equal balance of REITs and non-REITs, as represented by the FTSE EPRA Nareit index series. Some other countries in which REITs make up most of the index include Japan, the United Kingdom, Australia, and Singapore. In contrast, non-REIT property companies make up most of the real estate indexes in Hong Kong SAR, Germany, and Sweden.

EXHIBIT 29   REITs Make Up 50% of the Property Index Outside the United States

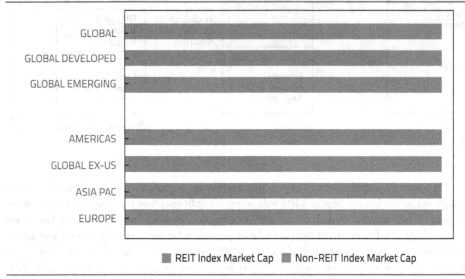

Exhibit 30 displays global and regional listed REIT returns. The table shows some disparity among regional returns and supports the importance of country-specific, regional, and local knowledge.

EXHIBIT 30   Historical Returns of Global REITs (Through 31 December 2019)

FTSE EPRA Nareit Developed Index Series, USD

Period	Global	North America	Asia Pacific	Europe
3 years	9.31%	7.76%	10.24%	13.05%
5 years	6.53%	6.63%	5.69%	7.40%
10 years	9.25%	11.39%	6.58%	8.66%
20 years	9.23%	11.06%	7.05%	9.38%
25 years	8.92%	11.13%	7.00%	8.88%
3-year volatility	8.24%	10.17%	9.05%	10.51%
10-year volatility	11.81%	13.05%	13.22%	15.16%
Dividend yield (Dec. 19)	3.83%	4.00%	3.60%	3.64%

Sources: FTSE, EPRA, Nareit.

A variety of indexes measure private investment performance, and they may report on private fund performance, underlying property values, or property operating performance. Funds that track listed REIT indexes make public REIT performance investable, but the same instruments are not available for private indexes. Real estate values are reported by property owners, advisers, and fund managers, and many private investors do not report results, giving rise to selection bias. The private fund and property indexes vary by property selection, valuation methodology, and longevity. Although in many cases private index property values are based on third-party property appraisal and, therefore, offer a measure of independence from owner/manager estimates, appraisals are nonetheless backward looking, subject to the biases of the appraisers, and likely to offer a smoothed-out picture of actual market volatility.

Industry associations, practitioners, and academics have developed *repeat sales indexes* that are transaction based rather than appraisal based. When repeat sales take place, the changing property prices are measured and used to construct the index. These indexes also suffer from a sample selection bias because the properties that sell in each period vary and may not be representative of the larger market. Also, the properties that change hands are not a random sample and may be biased toward those that have increased or decreased in value, depending on economic conditions. The higher the number of sales, the more reliable and relevant the index.

In the United States, NCREIF, in conjunction with the Pension Real Estate Association (PREA), collects fund and property data, maintains numerous indexes, and disseminates the results. The NCREIF Property Index (NPI), which has data going back to 1977, measures property-level performance each quarter. NCREIF also produces open-end diversified core equity (OEDCE) fund, open-end (OE) fund, closed-end value-add (CEVA) fund, and transaction-based repeat sales indexes. The European Association for Investors in Non-Listed Real Estate (INREV) and the Asian Association for Investors in Non-Listed Real Estate (ANREV) produce similar indexes for their respective regions. These three organizations also contribute data from their respective non-listed real estate vehicle indexes, which are rolled up into the quarterly Global Real Estate Fund Index (GREFI).

A wide range of indexes for public stocks and private real estate funds and properties are published by such organizations as Cambridge Associates, Bloomberg, FTSE, MSCI, Real Capital Analytics, Savills, and S&P Dow Jones Indices.

Although investors can benefit from this variety and may well identify an index that is relevant to them, they should be aware of how these indexes are constructed and the inherent limitations that result. Investors should also be aware that real estate's apparent low volatility and low correlation with other asset classes may result from these limitations.

7.4.2. Real Estate Investment Risks

Real estate investments, like any investment, may fail to perform in accordance with expectations. Property values are variable in the face of national and global economic conditions, local conditions, and interest rate levels. There are risks around the ability of the fund management teams to select, finance, and manage real properties and to account for changes in government regulation. Management of the underlying properties themselves includes handling rentals and leases, controlling expenses, directing maintenance and improvements, and ultimately disposing of the property. Expenses may increase because of circumstances beyond management's control or be covered by insurance. Returns to both debt and equity investors in real estate depend to a large extent on the ability of the owners or their agents to successfully operate the underlying properties.

Investments in distressed properties and in property development are subject to greater risks than investments in properties that are in sound financial condition or enjoy stable operations. Property development is subject to special risks, including regulatory issues, construction delays, and cost overruns. Environmental regulation is one regulatory hurdle, as is the failure to receive zoning, occupancy, and other approvals and permits. Because the development and disposition period of such projects can be very lengthy, economic conditions may change. All these moving pieces may conspire to increase construction time or delay successful leases, which increases construction costs and reduces the level of rents relative to initial expectations. And there is also financing risk: Long-term financing with acceptable terms simply might not be available, forcing real estate acquisitions and developments to be financed with lines of credit or other forms of temporary financing. Financing problems with one property may delay or limit further development of the owner's other projects.

It is important to recognize that the vast majority of direct investors, private funds, and public companies pursue leverage to increase returns for their investors. Leverage magnifies the effects of both gains and losses for equity investors and increases the risks that the real estate owner or investor will be left with insufficient funds to make interest payments or repay the debt at maturity. In that case, the lender or debt investor will receive less than the entire interest and principal balances. As the loan-to-value ratio increases and interest coverage weakens, the probability of default increases.

EXAMPLE 23

Fill in the blanks: Adding real estate to a portfolio has been demonstrated to increase portfolio _____ and reduce portfolio _____.

Solution: Adding real estate to a portfolio has been demonstrated to increase portfolio <u>diversification</u> and reduce portfolio <u>risk</u>.

7.5. Diversification Benefits

Many investors find the real estate sector attractive for providing high, steady current income. Although broad stock market gains are derived mostly from long-term capital appreciation, more than half of the returns from private core and listed real estate are derived from income. Throughout a market cycle, income is a more consistent source of return than capital appreciation, and hence, it is lower risk. The source of that consistency stems from the underlying medium- to long-term property leases: The longer the lease the more predictable the income. And the better the credit quality of a property's tenants, the more reliable the rents.

Are REITs equity, debt, or something else? In line with our categorization of all the assets in this chapter, many investors view REITs as alternative investments in the broader real estate category, and others see REITs as a fixed-income/equity hybrid, adding exposure simply for the incremental yield pickup over both high-grade bonds and equities. Others still have a different focus: Some institutional investors use their public equity department to analyze their REIT investments rather than engaging their real estate or alternative asset teams.

Real estate's moderate correlation with other asset classes adds to its attractiveness. Exhibit 31 lists the correlation of REITs with equity and debt securities during the 20-year period ended March 2020. The market capitalization of most REITs is on the smaller side, with the largest among them being notable exceptions.

EXHIBIT 31   REIT Allocation Can Improve Portfolio Diversification

Index	Correlation with the FTSE Nareit All Equity REITs Index
S&P 500	0.57
Russell 2000 Index	0.64
ICE BofAML Corp./Gov't.	0.19
ICE BofAML MBS	0.09
Bloomberg Barclays US Agg./Credit/Corp. High Yield	0.61

Sources: Nareit, using data from FactSet and Intercontinental Exchange (ICE).

There are periods when equity REIT correlations with other securities are elevated, and they are at their highest during steep market downturns, such as the 2007–08 financial crisis. These correlations remained high during the post-crisis recovery, which lifted the value of most asset classes.

Nevertheless, the diversification benefit persists, and including real estate has been demonstrated to reduce portfolio risk. Oxford Economics studied the expected performance of listed European real estate as an asset class, comparing it with equities, fixed income, and commodities.[9] "A substantial allocation to listed real estate," the authors concluded, "does enhance the risk-return characteristics of a multi-asset portfolio." They went on to recommend larger allocations to real estate for European investors.

Exhibit 32 contains a summary of the performance and correlations of major asset classes and shows that European investors would benefit from real estate allocations.

EXHIBIT 32   Total Returns by Asset Class, Jan. 1999–May 2019

	Total Return (CAGR)	Standard Deviation	Sharpe Ratio	Correlation with Listed Real Estate (Annual Returns)
Small-cap equities	8.2%	22.9%	0.47	0.60
Large-cap equities	2.2	21.3	0.21	0.55
Government bonds	3.8	3.9	1.02	0.15
Investment-grade corporate bonds	4.3	5.5	0.84	0.41
High-yield corporate bonds	7.1	18.0	0.45	0.44
Diversified commodities	1.8	18.9	0.19	0.14
Listed real estate	8.4	22.7	0.49	1.00

Source: Data sources are as follows: small-cap equities, S&P Europe SmallCap index; large-cap equities, STOXX Europe 50 Index; government bonds, Bloomberg Barclays Pan-European Aggregate Government A Index; investment-grade corporate bonds, Bloomberg Barclays Pan-European Aggregate Corporate Index; high-yield corporate bonds, Bloomberg Barclays Pan-European High Yield Total Return Index; diversified commodities, Bloomberg Commodity Index; listed real estate, FTSE EPRA Nareit Developed Europe Index.

---

[9]Listed Real Estate in A Multi-Asset Portfolio: A European Perspective, pg,. 2, Oxford Economics, EPRA, September 2019.

Whether listed real estate behaves like stocks or private real estate is a matter of ongoing debate. We know that listed REITs are priced continuously whereas private real estate is appraised perhaps once a year, and there are other indications that their correlation is weak. Listed equity investors will discount future cash flows, and appraisers place heavy emphasis on current market conditions and recent trends.

CEM Benchmarking, based in Toronto, has performed several studies looking at the role of listed and unlisted real estate in the portfolio of defined contribution pension funds. CEM Benchmarking also concludes that real estate improves the risk–return profile of funds diversified across equities, fixed income, and alternatives. CEM analyzed the performance of each asset class over 12 years, from 2005 to 2016, across €2 trillion of AUM at the end of 2016. The data covered 36% of European pension assets and provided a comprehensive view about how real estate performs relative to the pension funds' other assets. Exhibit 33 presents the asset correlations for Dutch and UK pension funds, which are among the deepest pension fund markets with real estate concentrations.

EXHIBIT 33   Correlations between Aggregate Asset Class Net Returns for Dutch and UK Pension Funds

Correlation Matrix	Public Equity	Private Equity	Fixed Income	Hedge Funds	Listed Real Estate	Unlisted Real Estate	Unlisted Infrastructure
Public equity	1.00						
Private equity	0.93	1.00					
Fixed income	0.12	0.06	1.00				
Hedge funds	0.91	0.77	0.16	1.00			
Listed real estate	0.86	0.83	0.28	0.81	1.00		
Unlisted real estate	0.76	0.86	0.37	0.64	0.88	1.00	
Unlisted infrastructure	0.73	0.67	0.56	0.62	0.66	0.67	1.00

Notes: The period spans 2005–2016. Unlisted real estate and private equity are adjusted for lagged and smoothed reporting. Actual, as-reported correlations would appear higher and standard deviations, lower.

CEM Benchmarking conducted another study addressing some of the differences between listed and unlisted real estate performance by comparing the returns, volatility, correlations, and Sharpe ratios for various private real estate investing styles. The study covered more than 200 US public and private defined benefit pension funds over 20 years through 2017. Unlisted real estate's correlation with listed real estate was 0.91, which supports the view that listed REITs behave more like stocks in the short term and more like real estate in the long term. The outperformance of listed real estate was primarily due to fees and carry charged by external managers in the unlisted markets.

8. INFRASTRUCTURE

8.1. Introduction and Overview

The assets underlying infrastructure investments are real, capital intensive, and long lived. These assets are intended for public use, and they provide essential services—for instance, airports, health care facilities, and power plants. Most infrastructure assets are financed, owned, and operated by governments. A 2017 World Bank/PPIAF study of infrastructure spending in developing countries reported that 83% came from public investment,[10] but more and more infrastructure is being financed privately, with the increasing use by local, regional, and national governments of public–private partnerships. PPPs are typically defined as a long-term contractual relationship between the public sector and the private sector for the purpose of having the private sector deliver a project or service traditionally provided by the public sector.

Allocations to infrastructure investments have increased not only because of increasing interest by investors (demand-side growth) but also because of governments providing more investment opportunities (supply-side growth) as they expand the financing of infrastructure assets and the privatization of services. By the end of 2019, according to Preqin, global infrastructure funds had raised more than US$98 billion for infrastructure projects, a year-over-year increase of approximately 15% and up from US$30 billion in 2012, with AUM of US$582 billion (as of the end of June 2019),[11] reflecting what is commonly considered a growth market. Indeed, Global Infrastructure Hub (a G–20 initiative) and Oxford Economics forecast an infrastructure investment gap of US$15 trillion in 2040, based on the US$79 trillion presently forecast to be spent. (A further $3.5 trillion is required by 2030 to meet the United Nations' Sustainable Development Goals for electricity and water).[12]

Infrastructure investors may intend to lease the assets back to the government, to sell newly constructed assets to the government, or to hold and operate the assets until they reach operational maturity or perhaps for even longer. Exhibit 34 shows the characteristics of a typical infrastructure investment.

EXHIBIT 34   Typical Infrastructure Investment Characteristics

From an investment perspective, if the assets are being held and operated, the relatively inelastic demand for the assets and services is advantageous; regulation and the high costs of the assets create high barriers to entry, which give the provider of the services a strong competitive position.

---

[10]World Bank Group and Public-Private Infrastructure Advisory Facility, "Who Sponsors Infrastructure Projects? Disentangling Public and Private Contributions" (2019).

[11]Preqin, "2020 Preqin Global Infrastructure Report" (4 February 2020).

[12]Global Infrastructure Hub and Oxford Economics, "Global Infrastructure Outlook" (2017).

(Regulation, conversely, deters adverse monopolistic behavior from the public perspective.) Maintenance, asset replacement, and operating costs are factored into the pricing of the services.

Investors expect these assets to generate stable long-term cash flows that adjust for economic growth and inflation. Well-defined contractual structures that allocate the risk and responsibilities of asset delivery, service provision, and legal and financial obligations contribute to such stability.

These structural aspects allow for relatively high levels of leverage, which is particularly important for funding given the typically high up-front capital investment. Leverage enhances investor returns, and with debt commonly issued on a non-recourse basis, the exposure of investors to their investment is capped.

An increasingly important theme of infrastructure investing is the incorporation of ESG criteria, whether through the application of technology (e.g., renewable energy sources), consideration of the project's impact on the surrounding environment, or how the criteria inform the business relationships and governance approach. All key infrastructure stakeholders are increasingly supporting this theme: the government/public procuring authority, by incorporating environmental and social impact assessments in the planning and permit processes; financiers, through, for instance, the application of the Equator Principles as a condition for advancing loan facilities; and investors, who consciously use ESG criteria to choose investments. The Equator Principles represent a risk management and due diligence framework that has been adopted by financial institutions globally to take account of environmental and social risk in projects.

8.2. Description

8.2.1. Categories of Infrastructure Investments

Infrastructure investments are frequently categorized on the basis of the underlying assets. The broadest categorization organizes investments into economic and social infrastructure assets.

Economic infrastructure assets support economic activity and include three broad types of assets: transportation assets, information and communication technology (ICT) assets, and utility and energy assets:

- *Transportation assets* include roads, bridges, tunnels, airports, seaports, and heavy and light/urban railway systems. Income will usually be linked to demand based on traffic, airport, and seaport charges, tolls, and rail fares and hence is deemed to carry market risk.
- *ICT assets* include infrastructure that stores, broadcasts, and transmits information or data, such as telecommunication towers and data centers.
- *Utility and energy assets* generate power and produce potable water; they transmit, store, and distribute gas, water, and electricity; and they treat solid waste.

Utility assets increasingly encompass environmentally sustainable development, with a greater focus on renewable technologies, including solar, wind, and waste-to-energy power generation. (The increasing rejection of less environmentally viable fuel sources, such as coal, is part of the story.) Other energy assets may encompass downstream oil and gas infrastructure, such as pipelines and liquefied natural gas (LNG) terminals, and also natural resource assets, such as mining assets. The income earned from utility assets may also carry demand risk as buyers' energy and natural resources needs fluctuate. Alternatively, utilities can institute "take-or-pay" arrangements that lock buyers into minimum purchases whether they need the supply or not. Buyers usually have recourse if the utility falls short on performance, delivering supplies that are late or of inferior quality.

Social infrastructure assets are directed toward human activities and include such assets as educational, health care, social housing, and correctional facilities, with the focus on providing, operating, and maintaining the asset infrastructure. The relevant services that are administered through those facilities, meanwhile, be they medical or schooling, are usually provided separately by the public authority or by a private service provider contracted by the public authority. In some countries, this model has been extended to other public infrastructure, such as courthouses and government and municipal buildings. Income from social infrastructure is typically derived from a type of lease payment that depends on assuring availability (often referred to as availability payments) and on managing and maintaining the asset according to predefined standards. For instance, an availability payment may be reduced or voided if a hospital operating room is not available because of an electromechanical fault.

Infrastructure investments may also be categorized by the underlying asset's stage of development. Investing in infrastructure assets *that are to be constructed* is generally referred to as **greenfield investment**. The intent may be to lease or sell the assets to the government after construction or to either hold and operate the assets over the long term or hold and operate them for a shorter period until operational maturity and then sell them to new investors, thus ensuring capital appreciation that reflects the construction and commissioning risk. Greenfield investors typically invest alongside strategic investors or developers who specialize in developing the underlying assets. Investing in *existing* infrastructure assets may be referred to as **brownfield investment**. Perhaps the assets are owned by a government that wants to privatize them, lease them out, or sell them and lease them back; or they may be owned by greenfield investors seeking to realize the value of their investment through a sale. Typically, some of the assets' financial and operating history is available. Brownfield investors may include strategic investors who specialize in the operation of the underlying assets, but particularly in the case of privatizations, there will be financial investors involved who focus on the long-term stable returns.

Finally, infrastructure may be categorized by location. Infrastructure investments are available globally, and the geographic location of the underlying assets will inform the political and macroeconomic risks, particularly in light of the government's relationship to the assets.

Risks and expected returns may differ on the basis of the underlying asset's category, stage of development, and geographic location. How the investment is actualized—its form—also affects the risks and expected returns.

EXAMPLE 24

Describe one of the three ways by which an infrastructure investment is typically categorized.

Solution: Infrastructure assets are frequently characterized on the basis of: (1) underlying assets, (2) the underlying asset's state of development, and (3) the geographic location on the underlying assets.

The first category comprises economic assets supporting economic activity, such as transportation and energy/utility assets. It also includes social infrastructure assets, which enable public services directed toward human activities, such as education, health care, and housing.

The second category refers to the relevant stages of the infrastructure asset's life cycle. These include a greenfield investment for a newly created asset and a brownfield investment for an established asset.

The third category highlights the specific place (local, regional, national) associated with the government entity directly involved with the assets.

8.2.2. Forms of Infrastructure Investments

As is the case with real estate investments, infrastructure investments take a variety of forms. The choice affects liquidity, cash flow, and income streams. Investing directly in the underlying assets provides control and the opportunity to capture full value. It entails a large investment, however, and results in concentration and liquidity risks while the assets have to be managed and operated. Hence, direct investment often happens in consortia, with strategic partners who are better placed to manage certain risks (e.g., operational) or with other financial/institutional investors to limit individual concentration risk. However, most investors invest indirectly.

Indirect investment vehicles include infrastructure funds (which are similar in structure to private equity funds and may be closed end or open end), infrastructure ETFs, and company shares. Different asset class strategies, including debt and mezzanine investment, are offered, but the vast majority of investors are focused on equity instruments. According to IJInvestor, equity is the preferred instrument for 77% of fund investors, with 10% looking for mixed strategies and 9% looking for debt and mezzanine strategies.[13]

Investors concerned about liquidity and diversification may choose publicly traded infra-structure securities or master limited partnerships. Publicly traded infrastructure securities provide the benefits not only of liquidity but also of reasonable fees, transparent governance, market prices, and the ability to diversify among underlying assets. An investor should be aware, however, that publicly traded infrastructure securities represent a small segment of the infrastructure investment universe and tend to be clustered in certain asset categories. Master limited partnerships (MLPs) trade on exchanges and are pass-through entities, similar to REITs. They also share with REITs applicable regulations that vary among countries, and income is passed through to the investors for taxation; MLPs generally distribute most free cash flow to their investors. Typically, the GP manages the partnership, receives a fee, and holds a small partnership interest, with LPs owning the remaining majority partnership interest.

8.3. Risk and Return Characteristics

The lowest-risk infrastructure investments have more stable cash flows and higher dividend payout ratios. They typically enjoy fewer growth opportunities, however, and lower expected returns. (See Exhibit 35.) For example, an MLP with an investment in a brownfield asset that

EXHIBIT 35   Typical Infrastructure Investment Risk–Return Profile

Early-Stage investments	Mid-Stage investments	Late-Stage investments
Investment in greenfield projects, with higher-risk profile (construction, commissioning, etc.), but typically deliver higher prospects for return through capital gain & yield	Investment in existing projects, which have been commissioned and commenced operations, thus also still delivering prospects for return through capital gain & yield (albeit generally at relatively lower level than early stage investments)	Investment in existing projects, which have been operational for a number of years, with returns generally yield driven

Risk profile decreases as investment moves from early to late stage Commensurate decrease in the level of return

[13]IJInvestor, "IJInvestor Funds & Investors Report - Q1 2020" (17 April).

is being leased back to a government represents a low-risk infrastructure investment, as does an investment in assets with a history of steady cash flows, such as certain established toll roads. An investment in a fund that is building a new power plant without any operating history (a greenfield investment) is riskier.

There is a risk that infrastructure revenues diverge meaningfully from expectations, leverage creates financing risk, and operational risk and construction risk are ever present. (See Exhibit 36.) As for regulatory risk, because the projects involve essential services, governments usually regulate the investments with strictures on the sale of the underlying assets, on operations and service quality, and on prices and profit margins. Global infrastructure investing introduces additional uncertainty, such as currency risk, political risk, and profit-repatriation risk. Hence, the fund manager must ensure these risks are appropriately managed and mitigated through insurance, financial instruments, and whatever other mechanisms are available.

EXHIBIT 36   Typical Infrastructure Risk Management

PERFORMANCE RISKS	**Demand/ volume risk**	Enter into take-or-pay arrangements, where payments are based upon the availability rather than the use of an asset
	Operational risk	Enter into operation and maintenance contracts with reputable and experienced operators who are incentivized to meet or exceed the minimum contractual performance standards through an appropriate regime
	Construction risk	Enter into fixed-price date-certain contracts with reputable and experienced contractors to minimize construction cost overruns and delays
STRUCTURAL RISKS	**Financing/ Interest rate risk**	Enter into interest rate swaps
	Regulatory risk	If regulation is by contract (e.g., PPP agreement), ensure clear, unambiguous provisions that govern such risks; if regulation is defined and enforced by a regulatory body, then ensure due diligence is undertaken on that body
	Political risk	Purchase political risk insurance for protection, as appropriate, against events such as expropriation, political violence, sovereign debt default, etc.
	Currency risk	Ensure PPP agreement incorporates appropriate mechanisms to permit an adjustment to tariffs when there are material foreign exchange fluctuations
	Tax/profit repatriation risks	Ensure PPP agreement incorporates appropriate mechanisms to permit an adjustment to tariffs and/or other compensation when there are significant changes in law/regulations affecting tax and profit repatriation

Returns, of course, depend on such factors as investment type. Exhibit 37 provides an illustrative range of returns for a private infrastructure fund according to different risk profiles, noting that returns may vary at an individual investment/asset level depending on its specific characteristics.

EXHIBIT 37   Private Infrastructure Fund Illustrative Target Returns

Higher-Risk Profile	Medium-Risk Profile	Lower-Risk Profile
Greenfield projects without guarantees of demand upon completion—e.g., variable electricity prices, uncertain traffic on roads and through ports	Mostly brownfield assets (with some capital expenditure requirements) and some greenfield assets (with limited construction and demand risk)	Brownfield assets with mitigated risks—e.g., fully constructed with contracted/regulated revenues
Located in OECD countries and emerging markets	Located primarily in OECD countries	Located in the most stable OECD countries
High weighting to capital appreciation	Mix of yield and capital appreciation	High weighting to current yield
Target equity returns of 14%+	**Target equity returns of 10%–12%**	**Target equity returns of 6%–8%**

Note: Target equity returns are net of fees.
Source: Cambridge Associates, "Digging In: Assessing the Private Infrastructure Opportunity Today," Research Note (April 2017).

Most infrastructure funds gravitate toward the medium- and lower-risk profiles. Rolling one-year-horizon returns have been around 10% annually since 2016.[14]

In summary, infrastructure investments generally provide investors with stable, long-term capital growth and cash distributions, according to the risks assumed, and these risks tend to be relatively well defined. Preqin maintains a return series of private funds investing in infrastructure deals. Standard & Poor's, FTSE Group, and other firms also publish indexes of publicly traded infrastructure companies.

EXAMPLE 25

Fill in the blank by choosing from among the following options:

_____ is an infrastructure investment characteristic *most likely* valuable to investors aiming to sell newly constructed assets to the government.

A. "Strategically important"
B. "Monopolistic and regulated"
C. "Significant capital investment"

Solution: A is the correct answer because the related priority will probably increase the demand of the public buyer to effectively provide essential services to its citizens. B would be more advantageous for investors holding and operating an asset and charging fees to the buyer, with the inelastic demand supporting pricing and regulations increasing the barriers to entry that improve the competitive position. C is more of a challenge than a benefit to the investor, requiring greater funding capability and potentially higher financial risks.

---

[14]Preqin, "2020 Preqin Global Infrastructure Report" 4 (February 2020).

8.4. Diversification Benefits

We have established that investors expect infrastructure assets to generate stable long-term cash flows that adjust for economic growth and inflation. Investors may also expect capital appreciation, depending on the type and timing of their investment.

Investing in infrastructure may allow for the addition of an income stream, for further portfolio diversification by adding an asset class with typically low correlation with existing investments, and for some protection against inflation. Low exposure to short-term GDP growth issues may also be a factor.

Infrastructure has proven to be relatively resilient to recent swings in the equity markets. According to Preqin, from December 2017 to December 2018 as equity returns fell from 22.8% to −9.6% and hedge fund returns fell from 12.2% to −3.05%, infrastructure returns dropped only from 11.4% to 9.6%.[15] Such resilience is a key factor for many institutional investors with an eye on portfolio construction.

Exhibit 38 provides an illustrative example of the low correlation of infrastructure—and in particular, unlisted Australian infrastructure—with other asset classes over the 10-year period through June 2019.

EXHIBIT 38   Quarterly Return Correlations for Selected Asset Classes, 2009–2019

	Global Treasury Bonds	Global Equities	Australian Equities	Global REITs	Listed Infrastructure	Unlisted Australian Infrastructure
Global Treasury bonds	1.00					
Global equities	−0.49	1.00				
Australian equities	−0.36	0.89	1.00			
Global REITs	0.18	0.64	0.70	1.00		
Listed infrastructure	−0.12	0.81	0.75	0.68	1.00	
Unlisted Australian infrastructure	−0.08	0.06	−0.05	−0.21	0.13	1.00

Notes: All data are for the period 31 March 2009–30 June 2019, except for the FTSE EPRA Nareit Developed Rental Net index (Global REITs), where data series began in May 2009.
• Global Treasury bonds: Bloomberg Barclays Global Treasury GDP Index
• Global equities: MSCI World Net Accumulation Index
• Australian equities: S&P/ASX 200
• Global REITs: FTSE EPRA Nareit Developed Rental Net index
• Listed infrastructure: Dow Jones Brookfield Global Infrastructure Net Accumulation Index
• Unlisted infrastructure: MSCI Australian Unlisted Infrastructure Index
Source: John Julian, "The Pros of Infrastructure Investment in a Lower-for-Longer Environment," AMP Capital (October 2019). www.ampcapital.com/au/en/insights-hub/articles/2019/october/the-pros-of-infrastructure-investment-in-a-lower-for-longer-environment.

Because these investments are placed in long-lived assets, infrastructure may better match the longer-term liability structure of certain investors, such as pension funds, superannuation schemes, and life insurance companies. It also suits the longer-term horizon of sovereign

---

[15]"2020 Preqin Global Infrastructure Report."

wealth funds, which tend to make the largest allocations to this asset class—around 5%–6% of total AUM, according to Preqin.[16]

EXAMPLE 26

To highlight typical risk management approaches on infrastructure projects, draw connecting lines to match a particular risk type with its appropriate mitigating mechanism:

Infrastructure Risk Type	Offsetting Mechanism
Construction	Incentivized maintenance contract
Operational	Insurance against debt default
Demand/volume	PPP agreement
Currency	Take-or-pay arrangement
Political	Fixed-price date-certain contract

Solution: The correct matches are as follows:

Infrastructure Risk Type	Offsetting Mechanism
Construction	Incentivized maintenance contract
Operational	Insurance against debt default
Demand/volume	PPP agreement
Currency	Take-or-pay arrangement
Political	Fixed-price date-certain contract

---

9. ISSUES IN PERFORMANCE APPRAISAL

9.1. Overview of Performance Appraisal for Alternative Investments

Portfolio managers invest in one of two basic ways to achieve returns: passively or actively. Passive investments focus on index or asset class coverage. Portfolios comprising real estate, commodity, and infrastructure instruments may be passively managed to provide exposure to these alternative asset classes. However, alternative investments are generally actively managed, aiming to achieve added portfolio benefits, but typically at a higher net cost for such active management.

Investors frequently look to alternative investments for diversification and a chance to earn relatively high returns on a risk-adjusted basis. They also value low correlation and a more risk-neutral source of alpha.

Evaluating an alternative investment can be a subtle qualitative exercise, one that depends on the initial objectives of the investor, as opposed to a purely quantitative, one-size-fits-all

---

[16]"2020 Preqin Global Infrastructure Report."

exercise. Much of the nuance revolves around not just the total net return created by an alternative investment but also the path and volatility (drawdown risk) required to create the total return and how an alternative investment fits into and benefits a larger portfolio of assets—in other words, its portfolio-level correlation benefit.

However, there is often a naive attraction to alternative investments based on their expected returns, which neglects to consider the atypical risks they present—risks we can examine on both a standalone and portfolio basis:

- Limited transparency
- Often low portfolio-level liquidity
- The active use of leverage (and, at times, derivatives)
- General strategy and product complexity
- Mark-to-market issues for a portfolio with niche specialized products
- Limited redemption availability and portfolio pressures from eventual redemption activities
- The general challenge of manager differentiation and diversification
- The fee drag associated with alternative investments, which can be non-trivial

In this section, we examine some of these issues in the context of applying traditional performance measurement tools to alternative investments, which is sometimes done incorrectly. In Section 10, we will delve into the impact of fee structures on alternative asset evaluation.

9.2. Common Approaches to Performance Appraisal and Application Challenges

9.2.1. Sharpe Ratio

The Sharpe ratio is probably the first basic intuitive metric that some people use to evaluate an alternative investment. It is often prominently displayed in marketing materials. The single biggest flaw, however, in a dependence on the Sharpe ratio is probably the underlying assumption of normally distributed returns.

In light of our list of atypical risks—leverage, illiquidity, mark-to-market smoothing, poor portfolio transparency—return profiles of alternative investments tend to be asymmetric and skewed, making the Sharpe ratio a less-than-ideal performance measure. For non-normal return distributions with significant skewness (fat tails in one direction or the other) and kurtosis (a measure of whether the data are heavy tailed or light tailed relative to a normal distribution), volatility is not a perfect measure of dispersion. Although still widely cited, the Sharpe ratio may not, therefore, be a good risk-adjusted performance measurement to rely on.

Given that caveat and taken by itself as a simple starting point, an attractive Sharpe ratio for an alternative strategy might be deemed to be anywhere between 1.0 and 2.0. Getting twice the return per unit of risk is generally quite attractive and hard to achieve; getting only a single unit of return for a unit of risk (a Sharpe ratio of 1.0) might be deemed acceptable but not overwhelmingly compelling, unless the strategy in question also has negative correlation attributes compared with other strategy areas in a portfolio, as with macro or CTA managers. In comparison, as of the end of 2019, the long-only S&P 500 equity index delivered an average annual return of around 10% over the past 32 years but with a relatively high annual standard deviation around the mean, 15%, yielding a Sharpe ratio close to 0.66. Alternative asset managers generally endeavor to offer a far superior risk–reward profile.

Ironically, if a Sharpe ratio for an alternative manager is too high—say, 3.0–4.0—extra caution in the evaluation of that manager may be warranted. These types of Sharpe ratios are typically only available if some degree of *return smoothing* is taking place. Illiquid securities that are hard to value and coupon return streams that might one day suddenly come to an end (sometimes along with a sudden loss of principal, as with a structured bond product that extinguishes itself or a short option strategy) can produce very high Sharpe ratios for a period of time that may deceive and then ultimately disappoint naive investors.

The ultimate test for a portfolio is really upon liquidation, but investment value at that point is frequently at odds with how accounting standards require alternative asset positions to be carried on the books. Furthermore, neither expected liquidation value nor reported value may account for the tail-risk aspects in an unfortunate macro environment.

The nature of the positions that a portfolio holds must be considered: Is the Sharpe ratio even the relevant metric?

9.2.2. Sortino Ratio

A second, arguably more valuable, quantitative measure of performance is return relative to downside volatility—the Sortino ratio. However, the Sharpe and Sortino risk measures alone still do not take into account the correlation of alternative assets with the traditional assets that their inclusion in the portfolio may be intended to hedge.

We have established that alternative investments' diversifying potential is part of the motivation for investing in them: Investors perceive an opportunity to improve the risk–return relationship in the portfolio context. Given the historical return, volatility, and correlation profiles of alternative investments, combining a portfolio of alternative investments with a portfolio of traditional investments should improve the overall portfolio's risk–return profile. Doing so can increase the risk-adjusted return of the overall portfolio because of potentially higher returns to the portfolio and a less-than-perfect correlation with traditional investments.

It is key for investors to consider how an alternative manager's investment choices will correlate with traditional assets and how the assets in question affect drawdown options and liquidity.

9.2.3. Treynor Ratio and Correlation Behavior

Alternative assets are generally deemed more valuable when they have a lower beta to traditional assets, and this is where the Treynor ratio proves useful: It is a measure of the excess average return of an investment relative to its beta to a relevant benchmark, such as a broad equity index.

The lower the beta of the alternative asset, the higher the Treynor ratio will be, and all else being equal, when comparing alternative investment possibilities, an asset with a higher Treynor ratio will be deemed more attractive than an asset with a low Treynor ratio.

The main limitation of the Treynor ratio is that it is based on historical beta data that may change in the future. The ratio also becomes less meaningful if the beta of the alternative asset to its systematic benchmark is negative, which is certainly possible for some alternative assets.

The Treynor ratio is the first ratio we have covered that encompasses the return of an alternative asset relative to its expected systematic risk. Examining an alternative asset's correlation coefficient with the overall market and with the other assets in the portfolio will also be instructive. All else being equal, less correlated alternative assets are generally deemed more attractive for portfolio diversification purposes than more correlated assets. It is nevertheless important to note that the expected diversification benefits from alternative investments are not always realized, even when they are most needed. Correlations between risky investments increase during periods of market stress and can approach 1.0 during financial crises.

For now, one easy proxy for measuring return relative to risk for alternative investments—and a far simpler calculation to observe and calculate—is to analyze the performance record for average return relative to the worst drawdown loss. A maximum drawdown (MDD) is the maximum observed loss from a peak to a trough of a portfolio, before a new peak is attained. The **Calmar ratio** is a comparison of the average annual compounded return to this maximum drawdown risk. The higher (lower) the Calmar ratio, the better (worse) an alternative asset performed on a risk-adjusted basis over a specified period of time. The Calmar ratio is typically calculated using the prior three years of performance, and it thus adjusts over time. Variations of the ratio exist: The **MAR ratio** uses a full investment history and the average drawdown. Both ratios help address the left-tailed return profile that sometimes characterizes alternative assets.

Other ratios are applied to specific alternative strategies and require more granular disclosure from investment managers. Some quantitative managers refer to the percentage of profitable trades (or "batting average") and their "slugging percentage," the magnitude of the gains from winning trades divided by the losses from losing trades. A manager who makes outsized gains on winning trades while incurring small losses on losing trades is worth considering.

EXAMPLE 27

True or false: The Sharpe ratio measures the amount of risk per unit of return.

A. True
B. False

Solution: B is correct; the statement is false. The Sharpe, Sortino, and Treynor ratios are risk-adjusted performance measurements. They are measures of return per unit of risk.

EXAMPLE 28

Is the following statement true or false? The Sharpe and Sortino ratios share the same denominator.

A. True
B. False

Solution: B is correct; the statement is false. The Sharpe and Sortino ratios share the same numerator—average annualized return net of the risk free-rate. Their denominators are different. The denominator for the Sharpe ratio is standard deviation of returns, and the denominator for the Sortino ratio is downside deviation of returns—a semi-deviation measure of volatility only during periods of loss for an alternative investment.

EXAMPLE 29

Which of the following performance measures uses beta as the risk measure?

A. Sharpe ratio
B. Treynor ratio
C. Sortino ratio

Solution: The correct answer is B. Both Sharpe ratio and Sortino ratio use standard deviation as a risk measure. Treynor ratio uses beta as a risk measure.

9.3. Private Equity and Real Estate Performance Evaluation

Unlike liquid hedge fund strategies, alternative investments that involve private equity and real estate tend to have variable cash flows.

Private equity investments generally involve an initial capital commitment, but actual capital flows often lag that commitment because capital "calls" are staggered over substantive periods of time. Private equity returns are frequently described in terms of the J-curve effect: a substantive initial capital commitment promise, followed by high initial fee drag (calculated on total committed capital, not the capital actually called), followed by the identification of longer-term growth or turnaround opportunities, and an eventual positive return (the investor hopes) when the staggered returns of the fund are realized. The component investments mature and are sold at various times, and the partnership finally closes—but usually only after six to eight years (often with two-year extensions allowed at the discretion of the general partner or after a vote of approval by a majority of limited partners). The line representing the return changes from downward sloping to positive and then to energetically upward sloping later in the investment's life (if all goes well).

The real estate pathway starts with initial property purchases, followed at times by substantive cash outlays for improvements, followed by instances of accounting depreciation that can influence after-tax performance, followed typically by the receipt of rents and then an eventual property sale (often at a long-term tax-advantaged tax rate).

The measurement of success in both instances depends far more on the timing and magnitude of cash flows in and out of the investments, and these are often hard to standardize, let alone always properly anticipate. Given the long time horizon, the application of different tax treatments can have a non-trivial impact on after-tax investment returns.

As a general rule, the best way to start evaluating such investments is with the IRR of the respective cash flows into an investment and the timing thereof, versus the magnitude and the timing of the cash flows returned by the investment (inclusive of tax benefits).

In an independent, fixed-life private equity fund, the decisions to raise money, take money in the form of capital calls, and distribute proceeds are all at the discretion of the private equity manager. Timing of cash flows is an important part of the investment decision process. The private equity manager should thus be rewarded or penalized for the results of those timing decisions, and the calculation of an IRR is a key metric for doing so.

Although the determination of an IRR involves certain assumptions about a financing rate to use for outgoing cash flows (typically a weighted average cost of capital) and a reinvestment rate to use for incoming cash flows (which must be assumed and may or may not actually be earned), the IRR is the key metric used to assess longer-term alternative investments in the private equity and real estate worlds.

Because of this complexity, a shortcut methodology often used by both private equity and real estate managers involves simply citing a **multiple of invested capital (MOIC)**, or money multiple, on total paid-in capital. Here, one simply measures the total value of all distributions and residual asset values (assets that may still be awaiting their ultimate sale) relative to an initial total investment. Although this shortcut valuation completely ignores the timing of cash flows, it is easier to calculate, and it is intuitively easier to understand when someone says they received two or three times their initial investment. But how long it takes to realize this value does matter. A 2× return on one's initial investment would be phenomenal if the return were collected over two years but far less compelling if it took 15 years to realize.

In general, because private equity and real estate investing involve longer holding periods, there is less emphasis on evaluating them in terms of shorter-term portfolio correlation benefits. After a private equity fund has fully drawn in its monetary commitments, interim accounting values for a private equity partnership become less critical for a period of time because no incoming or outgoing cash flows may immediately hinge on such valuations. During this "middle period" in the life of a private equity fund, accounting values may not always be particularly reflective of the future potential realizations (and hence the expected returns) of the fund. It is not that the value of the investments is not actually rising and falling in the face of economic influences; rather, accounting conventions simply leave longer-lived investments marked at their initial cost for some time or make only modest adjustments to carrying value until clearer impairments or realization events take place.

Ironically, many investors gravitate to private equity *because* they are not easily marked to market and can deliver somewhat smoothed returns over time—with less short-term mark-to-market angst. Although most private equity managers are conservative in their marks (awaiting actual realization events), a lagged mark-to-market process can at times offer a false sense of success, diminishing short-term investment worry but subsequently delivering the occasional back-end-loaded investment disappointment. Private equity interim valuations and real estate appraisals can certainly be inaccurate or skewed at times despite the best efforts of auditors to present a fair valuation.

The lagging impact of shorter-term economic events on the interim accounting valuations of these strategies makes them appear more resilient and less correlated than they really are. A more realistic picture may emerge when premature portfolio liquidations are forced on managers. The lack of transparency around such investments and the slowness to mark them to market can be incorrectly construed by investors as an overall lack of volatility.

Along this imperfect path and in an effort to benchmark how longer-term investments may be faring, private equity and real estate managers are generally judged by where they fall in terms of a *quartile ranking*, which depicts their performance against a cohort of peer investment vehicles constructed with similar investment attributes and funded around the same time, or what is often referred to as the same vintage year.

Real estate managers are also often judged by the **cap rate** being earned on their properties, which is simply the annual rent actually being earned (net of any vacancies) divided by the price originally paid for the property. This approach ignores the true values of properties should they need to be sold.

The large latitude around carried valuations for both private equity and real estate strategies makes any application of shorter-term risk metrics highly inappropriate.

Instead, the probability of permanent impairment on an investment is likely the best risk measure. Along these lines, an admittedly backward-looking metric of some interest and potential value that many private equity managers refer to is their historic **capital loss ratio**, defined as the percentage of capital in deals that have been realized below cost, net of any recovered proceeds, divided by total invested capital. Because markets have been generally buoyant for the past 30 years, investors can overestimate the true resilience of private equity and real estate. Having money tied up in longer-lived investments, for 7 to 10 years, should conceptually earn an illiquidity premium but may easily result in return disappointment given the wrong economic environment.

9.4. Hedge Funds: Leverage, Illiquidity, and Redemption Terms

9.4.1. Leverage

Hedge funds may use leverage to obtain higher returns on their investments. Leverage has the effect of magnifying gains and losses because it allows for taking a larger position relative to the capital committed. Hedge funds leverage their portfolios by using derivatives or borrowing capital from **prime brokers**, negotiating with them to establish margin requirements, interest, and fees in advance of trading. The hedge fund deposits cash or other collateral into a margin account with the prime broker, and the prime broker essentially lends the hedge fund the shares, bonds, or derivatives to make additional investments. The margin account represents the hedge fund's net equity in its positions. The minimum margin required depends on the riskiness of the investment portfolio and the creditworthiness of the hedge fund.

Leverage is a large part of the reason that some hedge funds either earn larger-than-normal returns or suffer significant losses. If the margin account or the hedge fund's equity in a position declines below a certain level, the lender initiates a margin call and requests that the hedge fund put up more collateral. An inability to meet margin calls can have the effect of magnifying or locking in losses because the hedge fund may have to liquidate (close) the losing position. This liquidation can lead to further losses if the order size is sufficiently large to move the security's market price before the fund can sufficiently eliminate the position.

Under normal conditions, the application of leverage may be necessary for yielding meaningful returns from given quantitative, arbitrage, or relative value strategies. But with added leverage comes increased risk. For example, in August 2007, a sudden cascade of problems arose from the application of leverage: so-called unattractive stocks rallied sharply over a 10-day period of short covering while stocks deemed fundamentally "attractive" declined as quantitative managers were forced to sell them. Many managers positioning themselves as market neutral and "safe" quickly lost 20%–25% of their portfolio value. The tail-risk aspect of such strategies was revealed to be the leverage and the "crowding" phenomenon of so many market participants holding similar positions that needed to be downsized when the market moved. Leverage can cause left-tailed events when mechanical downsizing and crowd psychology impacts come into play. Market watchers said that the source of the 2007 upheaval was no more than the butterfly effect of one levered quantitative manager after another deciding to de-lever at the same time.

The application of leverage to a strategy may not be revealed by studying the Sharpe ratio, the Sortino ratio, or another financial performance metric. Instead, it may underpin the strategy undetected. Understanding the impact of leverage on a portfolio is less about what the track record has been and more about *how* that track record was created. Analysts evaluating the alternative asset space should, therefore, scrutinize the returns of any alternative asset that relies on high leverage.

9.4.2. Illiquidity and Potential Redemption Pressures

A second qualitative issue for many hedge funds is the manner in which portfolios are marked to market. This issue is less important for traditional long–short managers trading only publicly traded equities, but it still can cause problems.

Consider the long–short equity manager involved in thinly traded small-capitalization stocks that see only a few thousand shares traded daily. Perhaps the manager was able at one point to source a block of stock from a retiring firm founder in order to establish the long exposure. An outside fund administrator uses a daily quoted price to value these shares, but the manager knows there is little chance of actually liquidating all the shares at that price.

This problem will be worse for a convertible bond manager, a credit-oriented manager, or a structured products manager who faces wider bid–offer spreads and deals in some securities that are particularly illiquid or that trade only "by appointment" (in other words, securities that trade so infrequently an appointment is almost necessary).

Proper valuations are important for calculating performance and meeting potential redemptions without incurring undue transaction costs for liquidating exposures. The frequency with which alternative assets are valued and how they are valued vary among funds. Hedge funds are generally valued by the manager internally, and these valuations are confirmed by an outside administrator on a daily or perhaps weekly basis; performance is reported to investors by the administrator on a monthly or quarterly basis. The valuation may use market values or estimated values of the underlying positions. When market prices or quotes are used for valuation, funds may differ in which price or quote they use (bid price, ask price, average quote, or median quote). A common practice is to use an average of the bid and the ask. A more conservative and theoretically more accurate approach is to use bid prices for long positions and ask prices for short positions because these are more realistic prices at which the positions could be closed.

In some instances, the underlying positions may be in highly illiquid or even non-traded investments, and since such securities may have no reliable market values, it becomes necessary to estimate values. Starting in 2006, with later amendments and modifications, GAAP accounting rules in the United States created a methodology that involves the categorization of investments into three buckets: Level 1, 2, and 3 asset pricing. Level 1 assets involve situations where an exchange-traded, publicly traded price is available and is mandated to be used for valuation purposes. When such pricing is not available, outside broker quotes, or Level 2 values, may be relied on. As a final recourse, when such broker quotes are deemed either unavailable or unreliable, assets may be computed using only internal models—a process referred to as Level 3 asset pricing. No matter the model used by a manager in such circumstances, it should be independently tested, benchmarked, and calibrated to industry-accepted standards to ensure a consistency of approach. Because of the potential for conflicts of interest when applying estimates of value, hedge funds must develop procedures for in-house valuation, communicate these procedures to clients, and adhere to them.

Notwithstanding best practice, the very nature of assets that can be valued only on a "mark-to-model" basis can and should be a concern for the alternative asset investor. A model may reflect an imperfect theoretical valuation and not a true liquidation value. The illiquid nature of these assets means that estimates, rather than observable transaction prices, may well have factored into any valuation. As a result, returns may be smoothed or overstated and the volatility of returns, understated. Any investor relying on a risk metric such as a Sharpe ratio for such illiquid strategy situations is basically involved in self-deception as to the true drawdown risk of the strategy. As a generalized statement, any investment vehicle that is heavily involved with Level 3–priced assets deserves increased scrutiny and due diligence.

EXAMPLE 30   Hedge Fund Valuation

A hedge fund with a market-neutral strategy restricts its investment universe to domestic publicly traded equity securities that are actively traded on an exchange or between over-the-counter brokers. In calculating net asset value, the fund is most likely to use which of the following to value underlying positions?

A. Exchange last-trade pricing and/or averaged quotes of any available over-the-counter bid–offer spreads
B. Average quotes adjusted for liquidity
C. Bid price for shorts and ask price for longs

Solution: A is correct. The fund is most likely to use exchange-traded last-trade pricing (Level 1 pricing) or averaged quotes of publicly available bid–offer spreads (Level 2 pricing). The securities are actively traded, so no liquidity adjustment is required.

If the fund uses bid–ask prices, it will use ask prices for shorts and bid prices for longs; these are the prices at which the positions are closed.

Understanding and evaluating "tail events"—low-probability, high-severity instances of stress—is an important yet extraordinarily difficult aspect of the risk management process, particularly when dealing with illiquid securities. Stress testing and scenario analysis are often used as a complement to other risk measures to develop a better understanding of a portfolio's potential loss under both normal and stressed market conditions. Stress testing involves estimating losses under extremely unfavorable conditions.

Another factor that can lock in or magnify losses for hedge funds is investor redemptions. Redemptions frequently occur when a hedge fund is performing poorly. Redemptions may require the hedge fund manager to liquidate some positions and potentially receive particularly disadvantageous prices when forced to do so by redemption pressures, while also incurring transaction costs. Funds sometimes charge redemption fees (typically payable to the remaining investors) to discourage redemption and to offset the transaction costs for remaining investors. Notice periods provide an opportunity for the hedge fund manager to liquidate a position in an orderly fashion without magnifying the losses. Lockup periods—time periods when investors cannot withdraw their capital—provide the hedge fund manager the required time to implement and potentially realize a strategy's expected results. If the hedge fund receives a drawdown request shortly after a new investment, the lockup period forces the investors who made the request to stay in the fund for a period of time rather than be allowed to immediately withdraw. A hedge fund's ability to demand a long lockup period while raising a significant amount of investment capital depends a great deal on the reputation of either the firm or the hedge fund manager. Funds of hedge funds may offer more redemption flexibility than is afforded to direct investors in hedge funds because of special redemption arrangements with the underlying hedge fund managers, the maintenance of added cash reserves, access to temporary bridge-loan financing, or the simple avoidance of less liquid hedge fund strategies.

Ideally, redemption terms should be designed to match the expected liquidity of the assets being invested in, but even with careful planning, an initial drawdown can turn into something far more serious when it involves illiquid and obscure assets. These left-tailed loss events are not easily modeled for hedge funds.

EXAMPLE 31 Effect of Redemption

A European credit hedge fund has a very short redemption notice period—one week— because the fund's managers believe it invests in highly liquid asset classes and is market neutral. The fund has a small number of holdings that represent a significant portion of the outstanding issue of each holding. The fund's lockup period has expired. Unfortunately, in one particular month, because of the downgrades of two large holdings, the hedge fund has a drawdown (decline in NAV) of more than 10%. The declines in value of the two holdings result in margin calls from their prime broker, and the drawdown results in requests to redeem 50% of total partnership interests. The combined requests are *most likely* to:

A. force the hedge fund to liquidate or unwind 50% of its positions in an orderly fashion throughout the week.
B. have little effect on the prices received when liquidating the positions because the hedge fund has a week before the partnership interests are redeemed.
C. result in a forced liquidation, which is likely to further drive down prices and result in ongoing pressures on the hedge fund as it tries to convince nervous investors to remain in the fund.

Solution: C is correct. One week may not be enough time to unwind such a large portion of the fund's positions in an orderly fashion that also does not further drive down prices. A downgrade is not likely to have a temporary effect, so even if other non-losing positions are liquidated to meet the redemption requests, it is unlikely that the two large holdings will return to previous or higher values in short order. Also, the hedge fund may have a week to satisfy the requests for redemptions, but the margin call must be met immediately. Overall, sudden redemptions at the fund level can have a cascading negative impact on a fund.

The previous discussion applies mostly to liquid alternative asset strategies, principally hedge funds. In the world of private equity and real estate alternative assets, other methodologies are used to measure relative performance. Here, we find more issues with lagged and smoothed pricing.

It is important to note that although the ratios we have considered are among the best performance and risk tools available, they can still lead to inappropriate conclusions, as shown in the following example.

EXAMPLE 32

Steamboat Structured Products LLC is a manager that specializes in the purchase and sale of residential mortgage-backed securities, sometimes hedged with other put option and short equity index exposures. For the most part, its strategy is geared to earn an attractive monthly mortgage payment on as low of a loan-to-value ratio of a secured property as possible. Steamboat managers are generally very good at sourcing such investments.

However, Steamboat's managers discover that in the wake of the 2008 financial crisis, many small pieces of "odd-lot" RMBS paper are being sold by financial institutions across the United States, sometimes with face values of just $200,000–$400,000. This paper is often offered at a 10% or 15% discount to the price a more sizable and significant "round-lot" block of $1 million–$2 million of the same type of paper might trade.

Steamboat managers know that their outside administrator will place only a single round-lot valuation on each security identifier (often referred to as a CUSIP) in their portfolio, and thus they can't resist starting to buy as many of these odd-lot offerings as possible. When they do, their administrator does indeed immediately mark them higher, which, as Steamboat continues this practice month after month, creates a lovely track record of constant "trading profits" on top of their natural coupon income. To the greatest extent possible, Steamboat hopes to create odd-lot "matchers" to eventually aggregate its exposures into larger tradable blocks. But what happens instead is that the firm ends up with 2,000 small-position line items in its book and a glorious track record.

This is a story of an illiquid asset class that is naturally hard to trade and mark. Steamboat's Sharpe ratio, Sortino ratio, and Calmar ratio all look stronger than they really should be, mostly because of accounting conventions. If Steamboat were ever forced to sell its portfolio, the odd-lot discount earned as trading revenue would largely disappear and be replaced by the true liquidation values that Steamboat would find in the market from others for its accumulated odd-lot portfolio.

Performance ratio analysis must, therefore, be discounted when dealing with illiquid securities as described here. Although not necessarily fraudulent, standard accounting practices can be purposefully gamed.

10. CALCULATING FEES AND RETURNS

Now that we have considered alternative assets, their risks and rewards, their investment characteristics, and headline strategies, performing a few calculations will take us close to the real-world evaluations made by investment managers and the investors who hire them.

10.1. Alternative Asset Fee Structures and Terms

EXAMPLE 33   Incentive Fees Relative to Waterfall Types

A PE fund invests $15 million in a nascent luxury yacht manufacturer and $17 million in a new casino venture. The yacht manufacturer generates a $9 million profit when the company is acquired by a larger competitor, but the casino venture turns out to be a flop when its state licensing is eventually denied and it generates a $10 million loss. If the manager's carried interest incentive fee is 20% of the profits, what would this incentive be with a European-style waterfall whole-of-fund approach, and what would it be if the incentive is paid on an American-style waterfall deal-by-deal basis (assuming no clawback applies)?

Solution: In aggregate, the fund lost money (+$9 million − $10 million = −$1 million), so with a European-style whole-of-fund waterfall and assuming the time period for the gain and the loss are the same, there is no incentive fee. With an American-style waterfall, the GP could still earn 20% × $9 million = $1.8 million on the yacht company, thereby further compounding the loss to the ultimate investor to −$2.8 million net of fees.

	Aggregate	Yacht Company	Casino Venture
Investment	$32 m	$15 m	$17 m
Profit/Loss	−$1 m	$9 m	−$10 m
Incentive by Deal		20% × $9m = $1.8m	$0 m
Total Incentive	$0 m	$1.8 m	

If the gain and loss in this example transpired sequentially over different years, perhaps with the yacht company gain occurring first and then the Casino venture loss later on, the outcome for a European-style waterfall would typically result in an initial accrued incentive fee for the yacht manufacturer gain, but if there is a clawback provision in place, then there would be a clawback of that fee for the investor in the subsequent year when the casino venture loss is eventually realized, still resulting in no overall incentive fee. Waterfall language and clawback provisions on fees are very important to study and understand in offering memorandums, and these terms can vary widely.

10.2. Custom Fee Arrangements

Although "2 and 20" and "1 and 10" are commonly quoted fee structures for hedge funds and funds of funds, respectively, many variations exist.

1. *Fees based on liquidity terms and asset size:* Hedge funds may charge different rates depending on the liquidity terms that an investor is willing to accept (longer lockups are generally associated with lower fees), and hedge fund managers may discount their fees for larger investors or for placement agents who introduced these investors. Different investors in the same fund may well face different fee structures. Hedge fund managers negotiate

terms, including fees and notice and lockup periods, with individual investors via side letters, which are special amendments to a standard offering memorandum's terms and conditions. For perspective, management fees for large LPs could range from 0.5% to 1.5%, with incentive fees reduced to 10%–15%, depending on the mandate. Such reductions can be meaningful in terms of net realized returns. However, some smaller hedge funds with strong performance (and capacity constraints) are able to maintain higher fees and may even turn down business from larger investors rather than agree to a lower fee.

2. *Founders' shares*: As a way to entice early participation in start-up and emerging hedge funds, managers have increasingly offered incentives known as founders' class shares. Founders' shares entitle investors to a lower fee structure, such as 1.5 and 10 rather than 2 and 20, and are typically available to be applied only to the first $100 million in assets, although cutoff thresholds vary. Another option is to reduce the fees for early founders' share investors once the fund achieves a critical mass of assets or performance targets. Both paths act as an incentive to spur investors to make faster investment commitments than might otherwise be the case.

3. *"Either/or" fees*: As a pushback against high hedge fund fees, institutional investors, such as the Teacher Retirement System of Texas, have recently requested a new fee model that some hedge fund managers have started to accept in return for substantive allocations. Managers agree *either* to charge a 1% management fee (simply to cover expenses during down years) *or* to receive a 30% incentive fee above a mutually agreed-on annual hurdle (to incentivize and reward managers during up years), whichever is greater. If a manager were to go without profits for a year or two, the 1% management fee becomes effectively an advance against an eventual 30% incentive-fee year (thereby reducing that future-year incentive fee by the prior years' advanced management fees. Although a far cry from the traditional 2 and 20, such novel fee structures, which are designed to reward performance and the delivery of true alpha above a benchmark, are likely to become even more in demand in the institutional hedge fund industry. Hedge funds will likely also endeavor to charge high-net-worth investors (with smaller commitment sizes) more traditional fees.

The following example demonstrates fee structures and their effect on the resulting returns to investors.

EXAMPLE 34   Fee and Return Calculations

AWJ Capital is a hedge fund with $100 million of initial investment capital. It charges a 2% management fee based on year-end AUM and a 20% incentive fee. In its first year, AWJ Capital has a 30% return. Assume management fees are calculated using end-of-period valuation.

1. What are the fees earned by AWJ if the incentive and management fees are calculated independently? What is an investor's effective return given this fee structure?
2. What are the fees earned by AWJ assuming that the incentive fee is calculated from the return net of the management fee? What is an investor's net return given this fee structure?

3. If the fee structure specifies a hurdle rate of 5% and the incentive fee is based on returns in excess of the hurdle rate, what are the fees earned by AWJ assuming the performance fee is calculated net of the management fee? What is an investor's net return given this fee structure?
4. In the second year, the fund value declines to $110 million. The fee structure is as specified for Question 1 but also includes the use of a high-water mark (computed net of fees). What are the fees earned by AWJ in the second year? What is an investor's net return for the second year given this fee structure?
5. In the third year, the fund value increases to $128 million. The fee structure is as specified in Questions 1 and 4. What are the fees earned by AWJ in the third year? What is an investor's net return for the third year given this fee structure?

Solution to 1:

AWJ fees

$$\$130 \text{ million} \times 2\% = \$2.6 \text{ million management fee.}$$

$$(\$130 - \$100) \text{ million} \times 20\% = \$6 \text{ million incentive fee.}$$

$$\text{Total fees to AWJ Capital} = \$8.6 \text{ million.}$$

$$\text{Investor return: } (\$130 - \$100 - \$8.6) \text{ million}/\$100 \text{ million} = 21.40\%.$$

Solution to 2:

$$\$130 \text{ million} \times 2\% = \$2.6 \text{ million management fee.}$$

$$(\$130 - \$100 - \$2.6) \text{ million} \times 20\% = \$5.48 \text{ million incentive fee.}$$

$$\text{Total fees to AWJ Capital} = \$8.08 \text{ million.}$$

$$\text{Investor return: } (\$130 - \$100 - \$8.08) \text{ million}/\$100 \text{ million} = 21.92\%.$$

Solution to 3:

$$\$130 \text{ million} \times 2\% = \$2.6 \text{ million management fee.}$$

$$(\$130 - \$100 - \$5 - \$2.6) \text{ million} \times 20\% = \$4.48 \text{ million incentive fee.}$$

$$\text{Total fees to AWJ Capital} = \$7.08 \text{ million.}$$

$$\text{Investor return: } (\$130 - \$100 - \$7.08) \text{ million}/\$100 \text{ million} = 22.92\%.$$

Solution to 4:

$$\$110 \text{ million} \times 2\% = \$2.2 \text{ million management fee.}$$

$$\text{No incentive fee because the fund has declined in value.}$$

$$\text{Total fees to AWJ Capital} = \$2.2 \text{ million.}$$

$$\text{Investor return: } (\$110 - \$2.2 - \$121.4) \text{ million}/\$121.4 \text{ million} = -11.20\%.$$

The beginning capital position in the second year for the investors is ($130 − $8.6) million = $121.4 million. The ending capital position at the end of the second year is ($110 − $2.2) million = $107.8 million.

Solution to 5:

$128 million × 2% = $2.56 million management fee.

($128 − $121.4) million × 20% = $1.32 million incentive fee.

The $121.4 million represents the high-water mark established at the end of Year 1.

Total fees to AWJ Capital = $3.88 million.

Investor return: ($128 − $3.88 − $107.8) million/$107.8 million = 15.14%.

The ending capital position at the end of Year 3 is $124.12 million. This amount is the new high-water mark.

As the previous example illustrates, the return to an LP investor in a fund may differ significantly from the quoted return for the fund as a whole, which generally reflects the return that a "Day 1" investor who made no capital movements would have earned. Hedge fund databases and indexes generally report performance net of fees. If fee structures vary, however, the actual net-of-fees returns earned by various investors often may vary from the one included in a given database or index.

The multi-layered fee structure of funds of hedge funds has the effect of further diluting returns to the investor, but as discussed, this disadvantage may be balanced by positive features, such as access to a diversified portfolio and to hedge funds that may otherwise be closed to direct investments, as well as expertise in due diligence in hedge fund selection. There is thus both added cost and added value.

Generally, over time many funds of funds have earned a reputation for being "fast" money because their managers tend to be the first to redeem their investment when a hedge fund performs poorly. They may also have negotiated more favorable redemption terms—a shorter lockup or notice period, for example. Because of the overall compression of hedge fund returns and issues of excessive fee layering, many fund-of-funds managers have been pressured to drop their incentive fees and simply charge a flat management fee.

EXAMPLE 35

Fill in the blank: Fund offering documents typically offer terms that include a _____, whereby incentive fees will accrue, and subsequently be paid, only on new earnings above and beyond the recoupment of any prior losses.

Solution: Fund offering documents typically offer terms that include a <u>high-water mark</u>, whereby incentive fees will accrue, and subsequently be paid, only on new earnings above and beyond the recoupment of any prior losses.

EXAMPLE 36

True or false: Advantages of funds-of-hedge funds include: due diligence in selecting individual hedge funds, access to hedge funds that may be closed to direct investments, and dilution of returns to the investor.

A. True
B. False

Solution: B is correct; the statement is false. Although these three attributes are indeed true of funds of hedge funds, the dilution of returns to the investor is a disadvantage for the investor, not an advantage. The "due diligence" and "access" attributes are advantages.

EXAMPLE 37   Comparison of Returns: Investment Directly into a Hedge Fund or through a Fund of Hedge Funds

An investor is contemplating investing €100 million in either the ABC Hedge Fund (ABC HF) or the XYZ Fund of Funds (XYZ FOF). XYZ FOF has a "1 and 10" fee structure and invests 10% of its AUM in ABC HF. ABC HF has a standard "2 and 20" fee structure with no hurdle rate. Management fees are calculated on an annual basis on AUM at the beginning of the year. For simplicity, assume that management fees and incentive fees are calculated independently. ABC HF has a 20% return for the year before management and incentive fees.

1. Calculate the return to the investor from investing directly in ABC HF.
2. Calculate the return to the investor from investing in XYZ FOF. Assume that the other investments in the XYZ FOF portfolio generate the same return before management fees as those of ABC HF and that XYZ FOF has the same fee structure as ABC HF.
3. Why would the investor choose to invest in a fund of funds instead of a hedge fund given the effect of the "double fee" demonstrated in the answers to Questions 1 and 2?

Solution to 1: ABC HF has a profit before fees on a €100 million investment of €20 million (= €100 million × 20%). The management fee is €2 million (= €100 million × 2%), and the incentive fee is €4 million (= €20 million × 20%). The return to the investor is 14% [= (20 − 2 − 4)/100].

Solution to 2: XYZ FOF earns a 14% return or €14 million profit after fees on €100 million invested with hedge funds. XYZ FOF charges the investor a management fee of €1 million (= €100 million × 1%) and an incentive fee of €1.4 million (= €14 million × 10%). The return to the investor is 11.6% [= (14 − 1 − 1.4)/100].

Solution to 3: This scenario assumes that returns are the same for all underlying hedge funds. In practice, this result will not likely be the case, and XYZ FOF may provide due diligence expertise and potentially valuable diversification.

10.3. Alignment of Interests and Survivorship Bias

The alternative asset business is attractive to portfolio managers because of how significant the fees can be if the fund performs well and AUM are significant. But as discussed previously, high fees destroy value and reduce the attractiveness of alternative investing. If a hedge fund manager can stay in business for just four to five years with acceptable returns, incentive fee allocations to the general partner can be substantive.

Comparatively, the commitment of a private equity or real estate manager to stay in business for 6–10 years (often with offering memorandum language that first attempts to return all capital to investors, then attempts in many instances to pay a preferred minimum return to investors, and then only belatedly allows a manager to crystalize, or realize, its own incentive fees) is arguably a more aligned overall incentive structure. However, the overall time commitment for the investor is obviously of a much longer duration. The investor runs a larger risk of being stuck in something that might be a disappointment, as opposed to an ability to simply move on, as with hedge funds. Landing a private equity commitment basically guarantees a manager a very attractive management fee runway for an extended period of time.

So, there remain these types of trade-offs that still make the alternative investing world overall quite lucrative regardless of the specific fund or fee format. Because of this generally lucrative incentive structure—particularly for hedge funds and their ability to crystalize incentive fees (even on gains that may still be unrealized) on an annualized basis—many new hedge funds launched in the late 1990s and early 2000s. Not all hedge funds, however, remain in business for very long. One study suggests that more than a quarter of all hedge funds fail within the first three years because of performance problems that result in investor defections and the ultimate failure to generate sufficient revenue to cover the fund's operating costs. This is one reason survivorship bias is a major problem with hedge fund indexes. *Backfill bias* is another problem: Certain surviving hedge funds may be added to databases and various hedge fund indexes only after they are initially successful and start to report their returns. Because of survivorship and backfill biases, hedge fund indexes may not reflect actual hedge fund performance but, rather, reflect only the performance of hedge funds that are performing well and thus "survived."

EXAMPLE 38

Clawbacks Due to Return Timing Differences

The Granite Rock Fund makes investments in leveraged-buyout Company A and start-up Company B, each for $10 million. One year later, the leveraged-buyout company returns a $14 million profit, and two years later, the start-up company turns into a complete bust, deemed to be worth zero.

If the GP's carried interest incentive fee is 20% of aggregate profits and there is a clawback provision, how much carried interest will the GP initially accrue and ultimately receive?

Solution: From leveraged-buyout Company A, the GP would initially accrue a 20% of $14 million profit at the end of the first year, equal to $2.8 million. Typically, this amount would be held in escrow for the benefit of the GP but not actually paid.

But then the GP loses $10 million of the initial $14 million gain, so the aggregate whole-of-fund gain at the end of the second year would be only $4 million; this amount times 20% would result in only an $800,000 incentive fee. The general partner would then have to return $2 million of the previously accrued incentive fees to the capital accounts of LP investors because of the clawback provision.

Soft and Hard Hurdles

A real estate investment fund has a $100 million initial drawdown structure in its first year and fully draws this capital to purchase a property. The fund has a soft hurdle preferred return to investors of 8% per annum and an 80%/20% carried interest incentive split thereafter. At the end of year two, the property is sold for a total of $160 million.

What are the correct distributions to the LPs and to the GP? And how would these have been different if the real estate investment fund had a hard hurdle of 8% per annum instead of a soft hurdle?

Solution: One needs to construct a waterfall of cash flows.

First, the LPs would be due their $100 million initial investment.

Then, they would be due $16 million (8% preferred return on initial capital for two years).

The soft hurdle has been met, and the GP is ultimately due 20% of $60 million, or $12 million, which would be paid to the GP next as a catch-up to the achieved hurdle return.

The residual amount would be $160 million − $100 million − $16 million − $12 million = $32 million. This amount would then be split 80% to the LPs and 20% to the GP, or $25.6 million and $6.4 million, respectively.

So, the total payout with a soft annual hurdle of 8% of the $160 million would end up with the following waterfall:

	LP	GP
Return of Capital	$100 m	
8% Preferred per Annum	$16 m	
GP Catch-Up 20%		$12 m
80%/20% Split	$25.6 m	$6.4 m
Total Payout	**$141.6 m**	18.4 m

If the fund instead had a hard hurdle rate, only the amount above the $100 return of capital and $16 million preferred return would be subject to the 20% carried interest incentive to the GP: 20% × $44 million = $8.8 million, quite a bit less than the carried interest payment with the soft hurdle. The LPs would be due the balance of $35.2 million ($44 million − $8.8 million incentive). This would result in the following total payout:

	LP	GP
Return of Capital	$100 m	
8% Preferred per Annum	$16 m	
80%/20% Split above Hurdle	$35.2 m	$8.8 m
Total Payout	**$151.2 m**	8.8 m

SUMMARY

This chapter provides a comprehensive introduction to alternative investments. Some key points of the chapter are as follows:

- Alternative investments are supplemental strategies to traditional long-only positions in stocks, bonds, and cash. Alternative investments include investments in five main categories: hedge funds, private capital, natural resources, real estate, and infrastructure.
- Alternative investment strategies are typically active, return-seeking strategies that also often have risk characteristics different from those of traditional long-only investments.
- Characteristics common to many alternative investments, when compared with traditional investments, include the following: lower liquidity, less regulation, lower transparency, higher fees, and limited and potentially problematic historical risk and return data.
- Alternative investments often have complex legal and tax considerations and may be highly leveraged.
- Alternative investments are attractive to investors because of the potential for portfolio diversification resulting in a higher risk-adjusted return for the portfolio.
- Investors can access alternative invests in three ways:
  1. Fund investment (such as a in a PE fund)
  2. Direct investment into a company or project (such as infrastructure or real estate)
  3. Co-investment into a portfolio company of a fund
- Investors conduct due diligence prior to investing in alternative investments. The due diligence approach depends on the investment method (direct, co-investing, or fund investing).
- Operational, financial, counterparty, and liquidity risks may be key considerations for those investing in alternative investments. These risks can be analyzed during the due diligence process. It is critical to perform fund due diligence to assess whether (a) the manager can effectively pursue the proposed investment strategy; (b) the appropriate organizational structure and policies for managing investments, operations, risk, and compliance are in place; and (c) the fund terms appear reasonable.
- Many alternative investments, such as hedge and private equity funds, use a partnership structure with a general partner that manages the business and limited partners (investors) who own fractional interests in the partnership.
- The general partner typically receives a management fee based on assets under management or committed capital (the former is common to hedge funds, and the latter is common to private equity funds) and an incentive fee based on realized profits.
- Hurdle rates, high-water marks, lockup and notice periods, and clawback provisions are often specified in the LPA.
- The fee structure affects the returns to investors (limited partners), with a waterfall representing the distribution method under which allocations are made to LPs and GPs. Waterfalls can be on a whole-of-fund basis (European) or deal-by-deal basis (American).
- Hedge funds are typically classified by strategy. One such classification includes four broad categories of strategies: equity hedge (e.g., market neutral), event driven (e.g., merger arbitrage), relative value (e.g., convertible bond arbitrage), macro and CTA strategies (e.g., commodity trading advisers).
- Funds-of-hedge-funds are funds that create a diversified portfolio of hedge funds. These vehicles are attractive to smaller investors that don't have the resources to select individual hedge funds and build a portfolio of them.

- Private capital is a broad term for funding provided to companies that is sourced from neither the public equity nor debt markets. Capital that is provided in the form of equity investments is called private equity, whereas capital that is provided as a loan or other form of debt is called private debt.
- Private equity refers to investment in privately owned companies or in public companies with the intent to take them private. Key private equity investment strategies include leveraged buyouts (e.g., MBOs and MBIs) and venture capital. Primary exit strategies include trade sale, IPO, and recapitalization.
- Private debt refers to various forms of debt provided by investors to private entities. Key private debt strategies include direct lending, mezzanine debt, and venture debt. Private debt also includes specialized strategies, such as CLOs, unitranche debt, real estate debt, and infrastructure debt.
- Natural resources include commodities (hard and soft), agricultural land (farmland), and timberland.
- Commodity investments may involve investing in actual physical commodities or in producers of commodities, but more typically, these investments are made using commodity derivatives (futures or swaps). One can also invest in commodities via a CTA (see hedge funds)
- Returns to commodity investing are based on changes in price and do not include an income stream, such as dividends, interest, or rent (apart from income earned on the collateral). However, timberland offers an income stream based on the sale of trees, wood, and other products. Timberland can be thought of as both a factory and a warehouse. Plus, timberland is a sustainable investment that mitigates climate-related risks.
- Farmland, like timberland, has an income component related to harvest quantities and agricultural commodity prices. However, farmland doesn't have the production flexibility of timberland, because farm products must be harvested when ripe.
- Real estate includes two major sectors: residential and commercial. Residential real estate is the largest sector, making up some 75% of the market globally. Commercial real estate primarily includes office buildings, shopping centers, and warehouses. Real estate property has some unique features compared with other asset classes, including heterogeneity (no two properties are identical) and fixed location.
- Real estate investments can be direct or indirect, in the public market (e.g., REITs) or private transactions, and in equity or debt.
- The assets underlying infrastructure investments are real, capital intensive, and long lived. These assets are intended for public use, and they provide essential services. Examples include airports, health care facilities, and power plants. Funding is often done on a public–private partnership basis.
- Social infrastructure assets are directed toward human activities and include such assets as educational, health care, social housing, and correctional facilities, with the focus on providing, operating, and maintaining the asset infrastructure.
- Infrastructure investments may also be categorized by the underlying asset's stage of development. Investing in infrastructure assets *that are to be constructed* is generally referred to as greenfield investment. Investing in *existing* infrastructure assets may be referred to as brownfield investment.
- Conducting performance appraisal on alternative investments can be challenging because these investments are often characterized by asymmetric risk–return profiles, limited portfolio transparency, illiquidity, product complexity, and complex fee structures.

- Traditional risk and return measures (such as mean return, standard deviation of returns, and beta) may provide an inadequate picture of alternative investments' risk and return characteristics. Moreover, these measures may be unreliable or not representative of specific investments.
- A variety of ratios can be calculated in order to review the performance of alternative investments, including the Sharpe ratio, Sortino ratio, Treynor ratio, Calmar ratio, and MAR ratio. In addition, batting average and slugging percentage can also be used. The IRR calculation is often used to evaluate private equity investments, and the cap rate is often used to evaluate real estate investments.
- Redemption rules and lockup periods can bring special challenges to performance appraisal of alternative investments.
- When comparing the performance of alternative investments versus an index, the analyst must be aware that indexes for alternative investments may be subject to a variety of biases, including survivorship and backfill biases.
- Analysts need to be aware of any custom fee arrangements in place that will affect the calculation of fees and performance. These can include such arrangements as fee discounts based on custom liquidity terms or significant asset size; special share classes, such as "founders' shares"; and a departure from the typical management fee + performance fee structure in favor of "either/or" fees.

PROBLEMS

1. Which of the following is *least likely* to be considered an alternative investment?
   A. Real estate
   B. Commodities
   C. Long-only equity funds
2. An investor is seeking an investment that can take long and short positions, may use multi-strategies, and historically exhibits low correlation with a traditional investment portfolio. The investor's goals will be *best* satisfied with an investment in:
   A. real estate.
   B. a hedge fund.
   C. a private equity fund.
3. Relative to traditional investments, alternative investments are *least likely* to be characterized by:
   A. high levels of transparency.
   B. limited historical return data.
   C. significant restrictions on redemptions.
4. Alternative investment funds are typically managed:
   A. actively.
   B. to generate positive beta return.
   C. assuming that markets are efficient.
5. Compared with traditional investments, alternative investments are *more likely* to have:
   A. greater use of leverage.
   B. long-only positions in liquid assets.
   C. more transparent and reliable risk and return data.

6. The potential benefits of allocating a portion of a portfolio to alternative investments include:
   A. ease of manager selection.
   B. improvement in the portfolio's risk–return relationship.
   C. accessible and reliable measures of risk and return.

7. From the perspective of the investor, the *most* active approach to investing in alternative investments is:
   A. co-investing.
   B. fund investing.
   C. direct investing.

8. In comparison to other alternative investment approaches, co-investing is *most likely*:
   A. more expensive.
   B. subject to adverse selection bias.
   C. the most flexible approach for the investor.

9. Relative to co-investing, direct investing due diligence is *most likely*:
   A. harder to control.
   B. more independent.
   C. equally thorough.

10. The investment method that typically requires the greatest amount of or most thorough due diligence from an investor is:
    A. fund investing.
    B. co-investing.
    C. direct investing.

11. An alternative investment fund's hurdle rate is a:
    A. rate unrelated to a catch-up clause.
    B. tool to protect clients from paying twice for the same performance.
    C. minimum rate of return the GP must exceed in order to earn a performance fee.

12. An investor in a private equity fund is concerned that the general partner can receive incentive fees in excess of the agreed-on incentive fees by making distributions over time based on profits earned rather than making distributions only at exit from investments of the fund. Which of the following is most likely to protect the investor from the general partner receiving excess fees?
    A. A high hurdle rate
    B. A clawback provision
    C. A lower capital commitment

13. Until the committed capital is fully drawn down and invested, the management fee for a private equity fund is based on:
    A. invested capital.
    B. committed capital.
    C. assets under management.

14. The distribution method by which profits generated by a fund are allocated between LPs and the GP is called:
    A. a waterfall.
    B. an 80/20 split.
    C. a fair division.

15. Fill in the blanks with the correct words: An American waterfall distributes performance fees on a(n) _____ basis and is more advantageous to the _____.
    A. deal-by-deal; LPs
    B. aggregate fund; LPs
    C. deal-by-deal; GP
16. Which approach is *most commonly* used by equity hedge strategies?
    A. Top down
    B. Bottom up
    C. Market timing
17. An investor may prefer a single hedge fund to a fund of funds if she seeks:
    A. due diligence expertise.
    B. better redemption terms.
    C. a less complex fee structure.
18. Hedge funds are similar to private equity funds in that both:
    A. are typically structured as partnerships.
    B. assess management fees based on assets under management.
    C. do not earn an incentive fee until the initial investment is repaid.
19. Both event-driven and macro hedge fund strategies use:
    A. long–short positions.
    B. a top-down approach.
    C. long-term market cycles.
20. Hedge fund losses are *most likely* to be magnified by a:
    A. margin call.
    B. lockup period.
    C. redemption notice period.
21. An equity hedge fund following a fundamental growth strategy uses fundamental analysis to identify companies that are *most likely* to:
    A. be undervalued.
    B. be either undervalued or overvalued.
    C. experience high growth and capital appreciation.
22. A collateralized loan obligation specialist is *most likely* to:
    A. sell its debt at a single interest rate.
    B. cater to niche borrowers in specific situations.
    C. rely on diverse risk profiles to complete deals.
23. Private capital is:
    A. accurately described by the generic term "private equity."
    B. a source of diversification benefits from both debt and equity.
    C. predisposed to invest in both the debt and equity of a client's firm.
24. The first stage of financing at which a venture capital fund *most likely* invests is the:
    A. seed stage.
    B. mezzanine stage.
    C. angel investing stage.
25. A private equity fund desiring to realize an immediate and complete cash exit from a portfolio company is *most likely* to pursue:
    A. an IPO.
    B. a trade sale.
    C. a recapitalization.

26. Angel investing capital is typically provided in which stage of financing?
    A. Later stage
    B. Formative stage
    C. Mezzanine stage

27. Private equity funds are *most likely* to use:
    A. merger arbitrage strategies.
    B. leveraged buyouts.
    C. market-neutral strategies.

28. A significant challenge to investing in timber is *most likely* its:
    A. high correlation with other asset classes.
    B. dependence on an international competitive context.
    C. return volatility compounded by financial market exposure.

29. A characteristic of farmland strongly distinguishing it from timberland is its:
    A. commodity price-driven returns.
    B. inherent rigidity of production for output.
    C. value as an offset to other human activities.

30. Which of the following statements about commodity investing is invalid?
    A. Few commodity investors trade actual physical commodities.
    B. Commodity producers and consumers both hedge and speculate.
    C. Commodity indexes are based on the price of physical commodities.

31. An investor seeks a current income stream as a component of total return and desires an investment that historically has low correlation with other asset classes. The investment *most likely* to achieve the investor's goals is:
    A. timberland.
    B. collectibles.
    C. commodities.

32. If a commodity's forward curve is downward sloping and there is little or no convenience yield, the market is said to be in:
    A. backwardation.
    B. contango.
    C. equilibrium.

33. The majority of real estate property may be classified as either:
    A. debt or equity.
    B. commercial or residential.
    C. direct ownership or indirect ownership.

34. Which of the following relates to a benefit when owning real estate directly?
    A. Taxes
    B. Capital requirements
    C. Portfolio concentration

35. Which of the following statements is true regarding mortgage-backed securities?
    A. Insurance companies prefer the first-loss tranche.
    B. When interest rates rise, prepayments will likely accelerate.
    C. When interest rates fall, the low-risk senior tranche will amortize more quickly.

36. Which of the following statements is true for REITs?
    A. According to GAAP, equity REITs are exempt from reporting earnings per share.
    B. Though equity REIT correlations with other asset classes are typically moderate, they are highest during steep market downturns.
    C. The REIT corporation pays taxes on income, and the REIT shareholder pays taxes on the REIT's dividend distribution of after-tax earnings.

37. What is the most significant drawback of a repeat sales index to measure returns to real estate?
    A. Sample selection bias
    B. Understatement of volatility
    C. Reliance on subjective appraisals

38. As the loan-to-value ratio increases for a real estate investment, risk *most likely* increases for:
    A. debt investors only.
    B. equity investors only.
    C. both debt and equity investors.

39. Compared with direct investment in infrastructure, publicly traded infrastructure securities are characterized by:
    A. higher concentration risk.
    B. more transparent governance.
    C. greater control over the infrastructure assets.

40. Which of the following forms of infrastructure investment is the most liquid?
    A. An unlisted infrastructure mutual fund
    B. A direct investment in a greenfield project
    C. An exchange-traded MLP

41. An investor chooses to invest in a brownfield, rather than a greenfield, infrastructure project. The investor is *most likely* motivated by:
    A. growth opportunities.
    B. predictable cash flows.
    C. higher expected returns.

42. The privatization of an existing hospital is best described as:
    A. a greenfield investment.
    B. a brownfield investment.
    C. an economic infrastructure investment.

43. Risks in infrastructure investing are *most likely* greatest when the project involves:
    A. construction of infrastructure assets.
    B. investment in existing infrastructure assets.
    C. investing in assets that will be leased back to a government.

44. The Sharpe ratio is a less-than-ideal performance measure for alternative investments because:
    A. it uses a semi-deviation measure of volatility.
    B. returns of alternative assets are not normally distributed.
    C. alternative assets exhibit low correlation with traditional asset classes.

45. Which of the following is true regarding private equity performance calculations?
    A. The money multiple calculation relies on the amount and timing of cash flows.
    B. The IRR calculation involves the assumption of two rates.
    C. Because private equity funds have low volatility, accounting conventions allow them to use a lagged mark-to-market process.

46. Which is *not* true of mark-to-model valuations?
    A. Return volatility may be understated.
    B. Returns may be smooth and overstated.
    C. A calibrated model will produce a reliable liquidation value.

47. An analyst wanting to assess the downside risk of an alternative investment is *least likely* to use the investment's:
    A. Sortino ratio.
    B. value at risk (VaR).
    C. standard deviation of returns.

48. United Capital is a hedge fund with $250 million of initial capital. United charges a 2% management fee based on assets under management at year end and a 20% incentive fee based on returns in excess of an 8% hurdle rate. In its first year, United appreciates 16%. Assume management fees are calculated using end-of-period valuation. The investor's net return assuming the performance fee is calculated net of the management fee is *closest* to:
    A. 11.58%.
    B. 12.54%.
    C. 12.80%.

49. Capricorn Fund of Funds invests GBP100 million in each of Alpha Hedge Fund and ABC Hedge Fund. Capricorn Fund of Funds has a "1 and 10" fee structure. Management fees and incentive fees are calculated independently at the end of each year. After one year, net of their respective management and incentive fees, Capricorn's investment in Alpha is valued at GBP80 million and Capricorn's investment in ABC is valued at GBP140 million. The annual return to an investor in Capricorn Fund of Funds, net of fees assessed at the fund-of-funds level, is *closest* to:
    A. 7.9%.
    B. 8.0%.
    C. 8.1%.

50. The following information applies to Rotunda Advisers, a hedge fund:
    - $288 million in AUM as of prior year end
    - 2% management fee (based on year-end AUM)
    - 20% incentive fee calculated:
      - net of management fee
      - using a 5% soft hurdle rate
      - using a high-water mark (high-water mark is $357 million)

    Current-year fund gross return is 25%.
    The total fee earned by Rotunda in the current year is *closest* to:
    A. $7.20 million.
    B. $20.16 million.
    C. $21.60 million.

51. A hedge fund has the following fee structure:

Annual management fee based on year-end AUM	2%
Incentive fee	20%
Hurdle rate before incentive fee collection starts	4%
Current high-water mark	$610 million

The fund has a value of $583.1 million at the beginning of the year. After one year, it has a value of $642 million before fees. The net percentage return to an investor for this year is *closest* to:

A. 6.72%.

B. 6.80%.

C. 7.64%.

CHAPTER 3

REAL ESTATE INVESTMENTS

Steven G. Bloom, CFA, Jeffrey D. Fisher, PhD, David Kruth,
CFA, Bryan D. MacGregor, PhD, MRICS, MRTPI,
Ian Rossa O'Reilly, CFA, and Anthony Paolone, CFA

LEARNING OUTCOMES

The candidate should be able to:

- compare the characteristics, classifications, principal risks, and basic forms of public and private real estate investments;
- explain portfolio roles and economic value determinants of real estate investments;
- discuss commercial property types, including their distinctive investment characteristics;
- explain the due diligence process for both private and public equity real estate investments;
- discuss real estate investment indexes, including their construction and potential biases;
- discuss the income, cost, and sales comparison approaches to valuing real estate properties;
- compare the direct capitalization and discounted cash flow valuation methods;
- estimate and interpret the inputs (for example, net operating income, capitalization rate, and discount rate) to the direct capitalization and discounted cash flow valuation methods;
- calculate the value of a property using the direct capitalization and discounted cash flow valuation methods;
- calculate and interpret financial ratios used to analyze and evaluate private real estate investments;
- discuss types of REITs;
- justify the use of net asset value per share (NAVPS) in REIT valuation and estimate NAVPS based on forecasted cash net operating income;
- describe the use of funds from operations (FFO) and adjusted funds from operations (AFFO) in REIT valuation;
- calculate and interpret the value of a REIT share using the net asset value, relative value (price-to-FFO and price-to-AFFO), and discounted cash flow approaches; and
- explain advantages and disadvantages of investing in real estate through publicly traded securities compared to private vehicles.

SECTION A. OVERVIEW OF TYPES OF REAL ESTATE INVESTMENT

Real estate is one of the largest and oldest investment asset classes, yet it is widely considered an alternative asset class. Nearly everyone has had experience with real estate, be it as a renter, homeowner and borrower, office space occupant, or retail shopper. Other than for homeowners, direct real estate investment has largely been beyond the reach of individual investors. The large amount of capital and expertise needed to invest in real estate, combined with its low liquidity, can be a deterrent that prevents most individuals and even many institutional investors from owning investment properties outright. During the last 20 years, however, investor acceptance of private fund vehicles and listed real estate securities, combined with the search for income during a period of declining and historically low interest rates, has contributed to steadily rising indirect real estate allocations and strong asset-class performance.

1. INTRODUCTION AND BASIC FORMS OF REAL ESTATE INVESTMENT

Real estate offers investors long-term stable income, some protection from inflation, and generally low correlations with stocks and bonds. High-quality, well-managed properties with low leverage are generally expected to provide higher returns than high-grade corporate debt (albeit with higher risk) and lower returns and risk than equity. Real estate investment can be an effective means of diversification in many balanced investment portfolios. Investors can choose to have the equity, or ownership, position in properties, or they may prefer to have exposure to real estate debt as a lender or owner of mortgage-backed securities. Residential real estate constitutes by far the largest portion of the real estate market, most of which is owner occupied. Nonetheless, we will focus almost exclusively on rental, or commercial, properties. These include office buildings, shopping centers, distribution facilities, and for-rent residential properties.

Private real estate investments often hold the greatest appeal for investors with long-term investment horizons and the ability to accept relatively lower liquidity. Pension funds, sovereign wealth funds, insurance companies, and high-net-worth individuals have been among the largest investors in private real estate. Securitized real estate ownership—shares of publicly traded, pooled real estate investments, such as real estate operating companies (REOCs), real estate investment trusts (REITs), and mortgage-backed securities (MBS)—has historically provided smaller investors with ready access to the asset class because of low share prices and the benefits of higher liquidity and professional management. Institutional investors also pursue securitized real estate when the market capitalization of the vehicles can accommodate large investor demand. In fact, institutional ownership of US REITs has increased from 6.6% in 1990 to 64.5% in 2015, according to a 2019 research paper (Huerta, Ngo, and Pyles 2019).

Regardless of vehicle type, the risk profile of the underlying investment can vary significantly. High-quality properties in leading markets with long-term leases and low leverage have a conservative risk profile, as do those **mortgages** that represent only slightly more than half of the asset's value. Older properties with short-term leases in suburban markets with ample room for new development and higher leverage constitute higher-risk properties. Below-investment-grade, non-rated, and mezzanine debt similarly carries higher risk. Development property is often considered the riskiest because of long lead times and the dependence on contractors, suppliers, regulators, and future tenants for success.

Section A presents real estate as an asset class, delves into its role in portfolios, and contrasts the different characteristics of the major property types. Sections B and C explore private and public investing, respectively, with particular attention to valuation. Investment valuation and performance can be analyzed at the property and vehicle level. The end of the chapter returns to the role of real estate in the portfolio and discusses whether investors' goals are best served by choosing private or public real estate vehicles.

1.1. Real Estate Market Size

The total value of the global real estate market dwarfs other asset classes. The value of real estate reached $281 trillion at the end of 2017, according to Savills World Research. Residential real estate accounted for nearly 80% of the total, at $220 trillion, making it by far the largest segment of the real estate market. Commercial buildings and agricultural/forestry totaled $33 trillion and $20 trillion, respectively. In comparison, traditional debt securities (bonds) stood at $105 trillion and equity securities (stocks) reached $83 trillion at the end of 2017. For further comparison, global GDP was $78 trillion at that time.

1.2. Real Estate Investment: Basic Forms

There are many different types of real estate property, capital position, and investment vehicle classifications. One simple way to classify property type distinguishes between residential and non-residential—typically, commercial—properties. Real estate can be categorized as either owner occupied or for rent. Real property type can further be classified as single-family residential, commercial, farmland, and timberland. Commercial real estate generally refers to the four largest rental property types: office buildings, shopping centers, industrial warehouses/distribution facilities, and for-rent residential, which can include multi-family rentals (i.e., buildings with multiple dwelling units/apartments/condominiums) and single-family detached home rentals. These four sectors make up the core property types because of market size, income stability, and low risk/return profile. In addition to the core property types, a **core real estate investment style** or strategy is further defined as investing in high-quality, well-leased, core property types with low leverage (no more than 30% of asset value) in the largest markets with strong, diversified economies. It is a conservative strategy designed to avoid real estate–specific risks, including leasing, development, and speculation in favor of steady returns. Hotel properties are excluded from the core categories because of the higher cash flow volatility resulting from single-night leases and the greater importance of property operations, brand, and marketing. Senior housing/assisted living properties represent a specialized real estate use. Other specialized and niche property types include medical offices and facilities, self-storage, data centers, manufactured housing communities, casinos, cell towers, movie theaters, billboards, and just about any other type of for-rent real property. These other property types would fit a non-core investment strategy.

Capital position describes whether the investment is structured as equity or debt. An equity investor has an ownership interest: Such an investor may be the sole or a joint owner of the real estate property or may invest in securities of a company that owns the real estate property. The owner of the real estate property controls such decisions as whether to obtain a mortgage loan on the real estate, who should handle property management, and when to sell the real estate. In the case of a REIT, that control is delegated to the managers of the REIT by the shareholders. A debt investor is in a position of lender: Such an investor may loan funds to the entity acquiring the real estate property or may invest in securities based on real estate lending. Typically, the real estate property is used as collateral for a mortgage loan. In such cases, the mortgage lender has a priority claim on the real estate. The value of the equity investor's interest in the real estate is equal to the value of the real estate less the amount owed to the mortgage lender.

Exhibit 1 presents the various property types along these two lines of classification

EXHIBIT 1   Commercial Real Estate Includes Any Type of Real Property That Can Be Rented

	Owner Occupied	For Rent (Commercial)
Residential*	Single-family homes, apartments/condominiums, manufactured housing	Single-family detached homes and multi-family buildings
Non-residential	Office, shopping centers, manufacturing facilities, warehouses, agricultural, other specialty real estate	Office, shopping centers, industrial warehouse/distribution, hotels, agricultural, other specialty real estate

*Section 2.4, "Classifications," goes into further detail about various types of residential real estate. Multi-family properties contain individual for-rent apartments or flats. Condominiums refer to owner-occupied units in multi-unit buildings.

The common investment distinction considers whether the real estate investment is made through a private or public vehicle. Private investment can be as simple as buying a property outright. Resident homeowners usually make their purchase without further structuring. Commercial property owners, whether as the sole owner or joint owner, are more likely to use a special vehicle to limit their liability. Property owners who accept capital from passive investors will form partnerships with the real estate professionals acting as the general partners (GPs) and the passive investors being admitted to the partnership as limited partners (LPs). The model commonly adopted by private equity investors has the entrepreneur/real estate professional taking the GP role and managing the partnership for the LPs. The LPs typically consist of insurance companies, pension funds, sovereign wealth funds, foundations, endowments, and high-net-worth individuals. Private investors may also invest through private companies.

Public investors can purchase common stock, partnership units, or trust units in entities that are listed on public exchanges and freely traded. By definition, investments in corporations, REITs, and other vehicles that, in turn, own properties are indirect investments. The key benefits to investing in publicly traded securities include access to professional management and a portfolio of properties combined with low minimum-purchase requirements.

Real estate operating companies are taxable corporations that operate and manage commercial real estate with few corporate-structure restrictions. They commonly own and often develop real estate. In contrast, REITs are restricted to primarily owning and operating rental properties and mortgages and are required to distribute nearly all or all of their earnings to investors to avoid paying corporate income. Mortgage-backed securities are often classified as public investments because there are often active secondary trading markets. There are some restrictions as to who is eligible to purchase the MBS and minimum trade sizes. MBS are indirect investments. The trust certificates typically own the right to receive cash flow from an underlying pool of mortgages, which, in turn, are secured by real property, rather than owning the mortgage outright.

Investment in real estate is often defined from a capital market perspective in the context of four quadrants, or areas, through which capital can be invested. The quadrants are a result of two dimensions of investment. The *first dimension* is whether the investment is made in the public or private market. The public market does not involve direct investment; rather, it involves investing in a security with claims on the underlying position(s)—for example, through investments in a REOC, a REIT, or a mortgage-backed security. The private market often involves investing directly in an asset—for example, purchasing a property or making or buying mortgages, which, in turn, have a claim on the asset. The private investment can also be made indirectly through a number of different investment vehicles that limit investor liability and tax leakage, such as a limited partnership or commingled real estate private equity fund. Regardless of the investment vehicle ownership structure, the transactions occur in the private market. The *second dimension* describes the investor's capital position in the underlying real estate. Property owners take the equity position and have rights to property profits, whereas debt investors lend capital to the owners subject to contractual interest payment and principal repayment terms or purchase mortgages or mortgage cash flow rights.

Combining the two dimensions, we have four quadrants: public equity, private equity, public debt, and private debt, as illustrated in Exhibit 2.

EXHIBIT 2   Examples of the Basic Forms of Real Estate Investment

	Public	Private
Equity	• Shares of REOCs • Shares of REITs, other listed trusts, exchange-traded funds (ETFs), and index funds	• Direct investments in real estate, including sole ownership and joint ventures • Indirect real estate ownership through limited partnerships, other forms of commingled funds, or private REITS and REOCs
Debt	• Mortgage REITs • MBS (residential and commercial) • Unsecured REIT debt	• Mortgages • Private debt • Bank debt

Equity investors generally expect a higher rate of return than lenders (debt investors) because they take on more risk. The lenders' claims on the cash flows and proceeds from sale must be satisfied before the equity investors can receive anything. As the amount of debt on a property, or financial leverage, increases, risk increases for both debt and equity; thus, an investor's debt or equity return expectations will increase. Of course, the risk is that the higher return will not materialize. The risk is even higher for an equity investor.

Debt investors in real estate, whether through private or public markets, expect to receive their return from promised cash flows and typically do not participate in any appreciation in value of the underlying real estate. Thus, debt investments in real estate are similar to other fixed-income investments, such as bonds. The returns to equity real estate investors have two components: an income stream resulting from such activities as renting the property and a capital appreciation component resulting from changes in the value of the underlying real estate. If the returns to equity real estate investors are less than perfectly positively correlated with the returns to stocks and bonds, then adding equity real estate investments to a traditional portfolio will potentially have diversification benefits.

Real estate markets in each of the four quadrants in Exhibit 2 have evolved and matured to create relatively efficient market structures for accessing all types of capital for real estate (i.e., public and private debt and equity). Such structures are critical for the success of the asset class for both lenders and equity investors. The categorization of real estate investment into the four quadrants helps investors identify the forms that best fit their objectives.

For example, some investors may prefer to own and manage real estate. Other investors may prefer the greater liquidity and professional management associated with purchasing publicly traded REITs. Other investors may prefer mortgage lending because it involves less risk than equity investment or unsecured lending; the mortgage lender has a priority claim on the real estate used as collateral for the mortgage. Still other investors may want to invest in each quadrant or allocate more capital to one quadrant or another over time as they perceive shifts in the relative value of each. Each quadrant offers differences in risk and expected return, including the impact of taxes on the return. So, investors should explore the risk and return characteristics of each quadrant as part of their investment decisions.

EXAMPLE 1   Form of Investment

An investor is interested in adding real estate to her portfolio of equity and fixed-income securities for the first time. She has no previous real estate experience but believes adding real estate will provide some diversification benefits. She is concerned about liquidity because she may need the money in a year or so. Which form of investment is *most likely* appropriate for her?

A. Shares of REITs
B. Mortgage-backed securities
C. Direct ownership of commercial real estate property

Solution: A is correct. She is probably better off investing in shares of publicly traded REITs, which provide liquidity, have professional management, and require a smaller investment than direct ownership of real estate. Using REITs, she may be able to put together a diversified real estate investment portfolio. Although REITs are more correlated with stocks than direct ownership of real estate, direct ownership is much less liquid and a lot of properties are needed to have a diversified real estate portfolio. Also, adding shares of REITs to her current portfolio should provide more diversification benefits than adding debt in the form of mortgage-backed securities and will allow her to benefit from any appreciation of the real estate. Debt investments in real estate, such as MBS, are similar to other fixed-income investments, such as bonds, and can be highly sensitive to changes in interest rates. The difference is that their income streams are secured on real estate assets, which means that the risks are default risks linked to the performance of the real estate assets and the ability of mortgagees to pay interest. In contrast, adding equity real estate investments to a traditional portfolio (of equity and fixed-income investments) will potentially have diversification benefits.

1.3. Characteristics

Some of the main characteristics of real estate investment that distinguish it from the other main investment asset classes and that complicate the measurement and assessment of performance include the following:

- *Unique asset and fixed location*: Whereas all bonds of a particular issue are identical, as are stocks of a particular type in a specific company, no two properties are the same. (In real estate economics, the terms heterogeneity or non-homogeneity are used to characterize real estate land, building, and location.) Buildings differ in use, size, location, age, type of construction, quality, and tenant and leasing arrangements. Even identically constructed buildings with the same tenants and leases will be at different locations. These factors are important in trying to establish value and in the amount of specific risk in a real estate investment.

- *High unit value*: The unit value of private real estate property is large. The amount required to make an investment in private real estate limits the number of potential investors and the ability to construct a diversified real estate portfolio. Even when private equity investors pool their capital, capital requirements are generally too high for individual investors. This factor contributed to the development of publicly traded securities, such as REITs, which allow partial ownership of an indivisible asset. Only when real estate is securitized, as with corporate debt through public bond offerings or company ownership via listed stocks, is ownership in the reach of most investors.

- *Management intensive*: An investor in bonds or stocks is not expected to be actively involved in managing the company, but a private real estate equity investor or direct owner of real estate has responsibility for management of the real estate, including maintaining the properties, negotiating leases, and collecting rents. This active management, whether carried out by the owner or by hired property managers, creates additional costs that must be taken into account when projecting returns.

- *High transaction costs*: Buying and selling real estate is also costly and time consuming because others—such as brokers, appraisers, lawyers, lenders, and construction professionals—are likely to be involved in the process until a transaction is completed.

- *Depreciation*: Buildings depreciate as a result of use and the passage of time. A building's value may also change as the desirability of its location and its design changes from the perspective of end users.

- *Need for debt capital*: Because of the large amounts required to purchase and develop real estate properties, the ability to access funds and the cost of funds in the credit markets are important. As a result, real estate values are sensitive to the cost and availability of debt capital. When debt capital is scarce or interest rates are high, the value of real estate tends to be lower than when debt capital is readily available or interest rates are low.

- *Illiquidity*: As a result of several of the listed factors, and because properties trade infrequently, real estate properties are relatively illiquid. They may take a significant amount of time to market and to sell at a price that is close to the owner's perceived fair market value. The initial spread between bid and asked prices is generally wide.

- *Price determination*: As a result of the wide differences in the characteristics of real estate properties and the low volume of transactions, estimates of value or appraisals rather than transaction prices are usually necessary to assess changes in value or expected selling price over time. However, the transaction prices of similar properties are often considered in estimating the value of or appraising a property. The limited number of participants in the market for a property, combined with the importance of local knowledge, makes it harder to know the market value of a property. In a less efficient market, those who have superior information and skill at evaluating properties may have an advantage. This situation is quite different from stocks in publicly traded companies, where many buyers and sellers with access to the same information value and transact in the shares in an active market.

These characteristics slowed widespread investor allocations to real estate. Securitization helped overcome some of these problems, especially investment size and illiquidity. In the United States, REITs were originally conceived of as a type of mutual fund to provide small investors with access to the asset class. The REIT provides or hires professional company and property managers. Similar to mutual funds, this vehicle does not pay income taxes and instead distributes dividends to investors. REITs typically allow exposure to a diversified portfolio of real estate. In regions without REIT structures or if property companies want greater flexibility, REOCs could also raise public capital. REIT and REOC shares are typically liquid, and active trading results in prices that are more likely to reflect market value. It is much easier to sell the shares of a listed company that owns real estate than to sell the underlying real estate.

EXAMPLE 2   Investment Characteristics

Question 1: An investor states that he likes investing in private real estate because he believes the market is less efficient than other liquid asset classes and, therefore, expects to earn a return premium. What are some of the sources of real estate market inefficiency?

Solution 1: It can be difficult to readily establish fair market value in real estate. Infrequent transactions, high transaction costs, and low transparency reduce market efficiency. There is evidence that real estate values are serially correlated, or autocorrelated, meaning prior-period values have a large influence on current-period values rather than price changes displaying the random-walk movement associated with efficient markets. When serial correlation is high, property values do not quickly incorporate new information. Market players who recognize the impact of new information on underlying property value cannot readily buy real estate when it is priced below intrinsic value and sell real estate when prices move above intrinsic value. In a less efficient market, an investor with superior knowledge and information or a better understanding of the appropriate price to pay for properties (superior valuation skills) may earn a higher return, provided that market prices adjust to intrinsic values, by making more informed investment decisions. However, there is also mounting evidence that real estate is efficient, or is at least becoming more efficient. Online data services provide real-time pricing transparency based on property location, type, size, and age. There is also information about commercial tenants, rents, lease terms, and lease expiration schedules. The large number and large size of real estate private equity funds with ample capital to deploy suggest numerous professional investors are scouring markets for the best opportunities. An investor buying relatively few properties may be able to take advantage of market inefficiencies. However, larger investors with broad real estate exposure are more likely to see diversification reduce idiosyncratic opportunities for above-market returns. Private real estate investors should expect to earn a return premium for illiquidity. Earning excess returns from market inefficiency becomes increasingly difficult as the number of knowledgeable, well-capitalized participants competing for acquisitions and spurring transaction activity increases.

Question 2: A portfolio manager believes the entire real estate sector is trading at cyclically depressed levels because of prior overbuilding, a jump in interest rates, and a recession. The manager wants tactical exposure to real estate for what the manager expects to be a three-year recovery cycle. What would be a good real estate investment strategy for the manager?

Solution 2: The portfolio manager could purchase the shares of a large, diversified REIT or REOC. REIT shares would provide exposure to underlying real estate, and REOCs could offer exposure to a combination of rental income, property management and brokerage income, and development profits. By investing in the shares of a larger, presumably liquid company, the portfolio manager should be able to exit the position if the sector recovers as expected or if the portfolio manager decides to raise cash. Geography- and sector-focused real estate companies (e.g., companies that own shopping centers in Australia) should be considered if the portfolio manager's views extend to specific markets.

Investing in private funds or companies may not offer as much liquidity, and entry/exit costs could be higher.

1.4. Risk Factors

Investors want an expected return that compensates them for incurring risk; the higher the risk, the higher the expected return. In this section, we consider risk factors associated with investing in commercial real estate. Most of the risk factors that follow affect the income and/or value of the real estate property and if investing indirectly, the income and value of the equity or debt investment.

The following are characteristic sources of risk or risk factors of real estate investment.

Property Demand and Supply

- *Business conditions*: Fundamentally, the real estate business involves renting space to users. The demand for space depends on a myriad of international, national, regional, and local economic conditions. GDP, employment, household income, interest rates, and inflation are particularly relevant to real estate. Changes in macroeconomic conditions will affect real estate investments because both current and expected income and real estate values may be affected.
- *Demographics*: Expanding on the already described macro factors are a variety of demographic factors, such as the size and age distribution of the population in the local market, the distribution of socioeconomic groups, and rates of new household formation. These demographic factors affect the demand for real estate.
- *Excess supply*: The real estate cycle is generally long, lasting approximately 17–18 years *on average*, albeit with a great deal of variance. Increases in the demand for space, which usually accompany the business cycle, will lead to higher occupancy, which, in turn, can support higher rents. New development usually begins once rents and property income increase to levels high enough to meet investor return requirements. Construction costs and property operating expenses generally increase later in the real estate cycle as increased competition for labor, materials, and land contribute to rising development costs, thereby increasing the minimum rent threshold required to justify new construction.

New development requires long lead times to secure capital, land, designs, permits, and zoning approval; to start and complete construction; to lease space; and to have tenants move in. If additions to real estate supply do not keep up with demand, rents will continue to rise, which encourages even more development. As the business cycle ages, recession risks increase. When the inevitable contraction in business activity occurs and demand for space moderates or declines, new supply continuing to come to market will contribute to a decline in market occupancy, which is accompanied by falling rents and declining returns to real estate investment. Rent price swings between the lows and highs can be dramatic. When rents and returns drop, new supply will contract and remain low until space demand rises high enough to absorb the excess space and contribute to higher rents.

Valuation

- *Cost and availability of capital*: Real estate must compete with other assets for debt and equity capital. The willingness of investors to invest in real estate depends on the availability of debt capital and the cost of that capital, as well as the expected return on other investments, such as stocks and bonds, which affects the availability of equity capital. A shortage of debt capital and high interest rates can significantly reduce the demand for real estate and lower prices. Alternatively, an environment of low interest rates and easy access to debt capital can lower investors' weighted average cost of capital and increase the amount investors are willing to pay for real estate investments. These capital market forces can cause prices to increase or decrease regardless of any changes in the underlying demand for real estate from tenants.
- *Availability of information*: Of increasing importance to investors, especially when investing globally, is having adequate information to make informed investment decisions. A lack of information to conduct the property analysis adds to the risk of the investment. The amount of data available on real estate space and capital markets has improved considerably. Although some countries have much more information available to investors than others, in general, the availability of information has been increasing on a global basis because real estate investment has become more global and investors want to evaluate investment alternatives on a comparable basis. Real estate indexes have become available in many countries around the world. These indexes allow investors to benchmark their properties' performance against that of peers and also provide a better understanding of the risk and return for real estate compared with other asset classes. Indexes are discussed in more detail in Section 4.
- *Lack of liquidity*: Liquidity is the ability to convert an asset to cash quickly without a significant price discount or loss of principal. Real estate is considered to have low liquidity (high liquidity risk) because of the large value of an individual investment and the time and cost it takes to sell a property at its current value. Buyers are unlikely to make large investments without conducting adequate due diligence, which takes both time and money. Therefore, buyers are not likely to agree to a quick purchase without a significant discount to the price. Illiquidity means both a longer time to realize cash and a risk that the market may move against the investor.
- *Rising interest rates*. Fixed-income securities are usually negatively affected by higher interest rates because higher discount rates reduce the present value of the instrument. Real estate values may also decline initially when interest rates rise. Unlike a fixed-rate bond with a fixed maturity price, however, property income, land prices, and real estate values may increase over time or at least through the latter part of the real estate cycle. Increasing land and property construction costs raise the rental threshold at which new development can generate target returns. Therefore, market rent can continue to rise up to the threshold before significant development begins.

Property Operations

- *Management*: Management involves the cost of monitoring an investment. Investment management can be categorized into two levels: asset management and property management. Asset management involves monitoring the investment's financial performance and making changes as needed. Property management is exclusive to real estate investments. It involves the overall day-to-day operation of the property and the physical maintenance of the property, including the buildings. Management risk reflects the ability of the property and asset managers to make the right decisions regarding the operation of the property, such as negotiating leases, maintaining the property, marketing the property, and making renovations when necessary.

- *Lease provisions:* Lease provisions may allow landlords to recover a portion or all of the loss in purchasing power from generally rising prices—that is, inflation—to preserve real returns through a combination of contractual rent bumps and expense passthroughs. Predetermined contractual rent step-ups may not be large enough to capture unexpected inflation unless they are tied to a consumer price or other inflation-linked index. Even then, regional increases in operating expenses, especially real estate taxes and insurance costs, can rise faster than general inflation. Real rental income after expenses would be penalized in such a scenario unless leases also require lessees to reimburse landlords for property operating expenses. Expense caps, which limit how much of the annual increase is passed along to the tenant, would not perfectly protect the lessor against unforeseen increases in expenses. Short-term leases (typically six months to two years) and leases in markets that allow the property owner to require periodic rent reviews present the landlord with the opportunity to frequently reset rents in response to changing market conditions. The longer the lease or the longer the period between rent reviews, the more difficult it is to anticipate rising costs and, therefore, the more important it is for lessors to require expense reimbursements from tenants. Following a real estate market downturn, however, high vacancy rates and low rents may prevent landlords from raising rents on new leases in line with inflation.

- *Leverage:* Leverage affects returns on investments in real estate but not the value of the underlying real estate property at any given point. Leverage is the use of borrowed funds to finance some of the purchase price of an investment. The ratio of borrowed funds to total purchase price is known as the loan-to-value (LTV) ratio. Higher LTV ratios mean greater amounts of leverage. Real estate transactions can be more highly leveraged than most other types of investments. But increasing leverage also increases risk because the lender has the first claim on the cash flow and on the value of the property if there is default on the loan. A small change in property income can result in a relatively large change in the amount of cash flow available to the equity investor after making the mortgage payment.

- *Environmental:* Real estate values can be affected by environmental conditions, including soil and groundwater contaminants related to a prior owner, prior tenants, or an adjacent property owner. Such problems can significantly reduce the value because of the costs incurred to correct them. Leaking fuel tanks that are discovered during buyer due diligence require removal and remediation.

- *Obsolescence:* Changes in tenant preferences, regulations, and technology affect space demand. Ceiling heights in older buildings may not be high enough to accommodate warehouse stacking requirements or office communication networking cables and equipment. Distribution facility docks may not work with larger trucks, and paved lots may not be deep enough to allow room for large trucks to turn. Internet shopping, department store closures and consolidation, and other retail shopping trends, especially in the United States, which has the largest amount of per capita retail space, have constrained demand for large shopping center space. At the same time, many delivery companies are looking at warehouse and inventory storage space much closer to retail clients. The forecasted shift to autonomous cars and trucks will further affect real estate in ways not imagined. It may not be economically viable to upgrade, reconfigure, or repurpose older buildings to comply with energy efficiency and other modernization requirements or changing business and consumer preferences.

- *Recent and ongoing market disruption:* Rising use of the internet, cloud computing services, and offsite IT backup systems have spurred the growth of data centers while reducing the space businesses need for onsite computer and server systems. Internet sales and delivery combined with increased attention to companies' carbon footprint are contributing to shifting trade and distribution patterns. Companies may prefer to locate warehouse distribution facilities closer to customers for faster and even same-day delivery. Large shopping center owners have been partially successful at replacing former department store anchor tenants with restaurants and other forms of entertainment to attract consumer traffic and converting retail space to local distribution space.

The COVID-19 pandemic caused tremendous shocks to the global economy. The quarantine and stay-at-home policies, which were still in effect in most Western countries at the time of this writing, inflicted great pain on the lodging and brick-and-mortar retail sectors in particular and accelerated such trends as retail consolidation and the rise of internet retailing. The prevalence of working from home during the pandemic may have helped the data center sector by increasing internet communication traffic and forcing companies to rely on business continuity services. At the same time, many employers realized they can get by with less office space by permitting some employees to work from home regularly, and many employees have grown accustomed to working from home and do not look to return to the office full time, at least until the pandemic ends. There is also evidence that urban residents are leaving large, expensive cities for suburban living. Rents across the residential, office, and retail sectors have been declining more than 10% in many gateway cities. Such events as the COVID-19 pandemic make it difficult to predict by how much and how fast demand for space will change during the next 2 to 10 years.

- *Other risk factors*: Many other risk factors exist, such as unobserved physical defects in the property, natural disasters (e.g., earthquakes and hurricanes, for which insurance and repair costs can be expensive), pandemics, acts of terrorism, and climate change. Unfortunately, the biggest risk may be one that was unidentified as a risk at the time of purchasing the property. Unidentified, difficult-to-forecast, and catastrophic risks can cause major disruptions and be devastating to investors.

Risks that are identified can be planned for to some extent and incorporated in investors' expectations. In some cases, a risk can be converted to a known dollar amount through insurance. In other cases, risk can be reduced through diversification or shifted to another party through contractual arrangements. For example, the risk of expenses increasing can be shifted to tenants by including expense reimbursement clauses in their leases. The risk that remains must be evaluated and reflected in contractual terms (e.g., rental prices) such that the expected return is equal to or greater than the required return necessary to make the investment.

EXAMPLE 3   Commercial Real Estate Risk

An investor wants to add real estate to her portfolio to benefit from its diversifying characteristics. She decides to buy a commercial property, financing at most 30% of the asset with debt in order to avoid incurring financial risk due to interest rate changes. This strategy is *most likely* to:

A. limit the risk due to leverage.
B. mitigate the risk due to inflation.
C. eliminate the risk due to interest rate changes.

Solution: A is correct. If less money is borrowed, there is less risk of cash flow and equity value volatility due to the use of financial leverage. C is not correct because the risk related to changes in interest rates remains. The investor may be able to accept slightly more leverage and mitigate the interest rate risk associated with debt by locking in the current interest rate with a long-term, fixed-rate amortizing loan. However, if interest rates rise, the value of real estate will likely be affected even if the investor did not borrow any money. Higher interest rates mean investors require a higher rate of return on all assets. In addition, the resale price of the property will likely depend on the cost of debt to the next buyer, who may be more likely to rely on higher leverage to finance the purchase. B is not correct because there is still risk of inflation, although real estate tends to have a low amount of inflation risk. But borrowing less money doesn't necessarily mean the property is less affected by inflation. Furthermore, inflation benefits fixed-rate borrowers who are able to repay debt in the future with cash that is worth less than cash borrowed today.

2. ECONOMIC VALUE DRIVERS, ROLE IN PORTFOLIO, AND RISK/RETURN OF REAL ESTATE INVESTMENTS RELATIVE TO STOCKS AND BONDS

2.1. Economic Drivers

Real estate return drivers are straightforward. Cash flow is a function of rental income, operating expenses, leverage, and capital spending. The contributors to cash flow are, in turn, driven by the supply of space, demand for space, and other economic factors. Investment vehicle valuation depends on the risk premium investors expect from real estate.

Exhibit 3 shows major economic factors that affect demand for the major property types. The list is by no means exhaustive. The relative importance of each measure can vary by market, property type, and timing of the business and real estate cycle, especially for rapid, extreme changes in the economic factors. Over the course of a full business cycle, however, each factor's relative importance for a market or property type tends to remain stable.

Risks tend to be greatest for those property-type sectors in which tenant/occupant demand for space can fluctuate most widely in the short term (notably, hotels), leases are shorter, and dislocations between supply and demand are most likely to occur (notably, office and hotel). However, the quality and locations of properties, leasing success, and financing status/access to capital are also extremely important factors in determining the investment risk profile.

EXHIBIT 3   Major Factors Affecting Real Estate Demand by Sector

	Retail	Office	Industrial	Multi-family	Hotel
GDP growth	x	x	x	x	x
Population growth	x	x	x	x	x
Job creation	x	x	x	x	x
Household formations	x			x	

Wage growth	x	x	x	x	x
Personal income growth	x			x	x
Consumer spending	x		x		
Retail sales growth	x		x		
Demographic trends	x			x	x
Consumer confidence	x			x	x
Consumer credit	x			x	x
Industrial production			x		
Trade and transportation			x		
Advances in logistics			x		
Changing supply routes			x		
Business formations		x	x	x	x
Business investment		x	x		x
Business confidence		x	x		x
Regulatory	x	x	x	x	x
Taxes	x	x	x	x	x

Growth in the economy or national GDP is generally the most important single economic factor affecting the outlook for all property types. Similarly, population growth, job creation, regulations, and taxes affect all the major sectors. Job creation tends to be reflected in increased demand for office space and in requirements for more retail space to cater to related increases in spending. Job creation also tends to be reflected in: (1) increased demand for multi-family accommodation as newly employed people gain the financial means to rent their own accommodations and (2) greater hotel room demand as leisure and business travel increase in response to an expanded workforce. Job creation is also a driver for many of the specialty sectors, including self-storage and data centers.

Household formation is one of the largest drivers of apartment demand. Income, wage growth, and consumer confidence all determine whether residents can afford to move to larger, higher-quality, better-located units or buy a home.

Wage growth, increases in income and disposable income, and improvements in consumer spending generally will support retail sales growth. Even as retail sales increase, online retailers have continued to pick up market share. During the 2019 holiday season, for example, US retail sales increased 4.1% annually whereas online and non-store sales rose 14.6% (excluding automobile dealers, gas stations, and restaurants, according to the National Retail Federation). Large regional shopping centers and department stores experienced the greatest pressure. Other retail categories, such as groceries, home furnishing stores, and drug/personal care stores saw modestly higher sales. Retailers' success or failure and landlords' ability to replace weak tenants with stronger tenants or reposition properties influence rental income and occupancy directly (through rental rates based on a percentage of sales) and indirectly (through tenants' ability to pay rent).

The share of sales claimed by online retailers jumped tremendously when shelter-at-home policies related to COVID-19 forced shopping centers, restaurants, and theaters to close in 2020. Only stores selling necessities (e.g., food and medicine) were allowed to remain open.

For the first time, the only way many consumers could purchase non-essential goods was online, and even online sales of groceries and personal care products rose.

Industrial manufacturing and warehouse distribution centers, which often include small offices, have seen increased demand from global trade in and near port cities. Online sales are shifting traditional transportation patterns as retailers look to store inventory closer to customers to speed delivery times. In addition, some brick-and-mortar retailers are allocating more retail space to holding inventory for delivery of online sales.

In contrast to the near- to medium-term trend in income and spending, long-term demographic trends, along with population growth, are major drivers of real estate demand. College graduates and non-child households moving to urban centers, new families moving to suburban markets, and elderly people moving to assisted living facilities are just a few of the demand drivers that have been widely reported on.

As discussed in Section 1.4, "Risk Factors," the supply side of the real estate economic cycle is driven by periods of oversupply, characterized by low occupancy and rental rates, and undersupply, when occupancy and rents are high. Property types with long development and construction periods are more prone to supply–demand dislocations because: (1) new construction typically commences in a booming economy when demand for space cannot be accommodated by existing supply and rents rise high enough to provide developers with an attractive return, (2) properties already under development continue to be completed for two or three years after a recession eventually arrives and depresses demand, and (3) the large size of many facilities (especially, trophy office properties), complicated mixed-use properties, or convention center hotels further exacerbates excess supply on completion.

EXAMPLE 4   Economic Value Drivers

1. Which of the following statistics is likely to be most relevant for all of the following: office, industrial, and hotel properties?
   A. Business confidence
   B. Household formation
   C. Industrial production
2. In addition to the market and property-specific analysis of occupancy, rental rate, lease expiry, and financing statistics, analysts of office properties are *most likely* to pay particular attention to trends in:
   A. retail sales growth.
   B. household formation.
   C. job creation.
3. Which of the following property sectors would be expected to experience the *greatest* cash flow volatility?
   A. Industrial
   B. Hotel
   C. Shopping center

Solution to 1: A is correct. Companies are more likely to expand their business and engage in business travel when business confidence is rising. Household formations have an indirect effect on these sectors and are most relevant to the multi-family sector. Changes in industrial production are less directly tied to the office and hotel markets.

Solution to 2: C is correct. Job creation is most significant for office REITs. Household formations are more significant for multi-family and retail REITs than for office REITs, whereas retail sales growth is more significant for shopping center/retail and industrial REITs than for office REITs.

Solution to 3: B is correct. Hotel room demand fluctuates with economic activity and business and consumer confidence; there are no long-term leases on hotel rooms to protect hotel REITs' revenue streams from changes in demand. Industrial and shopping center REITs benefit from long-term leases on their properties and from the relatively mild dislocations between supply and demand caused by the construction of new space in these subsectors.

2.2. Role of Real Estate in an Investment Portfolio

There are many different types of equity real estate investors, ranging from individual investors to large pension funds, sovereign wealth funds, and publicly traded real estate companies. Hereafter, for simplicity, the term *investor* will refer to an equity investor in real estate. Although there may be some differences in the motivations for each type of investor, they all hope to achieve one or more of the following benefits of equity real estate investment:

- *Current income*: Investors may expect to earn current income on the property through letting, leasing, or renting the property. Investors expect that market demand for space in the property will be sufficient to produce net income after collecting rents and paying operating expenses. This income constitutes part of an investor's return. The amount available to the investor will be affected by taxes and financing costs. Historically, income has been the largest component of investor return, with the main exception occurring during the steep decline in real interest rates after the 2008 global financial crisis.
- *Price appreciation (capital appreciation)*: Investors often expect prices to rise over time. Any price increase also contributes to an investor's total return. Investors may anticipate selling properties after holding them for a period of time and realizing the capital appreciation.
- *Inflation hedge*: Investors may expect both rents and real estate prices to rise in an inflationary environment. If rents and prices do, in fact, increase with inflation, then equity real estate investments provide investors with an inflationary hedge. This means that the real rate of return, as opposed to the nominal rate of return, may be less volatile for equity real estate investments.
- *Diversification*: Investors may anticipate diversification benefits. Real estate performance has not typically been highly correlated with the performance of other asset classes—such as stocks, bonds, or money market funds—so adding real estate to a portfolio may lower the risk of the portfolio (that is, the volatility of returns) relative to the expected return.

   Correlation data suggest that real estate property exposure, both private and listed, provides significant diversification benefits. Exhibit 4 shows correlations of annual returns for the 10-year period from 2010 through 2019 that are based on various US, European, and global indexes. Correlations for global private property, global private property funds, global listed real estate equities, and global listed equities are shown in addition to global consumer price index (CPI) data. Exhibit 4 also includes data for global investment-grade Treasuries and global investment-grade fixed-income securities.

EXHIBIT 4   10-Year Asset Class Correlations, 2010–2019

Category		CPI	Fixed Income		Property-Level Returns		Private Real Estate Funds			Listed Real Estate		Global Equities
	Indices	Global CPI	Bloomberg Barclays Global Treasury Index	Bloomberg Barclays Global Aggregate Index	MSCI Global Property Index	US NPI	GREFI	INREV Annual Fund Index	US ODCE, Net	MSCI Global Listed Property	FTSE EPRA Nareit Developed	MSCI Global World Equities
Category	Compound Annual Return	2.60%	3.90%	2.50%	8.30%	10.20%	8.10%	5.90%	10.40%	10.40%	9.20%	10.30%
CPI	Global CPI	1.00	0.42	0.42	-0.11	0.44	-0.53	-0.66	0.41	-0.03	0.05	-0.22
Fixed Income	Bloomberg Barclays Global Treasury Index	0.42	1.00	0.97	-0.35	-0.16	-0.31	-0.03	-0.21	0.16	0.30	0.08
	Bloomberg Barclays Global Aggregate Index	0.42	0.97	1.00	-0.45	-0.20	-0.46	-0.18	-0.29	0.37	0.50	0.28
Property-Level Returns	MSCI Global Property Index	-0.11	-0.35	-0.45	1.00	0.76	0.80	0.40	0.74	-0.28	-0.34	0.40
	US NPI	0.44	-0.16	-0.20	0.76	1.00	0.27	-0.22	0.96	-0.13	-0.14	-0.34
Private Real Estate Funds	GREFI	-0.53	-0.31	-0.46	0.80	0.27	1.00	0.84	0.32	-0.42	-0.47	-0.34
	INREV Annual Fund Index	-0.66	-0.03	-0.18	0.40	-0.22	0.84	1.00	-0.16	-0.32	-0.32	-0.21
	US ODCE, Net	0.41	-0.22	-0.29	0.75	0.96	0.32	-0.16	1.00	-0.25	-0.25	-0.36
Listed Real Estate	MSCI Global Listed Property	-0.03	0.16	0.37	-0.28	-0.13	-0.42	-0.32	-0.25	1.00	0.98	0.70
	FTSE EPRA Nareit Developed	0.05	0.30	0.50	-0.34	-0.14	-0.47	-0.32	-0.24	0.98	1.00	0.67
Global Equities	MSCI Global World Equities	-0.22	0.08	0.28	-0.40	-0.34	-0.34	-0.21	-0.36	0.70	0.67	1.00

Note that the correlation between the global private property and global listed property indexes is negative, as are the correlations between the private property indexes and bonds. This indicates the potential for diversification benefits of adding private equity real estate investment to a stock and bond portfolio. When real estate is publicly traded, it tends to behave more like the stock market than the real estate market, at least in the short run. Several studies have shown that listed real estate does perform similarly to private real estate in the medium term after adjusting for leverage and the lagged and smoothed performance of private real estate. However, some argue that because private real estate indexes are based on infrequent appraisals or market transactions, their performance lags changes in the listed markets, which dampens price volatility and correlations with stock indexes. In fact, the correlation between the MSCI global listed real estate index and the global private property index rises above 0.50, in comparison to a negative correlation, when the 10-year period for the listed real estate begins one year prior to the private real estate index. This issue is discussed in more detail in Section 4.1 which covers the uses and shortcomings of appraisal-based indexes.

- *Tax benefits*: A final reason for investing in real estate, which may be more important to some investors in certain countries than others, is the preferential tax benefits that may result. Private real estate investments may receive favorable tax treatment compared with other investments. In other words, the same before-tax return may result in a higher after-tax return on real estate investments compared with the after-tax return on other possible investments. For example, the preferential tax treatment in the United States comes from the fact that real estate can be depreciated for tax purposes over a shorter period (i.e., faster) than the period over which the property actually deteriorates. Although some real estate investors, such as pension funds, do not normally pay taxes, they compete with taxable investors who might be willing to pay more for the same property because of depreciation tax benefits to which they may be entitled. In many countries, REIT structures also offer tax benefits because in those countries, REITs do not pay corporate income taxes on real estate income as long as the income is distributed to shareholders. Exhibit 5 shows the minimum profit distribution obligation for various markets.

EXHIBIT 5   Most REITs Required to Distribute at Least 90% of Income

Market	Minimum Profit Distribution Obligation
United States	90% of taxable ordinary income
Japan	90% of distributable profits
Hong Kong SAR	90% of net income
United Kingdom	90% of property rental profits
Germany	90% of annual net income
Australia	100% of trust income
Singapore	90% of tax transparent income
Canada	100% of income
Sweden	No REIT regime
France	100% of taxable profit
Netherlands	100% of taxable profit

Source: European Public Real Estate Association, "EPRA Global REIT Survey 2019" (2019).

Notes: Ordered by market capitalization based on the FTSE EPRA Nareit Global Developed Real Estate Index Series. As of 31 December 2019. Exhibit 5 represents a simple view of dividend distribution requirements. Rates may vary depending on the source of income, such as capital gains on property sales, income from real estate securities, and non-real estate income.

EXAMPLE 5   Motivations for Investing in Real Estate

Why would an investor want to include real estate equity investments in a portfolio that already has a diversified mixture of stocks and bonds?

Solution: Real estate equity offers diversification benefits because it is less than perfectly correlated with stocks and bonds—for direct ownership (private equity investment) in particular. In other words, there are times when stocks and bonds may perform poorly while private equity real estate investments perform well, and vice versa. Thus, adding real estate equity investments may improve the risk-adjusted return of the portfolio.

2.3. Real Estate Risk and Return Relative to Stocks and Bonds

Total returns from investing in real estate have proved attractive on an absolute basis. US real estate began the 1990s at depressed values, following significant overbuilding and a weak economy. Many private companies and partnerships embraced REIT IPOs as the best way to recapitalize with equity capital and reduce crushing debt burdens. Investors appreciated that REITs with strong balance sheets could buy real estate for well below replacement cost while rents were generally increasing, which, in turn, supported higher dividends.

Listed REITs fell out of favor toward the end of the 1990s as dot-com mania captured investors' attention. Following the collapse of the dot-com bubble beginning in early 2000, investors turned back to REITs for high dividend yields and cash flow growth. The backdrop of declining interest rates contributed to the attractiveness of REITs. The public and private real estate sectors continued to gain institutional acceptance as investors worldwide increased their allocation to real estate in the early to mid-2000s.

The REIT sector in many markets outperformed listed equities generally through the mid-2000s. The large run-up in real estate stock values reversed when the US housing bubble burst and contributed to the global financial crisis (see Exhibit 6). Most major banks in the United States and Europe dramatically curtailed lending while they focused on improving their own balance sheets, often with government assistance or intervention. Although there was significant overbuilding in the housing market that would take years to absorb, non-residential commercial real estate supply growth remained moderate. Real estate stock values declined in 2007 and collapsed during 2008, wiping out four years of gains, with private fund values turning negative following a slight lag. For the non-residential market, the financial crisis was a liquidity crisis that continued into 2009, making it very difficult to refinance maturing debt, but it was not a real estate overbuilding/excess supply crisis. Still, many listed real estate companies cut dividends and sold equity at depressed prices to refinance maturing debt and strengthen balance sheets through the worst of the crisis.

Equity markets generally began to move higher in 2009 as governments in many countries stepped forward to support banks and sharply reduce interest rates. While housing markets continued to languish, private commercial real estate and real estate stocks, including the residential rental sector, recovered strongly in response to economic stabilization, improved access to capital, and very low interest rates. Real government bond yields turned negative in some

EXHIBIT 6   Global Listed Real Estate and Equities Plummeted in 2008

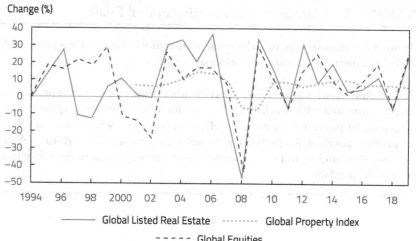

Change (%)

Sources: MSCI, MSCI Real Estate.

Notes: All indexes are in local currency. The MSCI World IMI Core Real Estate Index is a free-float-adjusted market capitalization index that consists of large-, mid-, and small-cap stocks across 23 developed markets engaged in the ownership, development, and management of specific core property-type real estate. The MSCI Global Annual Property Index (unfrozen; weighting: market size) measures unlevered total returns of directly held standing property investments from one valuation to the next. The index tracks the performance of 55,675 property investments, with a total capital value of USD1,775.5 billion as of December 2018. The MSCI ACWI Index (ACWI stands for "all country world index") captures large- and mid-cap global equities' representation across 23 developed markets and 26 emerging markets; with 2,849 constituents, it covers approximately 85% of the global investable equity opportunity set.

countries, which made dividend-paying stocks, such as REITs, that much more attractive. Real estate investments globally enjoyed as much as a 10-year run, from 2010 through 2019, during which property prices moved higher.

The run-up through 2019 came to an abrupt halt when the COVID-19 pandemic contributed to a collapse in stock values. The FTSE EPRA Nareit global REIT and real estate company index declined 43% from a peak in mid-February 2020 to a low on 23 March 2020 and ended the first quarter of 2020 with a 28% decline from year-end 2019. Through August 2020, the index recovered approximately two-thirds of the first-quarter decline as governments again lowered interest rates and increased fiscal spending.

Real estate investment has appealed to investors for providing income and being "better than bonds" by providing a higher current income with the possibility for income growth. The structure of leases, which are legal agreements requiring the tenant to make periodic payments to the space owner, and exposure to underlying tenant credits give real estate its bond-like characteristics. Like bond prices, real estate values are sensitive to changes in interest rates, inflation, and associated risk premiums.

At the end of the lease term, however, there will be uncertainty as to whether the tenant will renew the lease or the landlord will be required to find a new tenant and what the rental rate will be at that time. These issues depend on the availability of competing space and also on factors that affect the profitability of the companies leasing the space and the strength of the overall economy, in much the same way that stock prices are affected by the same factors. These factors give a stock market characteristic to the risk of real estate.

On balance, because of these two influences (bond-like and stock-like characteristics), core real estate, as an asset class, is expected to have a risk and return profile that falls between the risk and return profiles of stocks and bonds. By this, we mean the risk and return characteristics of a portfolio of real estate versus a portfolio of large-cap stocks and a portfolio of investment-grade bonds. Individual real estate investments or portfolios could certainly have risk that is greater or less than that of an individual stock or bond holdings or portfolios. The more aggressive real estate investment strategies, such as accepting high financial leverage or development risk, carry higher return expectations accompanied by higher volatility. Exhibit 7 illustrates the basic expected risk–return relationships of stocks, bonds, and core private real estate investments. In Exhibit 7, expected risk is measured by the standard deviation of expected returns. Given different correlations with stock and bond returns, it should be evident that adding real estate to a multi-asset-class portfolio expands the efficient frontier. Note that direct real estate won't have transparent (unambiguous) standard deviation and correlations with other, more liquid asset classes (stocks and bonds).

EXHIBIT 7   Expected Returns and Risks of Core Private Real Estate Compared with Stocks and Investment-Grade Bonds

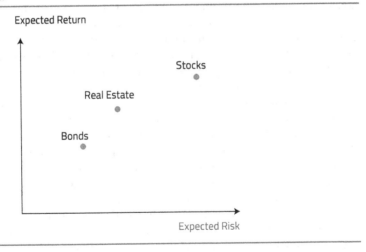

EXAMPLE 6   Investment Risk

Which is a riskier investment: core private real estate or investment-grade bonds? Explain why.

Solution: Historically, core private equity real estate with modest leverage is riskier than investment-grade bonds. Although real estate leases offer income streams somewhat

> like those of bonds, the income expected when leases renew can be uncertain and will depend on market conditions at that time—unlike the more certain face value of a bond at maturity.

2.4. Classifications

Section 1.2 introduced several basic real estate classifications and property types. In this section, we expand on the distinctions and characteristics of each property type.

Residential properties include *single-family detached houses* and *multi-family properties*, such as apartments. In general, residential properties are properties that provide housing for individuals or families. Single-family properties may be owner-occupied or rental properties. Multi-family properties contain multiple residential units that can be on the same floor or stacked within a single building; these can include attached townhouses. The names given to the individual units, such as apartments or flats, vary by region. A multi-unit building may be owned by one investor, or each unit may be owned by a separate investor, who may occupy or rent the unit. Individually owned units are referred to as condominiums, or condos, in the United States, Canada and many other countries. In some countries, the units are known as apartments, flats, cooperative houses, and a variety of other names. Multi-family housing is usually differentiated by location (urban or suburban), structure height (high-rise, mid-rise, low-rise, or garden apartments or townhouses), and amenities (pool, balcony, exercise facilities, concierge services, etc.). Residential real estate properties, particularly multi-family properties, purchased with the intent to let, lease, or rent (in other words, produce income) are typically included in the category of **commercial real estate properties** (sometimes called income-producing real estate properties).

Non-residential properties include commercial properties other than multi-family properties, farmland, and timberland. Commercial real estate is by far the largest class of real estate for investment and is the focus of this chapter. Commercial real estate properties are typically classified by end use. In addition to multi-family properties, core institutional commercial real estate properties include office, industrial and warehouse, and retail. Hospitality is sometimes included among the major commercial categories, but the higher cash flow volatility and the much greater importance of operations exclude it from being described as one of the core real estate sectors. Note, however, that the same *building* can serve more than one end use. For example, it can contain both office and retail space. In fact, the same building can contain residential as well as non-residential uses of space. A property that has a combination of end users is usually referred to as a *mixed-use development*. Thus, the classifications should be viewed mainly as a convenient way of categorizing the use of space for the purpose of analyzing the determinants of supply and demand and economic performance for each type of space.

- *Office* properties range from major multi-tenant office buildings found in the central business districts of most large cities to single-tenant office buildings. They are often built with the needs of specific tenants in mind (known in real estate terms as *build to suit* if it is for one occupant). Examples of properties developed and built considering the needs of prospective tenants would be a medical office building near a hospital or the office headquarters of a large company. At other times, new construction will begin after an anchor tenant has committed to occupy a large portion of the building and reduced the lease-up risk for the developer. Developments that are preleased to some or all of the tenants are easier to finance than "speculative" construction, which proceeds without tenant commitments. In some markets, speculative development is the norm. In general, speculative construction increases as the property cycle heats up. After a real estate bust, lenders may require preleasing as a condition for financing new development. As the cycle recovers, restrictions generally ease.

- *Industrial and warehouse* properties include wholesale and retail distribution centers, combination warehouse/showroom and office buildings, and light or heavy manufacturing facilities as well as associated warehouse space. Also included are special purpose buildings designed specifically for industrial use that would be difficult to convert to another use. Older buildings that originally had one use may be converted to another use. For example, office space may be converted to warehouse or light industrial space, and warehouse or light industrial space may be converted to residential or office space. Frequently, the conversion is based on the desirability of the area for the new use.

- *Retail* properties vary significantly in size and include the following: large regional shopping centers and malls with large department stores or big-box retailers as anchors and numerous smaller in-line stores between the anchors; neighborhood shopping centers with smaller anchor tenants and many in-line tenants; and stand-alone properties, such as a grocery store or restaurant. As indicated earlier, it is also common to find retail space combined with office space, particularly on the ground floor of office buildings in major cities, or residential space. Office tenants appreciate having restaurants, exercise facilities, and convenience stores in close proximity, and retailers benefit from the daily office-worker traffic.

- *Hospitality* properties vary considerably in size and available amenities. Motels and smaller hotels are used primarily as a place for business travelers and families to spend a night. These properties may have limited amenities and are often located very close to a major highway. Hotels designed for tourists who plan to stay longer usually have a restaurant, a swimming pool, and other amenities. They are also typically located near other attractions that tourists visit. Hotels at "destination resorts" provide the greatest number of amenities. These resorts are away from major cities, and the guests usually stay for several days or even several weeks. Facilities at these resort hotels can be quite luxurious, with several restaurants, swimming pools, nearby golf courses, and so on. Hotels that cater to convention business may be either in a popular destination resort or located near the center of a major city.

- *Other specialty types* of commercial real estate are almost too numerous to name. Investors' search for yield has led to the institutional acceptance of many property types, such as hospitals, medical office buildings, bioscience laboratories, self-storage, student housing, cell towers, and, recently, data centers. Investors can own parking facilities, restaurants, and recreational properties, such as country clubs, marinas, and sports complexes. Retail space that complements the recreational activity (such as gift and golf shops) is often associated with or part of these recreational real estate properties. Dining facilities and possibly hotel or residential facilities may also be present. The physical structure of a building intended for a specific use may be similar to the physical structure of buildings intended for other uses; for example, government office space is similar to other office space. In other cases, buildings intended for one use may not easily be adapted for other uses. For example, buildings used by universities and hospitals may not easily be adapted to other uses.

Some commercial property types are more management intensive than others. Of the main commercial property types, hotels require the most day-to-day management and are more like operating a business than multi-family, office, or retail space. Shopping centers (shopping malls) are also relatively management intensive because it is important for the owner to maintain the right tenant mix and promote the mall. Many of the "other" property types, such as recreational facilities, can also require significant management. Usually, investors consider properties that are more management intensive as riskier because of the operational risks. Therefore, investors typically require a higher rate of return on these management-intensive properties.

EXAMPLE 7   Commercial Real Estate Segments

Commercial real estate properties are *most likely* to include:

A. residential, industrial, hospitality, retail, and office.
B. multi-family, industrial, warehouse, retail, and office.
C. multi-family, industrial, hospitality, retail, and timberland.

Solution: B is correct. Commercial real estate properties include multi-family, industrial, warehouse, retail, and office, as well as hospitality and other. Residential properties include single-family, owner-occupied homes and income-producing (commercial) residential properties. Timberland is a unique category of real estate.

2.5. Investment Characteristics by Property Type

In this section, the main factors that influence property supply and demand and typical lease terms are discussed. It is important to discuss lease terms because they affect a property's value and the risk/return profile of the investment.

High-quality, well-leased office, retail, industrial/warehouse, and multi-family in strong markets are often considered the *core* property types used to create a portfolio that is relatively low risk. Hotels are usually considered riskier because there are no leases and their performance may be highly correlated with the business cycle—especially if they have a restaurant and depend on convention business. Specialty properties are excluded because the substitutability of the space is relatively low. It does not matter much what type of tenant occupies an office, retail, or distribution facility as long as the tenant blends well with the overall tenant mix and its credit quality is acceptable. Hospitals and cell towers have only one type of tenant, and the facilities are not easily converted to other uses.

For each property type, location is the critical factor in determining value. Properties with the highest value per unit of space are in the best locations and have modern features and functionality. Moderately valued properties are typically in adequate but not prime locations and/or have slightly outdated features. Properties with the lowest values per unit of space are in poor locations and have outdated features.

2.5.1. Common Types of Leases

An important consideration in commercial leases is whether the owner or tenant incurs the risk of operating expenses, such as utilities, increasing in the future. A **net lease** requires the tenant to be responsible for paying operating expenses, whereas a **gross lease** requires the owner to pay the operating expenses. Many apartment leases are gross leases, meaning the tenant pays one amount for use of the space and the property owner is responsible for operating expenses, including utilities and real estate taxes. It is also common to see residential tenants be responsible for their own energy (gas and electric) and telephone utilities, cable television costs, and internet access, in addition to the apartment's quoted rent.

Non-residential commercial properties that are net leased require tenants to pay a portion or all of the property's operating expenses in addition to the base or initial fixed rent. The amount varies by region and type of lease and is subject to negotiation. **Triple-net leases** (NNN leases) are common in the United States and Canada and require each tenant to pay its share of the following three operating expenses: common area maintenance (CAM) and repair expenses; property taxes; and building insurance costs. Tenants are also responsible for insuring their own furnishings, equipment, systems, and so on, against fire, water damage, and other perils. Triple-net leases are among several types of leases common in the Netherlands. In the United Kingdom, lessees may pay a service charge that covers common area expenses, and landlords may negotiate for the tenants to contribute to building insurance costs. In Hong Kong SAR, lessees may pay a management fee, which covers a portion of the common area maintenance and repair expenses. The longer the lease, the more likely that tenants will be responsible for property expenses.

A long-term single-tenant net lease requires the tenant to pay all the operating expenses directly and a base rent to the property owner. This setup is common with a **sale-leaseback** and other types of long-term real estate financings. In a sale-leaseback, a company sells the building it owns and occupies to a real estate investor and the company then signs a long-term lease with the buyer to continue to occupy the building. The tenant is responsible for all aspects of property ownership while it leases the space, including major repairs, such as roof replacement. At the end of the lease, use of the property reverts to the landlord. The tenant is not responsible for normal property depreciation.

The base rent for net leases is lower than that for an equivalent gross lease because the tenant must bear the operating expenses and the risk of expenses being higher than expected. Alternatively, the landlord must charge a higher rent to earn a profit when it is responsible for all property operating expenses.

Not all leases are structured as net or gross leases. For example, a lease may be structured such that in the first year of the lease, the owner is responsible for paying the operating expenses; then, for every year of the lease after that, the owner pays for expenses up to the amount paid in the first year. Any increase in expenses above that amount is passed through to the tenant as an expense reimbursement. That is, the tenant bears the risk of any increase in expenses, although the owner benefits from any decline in expenses. In a multi-tenant building, the expenses may be prorated among the tenants on the basis of the amount of space they are leasing. Although having a small number of tenants can simplify managing a property, it increases risk. If one tenant gets into financial trouble or decides not to renew a lease, it can have a significant effect on cash flows.

EXAMPLE 8   Net and Gross Leases

What is the net rent equivalent for an office building where the gross rent is $20 per square foot and operating expenses are currently $8 per square foot?

Solution: On a gross lease, the owner pays the operating expense, whereas on a net lease, the tenant pays. So, we might expect the rent on a net lease to be $12 per square foot (or \$20 psf – \$8 psf). With the gross lease, the owner bears the risk of rising operating expenses, whereas the same is true of the tenant with net leases. If expenses decline, the benefit under a gross lease accrues to the owner through improved operating margins because the tenant still would pay \$20. With the net lease, the tenant would benefit from a decline in operating expenses by paying a lower amount to the landlord, thereby reducing the tenant's total cost of occupancy.

Medium- to long-term leases frequently include contractual increases in rents known as rent bumps, rent step-ups, or step-up rents. The lease may specify a given step-up each year, such as 1% of the prior-period rent; a period step-up of, for example, 3% of the prior-period rent every five years; or occasionally an adjustment to mark rents to then-prevailing market rates. It is common to specify step-ups tied to CPI, either annually or cumulatively after several years. The higher a country's inflation rate, the more likely the tenant will pay a base rent plus annual CPI.

Long-term leases provide greater cash flow stability than short-term leases, especially when market-level rents are changing. When market vacancy is low and rents are rising, property owners benefit more from short-term leases because they can raise rents more frequently. The marking to market of rents hurts owners of properties with short-term leases when market rents decline. As above-market rent leases expire, tenants have greater ability to negotiate lower rates. Rental declines presumably occur when market vacancy increases, providing tenants with more space alternatives. When market rents decline, tenants cannot walk away from their leases in most countries unless they file for bankruptcy. When market rents increase, landlords cannot raise rents on existing leases (unless they negotiated a clause to reset rents from time to time on the basis of market conditions). Investors may prefer properties with long-term leases if they are risk averse or are concerned about declining market rents. Similarly, investors will expect greater returns from owning hotel properties, for example, than from a ground lease, at the other extreme, whereby a tenant has the right to develop and use the land property improvements for an extended period, with, say, 40 years remaining until lease expiration.

2.5.2. Office

The demand for office properties depends heavily on employment growth. The typical amount of space used per employee is also important because it tends to increase when the economy is strong and decline when the economy is weak. There also has been a tendency for the average amount of space per employee to decrease over time as technology has allowed more employees to spend more time working away from the office and less permanent space is needed.

The average length of an office building lease varies. Lease terms may depend on the desirability of the property and the financial strength of the tenant, as well as other terms in the lease, such as provisions for future rent changes and whether there are options to extend the lease. Smaller tenants tend to sign three- to five-year leases, whereas larger tenants more commonly sign five- to ten-year leases. Lease length, rent, renewal rights, and the tenant's ability to exit the lease vary by country, regulations, and culture and even through cycles and over time.

For example, in the United Kingdom since the early 1990s, lease terms have fallen. Rents are typically fixed for five years and then set at the higher of the then-market rent or contract rent upon review; these are known as upward-only rent reviews. Leases are typically on a full repairing and insuring (FRI) basis; the tenant is responsible for most costs. Therefore, detailed cost (expense) analysis is much less important in deriving net operating income—a critical measure in estimating the value of a commercial property—in the United Kingdom than in markets where operating costs are typically the responsibility of the owner.

2.5.3. Industrial and Warehouse

The demand for industrial and warehouse space heavily depends on the overall strength of the economy and economic growth. The demand for warehouse space also depends on import and export activity in the economy. Industrial leases are often long-term net leases, especially when the property is built specifically for the tenant, although gross leases or leases with expense reimbursements, as described for office properties, also exist.

Industrial and warehouse property values have shifted along with changing domestic and international trade routes. Developed economies outsourcing to low-cost manufacturing centers supported global trade centers. The opening of the wider Panama Canal in 2016, which can accommodate the much larger neo-Panamax container ships, has allowed US Gulf Coast and East Coast ports to accept more shipments from eastern Asia and take share from the US West Coast ports. In 2019 and 2020, various trade restrictions disrupted global trade and COVID-19 accelerated the penetration of online retail sales and e-commerce. The retail trend has increased demand for space closer to population centers. CBRE Research reported that in 2019 approximately 13.8 million square feet of retail shopping space had been or was in the process of being converted to 15.5 million square feet of warehouse space. If developed economies continue to increase domestic manufacturing, commodity and goods distribution routes will shift again.

2.5.4. Retail

The demand for retail space depends heavily on trends in consumer spending. Consumer spending, in turn, depends on the health of the economy, population growth, job growth, consumer confidence, and savings rates.

Retail lease terms, including length of leases and rental rates, vary not only on the basis of the quality of the property but also by the size and the importance of the tenant. For example, in the United States, the length of leases is typically shorter (three to five years) for the smaller tenants in a shopping center and is longer for larger, anchor tenants, such as department stores. Anchor tenants may be offered extremely favorable rental terms designed to attract them to the property. The quality of anchor tenants is often a key factor in attracting other tenants.

A unique aspect of many retail leases is the requirement that the tenants pay additional rent once their sales reach a certain level. This type of lease is referred to as a "percentage lease." The lease will typically specify a "minimum rent" or base rent that must be paid regardless of the tenant's sales and the basis for calculating percentage rent once the tenant's sales reach a certain level or breakpoint. For example, the lease may specify a minimum rent of $30 per square foot plus 10% of sales over $300 per square foot. Note that at the breakpoint of $300 per square foot in sales, we obtain the same rent per square foot based on either the minimum rent of $30 or 10% of $300. This is a typical way of structuring the breakpoint, and the sales level of $300 would be referred to as a "natural breakpoint."

EXAMPLE 9   Retail Rents

A retail lease specifies that the minimum rent is $40 per square foot plus 5% of sales revenue over $800 per square foot. What will the rent be if the tenant's sales are $1,000 per square foot?

Solution: The rent per square foot will be $40 + 5% × ($1,000 − $800), or $40 + $10 = $50. We get the same answer by multiplying 5% × $1,000 (= $50) because $800 is the "natural breakpoint," meaning that 5% of $800 results in the minimum rent of $40. A lease may not have the breakpoint set at this natural level, in which case it is important that the lease clearly define how to calculate the rent.

2.5.5. Multi-family

The demand for multi-family space depends on population growth, especially for the age segment most likely to rent apartments. In other words, population demographics are important. The relevant age segment can be very broad or very narrow, depending on the particular culture's propensity to rent. Homeownership rates vary from country to country. The relevant age segment for renters can also vary by type of property being rented or by locale. For example, the average age of a property renter in an area attractive to retirees may be higher.

Demand also depends on how the cost of renting compares with the cost of owning— that is, the ratio of home prices to rents. As home prices rise and become less affordable, more people will rent. Similarly, as home prices fall, there may be a shift from renting to owning. Mortgage markets also influence rental property and homeownership costs. Countries with well-developed or subsidized mortgage markets will see greater use of leverage. Home ownership usually receives greater subsidies and permits more leverage than investment properties. Higher interest rates will make homeownership more expensive. For owners that partially finance the purchase with debt, the financing cost will be higher, whereas for other homeowners, the opportunity cost of having funds tied up in a home will increase. This increase in the cost of ownership may cause a shift toward renting. If interest rates decrease, there may be a shift toward homeownership.

Multi-family rental properties typically have leases that range from six months to two years, with one year being most common. The tenant may or may not be responsible for paying expenses, such as utilities, depending on whether each unit has a separate meter. The owner is typically responsible for the upkeep of common property, insurance, repair, and maintenance of the property. The tenant is typically responsible for cleaning the space rented and for insurance on personal property.

EXAMPLE 10   Economic Value Determinants

1. The primary economic driver of the demand for office space is most likely:
   A. job growth.
   B. population growth.
   C. growth in savings rates.

2. The demand for which of the following types of real estate is likely most affected by population demographics?
   A. Office
   B. Multi-family
   C. Industrial and warehouse

Solution to 1: A is correct. Job growth is the main economic driver of office demand, especially for jobs in industries that are heavy users of office space, such as finance and insurance. As the number of jobs increases, companies need to provide office space for the new employees. Population growth may indirectly affect the demand for office space because it affects demand and job growth. Growth in savings rates affects consumer spending and the demand for retail space.

Solution to 2: B is correct. Population demographics are a primary determinant of the demand for multi-family space.

3. CONSIDERATIONS IN ANALYSIS AND DUE DILIGENCE

Direct real estate investors (individuals and companies), their advisers, appraisers, and lenders are well advised to perform thorough due diligence before acquiring or valuing properties or making secured loans. Property value will be based on the cash flow outlook, market conditions, and prices paid for recent properties. Therefore, due diligence should include an analysis of all the cash flow drivers, liabilities, and other qualitative factors, such as whether the seller/borrower has clear title to the property. Indirect investors should also perform due diligence on REITS and REOCs to determine whether the share valuation is appropriate before making buy/hold/sell decisions. Much of the information about public companies can be found in public filings of annual audited financial statements, quarterly reports, and investor presentations.

Property due diligence should include an examination of the following:

- Market review: Understand market trends, including local market population, job, and income growth; expected additions to supply; space absorption rates (how much net space is leased each year); tenant preferences; building amenities; market rents; and expense trends.
- Lease and rent review: Compare the tenant rents with market rent forecasts and lease length to determine how much rents will change when leases expire. A landlord who sets lease lengths from three to seven years on average may see approximately 20% of the leases expire in any given year. Or there may be some years with large lease expirations. Work into your review contractual step-ups and percentage rents, if any. Analyze the history of rental payments, late payments, and any defaults for the major tenants.
- Costs of re-leasing space: Look at lease renewal rates and incentives provided to both renewing and new tenants. Costs to lease space when a lease matures typically include brokerage commissions, allowances for tenants' improvements to their space, free rent, and downtime between leases. Such costs can be burdensome for landlords and are not usually included in annual operating income. Instead, these expenses are capitalized and amortized over the length of the lease.

- Seek underlying documentation. Get copies of bills for operating expenses, such as utility expenses and real estate taxes.
- Look at several years of audited financial statements. The seller's property-level cash flow statements should provide a perspective on operating expenses and revenue trends. Beware of underspending to boost operating income or free rent and other tenant incentives to lease vacant space and boost occupancy.
- Perform an environmental inspection to be sure there are no issues, such as a contaminant material at the site. Leaking fuel tanks can be a common problem.
- Have a physical/engineering inspection to be sure the property has no structural issues and to check the condition of the building systems, structures, and foundation and the adequacy of utilities.
- Have an attorney or appropriate party review the ownership history to be sure there are no issues related to the seller's ability to transfer free and clear title that is not subject to any previously unidentified liens.
- Review service and maintenance agreements to determine whether recurring problems exist.
- Have a property survey to determine whether the physical improvements are in the boundary lines of the site and to find out if any easements would affect the value.
- Verify that the property is compliant with zoning laws, environmental regulations, parking ratios, and so on.
- Verify that property taxes, insurance, special assessments, and so on, have been paid.

When differences in income, liabilities, property structural problems, permit issues, and the like are discovered, the investor should rework the cash flow forecast and include the cost to fix shortcomings into the valuation.

EXAMPLE 11   Due Diligence

What is the primary purpose of due diligence?

Solution: Due diligence is done to identify legal, environmental, physical, and other unanticipated problems that have not been disclosed by the seller that could be costly to remediate or that could negatively affect value. If identified, an issue or issues could result in negotiating a lower price or allow the investor to walk away from the transaction.

A company analysis will require a similar review process. Instead of examining one property, the investor will be evaluating the company's portfolio and potential for growth. The larger the portfolio, the easier it is to make simplifying assumptions, such as applying expected market rent and occupancy growth to the company's properties in the market. Cash flow growth can also increase because of completion and stabilization of properties recently developed, new developments, and acquisitions. The analysis must include the source of capital to finance the growth, be it from new equity, borrowing, or selling assets. Again, the company's audited financials will provide a sense of rent, occupancy, expense, margin, and spending trends over at least two to three years. The financial statements and accompanying notes will describe other assets and liabilities.

The investor's goal is to determine the value of the company and its shares. Two commonly used approaches compare: (1) the stock price with the net value per share and (2) cash flow multiples or dividend yields with market comparables, making adjustments for the quality of management, assets, the balance sheet, governance, the cash flow outlook, and so on.

4. INDEXES

An investor will find a variety of real estate indexes to choose from and may find one that seems representative of the market of interest to them. There are indexes that measure property income performance, property total return, investment fund performance, and listed security returns. Investors should be aware, however, of how the index is constructed and the inherent limitations resulting from the construction method. Investors should also be aware that the apparent low correlation of real estate with other asset classes may be due to limitations in real estate index construction.

4.1. Appraisal-Based Indexes

Many indexes rely on appraisals to estimate how the value of a portfolio of properties or the real estate market in general is changing over time. Property and private real estate investment indexes often rely on appraisals to estimate values because there usually are not sufficient transactions of the same property to rely on transactions to indicate value. Even though real estate transactions may be occurring, they are not for the same property; differences in sale prices (transaction prices) can be due to changes in the market or differences in the characteristics of the property (size, age, location, and so on). Appraisal-based indexes combine valuation information from individual properties and provide a measure of market movements. (Section 5 discusses common valuation techniques that appraisers also rely on in estimating property values.)

For example, a well-known index that measures the change in values of real estate held by institutional investors in the United States is the NCREIF Property Index (NPI). Members of NCREIF (National Council of Real Estate Investment Fiduciaries) who are investment managers and pension fund plan sponsors contribute to NCREIF every quarter information on appraised values, along with net operating income (NOI), capital expenditures, and other information, such as occupancy. This information is then used to create an index that measures the performance of these properties quarterly. The return for all the properties is calculated as follows:

$$\text{Return} = \frac{\begin{array}{c}\text{NOI} - \text{Capital expenditures} \\ +(\text{Ending market value} - \text{Beginning market value})\end{array}}{\text{Beginning market value}}$$

In this calculation, the beginning and ending market values are based on the appraisals of the properties.

The return calculated with this formula is commonly known as the *holding period return* and is equivalent to a single-period internal rate of return, or IRR (the IRR if the property were purchased at the beginning of the quarter at its beginning market value and sold at the end of the quarter at its ending market value). A similar equation is used to calculate the returns on stocks and bonds, but in those cases, an actual transaction price is typically used. Because this is not possible for real estate, the appraised value is used.

Note that the income return is not the same as cash flow, because cash flow is calculated after capital expenditures. That is, the amount of cash flow available each quarter is **net operating income** (or rental revenue less property operating expenses, including property taxes and insurance) minus capital expenditures. Thus, we can also think of the total return in the formula as measuring the cash flow (NOI – Capital expenditures) plus the change in value (Ending market value – Beginning market value).

An index like the one described allows us to compare the performance of real estate with other asset classes, such as stocks and bonds. The quarterly returns are also important for measuring risk, which is often measured as the volatility or standard deviation of the quarterly returns. A major drawback, however, is that *the income component of real estate returns does not represent distributions to investors in real estate funds or REITs.* The total return for equities is based on capital appreciation plus dividends, not on the underlying company's operating income. The index does succeed, however, as a benchmark to compare returns among individual real estate funds.

NCREIF, which began aggregating data and reporting property index-level returns in 1978, produces a variety of US real estate indexes based on such factors as property type and location. The European Association for Investors in Non-Listed Real Estate Vehicles (INREV), launched in 2003 and performs similar functions. The Asian Association for Investors in Non-Listed Real Estate Vehicles (ANREV) was formed in 2007 as a sister organization to INREV. All three of these organizations contribute data to produce the Global Real Estate Fund Index (GREFI), a capitalization-weighted index incorporating local currency returns. Released quarterly, GREFI launched in 2014, with values going back to 2009.

Several other appraisal-based indexes are also available. MSCI publishes a wide range of property indexes that cover markets worldwide, including emerging markets. These MSCI indexes, formerly called the MSCI IPD (Investment Property Databank) indexes, are calculated in a manner similar to that of the NPI.

EXAMPLE 12 Appraisal-Based Indexes

Why are appraisals often used to create real estate performance indexes?

Solution: Because properties do not transact very frequently, it is more difficult to create transaction-based indexes as is done for publicly traded securities. Appraisal-based indexes can be constructed even when there are no transactions by relying on quarterly or annual appraisals of the property. Of course, when no transactions occur, it is also difficult for appraisers to estimate value.

4.2. Transaction-Based Indexes

Some indexes are based on actual transactions rather than appraised values. These indexes have been made possible by companies that collect information on enough transactions to create an index based only on transactions. In fact, both NCREIF and MSCI have transaction information that can be used for this purpose. When creating a transaction-based index, the fact that the same property does not sell very frequently is still an issue. So, to develop an index that measures changes in value on a quarterly basis as discussed for appraisal indexes, the fact that different properties sell every quarter needs to be controlled for. Some econometric techniques, usually involving regression analysis, are used to address the issue and to create the index in two main ways. One is to create what is referred to as a **repeat sales index**, and the other is to create what is referred to as a **hedonic index**.

A repeat sales index, as the name implies, relies on repeat sales of the same property. A particular property may sell only twice during the entire period of the index. But if at least some properties have sold each quarter, the repeat sales regression methodology can use this information to create an index. Of course, the more sales, the more reliable the index. In general, the idea supporting this type of index is that because it is the same property that sold twice, the change in value between the two sale dates indicates how market conditions have changed over time. Property and tenant credit quality, the lease maturity schedule, and market conditions may have changed, depending on the amount of time between sales. The regression methodology allocates this change in value to each time period—that is, each quarter on the basis of the information from sales that occurred that quarter. The details of how the regression works are beyond the scope of this chapter. An example of a repeat sales index for commercial real estate in the United States is the suite of RCA Commercial Property Price Indices (RCA CPPI).

A hedonic index does not require repeat sales of the same property. It requires only one sale. The way it controls for the fact that different properties are selling each quarter is to include variables in the regression that control for differences in the characteristics of the property, such as size, age, quality of construction, and location. These independent variables in the regression reflect how differences in characteristics cause values to differ so that they can be separated from the differences in value due to changes in market conditions from quarter to quarter. Again, the details of this regression are beyond the scope of this chapter. The point is that indexes based only on transactions can be constructed. They require a lot of data and are usually most reliable at the national level for the major property types, but sometimes they are reliable at the regional level within a country if sufficient transactions are available.

EXAMPLE 13   Transaction-Based Indexes

Describe two main ways of creating transaction-based indexes.

Solution: The two main ways are: (1) a repeat sales index and (2) a hedonic index. A repeat sales index requires repeat sales of the same property; because it is the same property, controls for differences in property characteristics, such as its size and location, are not required. A hedonic index requires only one sale of a property and thus can usually include more properties than a repeat sales index; however, it must control for hedonic characteristics of the property, such as its size and location.

4.3. Advantages and Disadvantages of Appraisal-Based and Transaction-Based Indexes

All indexes, whether appraisal or transaction based, have advantages and disadvantages. Appraisal-based indexes are often criticized for having appraisal lag, which results from appraised values tending to lag when there are sudden shifts in the market. In an upward market, transaction prices usually start to rise first. Then as these higher prices are reflected in comparable sales and investor surveys, they are captured in appraised values. Thus, appraisal-based indexes may not capture the price increase until a quarter or more after it was reflected in transactions. The same lag would also occur in a down market, with appraised values not falling as soon as transaction prices. Another cause of appraisal lag is that all properties in an appraisal-based index may not be appraised every quarter. A manager may assume the value has stayed the same for several quarters until he or she goes through the appraisal process to estimate a new value. This situation causes a lag in the index. That being said, if the investment managers are all using appraised values to measure returns and if the index is based on appraised values, then it is an apples-to-apples comparison.

If the purpose of the index is for comparison with other asset classes that are publicly traded, however, appraisal lag is more of an issue. Appraisal lag tends to smooth the index, meaning that it has less volatility. It behaves somewhat like a moving average of what an index would look like if it were based on values obtained from transactions rather than appraisals. Thus, appraisal-based indexes may underestimate the volatility of real estate returns. Because of the lag in appraisal-based real estate indexes, they will also tend to have a lower correlation with other asset classes. (Exhibit 4 provides public and private real estate return correlations with fixed income and equities.) The smoothing effect will also overstate Sharpe ratios, which is problematic if the index is used in asset allocation models to determine how much of a portfolio should be allocated to real estate versus other asset classes. The appropriate allocation to and benefits from private real estate would likely be overestimated.

Appraisal lag can be adjusted for in two ways. The first is to "unsmooth" the appraisal-based index. Several techniques have been developed to do this, but they are beyond the scope of this chapter. In general, the resulting unsmoothed index will have more volatility and more correlation with other asset classes. The second way of adjusting for appraisal lag is to use a transaction-based index when comparing real estate with other asset classes.

Transaction-based indexes tend to lead appraisal-based indexes for the reasons discussed, but they can be noisy (that is, they include random elements in the observations) because of the need to use statistical techniques to estimate the index. So, there may be upward or downward movements from quarter to quarter that are somewhat random even though in general (viewed over a year or longer) the index is capturing the correct movements in the market. The challenge for those creating these indexes is to try to keep the noise to a minimum through the use of appropriate statistical techniques and collecting as much data as possible.

EXAMPLE 14   Comparing Appraisal-Based and Transaction-Based Indexes

What are the main differences between the performance of appraisal-based and transaction-based indexes?

Solution: An appraisal-based index will tend to have less volatility and lag a transaction-based index, resulting in a lower correlation with other asset classes being reported.

4.4. Real Estate Security Indexes

The major listed index providers, stock exchanges, and leading REIT trade organizations produce real estate equity security indexes. These include Bloomberg, FTSE Russell, MSCI, Nikkei, and S&P Dow Jones, among many others. There are also numerous real estate debt security indexes, such as the CMBX. FTSE and Nareit produce US REIT indexes; FTSE, EPRA, and Nareit publish European and Asia-Pacific listed real estate company indexes. FTSE, EPRA, and Nareit also provide a variety of global real estate securities indexes.

Depending on the split between REITs and REOCs, the indexes available from the various providers may contain equity REITs only, equity REITs and REOCs, or just REOCs. There are indexes based on market cap, country, property type, exchange listing, and major diversified index membership (e.g., S&P 500 REITs). In addition to total return, some indexes track capital appreciation and dividend yields.

SECTION B. INVESTMENTS IN REAL ESTATE THROUGH PRIVATE VEHICLES

Direct property ownership and investment through private vehicles has long been the preferred choice of institutional investors, including insurance companies, pension funds, sovereign wealth funds, foundations, endowments, and high-net-worth families and individuals. As mentioned previously, investors pursue private real estate for total return, income, tax benefits, and low correlation with other asset classes. Long-term investors expect to earn an illiquidity premium. Others like the control direct investments offer, which allows owners to decided where and when to invest and when to sell. Institutions may also seek private real estate for low volatility of returns stemming from appraisal-based valuations.

5. INTRODUCTION TO VALUATION APPROACHES

In general, appraisers, or surveyors as they are known in the United Kingdom, use three different approaches to estimate real estate value: the **income approach**, the **cost approach**, and the **sales comparison approach**.

The income approach considers what price an investor would pay for a property based on forecasted cash flows discounted by an expected rate of return that is commensurate with the risk of the investment. It commonly relies on a discounted cash flow (DCF) analysis to calculate the present value of the expected future income from the property, including proceeds from resale at the end of a typical investment holding period, although there are other methods. The concept is that value depends on the expected rate of return that investors would require to invest in the property. The two commonly used income approaches are discussed in detail in Sections 6 and 7, respectively.

The cost approach considers what it would cost to reproduce or replicate the asset and deducts depreciation and other factors that reduce the value of the property. **Replacement cost** includes the expense of buying the land and constructing a new property on the site that has the same utility or functionality as the property being appraised (referred to as the subject property). Adjustments are made if the subject property is older or not of a modern design, if it is not feasible to construct a new property in the current market, or if the location of the property is not ideal for its current use. The concept is that you should not pay more for a property than the cost of buying vacant land and developing a comparable property. The development cost should include the developer's expected profit that would compensate the developer for development risk, including time and complexity, and the cost of financing development.

The sales comparison approach considers what similar or comparable properties (comparables) transacted for in the current market. It is also referred to as the market approach. Recent property sales serve as the basis for establishing market comparables (market comps), or units of comparison. Price per square meter or square foot of leasable area or total area is the most common measure. The UK-based RICS (Royal Institute of Chartered Surveyors), which promotes international valuation standards, identifies other common units of measurement, many of which are used to value businesses and securities, such as price per gross or net rent per square meter, price-to-revenue, and price-to-earnings before interest, taxes, depreciation, and amortization. Adjustments are made to reflect comparables' differences from the subject property, such as size, age, location, and condition of the property, and to adjust for differences in market conditions at the times of sale. The most recent transactions should carry more weight than prior-period sales. The concept is that you would not pay more than others are paying for similar properties.

EXAMPLE 15   London Office Property Valuation

You have been asked to appraise an office property in London. The following table provides some characteristics about the property and details on three other properties that sold in the past three months. How would you estimate the property value using the information given, and what is your estimate?

Property/Market	Target Property	Taller Towers/ City of London	Fairview Ally/ Mayfair	Real Estate Road/ Knightsbridge
Size (square feet)	100,000	500,000	25,000	200,000
Occupancy	75%	85%	80%	80%
Market Net Rent	£80 psf	£65 psf	£90 psf	£75 psf
Property Net Rent	£72 psf	£75 psf	£95 psf	£65 psf
Annual Net Rent for Property	£5,400,000	£31,875,000	£1,900,000	£10,400,000
Annual Operating Income	£4,590,000	£28,687,500	£1,710,000	£8,840,000
Age	22 years	5 years	10 years	15 years
Quality	Class B	Class A	Class A	Class B
Market Rent Trend	Flat	+2%	+5%	Flat
Valuation Metrics				
Selling Price	?	£725,000,000	£40,000,000	£175,000,000
Price Per Square Foot		£1,150	£1,250	£735
Price/Rental Revenue		18.0×	16.3×	14.1×
Price/Operating Income		20.0×	18.0×	16.5×

Notes: Figures are rounded. Values are hypothetical.

Solution: The target property has more in common with the other Class B property based on quality, age, and rents trailing the market average. In contrast, the two Class A, or Grade A, properties, rent at a premium to the local market, and Taller Towers has the highest occupancy. As the appraiser, you may come up with a range of values based on the property in its current condition, with the in-place tenant leases and occupancy, and what the property would be worth if occupancy and income were higher. Using the most comparable property valuation metrics without any adjustments, values would range from a low of £73.5 million, based on a purchase price of £735 per square foot, to £76.3 million using the same price-to-revenue multiple. A discount to these multiples may be warranted because the target property is older. Alternatively, if the target property's occupancy were to readily increase to 80%, the upper range of the valuation could move to £80.5 million. It is beyond the scope of this example to consider how much it would cost to raise occupancy by spending capital to improve the vacant space and pay broker leasing commissions, nor are we considering the property potential if larger amounts were invested in renovating the property. If you were to estimate the property value following such a renovation, you would subtract the cost of the renovation from the post-renovation value.

These approaches are unlikely to result in the same value because they rely on different assumptions and availability of data to estimate the value. The idea is to try to triangulate on the market value by approaching the estimate three different ways. The appraiser may have more confidence in one or two of the approaches depending on the availability of data for each approach. Part of the appraisal process is trying to reconcile the differences in the estimates of value from each approach and coming up with a final estimate of value for the subject property.

5.1. Highest and Best Use

Before we elaborate on the three approaches to estimating value, it is helpful to understand an important concept known as **highest and best use**. The highest and best use of a vacant site is the use that would result in the highest value for the land. Presumably, the developer that could earn the highest risk-adjusted profit based on time, effort, construction and development cost, leasing, and exit value would be the one to pay the highest price for the land.

Developers commonly back into the cost of land by estimating the expected exit price for the to-be-completed property, subtracting the all-in development costs, exit costs, and their minimum profit requirement. The amount that remains represents the most the developer would be willing to pay for the land. Developers would consider all possible uses given zoning constraints or incorporating the cost paid and time spent securing rezoning approval. Developers might consider the potential profit and risk associated with residential, office, retail, mixed-use, and other property types. Note that the highest and best use is not the use with the highest total value; it is the use that provides the developer with the highest profit based on the return required to compensate it for all the risks associated with the project.

The theory is that the land value is based on its highest and best use *as if vacant* even if an existing building is on the site. If an existing building is on the site that is not the highest and best use of the site, then the value of the building—not the land—will be lower. For example, suppose that a site with an old warehouse on it would sell for $1.5 million as a warehouse (land

and building). If vacant, the land is worth $1 million. Thus, the value of the existing building (warehouse) is $500,000 (= $1,500,000 - $1,000,000). As long as the value under the existing use is more than the land value, the building should remain on the site. If another developer could build an office for an all-in cost of $2.5 million—*including its profit requirement*—and sell the property for $4.25 million, then the developer would be willing to pay as much as $2 million for the land. In that case, the value under the existing use falls below the land value ($1.5 million warehouse value minus $2.0 million for the land based on the highest and best use) and any buildings on the site will likely be demolished so the building that represents the highest and best use of the site can be constructed.

EXAMPLE 16   Highest and Best Use

Two uses have been identified for a property. One is an office building that would have a value after construction of $20 million. Development costs would be $16 million, including a profit for the developer. The second use is an apartment building that would have a value after construction of $25 million. Development costs, including a profit to the developer, would be $22 million. What is the highest and best use of the site and the implied land value?

Solution:

	Office	Apartment
Value on completion	$20,000,000	$25,000,000
Cost to construct building	(16,000,000)	(22,000,000)
Implied land value	$4,000,000	$3,000,000

An investor/developer could pay up to $4 million for the land to develop an office building but only $3 million for the land to develop an apartment building. The highest and best use of the site is an office building with a land value of $4 million. Of course, this answer assumes a competitive market with several potential developers who would bid for the land to develop an office building.

We will now discuss each of the approaches to estimating value in more detail and provide examples of each.

6. THE INCOME APPROACH TO VALUATION: DISCOUNT RATES AND THE DIRECT CAPITALIZATION OF NOI AND DCF METHODS

The **direct capitalization method** and the **discounted cash flow method** are income approaches used to appraise or estimate the value of a commercial (income-producing) property. The direct capitalization method estimates the value of an income-producing property based on the level and quality of its net operating income. The DCF method discounts future projected cash flows to arrive at a present value of the property. Net operating income, a measure of income and a *proxy for cash flow*, is a focus of both approaches.

6.1. Similarities in Approaches

Both income approaches focus on net operating income generated from a property. Recall, NOI is a measure of the income from the property after deducting operating expenses for such items as property taxes, insurance, maintenance, utilities, and repairs but before deducting any costs associated with financing (leverage) and before deducting federal income taxes. NOI in a real estate property context is similar to earnings before interest, taxes, depreciation, and amortization (EBITDA) in a financial reporting context. Note that neither property NOI nor EBITDA includes capital spending, financing costs, or taxes, and therefore, neither represents actual cash flow. That is not to say these considerations are unimportant. NOI is just the starting point.

Both income approaches consider growth and property quality. The first, the direct capitalization method, capitalizes the current NOI using an *implicit* growth **capitalization rate**, or cap rate. That is, properties expected to generate faster growth will use a capitalization rate that results in a higher value, and properties with slower growth will use a capitalization rate that results in a lower value. When the capitalization rate is applied to the forecasted first-year NOI for the property, the implicit assumption is that the first-year NOI is representative of what the typical first-year NOI would be for similar properties.

The second approach, the DCF method, applies an explicit growth rate to construct an NOI stream from which a present value can be derived. As we will see, there is some overlap because even for the second method, we generally estimate a terminal value by capitalizing NOI at some future date. Income can be projected either for the entire economic life of the property or for a typical holding period with the assumption that the property will be sold at the end of the holding period. The discount rate should reflect the risk characteristics of the property. It can be derived from market comparisons or from specific analysis; we will examine both cases.

6.2. The Direct Capitalization Method

The direct capitalization method capitalizes the current or expected NOI to calculate real estate value. If we think about the inverse of the cap rate as a multiplier, the approach is analogous to an income multiplier. The direct capitalization method differs from the DCF method, in which future operating income (a proxy for cash flow) is discounted at a discount rate to produce a present value.

6.2.1. The Capitalization Rate and the Discount Rate

The cap and discount rates are closely linked but are not the same. Briefly, the discount rate is the return required from an investment and comprises the risk-free rate plus a risk premium specific to the investment. The cap rate is lower than the discount rate because it is calculated using the current NOI. So, the cap rate is like a current yield for the property. The discount rate is applied to current and future NOI, which may be expected to grow. In general, when income and value are growing at a constant compound growth rate, we have

$$\text{Cap rate} = \text{Discount rate} - \text{Growth rate.} \qquad (3.1)$$

The growth rate is implicit in the cap rate in that the buyer incorporates cash flow growth into the value the buyer is willing to pay for the property, but we have to make it explicit for a DCF valuation. If the growth rate were negative, the cap rate would exceed the discount rate.

6.2.2. Defining the Capitalization Rate

The capitalization rate is a very important measure for valuing income-producing real estate property. The cap rate is defined as follows:

$$\text{Cap rate} = \text{NOI/Value}, \tag{3.2}$$

where NOI is usually based on what is expected during the current or first year of ownership of the property. Sometimes the term *going-in cap rate* is used to clarify that it is based on the first year of ownership when the investor is *going into* the deal. (Later, we will explain that the *terminal cap rate* is based on expected income for the year after the anticipated sale of the property.)

The value used in Equation 3.2 is an estimate of what the property is worth at the time of purchase. If we rearrange Equation 3.2 and solve for value, we get the following equation:

$$\text{Value} = \text{NOI/Cap rate}. \tag{3.3}$$

So, if we know the appropriate cap rate, we can estimate the value of the property by dividing its first-year NOI by the cap rate.

Where does the cap rate come from? That will be an important part of our discussion. A simple answer is that it is based on observing what other similar or comparable properties are selling for. Assuming that the sale price for a comparable property is a good indication of the value of the subject property, we have

$$\text{Cap rate of comparable} = \text{NOI of comparable/Sale price of comparable.} \tag{3.4}$$

We would not want to rely on the price for just one sale to indicate what the cap rate is. We want to observe several sales of similar properties before drawing conclusions about what cap rates investors are willing to accept for a property. As we will discuss later, there are also reasons why we would expect the cap rate to differ for different properties, such as what the future income potential is for the property—that is, how it is expected to change after the first year. This is important because the cap rate is only explicitly based on the first-year income. But the cap rate that investors are willing to accept depends on how they expect the income to change in the future and the risk of that income. These expectations are said to be implicit in the cap rate.

The cap rate is like a snapshot at a point in time of the relationship between NOI and value. It is somewhat analogous to the price–earnings multiple for a stock except that it is the reciprocal. The reciprocal of the cap rate is price divided by NOI. In the United Kingdom, the reciprocal of the cap rate is called the "years purchase" (YP). It is the number of years that it would take for income at the current level to be equal to the original purchase price. Just as stocks with greater earnings growth potential tend to have higher price–earnings multiples and, inversely, lower earnings yields, properties with greater income growth potential have higher ratios of price to current NOI and thus lower cap rates.

It is often necessary to make adjustments based on specific lease terms and characteristics of a market. For example, a similar approach is common in the United Kingdom, where the term "fully let property" is used to refer to a property that is leased at market rent because either it has a new tenant or the rent has just been reviewed. In such cases, the appraisal is undertaken by applying a capitalization rate to this rent rather than to NOI because leases usually require the tenant to pay all costs. The cap rate derived by dividing rent by the recent sale prices of comparables is often called the all-risks yield (ARY) and is shown in the following formula:

$$ARY = Rent/Recent\ sale\ prices\ of\ comparables. \qquad (3.5)$$

Note that the term "yield" in this case is used like a "current yield" based on first-year NOI. It is a cap rate and will differ from the total return that an investor might expect to get from future growth in NOI and value. If it is assumed, however, that the rent will be level in the foreseeable future (like a perpetuity), then the cap rate will be the same as the return and the all-risks yield will be an internal rate of return or yield to maturity.

In simple terms, the valuation is

$$Market\ value = Rent/ARY. \qquad (3.6)$$

Again, this valuation is essentially the same as dividing NOI by the cap rate as discussed earlier except the occupant is assumed to be responsible for all expenses, so the rent is divided by the ARY. In practice, management costs should also be considered—although operating costs falling on the landlord are typically much lower than in the United States. ARY is a cap rate and will differ from the required total return (the discount rate) an investor might expect to receive from future growth in NOI and value. When rents are expected to increase after every rent review, the investor's expected return will be higher than the cap rate. If rents are expected to increase at a constant compound rate, then the investor's expected return (discount rate) will equal the cap rate plus the growth rate, as was shown with Equation 3.1.

EXAMPLE 17   Capitalizing NOI

A property has just been let at an NOI of £250,000 for the first year, and the capitalization rate on comparable properties is 5%. What is the value of the property?

Solution:

$$Value = NOI/Cap\ rate = £250,000/0.05 = £5,000,000.$$

Suppose the rent review for the property in Example 17 occurs every year and rents are expected to increase 2% each year. *An approximation of the IRR would simply be the cap rate plus the growth rate*; in this case, a 5% cap rate plus 2% rent growth results in a 7% IRR. Of course, if the rent review were less frequent, as in the United Kingdom where it is typically every five years, then we could not simply add the growth rate to the cap rate to get the IRR. But the IRR would still be higher than the cap rate if rents were expected to increase.

6.2.3. Stabilized NOI

When the cap rate is applied to the forecasted first-year NOI for the property, the implicit assumption is that the first-year NOI is representative of what the typical first-year NOI would be for similar properties. In some cases, the appraiser might project an NOI to be used to estimate value that is different from what might actually be expected for the first year of ownership for the property if what is actually expected is not typical.

An example of this situation might be when a property is undergoing a renovation and has a temporarily higher-than-typical amount of vacancy until the renovation is complete. The purpose of the appraisal might be to estimate what the property will be worth once the renovation is complete. A cap rate will be used from properties that are not being renovated because they are more typical. Thus, the appraiser projects what is referred to as a **stabilized NOI**, which is what the NOI would be if the property were not being renovated—in other words, what the NOI will be once the renovation is complete. This NOI is used to estimate the value. Of course, if the property is being purchased before the renovation is complete, a slightly lower price will be paid because the purchaser has to wait for the renovation to be complete to get the higher NOI. Applying the cap rate to the lower NOI of the renovation period will understate the value of the property because it implicitly assumes that the lower NOI is expected to continue.

EXAMPLE 18   Value of a Property to Be Renovated

A property is being purchased that requires some renovation to be competitive with otherwise comparable properties. Renovations satisfactory to the purchaser will be completed by the seller at the seller's expense. If it were already renovated, it would have NOI of ¥9 million next year, which would be expected to increase by 3% per year thereafter. Investors would normally require a 12% IRR (discount rate) to purchase the property after it is renovated. Because of the renovation, the NOI will be only ¥4 million next year. But thereafter, the NOI is expected to be the same as it would be if it had already been renovated at the time of purchase. What is the value of or the price a typical investor is willing to pay for the property?

Solution: If the property were already renovated (and the NOI had stabilized), the value would be as follows:

$$\text{Value if renovated} = ¥9,000,000/(0.12 - 0.03) = ¥100,000,000.$$

But because of the renovation, there is a loss in income of ¥5 million during the first year. If for simplicity we assume that this amount would have been received at the end of the year, then the present value of the lost income at a 12% discount rate is as follows:

$$\text{Loss in value} = ¥5,000,000/(1.12) = ¥4,464,286.$$

Thus, the value of the property is as follows:

Value if renovated	¥100,000,000
Less loss in value	− ¥4,464,286
= Value	¥95,535,714

An alternative approach is to get the present value of the first year's income and the value in a year when renovated:

$$\{¥4{,}000{,}000 + [¥9{,}000{,}000(1.03)]/(0.12 - 0.03)]\}/(1.12) = ¥95{,}535{,}714.$$

6.2.4. Other Forms of the Income Approach

Direct capitalization usually uses NOI and a cap rate. However, there are some alternatives to the use of NOI and a cap rate. For example, a *gross income multiplier* might be used in some situations. The gross income multiplier is the ratio of the sale price to the gross income expected from the property in the first year after sale. It may be obtained from comparable sales in a way similar to what was illustrated for cap rates. The problem with using a gross income multiplier is that it does not explicitly consider vacancy rates and operating expenses. Thus, it implicitly assumes that the ratio of vacancy and expenses to gross income is similar for the comparable and subject properties. But if, for example, expenses were expected to be lower on one property versus another because it was more energy efficient, an investor would pay more for the same rent. Thus, its gross income multiplier should be higher. The use of a gross rent multiplier is also considered a form of direct capitalization but is generally not considered as reliable as using a capitalization rate.

7. THE DCF METHOD, THE RELATIONSHIP BETWEEN DISCOUNT RATE AND CAP RATE, AND THE TERMINAL CAPITALIZATION RATE

The direct capitalization method typically estimates value by capitalizing the first-year NOI at a cap rate derived from market evidence. The DCF method (sometimes referred to as a yield capitalization method) involves projecting income beyond the first year and discounting that income at a discount rate (yield rate). The terms *yield rate* and *discount rate* are used synonymously in this discussion, as are the terms *yield capitalization* and *discounted cash flow analysis*.

7.1. The Relationship between the Discount Rate and the Cap Rate

If the income and value for a property are expected to change over time at the same compound rate—for example, 3% per year—then the relationship between the cap rate and the discount rate is the same as in Equation 3.1:

$$\text{Cap rate} = \text{Discount rate} - \text{Growth rate.}$$

To see the intuition behind this, let us solve for the discount rate, which is the return that is required to invest in the property:

$$\text{Discount rate} = \text{Cap rate} + \text{Growth rate.}$$

Recall that the cap rate is based on first-year NOI. The growth rate captures how NOI will change in the future along with the property value. Thus, we can say that the investor's return (discount rate) comes from the return on first-year income (cap rate) plus the growth in income and value over time (growth rate). Although income and value may not always change at the same compound rate each year, this formula gives us insight into the relationship between the discount rate and the cap rate. Essentially, the difference between the discount and cap rates has to do with growth in income and value.

Intuitively, given that both methods start from the same NOI in the first year, you would pay more for an income stream that will grow than for one that will be constant. So, the price is higher and the cap rate is lower when the NOI is growing, which is what is meant by the growth being *implicit* in the cap rate. If the growth rate is constant, we can extend Equation 3.3 using Equation 3.1 to give

$$\text{Value of property} = \text{NOI}/(r - g), \tag{3.7}$$

where

$r =$ the discount rate (required return)

$g =$ the growth rate for income (given constant growth in income, value will grow at the same rate)

This equation is analogous to the dividend growth model applied to stocks. If NOI is not expected to grow at a constant rate, then NOIs are projected into the future and each period's NOI is discounted to arrive at a value of the property. Rather than project NOIs into infinity, NOIs typically are projected for a specified holding period, and a terminal value (estimated sale price) at the end of the holding period is estimated.

EXAMPLE 19   Growth Explicit Appraisal

NOI is expected to be $100,000 the first year, and after that, NOI is expected to increase at 2% per year for the foreseeable future. The property value is also expected to increase by 2% per year. Investors expect to get a 12% IRR given the level of risk; therefore, the value is estimated using a 12% discount rate. What is the value of the property today (at the beginning of the first year)?

Solution:
$$V = \text{NOI}/(r - g)$$
$$= \$100,000/(0.12 - 0.02)$$
$$= \$100,000/0.10$$
$$= \$1,000,000.$$

The property value growth rate is not required to calculate the value of the property after the first year. However, it would be used in a DCF calculation to determine the property's terminal value.

7.2. The Terminal Capitalization Rate

When a DCF methodology is used to value a property, one of the important inputs is generally the estimated sale price of the property at the end of a typical holding period. This input is often referred to as the estimated terminal value. Estimating the terminal value of a property can be quite challenging in practice, especially given that the purpose of the analysis is to estimate the value of the property today. But if we do not know the value of the property today, how can we know what it will be worth in the future when sold to another investor? We must also use some method for estimating what the property will be worth when sold in the future.

In theory, this value is based on the present value of income to be received by the *next* investor. But we usually do not try to project NOI for another holding period beyond the initial one. Rather, we rely on the direct capitalization method using the NOI of the first year of ownership for the next investor and a cap rate. The cap rate used to estimate the resale price or terminal value is referred to as a *terminal cap rate* or *residual cap rate*. It is a cap rate that is selected at the time of valuation to be applied to the NOI earned in the first year after the property is expected to be sold to a new buyer.

Selecting a terminal cap rate is challenging. Recall that the cap rate equals the discount rate less the growth rate when income and value are growing constantly at the same rate. Whether constant growth is realistic or not, we know that the cap rate will be higher (lower) if the discount rate is higher (lower). Similarly, the cap rate will be lower if the growth rate is expected to be higher, and vice versa. These relationships also apply to the terminal cap rate and the going-in cap rate.

The terminal cap rate could be the same, higher, or lower than the going-in cap rate, depending on the expected discount and growth rates at the time of sale. If interest rates are expected to be higher in the future, pushing up discount rates, then terminal cap rates might be higher. The growth rate is often assumed to be a little lower because the property is older at the time of sale and may not be as competitive. This situation would result in a slightly higher terminal cap rate. Uncertainty about what the NOI will be in the future may also result in selecting a higher terminal cap rate. The point is that the terminal cap rate is not necessarily the same as the going-in cap rate at the time of the appraisal.

EXAMPLE 20   Appraisal with a Terminal Value

Net operating income is expected to be level at $100,000 per year for the next five years because of existing leases. Starting in Year 6, the NOI is expected to increase to $120,000 because of lease rollovers and increase at 2% per year thereafter. The property value is also expected to increase at 2% per year after Year 5. The investors in the property require a 12% return and expect to hold the property for five years. What is the current value of the property?

Solution: Exhibit 8 shows the projected NOI for this example. Because NOI and property value are expected to grow at the same constant rate after Year 5, we can calculate the cap rate at that time based on the discount rate less the growth rate. That gives us a terminal cap rate that can be used to estimate the value that the property could be sold for at the end of Year 5 (based on the income a buyer would get after that). We can then discount this value along with the income for Years 1–5 to get the present value.

EXHIBIT 8   Projected Income

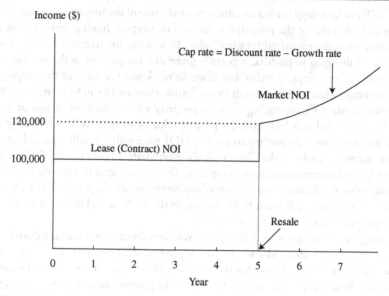

Step 1: Estimate resale price after five years.

$$\text{Resale (residual) or “terminal” cap rate} = 12\% - 2\% = 10\%.$$

Apply this to NOI in Year 6:

$$\text{Resale} = \$120,000/0.10 = \$1,200,000.$$

Note that the value that can be obtained by selling the property at some point in the future is often referred to as the "reversion" by real estate professionals.

Step 2: Discount the level NOI for the first five years and the resale price.

$$PMT = \$100,000.$$
$$FV = \$1,200,000.$$
$$n = 5.$$
$$i = 12\%.$$

Solving for PV, the current value of the property is estimated to be $1,041,390.
Note that the implied going-in cap rate is $100,000/$1,041,390 = 9.60%.

In Example 20, the going-in cap rate is lower than the terminal cap rate. Investors would be willing to pay a higher price for the current NOI because they know that it will increase when the lease is renewed at market rents in five years. The expected rent jump on lease renewal is implicit in the cap rate.

As noted earlier, we often expect the terminal cap rate to be higher than the going-in cap rate because it is being applied to income that is more uncertain. Also, the property will be older and may have less growth potential or require increased spending. Finding a lower implied going-in cap rate in this example is consistent with this. At certain times, however, we would expect the terminal cap rate to be lower than the going-in cap rate—for example, if we thought that interest rates and thus discount rates would be lower when the property is sold in the future or we expected that markets would be a lot stronger in the future, with expectations for higher rental growth than in the current market. In general, the higher the risk, the higher the cap rate required to lift the investment return commensurately.

EXAMPLE 21   Appraisal with Level NOI

Suppose the NOI from a property is expected to be level at $600,000 per year for a long period of time such that, for all practical purposes, it can be assumed to be a perpetuity. What is the value of the property assuming investors want a 12% rate of return?

Solution: In this case, the growth rate is zero, so we have

$$\text{Value} = \text{NOI}/\text{Discount rate.}$$

$$\text{Value} = \$600,000/0.12 = \$5,000,000.$$

Note that in this case, the cap rate will be the same as the discount rate. This is true when there is no expected change in income and value over time.

EXAMPLE 22   Discounted Cash Flow Analysis

You work for a real estate investment firm that has been presented with the opportunity to purchase a 10-year-old warehouse distribution facility in Perth, Australia. The property contains 20,000 square meters (m^2) of leasable area that is 100% leased to three tenants. Two of the tenants have 10 years remaining on their respective leases. The third tenant has only three years left on its lease and has already indicated it will not renew the lease at expiration. One of the other tenants has indicated it would like to lease the space as soon as it becomes available as long as the property owner makes material improvements to the building.

Part 1: Your manager has asked you to prepare a discounted cash flow analysis to determine whether the acquisition would meet the company's return targets. Based on the assumptions provided, calculate the first-year NOI, the purchase price, and the terminal value. Note that the rent presented is net of all operating expenses.

Assumptions

Annual Net Rent per Square Meter	AUD 145.00	Initial Cap Rate	6.0%
Leasable Area (square meters)	20,000	Terminal Cap Rate	7.0%
Lease 1 (m^2)	6,897	Exit Year	7
Lease 2 (m^2)	6,897	NOI in Year 9 (millions)	AUD 3.79
Lease 3 (m^2)	6,207		

Solution:
> First-year NOI = AUD145/m² × 20,000 m² of leasable area
> = AUD2.9 million.
> Purchase price = Year 1 NOI/Cap rate = AUD2.9 million/6.0%
> = AUD48.3 million.
> Terminal value at the end of Year 7 = AUD3.79 million/7.0%
> = AUD54.1 million.

Part 2: Why do you think your manager asked you to use a 6.0% acquisition cap rate and a 7.0% terminal cap rate?

Solution: The 6.0% cap rate would be based on the cap rate from recent property sales adjusted for location, property age and quality, and tenant/lease composition. The 7.0% terminal cap rate is 100 bps higher than the initial cap rate because of a combination of the following: The property will be older and, besides the renovation of one building, will have continued to depreciate; the government benchmark rate, which is approximately 2.0%, could increase over the next seven years; and a measure of conservatism is advisable. A higher cap rate implies a lower *relative* price based on future earnings.

Part 3: This part of the example illustrates the cash flow forecast, the DCF, and NPV/return analysis.

Net property income increases at a 3.0% annual rate based on lease terms, which is consistent with the market. Additional capital spending and other below-the-line expenses that are not reported on the income statement are estimated at 3.5% of NOI. The forecast includes the large renovation during Year 4 to prepare the space vacated by the tenant whose lease expires at the end of Year 3 for one of the remaining tenants. Year 4 NOI includes a 20% increase above the 3.0% trend, which was negotiated with the tenant for the new lease, offset by six months of forgone rent during the renovation as incentive for the expanding tenant. Capital spending is also assumed to be lower in the year immediately preceding and the year following the renovation before returning to the steady-state trend. Recall that the NOI forecast needs to extend one year past the exit year to calculate the forward income that the next property buyer would use to value the property and present its own bid.

Cash Flow Forecast (AUD thousands)

Property Net Operating Income:	Year 0	Year 1	Year 2	Year 3	Year 4	Year 5	Year 6	Year 7	Year 8
Lease 1		1,000.0	1,030.0	1,060.9	1,092.7	1,125.5	1,159.3	1,194.1	1,229.9
Lease 2		1,000.0	1,030.0	1,060.9	1,092.7	1,125.5	1,159.3	1,194.1	1,229.9
Lease 3		900.0	927.0	954.8	590.1	1,215.5	1,242.0	1,289.6	1,328.3
Net Property NOI		2,900.0	2,987.0	3,076.6	2,775.5	3,466.6	3,570.6	3,677.7	3,788.0
Capital Spending and Leasing Expense		(101.5)	(104.5)	(74.3)	(1,094.4)	(78.8)	(125.0)	(128.7)	(132.6)
Property Cash Flow		2,798.5	2,882.5	3,002.3	1,681.2	3,387.8	3,445.6	3,549.0	3,655.4

The next table presents the unlevered discounted cash flow. Your manager suggests using a 7.0% discount rate for the investment based on the attractive, lower-risk-location, 10-year leases; the likelihood that an existing tenant will expand into the to-be-vacated space; and strong market fundamentals. The present value of the future cash flows is then compared with the acquisition price. (It is only a coincidence that the discount rate equals the terminal cap rate.) If the net present value is positive, the investment would create some value over the hurdle rate of return represented by the discount rate.

Discounted Cash Flow Analysis (AUD thousands)

	Year 0	Year 1	Year 2	Year 3	Year 4	Year 5	Year 6	Year 7
Initial outlay	−48,333							
Annual property cash flow		2,799	2,882	3,002	1,681	3,388	3,446	3,549
Exit value								54,114
Total cash flow	(48,333)	2,799	2,882	3,002	1,681	3,388	3,446	57,663
Discount rate (input)	7.0%	$1/(1+0.07)^1$	$1/(1+0.07)^2$	$1/(1+0.07)^3$	$1/(1+0.07)^4$	$1/(1+0.07)^5$	$1/(1+0.07)^6$	$1/(1+0.07)^7$
Present value factor		0.9346	0.8734	0.8163	0.7629	0.7130	0.6663	0.6227
Present value of property cash flows		2,615	2,518	2,451	1,283	2,415	2,296	35,910

NPV and Return Analysis	
Sum of present value of cash inflows	49,488
Cash outlay	(48,333)
Net present value of future CF	1,154
IRR (Output)	7.4%

The NPV of the property exceeds the acquisition price by AUD1.2 million. The positive net present value demonstrates that the investment would create value and excess return relative to the risk-adjusted cost of capital. The 7.4% expected IRR further confirms that the forecasted return would exceed the 7.0% discount rate.

Part 4: This part of the example provides two sensitivity tables: (1) a sensitivity analysis on the entry cap rate and (2) a sensitivity analysis on the exit cap rate.

Sensitivity Tables (AUD thousands)

	Initial Capitalization Rate				
	7.0%	6.5%	6.0%	5.5%	5.0%
Purchase price	41,429	44,615	48,333	52,727	58,000
NPV	3,847	2,626	1,154	(647)	(2,896)

	Terminal Capitalization Rate				
	8.0%	7.5%	7.0%	6.5%	6.0%
Exit price	47,350	50,507	54,114	58,277	63,134
NPV	(3,058)	(1,092)	1,154	3,747	6,771

The preceding sensitivity tables present the range of net present values in thousands of Australian dollars for several entry and exit cap rates. The corresponding purchase and exit prices, also in thousands, are presented alongside the cap rates. The acquisition table is presented from lower asset price/higher cap rate to higher asset price/lower cap rate. The table indicates that the investor could pay more than AUD48.3 million, or the 6.0% cap rate on Year 1 NOI, and still exceed the cost of capital but not as much as AUD52.7 million, which equates to a 5.5% cap rate. In fact, the investor could pay approximately AUD51.1 million, the equivalent of a 5.67% cap rate, and still break even on the basis of the given discount rate. The breakeven purchase price represents the maximum value the investor could pay for the acquisition while holding all other factors constant without the net present value turning negative.

8. PRIVATE MARKET REAL ESTATE DEBT

Thus far, our focus has been on analyzing a property without considering whether debt financing would be on the property or whether it would be purchased on an all-cash basis. The reason is that the way a property is financed should not affect the property's value. This does not mean that the overall level of interest rates and the availability of debt in the market do not affect values. It means that for a given property, the investor paying all cash should be paying the same price as one who decides to use some debt financing. Of course, investors who do use debt financing will normally expect to earn a higher rate of return on their equity investment because they expect to earn a greater return on the property than what they will be paying the lender. Thus, there will be positive financial leverage. By borrowing money, the investor is taking on more risk in anticipation of a higher return on equity invested. The risk is higher because with debt comes more uncertainty as to what return the investor will actually earn on equity, since the investor gets what is left over after paying the lender. A small drop in property value can result in a large decrease in the investor's return if a high amount of debt was used to finance the property. When a property is valued without explicitly considering financing, the discount rate can be thought of as a weighted average of the rate of return an equity investor would want and the interest rate on the debt.

The maximum amount of debt that an investor can obtain on commercial real estate is usually limited by either the ratio of the loan to the appraised value of the property (loan to value, or LTV) or the debt service coverage ratio (DSCR), depending on which measure results in the lowest loan amount. The debt service coverage ratio is the ratio of the first-year NOI to the loan payment (referred to as debt service for commercial real estate). That is,

$$DSCR = NOI/Debt \; service. \tag{3.8}$$

The debt service includes both interest and principal payments on the mortgage. The principal payments are the portion of the loan payment that amortizes the loan over the loan term. An interest-only loan is one that has no principal payments, so the loan balance will remain constant over time. Interest-only loans typically either revert to amortizing loans at some point or have a specified maturity date. For example, an interest-only loan might be made that requires the entire balance of the loan to be repaid after 7–10 years (referred to as a "balloon payment"). Lenders typically require a DSCR of 1.25–1.5 depending on the property type to provide a margin of safety that the NOI from the property can cover the debt service.

EXAMPLE 23   Loans on Real Estate

A property has been appraised for $5 million and is expected to have NOI of $400,000 in the first year. The lender is willing to make an interest-only loan at an 8% interest rate as long as the loan-to-value ratio does not exceed 80% and the DSCR is at least 1.25. The balance of the loan will be due after seven years. How much of a loan can be obtained?

Solution: Based on the loan-to-value ratio, the loan would be 80% of $5 million, or $4 million. With a DSCR of 1.25, the maximum debt service would be $400,000/1.25 = $320,000. This amount is the mortgage payment that would result in a 1.25 DSCR for an interest-only loan.

If the loan is interest only, then we can obtain the loan amount by simply dividing the mortgage payment by the interest rate. Therefore, the loan amount would be $320,000/0.08 = $4,000,000.

In this case, we obtain the same loan amount from either the LTV or the DSCR requirements of the lender. If one ratio had resulted in a lower loan amount, that would normally be the maximum that could be borrowed.

When financing is used on a property, equity investors often look at their first-year return on equity or the "equity dividend rate" as a measure of how much cash flow they are getting as a percentage of their equity investment. This measure is sometimes referred to as a *cash-on-cash return* because it measures how much cash they are receiving as a percentage of the cash equity they put into the investment.

EXAMPLE 24   Equity Dividend Rate

Using the information in Example 23, what is the equity dividend rate, or cash-on-cash return, assuming the property is purchased at its appraised value?

Solution: The first-year cash flow is the NOI less the mortgage payment.

NOI	$400,000
Debt service	$320,000
Cash flow	$80,000

The amount of equity is the purchase price less the loan amount.

Price	$5,000,000
Mortgage	$4,000,000
Equity	$1,000,000

The equity yield rate is the cash flow divided by equity: $80,000/$1,000,000 = 8\%$. Keep in mind that this is not an IRR that would be earned over a holding period until the property is sold. The equity investor does not share any of the price appreciation in the value of the property with the lender.

For loans called "participation" loans, the lender might receive some of the price appreciation, but it would be in exchange for a lower interest rate on the loan.

EXAMPLE 25   Leveraged IRR

Refer to Examples 23 and 24. Suppose the same property is sold for $6 million after five years. What IRR will the equity investor receive on his or her investment?

Solution: The cash flow received by the equity investor from the sale will be the sale price less the mortgage balance, or $6 million − $4 million = $2 million. Using a financial calculator,

> PV = −$1,000,000 (using a calculator, this is input as a negative to indicate the negative cash flow at the beginning of the investment).
> PMT = $80,000.
> $n = 5$.
> FV = $2,000,000.
> Solving for i gives 21.14%.

This IRR is based on the equity invested in the property.

EXAMPLE 26   Unleveraged IRR

Refer to Examples 23, 24, and 25. What would the IRR be if the property were purchased on an all-cash basis (no loan)?

Solution: Now the equity investor will receive all the cash flow from the sale ($6 million) and the NOI ($400,000). The initial investment will be $5 million. Using a financial calculator,

$$PV = -\$5,000,000.$$
$$PMT = \$400,000.$$

$$n = 5.$$
$$FV = \$6,000,000.$$
Solving for i gives 11.20%.

This IRR is based on an unleveraged (all-cash) investment in the property. The difference between this IRR (11.20%) and the IRR the equity investor receives with the loan calculated in Example 25 (21.14%) reflects positive financial leverage. The property earns 11.20% before adding a loan, and the loan is at 8%. So, the investor is benefiting from the spread between 11.20% and 8%.

SECTION C. INVESTMENTS IN REAL ESTATE THROUGH PUBLICLY TRADED SECURITIES

Real estate investment trusts were initially conceived of as a way for small investors to gain exposure to a professionally managed, diversified real estate portfolio. REITs were viewed as a type of (closed-end) mutual fund and income passthrough vehicle through which the portfolio manager would acquire attractively valued properties, occasionally sell fully valued properties, and distribute property earnings to the trust's investors. Until legislation was passed in the United States in 1960 to authorize REITs, real estate investing was reserved for the wealthy and institutions. The Netherlands followed suit in 1969. The US model and other types of tax-advantaged real estate investment vehicles have been adopted worldwide. Subsequent liberalization of US REIT restrictions made it easier for pension funds to invest in REITs. The S&P 500 added REITs as a separate GICS sector in 2016.

Today, more than 35 countries have REITs or REIT-like structures, more are considering adopting similar vehicles, and REITs are held by individuals and institutions alike. The FTSE EPRA Nareit Developed Index had a market cap of $1.45 trillion as of March 2020, and 30 REITs are members of the S&P 500.

9. TYPES OF PUBLICLY TRADED REAL ESTATE SECURITIES

Publicly traded real estate securities allow investors to gain indirect exposure to real estate equity and debt, primarily mortgages, by purchasing shares of companies that own real estate, real estate loans, or both. The very definition of securitization—transforming an illiquid asset into a financial product—makes it possible for investors of all sizes to access an asset class that was once available only to the largest investors and the diversification of the underlying asset pool. Globally, the principal types of publicly traded real estate securities are real estate investment trusts, real estate operating companies, and mortgage-backed securities.

- **Real estate investment trusts** are companies or trusts that own, finance, and—to a limited extent—develop income-producing real estate property. REITs that own real estate are called **equity REITs**. Those that make or invest in loans secured by real estate are categorized as mortgage REITs. The companies' tax advantages result from being allowed to deduct dividends paid from income, which effectively exempts REITs from corporate income tax in many countries. In many jurisdictions, qualifying REITs are simply exempt from corporate income tax. Most REITs are required to distribute 90%–100% of their taxable income to shareholders.

- **Real estate operating companies** are ordinary taxable real estate ownership companies. Businesses are organized as REOCs, as opposed to REITs, if they are located in countries that do not have a tax-advantaged REIT regime in place, if they engage to a large extent in the development of for-sale real estate properties, or if they offer other non-qualifying services, such as brokerage and third-party property management. The primary cash inflows for merchant developers are from sales of developed or improved properties rather than from recurring lease or rental income. Other companies prefer the more flexible operating company structure, even when they develop, own, and operate qualifying rental properties, because the REIT prohibitions may be too restrictive or they may prefer to retain earnings for reinvestment.

- Mortgage-backed securities are asset-backed securitized debt obligations that represent rights to receive cash flows from portfolios of mortgage loans—mortgage loans on commercial properties in the case of commercial mortgage-backed securities (CMBS) and mortgage loans on residential properties in the case of residential mortgage-backed securities (RMBS). The market capitalization of publicly traded real estate equity securities is greatly exceeded by the market value of real estate debt securities—in particular, RMBS. Whereas residential mortgage pools may contain thousands of loans, commercial mortgage pools may contain more than 100 loans or as few as 1 loan when the asset is very large.

In addition to publicly traded real estate securities, there are privately held real estate securities, including private REITs and REOCs, privately held mortgages, private debt issues, and bank debt. Many real estate private equity partnerships create private REITs to own income-producing properties.

9.1. REIT Structures

REITs are tax-efficient conduits for distributing earnings from rental income to shareholders. Most are structured as corporations or trusts. There are numerous requirements for a company to qualify as a REIT. In most countries, REITs are required to distribute 90%–100% of their otherwise taxable earnings, invest at least 75% of their assets in real estate, and derive at least 75% of income from real estate rental income or interest on mortgages. Countries may specify a minimum number of shareholders, maximum share ownership by a single shareholder, a minimum number of properties/maximum asset concentration, a maximum level of non-rental income, a maximum amount of development, and limits on leverage and types of loans. In the United States, a REIT must have at least 100 shareholders, and no fewer than 5 shareholders can own more than 50% of the shares (the five-or-fewer rule). There are numerous other requirements as well. The restrictions effectively bar an individual or small group from creating REITs to own individual assets.

Most REITs in the United States are self-managed and self-advised. Senior executives are company employees who report to trustees or the board of directors, who, in turn, are elected by shareholders. Fully integrated REITs generally have fewer conflicts than REITs that are externally advised or externally managed. Externally managed REITs pay asset management fees to the third-party adviser, which has an inherent incentive to increase the size of the REIT if fees are based on total assets. External managers may require REITs to pay for other services that are provided by affiliates of the manager, such as property management, acquisitions, and debt placement.

That is not to say all externally managed REITs should be avoided. Management quality, governance, alignment, reputation, and transparency clearly matter. Several services rate the quality of governance, transparency, and so forth, to assist in the investment valuation, for both externally managed and self-managed REITs.

In the United States, shareholder taxation of REIT dividends received may vary according to the underlying source of income. The portion of the distribution derived from ordinary rental income is classified as ordinary income and taxed at investors' top marginal tax rates. The portion of distributions in excess of a REIT's earnings is categorized as return of capital and is deducted from the investor's share cost basis for tax purposes (if an investor later sells shares at a higher price than the reduced cost basis and generates a long-term capital gain, the profit would qualify for lower capital-gains tax treatment). REIT distributions of capital gains on property sales may also be taxed at shareholders' capital gains tax rate. There are other classifications, such as recaptured depreciation, that are beyond the scope of this chapter. In any country, foreign investors are likely to be subject to the host country's withholding tax rate.

9.2. Market Size

As of May 2019, the market value of publicly traded real estate investment trusts and real estate operating companies globally was approximately US$2.6 trillion for the developed markets, whereas the total face value of residential and commercial mortgage-related securities outstanding in the United States alone was approximately US$9.8 trillion. Details about the market's relative size by geographic area and security type are shown in Exhibit 9.

EXHIBIT 9   Relative Size and Composition of Publicly Traded Real Estate Equity Security Markets

A. Percentage of market value of publicly traded real estate equity securities (REITs and REOCs) in developed markets as of 31 May 2019

By Region (%)		By Market (%)	
North America	56.7	United States	53.9
Asia Pacific	26.4	Japan	11.3
Europe	16.8	Hong Kong SAR	7.9
Middle East, Africa	0.1	Australia	4.7
		Germany	4.7
		United Kingdom	4.6
		Canada	2.8
		Singapore	2.5
		Sweden	1.7
		Netherlands	1.6
		France	1.5
		Others	2.8

B. Percentage of market value of publicly traded equity real estate equity securities in developed markets by type of structure as of 29 March 2019

	Global	North America	Europe	Asia Pacific
REITs	68	96	43	42
Non-REITs, REOCs	32	4	57	58

Sources: www.ftserussell.com and www.epra.com. Based on data from the FTSE EPRA Nareit Developed Index.

As an investment asset class, income-producing real estate offers the advantages of stable income based on its contractual revenue from leases and a measure of long-term inflation protection because, over the long term, rents tend to rise with inflation. For example, in the United States over 1998–2018, the FTSE Nareit All Equity REITs Index achieved a compounded annual total return of 10.0%, compared with 5.6% for the S&P 500 and 4.5% for the Bloomberg Barclays US Aggregate Bond Index. The US Consumer Price Index increased by an average of 2.2% annually over the same period.

9.3. Benefits and Disadvantages of Investing in REITs

The benefits of investing in public real estate companies as compared with private real estate investments include the following:

1. *Liquidity*: Ability to buy and sell shares of almost any amount on major exchanges
2. *Transparency*: Readily available share prices and transaction histories
3. *Diversification*: By property type, geography, and underlying tenant credit when medium-sized and larger companies own several dozen properties, thousands of rental apartment units, and millions of square feet of leasable office space, retail space, industrial space, and so on
4. *High-quality portfolios*: Many companies own high-quality assets in leading markets
5. *Active professional management*: Most companies have strong executive management overseeing dedicated property management teams and achieve economies of scale and operating efficiencies
6. *High, stable income*: Well occupied properties subject to long-term leases generate predictable property income, sometimes with distributions occurring monthly
7. *Tax efficiency*: REIT and passthrough structures avoid corporate income taxation, leaving only the investor to pay taxes on dividends received

The largest disadvantage for REITs that seek to expand their portfolios is the lack of retained earnings. These companies need to access capital markets for equity and debt to fund growth. The faster the expansion, the more often the company must raise new capital. REITs are also constrained in the types of assets they own. Consequently, many REITs form **taxable REIT subsidiaries** (TRS), which pay income taxes on earnings from non-REIT-qualifying activities, such as merchant development or third-party property management.

EXAMPLE 27   Advantages of Publicly Traded Real Estate Investments

1. Which of the following assets requires the *most* expertise in real estate on the part of the investor?
   A. A REOC share
   B. An equity REIT share
   C. A direct investment in a single property
2. Which of the following has the *most* operating and financial flexibility?
   A. A REOC
   B. An equity REIT
   C. A direct investment in a single property
3. Investors seeking broad diversification would invest in the securities of which of the following companies?
   A. A company that owns multi-family rental properties in Hong Kong SAR
   B. A company that owns large office properties in New York City, San Francisco, Los Angeles, and Chicago
   C. A company with a mix of office and retail properties in urban and suburban markets

Solution to 1: C is correct. Direct investment in a single property requires a high level of real estate expertise. Investment in publicly traded equity investments (in REITs or REOCs) requires much less expertise because investors benefit from having their property interests actively managed on their behalf by professional managers and from having their business interests overseen and guided by boards of directors, as in the case of all public corporations.

Solution to 2: A is correct. REOCs are free to invest in any kind of real estate or related activity without limitation. This freedom gives management the opportunity to create more value in development activity and in trading real estate and to retain as much of their income as they believe is appropriate. A wider range of capital structures and degrees of financial leverage may be used in the process. In contrast to REOCs, REITs face restrictions on the amount of income and assets accounted for by activities other than collecting rent and interest payments. Direct investment is less liquid and divisible than REOC and REIT shares, which limits the operational flexibility of such investment.

Solution to 3: C is correct. It should be clear that a company with a mix of assets—office and retail—with exposure to urban and suburban markets offers the best diversification. A is incorrect because the company has only one type of asset, multi-family rentals, in one market, Hong Kong SAR. The systematic risk is high for that portfolio. B is incorrect because the company owns only one asset type, office properties, and the economic activity correlation may be high among urban cities with exposure to global trade and the financial sector.

Alternatively, investors looking for property and market diversification might, instead of the solutions provided, consider investing in fewer, large companies that own different asset types in multiple cities or several pure-play companies, each of which concentrates on a single asset type in its given region, as long as the companies' regions and product type do not overlap to a large extent.

EXAMPLE 28   Publicly Traded Real Estate Investments

Which of the following best represents an advantage of REITs over a direct investment in an income-producing property?
A. Diversification
B. Operating flexibility
C. Income growth potential

Solution: A is correct. REITs provide diversification of property holdings. B is incorrect because REITs do face restrictions on the amount of income and assets accounted for by activities other than collecting rent and interest payments; these restrictions can prevent a REIT from maximizing its returns. C is incorrect because the relatively low rates of income retention that are required to maintain a REIT's tax-free status can detract from income growth potential.

EXAMPLE 29   Investment Objectives

Two real estate investors are each choosing from among the following investment types: a REOC, an equity REIT, or a direct investment in an income-producing property. Investor A's primary objective is liquidity, and Investor B's primary objective is maximum growth/capital gain potential. State and explain which real estate investment type best suits:

1. Investor A.
2. Investor B.

Solution to 1: For Investor A, with a liquidity objective, REOC and REIT investments are most appropriate because REOCs and REITs are traded on stock exchanges and are more liquid. Direct investments in income-producing property are generally less liquid.

Solution to 2: For Investor B, with a maximum growth objective, REOCs and direct property investment are most appropriate because REOCs and direct investors are free to invest in any kind of real estate or related activity without limitation and to reinvest as much of their income as they believe is appropriate for their objectives. This freedom gives them the opportunity to create more value in development activity and in trading real estate. REITs' constraints prevent them from retaining earnings to reinvest, so their growth opportunities are more limited.

There are several caveats to note for each generalized solution. Shares of closely held listed companies with low market float that trade infrequently may not offer the desired liquidity. Management quality, corporate governance, balance-sheet capacity and leverage, attractive investment and reinvestment opportunities, and many other considerations matter greatly when it comes to selecting the vehicle and company that are best at delivering growth and value to shareholders. There are many REITs that offer dividend reinvestment programs (DRIPs), and there are some REOCs that continuously develop without selling assets when real estate valuations are high.

10. VALUATION: NET ASSET VALUE APPROACH

The approaches analysts take in valuing equity include those based on asset value estimates, price multiple comparisons, and discounted cash flow.

Two possible measures of value that analysts might use are book value per share (BVPS) and net asset value per share (NAVPS) based on reported accounting values and market values for assets, respectively. In this chapter, BVPS refers to depreciated real estate value rather than total shareholders' equity per share. NAVPS is the relevant market-based valuation measure for valuing REITs and REOCs.

NAVPS is a fundamental benchmark for the value of a REIT or REOC. In Europe and Asia, the price-to-NAV multiple is the primary measure that analysts use to value real estate companies. (US analysts more commonly report on price multiples of gross cash flow, as discussed in Section 11.) Real estate **net asset value** may be viewed as the largest component of the intrinsic value of a REIT or REOC. NAVPS should also include investors' assessments of the value of any non-asset-based income streams (e.g., fee or management income); the value of non–real estate assets, including cash, net of the value of any contingent liabilities; and the value added by management of the REIT or REOC.

Shares priced at discounts to NAVPS are interpreted as indications of potential undervaluation, and shares priced at premiums to NAVPS, in the absence of indications of positive future events, such as a successful property development completion or expected high value creation by a management team, suggest potential overvaluation. However, these assessments must be made in the context of the stock market's tendency to be forward looking in its valuations and at times to have different investment criteria from property markets. In addition, the stock price discount or premium to NAVPS may be explained by investors' view of management's added value, leverage, and company governance. REITs whose shares trade below NAVPS or have high leverage may have a more difficult time raising new capital to fund acquisitions and development, which, in turn, may limit long-term growth, in contrast to REITs that trade at or above NAVPS. Selling equity below NAVPS can be dilutive for investors.

10.1. Accounting for Investment Properties

If accounting is on a fair value basis, accounting values may be relevant for asset-based valuation. If historical cost values are used, however, accounting values are generally not relevant.

Under International Financial Reporting Standards (IFRS), companies are allowed to value investment properties using either a cost model or a fair value model. The cost model is identical to the cost model used for property, plant, and equipment. Under the fair value model, all changes in the asset's fair value affect net income. To use the fair value model, a company must be able to reliably determine the property's fair value on a continuing basis.

In general, a company must consistently apply its chosen model (cost or fair value) to all of its investment property. If a company chooses the fair value model for its investment property, it must continue to use the fair value model until it disposes of the property or changes its use such that it is no longer considered investment property (e.g., it becomes owner-occupied property or part of inventory). The company must continue to use the fair value model for that property even if transactions on comparable properties, used to estimate fair value, become less frequent.

Investment property appears as a separate line item on the balance sheet. Companies are required to disclose whether they use the fair value model or the cost model for their investment property. If the company uses the fair value model, it must make additional disclosures about how it determines fair value and must provide reconciliation between the beginning and ending carrying amounts of the investment property. If the company uses the cost model, it must make additional disclosures—for example, the depreciation method and useful lives must be disclosed. In addition, if the company uses the cost model, it must also disclose the fair value of investment property.

In contrast to IFRS, under US GAAP, most US real estate owners use the historical cost accounting model, which values an asset at its original purchase price plus capital investment less historical depreciation. This model does not accurately represent the economic values of assets and liabilities in environments of significant operating income and asset price changes or long-term inflation. Net asset values can be written down when there is a permanent impairment in economic value, but they can be written up only under exceptional circumstances, such as mergers, acquisitions, or reorganizations. US GAAP historical cost accounting practices tend to distort the measure of economic income and asset value by: (1) understating carrying values on long-held property assets that are often appreciating in value because of general price inflation or other property-specific reasons and (2) overstating depreciation when companies use accelerated depreciation.

10.2. Net Asset Value per Share: Calculation

As a result of shortcomings in accounting reported values, investment analysts and investors use estimates of **net asset value per share**. NAVPS is the difference between a real estate company's assets and its liabilities, *all taken at current market values instead of accounting book values*, divided by the number of shares outstanding. NAVPS is a superior measure of a company's net worth compared with historical book value per share.

In valuing a REIT's or REOC's real estate portfolio, analysts will look for the results of existing appraisals if they are available (such as those provided by companies reporting under IFRS). If such appraisals are unavailable or if they disagree with the assumptions or methodology of those appraisals, analysts will often capitalize the rental streams—represented by net operating income—produced by a REIT's or REOC's properties, using a market-required rate of return. NOI is defined as gross rental revenue minus operating costs (which include estimated vacancy and collection losses, insurance costs, taxes, utilities, and repair and maintenance expenses) before deducting depreciation, general and administrative (G&A) expenses, and interest expense. After deducting G&A expenses from NOI, the figure obtained is analogous to earnings before interest, depreciation, and amortization (EBITDA). Recall that this approach is similar to the valuation of private real estate covered in Sections 5–7. These estimated asset values will be substituted for the book values of the properties on the balance sheet and adjustments made to any related accounting assets, such as capitalized leases, to avoid double counting.

Generally, goodwill, deferred financing expenses, and deferred tax assets will be excluded to arrive at a "hard" economic value for total assets. Liabilities will be similarly adjusted to replace the face value of debt with market values if these are significantly different (e.g., as a result of changes in interest rates), and any such "soft" liabilities as deferred tax liabilities will be removed. The revised net worth of the company divided by the number of shares outstanding is the NAV. Although this figure is calculated before provision for any income or capital gains taxes that might be payable on liquidation, the inability to predict how the company or its assets might be sold and the prospect that it might be kept intact in an acquisition cause investors to look to the pre-tax asset value as their primary net worth benchmark. If a company has held its assets for many years and has a very low remaining depreciable value for its assets for tax purposes, it can affect investors' perspectives on valuation. Quantifying the effects of a low adjusted cost base, however, is impeded by lack of knowledge of the tax circumstances and strategies of a would-be acquirer.

Exhibit 10 provides an example of the calculations involved in estimating NAV based on capitalizing rental streams. Because the book values of assets are based on historical costs, the analyst estimates NAVPS. First, by capitalizing NOI with certain adjustments, the analyst obtains an estimate of the value of rental properties; then, the value of other tangible assets is added and the total is netted of liabilities. This net amount, NAV, is then divided by the number of shares outstanding to obtain NAVPS.

EXHIBIT 10   Analyst Adjustments to REIT Financials to Obtain NAVPS

Last-12-month real estate NOI	$270,432
Less: Non-cash rent	7,667
Plus: Adjustment for full impact of acquisitions (1)	4,534
Pro forma cash NOI for last 12 months	$267,299
Plus: Next-12-month growth in NOI (2)	$4,009
Estimated next-12-month cash NOI	$271,308
Assumed cap rate (3)	7.00%
Estimated value of operating real estate	$3,875,829
Plus: Cash and equivalents	65,554
Plus: Land held for future development	34,566
Plus: Accounts receivable	45,667
Plus: Prepaid/other assets (4)	23,456
Estimated gross asset value	$4,045,072
Less: Total debt	1,010,988
Less: Other liabilities	119,886
Net asset value	$2,914,198
Shares outstanding	55,689

1. An incremental 50% of the annual expected return on acquisitions that were completed midway through 2020.

2. Growth is estimated at 1.5%.

3. Cap rate is based on recent comparable transactions in the property market.

4. This figure does not include intangible assets.

NAVPS is calculated to be $2,914,198 divided by 55,689 shares, which equals $52.33 per share.

The second line in Exhibit 10 shows the adjustment to remove **non-cash rent**; these are the result of the accounting practice of "straight lining" the rental revenue from long-term leases with contractual step-ups. When the real estate company reports the average contractual rent it expects to receive over the course of each lease, rent received from the tenant is less than the average revenue booked during the early years of the lease, and the tenant pays more rent than the company reports during the latter years of the lease term. (The amount of this deduction is the difference between the average contractual rent over the leases' terms and the cash rent actually paid.) NOI is also increased to reflect a full year's rent for properties acquired during the course of the year, resulting in pro forma "cash NOI" for the previous 12 months of $267,299,000. This amount is then increased to include expected growth for the next 12 months at 1.5%, resulting in expected next-12-month cash NOI of $271,308,000.

An appropriate capitalization rate is then estimated on the basis of recent transactions for comparable properties in the property market. An estimated value for the REIT's operating real estate is obtained by dividing expected next-12-month cash NOI by the decimalized capitalization rate (in this case, 0.07). The book values of the REIT's other tangible assets, including cash, accounts receivable, land for future development, and prepaid expenses, are added to obtain estimated gross asset value. (Land is sometimes taken at market value if this amount can be determined reliably; but because land is often difficult to value and of low liquidity, analysts tend to use book values.) From this figure, debt and other liabilities (but not deferred taxes, because this item is an accounting provision rather than an economic liability) are subtracted to obtain net asset value. Division by the number of shares outstanding produces NAVPS.

10.3. Net Asset Value per Share: Application

NAVPS can be reasonably estimated when there are ample market transactions to provide property comparables. Investors can make observations about how such properties trade on the basis of the capitalization rate (the rate obtained by dividing net operating income by total value) or on the basis of price per square foot. Broker reports and private real estate research companies also track rental rates by property and other tenant incentives, such as free rent or capital to improve the space, and then apply these valuations to the assets of a public company. In the United States, close to 15% of commercial real estate is held by publicly traded REITs, according to EPRA (www.epra.com). In Europe, only 7% of the commercial real estate market is owned by listed real estate companies (REITs and REOCs), and in Singapore, 34% of the commercial market is owned by listed real estate companies

Over time, REITs and REOCs in the United States and globally have at times traded at premiums to NAV of more than 25% and at other times at discounts to NAV exceeding 25%. Thus, if the NAV of a REIT was $20 per share, the stock might trade as low as $15 per share or as high as $25 per share, depending on a range of factors.

10.3.1. Important Considerations in a NAV-Based Approach to Valuing REITs
Although NAV estimates provide investors with a specific value, a number of important considerations should be taken into account when using this approach to value REITs and REOCs. First, investors must understand the implications of using a private market valuation tool on a publicly traded security. In this context, it is useful to examine how NAVs are calculated.

The methods most commonly used to calculate NAV are: (1) using the cap rate approach to valuing the NOI of a property or portfolio of properties, (2) applying value per square foot (or unit) to a property or portfolio of properties, and (3) using appraised values disclosed in the company's financial statements. An analyst may adjust these appraised values reported by the company if she does not agree with the underlying assumptions and if there is sufficient information to do so. In the first two instances, the cap rates and values per square foot are derived from observing transactions that have occurred in the marketplace. In contrast, most sophisticated direct purchasers of commercial real estate arrive at a purchase price after performing detailed forecasting of the cash flows they expect to achieve from owning and operating a specific property over their investment time horizon. These cash flows are then discounted to a present value or purchase price. Whatever that present value or purchase price is, an analyst can estimate value by dividing an estimate of NOI by the cap rate—essentially, the required rate of current return for income streams of that risk. In addition, an analyst can take the present value or purchase price and divide by the property's rentable area for a value per square foot. The point is that cap rates and values per square foot result from a more detailed analysis and discounted cash flow process. The discount rate used by a private owner/operator of commercial real estate could differ from the discount rate used by investors purchasing shares of REITs.

Real estate stocks trade at premiums and discounts to NAV. The price-to-NAV ratio will vary by market, sector, outlook, and perceived quality of management and governance. Private property investors may or may not value individual assets the same way public equity investors value listed real estate companies. Property buyers frequently consider the long-term prospects and valuation for an asset when making an investment. Appraisal-based NAV estimates, however, often lag changes in market conditions. Stock investors tend to focus more on the near-term projected outlook for changes in income and asset value. These factors help explain why share valuation may differ from NAV. As alluded to earlier, it is possible that REITs and REOCs can trade at some premium or discount to NAV until the premium/discount becomes wide enough for market forces to close the arbitrage gap.

Another factor to consider when using a NAV approach to REIT/REOC valuation is that NAV implicitly treats a company as an individual asset or static pool of assets. In reality, such treatment is not consistent with a going-concern assumption. Management teams have different track records and abilities to produce value over time, assets can be purchased and sold, and capital market decisions can add or subtract value. An investor must thus consider how much value a management team can add to (or subtract from) current NAV. For instance, an investor may be willing to purchase REIT A trading at a 10% premium to NAV versus REIT B trading at a small discount to NAV because the management team of REIT A has a stronger track record and better opportunities to grow the NAV compared with REIT B, thus justifying the premium at which REIT A trades relative to REIT B.

NAV estimates can also become quite subjective when property markets become illiquid and few transactions are observable or when REITs and REOCs own hundreds of properties, making it difficult for an investor to estimate exactly how much the portfolio would be worth if the assets were sold individually. There may also be a large-portfolio premium in good economic environments when prospective strategic purchasers may be willing to pay a premium to acquire a large amount of desired property at once or a large-portfolio discount when there are few buyers for the kind of property in question. In addition, such assets as undeveloped land, very large properties with few comparable assets, properties with specific uses, service businesses, and joint ventures complicate the process of estimating NAV with accuracy and confidence.

10.3.2. Further Observations on NAV

Among institutional investors, the most common view is that if REIT management is performing well in the sense of creating value, REITs and REOCs should trade at premiums to underlying NAVPS. This rationale is based on the following:

1. Investors in the stocks have liquidity on a day-to-day basis, whereas a private investor in real estate does not, thus warranting a lower required return rate (higher value) in the public market than in the private market for the same assets.
2. The competitive nature of the public markets and the size of the organizations should attract above-average management teams, which should produce better real estate operating performance and lead to better investment decisions than the average private real estate concern.

In conclusion, although NAV is by its nature an absolute valuation metric, in practice it is often more useful as a relative valuation tool. If all REITs are trading above or below NAV, selecting individual REITs could become a relative exercise—that is, purchasing the REIT stock trading at the smallest premium to NAV when REITs are trading above NAV or selling the REIT trading at the smallest discount to NAV when REITs are all trading at a discount to NAV. In practice, NAV is also used as a relative metric by investors looking at implied cap rates. To calculate the implied cap rate of a REIT or REOC, the current price is used in a NAV model to work backward and solve for the cap rate. By doing so, an investor looking at two similar portfolios of real estate could ascertain whether the market is valuing these portfolios differently on the basis of the implied cap rates.

11. VALUATION: RELATIVE VALUE (PRICE MULTIPLE) APPROACH

Conventional equity valuation approaches, including market-based or relative value approaches, are used with some adaptations to value REITs and REOCs. Such multiples as the price-to-funds from operations ratio (P/FFO), the price-to-adjusted funds from operations ratio (P/AFFO), and the enterprise value-to-EBITDA ratio (EV/EBITDA) are used for valuing shares of REITs and REOCs in much the same way as for valuing shares in other industries.

11.1. Relative Value Approach to Valuing REIT Stocks

REIT analysts and investors make extensive use of two measures of operating performance that are specific to REITs. **Funds from operations (FFO)** is defined as net income plus depreciation and amortization less gains or losses on the sale of real property. It is one of the most commonly used metrics in the United States. (In Europe and Asia, NAVPS is more commonly used, as discussed in Section 10.) **Adjusted funds from operations (AFFO)** subtracts recurring capital expenditure and the difference between reported rents and cash rents (i.e., rent straight lining). AFFO better approximates a company's sustainable dividend-paying capacity. These definitions are discussed in greater detail in Section 11.2.

The relative value measures most frequently used in valuing REIT shares are P/FFO and P/AFFO. The ratio EV/EBITDA is used to a lesser extent. Similar to the P/E and P/CF multiples used for valuing equities in other industries, P/FFO and P/AFFO multiples allow investors to quickly ascertain the value of a given REIT's shares compared with that of other REIT shares or to compare the current valuation level of a REIT's shares with historical levels. Within the REIT sector, P/FFO and P/AFFO multiples are also often compared with the average multiple of companies owning

similar properties—for example, comparing the P/FFO multiple of a REIT that owns office properties with the average P/FFO multiple for all REITs owning office properties. These multiples are
typically calculated using current stock prices and year-ahead estimated FFO or AFFO.

FFO and AFFO are based on net income available to equity and thus represent levered
income. P/FFO multiples are generally lower for companies with higher leverage, all things
equal. EBITDA, by definition, measures income before the leveraging effect of debt. Not only
do EV/EBITDA multiples facilitate like-for-like valuation comparisons; they also better approximate how investors evaluate real estate. Recall that the inverse of the multiple, EBITDA/EV,
closely approximates the real estate capitalization rate formula (NOI/market value).

There are three main drivers that differentiate P/FFO, P/AFFO, and EV/EBITDA multiples among most REITs and REOCs:

1. *Expectation for growth in FFO and AFFO*: The higher the expected growth, the higher
   the multiple or relative valuation. Growth can be driven by business model (e.g., REITs
   and REOCs successful in real estate development often generate above-average FFO and
   AFFO growth over time); geography (e.g., having a concentration of properties in primary, supply-constrained markets, such as New York City or London, can give landlords
   more pricing power and higher cash flow growth than can be obtained in secondary markets); and other factors (e.g., management skill or lease structure).
2. *Risk associated with the underlying real estate*: Cash flow volatility related to asset type,
   quality, and age; market conditions; lease types; and submarket location also affect valuation. For example, owning apartments is viewed as having less cash flow variability than
   owning hotels. As such, apartment-focused REITs have tended to trade at relatively high
   multiples compared with hotel REITs. Likewise, shares of companies with younger, well-
   maintained portfolios generally trade at higher multiples than stocks of companies with
   older or out-of-date properties with deferred maintenance that will require higher capital
   expenditures to sustain rent growth.
3. *Risks associated with the company's capital structures and access to capital*: As financial leverage
   increases, equities' FFO and AFFO multiples decrease because required return increases as risk
   increases. Higher leverage constrains a company's incremental borrowing capacity and may create a stock overhang if investors avoid buying shares in anticipation of future equity offerings.

There are many other factors that affect valuation, as with any investment, including
investor perceptions of management, asset types or markets being in or out of favor, complexity, quality of financial disclosure, transparency, and governance.

FFO has some shortcomings, but because it is the most standardized measure of a REIT's
or REOC's earning power, P/FFO is the most frequently used multiple in analyzing the sector.
It is, in essence, the REIT sector equivalent of P/E. Investors can derive a quick "cash flow"
multiple by looking at P/AFFO because AFFO makes a variety of adjustments to FFO that
result in an approximation of cash earnings.

11.2. Funds from Operations and Adjusted Funds from Operations

FFO has long been the standard measure of REIT performance. The National Association of
Real Estate Investment Trusts (Nareit) took steps to standardize and promote the definition.
FFO is an SEC-accepted non-GAAP financial measure (as is EBITDA), which, according to
the SEC and as specified in updated guidance from Nareit (2018), must be reconciled with
GAAP net income. The SEC also recommends that companies that report adjustments to FFO
reconcile those figures with the Nareit-defined FFO, sometimes referred to as Nareit FFO.

FFO attempts to approximate continuing operating performance. The more complete definition of FFO is as follows: net income (computed in accordance with GAAP) plus losses (minus gains) from sales of properties, plus depreciation and amortization related to real estate, plus real estate impairments and write-downs unrelated to depreciation.

Why is depreciation added back to net income? Investors believe that real estate maintains its value to a greater extent than other business assets, often appreciating in value over the long term, and that depreciation deductions under IFRS and US GAAP do not represent economic reality. A taxable REOC that uses a moderate degree of leverage and regularly chooses to reinvest most of its income in its business usually will be able to defer a large part of its annual tax liability—that is, its cash income taxes will be low as a result of the accelerated depreciation rates for tax purposes permitted in most countries, and reinvesting continues to add to the depreciable real estate base. (Section 2.2 highlights the tax benefits derived from investing in real estate.)

Net income is adjusted for gains and losses from sales of previously depreciated operating properties on the grounds that they do not represent sustainable, normal income. The amortization add-back includes amortization of leasing commissions, tenant improvements, and tenant allowances.

Similar to cash flow from operations, FFO is not a measure of cash flow. It does not include investment and spending necessary to sustain cash flow growth or cash flow related to financing activities. FFO also includes FFO from unconsolidated businesses.

Adjusted funds from operations, also known as **funds available for distribution (FAD)** or **cash available for distribution**, is a refinement of FFO that is designed to be a more accurate measure of current economic income. AFFO is most often defined as FFO adjusted to remove any non-cash rent and to subtract maintenance-type capital expenditures and leasing costs (including leasing agents' commissions and tenants' improvement allowances). So-called **straight-line rent** is the average contractual rent over a lease term, and this figure is recognized as revenue under IFRS and US GAAP. The difference between this figure and the cash rent paid during the period is the amount of the non-cash rent or **straight-line rent adjustment**. Because most long-term leases contain escalating rental rates, this difference in rental revenue recognition can be significant. Also, deductions from FFO for capital expenditures related to maintenance and for leasing the space in properties reflect costs that need to be incurred to maintain the value of properties.

The purpose of the adjustments to net earnings made in computing FFO and AFFO is to obtain a more tangible, cash-focused measure of sustainable economic income that reduces reliance on non-cash accounting estimates and excludes non-economic, non-cash charges.

AFFO is superior to FFO as a measure of economic income and thus economic return because it takes into account the capital expenditures necessary to maintain the economic income of a property portfolio. AFFO is also more reflective of a REIT's dividend-paying ability than FFO. It is open, however, to more variation and error in estimation than FFO. The precise annual provision required to maintain and lease the space in a property is difficult to predict, and the actual expense in any single year may be significantly more or less than the norm because of the timing of capital expenditure programs and the uneven expiration schedule of leases. Consequently, estimates of FFO are more frequently referenced measures, although analysts and investors will tend to base their investment judgments to a significant degree on their AFFO estimates. Although many REITs and REOCs compute and refer to AFFO in their disclosures, their methods of computation and their assumptions vary. Firms that compile statistics and estimates of publicly traded enterprises for publications, such as Bloomberg and Refinitiv, tend not to gather AFFO estimates because of the absence of a universally accepted methodology for computing AFFO and inconsistent corporate reporting of actual AFFO figures, which hinders corroboration of analysts' estimates. An example of FFO data compiled for US equity REITs by property classification is shown in Exhibit 11.

Funds from Operations

All listed U.S. equity REITs

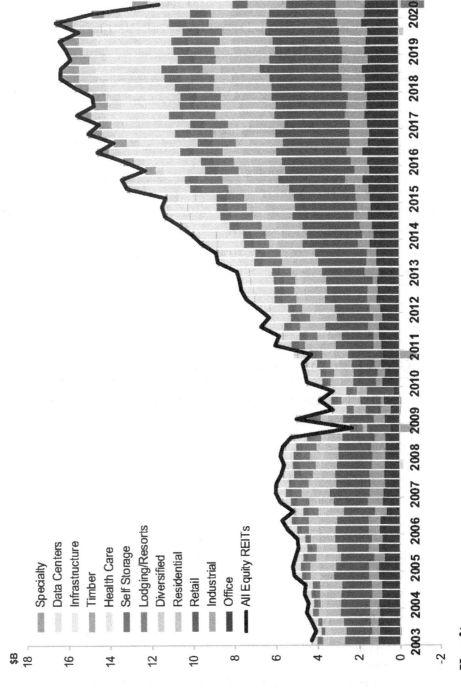

Legend:
- Specialty
- Data Centers
- Infrastructure
- Timber
- Health Care
- Self Storage
- Lodging/Resorts
- Diversified
- Residential
- Retail
- Industrial
- Office
- All Equity REITs

$B axis: 18, 16, 14, 12, 10, 8, 6, 4, 2, 0, -2

Years: 2003 2004 2005 2006 2007 2008 2009 2010 2011 2012 2013 2014 2015 2016 2017 2018 2019 2020

Nareit.   Source: S&P Global Market Intelligence, Nareit T-Tracker®

5

Exhibit 12 illustrates the most straightforward, convenient way of calculating FFO and AFFO for a hypothetical firm, Office Equity REIT Inc.

EXHIBIT 12   Calculation of FFO and AFFO for Office Equity REIT Inc.
(SGD thousands, except per-share data)

A. Calculation of funds from operations	
Net income	160,638
Add: Depreciation and amortization	76,100
Add: (Gains)/losses from sale of depreciable real estate	25,000
Funds from operations	261,738
FFO per share (55,689 shares outstanding)	4.70
B. Calculation of adjusted funds from operations	
Funds from operations	261,738
Less: Non-cash (straight-line) rent adjustment	21,103
Less: Recurring maintenance-type capital expenditures and leasing commissions	55,765
Adjusted funds from operations	184,870
AFFO per share (55,689 shares outstanding)	3.32

EXAMPLE 30   Analyst Adjustments (I)

1. Which of the following is the *best* measure of a REIT's current economic return to shareholders?
   A. FFO
   B. AFFO
   C. Net income

2. An analyst gathers the following information for a REIT:

Net operating income	$ 115 million
USD	$1,005 million
Market value of debt outstanding	$ 505 million
Market cap rate	7%
Shares outstanding	100 million
Book value per share	$ 5.00

   The REIT's NAV per share is *closest* to:
   A. $10.05.
   B. $11.38.
   C. $16.42.

3. All else equal, estimated NAV per share will decrease with an increase in the:
   A. capitalization rate.
   B. estimated growth rate.
   C. deferred tax liabilities.

Solution to 1: B is correct. AFFO is calculated from FFO by deducting non-cash rent, capital expenditures for maintenance, and leasing costs.

A is incorrect because it does not account for non-cash rent, capital expenditures for maintenance, and leasing costs. C is incorrect because it includes non-cash depreciation and amortization expense and does not account for non-cash rent, capital expenditures, and capitalized leasing costs, which are appropriate adjustments to net income in calculating current economic return.

Solution to 2: B is correct. NAVPS estimates real estate values by capitalizing NOI. Valuing $115 million of NOI with a capitalization rate of 7% yields a value for the properties of $1,642,857,000. After deducting $505 million of debt at market value, NAV is $1,137,857,000; NAVPS equals NAV divided by 100 million shares outstanding, or $11.38.

A is incorrect because it is the book value of the assets (not the net assets) per share: $1,005 million divided by 100 million shares = $10.05 per share. It does not take into account the market value of the assets and does not deduct debt. C is incorrect because it is the market value of the real estate—that is, NOI capitalized at 7%, divided by 100 million shares: $1,642,857,000/100,000,000 = $16.42. This calculation excludes the liabilities of the entity.

Solution to 3: A is correct. The capitalization rate is used to calculate the estimated value of operating real estate because it is the NOI as a percentage of the value of operating real estate: NOI/Capitalization rate = Estimated value. As the capitalization rate increases, the estimated value of operating real estate and thus NAV will decrease.

B is incorrect because an increase in the estimated growth rate would increase the estimated NOI and the estimated value of operating income. C is incorrect because deferred liabilities are not counted as "hard" liabilities and are not subtracted from the NAV.

EXAMPLE 31   Analyst Adjustments (II)

1. An increase in the capitalization rate will *most likely* decrease a REIT's:
   A. cost of debt.
   B. estimated NOI.
   C. estimated NAV.
2. An analyst gathers the following information for a REIT:

Non-cash (straight-line) rent	€ 207,430
Depreciation	€ 611,900
Recurring maintenance-type capital expenditures and leasing commissions	€ 550,750
Adjusted funds from operations	€3,320,000
AFFO per share	€ 3.32

The REIT's FFO per share is *closest* to:
A. €3.93.
B. €4.08.
C. €4.48.

3. Which of the following estimates is *least likely* to be compiled by firms that publish REIT analysts' estimates?
A. FFO
B. AFFO
C. NAV

Solution to 1: C is correct. The capitalization rate is used to estimate the market value of real estate, which is then used to calculate NAV.

A is incorrect because a higher capitalization rate does not decrease the REIT's cost of debt. B is incorrect because the estimated NOI is based on income growth, not the capitalization rate.

Solution to 2: B is correct. FFO = AFFO + Non-cash (straight-line) rent + Recurring maintenance-type capital expenditures and leasing commissions = 3,320,000 + 550,750 + 207,430 = €4,078,180. The number of shares outstanding = 3,320,000/3.32 = 1,000,000. FFO per share = 4,078,180/1,000,000 ≈ €4.08.

A is incorrect because it adds depreciation to AFFO (3,320,000 + 611,900 = €3,931,900; 3,931,900/1,000,000 ≈ €3.93 per share). C is incorrect because it also adds depreciation to AFFO + Non-cash (straight-line) rent + Recurring maintenance-type capital expenditures and leasing commissions.

Solution to 3: B is correct. Firms that compile statistics and estimates of REITs tend not to gather AFFO estimates because of the absence of a universally accepted methodology for computing AFFO and inconsistent corporate reporting of actual AFFO figures. FFO is commonly tracked in the United States, and NAV is the standard measure in Europe and Asia.

11.3. P/FFO and P/AFFO Multiples: Advantages and Drawbacks

The key benefits of using P/FFO and P/AFFO multiples in the valuation of REITs and REOCs are as follows:

1. Multiples of earnings measures of this kind are widely accepted in evaluating shares across global stock markets and industries.
2. In light of this acceptance, portfolio managers can put the valuation of REITs and REOCs into context with other investment alternatives.
3. FFO estimates are readily available through market data providers, such as Bloomberg and Refinitiv, which facilitates calculating P/FFO multiples.
4. Multiples can be used in conjunction with such items as expected growth and leverage levels to deepen the relative analysis among REITs and REOCs. Because FFO and AFFO do not take into account differences in leverage, leverage ratios can be used to adjust for leverage differences among REITs when using these multiples to compare valuations.

There are also drawbacks. Multiples are not a perfect basis for valuation because of the following:

1. Applying a multiple to FFO or AFFO may not capture the intrinsic value of all real estate assets held by the REIT or REOC, such as non-income-producing assets (for example, land held for development, vacant buildings, and properties under development), underused assets (current use may not represent highest and best use), or assets with below-market rents.
2. P/FFO does not adjust for the impact of recurring capital expenditures needed to keep properties operating smoothly. Although P/AFFO should do so, wide variations in estimates and assumptions are incorporated into the calculation of AFFO.
3. An increased level of such one-time items as gains and accounting charges, as well as new revenue recognition rules, has affected the income statement, thus making P/FFO and P/AFFO more difficult to compute and complicating comparisons between companies.

12. REIT MINI CASE STUDY: EXAMPLE OF DISCLOSURES AND VALUATION ANALYSIS

In this section, we undertake the valuation of a REIT by using the previously outlined approaches for valuation. The REIT in our example is Capitol Shopping Center REIT Inc. (CRE), a fictitious company that owns and operates retail shopping centers primarily in the Washington, DC, metropolitan area. Exhibit 13 shows CRE's income statements, balance sheets, and cash flow statements for 2019 and 2020.

EXHIBIT 13   Capitol Shopping Center REIT Inc. Financial Statements (USD thousands, except per-share data)

A. Income statements

	Three Months Ending 31 December		Year Ending 31 December	
	2020	2019	2020	2019
Rental revenue	133,700	130,300	517,546	501,600
Other property income	3,600	2,100	14,850	13,450
Total property revenue	137,300	132,400	532,396	515,050
Rental expenses	29,813	28,725	112,571	109,775
Property taxes	15,050	14,850	57,418	55,375
Total property expenses	44,863	43,575	169,989	165,150
Property net operating income	92,437	88,825	362,407	349,900
Other income	450	385	1,840	1,675
General and administrative expenses	6,150	7,280	23,860	26,415
EBITDA	86,737	81,930	340,387	325,160
Depreciation and amortization	28,460	27,316	115,110	111,020
Net interest expense	25,867	25,015	100,823	99,173
Net income available to common	32,410	29,599	124,454	114,967

Weighted average common shares	61,100	60,100	60,600	60,100
Earnings per share	0.53	0.49	2.05	1.91

B. Balance sheets

	Year Ending 31 December	
	2020	2019
Assets		
Real estate, at cost		
Operating real estate	3,627,576	3,496,370
Land held for future development	133,785	133,785
	3,761,361	3,630,155
Less accumulated depreciation	(938,097)	(822,987)
Net real estate	2,823,264	2,807,168
Cash and equivalents	85,736	23,856
Accounts receivable, net	72,191	73,699
Deferred rent receivable, net	38,165	33,053
Prepaid expenses and other assets	106,913	101,604
Total assets	3,126,269	3,039,380
Liabilities and shareholders' equity		
Liabilities		
Mortgages payable	701,884	647,253
Notes payable	1,090,745	1,090,745
Accounts payable and other liabilities	219,498	200,439
Total liabilities	2,012,127	1,938,437
Common shares and equity	1,114,142	1,100,943
Total liabilities and shareholders' equity	3,126,269	3,039,380

C. Cash flow statements

	Year Ending 31 December	
	2020	2019
Operating activities		
Net income	124,454	114,967
Depreciation and amortization	115,110	111,020
Change in accounts receivable	1,508	452
Change in deferred rents	(5,112)	(4,981)
Change in prepaid expenses and other assets	(5,309)	1,237
Change in accounts payable and other liabilities	19,059	(11,584)
Net cash provided by operating activities	249,710	211,111

Investing activities		
Acquisition of real estate	(111,200)	(22,846)
Capital expenditures on operating real estate	(20,006)	(18,965)
Net cash used in investing activities	(131,206)	(41,811)
Financing activities		
Issuance of mortgages	54,631	14,213
Issuance of common shares	58,425	0
Dividends paid to common shareholders	(169,680)	(165,275)
Net cash used in financing activities	(56,624)	(151,062)
Increase (decrease) in cash and equivalents	61,880	18,238
Cash and cash equivalents, beginning of year	23,856	5,618
Cash and cash equivalents, end of year	85,736	23,856

CRE also publishes a supplemental investor packet that provides further disclosures used by the investment community to analyze the company. Exhibit 14 shows its adjustments to arrive at FFO and AFFO, as well as its calculation of dividend payouts based on dividends paid.

EXHIBIT 14   Capitol Shopping Center REIT Inc. FFO, AFFO, and Dividend Payouts (USD thousands, except per-share data)

	Three Months Ending 31 December		Year Ending 31 December	
	2020	2019	2020	2019
Funds from operations				
Net income	32,410	29,599	124,454	114,967
Depreciation and amortization	28,460	27,316	115,110	111,020
Funds from operations	60,870	56,915	239,564	225,987
FFO/share	1.00	0.95	3.95	3.76
Adjusted funds from operations				
Funds from operations	60,870	56,915	239,564	225,987
Less non-cash rents (1)	(1,469)	(1,325)	(5,112)	(4,981)
Less recurring capital expenditures (2)	(5,638)	(5,101)	(20,006)	(18,965)
Adjusted funds from operations	53,763	50,489	214,446	202,041
AFFO/share	0.88	0.84	3.54	3.36
Dividends/share	0.70	0.69	2.80	2.75

Dividend payout ratios				
On FFO	70.0%	72.6%	70.9%	73.1%
On AFFO	79.6%	82.1%	79.1%	81.8%
Weighted average common shares	61,100	60,100	60,600	60,100

1. Non-cash rents include the impact of straight lining contractual rent increases in leases, per accounting rules. The change in deferred rents can often provide the impact of this accounting on rental revenues.

2. Recurring capital expenditures include those costs needed to maintain the revenue-producing ability of existing assets, such as leasing commissions to keep or attract new tenants, such maintenance items as roofs and parking lot repairs, and basic buildouts of space as an inducement to attract tenants.

The historical stock price and the company's financial statements, including disclosures, are used to complete a simple analysis of the balance sheet, as shown in Exhibit 15.

EXHIBIT 15   Capitol Shopping Center REIT Inc. Balance Sheet Analysis (USD thousands, except per-share data)

	Year Ending 31 December	
	2020	2019
Ending debt	1,792,629	1,737,998
Ending stock price	72.36	61.50
Ending shares	61,100	60,100
Ending market capitalization	4,421,196	3,696,150
Debt/total market capitalization	*40.5%*	*47.0%*
Peer group debt/total market capitalization	47.1%	56.7%
All REITs debt/total market capitalization	42.8%	49.6%
EBITDA	340,387	325,160
Interest expense	100,823	99,173
Interest coverage	*3.38x*	*3.28x*
Peer group interest coverage	2.35×	2.16×
All REITs interest coverage	2.58×	2.27×
Ending net debt	1,706,893	1,714,142
EBITDA	340,387	325,160
Net debt-to-EBITDA	*5.01×*	*5.27×*
Peer group net debt-to-EBITDA	7.10×	8.60×
All REITs net debt-to-EBITDA	6.70×	7.80×
Ending net debt	1,706,893	1,714,142
Ending gross real estate	3,761,361	3,630,155
Net debt/gross real estate (book)	*45.4%*	*47.2%*
Peer group net debt/gross real estate (book)	52.8%	55.1%
All REITs net debt/gross real estate (book)	49.6%	52.6%

The exhibits provide a historical picture of CRE's financial performance and balance sheet. Some key points about the company's properties, operations, dividend policy, recent business activity, and historical trading attributes follow.

- CRE owns properties that are generally considered defensive in the commercial real estate sector because many of its properties are tenanted by basic necessity goods retailers such as grocery stores and drug stores.
- CRE's location in the Washington, DC, metropolitan area is generally viewed as favorable for two key reasons: (1) Washington, DC, is the capital of the United States, and the government is the largest driver of employment and has historically provided more stability compared with the private sector; and (2) the city is a fairly dense area with strict zoning restrictions that make new construction of shopping centers difficult, which limits competing new supply.
- CRE has been able to increase its rents and net operating income by 2%–3% each year, on average, in the past decade.
- The past two reported years (2019 and 2020) were difficult for the broader commercial real estate markets. CRE was able to achieve positive growth while many of its peers saw FFO and AFFO decline. Because forecasts now call for improving fundamental property-level conditions, CRE's portfolio may not have as much upside because it did not experience the decline in occupancy and rents that other REITs did.
- In the middle of 2020, the company purchased a portfolio of three shopping centers from a local developer for a total price of $111.2 million. The return on these assets in the first year is an estimated 6.75%. The company was able to achieve a better going-in cap rate on this acquisition than the market averages of 6.0%–6.25% because of its strong relationships and reputation with tenants, commercial property brokers, and competitors, as well as its ability to act quickly because of its strong balance sheet. In addition, the property is not fully leased, leaving the potential to increase net operating income if CRE can attract additional tenants. CRE funded the purchase with a $54.6 million mortgage at a 6% interest rate and cash from a common stock offering of 1 million shares and from cash on hand.
- The company intends to make additional acquisitions in the future as part of its growth plan. It intends to use a combination of debt, common equity, and internally generated cash to make these purchases. It typically requires the properties it acquires to generate an unleveraged internal rate of return of 9.5% in the form of current yield and capital appreciation over time.
- CRE's balance sheet strategy is to operate at less than 50% debt/market capitalization, with a preference for leverage to be closer to 40%. At year-end 2018, CRE's debt/market capitalization was 40.5% and its interest coverage was 3.38×. The company's current in-place average debt cost is 5.7%. In comparison, CRE's peers operate at an average leverage level of 47.1% and have an interest coverage ratio of 2.35×.
- CRE's board has chosen a dividend policy that provides an approximate 80% payout of cash flow, or AFFO. This level allows the company to pay an attractive dividend to shareholders, retain some cash flow, provide a cushion in the event of a downturn, and remain in compliance with REIT payout requirements in the United States. It is easily able to meet these REIT payout requirements because the requirements are based on taxable net income, which is calculated after deducting depreciation. In fact, CRE's dividend level has run well in excess of taxable net income, according to comments made by its management.
- Over the last decade, CRE has traded between 9× and 19× FFO, while its peers have traded between 8× and 18×, and all REITs have traded between 7× and 20×. On an AFFO basis,

CRE's historical multiple has been 10×–21×, with its peers trading between 9×–19× and all REITs being in the 9×–24× range.
- Currently, shopping center REITs are estimated to be trading at 7.6% above analyst estimates of NAV. The overall REIT sector is estimated to be trading at a 14.8% premium to estimated NAV.
- CRE's historical beta to the broader equity market is 0.80. The current risk-free rate of return is 4.0%, and the market risk premium is estimated at 5.0%.

Investors and analysts who cover CRE have published estimates for its FFO per share, AFFO per share, and dividends per share for the next three years. Putting the average, or "consensus," of these estimates together with the company's reported results reveals the FFO/AFFO and dividend snapshot shown in Exhibit 16.

EXHIBIT 16   Capitol Shopping Center REIT Inc. Historical and Forecast Earnings and Dividends (all amounts are per share)

	Year Ending 31 December				
	2019A	2020A	2021E	2022E	2023E
CRE's FFO/share	$3.76	$3.95	$4.23	$4.59	$4.80
Growth	—	5.1%	7.1%	8.5%	4.6%
Peer group FFO/share growth	—	3.4%	6.8%	8.2%	4.2%
All REITs FFO/share growth	—	1.2%	7.9%	9.8%	10.2%
CRE's AFFO/share	$3.36	$3.54	$3.76	$4.09	$4.31
Growth	—	5.4%	6.2%	8.8%	5.4%
Peer group AFFO/share growth	—	–1.0%	6.2%	9.1%	4.8%
All REITs AFFO/share growth	—	–3.0%	8.1%	9.7%	10.8%
CRE's dividends/share	$2.75	$2.80	$2.98	$3.25	$3.40
Growth	—	1.8%	6.4%	9.1%	4.6%
Peer group dividends/share growth	—	–2.0%	5.6%	7.9%	5.1%
All REITs dividends/share growth	—	–5.0%	7.8%	8.9%	6.0%
CRE's dividend payout on AFFO	81.8%	79.1%	79.3%	79.5%	78.9%

Taking the recent stock price of $69.85 per share and focusing on the next two years (as most analysts looking at multiples do), we can determine comparative FFO and AFFO multiples for CRE. Exhibit 17 also includes the multiples of its direct peers and the entire REIT industry.

EXHIBIT 17   Comparative Multiple Analysis

	P/FFO		P/AFFO	
	2021E	2022E	2021E	2022E
Capitol Shopping Center REIT Inc. (CRE)[a]	16.5×	15.2×	18.6×	17.1×
Shopping center–oriented REITs	14.5×	13.3×	16.1×	14.5×
All REITs	14.2×	12.8×	16.5×	14.6×

CRE's premium/(discount) to:				
Shopping center REITs	13.8%	14.3%	15.5%	17.9%
All REITs	16.2%	18.8%	12.7%	17.1%

ᵃBased on a current stock price of $69.85.

12.1. Selection of Valuation Methods

As this discussion demonstrates, different valuation methods can yield different results. Under such circumstances, an analyst should re-examine the assumptions made to investigate why the approaches are generating such different results. The methods selected by an analyst may depend on which ones the analyst believes use the most reliable assumptions, which ones the analyst believes will be used by other investors, or which ones best reflect the analyst's own investment philosophy or view of value. The analyst may choose to use a single valuation approach, a midpoint in the range of values obtained by using several approaches, or a weighted average of the values obtained based on the analyst's view of the relative reliability of the models used to arrive at the values.

EXAMPLE 32   Valuation (I)

1. If the outlook for economic growth turns negative and property market transaction volumes decline, it is *least likely* that CRE's:
   A. P/FFO and P/AFFO would be lower.
   B. relative P/FFO and P/AFFO multiples would be higher than those of peers.
   C. NAV becomes the most useful valuation method.
2. If other REITs have no land on their balance sheets, how is CRE's "Land held for future development" *best* factored into a relative P/FFO or P/AFFO multiple valuation?
   A. There should be no impact on multiples as a result of land value.
   B. CRE would warrant lower multiples to account for land value.
   C. CRE would warrant higher multiples to account for land value.
3. An analyst speaks with private market real estate investors and learns that because interest rates have just increased 200 bps, buyers will require future property acquisitions to have going-in cap rates that are 100 bps to 200 bps higher than those on recent property market transactions. The analyst's estimate of NAV for CRE *most likely*:
   A. increases as cap rates are higher.
   B. decreases as cap rates are higher.
   C. remains the same unless CRE has debt maturing in the near term.
4. An analyst determines that CRE purchased its "Land held for future development" 15 years ago and that on average, land values at that time were one-third of what they are today. Which of the following *best* adjusts NAV to reflect this consideration?
   A. The cap rate on operating assets should be changed.
   B. Land value and thus NAV should be adjusted higher to reflect today's valuations.
   C. NAV is still mainly a representation of book values; thus, there should be no adjustments.

5. Zoning in CRE's real estate markets is changed to allow more new space in the future, dampening CRE's long-term FFO growth by about 0.5%. The effect on CRE's valuation using a dividend discount model is *most likely* that the present value of the dividend stream:
   A. decreases because of lower growth.
   B. remains the same.
   C. increases because of the new supply.

Solution to 1: C is correct. NAV becomes more subjective in a negative and less liquid market with fewer observable transactions, and thus this basis of valuation becomes less useful and reliable.

A and B are incorrect because P/FFO and P/AFFO are likely to fall in a negative economic environment, but investors may be willing to pay a relative premium for CRE's stock based on its superior stability in economically challenging times. Thus, P/FFO and P/AFFO are likely to be higher than those of peers.

Solution to 2: C is correct. Although it may not produce income that contributes to FFO or AFFO, the land has value and represents a source of greater internal growth potential. For that reason, A and B are incorrect.

Solution to 3: B is correct. Estimated real estate value decreases as the cap rate increases. Because NAV is derived directly from estimated real estate value, it also decreases. For this reason, A is incorrect. C is incorrect because an increase in cap rates decreases asset values. The fact that CRE has debt maturing in the near term is not a key factor influencing NAV.

Solution to 4: B is correct. An analyst tries to attribute market values to real property owned.

A is incorrect because the cap rate used by analysts in calculating NAVs represents the return on only the income-producing asset portfolio and does not relate to land holdings that are not currently producing any income. C is incorrect because NAV is not a representation of book values, which rely on accounting methodology rather than market values.

Solution to 5: A is correct. Lower growth affects the projected dividend stream, decreasing its present value. For that reason, B and C are incorrect.

EXAMPLE 33   Valuation (II)

1. An analyst gathers the following information for two REITs:

	Price/NAV	Capitalization Rate Used in NAV
REIT A	100%	6%
REIT B	99%	8%

If the REITs have similar property portfolio values, interest expense, and corporate overhead, which REIT *most likely* has the higher price/FFO?

A. REIT A

B. REIT B

C. They will have similar P/FFO because their ratios of price to NAV are almost identical.

Solution to 1: A is correct. If both companies have similar portfolio values as indicated in the text and by the similar P/NAV, then the company with the lower capitalization rate is more expensive, which results in lower FFO and hence a higher P/FFO. If each company were worth ¥100, then REIT A, which is valued at a 6% cap rate, would have ¥6 of NOI and REIT B would have ¥8 of NOI. Because interest expense and overhead are similar for both companies, REIT A would also have lower FFO and a correspondingly higher P/FFO multiple.

B is incorrect because A has a lower capitalization rate, implying a lower FFO and hence a higher P/FFO if P/NAV for each company is similar, which is the case here.

C is incorrect because it neglects the effect of the lower capitalization rate of REIT A.

13. PRIVATE VERSUS PUBLIC: A COMPARISON

Large institutional and high-net-worth investors have historically pursued private real estate investments through direct ownership, joint ventures, and private fund investments, whereas individual investors, without the resources to invest directly, typically invested in listed property companies. As more real estate companies went public and continued to issue equity to fund acquisitions, developments, and mergers, the market cap of the publicly listed real estate sector rose significantly. This larger market float and liquidity permitted institutional investors to add to their real estate exposure by creating allocations to public real estate companies

Should investors with the ability to pursue both public *and* private real estate investments choose one over the other? The answer depends on investor objectives, including total return requirements, volatility (risk) tolerance, diversification goals, and the expected returns from each investment. Many institutional investors such as pension funds and endowments have chosen to allocate to both.

Both public and private real estate equity investments provide exposure to real estate properties, potentially hedge inflation, deliver attractive risk-adjusted returns, and provide some diversification benefits to stock and bond portfolios.

Listed real estate can play a complementary role in private real estate. Listed real estate's liquidity makes it easier to express a short-term view, such as when markets become too negative on retail and drive shares of public companies below net asset value. When there are sustained valuation differences between public and private real estate, fund and company managers can capture opportunities. If public companies trade well below net asset value, the public companies may choose to go private or sell to private real estate funds. When real estate values are high, public companies can sell real estate to realize gains and private funds may seek exits through the IPO market.

Private real estate investors have the ability to pursue a variety of strategies, such as merchant (for sale) development, which is highly restricted for REITs. In some countries, REITs were early movers in specialty sectors, such as self-storage and data centers. Investors wanting exposure to some of these niches had to seek out listed company exposure until the private funds moved into these sectors, often in the search for higher yield.

Private and public real estate investments both have something to offer investors, and each has its drawbacks. Exhibit 18 summarizes some of the key differences, advantages, and disadvantages of public and private real estate investing.

EXHIBIT 18   Advantages and Disadvantages of Private and Public Real Estate

Private Real Estate (Direct Investment)	Public Real Estate (Equity REITs and Real Estate Operating Companies)
Advantages	
• Direct exposure to real estate fundamentals • Stable returns/low volatility • Income and capital appreciation • Property performance drives returns • Low correlations with other asset classes • Potential inflation hedge • Control (direct real estate and separate accounts) • Potential to earn illiquidity premium • Wide variety of strategies/few restrictions • Tax benefits (e.g., accelerated depreciation, deferred taxes in some markets when sales are reinvested in other real estate)	• Tracks real estate fundamentals over the long term • Liquidity • Access to professional management • Potential inflation hedge • Potential for strong alignment of interests • Tax-efficient structure avoids double taxation (REITs only) • Potential for exposure to diversified portfolios • Access to diverse sectors, including data centers, medical offices, and self-storage • Low investment requirements • Low entry/exit costs • No special investor qualifications beyond equity investing generally • Limited liability • Greater regulation and investor protections • High transparency
• *Disadvantages*	
• Low liquidity • Difficult-to-exit funds' redemption activity is high • High fees and expenses • Appraisal valuations commonly lag changes in market conditions • Fewer regulations to protect investors • Some managers focus on asset gathering over high profitability • High investment minimums and high net-worth requirements • Low transparency • High returns often derived from leverage	• High volatility (compared with private real estate) • Equity market correlation is high in short term • REIT structure limits possible activities • Stock prices may not reflect underlying property values (i.e., trade at discount to NAV) • Dividends taxed at high current income tax rates • Regulatory compliance costs are prohibitive for small companies • Poor governance/mis-aligned interests can penalize stock performance • Equity markets often penalize companies with high leverage

SUMMARY

Real estate property is an asset class that plays a significant role in many investment portfolios and is an attractive source of current income. Investor allocations to public and private real estate have increased significantly over the last 20 years. Because of the unique characteristics of real estate property, real estate investments tend to behave differently from other asset classes—such as stocks, bonds, and commodities—and thus have different risks and diversification benefits. Private real estate investments are further differentiated because the investments are not publicly traded and require analytic techniques different from those of publicly traded assets. Because of the lack of transactions, the appraisal process is required to value real estate property. Many of the indexes and benchmarks used for private real estate also rely on appraisals, and because of this characteristic, they behave differently from indexes for publicly traded equities, such as the S&P 500, MSCI Europe, FTSE Asia Pacific, and many other regional and global indexes.

General Characteristics of Real Estate

- Real estate investments make up a significant portion of the portfolios of many investors.
- Real estate investments can occur in four basic forms: private equity (direct ownership), publicly traded equity (indirect ownership claim), private debt (direct mortgage lending), and publicly traded debt (securitized mortgages).
- Each of the basic forms of real estate investment has its own risks, expected returns, regulations, legal structures, and market structures.
- Equity investors generally expect a higher rate of return than lenders (debt investors) because they take on more risk. The returns to equity real estate investors have two components: an income stream and capital appreciation.
- Many motivations exist for investing in real estate income property. The key ones are current income, price appreciation, inflation hedge, diversification, and tax benefits.
- Adding equity real estate investments to a traditional portfolio will potentially have diversification benefits because of the less-than-perfect correlation of equity real estate returns with returns to stocks and bonds.
- If the income stream can be adjusted for inflation and real estate prices increase with inflation, then equity real estate investments may provide an inflation hedge.
- Debt investors in real estate expect to receive their return from promised cash flows and typically do not participate in any appreciation in value of the underlying real estate. Thus, debt investments in real estate are similar to other fixed-income investments, such as bonds.
- Regardless of the form of real estate investment, the value of the underlying real estate property can affect the performance of the investment. Location is a critical factor in determining the value of a real estate property.
- Real estate property has some unique characteristics compared with other investment asset classes. These characteristics include heterogeneity and fixed location, high unit value, management intensiveness, high transaction costs, depreciation, sensitivity to the credit market, illiquidity, and difficulty of value and price determination.
- There are many different types of real estate properties in which to invest. The main commercial (income-producing) real estate property types are office, industrial and warehouse, retail, and multi-family. Other types of commercial properties are typically classified by their specific use.
- Certain risk factors are common to commercial property, but each property type is likely to have a different susceptibility to these factors. The key risk factors that can affect commercial real estate include business conditions, lead time for new development, excess supply, cost and availability of capital, unexpected inflation, demographics, lack of liquidity, environmental issues, availability of information, management expertise, and leverage.

- Location, lease structures, and economic factors—such as economic growth, population growth, employment growth, and consumer spending—affect the value of each property type.
- An understanding of the lease structure is important when analyzing a real estate investment.
- Appraisals estimate the value of real estate income property. Definitions of value include market value, investment value, value in use, and mortgage lending value.
- Due diligence investigates factors that might affect the value of a property prior to making or closing on an investment. These factors include leases and lease history, operating expenses, environmental issues, structural integrity, lien/proof of ownership, property tax history, and compliance with relevant laws and regulations.
- Appraisal-based and transaction-based indexes are used to track the performance of private real estate. Appraisal-based indexes tend to lag transaction-based indexes and appear to have lower volatility and lower correlation with other asset classes than transaction-based indexes.

Private Equity Real Estate

- Generally, three different approaches are used by appraisers to estimate value: income, cost, and sales comparison.
- The income approach includes direct capitalization and discounted cash flow methods. Both methods focus on net operating income as an input to the value of a property and indirectly or directly factor in expected growth.
- The cost approach estimates the value of a property based on adjusted replacement cost. This approach is typically used for unusual properties for which market comparables are difficult to obtain.
- The sales comparison approach estimates the value of a property based on what price comparable properties are selling for in the current market.
- When debt financing is used to purchase a property, additional ratios and returns calculated and interpreted by debt and equity investors include the loan-to-value ratio, the debt service coverage ratio, and leveraged and unleveraged internal rates of return.

Publicly Traded Real Estate Securities

- The principal types of publicly traded real estate securities available globally are real estate investment trusts, real estate operating companies, and residential and commercial mortgage-backed securities.
- Publicly traded equity real estate securities offer investors participation in the returns from investment real estate with the advantages of superior liquidity; greater potential for diversification by property, geography, and property type; access to a larger range of properties; the benefit of management services; limited liability; protection accorded by corporate governance, disclosure, and other securities regulations; and in the case of REITs, exemption from corporate income taxation within the REIT if prescribed requirements are met.
- Disadvantages include the costs of maintaining a publicly traded corporate structure and complying with regulatory filings, pricing determined by the stock market and returns that can be volatile, the potential for structural conflicts of interest, and tax differences compared with direct ownership of property that can be disadvantageous under some circumstances.

- Compared with other publicly traded shares, REITs offer higher-than-average yields and greater stability of income and returns. They are amenable to a net asset value approach to valuation because of the existence of active private markets for their real estate assets. Compared with REOCs, REITs offer higher yields and income tax exemptions but have less operating flexibility to invest in a broad range of real estate activities and less potential for growth from reinvesting their operating cash flows because of their high income-to-payout ratios.
- In assessing the investment merits of REITs, investors analyze the effects of trends in general economic activity, retail sales, job creation, population growth, and new supply and demand for specific types of space. They also pay particular attention to occupancies, leasing activity, rental rates, remaining lease terms, in-place rents compared with market rents, costs to maintain space and re-lease space, tenants' financial health and tenant concentration in the portfolio, financial leverage, debt maturities and costs, and the quality of management and governance.
- Analysts make adjustments to the historical cost-based financial statements of REITs and REOCs to obtain better measures of current income and net worth. The three principal figures they calculate and use are (1) funds from operations or accounting net earnings, excluding depreciation, deferred tax charges, and gains or losses on sales of property and debt restructuring; (2) adjusted funds from operations, or funds from operations adjusted to remove straight-line rent and to provide for maintenance-type capital expenditures and leasing costs, including leasing agents' commissions and tenants' improvement allowances; and (3) net asset value or the difference between a real estate company's asset and liability ranking prior to shareholders' equity, all valued at market values instead of accounting book values.
- REITs and some REOCs generally return a significant portion of their income to their investors and, as a result, tend to pay high dividends. Thus, dividend discount or discounted cash flow models for valuation are also applicable. These valuation approaches are applied in the same manner as they are for shares in other industries. Usually, investors use two- or three-step dividend discount models with near-term, intermediate-term, and/or long-term growth assumptions. In discounted cash flow models, investors often use intermediate-term cash flow projections and a terminal value based on historical cash flow multiples.

REFERENCES

Huerta, Daniel, Thanh Ngo, and Mark Pyles. 2019. "The Role of Institutional Ownership in REIT Acquisitions." Working paper (August): 3. www.fmaconferences.org/NewOrleans/Papers/TheRoleofInstitutionalOwnershipinREITAcquisitions.pdf.

Nareit. 2018. "Nareit Funds from Operations White Paper—2018 Restatement." White paper (December). www.reit.com/sites/default/files/2018-FFO-white-paper-(11-27-18).pdf.

PROBLEMS

The following information relates to Questions 1–12.

Amanda Rodriguez is an alternative investment analyst for a US investment management firm, Delphinus Brothers. Delphinus's chief investment officer, Michael Tang, has informed Rodriguez that he wants to reduce the amount invested in traditional asset classes and gain exposure to the real estate sector by acquiring commercial property in the United States. Rodriguez is asked to analyze potential commercial real estate investments for Delphinus Brothers. Selected data on three commercial real estate properties are presented in Exhibit 1.

EXHIBIT 1   Selected Property Data

	Property 1	Property 2	Property 3
Property Type	Downtown Office Building	Grocery-Anchored Retail Center	Multi-Family Building
Location	New York City	Miami	Boston
Occupancy	90.00%	93.00%	95.00%
Square Feet or Number of Units	100,000 sf	205,000 sf	300 units
Gross Potential Rent	$4,750,000	$1,800,000	$3,100,000
Expense Reimbursement Revenue	$333,333	$426,248	$0
Other Income (includes % rent)	$560,000	$15,000	$45,000
Potential Gross Income	$5,643,333	$2,241,248	$3,145,000
Vacancy Loss	($564,333)	($156,887)	($157,250)
Effective Gross Income	$5,079,000	$2,084,361	$2,987,750
Property Management Fees	($203,160)	($83,374)	($119,510)
Other Operating Expenses	($2,100,000)	($342,874)	($1,175,000)
Net Operating Income	$2,775,840	$1,658,113	$1,693,240

Rodriguez reviews the three properties with Tang, who indicates that he would like her to focus on Property 1 because of his prediction of robust job growth in New York City over the next 10 years. To complete her analysis, Rodriquez assembles additional data on Property 1, which is presented in Exhibits 2, 3, and 4.

As part of the review, Tang asks Rodriguez to evaluate financing alternatives to determine whether it would be better to use debt financing or to make an all-cash purchase. Tang directs Rodriguez to inquire about terms with Richmond Life Insurance Company, a publicly traded company that is an active lender on commercial real estate property. Rodriguez obtains the following information from Richmond Life for a loan on Property 1: loan term of five years, interest rate of 5.75% interest only, maximum loan to value of 75%, and minimum debt service coverage ratio of 1.5×. Data on Property 1 are provided in Exhibit 2, Exhibit 3, and Exhibit 4.

EXHIBIT 2   Six-Year Net Operating Income (NOI) and DCF Assumptions for Property 1

	Year 1	Year 2	Year 3	Year 4	Year 5	Year 6
NOI	$2,775,840	$2,859,119	$2,944,889	$3,033,235	$3,124,232	$3,217,959

DCF Assumptions

Investment Hold Period	5 years
Going-In Cap Rate	5.25%
Terminal Cap Rate	6.00%
Discount Rate	7.25%
Income/Value Growth Rate	Constant

EXHIBIT 3   Sales Comparison Data for Property 1

Variable	Property 1	Sales Comp A	Sales Comp B	Sales Comp C
Age (years)	10	5	12	25
Condition	Good	Excellent	Good	Average
Location	Prime	Secondary	Secondary	Prime
Sale Price psf		$415 psf	$395 psf	$400 psf
Adjustments				
Age (years)		−10%	2%	10%
Condition		−10%	0%	10%
Location		15%	15%	0%
Total Adjustments		**−5%**	**17%**	**20%**

EXHIBIT 4   Other Selected Data for Property 1

Land Value	$7,000,000
Replacement Cost	$59,000,000
Total Depreciation	$5,000,000

After reviewing her research materials, Rodriguez formulates the following two conclusions:

Conclusion 1: Benefits of private equity real estate investments include the owners' ability to attain diversification benefits, to earn current income, and to achieve tax benefits.

Conclusion 2: Risk factors of private equity real estate investments include business conditions, demographics, the cost of debt and equity capital, and financial leverage.

1. Which of the following is *most likely* accurate regarding Property 2, described in Exhibit 1?
   A. Operating expense risk is borne by the owner.
   B. The lease term for the largest tenant is longer than three years.
   C. A significant amount of percentage rent is linked to sales levels.
2. Based on Exhibits 2, 3, and 4, which of the following statements is *most* accurate regarding the valuation of Property 1?
   A. The cost approach valuation is $71 million.
   B. The adjusted price psf for Sales Comp B is $423 psf.
   C. The terminal value at the end of Year 5 in the income approach is $53,632,650.
3. Based on Exhibit 2, the growth rate of Property 1 is *closest* to:
   A. 0.75%.
   B. 1.25%.
   C. 2.00%.
4. Based on Exhibit 2, the value of Property 1 using the discounted cash flow method is *closest* to:
   A. $48,650,100.
   B. $49,750,900.
   C. $55,150,300.

5. Based on Exhibit 2, relative to the estimated value of Property 1 under the discounted cash flow method, the estimated value of Property 1 using the direct capitalization method is:
   A. the same.
   B. lower.
   C. higher.

6. Based on Exhibits 1 and 3, the estimated value of Property 1 using the sales comparison approach (assigning equal weight to each comparable) is *closest* to:
   A. 40,050,000.
   B. 40,300,000.
   C. 44,500,000.

7. In the event that Delphinus purchases Property 2, the due diligence process would *most likely* require a review of:
   A. all tenant leases.
   B. tenant sales data.
   C. the grocery anchor lease.

8. Compared with an all-cash purchase, a mortgage on Property 1 through Richmond Life would *most likely* result in Delphinus earning:
   A. a lower return on equity.
   B. a higher return on equity.
   C. the same return on equity.

9. Assuming an appraised value of $48 million, Richmond Life Insurance Company's maximum loan amount on Property 1 would be *closest* to:
   A. $32 million.
   B. $36 million.
   C. $45 million.

10. Rodriguez's Conclusion 1 is:
    A. correct.
    B. incorrect, because tax benefits do not apply to tax-exempt entities.
    C. incorrect, because private real estate is highly correlated with stocks.

11. Rodriguez's Conclusion 2 is:
    A. correct.
    B. incorrect, because inflation is not a risk factor.
    C. incorrect, because the cost of equity capital is not a risk factor.

12. Richmond Life Insurance Company's potential investment would *most likely* be described as:
    A. private real estate debt.
    B. private real estate equity.
    C. publicly traded real estate debt.

The following information relates to Questions 13–28.

First Life Insurance Company, Ltd., a life insurance company located in the United Kingdom, maintains a stock and bond portfolio and also invests in all four quadrants of the real estate market: private equity, public equity, private debt, and public debt. Each of the four real estate quadrants has a manager assigned to it. First Life intends to increase its allocation to real estate. The chief investment officer (CIO) has scheduled a meeting with the four real estate managers to discuss the allocation to real estate and to each real estate quadrant. Leslie Green, who manages the private equity quadrant, believes her quadrant offers the greatest potential and has identified three investment properties to consider for acquisition. Selected information for the three properties is presented in Exhibit 5.

EXHIBIT 5   Selected Information on Potential Private Equity Real Estate Investments

	Property		
	A	B	C
Property description	Single-Tenant Office	Shopping Center	Warehouse
Size (square meters)	3,000	5,000	9,000
Lease type	Net	Gross	Net
Expected loan-to-value ratio	70%	75%	80%
Total economic life	50 years	30 years	50 years
Remaining economic life	30 years	23 years	20 years
Rental income (at full occupancy)	£575,000	£610,000	£590,000
Other income	£27,000	£183,000	£29,500
Vacancy and collection loss	£0	£61,000	£59,000
Property management fee	£21,500	£35,000	£22,000
Other operating expenses	£0	£234,000	£0
Discount rate	11.5%	9.25%	11.25%
Growth rate	2.0%	See Assumption 2	3.0%
Terminal cap rate		11.00%	
Market value of land	£1,500,000	£1,750,000	£4,000,000
Replacement costs			
• Building costs	£8,725,000	£4,500,000	£12,500,000
• Developer's profit	£410,000	£210,000	£585,000
Deterioration—curable and incurable	£4,104,000	£1,329,000	£8,021,000
Obsolescence			
• Functional	£250,000	£50,000	£750,000
• Locational	£500,000	£200,000	£1,000,000
• Economic	£500,000	£100,000	£1,000,000
Comparable adjusted price per square meter			
• Comparable Property 1	£1,750	£950	£730
• Comparable Property 2	£1,825	£1,090	£680
• Comparable Property 3	£1,675	£875	£725

To prepare for the upcoming meeting, Green has asked her research analyst, Ian Cook, for a valuation of each of these properties under the income, cost, and sales comparison approaches using the information provided in Exhibit 5 and the following two assumptions:

Assumption 1: The holding period for each property is expected to be five years.

Assumption 2: Property B is expected to have the same net operating income for the holding period because of existing leases and a one-time 20% increase in Year 6 because of lease rollovers. No further growth is assumed thereafter.

In reviewing Exhibit 5, Green notes the disproportionate estimated obsolescence charges for Property C relative to the other properties and asks Cook to verify the reasonableness of these estimates. Green also reminds Cook that they will need to conduct proper due diligence. In that regard, Green indicates that she is concerned whether a covered parking lot that was added to Property A encroaches (is partially located) on adjoining properties. Green would like for Cook to identify an expert and present documentation to address her concerns regarding the parking lot.

In addition to discussing the new allocation, the CIO informs Green that she wants to discuss the appropriate real estate index for the private equity real estate quadrant at the upcoming meeting. The CIO believes that the current index may result in over-allocating resources to the private equity real estate quadrant.

13. The *most* effective justification that Green could present for directing the increased allocation to her quadrant would be that relative to the other quadrants, her quadrant of real estate investments:
   A. provides greater liquidity.
   B. requires less professional management.
   C. enables greater decision-making control.

14. Relative to the expected correlation between First Life's portfolio of public REIT holdings and its stock and bond portfolio, the expected correlation between First Life's private equity real estate portfolio and its stock and bond portfolio is *most likely* to be:
   A. lower.
   B. higher.
   C. the same.

15. Which of the properties in Exhibit 5 exposes the owner to the greatest risk related to operating expenses?
   A. Property A
   B. Property B
   C. Property C

16. Which property in Exhibit 5 is *most likely* to be affected by import and export activity?
   A. Property A
   B. Property B
   C. Property C

17. Which property in Exhibit 5 would *most likely* require the greatest amount of active management?
   A. Property A
   B. Property B
   C. Property C

18. Which property in Exhibit 5 is *most likely* to have a percentage lease?
    A. Property A
    B. Property B
    C. Property C

19. The disproportionate charges for Property C noted by Green are *least likely* to explicitly factor into the estimate of property value using the:
    A. cost approach.
    B. income approach.
    C. sales comparison approach.

20. Based on Exhibit 5, which of the following statements regarding Property A is *most* accurate?
    A. The going-in capitalization rate is 13.5%.
    B. It appears to be the riskiest of the three properties.
    C. The net operating income in the first year is £298,000.

21. Based on Exhibit 5, the value of Property C using the direct capitalization method is *closest* to:
    A. £3,778,900.
    B. £4,786,700.
    C. £6,527,300.

22. Based on Exhibit 5 and Assumptions 1 and 2, the value of Property B using the discounted cash flow method, assuming a five-year holding period, is *closest* to:
    A. £4,708,700.
    B. £5,034,600.
    C. £5,050,900.

23. Which method under the income approach is *least likely* to provide a realistic valuation for Property B?
    A. Layer method
    B. Direct capitalization method
    C. Discounted cash flow method

24. Based on Exhibit 5, the value of Property A using the cost approach is *closest* to:
    A. £5,281,000.
    B. £6,531,000.
    C. £9,385,000.

25. Based on Exhibit 5, the value of Property B using the sales comparison approach is *closest* to:
    A. £4,781,000.
    B. £4,858,000.
    C. £6,110,000.

26. Which due diligence item would be *most* useful in addressing Green's concerns regarding Property A?
    A. Property survey
    B. Engineering inspection
    C. Environmental inspection

27. The real estate index currently being used by First Life to evaluate private equity real estate investments is *most likely:*
    A. an appraisal-based index.
    B. a transaction-based index.
    C. the NCREIF Property Index.

28. Based on Exhibit 5, the property expected to be most highly leveraged is:
    A. Property A.
    B. Property B.
    C. Property C.

The following information relates to Questions 29–34.

Hui Lin, CFA, is an investment manager looking to diversify his portfolio by adding equity real estate investments. Lin and his investment analyst, Maria Nowak, are discussing whether they should invest in publicly traded real estate investment trusts or public real estate operating companies. Nowak expresses a strong preference for investing in public REITs in taxable accounts.

Lin schedules a meeting to discuss this matter, and for the meeting, Lin asks Nowak to gather data on three specific REITs and come prepared to explain her preference for public REITs over public REOCs. At the meeting, Lin asks Nowak,

> Why do you prefer to invest in public REITs over public REOCs for taxable accounts?

Nowak provides Lin with an explanation for her preference of public REITs and provides Lin with data on the three REITs shown in Exhibits 6 and 7.

The meeting concludes with Lin directing Nowak to identify the key investment characteristics along with the principal risks of each REIT and to investigate the valuation of the three REITs. Specifically, Lin asks Nowak to value each REIT using four different methodologies:

Method 1: Net asset value
Method 2: Discounted cash flow valuation using a two-step dividend model
Method 3: Relative valuation using property subsector average P/FFO multiple
Method 4: Relative valuation using property subsector average P/AFFO multiple

EXHIBIT 6   Select REIT Financial Information

	REIT A	REIT B	REIT C
Property subsector	Office	Storage	Health Care
Estimated 12-month cash net operating income	$ 350,000	$ 267,000	$ 425,000
Funds from operations	$ 316,965	$ 290,612	$ 368,007
Cash and equivalents	$ 308,700	$ 230,850	$ 341,000
Accounts receivable	$ 205,800	$ 282,150	$ 279,000
Debt and other liabilities	$2,014,000	$2,013,500	$2,010,000
Non-cash rents	$ 25,991	$ 24,702	$ 29,808
Recurring maintenance-type capital expenditures	$ 63,769	$ 60,852	$ 80,961
Shares outstanding	56,100	67,900	72,300

EXHIBIT 7   REIT Dividend Forecasts and Average Price Multiples

	REIT A	REIT B	REIT C
Expected annual dividend next year	$3.80	$2.25	$4.00
Dividend growth rate in Years 2 and 3	4.0%	5.0%	4.5%
Dividend growth rate (after Year 3 into perpetuity)	3.5%	4.5%	4.0%
Assumed cap rate	7.0%	6.25%	6.5%
Property subsector average P/FFO multiple	14.4×	13.5×	15.1×
Property subsector average P/AFFO multiple	18.3×	17.1×	18.9×

Note: Nowak estimates an 8% cost of equity capital for all REITs and a risk-free rate of 4.0%.

29. Nowak's *most likely* response to Lin's question is that the type of real estate security she prefers:
    A. offers a high degree of operating flexibility.
    B. provides dividend income that is exempt from double taxation.
    C. has below-average correlations with overall stock market returns.

30. Based on Exhibits 6 and 7, the value per share for REIT A using valuation Method 1 is *closest* to:
    A. $51.26.
    B. $62.40.
    C. $98.30.

31. Based on Exhibits 6 and 7, the value per share of REIT B using valuation Method 3 is *closest* to:
    A. $40.77.
    B. $57.78.
    C. $73.19.

32. Based on Exhibit 7, the value per share of REIT C using valuation Method 2 is *closest* to:
    A. $55.83.
    B. $97.57.
    C. $100.91.

33. Based on Exhibits 6 and 7, the value per share of REIT A using valuation Method 4 is *closest* to:
    A. $58.32.
    B. $74.12.
    C. $103.40.

34. The risk factor *most likely* to adversely affect an investment in REIT B is:
    A. new competitive facilities.
    B. tenants' sales per square foot.
    C. obsolescence of existing space.

The following information relates to Questions 35–40.

Tim Wang is a financial adviser specializing in commercial real estate investing. He is meeting with Mark Caudill, a new client who is looking to diversify his investment portfolio by adding real estate investments. Caudill has heard about various investment vehicles related to real estate from his friends and is seeking a more in-depth understanding of these investments from Wang.

Wang begins the meeting by advising Caudill of the many options that are available when investing in real estate, including the following:

Option 1: Direct ownership in real estate
Option 2: Publicly traded real estate investment trusts
Option 3: Publicly traded real estate operating companies
Option 4: Publicly traded residential mortgage-backed securities

Wang next asks Caudill about his investment preferences. Caudill responds by telling Wang that he prefers to invest in equity securities that are highly liquid, provide high income, and are not subject to double taxation.

Caudill asks Wang how the economic performance of REITs and REOCs is evaluated and how their shares are valued. Wang advises Caudill there are multiple measures of economic performance for REITs and REOCs, including the following:

Measure 1: Net operating income
Measure 2: Funds from operations
Measure 3: Adjusted funds from operations

In response, Caudill asks Wang,

> *"Which of the three measures is the best measure of a REIT's current economic return to shareholders?"*

To help Caudill's understanding of valuation, Wang presents Caudill with data on Baldwin, a health care REIT that primarily invests in independent and assisted senior housing communities in large cities across the United States. Selected financial data on Baldwin for the past two years are provided in Exhibit 8.

EXHIBIT 8   Baldwin REIT Summarized Income Statement (USD thousands, except per-share data)

	Year Ending 31 December	
	2019	2018
Rental income	339,009	296,777
Other property income	6,112	4,033
Total income	345,121	300,810
Rental expenses		
Property operating expenses	19,195	14,273
Property taxes	3,610	3,327
Total property expenses	22,805	17,600
Net operating income	322,316	283,210
Other income (gains on sale of properties)	2,162	1,003
General and administrative expenses	21,865	19,899

Depreciation and amortization	90,409	78,583
Net interest expenses	70,017	56,404
Net income	142,187	129,327
Weighted average shares outstanding	121,944	121,863
Earnings per share	1.17	1.06
Dividend per share	0.93	0.85
Price/FFO, based on year-end stock price	11.5×	12.7×

Before the meeting, Wang had put together some valuation assumptions for Baldwin in anticipation of discussing valuation with Caudill. Wang explains the process of valuing a REIT share using discounted cash flow analysis, and he proceeds to estimate the value of Baldwin on a per-share basis using a two-step dividend discount model using the data provided in Exhibit 9.

EXHIBIT 9   Baldwin Valuation Projections and Assumptions

Current risk-free rate	4.0%
Baldwin beta	0.90
Market risk premium	5.0%
Appropriate discount rate (CAPM)	8.5%
Expected dividend per share, 1 year from today	$1.00
Expected dividend per share, 2 years from today	$1.06
Long-term growth rate in dividends, starting in Year 3	5.0%

35. Based on Caudill's investment preferences, the type of real estate investment Wang is *most likely* to recommend to Caudill is:
    A. Option 2.
    B. Option 3.
    C. Option 4.
36. Relative to Option 2 and Option 3, an advantage of investing in Option 1 is:
    A. greater liquidity.
    B. lower investment requirements.
    C. greater control over property-level investment decisions.
37. The Baldwin REIT is *least likely* to experience long-run negative effects from:
    A. an economic recession.
    B. an unfavorable change in population demographics.
    C. a major reduction in government funding of health care.
38. The *most appropriate* response to Caudill's question is:
    A. Measure 1.
    B. Measure 2.
    C. Measure 3.

39. Based on Exhibit 8, the 2019 year-end share price of Baldwin was *closest* to:
    A. $13.23.
    B. $21.73.
    C. $30.36.
40. Based on Exhibit 9, the intrinsic value of the Baldwin REIT on a per share basis using the two-step dividend discount model is *closest* to:
    A. $26.72.
    B. $27.59.
    C. $28.76.

CHAPTER 4

PRIVATE EQUITY INVESTMENTS

Yves Courtois, CMT, MRICS, CFA, and Tim Jenkinson, PhD

LEARNING OUTCOMES

The candidate should be able to:

- explain sources of value creation in private equity;
- explain how private equity firms align their interests with those of the managers of portfolio companies;
- compare and contrast characteristics of buyout and venture capital investments;
- interpret LBO model and VC method output;
- explain alternative exit routes in private equity and their impact on value;
- explain risks and costs of investing in private equity;
- explain private equity fund structures, terms, due diligence, and valuation in the context of an analysis of private equity fund returns;
- interpret and compare financial performance of private equity funds from the perspective of an investor;
- calculate management fees, carried interest, net asset value, distributed to paid in (DPI), residual value to paid in (RVPI), and total value to paid in (TVPI) of a private equity fund.

1. INTRODUCTION

Private equity's shift from a niche activity to a critical component of the financial system is evident from investors' financial commitment: around $2.8 trillion globally as of mid-2018. And that's just the equity portion. The use of debt means transaction value is often two or three times the actual equity raised. Blackstone, Carlyle, and KKR are household names and publicly traded companies of significant size. Private equity funds may account for 15%–18% of the value of all mergers and acquisitions, and the market capitalization of Alibaba, Amazon, Facebook, and Google has raised the profile of venture capital investing.

We take two approaches to illuminate our subject: In Sections 2–6 the perspective is primarily that of the private equity firm evaluating potential investments. Valuing acquisitions is particularly complex; except for public-to-private transactions, there will be no market prices to refer to, and the challenges are considerable. In Sections 7–9 we take the perspective of an outside investor investing in a fund sponsored by the private equity firm.

Definitions of private equity differ, but here we include the entire asset class of equity investments that are not quoted on stock markets. Private equity stretches from venture capital (VC)—working with early-stage companies that may be without revenues but that possess good ideas or technology—to growth equity, providing capital to expand established private businesses often by taking a minority interest, all the way to large buyouts (leveraged buyouts, or LBOs), in which the private equity firm buys the entire company. When the target is publicly traded, the private equity fund performs a public-to-private transaction, removing the target from the stock market. But buyout transactions usually involve private companies and very often a particular division of an existing company.

Some exclude venture capital from the private equity universe because of the higher risk profile of backing new companies as opposed to mature ones. For this chapter, we refer simply to *venture capital* and *buyouts* as the two main forms of private equity.

Many classifications of private equity are available. Classifications proposed by the European and Private Equity Venture Capital Association (EVCA) are displayed in Exhibit 1.

EXHIBIT 1   Classification of Private Equity in Terms of Stage and Type of Financing of Portfolio Companies

Broad Category	Subcategory	Brief Description
Venture capital	Seed stage	Financing provided to research business ideas, develop prototype products, or conduct market research
	Startup stage	Financing to recently created companies with well-articulated business and marketing plans
	Later (expansion) stage	Financing to companies that have started their selling effort and may already be covering costs: Financing may serve to expand production capacity, product development, or provide working capital.
	Replacement capital	Financing provided to purchase shares from other existing venture capital investors or to reduce financial leverage.
Growth	Expansion capital	Financing to established and mature companies in exchange for equity, often a minority stake, to expand into new markets and/or improve operations
Buyout	Acquisition capital	Financing in the form of debt, equity, or quasi-equity provided to a company to acquire another company
	Leveraged buyout	Financing provided by an LBO firm to acquire a company
	Management buyout	Financing provided to the management to acquire a company, specific product line, or division (carve-out)

Broad Category	Subcategory	Brief Description
Special situations	Mezzanine finance	Financing generally provided in the form of subordinated debt and an equity kicker (warrants, equity, etc.) frequently in the context of LBO transactions
	Distressed/turnaround	Financing of companies in need of restructuring or facing financial distress
	One-time opportunities	Financing in relation to changing industry trends and new government regulations
	Other	Other forms of private equity financing are also possible—for example, activist investing, funds of funds, and secondaries.

Private equity funds may also be classified geographically, by sector, or both. Certain specialists target real asset classes, such as real estate, infrastructure, energy, and timber, or they seek out emerging or niche sectors, such as agribusiness or royalties in pharmaceuticals, music, film, or TV.

US private equity enjoyed a far larger market size historically than private equity in other regions, with few restrictions on hostile takeovers. Buyouts subsequently expanded to Europe and then Asia as friendly deals became commonplace. In broad terms, around four-fifths of the money has been flowing into buyout, growth, and other types of private equity in both the United States and Europe, with buyout amounts far exceeding other types. The sheer scale of buyouts means that an individual deal can absorb billions of dollars in capital. Buyout funds have benefited from increased allocations given their ability to absorb far higher capital amounts and to deliver historically higher-than-average returns.

Venture capital deals, in contrast, tend to drip, providing small amounts of feed money. Still, advances in technology and communications are causing the number of venture capital funds and the availability of startup capital to grow. Investor attention started to shift to China in 2015, an especially active year for raising capital. VC funds targeting Asia had more than US$200 billion in 2017, up from US$50 billion in 2010.

Most private equity money comes from institutional investors, such as pension funds, sovereign wealth funds, endowments, and insurance companies, although many family offices and high-net-worth individuals also invest directly or through fund-of-funds intermediaries. Venture capital investors include government agencies and corporations seeking to promote regional investment or gain insight into, and possibly control of, emerging businesses and technologies.

Private equity investment is characterized by a buy-to-sell orientation: Investors typically expect their money to be returned, with a handsome profit, within 10 years of committing their funds. The economic incentives of the funds are aligned with this goal.

2. INTRODUCTION TO VALUATION TECHNIQUES IN PRIVATE EQUITY TRANSACTIONS

This chapter is not intended to be a comprehensive review of valuation techniques. Instead, we highlight some essential considerations specific to private equity. Private equity firms serve as a rich laboratory for applying the principles of asset and equity valuation.

First and foremost, we must distinguish between the price paid for a private equity stake and the valuation of that same private equity stake. The price paid for a private equity stake is the outcome of a negotiation process in which each party may assign a different value to the same stake. Whereas public company shares are traded on a regulated market and their prices are transparent, the buyers and sellers of private equity interests generally make greater efforts to uncover their value. Private equity valuation is thus time-bound and dependent on the respective motives of buyers and sellers.

Selecting a valuation methodology for a private equity (PE) portfolio company depends largely on its stage of development. Common methodologies appear in Exhibit 2, along with the stages in which they may apply.

EXHIBIT 2   Overview of Selected Valuation Methodologies and Their Possible Application in Private Equity

Valuation Technique	Brief Description	Application
Income approach: discounted cash flow (DCF)	Value is obtained by discounting expected future cash flows at an appropriate cost of capital.	Generally applies across the broad spectrum of company stages. Given the emphasis on expected cash flows, DCF provides the most relevant results when applied to companies with a sufficient operating history. It is most applicable to companies operating from the expansion phase up to the maturity phase.
Relative value: earnings multiples	Application of an earnings multiple to the earnings of a portfolio company. The earnings multiple is frequently obtained from the average of a group of public companies operating in a similar business and of comparable size. Commonly used multiples include price/earnings (P/E), enterprise value/ EBITDA, enterprise value/ sales.	Generally applies to companies with a significant operating history and a predictable stream of cash flows. May also apply (with caution) to companies operating at the expansion stage. Rarely applies to early-stage or startup companies.
Real option	The right to undertake a business decision (call or put option). Requires judgmental assumptions about key option parameters.	Generally applies to situations in which the management or shareholders have significant flexibility in making radically different strategic decisions (i.e., option to undertake or abandon a high-risk, high-return project). Therefore, generally applies to some companies operating at the seed or startup phase.

Valuation Technique	Brief Description	Application
Replacement cost	Estimated cost to recreate the business as it stands as of the valuation date.	Generally applies to early-stage (seed and startup) companies, companies operating at the development stage and generating negative cash flows, or asset-rich companies.
		Rarely applies to mature companies because it is difficult to estimate the cost to recreate a company with a long operating history. For example, it would be difficult to estimate the cost to recreate a long-established brand, such as Coca-Cola, whereas the replacement cost methodology may be used to estimate the brand value for a recently launched beverage (R&D expenses, marketing costs, etc.).

In a vibrant and booming private equity market, there is a natural tendency among participants to focus on the earnings approach to determine value. The benchmark value it offers is perceived as corresponding best to the market's present state, but given the lack of liquidity of private equity investments, the concurrent use of other metrics is strongly recommended.

In most transactions, private equity investors are faced with a set of investment decisions that are based on an assessment of prospective returns and associated probabilities. Private equity firms are confronted generally with a large flow of information arising from detailed due diligence investigations and from complex financial models. It is essential to understand the potential upside and downside impact of internal and external factors on the business, net income, and cash flows. The interplay between exogenous factors (such as favorable and unfavorable macroeconomic conditions, interest rates, and exchange rates) and value drivers for the business (such as sales margins and required investments) should also be considered carefully. For example, what will be the sales growth if competition increases or if competing new technologies are introduced?

When building financial forecasts, variables in the financial projections should be linked to key business drivers with assigned subjective probabilities. The use of Monte Carlo simulation can further enhance the analysis and identify significant financial upsides and downsides to the business. In a Monte Carlo simulation, the analyst must model the fundamental value drivers of the portfolio company, which are in turn linked to a valuation model. The objective is to ensure that the simulation is as close as possible to the realities of the business and encompasses the range of possible outcomes, including base-case, worst-case, and best-case scenarios (sometimes called a triangular approach).

Other key considerations when evaluating a private equity transaction include the value of control, the impact of illiquidity, and the extent of any country risk. Estimating the discount for illiquidity and marketability and a premium for control are among the most subjective decisions in private equity valuation. The control premium is an incremental value associated with a bloc of shares that will be instrumental in gaining control of a company. In most buyouts, the entire equity capital is acquired by the private equity purchasers. But in venture capital deals, investors often acquire minority positions. In this case, the control premium (if any) largely depends on the relative strength and alignment of interest of shareholders willing to gain control. For example, in a situation with only a limited number of investors able to acquire control, the control premium is likely to be much more significant relative to a situation with a dominant controlling shareholder invested along with a large number of much smaller shareholders.

The distinction between marketability and liquidity is more subtle. The cost of illiquidity may be defined as the cost of finding prospective buyers and represents the speed of conversion of the assets to cash, whereas the cost of marketability is closely related to the right to sell the assets. In practice, the marketability and liquidity discounts are frequently lumped together.

The cost for illiquidity and premium for control may be closely related because illiquidity may be more acute when there is a fierce battle for control. But there are many dimensions to illiquidity. The size of the illiquidity discount may be influenced by such factors as the shareholding structure, the level of profitability and its expected sustainability, the possibility of an initial public offering (IPO) in the near future, and the size of the private company. Because determining the relative importance of each factor may be difficult, the illiquidity discount is frequently assessed overall on a judgmental basis. In practice, the discount for illiquidity and premium for control are both adjustments to the preliminary value estimate instead of being factored into the cost of capital.

When valuing private equity portfolio companies in emerging markets, country and currency risk represent additional sources of risk frequently added to a modified version of the standard CAPM. Estimating the appropriate country risk premium represents a significant challenge in emerging market private equity valuation, and numerous estimation approaches exist.

All of this is to say that PE valuation is highly challenging and valuation does not simply involve a net present value calculation based on a static set of future profit projections. Using a combination of valuation methodologies, supplemented by stress testing and scenario analysis, provides the strongest support to estimating value. One of the key ways private equity firms add value is by challenging the way businesses are run. Should the PE firm manage to improve the business's finances, operations, management, or marketing, we can expect additional value.

2.1. How Is Value Created in Private Equity?

How private equity funds actually create value has been the subject of much debate. Rather than ownership and control being separate, as in most publicly quoted companies, private equity concentrates ownership and control. Many view the combining of ownership and control as a fundamental source of the returns earned by the best private equity funds. The survival of the private equity governance model depends on economic advantages it may have over the public equity governance model, including (1) the ability to re-engineer the private firm to generate superior returns, (2) financial leverage and the ability to access credit markets on favorable terms, and (3) a better alignment of interests between private equity firm owners and the managers of the firms they control.

Do private equity houses have a superior ability to re-engineer companies and therefore generate superior returns? Some of the largest PE organizations, such as Ardian, Blackstone Group, Carlyle Group, CVC Capital Partners, KKR, and Partners Group, have developed high-end consulting capabilities supported frequently by seasoned industry veterans, such as former CEOs, chief financial officers, and senior advisers. They have proven their ability to execute deals on a global basis. Irrespective of their size, some of the very best firms have developed effective re-engineering capabilities to add value to their investments. But it is hard to believe that this factor, all else being equal, is the main driver of added value. Assuming that private equity houses have a superior ability to re-engineer companies, this would mean that public companies have inherently less ability to do so. Many public companies, however, such as Apple, Berkshire Hathaway, Samsung, Tencent Holdings, Toyota, and Unilever, have long track records of creating value through organizational changes and re-engineering. Only a portion of the value added by private equity houses may be explained by superior capabilities in this sphere.

Is financial leverage the main driver of private equity returns in buyouts? In private equity, target companies are rarely purchased using only the equity of the buyout company. Relative to comparable publicly quoted companies, there is a much greater use of debt in a typical buyout transaction. The use of debt is central to the structure and feasibility of buyouts, and private equity firms use significant proportions of debt to finance each deal. The leverage increases equity returns and the number of transactions a particular fund can make. A private equity firm may invest equity representing 30% of the buyout purchase price and raise the rest in the debt markets. It may use a combination of bank loans—often called leveraged loans because of the prominent proportion of the company's capital structure they represent—and high-yield bonds.

Leveraged Loan Covenants

To protect investors, leveraged loans often carry covenants that may require or restrict certain actions. For instance, the covenants may require the company: (1) to maintain specified financial ratios, (2) within certain limits, to submit information regularly so that the bank can monitor performance, or (3) to operate within certain parameters. The covenants may restrict the company from further borrowing (in other words, no additional bonds can be issued and no additional funds can be borrowed from banks or other sources), or they may impose limits on paying dividends or even making certain operating decisions.

Similarly, bond terms may include covenants intended to protect the bondholders. One of the key differences between leveraged loans and high-yield bonds, however, is that leveraged loans are generally senior secured debt whereas the bonds are unsecured in the case of bankruptcy. Even given covenants on the bonds, the bonds issued to finance an LBO are usually high-yield bonds that receive low-quality ratings and must offer high coupons to attract investors because of the amount of leverage used.

The ample availability of credit at favorable terms—think low credit spreads and fewer covenants—before the 2007 global financial crisis and a resumption of covenant-lite terms combined with low interest rates during much of the 2010s contributed to a significant increase in available leverage for buyouts. Borrowing six to eight times EBITDA has been common for large buyout transactions. Note that in private equity, leverage is typically measured as a multiple of EBITDA instead of equity.

When considering the impact of leverage on value, we should naturally turn to one of the foundations of modern finance: the Modigliani–Miller (1958) theorem. This theorem, in its basic form, states that in the absence of taxes, asymmetric information, and bankruptcy costs and assuming efficient markets, the value of a firm is not affected by how the firm is financed. In other words, it should not matter if the firm is financed by equity or debt as far as firm value is concerned. The relaxing of the no-tax assumption raises interesting questions in leveraged buyouts, as the tax shield on the acquisition debt creates value because of the tax-deductibility of interest. One would also expect that the financial leverage of a firm would be set at a level where bankruptcy costs do not outweigh these tax benefits. PE firms may have a better ability than public companies to raise high levels of debt as a result of their better control over management but also as a result of their reputation for having raised and repaid such high levels of debt in previous transactions.

Such debt financing is raised initially from the syndicated loan market but then is frequently repackaged via sophisticated structured products, such as collateralized loan obligations (CLOs), which typically consist of a portfolio of secured floating-rate leveraged loans issued by non-investment-grade companies. In some cases, the private equity funds issue high-yield bonds as a way of financing the portfolio company, and these often are sold to funds that create collateralized debt obligations (CDOs).

This raises the question of whether a massive transfer of risk to the credit markets is taking place in private equity. If the answer to this question is yes, then one would expect that it will self-correct during the next economic downturn. During early 2008, the CDO and CLO markets were undergoing a significant slowdown as a result of the credit market turmoil that started in the summer of 2007, triggered by the subprime mortgage crisis. As a result, the LBO market for very large transactions ("mega-buyouts") was affected by a lack of financing. Global equity market declines beginning in mid- to late 2015, which accompanied or responded to the Brexit referendum, the Asian currency weakness, and changing regulatory capital rules, further interrupted LBO and leveraged debt activity. The pause ended up being short-lived; market volumes resumed their upward growth in 2017.

Additional leverage is also gained by means of equity-like instruments at the acquisition vehicle level, which are frequently located in a favorable jurisdictions, such as Luxembourg, the Channel Islands, the Cayman Islands, the British Virgin Islands, or Malta. Acquisitions by large buyout private equity firms are generally held by a top holding company in a favorable tax jurisdiction. The top holding company's share capital and equity-like instruments are held in turn by investment funds run by a general partner who is controlled by the private equity buyout firm. These instruments are treated as debt for tax purposes in certain jurisdictions.

The effect of leverage may be analyzed through Jensen's (1986, 1989) free cash flow hypothesis. According to Jensen, low-growth companies generating high free cash flows tend to invest in projects that destroy value (i.e., with a negative net present value) instead of distributing excess cash to shareholders. This is a possible explanation for why an LBO transaction generates value, because excess cash is used to repay the senior debt tranche, effectively removing management's discretionary use of cash. Here, too, financial leverage may explain part of the value added by private equity investment.

Examining the value created via the re-engineering of private firms and the availability and effects of leverage is informative. Now we turn to the alignment of economic interests between private equity owners and the managers of the companies they control to ensure the latter's efforts to achieve the ambitious milestones set by the former. Results-driven pay packages and contractual clauses ensure that managers are incentivized to reach their targets and that they will not be left behind after the private equity house exits the investment. One common clause stipulates that any offer made by a future acquirer of the company be extended to all shareholders, including company management.

Consider the managers of public companies subsequently acquired by private equity groups. Empirical evidence shows that managers tend to acknowledge an increased level of directness and intensity of input after the takeover, which enables them to conduct higher-value-added projects. Crucially, these projects can be implemented over a longer time frame after the buyout; this situation is in contrast to the short-termism that prevailed during their public market period. This short-termism is mostly driven by shareholders' expectations, the analyst community, and market participants more broadly who place significant emphasis on meeting quarterly earnings targets. Private equity firms have a longer time horizon, so they attract talented managers with the ability to implement sometimes profound restructuring plans, isolated against short-term market consequences.

Private equity firms are not, however, the sole catalysts of change at large companies. Some large organizations, such as Google, SAP, and Tencent, have proven their ability to inspire entrepreneurship at all levels within their ranks while generating substantial value over the long term.

A balance of rights and obligations between the private equity firm and the management team requires effective structuring. The following matters are covered by the contractual clauses that private equity firms use to ensure that the management team is focused on achieving the business plan. If the agreed objectives are not met, the control and equity allocation held by the private equity firm may increase.

- *Corporate board seats*: A seat ensures some degree of private equity control in the case of major corporate events, such as a company sale, takeover, restructuring, IPO, bankruptcy, or liquidation.
- *Noncompete clause*: This is generally imposed on founders, preventing them from restarting the same activity during a predefined period of time.
- *Preferred dividends and liquidation preference*: Private equity firms generally come first when distributions take place, and they may be guaranteed a minimum multiple of their original investment before other shareholders receive their returns.
- *Reserved matters*: Some domains of strategic importance (such as changes in the business plan, acquisitions, or divestitures) are subject to approval or veto by the private equity firm.
- *Earnouts (mostly in venture capital)*: These are agreements that the acquisition price paid by the private equity firm is contingent on company management achieving predefined financial performance over a specified future time period (e.g., over one or two years). Earnouts are not specific to private equity.

How the PE firm structures the investment contract can have a major bearing on the returns. Venture capital firms, in particular, whose investee companies face considerable uncertainties, can set terms that increase their level of control over time or can even seize control if too many targets are missed.

2.2. Using Market Data in Valuation

With the exception of public-to-private transactions, there is no direct market evidence of company valuation with most private equity deals. But virtually all valuation techniques use evidence from the market at different stages in the calculation rather than relying entirely on accounting data and management forecasts.

The two most important ways in which market data are used to infer the value of the entity being acquired are: (1) by analyzing publicly traded comparison companies and (2) by considering the valuations that are implied by recent transactions involving similar entities. Typically, these techniques involve trading or acquisition multiples. Suppose we need a valuation for a privately owned company in the food-retail sector. The comparison-company approach would look at the trading multiples—such as enterprise value to EBITDA—of comparable public food-retail companies and use this multiple to value the target. Similarly, the transaction multiples that were paid in recent food-retail M&A transactions can inform the market value of our target. It is very important, of course, to make sure that the comparisons are appropriate, and this is simply not always possible, especially for niche businesses or targets that are pioneering products and services.

Market data come into play for DCF approaches, in particular when estimating the discount rate. The same weighted average cost of capital (WACC) formula we use for public companies is used to establish the cost of capital for private companies. We face a serious challenge, however, in assessing the cost of equity in PE settings: the lack of public historical data on share prices and returns. Therefore, beta (β), which represents the relative exposure of company shares to the market, must be estimated by means of a proxy. Typically the proxy is the result of estimating the beta for comparable companies and then adjusting it for financial and operating leverage. This benchmark exercise calls for analyst judgment: To what extent are the comparable public firms genuinely comparable to the target firm? Should outlying companies be excluded? What is the target debt-to-equity ratio of the target firm versus the industry average? What comparable public companies are appropriate if the target firm operates in several business segments?

Given that forecasts of future financial performance are usually only available for a few years ahead, when it comes to DCF valuation it is almost always necessary to estimate the terminal value of the company beyond this forecasting horizon. It is possible to apply a perpetual growth rate assumption, although small changes in the assumed growth rate, which itself is very difficult to predict, can have a significant impact on the valuation. An alternative is to use a trading multiple that exists (or is predicted to exist) in public markets and apply this to the final-year forecasted values. For instance, if the average enterprise-value-to-EBITDA ratio for comparable publicly quoted companies is 10, then this might be applied to the private target's final forecast EBITDA value as a way of estimating the terminal value.

3. CONTRASTING VENTURE CAPITAL AND BUYOUT INVESTMENTS

Our two main categories of private equity investments, buyout and venture capital funds, dominate in terms of number of funds and invested amounts. Whereas a VC firm may have a specialized industry focus—seeking the next rising star in technology or life sciences—LBO firms generally invest in a portfolio of firms with more predictable cash flow. VC firms seek revenue growth from new enterprise and technology; buyout firms focus more on EBIT or EBITDA growth by established companies. Valuation is thus fundamentally different, and Exhibit 3 presents certain key distinctions.

EXHIBIT 3   Characteristics of Buyout and Venture Capital Investments

Buyout Investments:	Venture Capital Investments:
• Steady and predictable cash flows.	• Low cash flow predictability; cash flow projections may not be realistic.
• Excellent market position (can be a niche player).	• Lack of market history; new market and possibly an unproven future market (early-stage venture).
• Significant asset base (may serve as a basis for collateral lending).	• Weak asset base.
• Strong and experienced management team.	• Newly formed management team with strong individual track record as entrepreneurs.
• Extensive use of leverage consisting of a large proportion of senior debt and a significant layer of junior and/or mezzanine debt.	• Primarily equity funded; the use of leverage is rare and very limited.

Buyout Investments:	Venture Capital Investments:
• Risk is measurable; investments are in mature businesses with long operating histories.	• The assessment of risk is difficult because of new technologies, new markets, and a lack of operating history.
• Predictable exit (secondary buyout, sale to a strategic buyer, IPO).	• Exits are difficult to anticipate (secondary venture sale, sale to strategic/financial buyer, IPO).
• Established products.	• Technological breakthrough but the route to market is yet unproven.
• Potential for restructuring and cost reduction.	• Significant cash burn rate required to ensure company development and commercial viability.
• Low working capital requirement.	• Expanding capital requirement if in the growth phase.
• Buyout firms typically conduct full-blown due diligence before investing in the target firm (financial, strategic, commercial, legal, tax, environmental).	• VC firms tend to conduct technology and commercial due diligence before investing; financial due diligence is limited as portfolio companies have no or very little operating history.
• Buyout firms monitor cash flow management and strategic and business planning.	• VC firms monitor the achievement of milestones defined in the business plan.
• Investment portfolio returns are generally characterized by a lower variance across returns from underlying investments; bankruptcies are rare.	• Investment portfolio returns are generally characterized by very high returns from a limited number of highly successful investments and a significant number of write-offs from poor-performing investments or failures.
• Large buyout firms are generally significant players in the capital markets.	• VC firms tend to be much less active in the capital markets.
• Most transactions are auctions involving multiple potential acquirers.	• Many transactions are "proprietary," arising from relationships between venture capitalists and entrepreneurs.
• High-performing buyout firms tend to have a better ability to secure larger pools of financing given their track record.	• VC firms tend to be less scalable relative to buyout firms; the increase in size of subsequent funds tends to be less significant.
• Variable revenue to the general partner (GP) at buyout firms generally comes in the form of carried interest, transaction fees, and monitoring fees.	• Carried interest (participation in profits) is generally the main source of variable revenue to the general partner at VC firms; transaction and monitoring fees are rare in practice.

4. LBO MODEL FOR VALUATION OF BUYOUT TRANSACTIONS

When the buyer in a private equity transaction acquires from the seller a controlling stake in the equity capital of a target company, it is called a buyout. The generic term "buyout" refers explicitly to the notion of acquiring control. It denotes a wide range of techniques, including but not limited to management buyouts (MBOs), leveraged buyouts (LBOs), and takeovers. In this chapter, we focus on LBOs, using borrowed money to finance a significant portion of the acquisition price.

Given their target sector, private equity firms look for characteristics that make a company particularly attractive as an LBO target:

Undervalued/depressed stock price. The private equity firm perceives that the company's intrinsic value exceeds its market price. Firms are therefore willing to pay a premium to the market price in order to secure approval by the seller's shareholders. In other circumstances, firms see a chance to make an acquisition cheaply, and the stock prices of out-of-favor public companies may make them attractive.

Willing management and shareholders. Company management is looking for a deal. They may have opportunities to increase value, but they lack the resources to make investments in the processes, personnel, equipment, and so on, that would drive long-term growth. Company shareholders may have insufficient access to capital and so welcome a private equity partner. Family business owners may want to cash out. PE firms can provide the time and capital to expand a company or turn it around.

Inefficient companies. Private equity firms seek to generate attractive returns by identifying companies that are inefficiently managed and have the potential to perform well if managed better.

Strong and sustainable cash flow. Companies that generate strong cash flow are attractive because LBO transactions have the target company taking on significant debt. Cash flow is necessary to make interest payments.

Low leverage. Private equity firms focus on target companies that have no significant debt on their balance sheets because then it's easier to use debt to finance a large portion of the purchase price.

Assets. Private equity managers like companies that have a significant amount of unencumbered physical assets. These physical assets can be used as security, and secured debt is cheaper than unsecured debt.

Earlier we considered a typical LBO capital structure that entailed 30% equity along with leveraged loans and high-yield bonds to make up the rest of the purchase price. Leveraged loans are often the source of a larger amount of capital than either equity or high-yield bonds. As an alternative to high-yield bonds, mezzanine financing may be used. Mezzanine financing refers to debt or preferred shares with a relationship to common equity that results from a feature such as attached warrants or conversion options. Being subordinate to both senior and high-yield debt, mezzanine financing typically pays a higher coupon rate. In addition to interest or dividends, this type of financing offers a potential return based on increases in the value of common equity and is generally customized to fit the specific requirements of the transaction in question.

4.1. The LBO Model

The LBO model is not a separate valuation technique but, rather, a way of determining the impact of the capital structure, purchase price, and other parameters on the returns expected by the private equity firm from the deal.

The LBO model has three main input parameters: the cash flow forecasts of the target company, the return that the providers of financing (equity, senior debt, high-yield bonds, mezzanine) are expecting, and the amount of financing available for the transaction. The free cash flow forecasts of the target company are generally prepared by its management and are subject to an extensive due diligence process (strategic, commercial, financial, legal, and environmental) to determine their reliability. The forecasts assume an explicit horizon that generally corresponds to the expected holding period (i.e., investment period) of the private equity firm.

The exit year is typically considered to determine the expected IRR sensitivity of the equity capital around the anticipated exit date. The exit value is determined most frequently by reference to an expected range of exit multiples determined on the basis of a peer group of comparable companies (enterprise value-to-EBITDA ratio).

Given the significant predictability of cash flows in buyout transactions, the income-based approach (discounted cash flows, adjusted present value, LBO model, target IRR) is frequently used as a primary method to determine the value of equity, considering the expected change in leverage until the time of exit of the investment. The initial high and declining financial leverage is the main technical valuation issue that needs to be adequately factored into the income approach when applied to a buyout valuation. The value is also frequently corroborated by an analysis of the peer group of comparable publicly traded companies.

On the basis of the input parameters, the LBO model provides the maximum price that can be paid to the seller while satisfying the target returns for the providers of financing. This is why the LBO model is not a valuation methodology per se. It is a negotiation tool that helps develop a range of acceptable prices to conclude the transaction.

Exhibit 4 is a value-creation chart that illustrates the sources of the additional value between the original cost and the exit value. Value creation comes from a combination of factors: earnings growth arising from operational improvements and enhanced corporate governance, multiple expansion depending on pre-identified potential exits, and the optimization of financial leverage and repayment of part of the debt with operational cash flows before the exit. Each component of the value creation chart should be carefully considered and backed by supporting analyses, which frequently come from the lengthy due diligence process (especially commercial, tax, and financial analysis) and also from a strategic review that quantifies the range of plausible value creation.

EXHIBIT 4   Typical Leveraged Buyout Value-Creation Chart

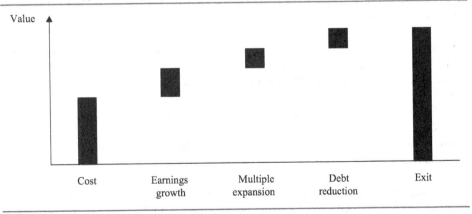

Exhibit 5 provides an example of a €5,000 (amounts in millions) investment in a private equity transaction. The transaction is financed with 50% debt and 50% equity. The €2,500 equity investment is further broken into €2,400 of preference shares owned by the private equity fund, €95 of equity owned by the private equity fund, and €5 of management equity. The preference shares are promised a 12% annual return (paid at exit). The private equity fund's equity is promised 95% of the residual value of the firm after creditors and preference shares are paid, and management equity holders are promised the remaining 5%.

EXHIBIT 5   Stakeholder Payoffs

	Invested	Proceeds	Multiple	IRR
Management	€5m	€109m	21.8x	85%
PE fund	€2,495m	€6,291m	2.5x	20%

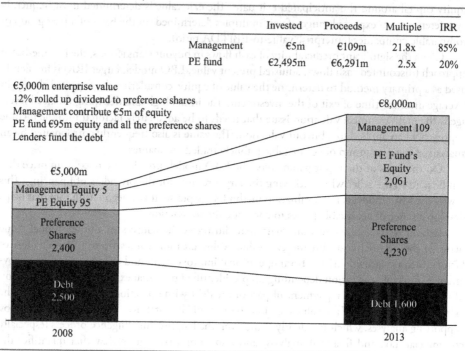

€5,000m enterprise value
12% rolled up dividend to preference shares
Management contribute €5m of equity
PE fund €95m equity and all the preference shares
Lenders fund the debt

Assume that the exit value, five years after investment, is 1.6 times the original cost. The initial investment of €5,000 has an exit value of €8,000. The specific payoffs for the four claimants are as follows:

- Senior debt has been partially retired with operational cash flows, reducing debt from €2,500 to €1,600. So debtholders get €1,600.
- Preference shares are paid a 12% return for five years, so they receive €2,400 × $(1.12)^5$ = €4,230.
- PE fund equity receives 95% of the terminal equity value, or 0.95 × [8,000 – (4,230 + 1,600)] = €2,061.
- Management equity receives 5% of the terminal equity value, or 0.05 × [8,000 – (4,230 + 1,600)] = €109.

As you can see, preference shares increase in value over time as a result of their preferred dividend being capitalized, and the equity held by the PE fund and by the management is expected to increase significantly depending on the total enterprise value upon exit. Both the equity sold to managers, frequently known as the management equity program (MEP), and the equity held by the private equity firm are most sensitive to the level of the exit. The larger the exit multiple, the larger the upside potential for both the MEP and the equity held by the private equity firm. In the example, assuming that an exit of 1.6 times cash may be achieved at the anticipated exit date (five years from investment), the management would realize an IRR of 85% per annum on its investment and the private equity fund equity holders an IRR of 20% per annum. The private equity firm also earns 12% per annum on its preference shares.

This chart also demonstrates the critical importance of leverage in buyout transactions. A reduction in financial leverage over time is instrumental in magnifying the returns available to shareholders. Note that the bulk of financial leverage in LBOs consists of senior debt, much of which will be amortizing. Therefore, the reduction in financial leverage gradually increases over time as a proportion of principal is paid back to senior lenders on an annual or semi-annual basis depending on the terms of the senior debt. As a result of the gradual repayment of senior debt over time, a larger proportion of operating cash flows becomes available to equity holders. Of course, this mechanism works well as long as no significant adverse economic factors impact the business of the target LBO company and also as long as a successful exit can be secured in the foreseeable future. It should be remembered that these high levels of debt increase the risks borne by the equity investors significantly. Such risks should be accounted for when comparing the expected returns with alternative investment classes, such as investments in the stock market.

Typically, a series of scenarios with varying levels of cash exits, growth assumptions, and debt levels are engineered with the use of an LBO model, using as inputs the required rate of return from each stakeholder (equity, mezzanine, senior debtholders) to gain a sound understanding of the buyout firm's flexibility in conducting the deal.

5. VC METHOD FOR VALUATION OF VENTURE CAPITAL TRANSACTIONS[1]

The primary difficulty of venture capital investing is the substantial uncertainty about the company's future prospects. Traditional valuation tools, such as discounted cash flow, earnings multiples, and the LBO model, are not usually practical in the VC context. Moreover, due to the uncertainty, VC financing is done in stages—financing rounds referred to as Series A, Series B, and so on—and it is essential to understand the effects of ownership dilution. So, we turn to the VC method.

Imagine a startup company is worth $16 million, and its shareholders own 100% of the equity. The company decides to raise $4 million in additional equity capital from a venture capital firm. The value of the startup company after the financing is $20 million (= $16 million + $4 million).

According to the VC method, $16 million is known as the pre-money (i.e., pre-financing) valuation, $4 million is the amount of new equity Series A investment, and $20 million is known as the post-money (i.e., post-financing) valuation. That is,

Pre-money valuation + New equity investment = Post-money valuation.

What is the total equity stake owned by the VC firm if it were to make the $4 million investment? After the transaction, the VC firm will own 20% (= $4 million/$20 million) of the equity stake or, in VC terms, will have 20% fractional ownership of the startup. The original

---

[1]Authored by Victoria Ivashina, PhD, Harvard Business School.

shareholder equity stake gets diluted to 80%. This basic example is central to understanding the VC method.

The central challenge of the VC method is determining the pre-money valuation. The closer you are to the inception date of the company, the harder it is to assess its pre-money valuation. Indeed, in early-stage venture capital, the investor might be backing an idea with no tangible proof of commercial viability. At the heart of a successful VC investment is a fundamentally novel and uncertain idea; otherwise, existing firms would easily replicate it. It is hard to envision a comparable company in the public domain or even comparable VC investments when you are early in the process. So the VC method works backwards to come up with the pre-money valuation, taking as inputs the expected exit valuation and the required return on investment.

5.1. Expected Exit Valuation

VC investments are typically financed through a closed-end fund with a finite life horizon; 10 years is very common in private equity. The average holding period for individual investments within the fund is between five and eight years. Performance metrics for the firm, measuring its progress toward commercial success, are identified at the end of the expected investment period. The performance metric could be, for example, revenues or number of users. For early-stage VC investments, it might be ambitious to expect that the company becomes profitable, but if that is the expectation, one could also use earnings per share or EBITDA. Choosing the right multiple to apply depends on the specifics of the industry, and the general idea is that, whatever the performance metrics, the value of the VC investment at exit can be determined based on projected performance metrics at anticipated exit and an appropriate industry multiple.

5.2. Required Rate of Return

VC firms target an expected hurdle return. The failure rate of VC investments, especially early-stage VC investments, is much higher than that of growth equity or buyouts. Thus, the target return on investment tends to be 10× to 30×, compared with 2.0× to 2.5× in the buyout space.

Armed with the hurdle return and the value of the equity at exit, we can compute the post-money valuation:

$$ROI = \frac{\text{Value of equity at exit}}{\text{Post-money valuation}},$$

so,

$$\text{Post-money valuation} = \frac{\text{Value of equity at exit}}{ROI}.$$

Given the capital needs of the company, we know that the pre-money valuation is as follows:

$$\text{Pre-money valuation} = \text{Post-money valuation} - \text{New equity injection}.$$

Take an entrepreneur who is looking to raise $500,000. Given the size of its market and the industry, the entrepreneur's company expects to reach sales of $80 million over the investment horizon. A typical revenue multiple for a revenue-generating business in its industry is 2×.

If the VC firm's ROI is 20× and the entrepreneur's company has no debt, then what is the pre-money valuation? And what is the VC firm's fractional ownership?

$$\text{Pre-money valuation} = \frac{\$80 \text{ million} \times 2}{20} - \$0.5 \text{ million} = \$7.5 \text{ million}.$$

$$\text{VC fractional ownership} = \frac{\$0.5 \text{ million}}{\$7.5 \text{ million} + \$0.5 \text{ million}} = 6.25\%.$$

These numbers are sensitive to the revenue figure. The required ROI will be dictated by the competition and the cost of capital. Although ROI is not sensitive to the length of the holding period, an expected holding period of five to eight years is generally the assumption in the VC fund structure. The previous example could also be reframed in terms of required internal rate of return (IRR) to equity. Over a five-year period, 20× ROI is equivalent to an 82% IRR. In general,

$$(1 + \text{IRR})^t = \text{ROI} = \frac{\text{Value of equity at exit}}{\text{Post-money valuation}},$$

or in this case,

$$(1 + \text{IRR})^5 = 20 = \frac{\$80 \text{ million} \times 2}{\$8 \text{ million}}.$$

5.3. Option Pools

Returning to the first example, if the startup were owned by the founders, they held a total of 10 million shares, and there is no option pool, what is the number of new shares that the company needs to issue? And at what price?
We know that

$$\frac{N(\text{new shares})}{N(\text{total shares after financing})} = \frac{N(\text{new shares})}{N(\text{old shares}) + N(\text{new shares})} = 20\%.$$

This means that 2.5 million new shares [= (0.2 × 10 million)/0.8] will have to be issued. Based on the $4 million of new equity raised, the shares would be issued at $4 million/2.5 million = $1.60 per share.

Scenarios without an outstanding option pool, however, are unrealistic. To attract and incentivize employees, startups grant their employees the option to purchase shares. When these options are exercised, they will naturally have a dilutive effect, so VC firms tend to calculate the per-share price on a fully diluted basis.

The basis of the dilution is contractually defined. The central question is about who assumes the effect of future dilution: original shareholders or new investors? There is tension between what benefits the VC investors and what benefits the founders, which is why this is important. By calculating the share price on a fully diluted basis, VC investors are effectively left untouched by the dilution effect. Instead, the original shareholders, our founders, absorb the effects of dilution. We will return to this concept when we examine follow-up financing series.

Back to our startup example, let's say that in addition to the founders holding 10 million shares, there is an outstanding option pool of 2 million shares. How many shares need to be issued? And at what price per share? (Recall that the default is to make calculations on a fully diluted basis.) What is the starting equity stake of the VC firm? What is the VC firm's equity stake after dilution?

- The number of existing or original shares on a fully diluted basis now is 12 million. This means that 3 million new shares [= $(0.2 \times 12 \text{ million})/0.8$] will have to be issued.
- The new price per share is \$4 million/\$3 million = \$1.33.
- The VC firm's starting ownership is 3 million/13 million = 23.08%, but as options are exercised, this ownership will be diluted to 20%.
- The VC fractional ownership on a post-dilution basis is not affected and is equal to 20% = \$4 million/\$20 million. The ownership structure should not affect the value of the assets—the key insight of the Modigliani–Miller theorem. If the pre-money valuation is \$4 million, it should remain at \$4 million regardless of how many options the firm issues.

5.4. Stage Financing

We've established that VC financing is usually executed in stages, largely due to the uncertainty that surrounds VC investments.

As an example, let's take Facebook and its initial financing rounds. The first external investment in the company took place in 2004, shortly after the platform launched, in the amount of \$500,000. Just a year later, Facebook raised \$12.7 million. In 2006, it raised \$27.5 million, followed by \$300 million in 2007. Behind this astonishing growth in fundraising sits an even more impressive rise in company valuation. So what changed for Facebook in the three years between 2004 and 2007? Why were the initial rounds so small by comparison? The answer is uncertainty about the company's future, and this illustrates that even one year out, company valuation can fluctuate dramatically. This is despite the fact that Facebook was a sought-after company with multiple veteran VC investors pursuing it. As the Facebook user base grew, so did their investment and investors' visibility into the company's future commercial success. Stage financing, thus, is a key mitigator of the risk that is fundamental to venture capital: significant uncertainty about growth and profitability prospects.

How do the different series of financing relate to each other? Because the earlier-stage investors take on higher risk, the return for those investors has to be higher. Valuations, specifically pre-money valuations, at which later rounds of financing are raised, provide insight into the performance of an otherwise illiquid asset class.

Let's assume that our earlier example—a VC firm raising \$500,000 for a startup company in exchange for a 6.25% stake—describes a Series A financing. Imagine that one year later the firm raises \$2 million in a Series B financing at 10× ROI. The exit of all investors is expected to occur simultaneously, and Series B investors were projecting an exit valuation of \$300 million. We can compute the ownership structure in each of the financing rounds along with the implied ROI for the Series A and B financings.

For Series B investors,

$$\text{Post-money valuation} = \frac{\$300 \text{ million}}{10} = \$30 \text{ million}.$$

$$\text{Pre-money valuation} = \frac{\$300 \text{ million}}{10} - \$2 \text{ million} = \$28 \text{ million}.$$

$$\text{VC fractional ownership} = \frac{\$2 \text{ million}}{\$28 \text{ million} + \$2 \text{ million}} = 6.67\%.$$

$$\text{ROI} = (1 + \text{IRR})^5 = 10 = \frac{\$300 \text{ million}}{\$30 \text{ million}}.$$

These figures are summarized in Exhibit 6.

EXHIBIT 6   Stage Financing Example

(in thousands)	Series A	Series B
Required ROI	20.0	10.0
Investment	500	2,000
Exit valuation	160,000	300,000
Post-money valuation	8,000	30,000
Pre-money valuation	7,500	28,000
Fractional ownership required	6.25%	6.67%
Ownership:		
Entrepreneurs	93.75%	87.50%
Series A investors	6.25%	5.83%
Series B investors	—	6.67%
Total	100.00%	100.00%
Implied ROI		
Series A investors	20.0	35.0
Series B investors	—	10.0

This example illustrates that the pre-money valuation implied by Series B indicates a substantial appreciation of the Series A investment. Instead of 20× ROI, Series A now has an implied ROI of 35×, although no exits occurred, and despite dilution of the Series A stake from 6.25% to 5.83%.

For Series A investors, the implied ROI, which was originally 20×, or

$$\text{ROI} = 20 = \frac{\$160 \text{ million} \times 6.25\%}{\$0.5 \text{ million}},$$

increases to 35× at the time of the Series B financing one year later, or

$$\text{ROI} = 35 = \frac{\$300 \text{ million} \times 5.83\%}{\$0.5 \text{ million}}.$$

The entry of new investors with Series B dilutes ownership for both Series A investors and the entrepreneurs on a proportionate basis. That is,

$$\text{Entrepreneurs' ownership} = [(1 - 6.67\%) \times 93.75\%] = 87.50\%.$$
$$\text{Series A investors' ownership} = [(1 - 6.67\%) \times 6.25\%] = 5.83\%.$$

Venture capital investments tend to be minority stake investments. This is partly because the founders might not be willing to give up control but also because entrepreneurs are essential in the initial stages of business development. So, the dilution of initial investors through the subsequent financing rounds is common. In the previous example, the dilution from Series B was absorbed pro rata by the entrepreneurs and the Series A investors. Because control is not essential, this arrangement is typical. If an alternative economic arrangement is sought, however—as in the earlier example of employees' stock options—designing an arrangement whereby the dilution is absorbed disproportionately by entrepreneurs is possible.

Whereas our example treated Series A and Series B shares as common stock, it is typical to use convertible preferred equity in later-stage financing. The capital that comes in later stages is less risky than earlier-stage financing. In addition, to mitigate risk further, later-stage capital tends to have a preferred dividend. Series B shares could entitle shareholders to a preferred dividend of 5%, for example. On an investment of $2 million over three years, the cumulative dividend is $315,250. If the investee company performance is as expected and the returns are high, the preference shares will be irrelevant. However, if things do not go as planned, the accumulated dividend is treated as junior debt, diminishing the value held by earlier equity investors while preserving the value for Series B. Clearly, this makes Series B more valuable than if it had been just common equity. Importantly, the value comes at the expense of earlier investors. These adjustments are rarely accounted for in practice, however.

6. EXIT ROUTES: RETURN CASH TO INVESTORS

The exit is a critical mechanism for unlocking value in private equity. Most private equity firms consider their exit options prior to investing, and they factor their assessment of the exit outcome into their IRR analysis.

Generally, PE investors have access to the following four exit routes:

- *Initial public offering (IPO)*: Going public offers significant advantages, including higher valuation multiples as a result of enhanced liquidity, access to large amounts of capital, and the possibility of attracting higher-caliber managers. But the process is cumbersome and less flexible and entails significant costs. Therefore, an IPO is an appropriate exit route for private companies that are of a sufficient size with an established operating history and excellent growth prospects. Timing is important and heavily dependent on public equity market conditions. IPO markets have shut down for long periods following major events, such as the internet bubble collapse that began in March 2000 and the global financial crisis, starting in 2007. Regional economic concerns and regulatory issues, such as uncertainty around Britain's plan to exit the European Union, have had negative ramifications for equity and IPO markets worldwide. In fact, any extended market downturn can limit the ability of new companies to come to market. IPO exits are more common for VC-backed companies, but they are not the largest divestment alternative.
- *Secondary market*: The sale of an investor's stake to other financial investors or to strategic investors (think companies that operate in the same sector or are keen to try). As private equity has become increasingly segmented, secondary market transactions tend to occur within each segment—that is, buyout firms tend to sell to other buyout firms (secondary buyouts) and venture firms to other venture firms (secondary venture capital transactions). These secondary market transactions account for a significant proportion of exits, especially in the buyout segment. Venture capital exits by means of a buyout are also possible but are rare in practice, because buyout firms are reluctant to finance development-stage companies with a significant amount of leverage. The main advantages of secondary market transactions are: (1) the possibility of achieving the highest valuation multiples in the absence of an IPO

and (2) the fact that given the segmentation of private equity firms, specialized firms have the skill to bring their portfolio companies to the next level—say, through a restructuring or merger or by bringing them to a new market—and then to sell, either to a strategic investor seeking to exploit synergies or to another private equity firm with another set of skills to further add value to the portfolio company.

- *Management buyout (MBO)*: These takeovers by company management use significant amounts of leverage to finance the acquisition. Alignment of interest between management and investors is optimal under this exit scenario, but it may come at the expense of excessive leverage that significantly reduces the company's flexibility.
- *Liquidation*: Controlling shareholders have the power to liquidate the company if it is no longer viable. This exit mechanism generally results in a floor value for the company but may come at a cost of very negative publicity for the private equity firm if the company is large and the employee count is significant.

Timing the exit and determining the optimal exit route are important. Even carefully planned exits face the unexpected, however, and may be delayed or accelerated depending on market conditions or purely opportunistic circumstances.

Suppose, for example, that an LBO firm is planning to exit one of its portfolio companies, but the public market and economic conditions have collapsed, rendering any exit via a trade sale or an IPO unprofitable. Instead, the LBO firm exploits the depressed pricing environment to conduct another acquisition and merges the target with the original portfolio company in order to strengthen its market position and product range. Then it waits for better market conditions before conducting the sale. Such flexibility is critical for private equity firms during hard times and underlines the importance of PE firms maintaining sufficient financial strength.

There seems to be no boundary to the size of buyout transactions, as expectations have consistently been exceeded. Three of the largest buyout transactions—TXU Energy ($32.1 billion), First Data ($25.7 billion), and Alltel ($25.1 billion)—all took place in 2007 immediately prior to the global financial crisis. Strength in capital markets combined with the increasing prevalence of megafunds suggest even larger transactions may be in store for the biggest buyout firms. Private equity firms appear to be moving into uncharted territory by managing exits at such levels. The central question about these mega-buyout transactions is how the exits will take place given that the possibilities are much more limited relative to smaller deals. IPOs, for example, raise significantly more challenges, restricting sellers to a gradual exit (only a single block of shares can be sold initially) and proving excessively risky when market conditions are suboptimal. And a real challenge exists for large, unified companies for which a single exit is the only way out. This is in contrast to the type of large companies that may be viewed as holding companies for a portfolio of real assets, which can be sold in tranches.

When an exit is anticipated within one or two years, the multiples observed from comparable publicly quoted firms provide good guidance for an expected exit multiple, and stress tests on that value may be conducted for small incremental changes and based on market knowledge. When the exit horizon is much further out, these multiples are less reliable, and stress tests may be performed on valuation model inputs, such as discount factor and terminal growth rates, and on financial forecasts, such as sales growth and operating margins.

6.1. Exit Routes: Summary

Valuation is the most critical aspect of private equity transactions. The investment decision-making process typically flows from the screening of investment opportunities to preparing a proposal, appraising the investment, and structuring the deal and finally to the negotiating phase. Along with the various due diligence investigations (commercial or strategic, financial, legal, tax, environmental) that are generally conducted on private equity investment opportunities, valuation serves to assess a company's ability to generate superior cash flows from a distinctive competitive advantage and as a benchmark for negotiations with the seller. Because of the difficulties in valuing private companies, a variety of alternative valuation methods are typically used to provide guidance. Private equity valuation is a process that starts as a support for decision making at the transaction phase but also serves as a monitoring tool to capture new opportunities, create value, or protect from losses during the investment period and as a performance reporting tool for investors.

7. RISKS AND COSTS OF INVESTING IN PRIVATE EQUITY

We turn now to the perspective of a private equity fund investor.

7.1. What Are the Risks and Costs of Investing in Private Equity?

Most jurisdictions restrict private equity investing to "qualified investors"—typically, institutions and high-net-worth individuals who meet certain criteria. These restrictions are a product of the high levels of risk associated with private equity investing, which are generally subject to disclosure in the private equity fund prospectus. Such risks may be categorized as general private equity risk factors, investment strategy–specific risk factors (buyout, venture capital, mezzanine), industry-specific risk factors, risk factors specific to the investment vehicle, or regional or emerging market risks when applicable.

The following are some general private equity risk factors:

- *Illiquidity of investments*: Because private equity investments are generally not traded on any securities market, the exit of investments may not end up being conducted on a timely basis.
- *Unquoted investments*: Investing in unquoted securities may be risky relative to investing in securities quoted on a regulated securities exchange.
- *Competition for attractive investment opportunities*: Competition for investment opportunities on attractive terms may be high.
- *Reliance on the management of investee companies (agency risk)*: There is no assurance that the management of the investee companies will run the company in the best interests of the private equity firm, particularly in earlier-stage deals in which the management retains a controlling stake in the company and enjoys certain private benefits of control.
- *Loss of capital*: High business and financial risks may result in a substantial loss of capital.
- *Government regulations*: Investee companies' products and services may be subject to changes in government regulations that adversely affect their business model.
- *Taxation risk*: The tax treatment of capital gains, dividends, or limited partnerships may change over time.
- *Valuation of investments*: The valuation of private equity investments is subject to significant judgment. When valuations are not conducted by an independent party, they may be subject to bias.
- *Lack of investment capital*: Investee companies may require additional future financing that may not be available.

- *Lack of diversification*: Highly concentrated investment portfolios may be exposed to significant losses. Instead, private equity investors should consider a mix of funds of different vintage, portfolio companies at different stages of development, and investing across private equity strategies, such as large and mid-market buyouts, venture capital, mezzanine finance, and restructuring.
- *Market risk*: Changes in general market conditions (interest rates, currency exchange rates) may adversely affect private equity investments. The impact of market risk is, however, long-term in nature given the long-term horizon of private equity funds. Temporary short-term market fluctuations are generally irrelevant.

The costs associated with private equity are substantially higher than the costs of public market investing. We break them down here:

- *Transaction fees*: These arise from due diligence work, bank financing costs, the legal fees of arranging an acquisition, and the costs of arranging the sale of an investee company.
- *Fund setup costs*: These are mainly the legal costs of setting up the investment vehicle, and they are typically amortized over the life of the investment vehicle.
- *Administrative costs*: Custodian, accounting, and transfer-agent costs are generally charged yearly as a fraction of the investment vehicle's net asset value.
- *Audit costs*: This is a fixed annual fee.
- *Management and performance fees*: 2% management fees and 20% performance fees, which are generally more significant than the fees charged by regular investment funds.
- *Dilution*: A more subtle cost—from our preceding examples we know that dilution comes from the stock options granted to management and the PE firm itself, as well as from additional rounds of financing.
- *Placement fees*: Fundraising fees may be charged up front—2% is not uncommon in private equity—or by means of a trailer fee. A trailer fee is generally charged annually and figures as a fraction of the amount invested by limited partners as long as these amounts remain invested in the investment vehicle.

8. PRIVATE EQUITY FUND STRUCTURES AND TERMS

When analyzing an investment in a private equity fund, a solid understanding of PE fund structures, terms of investment, due diligence, and PE fund valuation are an absolute prerequisite for investors. When interpreting financial performance, private equity raises many more challenges than public equities do. In addition to the structure and terms, two of the main differentiating characteristics relate to the nature of the subscriptions investors make in private equity structures and to the J-curve effect. Investors initially commit a certain amount to the private equity fund that is subsequently drawn by the fund as the fund's capital is deployed to portfolio companies. This contrasts with public market investing in which investment orders are typically fully disbursed at the time the orders are settled on the markets. The J-curve effect refers to the typical profile of reported PE fund returns, whereby low or negative returns are reported in the early years of a private equity fund (in large part as a result of the fees' impact on net returns), followed by increased returns thereafter as the private equity firm manages portfolio companies toward the exit.

The limited partnership has emerged as the dominant form in most jurisdictions. Funds that are structured as limited partnerships are governed by a limited partnership agreement between the fund manager, called the general partner (GP), and the fund's investors, called limited partners (LPs). Whereas the GP has management control over the fund and is jointly liable for all debts, LPs have limited liability; that is, they do not risk more than the amount of their investment in the fund.

The main alternative to the limited partnership is a corporate structure called a company limited by shares, which mirrors in its functioning the limited partnership but offers better legal protection to the GP and to some extent the LPs, depending on the jurisdiction. Some fund structures are subject to light regulatory oversight, which offers enhanced protection to LPs.

The vast majority of these private equity fund structures are closed-end, meaning they restrict existing investors from redeeming their shares over the lifetime of the fund and limit new investors to entering the fund at predefined time periods, at the discretion of the GP.

Private equity firms operate effectively in two spheres: the business of managing private equity investments and the business of raising funds. Their marketing efforts tend to be planned well in advance of the launch of their funds to ensure that the announced target fund size will be met once the fund is effectively started. The marketing phase of a private equity fund, depending on whether it is a first fund or a following fund, may take between one and two years. Once investors have committed their investment to the fund, private equity managers draw on investors' commitments—this action is called a drawdown or capital call—as the fund is being deployed and invested in portfolio companies. After commitment, private equity funds tend to have a duration of 10–12 years, generally extendable to an additional 2–3 years. Exhibit 7 illustrates structuring and stages in the life cycle for a PE fund.

EXHIBIT 7   Structuring and Life Cycle Stages for a Private Equity Fund

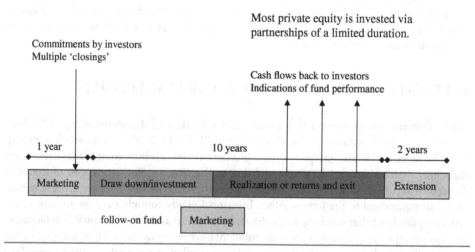

How are private equity funds structured?

Fund terms are contractually defined in a fund prospectus or limited partnership agreement, which is available to qualified prospective investors. The definition of qualified investors depends on the jurisdiction. Typically, wealth criteria (e.g., exceeding US$1 million) and/or a minimum subscription threshold (e.g., a minimum of €125,000) apply. The terms are frequently the result of the balance of negotiation power between GPs and LPs. Although the balance of negotiation power shifted in favor of LPs during and immediately following the global financial crisis, it turned back in favor of GPs as the largest sponsor continued to increase in size and gain market share. Any significant downturn in private equity's fortunes may change the balance of power in favor of LPs once again. In any event, the negotiation of terms informs an alignment of interests between the GP and LPs and defines GP incentives, such as transaction fees and profit sharing. The most significant fund terms may be categorized into economic and corporate governance terms.

8.1. Economic Terms

- *Management fees* represent an annual percentage of committed capital, which is paid quarterly to the GP during the fund investment period. Fees of 1.5%–2.5% are common, and some of the most successful funds charge even more. After the investment period, fees may decline somewhat and be calculated based on invested capital. Less frequently, management fees may continue to be calculated based on capital commitment or net asset value.
- *Transaction fees* are fees paid to GPs in their advisory capacity when they provide investment banking services for transactions (mergers and acquisitions, IPOs) that benefit the fund. These fees may be subject to sharing agreements with LPs, typically a 50/50 split. When such fee-sharing agreements apply, they generally come as a deduction to the management fees.
- *Carried interest* represents the general partner's share of the profits generated by a private equity fund. Carried interest is frequently in the range of 20% of the fund's profits (after management fees).
- *Ratchet* is a mechanism that determines the allocation of equity between shareholders and the management team of the PE-controlled company. A ratchet enables the management team to increase its equity allocation depending on the company's actual performance and the return achieved by the PE firm.
- *Hurdle rate* is the internal rate of return that a private equity fund must achieve before the GP receives any carried interest. The hurdle rate is typically in the range of 7%–10%. The objective is to align the interests of the GP with those of LPs by giving additional incentives to the GP to outperform traditional investment benchmarks and to protect against LP downside.

EXAMPLE 1   Calculation of Carried Interest

Suppose that a LBO fund has committed capital of US$100 million, carried interest of 20%, and a hurdle rate of 8%. The fund called 75% of its commitments from investors at the beginning of Year 1, which was invested at the beginning of Year 1 in target company A for $40 million and target company B for $35 million. Suppose that at the end of Year 2, a profit of $5 million has been realized by the GP upon exit of the investment in company A, and the value of the investment in company B has remained unchanged. Suppose also that the GP is entitled to carried interest on a deal-by-deal basis; that is, the IRR used to calculate carried interest is calculated for each investment upon exit. A theoretical carried interest of $1 million (20% of $5 million) could be granted to the GP, but the IRR upon exit of investment in company A is only 6.1%. Unless the IRR exceeds the hurdle rate, no carried interest may be paid to the GP.

- *Target fund size* is expressed as an absolute amount in the fund prospectus or information memorandum (also called the private placement memorandum, or PPM; offering memorandum, or OM; or offering circular, or OC). Target fund size is critical investor information because it signals the GP's capacity to manage a portfolio of a predefined size and also the GP's ability to raise funds. A fund that closed with a significantly lower size relative to the target size is perceived as a negative signal.
- *Vintage year* is the year the private equity fund is launched. Reference to the vintage year allows performance comparison of funds operating at the same stage and under the same market conditions.
- *Term of the fund* is typically 10 years, which is extendable for additional shorter periods by agreement with the investors. Although infrequently observed, funds can also be of unlimited duration, and in this case they are often quoted on stock markets—for example, investment trusts.

8.2. Corporate Governance Terms

- *Key man clause.* Under the key man clause, a certain number of key named executives are expected to play an active role in the management of the fund. In case of the departure of such a key executive or insufficient time spent in the management of the fund, the clause provides that the GP may be prohibited from making any new investments until a new key executive is appointed.
- *Disclosure and confidentiality.* Private equity firms have no obligations to publicly disclose their financial performance. Following a 2002 court ruling requiring the California Public Employees' Retirement System (CalPERS) to publicly report its returns on private equity investments, the Freedom of Information Act (FOIA) in the United States and similar legislation in some European countries led public pension funds to report on their private equity investments. Disclosable information relates to the financial performance of the underlying funds but does not extend to information on the companies in which the funds invest, which is not typically disclosed. The reporting by CalPERS is a prominent example of the application of this clause. Some PE fund terms may be more restrictive on confidentiality and disclosure, subject to FOIA.
- *Distribution waterfall.* This is a mechanism that delineates how distributions are allocated to LPs and GPs. The predominant mechanisms are deal-by-deal waterfalls, which allow earlier distribution of carried interest to the GP after each individual deal (also known as an American waterfall), and total return waterfalls, which result in earlier distributions to LPs because carried interest is calculated on the profits of the entire portfolio (also known as a European waterfall). Two alternatives for calculating carried interest exist under the total return method. In the first alternative, the GP receives carried interest only after the fund has returned the entire committed capital to LPs; in the second alternative, the GP receives carried interest on any distribution as long as the value of the investment portfolio exceeds a certain threshold above invested capital, usually 20%. The European waterfall has become prevalent among large funds marketed to institutional investors.
- *Clawback provision.* A clawback provision requires the GP to return a portion or all of the carried interest to LPs if it turns out the GP has received more than its share of profits. This provision ensures that when an LP exits a highly profitable investment early in the fund's life and subsequent exits are less profitable, the GP pays back capital contributions, fees, expenses, and carried interest profits to the LPs in order to ensure that the profit split is in

line with the fund's prospectus. The clawback is normally due on termination of the fund but may be subject to an annual reconciliation or true-up).

EXAMPLE 2   Distribution Waterfalls

Suppose a private equity fund has committed capital of £300 million and a carried interest of 20%. After a first investment of £30 million, the fund exits the investment nine months later with a £15 million profit. Under the deal-by-deal method, the GP would be entitled to 20% of the profit—that is, £3 million. In the first alternative for calculating carried interest under the total return method, the LPs are entitled to the entire proceeds of the sale—that is, £45 million—and the GP is entitled to nothing (yet). Under the second alternative, the exit value of £45 million exceeds the invested value of £30 million by more than 20%. The GP would thus be entitled to £3 million.

Continuing this example with a clawback provision with an annual true-up, suppose that the deal-by-deal method applies and that a second investment of £25 million is concluded with a loss of £5 million one year later. At the annual true-up, the GP would have to pay back £1 million to LPs. In practice, an escrow account is used to regulate these fluctuations until termination of the fund.

- *Tag-along, drag along rights* are contractual provisions in share-purchase agreements. Tag-along rights ensure that minority shareholders have the right to join in a sale entered into by a majority shareholder at the same terms offered to the majority shareholder. Essentially the buyer cannot acquire control without extending its offer to all shareholders, including the management of the company. Drag-along rights allow majority shareholders who have negotiated an exit to require the minority investors to participate in the sale at the same terms, preventing minority investors from vetoing a sale.
- *No-fault divorce.* A GP may be removed both with and without cause provided that a super-majority (generally above 75%) of LPs approve the removal. In practice it is unusual for investors to succeed in removing the GP.
- *Removal for cause* is a clause that allows for removal of the GP or an earlier termination of the fund for "cause." Cause may include gross negligence on the part of the GP, a key person event, the felony conviction of a key person, bankruptcy of the GP, or a material breach of the fund prospectus. It is difficult for LPs to remove the GP for cause because when there is an allegation of wrongdoing, the GP will often agree to an out-of-court settlement and pay a fine without having to admit guilt. Moreover, it may be many years until a final court hearing takes place.
- *Investment restrictions* generally impose a minimum level of diversification on the fund's investments, a geographic and/or sector focus, or limits on borrowing.
- *Co-investment.* LPs generally have a first right of co-investing along with the GP. This can be advantageous for the LPs as fees and profit share are likely to be lower (or zero) on co-invested capital. The GP and affiliated parties are also typically restricted in their co-investments to prevent conflicts of interest with their LPs. Crossover co-investments are a classic example of a conflict of interest. A crossover co-investment occurs when

a subsequent fund launched by the same GP invests in a portfolio company that has received funding from a previous fund.

8.3. Due Diligence Investigations by Potential Investors

Prior to investing in a private equity fund, prospective investors generally conduct thorough due diligence. Outlining several fundamental characteristics of PE funds will underline how important the due diligence process is:

- Private equity funds tend to exhibit a strong persistence of returns over time. This means that, typically, top-performing funds continue to outperform and poorly performing funds continue to perform poorly or disappear.
- The performance range between funds varies widely. For example, the difference between top-quartile and third-quartile fund IRRs can be 20 percentage points.
- Liquidity in private equity is typically very limited, and thus LPs are locked in for the long term. However, when private equity funds exit an investment, they return the cash to the investors immediately. Therefore, the duration of an investment in private equity is typically shorter than the maximum life of the fund.

Standard due diligence questionnaires (DDQs) have been developed by numerous international and country trade organizations. The Institutional Limited Partners Association (ILPA) publishes and makes available a DDQ on its website. These guides are not a substitute for the due diligence process that is conducted by LPs before investing in a venture capital or private equity fund.

8.4. Private Equity Fund Valuation

The description of private equity valuation in a fund prospectus is generally associated with the fund's calculation of net asset value (NAV), which itself is generally defined as the value of the fund assets less liabilities corresponding to the accrued expenses of the fund. The fund's assets are frequently valued by GPs, depending on their valuation policies, in the following ways:

1. At cost with significant adjustments for subsequent financing events or deterioration
2. At the lower of cost or market value
3. By the revaluation of a portfolio company whenever a new financing round involving new investors takes place
4. At cost with no interim adjustment until the exit
5. With a discount for restricted securities—for example, Reg. 144 securities
6. More rarely, marked to market by reference to a peer group of public comparables and applying illiquidity discounts

Private equity valuation standards, such as those originally produced by British, French, and European industry associations, have been adopted by funds operating in numerous jurisdictions.

Because the fund's valuation is adjusted with each new round of financing, the NAV may be more stale in down markets when there is a long gap between funding rounds. This mechanism is similar to the valuation of investment funds of publicly quoted securities. There is thus a fundamental implicit break-up assumption whereby the fund may be broken up at any time, the funds underlying investments may be liquidated individually and immediately, and the proceeds returned to LPs. Whereas this fundamental break-up assumption may hold for publicly traded securities, which are marked to market, this assumption may be more questionable for private equity investment portfolios typically held over a long period of time. At what value should investments in portfolio companies be reported prior to the private equity fund exiting the investment and returning the proceeds to the LPs? There is no clear answer to that question, because there is no market for securities issued by private equity companies.

Undrawn LP commitments represent legal obligations to meet capital calls in the future. They are not accounted for in the NAV calculation and should be viewed as unfunded liabilities by each LP for as long as they are callable.

Given that PE funds have different investment strategies, an understanding of their respective valuation policies will prevent biases. Whereas an early-stage VC fund may record its investments at cost, a late-stage VC fund may mark its portfolio companies to market by reference to public market comparables. When market bubbles form, as they did in the year leading up to the global financial crisis, public market comparables may distort the valuation of portfolio companies and thus reported fund returns.

Private equity valuations are mostly performed by GPs. Under pressure from LPs, an increasing number of annual and semi-annual valuations are performed by independent valuers that are mandated by GPs. Although auditors sign off on annual results, their responsibility does not extend much beyond testing the reasonableness and allocation of the GP's model for illiquid investment values.

9. EVALUATING FUND PERFORMANCE AND CONCEPT IN ACTION: EVALUATING A PRIVATE EQUITY FUND

Because each private equity fund is unique, assessing financial performance depends on good knowledge of a fund's objectives, structure, terms, and valuation policies. Typically an analysis of a private equity fund's financial performance includes a detailed examination of each investment's and the fund's return using IRR and multiples.

9.1. Analysis of IRR since Inception

Here, *net of fees* means net of management fees, carried interest, or any other financial arrangements that accrue to the GP. The IRR, a cash flow–weighted rate of return, is deemed the most appropriate measure of private equity performance by the Global Investment Performance Standards (GIPS), by the International Private Equity and Venture Capital Valuation Guidelines (2018 Guidelines), and by other venture capital and private equity standards. The interpretation of IRR in private equity is subject to caution, however, because an implicit assumption behind the IRR calculation is that the fund is fully liquid, whereas a significant portion of the fund's underlying investments is illiquid during much of a private equity fund's life. Therefore, valuation of portfolio companies according to industry standards is important to ensure the quality of the IRR figures.

Gross IRR is a function of the cash flows between the portfolio companies and the PE fund and is often considered a good measure of the PE firm's track record in creating value. Net IRR is a function of the cash flows between the PE fund and LPs, capturing the returns to investors. Fees and profit sharing create significant deviations between gross and net IRR. IRR analysis is often combined with a benchmark IRR analysis—that is, the median IRR for the relevant peer group of comparable private equity funds operating with a similar investment strategy and vintage year. This is particularly important because there are clear trends in private equity returns, with some vintage years producing much higher returns than others.

Despite the widespread prevalence of IRR as a performance measure and a hurdle for GP profit participation, it has its drawbacks. One drawback is that it can be easily manipulated. Imagine that a GP delays investor capital calls by using a fund's line of credit or bridge financing to make an initial investment instead or that the GP refinances an investment in order to return capital to investors prior to an exit. Both strategies reduce the time that investors' capital is outstanding, which boosts IRR independently of the investment holding period. In some cases, the only reason the GP may be entitled to its carried interest in the end is the manipulation and timing of leverage. Another problem with IRR is that it provides no information about the size of the return.

9.2. Analysis of Return Multiples

Return multiples simply measure the total return to investors relative to the total sum invested. Although multiples ignore the time value of money, their ease of calculation and their ability to differentiate between "realized" actual proceeds from divestments and the "unrealized" portfolio subject to the GP's valuation make these ratios very popular among LPs. The return multiples used most frequently by LPs and also defined by GIPS that provide additional information about fund performance are as follows:

- PIC (paid-in capital): The ratio of paid-in capital, which is the proportion of the LPs' total committed capital that the GP has so far deployed following any capital calls, to total committed capital.
- DPI (distributed to paid-in): The ratio of the cumulative distributions, which is the amount of cash and stock that has already been paid out to LPs from the fund, to the paid-in capital. This ratio indicates the fund's realized return on investment and is often called the cash-on-cash return. DPI is presented net of management fees and carried interest.
- RVPI (residual value to paid-in): This is the value of LPs' shareholding held with the private equity fund as a proportion of the cumulative invested capital (i.e., the paid-in capital). The numerator is the value that the GP assigns to the remaining portfolio companies. This ratio is a measure of the private equity fund's unrealized return on investment. RVPI is presented net of management fees and carried interest.
- TVPI (total value to paid-in): This ratio is the portfolio companies' distributed (or realized) and undistributed (or unrealized) value as a proportion of the cumulative invested capital. TVPI is the sum of DPI and RVPI and is presented net of management fees and carried interest.

In addition to quantitative measures of return, an analysis of fund financial performance includes:

- an analysis of realized investments since inception, with comments on all successes and failures;
- an analysis of unrealized investments, highlighting all red flags in the portfolio and the expected time to exit for each portfolio company;
- a cash flow forecast for each portfolio company and for the aggregate portfolio; and
- an analysis of portfolio valuation, audited financial statements, and the NAV.

EXAMPLE 3   Calculating and Interpreting Private Equity Fund Performance

Suppose that a private equity fund has a DPI of 0.07 and an RVPI of 0.62 after five years. The IRR is -17%. The fund follows a venture capital strategy in high technology and has a vintage year of 2006 and a term of 10 years. A DPI of 7% indicates that few successful exits were made. An RVPI of 62% points to an extended J-curve effect for the fund, as TVPI amounts to 69% at the midlife of the fund. A vintage year of 2006 hints that the fund was started before the 2007 global financial crisis and that the routes to exit for portfolio companies have been dramatically changed. During the financial crisis, the investment portfolio probably suffered a number of complete write-offs. LPs should thus consider the state of the portfolio and examine the number of write-offs and other signals of ailing companies. The risk of not recovering the invested amount at termination of the fund is significant. The GP's compliance with valuation policies should also be closely monitored by LPs in order to ensure that the GP's expectations are not excessive given the state of the portfolio.

With increased allocations to private equity, performance comparisons across asset classes are often misinterpreted. The IRR, a standard measure of private equity returns, is cash flow weighted, whereas the performance of most other asset classes is measured in terms of a time-weighted rate of return.

There have been ongoing attempts to solve performance-comparison issues. The public market equivalent (PME) compares a fund's IRR to a public market index (e.g., the MSCI World, the S&P 500 Index, and the FTSE All-Share Index) by assuming the fund's cash flows were invested and disinvested in the public index at the same amount and time. The PME, sometimes referred to as the Long Nickels PME for its developers Austin Long and Craig Nickels or as the index comparison method (ICM), often calculates the IRR based on public index values. The PME facilitates a direct comparison of the fund's IRR to public markets, but it breaks down when the fund significantly outperforms the public index, resulting in a negative NAV and IRR. The PME+ (developed by Christophe Rouvinez in 2003), the modified PME (created by Cambridge Associates in 2013), and several other approaches attempt to address the shortcomings of the Long Nickels PME.

9.3. Concept in Action: Evaluating Private Equity Fund Performance

Michael Hornsby, CFA, is a senior investment officer at Icarus, a UK-based institutional investor in private equity. He is contemplating an investment in Europa Venture Partners III, a new late-stage technology venture capital fund, after thorough due diligence was performed both on the fund and on the GP. Icarus has been an investor in Europa Venture Partners' (EVPs') previous two funds, EVP I and EVP II, and has been satisfied with performance so far. Icarus is seeking to further expand its relationship with this GP because it sees it as a niche venture capital firm operating in a less crowded segment of the pan-European technology markets. In light of its past success, EVP is increasing its carried interest for the third fund to 25% from

20% for the previous two funds. Hornsby has received information about the fund's financial performance and is seeking assistance in calculating and interpreting financial performance for a number of specific queries as outlined below.

Europa Venture Partners (EVP)

General Partner	Europa Venture Partners (EVP) was established to provide equity financing to later-stage European technology companies in need of development capital. The GP seeks to provide strategic support to seasoned entrepreneurial teams and to bring proven new technologies to the market. The GP targets investment in portfolio companies between €2 million and €10 million.

Established in 2012			Type: Development Capital				
Fund	Vintage	Actual Fund Size (€ Millions)	Capital Called (%)	Mgmt. Fees (%)	Carried Interest (%)	Hurdle Rate (%)	Term	Report Date
EVP I	2014	125	92	2	20	8	2012	31 Dec 2019
EVP II	2016	360	48	2	20	8	2025	31 Dec 2019

The financial performance for Icarus' investments in EVP funds follows.

Fund	Committed Capital (€ Millions)	Capital Called Down (€ Millions)	Gross IRR (%)	Net IRR (%)	DPI (×)	RVPI (×)	TVPI (×)	Quartile
EVP I	10	9.2	16.1	11.3	1.26	1.29	2.55	1
EVP II	25	12.0	1.6	(0.4)	0.35	1.13	1.48	2

Hornsby is also interested in verifying management fees, carried interest, and the NAV of EVP I. He has the following information about yearly capital calls (assumed to occur on 1 January of the given year), operating results, and annual distributions (as of 31 December of the given year).

Calls, Operating Results, and Distributions (€ Millions)

	2014	2015	2016	2017	2018	2019
Called down	50	15	10	25	10	5
Realized results	0	0	10	35	40	80
Unrealized results	−5	−15	15	10	15	25
Distributions	—	—	—	25	45	75

Operating results are the sum of realized results from exiting portfolio companies and unrealized results from the revaluation of investments presently held in portfolio companies. In addition to the information available on EVP I, Hornsby also knows from the fund prospectus that the distribution waterfall is calculated according to the total return method, in which the GP receives carried interest only after the fund has returned the entire committed capital to LPs. Management fees are calculated on the basis of the paid-in capital. Hornsby also wants to calculate DPI, RVPI, and TVPI of EVP I for 2019, and he is interested in understanding how to calculate gross and net IRRs.

1. Interpret and compare the financial performance of EVP I and EVP II.
2. Calculate the management fees, the carried interest, and the NAV of EVP I. Also calculate DPI, RVPI, and TVPI of EVP I for 2019. Explain on the basis of EVP I how gross and net IRRs are calculated.

Solution to 1: In the table above, the first venture capital fund (EVP I) made its initial capital call in 2014 and returned to LPs €1.26 (all amounts in millions) for every €1 that had been drawn down two years ahead of the termination of the fund. EVP I residual value remains high, at 1.29 times capital drawn down, which is a good signal about the profitability of the fund at termination. The fund ranks in the first quartile, which means it belongs to the best-performing funds of that category and vintage year. Gross IRR of 16.1% after six years of operations and 11.3% net of fees represents good performance.

The second fund exhibits very modest performance to date in terms of gross and net IRR, which indicates that the fund is still experiencing the J-curve effect. EVP II has returned to LPs 35% of capital drawn down and a residual value of 113% of the capital drawn down, which indicates that despite the fund being in its early years, the GP has already managed a number of profitable exits and increased the value of the investment portfolio halfway through the termination of the fund. Actual fund size significantly exceeds previous fund size and is an indication that the GP is gaining momentum in terms of fundraising, probably partly attributable to the strong performance of the first fund.

Solution to 2: Cash Flows and Distributions (€ Millions)

Year	Called Down (1)	Paid-In Capital (2)	Mgmt. Fees (3)	Operating Results (4)	NAV before Distributions (5)	Carried Interest (6)	Distributions (7)	NAV after Distributions (8)
2014	50	50	1.0	−5	44.0			44.0
2015	15	65	1.3	−15	42.7			42.7
2016	10	75	1.5	25	76.2			76.2
2017	25	100	2.0	45	144.2	3.8	25	115.4
2018	10	110	2.2	55	178.2	6.8	45	126.4
2019	5	115	2.3	105	234.1	11.2	75	147.9

Based on this table, the calculations of DPI, RVPI, and TVPI can be derived as follows:

- Paid-in capital = Cumulative capital called down (Column 2).
- Management fees = (2%) × (Column 2).
- Carried interest: The first year that NAV is higher than committed capital (€125 million), carried interest is 20% of the excess, or (20%) [(NAV in Column 5) − €125 million].

Thereafter, provided that NAV before distribution exceeds committed capital, carried interest is (20%) × (Increase in NAV before distributions). Carried interest in 2019 is calculated as follows: (20%) × (€234.1 million − €178.2 million).

- NAV before distributions = NAV after distributions$_{t-1}$ + (Column 1) − (Column 3) + (Column 4).
- NAV after distributions = (Column 5) − (Column 6) − (Column 7).
- DPI = (€25 + €45 + €75)/€115, or 1.26×.
- RVPI = €147.9/€115, or 1.29×.
- TVPI = 1.26× + 1.29× = 2.55×.

The IRRs may be developed as follows:

- Gross IRRs are estimated by calculating the internal rate of return for the following cash flows: called-down capital at the beginning of period (Column 1) and the previous year's operating results (Column 4).
- Net IRRs are estimated by calculating the internal rate of return for the following cash flows: called-down capital at the beginning of period (Column 1) and the previous year's operating results (Column 4), net of management fees (Column 3) and carried interest (Column 6). Cash flows for gross and net IRRs are shown in the following table. Gross IRR and net IRR are shown in the bottom row.

Year End	Called Down	Operating Results	Cash Flows Gross IRR	Mgmt. Fees	Carried Interest	Cash Flows Net IRR
2013	50		−50			−50.0
2014	15	−5	−20	1.0		−21.0
2015	10	−15	−25	1.3		−26.3
2016	25	25	0	1.5		−1.5
2017	10	45	35	2.0	3.8	29.2
2018	5	55	50	2.2	6.8	41.0
2019		105	105	2.3	11.2	91.5
IRR			16.1%			11.3%

SUMMARY

- Private equity funds seek to add value by various means, including optimizing financial structures, incentivizing management, and creating operational improvements.
- Private equity can be thought of as an alternative system of governance for corporations. Rather than ownership and control being separated as in most publicly quoted companies, private equity concentrates ownership and control. Many view the combination of ownership and control as a fundamental source of the returns earned by the best private equity funds.
- A critical role for the GP is valuation of potential investments. But because these investments are usually privately owned, valuation encounters many challenges.
- Valuation techniques differ according to the nature of the investment. Early-stage ventures require very different techniques than leveraged buyouts. Private equity professionals tend

to use multiple techniques when performing a valuation, and they explore many different scenarios for the future development of the business.

* In buyouts, the availability of debt financing can have a big impact on the scale of private equity activity, and it seems to impact valuations observed in the market.
* Because private equity funds are incentivized to acquire, add value, and then exit within the lifetime of the fund, they are considered buy-to-sell investors. Planning the exit route for the investment is a critical role for the GP, and a well-timed and well-executed investment can be a significant source of realized value.
* In addition to the problems encountered by the private equity funds in valuing potential portfolio investments, challenges exist in valuing the investment portfolio on an ongoing basis. This is because the investments have no easily observed market value and there is a large element of judgment involved in valuing each of the portfolio companies prior to their sale by the fund.
* The two main metrics for measuring the ongoing and ultimate performance of private equity funds are IRR and multiples. Comparisons of PE returns across funds and with other assets are demanding because it is important to control for the timing of cash flows, differences in risk and portfolio composition, and vintage-year effects.

REFERENCES

Jensen, M. 1986. "Agency Costs of Free Cash Flow, Corporate Finance, and Takeovers." *American Economic Review* 76 (2): 323–29.
Jensen, M. 1989. "Eclipse of the Public Corporation." *Harvard Business Review* 67 (September–October).
Modigliani, F., and M. Miller. 1958. "The Cost of Capital, Corporation Finance and the Theory of Investment." *American Economic Review* 48 (3): 261–97.
Rouvinez, C. 2003. "Private Equity Benchmarking with PME+." *Venture Capital Journal* (1 August).

PROBLEMS

1. Jo Ann Ng is a senior analyst at SING INVEST, a large regional mid-market buyout manager in Singapore. She is considering the exit possibilities for an existing investment in a mature automotive parts manufacturer that was acquired three years ago at a multiple of 7.5 times EBITDA. SING INVEST originally anticipated exiting its investment in China Auto Parts, Inc., within three to six years. Ng noted that market conditions have deteriorated and that companies operating in a similar business trade at an average multiple of 5.5 times EBITDA. She expects, however, based on analyst reports and industry knowledge, that the market will recover strongly within the next two years because of the fast-increasing demand for cars in emerging markets. Upon review of market opportunities, Ng also noted that China Gear Box, Inc., a smaller Chinese automotive parts manufacturer that presents strong potential synergies with China Auto Parts, Inc., is available for sale at an EBITDA multiple of 4.5. Exits by means of an IPO or a trade sale to a financial or strategic (company) buyer are possible in China. How would you advise Ng to enhance value upon exit of China Auto Parts?

2. Wenda Lee, CFA, is a portfolio manager at a UK-based private equity institutional investor. She is considering an investment in a mid-market European buyout fund to achieve better diversification for her firm's private equity portfolio. She short-listed two funds that she sees as having similar risk–return profiles. Before deciding which one to invest in, she is carefully reviewing and comparing the terms of each fund.

	Mid-market Fund A	Mid-market Fund B
Management fees	2.5%	1.5%
Transaction fees	100% to the GP	50–50% split
Carried interest	15%	20%
Hurdle rate	6%	9%
Clawback provision	No	Yes
Distribution waterfall	Deal by deal	Total return

Based on the analysis of terms, which fund would you recommend to Lee?

3. Jean-Pierre Dupont is the chief investment officer (CIO) of a French pension fund that allocates a substantial portion of its assets to private equity. The fund's PE portfolio comprises mainly large buyout funds and mezzanine funds with a limited allocation to a special situations fund. A decision has been made to increase allocations to European venture capital. The investment committee of the pension fund requested that Dupont present an analysis of five key investment characteristics specific to venture capital relative to buyout investing. Can you assist Dupont in this request?

4. Discuss the ways that private equity funds can create value.

5. What problems are encountered when using comparable publicly traded companies to value private acquisition targets?

6. What are the main ways that the performance of private equity limited partnerships can be measured (A) during the life of the fund and (B) once all investments have been exited?

The following information relates to Questions 7–12.

Martha Brady is the CIO of the Upper Darby County (UDC) public employees' pension system. Brady is considering an allocation of the pension system's assets to private equity. She has asked two of her analysts, Jennifer Chau, CFA, and Matthew Hermansky, to provide more information about the workings of the private equity market.

Brady recognizes that the private equity asset class covers a broad spectrum of equity investments that are not traded in public markets. She asks Chau to describe the major differences between assets within this asset class. Chau notes that private equity ranges from venture capital financing of early-stage companies to complete buyouts of large publicly traded or even privately held companies. Chau describes some of the characteristics of venture capital and buyout investments.

Chau mentions that private equity firms take care to align the economic interests of the managers of the investments they control with their own. Various contractual clauses are inserted in the compensation contracts of the management team in order to reward or punish managers who meet or do not meet agreed-upon target objectives.

One concern Chau highlights is the illiquidity of private equity investments over time. Some funds are returned to investors, however, over the life of the fund because a number of investment opportunities are exited early. Provisions in a fund's prospectus describe the distribution of returns to investors, some of which favor the limited partners. One such provision is the distribution waterfall mechanism that provides distributions to limited partners (LPs) before the general partner (GP) receives the carried interest. This distribution mechanism is called the total return waterfall.

Chau prepares the following data to illustrate the distribution waterfall mechanism and the funds provided to limited partners when a private equity fund with a zero hurdle rate exits from its first three projects during a three-year period.

EXHIBIT 1   Investment Returns and Distribution Waterfalls

Private equity committed capital	$400 million
Carried interest	20%
First project investment capital	$20 million
Second project investment capital	$45 million
Third project investment capital	$50 million
Proceeds from first project	$25 million
Proceeds from second project	$35 million
Proceeds from third project	$65 million

Chau cautions that investors must understand the terminology used to describe the performance of private equity funds. Interpretation of performance numbers should be made with the awareness that much of the fund assets are illiquid during a substantial part of the fund's life. She provides the latest data in Exhibit 2 for the Alpha, Beta, and Gamma Funds, diversified high-technology venture capital funds formed five years ago, each with five years remaining to termination.

EXHIBIT 2   Financial Performance of Alpha, Beta, and Gamma Funds

Fund	PIC	DPI	RVPI
Alpha	0.30	0.10	0.65
Beta	0.85	0.10	1.25
Gamma	0.85	1.25	0.75

Chau studies the data and comments that of the three funds, the Alpha Fund has the best chance to outperform over the remaining life. First, it's because the management has earned such a relatively high residual value on capital and will be able to earn a high return on the remaining funds called down. At termination, the RVPI will be double the 0.65 value when the rest of the funds are called down. Second, its cash-on-cash return as measured by DPI is already as high as that of the Beta Fund. The PIC (or paid-in capital) ratio indicates the proportion of capital already called by the GP. The PIC of Alpha is relatively low relative to Beta and Gamma.

Hermansky notes that a private equity fund's ability to properly plan and execute its exit from an investment is vital for the fund's success. Venture funds, such as Alpha, Beta, and Gamma, take special care to plan their exits.

Brady then asks the analysts what procedures private equity firms would use to value investments in their portfolios as well as investments that are added later. She is concerned about buying into a fund with existing assets that do not have public market prices that can be used to ascertain value. In such cases, she worries, what if a GP overvalues the assets and new investors in the fund pay more for the fund assets than they are worth?

Hermansky makes three statements regarding the valuation methods used in private equity transactions during the early stages of selling a fund to investors:

Statement 1: For venture capital investment in the early stages of analysis, emphasis is placed on the discounted cash flow approach to valuation.

Statement 2: For buyout investments, income-based approaches are used frequently as a primary method of valuation.

Statement 3: If a comparable group of companies exist, multiples of revenues or earnings are used frequently to derive a value for venture capital investments.

7. The characteristic that is *most likely* common to both the venture capital and buyout private equity investment is:
   A. measurable and assessable risk.
   B. the extensive use of financial leverage.
   C. the strength of the individual track record and ability of members of management.

8. The contractual term enabling management of the private equity–controlled company to be rewarded with increased equity ownership as a result of meeting performance targets is called:
   A. a ratchet.
   B. the tag-along right.
   C. the clawback provision.

9. For the projects described in Exhibit 1, under a deal-by-deal method with a clawback provision and true-up every three years, the cumulative dollar amount the GP receives by the end of the three years is equal to:
   A. 1 million.
   B. 2 million.
   C. 3 million.

10. Are Chau's two reasons for interpreting Alpha Fund as the best-performing fund over the remaining life correct?
   A. No
   B. Yes
   C. The first reason is correct, but the second reason is incorrect.

11. The exit route for a venture capital investment is *least likely* to be in the form of a(n):
   A. initial public offering (IPO).
   B. sale to other venture funds targeting the same sector.
   C. buyout by the management of the venture investment.

12. Which statement by Hermansky is the *least* valid?
   A. Statement 1
   B. Statement 2
   C. Statement 3

The following information relates to questions 13–18.

Daniel Collin is a junior analyst at JRR Equity Partners (JRR), a private equity firm. Collin is assigned to work with Susan Tseng, a senior portfolio manager. Tseng and Collin meet to discuss existing and potential investments.

Tseng starts the meeting with a discussion of LBO firms and VC firms. Collin tells Tseng,

> *LBO firms tend to invest in companies with predictable cash flows and experienced management teams, whereas VC firms tend to invest in companies with high EBITDA or EBIT growth and where an exit is fairly predictable.*

Tseng and Collin next analyze a potential investment in the leveraged buyout of Stoneham Industries. Specifically, they assess the expected gain if they elect to purchase all of the preference shares and 90% of the common equity through the LBO. Details of the LBO include the following:

- The buyout requires an initial investment of $10 million.
- Financing for the deal includes $6 million in debt, $3.6 million in preference shares that promise a 15% annual return paid at exit, and $0.4 million in common equity.

The expected exit value in six years is $15 million, with an estimated reduction in debt of $2.8 million over the six years prior to exit.

Tseng and Collin next discuss JRR's investment in Venture Holdings, a private equity fund. Selected details on the Venture Holdings fund include the following:

- Total committed capital is $115 million.
- The distribution waterfall follows the deal-by-deal method, and carried interest is 20%.
- On its first exit event a few years ago, the fund generated a $10 million profit.

At the end of the most recent year, cumulative paid-in capital was $98 million, cumulative distributions paid out to LPs were $28 million, and the year-end NAV, before and after distributions, was $170.52 million and $131.42 million, respectively.
Tseng and Collin estimate that the fund's NAV before distributions will be $242.32 million at the end of next year.

Finally, Tseng and Collin evaluate two venture capital funds for potential investment: the Squire Fund and the Treble Fund. Both funds are in Year 7 of an estimated 10-year term. Selected data for the two funds are presented in Exhibit 3.

EXHIBIT 3   Selected Data for the Squire Fund and the Treble Fund

	Squire Fund	Treble Fund
DPI	0.11	0.55
RVPI	0.95	0.51
Gross IRR	−11%	10%
Net IRR	−20%	8%

After reviewing the performance data in Exhibit 3, Collin draws the following conclusions:

Conclusion 1:   The unrealized return on investment for the Squire Fund is greater than the unrealized return on investment for the Treble Fund.

Conclusion 2:   The TVPI for the Treble Fund is higher than the TVPI for the Squire Fund because the Treble Fund has a higher gross IRR.

13. Is Collin's statement about LBO firms and VC firms correct?
    A. Yes
    B. No, because he is wrong with respect to VC firms
    C. No, because he is wrong with respect to LBO firms

14. The multiple of expected proceeds at exit to invested funds for JRR's Stoneham LBO investment is *closest* to:
    A. 2.77.
    B. 2.89.
    C. 2.98.

15. The distribution available to the limited partners of the Venture Holdings fund from the first exit is *closest* to:
    A. $2 million.
    B. $8 million.
    C. $10 million.

16. At the end of the most recent year, the ratio of total value to paid-in capital (TVPI) for the Venture Holdings fund was *closest* to:
    A. 0.29.
    B. 1.34.
    C. 1.63.

17. Based on Tseng and Collin's estimate of NAV next year, the estimate of carried interest next year is *closest* to:
    A. $14.36 million.
    B. $22 million.
    C. $25.46 million.

18. Which of Collin's conclusions regarding the Squire Fund and the Treble Fund is correct?
    A. Only Conclusion 1
    B. Only Conclusion 2
    C. Both Conclusion 1 and Conclusion 2

CHAPTER 5

INTRODUCTION TO COMMODITIES AND COMMODITY DERIVATIVES

David Burkart, CFA, and James Alan Finnegan, CAIA, RMA, CFA

LEARNING OUTCOMES

The candidate should be able to:

- compare characteristics of commodity sectors;
- compare the life cycle of commodity sectors from production through trading or consumption;
- contrast the valuation of commodities with the valuation of equities and bonds;
- describe types of participants in commodity futures markets;
- analyze the relationship between spot prices and futures prices in markets in contango and markets in backwardation;
- compare theories of commodity futures returns;
- describe, calculate, and interpret the components of total return for a fully collateralized commodity futures contract;
- contrast roll return in markets in contango and markets in backwardation;
- describe how commodity swaps are used to obtain or modify exposure to commodities;
- describe how the construction of commodity indexes affects index returns.

1. INTRODUCTION

In the upcoming sections, we present the characteristics and valuation of commodities and commodity derivatives. Given that investment in commodities is conducted primarily through futures markets, the concepts and theories behind commodity futures is a primary focus of the chapter. In particular, the relationship between spot and futures prices, as well as the underlying components of futures returns, are key analytical considerations.

What do we mean when we talk about investing in commodities? A basic economic definition is that a commodity is a physical good attributable to a natural resource that is tradable and supplied without substantial differentiation by the general public.

Commodities trade in physical (spot) markets and in futures and forward markets. Spot markets involve the physical transfer of goods between buyers and sellers; prices in these markets reflect current (or very near term) supply and demand conditions. Global commodity futures markets constitute financial exchanges of standardized futures contracts in which a price is established in the market today for the sale of some defined quantity and quality of a commodity at a future date of delivery; completion of the contract may permit cash settlement or require physical delivery.

Commodity futures exchanges allow for risk transfer and provide a valuable price discovery mechanism that reflects the collective views of all market participants with regard to the future supply and demand prospects of a commodity. Given the financial (versus physical) nature of their contract execution, commodity exchanges allow important parties beyond traditional suppliers and buyers—speculators, arbitrageurs, private equity, endowments, and other institutional investors—to participate in these price discovery and risk transfer processes. Standardized contracts and organized exchanges also offer liquidity (i.e., trading volumes) to facilitate closing, reducing, expanding, or opening new hedges or exposures as circumstances change on a daily basis.

Forward markets exist alongside futures markets in certain commodities for use by entities that require customization in contract terms. Forwards are largely outside the scope of this reading and are discussed only briefly. Exposure to commodities is also traded in the swap markets for both speculative and hedging purposes. Investment managers may want to establish swap positions to match certain portfolio needs, whereas producers may want to more precisely adjust their commodity risk (e.g., the origin of their cattle or the chemical specifications of their crude oil).

Commodities offer the potential for diversification benefits in a multi-asset class portfolio because of historically low average return correlation with stocks and bonds. In addition, certain academic studies (e.g., Gorton and Rouwenhorst 2006; Erb and Harvey 2006) demonstrate that some commodities have historically had inflation hedging qualities.

Our coverage of the commodities topic is organized as follows: We provide an overview of physical commodity markets, including the major sectors, their life cycles, and their valuation. We then describe futures market participants, commodity futures pricing, and the analysis of commodity returns, including the concepts of contango and backwardation. The subsequent section reviews the use of swap instruments rather than futures to gain exposure to commodities. We then review the various commodity indexes given their importance as benchmarks for the asset class and investment vehicles. Finally, we conclude with a summary of the major points.

2. COMMODITY SECTORS

Commodities are an asset class inherently different from traditional financial assets, such as equities and bonds. These latter assets are securities that are claims on productive capital assets and/or financial assets and thus are expected to generate cash flows for their owners. The intrinsic value of these securities is the present discounted value of their expected future cash flows. Commodities are valued differently. Commodities' value derives from either their use as consumables or as inputs to the production of goods and services. Because a number of commodities need to be processed or have a limited life before spoiling or decaying, an astute analyst will take into account the growth and extraction patterns of the various commodities as well as the logistics associated with transporting these physical goods. Therefore, commodities, while seemingly familiar from everyday life, offer distinct sets of risk exposures for investors.

Fundamental analysis of commodities relies on analyzing supply and demand for each of the products as well as estimating the reaction to the inevitable shocks to their equilibrium or underlying direction. For example, a growing world population demands more crude oil or related products as transportation of goods and people increases. However, technological improvements (e.g., shale drilling or electric vehicles) can disrupt that trend and in the case of armed conflict or adverse weather, for example, may alter it on very short notice! This means that the quantitative analysis of commodities is often imperfect because of high degrees of non-normalcy and shifting correlations. Furthermore, the coefficients to underlying variables are often non-stationary; for example, much corn today is genetically modified to resist heat, rendering drought impact estimates derived from history less predictive. Much of the raw data are held off market by private firms engaged in the commodity industry (such as oil or agricultural companies), which also hinders a purely quantitative approach. Therefore, the framework offered here will be at a high level. We will later provide a breakdown of individual areas for the investor to apply discretionary or quantitative techniques, as circumstances allow. Because the framework can be applied to both supply and demand, we shall set that distinction aside until we focus on individual sectors and commodities. The tools and considerations in fundamental analysis are as follows:

A. Direct announcements: Various government agencies and private companies broadcast production and inventory data that can be used to infer demand, which is often unobservable. Possible public sources include the USDA (US Department of Agriculture), OPEC (Organization of the Petroleum Exporting Countries), the NBS (National Bureau of Statistics of China), and the IEA (International Energy Agency). Setting aside questions of reliability, sometimes estimating current conditions is as straightforward as monitoring official announcements, even with a lag.

B. Component analysis: The more diligent analyst will attempt to break down high-level supply and demand into various components. Applying a stock and flow approach is a logical method. The stock or potential production or demand attempts to set boundaries around what is actually produced or wanted. This can be as general as the amount of arable land in all of Europe or as specific as the current capacity of the Ghawar oil field in Saudi Arabia. The flow considers the utilization of that stock of raw material. Examples include understanding the oil tanker traffic heading to China, estimating the historical yields of US cotton (the amount of fiber per unit of land) in various weather conditions, and estimating the number of piglets per mother hog in Canada.

These examples lend themselves to historical quantitative or conditional analysis. However, care needs to be taken regarding the qualitative aspects of supply and demand; a new policy such as stricter emissions standards can affect both supply (higher standards often strand lower-quality materials) and demand (not all consumers may be properly equipped to utilize a changing standard). Political unrest may not touch an isolated farm but may disrupt consumption.

C. Timing considerations: Stocks and flows from (b) can be further affected by timing issues—such as seasonality and logistics—and, therefore, price reaction. A shock, by definition, is a sudden timing switch; an earthquake that destroys a pipeline does not affect the stock, but it does halt the flow. A more common consideration is seasonality, such as the growing period for crops and people's demand for winter heat generated from natural gas. This last aspect in particular feeds into the shape of the commodity futures curve, as discussed later.

D. Money flow: Short-term and long-term prices can be affected by sentiment and macro monetary conditions, such as inflation. If investor risk tolerance is particularly high or low, then expecting exaggerated price movements would be rational as fundamental conditions are hyped up or beaten down. Alternatively, capital availability from low interest rates can help trigger the building of new mines and affect future supply. Government subsidies of substitute technologies can limit commodity price appreciation (e.g., available funds for electric cars indirectly affect the price of gasoline).

In summary, although the casual investor can perhaps focus solely on public summary statements, the engaged researcher will apply a framework of examining the stock and flow components and their related timing to better understand and weigh the pressures leading to higher or lower prices.

2.1. Commodity Sectors

The world of commodities is relatively broad but can be defined and separated in a reasonable manner. Although there are several ways to segment the asset class by sector, here we use the approach that is the basis for the Bloomberg Commodity Index: energy, grains, industrial (base) metals, livestock, precious metals, and softs (cash crops). This segmentation is more granular than some other indexes but is reasonably consistent with the breakdown in the specialties of most market participants. As noted previously, each sector has a number of individual characteristics that are important in determining the supply and demand for each commodity. A key concept is how easily and cost-effectively the commodity can be produced and stored, as well as such related issues as frequency/timing of consumption, spoilage, insurance, and ease of transportation to consumers. Note that many commodities, such as uranium or water, are traded only in thin, private markets. They are really just individual transactions, as opposed to the markets we are discussing. For the purposes of our coverage, we have to constrain ourselves to primary commodities, recognizing that there are many others that may offer investment opportunities or require hedging. Exhibit 1 reviews each sector and its main characteristics and influences.

EXHIBIT 1   A Description of Commodity Sectors and Factors

	Energy: Fuel transportation, industrial production, and electrical generation. Primary commodities include crude oil, natural gas, coal, and refined products, such as gasoline and heating oil.	
Primary Influences	Stocks: Discovery and depletion of new fields, economic and political costs/ certainty of access to those fields, refinery technology and maintenance, power plant type and construction, economic (GDP) size	Flows: Pipeline and tanker reliability, seasonality (summer/winter), adverse weather (cold, hurricanes), automobile/ truck sales, geopolitical instability, environmental requirements, economic (GDP) growth
	Grains: Provide human and animal sustenance but also can be distilled into fuel (e.g., ethanol). Primary commodities include corn, soy, wheat, and rice.	

Primary Influences	Stocks: Arable farmland, storage/port facilities (infrastructure), human and animal population size	Flows: Weather (moisture, temperature), disease, consumer preferences, genetic modification, biofuel substitution, population growth

Industrial/Base Metals: Materials for durable consumer goods, industry, and construction. Primary commodities include copper, aluminum, nickel, zinc, lead, tin, and iron.

Primary Influences	Stocks: Mined acreage, smelter capacity, economic (GDP) stage of industrial/consumer development	Flows: Government industrial and environmental policies, economic (GDP) growth, automobile/truck sales, infrastructure investment

Livestock: Animals raised for human consumption. Primary commodities include hogs, cattle, sheep, and poultry.

Primary Influences	Stocks: Herd size, processing plant capacity, consumer preferences, feed availability/cost	Flows: Speed of maturation to slaughter weight, economic (GDP) growth/consumer income, disease, adverse weather

Precious Metals: Certain metals that act as monetary stores of value (as well as industrial uses). Primary commodities include gold, silver, and platinum.

Primary Influences	Stocks: Mined acreage, smelter capacity, fiat money supply/banking development	Flows: Central bank monetary policy, geopolitics, economic (GDP) growth

Softs (Cash Crops): Crops sold for income—as opposed to consumed for subsistence—and often originally seen as luxuries. Primary commodities include cotton, cocoa, sugar, and coffee.

Primary Influences	Stocks: Arable farmland, storage/port facilities (infrastructure), economic (GDP) size	Flows: Weather (moisture, temperature), disease, consumer preferences, biofuel substitution, economic (GDP) growth/consumer income

As noted in this section, each commodity sector is unique in its fundamental drivers but with the overlapping context of economic and monetary data. With this context in mind, we will now examine the life cycle of the sectors from production to consumption—and their interaction—in more detail.

EXAMPLE 1   Commodity Sector Demand

Industrial activity *most likely* affects the demand for which of the following commodities?

A. Copper
B. Natural gas
C. Softs (e.g., cotton, coffee, sugar and cocoa)

Solution: A is correct. Copper is used for construction, infrastructure development, and the manufacture of durable goods, all of which are economically sensitive. B is incorrect because demand for natural gas is driven primarily by weather conditions (heating or cooling) and only secondarily by industrial activity. C is incorrect because demand for softs is driven primarily by global income.

EXAMPLE 2   Commodity Sector Risks

Which of the following commodity sectors are *least* affected in the short term by weather-related risks?

A. Energy
B. Livestock
C. Precious metals

Solution: C is correct. Weather has very little impact on the availability of precious metals given their ease of storage. Inflation expectations, fund flows, and industrial production are more important factors. A is incorrect because energy demand is strongly influenced by weather (e.g., heating demand in the winter or transportation demand in the summer). B is incorrect because the health of livestock is vulnerable to unfavorable weather conditions increasing the risks of death and disease by extreme cold, wet, and heat.

---

3. LIFE CYCLE OF COMMODITIES

The life cycle of commodities varies considerably depending on the economic, technical, and structural (i.e., industry, value chain) profile of each commodity, as well as the sector. Conceptually, the commodity production life cycle reflects and amplifies the changes in storage, weather, and political/economic events that shift supply and demand. Recall from the earlier discussion that timing/seasonality is, in effect, an overlay on top of the underlying supply/demand factors. A short life cycle allows for relatively rapid adjustment to outside events, whereas a long life cycle generally limits the ability of supply or demand to react to new conditions. These shifts, in turn, feed into the economics for the valuation and shape of the commodity supply and demand curves, plus their respective price elasticities of demand and supply. Understanding the life cycle builds understanding of, and ideally ability to forecast, what drives market actions and commodity returns.

Among the food commodities, agriculture and livestock have well-defined seasons and growth cycles that are specific to geographic regions. For example, by March of each year, corn planting may be finished in the southern United States but not yet started in Canada. Meanwhile, the corn harvest may be underway in Brazil and Argentina given their reverse seasonal cycle in the Southern Hemisphere. Each geographic location also represents local markets that have different domestic and export demand. These differences affect the nature (level and reliability) of demand and the power of buyers to extend or contract the life cycle.

In comparison, commodities in the energy and metals sectors are extracted all year round. Their life cycle changes are generally at the margin of a continuous process, as opposed to being centered at a discrete time or season. But the products from crude oil and metal ore have seasonal demands depending on weather (e.g., gasoline demand in the summer and heating oil demand in the winter) that affect the life cycle and usage of the underlying commodity. And with all the differences between the varieties even within the same sector, the life cycles depicted have to be representative and selective. The life cycles of several key commodity sectors are as follows.

3.1. Energy

For an example of the differences within a sector, one need look no further than energy. Natural gas can be consumed almost immediately after extraction from the ground. Crude oil, in contrast, has to be transformed into something else; crude is useless in its innate form. The refined products (e.g., gasoline and heating oil), in turn, have a number of potential processing steps depending on the quality of crude oil input and the relative demand for the various products. The steps for the energy complex can be summarized as shown in Exhibit 2.

EXHIBIT 2   Steps for the Energy Complex

Step	Title	Description
1.	Extraction	A drilling location is selected after surveys, and the well is dug. Enough underground pressure for the hydrocarbons to come out naturally may exist, or water or other tools may be required to create such pressure. Water is also used for the fracturing process known as fracking, which breaks up shale formations to allow for oil or gas to be extracted.
2.	Storage	After extraction, crude oil is commercially stored for a few months on average in the United States, Singapore, and northern Europe and is strategically stored by many countries. In addition, oil may temporarily be stored on tanker ships. Natural gas may be delivered directly to the end consumer. Summer-extracted natural gas is often injected into storage for the winter months.
3.	Consumption Stage	Only natural gas is consumed at this stage because it does not need to be refined. Crude oil requires further processing.
4.	Refining	Crude oil is distilled into its component parts via a process called cracking. Heat is used to successively boil off the components that are, in turn, cooled down and collected (e.g., gasoline, kerosene), until only the remnants (e.g., asphalt) are left.
5.	Consumption Stage	The distilled products are separated and shipped to their various locations—by ship, pipe, train, or truck—for use by the end consumer.

Sources: Based on information from www.eia.gov/energyexplained/index.php?page=oil_refining#tab1, https://en.wikipedia.org/wiki/Petroleum_refining_processes (accessed 23 April 2019), and authors' research.

Refineries are extraordinarily expensive to build—typically costing several billion US dollars—depending on the processes required to purify and distill the oil. Part of the cost depends on the expected specifications of the crude oil input. Generally speaking, a low-grade, high sulfur source would require more investment than one with an assured lighter, "sweeter" source. Pipelines are also very costly. For example, the Keystone XL pipeline expansion between Canada and the United States was originally estimated to cost $5 billion in 2010, but the estimate was doubled to $10 billion in 2014. Even in countries dealing with violent insurrections (e.g., Libya, Iraq, Nigeria), damage to refineries has been generally modest because of their value to all parties. Pipelines, however, are often destroyed or cut off. Although these costs may appear staggering, they actually pale in comparison with the costs (and risks) of oil exploration, especially in deep offshore locations or geographically remote (or geopolitically risky) regions.

The crude oil market has a number of futures contracts and indexes that follow local grades and origins, but the two most commonly traded set of contracts follow the US-based crude oil (West Texas Intermediate, or WTI, crude oil) and the UK-located Brent crude oil from the North Sea. Likewise, there are futures for natural gas, gasoil, gasoline, and heating oil. Each has different delivery locations and standards, but the WTI and Brent contracts represent a high-quality refinery input that exploration and production companies can use as a hedging device.

EXAMPLE 3   Energy Life Cycle

Which of the following is a primary difference in the production life cycle between crude oil and natural gas?

A. Only crude oil needs to be stored.
B. European companies are the only ones that store crude oil.
C. Natural gas requires very little additional processing after extraction compared with crude oil.

Solution: C is correct. Natural gas can be used after it is extracted from the ground upon delivery, but crude oil must first be processed for later use. A is incorrect because both oil and natural gas are stored before usage. B is incorrect because many countries around the world store crude oil, both commercially and strategically.

3.2. Industrial/Precious Metals

The life cycle of both precious and industrial metals is probably the most flexible because the ore, as well as the finished products, can be stored for months (if not years) given the relative resistance to spoilage of metals (assuming proper storage). Otherwise, the life cycle parallels the energy one outlined previously, as shown in Exhibit 3.

EXHIBIT 3   Copper Purification Process

	Step Name	Description
1.	Extracting and Preparing	Ore (raw earth with ~2% metal content) is removed via a mine or open pit. Ore is then ground into powder and concentrated to roughly 25% purity.
2.	Smelting	The purified ore is heated, and more impurities are removed as slag, increasing the metal content to 60%. Further processes increase the concentration to 99.99%.
3.	Storage/Logistics	The purified metal is held typically in a bonded warehouse until it is shipped to an end user.

Sources: Based on information from http://resources.schoolscience.co.uk/CDA/14-16/cumining/copch2pg1.html (accessed 23 April 2019), www.madehow.com/Volume-4/Copper.html (accessed 23 April 2019), and authors' research.

Similar to refining crude oil, creating the economies of scale involved in the smelter and ore processing plants is critical. These are huge facilities for which marginal costs (i.e., the cost to convert the last pound or kilogram of processed ore into a useful metal) decline substantially with both the scale of the facility and its utilization (output as a percentage of capacity). As a result, when supply exceeds demand for a given industrial metal, it is difficult for suppliers to either cut back production or halt it entirely. Overproduction often continues until smaller or financially weaker competitors are forced to shut down. Because demand for industrial metals fluctuates with overall economic growth, as was discussed previously, there are substantial incentives for metals producers to invest in new capacity when their utilization (and profit) is high but huge economic and financial penalties for operating these facilities when demand falls off during an economic downturn. Ironically, given the typical economic cycle and the time lag involved after deciding to expand capacity, new supply often arrives just as demand is declining—which exacerbates pricing and profit declines.

With the lack of annual seasonality in the production of metals and ease of storage without spoilage, much of time variability comes from the demand side of the equation (e.g., construction and economic growth).

EXAMPLE 4   Industrial Metals Life Cycle

Because of large economies of scale for processing industrial metals, producers:

A. immediately shut down new capacity when supply exceeds demand.
B. have an incentive to maintain maximum operating production levels when demand declines.
C. find it difficult to cut back production or capacity even when supply exceeds demand or demand slows.

Solution: C is correct. Given the sizable facilities in which metals are produced and their capital requirements, reducing capacity is difficult when demand slows. A is incorrect because of the time lag involved in responding to reduced demand conditions. B is incorrect because producers would face financial losses if they maintained maximum production levels when there is a decline in demand.

3.3. Livestock

Livestock grows year round, but good weather and access to high-quality pasture and feed accelerate weight gain. As a result, there is fluctuation in the availability of animals ready for slaughter. The timing to maturity typically increases with size, with poultry maturing in a matter of weeks, hogs in months, and cattle in a few years. Taking the example of a hog, the life cycle begins with a sow (female hog) giving birth. Normally it takes about six months to raise a piglet to slaughter weight, and during that time it can be fed almost anything to get it up to proper bulk. In mass-scale production, soymeal and cornmeal are the most common foods. In contrast, cattle take longer to raise. For mass-scale breeding, the first one to two years are spent as feeder cattle, first eating a grass diet in pasture. The next phase covers an additional

6–12 months whereby cattle are in a feed lot being fattened to slaughter weight, generally on a corn-based diet. Note that the various types of feed for these animals are other traded commodities.

The livestock industry in the United States has historically been among the least export-oriented of all the commodities because of the high risk of spoilage once an animal is slaughtered. However, advances in cryogenics (freezing) technologies with regard to chicken, beef, and pork mean that increasingly these products are moving from one part of the world to another in response to differences in production costs and demand. And as emerging and frontier market countries develop middle class consumers capable of purchasing meat protein as a regular part of their diet, there has been increased investment in the livestock and meatpacking industries in such countries as the United States and Brazil. These industries combine low-cost sources of animal feed, large grazing acreage, and strong domestic demand (leading to facilities with substantial economies of scale) as key export points to supply global demand.

Ranchers and slaughterhouses trade hog and cattle futures to hedge against their commitments. Ranchers can hedge both young cattle that are still in pasture (called feeder cattle) and animals being fattened for butchering (called live cattle).

EXAMPLE 5   Livestock Life Cycle

The US livestock sector has been among the least export-oriented commodity sectors because of:

A. low technological innovation in the sector.
B. high risk of spoilage once animals are slaughtered.
C. little or no demand for US livestock from outside the United States.

Solution: B is correct. Livestock incur a high risk of spoilage once they are slaughtered unless the meat is frozen. A is incorrect because advances in cryogenics have improved the ability to export from the United States. C is incorrect because demand for US livestock has expanded internationally, particularly in emerging market countries that are experiencing economic growth.

3.4. Grains

Grains in the Northern Hemisphere follow a similar growth cycle, with an analogous but opposite growth cycle in the Southern Hemisphere. Plants mature according to the following steps: (1) planting (placing the seeds in the ground after preparation/fertilization work); (2) growth (the emerging of the seedling to full height); (3) pod/ear/head formation (the food grain is created by the plant); and (4) harvest (the collection of the grain by the farmer). The timing in North America is shown in Exhibit 4 to illustrate the time it takes to grow each crop.

EXHIBIT 4   Timing for Grain Production in North America

	Corn	Soybeans	Wheat*
Planting	April–May	May–June	Sep.–Oct.
Growth	June–Aug.	July–Aug.	Nov.–March
Pod/Ear/Head Formation	Aug.–Sep.	Sep.	April–May
Harvest	Sep.–Nov.	Sep.–Oct.	June–July

*The hard winter wheat variety, which has a higher protein content, is used here.

Source: Authors' research.

Because demand for grains is year round, they are regularly stored in silos and warehouses globally. Some countries have a central purchasing bureau, and others depend on local or international trading companies to maintain stockpiles. Poor hygienic standards and logistics can result in a substantial loss of value to grains due to mold or insect/animal infestation. Monitoring the purchasing patterns of these government tenders can assist a research analyst in determining grain demand.

Farmers and consumers can trade futures to hedge their exposure to the crop in question, and the contract delivery months reflect the different times of the growing cycle outlined earlier. Ranchers also can use grain futures to hedge against the cost of feeding an animal.

3.5. Softs

Coffee, cocoa, cotton, and sugar are very different soft commodities in this sector, so we will focus on one that is grown and enjoyed broadly—coffee. Coffee is harvested somewhere all year round in the various countries that circle the equator. After the coffee cherries are picked (still often by hand, to ensure that only ripe ones are taken), the husk and fruit are removed and the remaining bean dried. More than half of coffee uses the dry method in which the harvested cherries are laid out in the sun for two to three weeks. The wet method uses fresh water to soak the cherries, the soft pulp is removed, the bean is fermented for 12–48 hours, and then the bean is dried. The "green" beans are then hulled, sorted, and bagged for their final markets. With most of the consumption in faraway foreign markets, ships are commonly used to transport the beans to their buyer, which may store them in a bonded warehouse. The local buyer roasts the beans and ships them to the retail location (e.g., coffeehouse or supermarket) for purchase or brewing.

Coffee comes in two main varieties, robusta and arabica, although there are many others. Generally speaking, robusta beans are lower quality with less flavor than the arabica. There are two futures contracts associated with coffee: The robusta variety is traded in London, and the arabica variety is traded in New York. Note that the contracts are for the unroasted or "green" beans. The physical delivery aspect of these contracts allows for sellers to deliver the beans to an authorized bonded warehouse as fulfillment of the contract at expiration. Therefore, farmers and distributors can sell futures contracts to hedge the sales price of production, and coffee roasters can buy futures contracts to hedge coffee bean purchase costs; contract maturities can be selected by each to match their product delivery schedules.

4. VALUATION OF COMMODITIES

The valuation of commodities compared with that of equities and bonds can be summarized by the fact that stocks and bonds represent financial assets and are claims on the economic output of a business, a government, or an individual. Commodities, however, are almost always physical assets. We say "almost always" because some newer classes of commodities, such as electricity or weather, are not physical assets in the sense that you can touch or store them.

Commodities are typically tangible items with an intrinsic (but variable) economic value (e.g., a nugget of gold, a pile of coal, a bushel of corn). They do not generate future cash flows beyond what can be realized through their purchase and sale. In addition, the standard financial instruments that are based on commodities are not financial assets (like a stock or bond) but are derivative contracts with finite lifetimes, such as futures contracts. As with other types of derivatives, commodity derivative contracts can and do have value, but they are contingent on some other factors, such as the price of the underlying commodity. Hence, the valuation of commodities is based not on the estimation of future profitability and cash flows but on a discounted forecast of future possible prices based on such factors as the supply and demand of the physical item or the expected volatility of future prices. On the one hand, this forecast may be quite formal and elaborately estimated by a producer or consumer. One can imagine the detailed inputs available to an oil company based on the labor and capital expenses needed to extract oil, refine it, and transport it to final sale as gasoline in your automobile. On the other hand, this forecast may be instinctively made by a floor trader with little fundamental analysis but instead with professional judgment based on years of experience and perhaps some technical analysis.

As opposed to a stock or bond that receives periodic income, owning a commodity incurs transportation and storage costs. These ongoing expenditures affect the shape of the forward price curve of the commodity derivative contracts with different expiration dates. If storage and transportation costs are substantial, the prices for a commodity futures contract will likely be incrementally higher as one looks farther into the future. However, sometimes the current demand for the commodity can move the spot price higher than the futures price. The spot price reflects the fact that, instead of going long a futures contract, one could buy the commodity today and store it until a future date for use. The expenditure would be the outlay/investment at today's spot price for the commodity along with (or net of) the future costs one would incur to store and hold it. This time element of commodity storage and supply and demand can generate "roll return" and affect investment returns. These and other factors figure into the assessment of futures pricing, which we will cover later.

Some commodity contracts require actual delivery of the physical commodity at the end of the contract versus settlement in a cash payment (based on the difference between the contract futures price and the spot price prevailing at the time of contract expiration). The force of arbitrage—which reflects the law of one price—may not be entirely enforced by arbitrageurs because some participants do not have the ability to make or take delivery of the physical commodity. In these situations, the relationships that link spot and futures prices are not an equality but are a range that only indicates the limit or boundary of value differences that can occur.

There is an important additional consideration concerning the link between spot and futures prices in commodities. Some of the largest users of commodity futures are businesses seeking to hedge price risk when that price is a critical source of either revenue or cost in their business operations. For example, the airline industry is very dependent on the cost of jet fuel for operating planes. The highly competitive nature of the industry results in tremendous price pressure on airfares, with a need for airlines to fill each flight with as many passengers as possible. The futures and swap markets for jet fuel allow airlines to lower the risk of higher fuel costs by hedging the price of future fuel purchases (particularly against surprise shocks in oil prices).

In addition, the price discovery process of the commodity futures markets provides airlines with insights about future fuel prices that help determine what prices to offer their customers for future flights while still making a profit. In fact, airline ticket sales are—in effect—selling a contract at a price set today for future delivery of a service—namely, a plane flight. In this case, the airlines will typically hedge their price risk and uncertainty about future fuel costs by purchasing ("going long") energy futures contracts.

EXAMPLE 6 Commodities versus Stocks and Bonds

In contrast to financial assets, such as stocks and bonds:

A. commodities are always physical goods.
B. commodities generate periodic cash flows.
C. commodity investment is primarily via derivatives.

Solution: C is correct. The most common way to invest in commodities is via derivatives. A is incorrect because although most commodities are physical goods, certain newer classes, such as electricity or weather, are not tangible. B is incorrect because commodities may incur, rather than generate, periodic cash flow through transportation and storage costs (when the commodities are physically owned).

EXAMPLE 7 Spot Commodity Valuation

What is a key distinction between the valuation of commodities compared with the valuation of stocks and bonds?

A. Valuation of commodities cannot be conducted using technical analysis.
B. Valuation of commodities focuses on supply and demand, whereas valuation of stocks and bonds focuses on discounted cash flows.
C. Valuation of stocks and bonds focuses on future supply and demand, whereas commodity valuation focuses on future profit margins and cash flow.

Solution: B is correct. The valuation of commodities is based on a forecast of future prices based on supply and demand factors, as well as expected price volatility. In contrast, the valuation of stocks and bonds is based on estimating future profitability and/or cash flow. A is incorrect because technical analysis is sometimes applied to valuing commodities. C is incorrect for the reasons stated for choice B.

5. COMMODITIES FUTURES MARKETS: PARTICIPANTS

Public commodity markets are structured as futures markets—that is, as a central exchange where participants trade standardized contracts to make and take delivery at a specified place at a specified future time. As mentioned, futures contracts are derivatives because the value of the contract is derived from another asset. Both futures and forward contracts are binding agreements that establish a price today for delivery of a commodity in the future (or settlement of the contract in cash at expiration). As mentioned at the beginning of the reading, the focus of this reading is on futures, with forwards discussed only briefly.

5.1. Futures Market Participants

The key differences between futures and forward contracts is that futures contracts are standardized agreements traded on public exchanges, such as the Chicago Mercantile Exchange (CME), Intercontinental Exchange (ICE), and the Shanghai Futures Exchange (SHFE), and gains/losses are marked to market every day. Standardization allows a participant to enter into a contract without ever knowing who the counterparty is. In addition, the exchange oversees trading and margin requirements and provides some degree of self-imposed regulatory oversight. In contrast, forward contracts are commonly bilateral agreements between a known party that wants to go long and one that wants to go short. Because of their bilateral nature, forwards are considered to be OTC (over-the-counter) contracts with less regulatory oversight and much more customization to the specific needs of the hedging (or speculating) party. Often, the counterparty for a forward contract is a financial institution that is providing liquidity or customization in exchange for a fee. Although futures markets require that daily cash movements in the futures price be paid from the losing positions to the winning positions, forward contracts are usually only settled upon expiration or with some custom frequency dictated by the contract.

Early commodity exchanges operated as forward markets, but too often participants would go bankrupt when unrealized losses became realized at the end of the contract. The futures process was introduced to minimize this risk, with the exchange acting as payment guarantor. The first modern organized futures exchange was the Dojima Rice Exchange in Osaka, Japan, which was founded in 1710, although futures contracts were traded in England during the 16th century. The structure of futures markets is important to understand as a way of understanding the goals and roles of the various participants. When we consider any commodity, for every producer of that commodity there is a consumer. Thus, for participants who are long the physical commodity and want to sell it, there are also participants who are short the physical commodity and want to buy it. Therefore, for fairness between the two sets of participants, longs and shorts need to operate on an equal basis. As a coincident observation, the commodity markets are net zero in terms of aggregate futures positions (futures contract longs equal futures contract shorts). In contrast, in markets for stocks and bonds, there is a net long position because the issued stocks' and bonds' market values are equal to the net aggregate positions at the end of each day. Shorting an equity is constrained by the short seller's need to locate shares to short, the requirement to reimburse dividends on borrowed shares, and requirements to post and pay interest on margin that generally exceeds the margin required for long equity positions (as in the United States under Regulation T). In contrast, shorting commodity futures is much simpler, with short investors selling to long investors directly, and thus short investors post the same margin required of long investors.

There are a number of participants in commodity futures markets. First are *hedgers*, who trade in the markets to hedge their exposures related to the commodity. The second are long-term and short-term *traders* and *investors* (including index investors), who speculate on market direction or volatility and provide liquidity and price discovery for the markets in exchange for the expectation of making a profit. Third are the *exchanges* (or clearing houses), which set trading rules and provide the infrastructure of transmitting prices and payments. Fourth are *analysts*, who use the exchange information for non-trading purposes, such as evaluating commodity businesses, creating products that are based on commodity futures (e.g., exchange-traded funds, swaps, and notes), and making public policy decisions. Analysts also include brokers and other financial intermediaries who participate in the markets but do not take a position. Finally, *regulators* of both the exchange and traders exist to monitor and police the markets, investigate malfeasance, and provide a venue for complaints.

5.1.1. Commodity Hedgers

Hedgers tend to be knowledgeable market participants. One would expect that a company that drills for oil knows something about the supply and demand for oil and related forms of energy (at least in the long run). However, hedgers may not be accurate predictors of the future supply and demand for their product. Consider a baker who buys wheat for future delivery and benefits from a surprise drought (has locked in a low price in a supply-constrained market). However, the baker is hurt if the weather is beneficial (has effectively overpaid during a bumper crop). Given that a hedger can make delivery (if short the futures contract) or take delivery (if long the futures contract), he or she is generally motivated by risk mitigation with regard to cash flow, so the risk is more of an opportunity cost than an actual one.

It is important to keep in mind that hedging and speculating are not synonymous with being (respectively) long or short. As Exhibit 5 illustrates with some examples, both long and short positions can be associated with either hedging or speculating.

EXHIBIT 5   Examples of Hedging and Speculating Positions

	Long Position	Short Position
Hedging	Food manufacturer seeking to hedge the price of corn needed for snack chips	Gold mining company seeking to hedge the future price of gold against potential declines
Speculating	Integrated oil company seeking to capitalize on its knowledge of physical oil markets by making bets on future price movements	Commodity trading adviser (CTA) seeking to earn a profit for clients via a macro-commodity investment fund

Note also that hedgers tend to speculate based on their perceived unique insight into market conditions and determine the amount of hedging that is appropriate. From a regulatory standpoint in the United States, the difficulty in clearly distinguishing between hedging and speculating, therefore, has resulted in the separation of commodity producers and consumers from other trading participants regardless of whether commercial participants are actually speculating.

5.1.2. Commodity Traders and Investors

The commodity trading community, like other groups of traders, consists of three primary types: (1) informed investors, (2) liquidity providers, and (3) arbitrageurs. Informed investors largely represent the aforementioned hedgers and speculators, including index and institutional investors. With regard to the hedger, as mentioned previously, a company that drills for oil clearly is familiar with the supply and demand for oil and related forms of energy (at least in the long run). But hedgers may not be accurate predictors of the *future* supply and demand for their product.

Speculators, who believe that they have an information advantage, seek to outperform the hedger by buying or selling futures contracts in conjunction with—or opposite from—the hedger. This trading may be on a micro-second time scale or a multi-month perspective. For example, if a speculator has a superior weather prediction process, he or she has an information advantage and will trade accordingly. Alternatively, a speculator may be willing to act as a liquidity provider, knowing that producers and consumers may not be in the market at the same time. By buying when the producer wants to sell and selling when the consumer is ready to buy, speculators may be able to make a profit. In this sense, speculators are willing to step in, under the right pricing circumstances, to provide insurance to hedgers in return for an expected (albeit not guaranteed) profit.

Finally, arbitrageurs who have the ability to inventory physical commodities can attempt to capitalize on mispricing between the commodity (along with related storage and financing cost) and the futures price. They may own the storage facilities (bonded warehouses, grain silos, feedlots) and work to manage that inventory in conjunction with the futures prices to attempt to make arbitrage-style profits.

5.1.3. Commodity Exchanges
Commodity futures markets are found throughout the world. The CME and ICE are the primary US markets, having consolidated the bulk of the various specialist exchanges. Elsewhere in the Americas, the primary commodity exchange is in Brazil, where B3 trades softs, grains, and livestock. In Europe, the London Metal Exchange (owned by Hong Kong Exchanges and Clearing Limited (HKEX) is the main industrial metals location globally. Energy and shipping are also traded out of London. In Asia, major commodity exchanges include China's Dalian Commodity Exchange and Shanghai Futures Exchange and Japan's Tokyo Commodity Exchange, among others. Finally, Indonesia (palm oil), Singapore (rubber), and Australia (energy, grains, wool) have supplementary commodity futures markets. Given that people all over the world need food, energy, and materials, exchanges have formed globally to meet those needs.

5.1.4. Commodity Market Analysts
Non-market participants use the exchange information to perform research and conduct policy as well as to facilitate market participation. Their activities affect market behavior, albeit in an indirect manner. Research may be commercially based. For example, a manufacturer may want to project and forecast the energy cost of a new process or product as part of an academic study comparing one market structure with another. Commodity prices are a key component in understanding sources of inflation and are used in other indexes that indicate quality of life for consumers and households. Governments that control natural resource extraction (e.g., nationalized oil companies) or tax commodity extraction by private entities are also interested in understanding futures markets to promote or discourage investment and/or raise revenue.

5.1.5. Commodity Regulators
Finally, various regulatory bodies monitor the global commodity markets. In the United States, commodity and futures regulation falls under the Commodity Futures Trading Commission (CFTC), which is a regulatory body separate from the better-known Securities and Exchange

Commission. The CFTC delegates much of the direct monitoring to the National Futures Association (NFA)—a self-regulatory body—whose members are the authorized direct participants in the markets with customer responsibilities (e.g., clearing firms, brokers, advisers).

Outside the United States, most other countries have a unified regulatory structure. For example, the China Securities Regulatory Commission regulates both futures and securities (i.e., stocks and bonds). In Europe, most legislation in the area of financial services is initiated at the European Union (EU) level primarily through the European Securities and Markets Authority (ESMA). The Markets in Financial Instruments Directive (MiFID, and subsequently MiFID II), which first came into force in 2007, was a key element of EU financial market integration that focused largely on deregulation (MiFID II took effect in January 2018). Since 2009, existing legislative instruments, particularly for commodity derivative markets, have been revised and new regulations have been introduced with the aim to strengthen oversight and regulation, and they are subject to G–20 commitments. Harmonizing these different regulatory bodies is the International Organization of Securities Commissions (IOSCO), which is the international association of the world's securities and futures markets.

In all regions, the interests of the financial sector strongly influence debates and legislation on financial market regulation, including that of commodities.

EXAMPLE 8   Commodity Market Participants

Commodity traders that often provide insurance to hedgers are *best* described as:

A. arbitrageurs.
B. liquidity providers.
C. informed investors.

Solution: B is correct. Liquidity providers often play the role of providing an insurance service to hedgers who need to unload and transfer price risk by entering into futures contracts. A is incorrect because arbitrageurs typically seek to capitalize and profit on mispricing due to a lack of information in the marketplace. C is incorrect because informed investors predominantly keep commodity futures markets efficient by capitalizing on mispricing attributable to a lack of information in the marketplace.

---

6. COMMODITY SPOT AND FUTURES PRICING

Commodity prices are typically represented by: (1) spot prices in the physical markets and (2) futures **prices for** later delivery. The **spot price** is simply the current price to deliver a physical commodity to a specific location or purchase it and transport it away from a designated location. Examples of a spot price may be the price quoted at a grain silo, a natural gas pipeline, an oil storage tank, or a sugar refinery.

A **futures price** is a price agreed on to deliver or receive a defined quantity (and often quality) of a commodity at a future date. Although a producer and a consumer can enter into a bilateral contract to exchange a commodity for money in the future, there are (conveniently) many standardized contracts that trade on exchanges for buyers and sellers to use. Recall that a bilateral agreement is a forward contract, compared with a futures contract that is standardized and trades on a futures exchange. One benefit of futures markets is that information regarding contracts (number, price, etc.) is publicly available. In this way, the price discovery process that brings buyers and sellers into agreement is shared broadly and efficiently (in real time) with a global marketplace among the aforementioned market participants. The longest-maturity futures contract outstanding can have maturity extending from about a year (e.g., livestock) to several years (e.g., crude oil).

The difference between spot and futures prices is generally called the **basis**. Depending on the specified commodity and its current circumstances (e.g., supply and demand outlook), the spot price may be higher or lower than the futures price. When the spot price exceeds the futures price, the situation is called **backwardation**, and the opposite case is called **contango**. The origin of the word "contango" is a bit murky, but one theory is that it came from the word "continuation" used in the context of the London Stock Exchange in the mid-1800s. During this period, contango was a fee paid by the buyer to the seller to defer settlement of a trade (hence the near-term price would be less expensive than the longer-term price). The term "backwardation" describes the same arrangement if it were "backward," or reversed (i.e., payment to defer settlement was made by the seller to the buyer).

Backwardation and contango are also used to describe the relationship between two futures contracts of the same commodity. When the near-term (i.e., closer to expiration) futures contract price is higher than the longer-term futures contract price, the futures market for the commodity is in backwardation. In contrast, when the near-term futures contract price is lower than the longer-term futures contract price, the futures market for the commodity is in contango. The price difference (whether in backwardation or contango) is called the calendar spread. Generally speaking and assuming stable spot prices, the producer is willing to take a price in the future that is lower than the current spot price because it provides a level of certainty for the producer's business. The seller of that insurance on the other side of the trade profits because the lower futures price converges to the higher spot price over time. This relationship occurs when future commodity prices are expected to be higher because of a variety of reasons related to economic growth, weather, geopolitical risks, supply disruptions, and so on. As a long owner of a futures contract in contango, value will erode over time as the contract pricing moves closer to the spot price, assuming all else is unchanged. This relationship can be very costly for long holders of contracts if they roll futures positions over time. Although backwardation is "normal" for some contracts, there are other commodities that often trade in contango.

Exhibit 6 is a stylized representation of backwardation in West Texas Intermediate crude oil on CME Group's New York Mercantile Exchange (NYMEX).

For contracts in a single (common) commodity, such as lean hogs or crude oil, the price differences may be traded as a spread rather than individually.

EXHIBIT 6   Backwardation

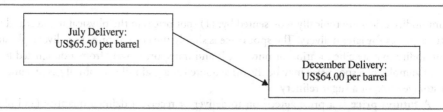

Exhibit 7 is a stylized representation of contango in lean hogs on the CME.

EXHIBIT 7   Contango

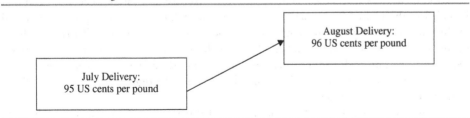

From these examples, the lean hogs July–August calendar spread is −1.0 cent per pound (95 − 96) and the crude oil July–December calendar spread is $1.50 per barrel (65.50 − 64.00).

A positive calendar spread is associated with futures markets that are in backwardation, whereas a negative calendar spread in commodities is associated with futures markets that are in contango. These calendar spreads are traded with their own bid–ask prices, trading range, and order book, similar to the single-month (i.e., nearest to expiration) futures contracts. Note that from this one trade, two contracts (one for each side, or "leg", of the spread) appear on an exchange's trading account and use their respective closing prices to determine profit or loss. Therefore, in the end, all trades and positions are valued at the close-of-day prices.

Commodity futures are settled by either cash or physical delivery. Cash-settled contracts, such as feeder cattle traded on the CME, have no value after the maturity date. Cash settlement is an important innovation in the evolution and development of commodity futures markets. To a certain extent, cash settlement enabled more involvement of two key participants in today's futures markets: speculators and arbitrageurs. It also introduced an entirely new way that hedgers (long or short) could participate in the market to transfer the future price risk of having to sell or buy a commodity without the complications associated with requiring physical delivery. Physical-settled commodity futures contracts require that the title of the actual commodity be transferred by the seller of the futures contract to the buyer at a particular place, on or by a particular date, and of a particular quality specification. For example, under a futures contract with West Texas Intermediate crude oil as the underlying physical commodity, crude oil meeting minimum specifications must be delivered to a particular set of tanks at Cushing, Oklahoma, in the United States. Meanwhile, a similar futures contract with Brent crude oil as the underlying physical commodity has delivery points in the North Sea off the coast of the United Kingdom and Norway. Supply and demand differences at these two faraway geographic locations can cause price divergences despite otherwise similar specifications.

Physical delivery also ensures a convergence of the futures and spot markets, which may not necessarily occur in a cash-settled market. Note that this statement does not imply market manipulation in cash-settled markets, because trading costs or other factors may limit complete convergence. The emergence of central exchanges for trading commodity futures facilitated this convergence with standardized contracts. In addition, these exchanges provided centrally established, publicly available pricing, which quickly replaced private pricing that was dependent on both contract terms and the location where transactions occurred.

Physical delivery can become complicated by such factors as quality or variety differences in the commodity. For example, robusta coffee (traded in the United Kingdom) cannot be delivered for arabica coffee (traded in the United States) because it is a different variety of coffee with a different venue for delivery. Likewise, raw (or unprocessed) sugar that is traded in the United States cannot be delivered for white processed sugar that is traded in the United Kingdom. Futures markets can address some of these peculiarities involving quality or differences in supply. When physical delivery is required, some futures contracts require a premium or discount associated with specifications. For example, arabica coffee prices are automatically adjusted based on the country of origin and the location of the warehouse where delivery is made.

In summary, spot prices are highly localized and associated with physical delivery, limiting the degree to which interested participants can seek to hedge or speculate on their future direction. In contrast, futures prices can be global (and if not, at least regional or national) in scope. They also are standardized for trading on exchanges to promote liquidity; act as a reference price point for customized (i.e., forward) contracts; and generate widely available, minimally biased data for market participants and governments to judge supply and demand and to make planning decisions.

In this manner, futures can be used to allocate risk and generate returns for market participants. On the surface, futures trading may seem muddled and chaotic on a micro level but serves as an overall social benefit by sending signals to producers and consumers for hedging and inventory-sizing purposes and to governments for the potential impact of policy decisions.

EXAMPLE 9   Spot and Futures Pricing (1)

The current price of the futures contract nearest to expiration for West Texas Intermediate (WTI) crude oil is $65.00 per barrel, whereas the six-month futures contract for WTI is priced at $60.75 per barrel. Based on this information:

A. the futures market for WTI crude oil is currently in a state of contango.
B. the futures market for WTI crude oil is currently in a state of backwardation.
C. the shipping and delivery cost of WTI crude oil for a futures contract expiring in six months with physical delivery to Cushing, Texas, is $4.25 per barrel.

Solution: B is correct. Commodity futures markets are in a state of backwardation when the spot price is greater than the price of near-term (i.e., nearest to expiration) futures contracts, and correspondingly, the price of near-term futures contracts is greater than longer-term contracts. A is incorrect because the market would be in contango only if the deferred futures price exceeded that of the nearby futures price. C is incorrect because the shipping and delivery costs associated with physical delivery of a commodity are only one component in determining a commodity futures contract price. Geopolitical, seasonal, and other factors also influence the difference in delivery months.

EXAMPLE 10   Spot and Futures Pricing (2)

An important distinction between spot and futures prices for commodities is that:

A. spot prices are universal across regions, but futures prices vary by location.
B. futures prices do not reflect differences in quality or composition for a commodity.
C. spot prices vary across region based on quality/composition and local supply and demand factors.

Solution: C is correct. Spot prices of commodities vary across regions, reflecting logistical constraints and supply and demand imbalances that hinder the movement of materials. A is incorrect because spot prices tend to vary by region while futures are purposely standardized to facilitate trading. B is incorrect because while futures contracts are based on standardized specifications, composition and quality can be assigned premiums or discounts for delivery.

EXAMPLE 11   Spot and Futures Pricing (3)

An arbitrageur has two active positions in the commodity futures markets—one for lean hogs and the other for natural gas. The calendar spread on the lean hogs contract is quoted at −50 cents per pound, and the calendar spread on the natural gas contract is +$1.10 per million BTU (British thermal units). Based on this information, we can say that:

A. only the spreads of these commodities, and not the individual prices, can be traded in commodity markets.
B. the lean hogs futures market is in a state of backwardation and the natural gas futures market is in a state of contango.
C. the lean hogs futures market is in a state of contango and the natural gas futures market is in a state of backwardation.

Solution: C is correct. The spread is the difference between the current spot price for a commodity and the futures contract price. Because futures markets in a state of contango will have futures prices that exceed the spot price, the spread for these markets is negative. Conversely, in a state of backwardation, the spread is positive. A is incorrect because either the individual contract prices or the combined spreads can be traded. B is incorrect because, as mentioned earlier, the negative sign of the spread of lean hogs futures indicates a state of contango, whereas the positive sign of the spread of natural gas futures indicates a state of backwardation.

EXAMPLE 12   Spot and Futures Pricing (4)

A futures price curve for commodities in backwardation:

A. always remains in backwardation in the long term.
B. can fluctuate between contango and backwardation in the long term.
C. reflects structural long-term industry factors, as opposed to dynamic market supply and demand pressures.

Solution: B is correct. During periods of market stress or fundamental structural change in market conditions, some commodity futures price curves can rapidly shift from contango to backwardation or vice versa. A is incorrect because futures price curves can vacillate between contango and backwardation. C is incorrect because the shape of a commodity futures price curve reflects both long-term industry factors as well as market expectations of future supply and demand of the underlying commodity(ies).

---

7. THEORIES OF FUTURES RETURNS

Commodity futures markets have a reputation for volatility, but similar to other asset classes, there are theoretical bases for their long-run behavior. The original purpose of futures markets is for producers and consumers to hedge physical raw materials. In this section, we will discuss the underpinning theories of commodity futures returns, deconstruct the components of futures returns (i.e., at an index level), and close with thoughts on term structure (i.e., contango versus backwardation and implications of rolling futures contracts).

7.1. Theories of Futures Returns

Several theories have been proposed to explain the shape of the futures price curve, which has a dramatic impact on commodity futures returns. This reading covers three of the most important theories: (1) insurance theory, (2) hedging pressure hypothesis, and (3) theory of storage.

7.1.1. Insurance Theory
Keynes (1930), the noted economist and market speculator, proposed one of the earliest known theories on the shape of a commodity futures price curve. Also known as his theory of "normal backwardation," Keynes, in his 1930 tome *A Treatise on Money*, proposed that producers use commodity futures markets for insurance by locking in prices and thus make their revenues more predictable. A commodity producer is long the physical good and thus would be motivated to sell the commodity for future delivery to hedge its sales price. Imagine a farmer who thinks that next year she will grow a certain amount of soybeans on her land. She can sell a portion of her crop today that will be harvested months later to lock in those prices. She can then spend money on fertilizer and seed with more confidence about her budget. She may not be locking in a profit, but she would better understand her financial condition. Keynes's theory assumes that the futures curve is in backwardation "normally" because our farmer would persistently sell forward, pushing down prices in the future. Alternatively, this theory posits that the futures price has to be lower than the current spot price as a form of payment or remuneration to the speculator who takes

on the price risk and provides price insurance to the commodity seller. The concept of normal backwardation is illustrated in Exhibit 8, using cotton prices pre- and post-harvest.

EXHIBIT 8   Normal Backwardation

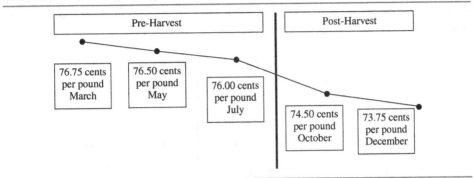

In terms of returns, if the front price is stable (in our example, 76.75 cents), then an investor can buy a further-dated contract (e.g., October) at 74.50 cents and wait for that contract to become the current contract. As the month of October approaches (and assuming no change in front prices), the October contract will reach 76.75 cents at maturity, and the speculator will make a profit of 2.25 cents per pound (note that a contract is 50,000 pounds, so that is a total profit of $1,125 per contract). Even if the contract does not fully converge, this theory holds that there should be positive excess returns (sometimes referred to as the risk premium) via this process to induce buying. As noted earlier, this process acts as a type of insurance for the farmer as well as a return for the investor providing such insurance.

Looking at the evidence, however, markets failed to match Keynes's hypothesis. Kolb (1992) looked at 29 futures contracts and concluded (with some humor) that "normal backwardation is not normal." That is, the presence of backwardation does not necessarily generate positive returns in a statistically significant fashion for the investor (or that contango leads to negative returns, for that matter). This result confirmed other studies, including one by Fama and French (1987). Therefore, a more sophisticated view developed to explain futures markets in contango (i.e., when the shape of the futures price curve is upward sloping with more distant contract dates), recognizing that certain commodity futures markets often show persistently higher prices in the future as opposed to the backwardation outlined by Keynes. This view is called the hedging pressure hypothesis.

7.1.2. Hedging Pressure Hypothesis

This perspective stemmed from multiple works, most notably outlined by De Roon, Nijman, and Veld (2000), who drew from Cootner (1960). Their research analyzed 20 futures markets from 1986 to 1994 and concluded that hedging pressure plays an important role in explaining futures returns. Hedging pressure occurs when both producers and consumers seek to protect themselves from commodity market price volatility by entering into price hedges to stabilize their projected profits and cash flow. Producers of commodities will tend or want to sell commodities forward and thus sell commodity futures. On the other side, consumers of commodities want to lock in prices of their commodity purchases and buy commodity futures. This theory applies to the aforementioned farmer selling a portion of next year's crop today. It can also apply to a central bank that wants to buy gold during each of the next 12 months as part of its monetary operations or a refinery that may want to lock in the price of its oil purchases and, conversely, the prices of its gasoline and heating oil production.

If the two forces of producers and consumers both seeking price protection are equal in weight, then one can envision a flat commodity curve, such as Exhibit 9 illustrates. In this idealized situation, the natural needs for price insurance by commodity buyers and sellers offset each other. There is no discount on the commodity futures price required to induce speculators to accept the commodity price risk because the hedging needs of both the buyer and seller complement and offset each other.

EXHIBIT 9   Balanced Hedging between Producers and Consumers

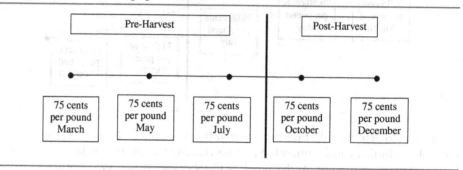

To use a different example, consider the problem of snowfall in the New England region of the United States. On one hand, small municipalities in Vermont, New Hampshire, or Maine may experience high levels of annual snowfall that are a risk to their snow removal budgets. On the other hand, ski resorts in New England have an opposite risk challenge: Low snowfall creates skiing revenue shortfalls (or adds to costs because of the need for man-made snow), whereas high snowfall winters are a potential bonanza for both higher revenue and lower operating costs. This situation is another example of when the hedging needs of two parties can offset each other and create a mutually beneficial outcome.

If commodity producers as a group are more interested in selling forward (seeking price insurance) than commodity consumers (as per the concept of normal backwardation), then the relative imbalance in demand for price protection will lead to the need for speculators to complete the market. But speculators will only do so when futures prices trade at a sufficient discount to compensate for the price risk they will take on. In this case, the shape and structure of the futures price curve can be illustrated as backwardation, as shown in Exhibit 10, which is consistent with Keynes's insurance theory.

EXHIBIT 10   Commodity Producers Exceed Consumers (Backwardation)

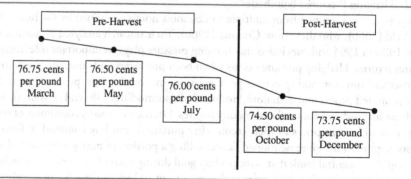

Finally, if the buyers of soybeans (as a group) are especially worried about the availability of the crop in the next harvest but producers of soybeans are less concerned about crop prices, there would be an imbalance in the demand for price insurance away from producers and toward buyers. This situation would lead to a futures price curve that represents a market in contango, as illustrated in Exhibit 11. In this case, the additional demand for price insurance among buyers (versus sellers) of the commodity will lead them to bid up the futures price to induce speculators to take on this price uncertainty risk.

EXHIBIT 11   Commodity Consumers Exceed Producers (Contango)

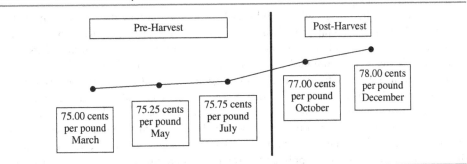

Although this theory is more robust than the Keynes's insurance theory, it is still incomplete. One issue is that producers generally have greater exposure to commodity price risk than consumers do (Hicks 1939). There are companies (as well as countries) that are almost entirely dependent on commodity production and thus are very concentrated in one sector, such as energy (e.g., British Petroleum, ExxonMobil), grains (e.g., Cargill, Louis Dreyfus), and metals (e.g., BHP Billiton, Vale, Rio Tinto, Shenhua).

Commodity consumers, in contrast, are very diffuse and often have other priorities (i.e., few if any individual people hedge their meat consumption or gasoline spending). Companies that purchase and use commodities in their products have a mixed record of price hedging, depending on the importance of the commodities in their cost structure. Clothing companies (e.g., Gap) generally do not hedge cotton because the spending is only a few percentage points of their expense base. Marketing and store experience (seen in rent, occupancy, and depreciation expenses) are much more important. But fast food companies hedge a wide variety of commodity inputs (e.g., livestock, grains, energy) because of the high degree of competition for prepared food at a low price point (e.g., McDonald's, Burger King, Wendy's).

In addition, both producers and consumers speculate on commodity prices, whether it is intended or unintended. Corporate treasury departments that serve as profit centers may adjust their hedges based on their views of the commodity markets. Their primary function may be to hedge, but a profit incentive can lead them to speculate. Individual farmers may not be overly aware of the commodity markets and thus have an inconsistent hedging approach. Trading companies actively trade the futures and physical markets in energy, metals, and grains. The very nature of trading companies is to know what is happening at all times along the value chain of any commodity market and profit from that informational advantage while bringing together buyers and sellers. In their case, profit maximization does not come from the production of commodities but trading around that production. In all of these examples, attempts to hedge may result instead in unintended speculative positions in which a company is not transferring price risk away but instead taking on more risk. The collapse in 1993 of

Metallgesellschaft AG, one of Germany's largest industrial conglomerates at the time, from a poorly constructed gasoline, fuel oil, and heating oil hedge is a defining example of flawed commercial hedging.

In summary, despite its intuitive logic, applying the hedging pressure hypothesis remains a challenge because measuring the asymmetry in hedging pressure between buyers and sellers of a commodity is very difficult.

7.1.3. Theory of Storage

This theory, originally postulated by Kaldor (1939), focuses on how the level of commodity inventories helps shape commodity futures price curves. The key issue this theory attempts to address is whether supply or demand of the commodity dominates in terms of its price economics. Recall that commodities are physical assets, not virtual assets like stocks and bonds. Physical assets have to be stored, and storage incurs costs (rent, insurance, inspections, spoilage, etc.). Therefore, a commodity that is regularly stored should have a higher price in the future (contango) to account for those storage costs. In other words, supply dominates demand. In contrast, a commodity that is consumed along a value chain that allows for just-in-time delivery and use (i.e., minimal inventories and storage) can avoid these costs. In this situation, demand dominates supply and current prices are higher than futures prices (i.e., backwardation).

In theoretical terms, available inventory generates a benefit called a convenience yield. Having a physical supply of the commodity available is convenient for consumers of the commodity (e.g., individuals, bread companies, meat processors, refiners) because it acts as a buffer to a potential supply disruption that could otherwise force a shutdown of their operations. Because this type of risk/concern is inversely related to the inventory size and the general availability of the commodity (and confidence in its continued availability), the convenience yield is low when stock is abundant. However, the yield rises as inventories diminish and concerns regarding future availability of the commodity increase.

As a result, the theory of storage states that futures prices can be written this way:

$$\text{Futures price} = \text{Spot price of the physical commodity} + \text{Direct storage} \\ \text{costs (such as rent and insurance)} - \text{Convenience yield.}$$

This equation indicates that price returns and the shape of the curve can move in conjunction with the changes in the available inventory as well as actual and expected supply and demand. For example, when civil war broke out in Libya in 2011, the production of that country's high-quality crude oil was placed in jeopardy, constricting supply. In reaction, the spot price for high-quality crude oil increased. At the same time, the convenience yield increased in the futures contracts closer to expiration because there was a scramble to tap into alternative oil supplies for European refiners. The high quality of Libyan crude oil also restricted which substitute crude oil supplies could be used to replace production from the blocked oil fields and how soon these replacements could be available. The real-world constraints and complications imposed by geography and the logistics of the oil industry resulted in a multi-month delay for replacement supplies. As a result, in the further-out (i.e., longer time to expiration) futures contracts, the reaction was muted as traders assumed that such replacement supplies would be available. Thus the convenience yield remained lower in the deferred months. For this and other reasons, crude oil was pressured to trade in backwardation during 2011.

Unfortunately, while all these theories are reasonable and attractive, they have components that are unobservable or highly volatile and, therefore, not reliably calculable. Commodity producers and consumers regard storage costs as proprietary information. Events (weather, war, technology) can radically adjust convenience yield in a short time with unknown magnitude. Corn suitable for feed may not be suitable for human consumption, so defining inventories is tricky. In the end, we have frameworks and theories, but they are not easily applied and require judgment and analysis by a trader or a valuation system.

EXAMPLE 13 Theories of Commodity Futures Returns (1)

Which of the following *best* describes the insurance theory of futures returns?

A. Speculators will not provide insurance unless the futures price exceeds the spot price.
B. Producers of a commodity will accept a lower future price (versus the spot price) in exchange for the certainty of locking in that price.
C. Commodity futures markets result in a state of contango because of speculators insisting on a risk premium in exchange for accepting price risk.

Solution: B is correct. Under the insurance theory of futures returns, Keynes stated that producers of a commodity would prefer to accept a discount on the potential future spot price in return for the certainty of knowing the future selling price in advance. A is incorrect because the futures price must be below the spot price (normal backwardation) under the insurance theory of futures returns. C is incorrect because the insurance theory of futures returns implies markets are in backwardation, not contango.

EXAMPLE 14 Theories of Commodity Futures Returns (2)

Under the hedging pressure hypothesis, when hedging activity of commodity futures buyers exceeds that of commodity futures sellers, that futures market is *most likely*:

A. flat.
B. in contango.
C. in backwardation.

Solution: B is correct. Under the hedging pressure hypothesis, a market in contango typically results when excess demand for price insurance among commodity futures buyers drives up the futures price to induce speculators to take on price uncertainty risk. A is incorrect because a flat market would likely exist if futures demand activity largely equaled that of supply. C is incorrect because under this scenario, the futures market would be in contango, not backwardation.

EXAMPLE 15   Theories of Commodity Futures Returns (3)

Under the theory of storage, the convenience yield is:

A. not affected by the supply of a commodity.
B. typically low when the supply of a commodity is scarce.
C. typically high when the supply of a commodity is scarce.

Solution: C is correct. Under the theory of storage, the convenience yield of a commodity increases as supply (inventories) diminish and concerns about the future availability increase. A is incorrect because supply levels have a discernible effect on the convenience yield, as mentioned. B is incorrect because the convenience yield would likely be high, as opposed to low, when supply is limited.

EXAMPLE 16   Theories of Commodity Futures Returns (4)

Which of the following represents the formula for a futures price according to the theory of storage?

A. Futures price = Spot price of the physical commodity + Direct storage costs − Convenience yield.
B. Futures price = Spot price of the physical commodity + Direct storage costs + Convenience yield.
C. Futures price = Spot price of the physical commodity − Direct storage costs + Convenience yield.

Solution: A is correct. According to the theory of storage, the futures price reflects the current spot price as well as costs incurred in actually holding the commodity until its delivery. Such costs include direct storage, such as inventory and insurance costs. Finally, because there is a convenience yield (or benefit) to owning a commodity as a form of insurance against potential supply disruptions, this term is subtracted from the current price of the commodity.

---

8. COMPONENTS OF FUTURES RETURNS

The total return on a commodity investment in futures is different from a total return on the physical assets. So, why do investors tend to use futures to gain their exposure to commodities? Building on the previous section, one can see that physical commodities need to be stored, fed, or perhaps treated against spoilage. Each commodity can be very different in its maintenance requirements; sustaining a hog in Mexico would be very different from storing crude oil in Nigeria.

The total return on commodity futures is traditionally broken into three components:

1. the price return (or spot yield),
2. the roll return (or roll yield), and
3. the collateral return (or collateral yield).

The price return is the change in commodity futures prices, generally the front month contract. Note that this change is different from the change in the price of the physical commodity because lack of standardization of the physical markets makes that a difficult task. Calculating the price return is straightforward, as shown in the following equation:

Price return = (Current price − Previous price)/Previous price.

In addition, as investors move from futures contract to futures contract, they must "roll" that exposure by selling the current contract as it approaches expiration and buying the next contract (assuming a long position). Depending on the shape of the futures curve, there is likely a difference between the two prices. Thus, a portfolio may require buying more far contracts than the near contracts being sold. Investors can observe this scenario if backwardation is driving the shape of the commodity futures price curve.

Example (stylized): Assume an investor has £110 of exposure in wheat futures and the near contract is worth £10 of exposure (so, the investor has £110 exposure divided by £10 per contract, or 11 contracts), but the far (i.e., longer expiration date) contract is worth only £9 of exposure. Therefore, for the investor to roll forward his contracts and maintain a constant level of exposure, he needs to roll the 11 contracts forward and also buy an additional 1 contract to keep the post-roll exposure close to the pre-roll exposure (£110 exposure divided by £9 per contract equals 12.2, or 12 contracts rounded).

In the opposite case, if the futures price curve shape is being driven by contango—with a higher futures price in the far contract—this scenario will require the purchase of fewer commodity contracts than in the near position.

Example: Assume an investor has £108 of exposure in regular unleaded gasoline (or petrol) futures and the near contract is worth £9 of exposure (so, the investor has £108 exposure divided by £9 per contract, or 12 contracts), but the far contract is worth £10 of exposure. Therefore, for the investor to roll forward her contracts and maintain a constant level of exposure, she needs to roll only 11 contracts and sell the extra 1 near contract to keep the post-roll exposure close to the pre-roll exposure (£108 exposure divided by £10 per contract equals 10.8, or 11 contracts rounded).

Note that this roll return is not a return in the sense that it can be independently captured; investors cannot construct a portfolio consisting of only roll returns. Instead, roll return is an accounting calculation used to replicate a portion of the total return for a fully collateralized (i.e., with no leverage) commodity index. As defined, the roll return is effectively the accounting difference (in percentage terms) between the near-term commodity futures contract price and the farther-term commodity futures contract price (note that roll return is sometimes defined in monetary terms rather than as a percentage):

Roll return = [(Near-term futures contract closing price − Farther-term
futures contract closing price)/Near-term futures contract closing price] ×
Percentage of the position in the futures contract being rolled.

As an example, consider the roll from the March contract to the April contract for WTI crude oil on 7 February 2019 using the S&P GSCI methodology, which rolls its positions over a five-day period (so 1/5 = 20% per day):

March contract closing price: $52.64/barrel
April contract closing price: $53.00/barrel

$$($52.64 - $53.00)/$52.64 = -0.68\% \text{ gross roll return} \times 20\% \text{ rollover portion}$$
$$= -0.13\% \text{ net roll return (note the negative return in contango).}$$

Note that different indexes use different periods and/or weights in their "rolling methodology." In Section 11, we will further discuss the rolling methodology of various indexes.

In his book *Expected Returns*, Ilmanen (2011) made the argument (challenged by others) that roll return is approximately equal to a risk premium. This concept relates back to Keynes and his theory of "normal backwardation." Keynes proposed that speculators take the other side of the transaction from commodity producers—who sell forward to lock in their cash flows—in an attempt to earn an excess return as compensation for providing price insurance to producers. Ilmanen attempted to demonstrate that positive long-run average returns are associated with positive roll return (i.e., in commodities for which futures prices are in backwardation) and negative long-run average returns are associated with negative roll return. However, because 40% of the commodities examined by Ilmanen (p. 255) had negative roll returns but positive total returns, one cannot directly conclude that backwardation earns a positive total return.

The **collateral return** is the yield (e.g., interest rate) for the bonds or cash used to maintain the investor's futures position(s). The minimum amount of funds is called the initial margin. If an investor has less cash than required by the exchange to maintain the position, the broker who acts as custodian will require more funds (a margin call) or close the position (buying to cover a short position or selling to eliminate a long position). Collateral thus acts as insurance for the exchange that the investor can pay for losses.

For return calculations on indexed investments, the amount of cash would be considered equal to the notional value of the futures. This approach means no leverage. For expected returns, commonly, investors should use a risk-free government bond that most closely matches the term projected. Most commodity indexes use short-term US Treasury bills, but if one is forecasting 10-year returns, then for collateral return purposes, a 10-year constant maturity government bond would have a more appropriate term.

Although indexes will be discussed more fully later in the reading, to illustrate the commodity return elements just discussed, one can use an index—in this case, the aforementioned S&P GSCI, which has one of the longest backtested and live history of the investable commodity indexes. Exhibit 12 shows the disaggregation of its return components.

As can be seen in the table, over the past 40+ years, the S&P GSCI generated 6.8% in geometrically compounded annualized returns, with about three-quarters derived from interest rates (collateral return). The commodity price spot return component of the index (which has varied over time) contributed to approximately 45% of the total return (3.0% out of 6.8%), whereas the roll return subtracted from the overall return by –1.3% (or 130 bps) on an annualized basis. Investors can see the effect of commodities on inflation via the price return.

The volatility and correlations of the components of index returns are driven by the changes in the spot price return (effectively the same annualized standard deviation of 19.8% as the S&P GSCI with a 97% correlation). The roll return and collateral return do not drive, in general, the

EXHIBIT 12   Average Annual Return Components of the S&P GSCI, January 1970–March 2019

S&P GSCI Return	Total Return	Spot Return	Roll Return[1]	Collateral Return[1]
Return[2]	6.8%	3.0%	–1.3%	5.0%
Risk[3]	19.8%	19.8%	4.2%	1.1%
Correlation[4]		0.97	–0.11	–0.14

[1] Roll return is defined as the excess return on the S&P GSCI minus the spot of the S&P GSCI. Collateral return is defined as the total return on the S&P GSCI minus the excess return of the S&P GSCI. The excess return measures the returns accrued from investing in uncollateralized nearby commodity futures.
[2] Monthly returns are used.
[3] Risk is defined as annualized standard deviation.
[4] Correlation with the S&P GSCI Total Return.
Source: Author's research based on data from S&P Dow Jones Indices.

monthly returns historically. This link between commodity futures prices and commodity total return indexes helps to define commodities as a separate and investable asset class.

In summary, the total return on a fully collateralized commodity futures contract can be described as the spot price return plus the roll return plus collateral return (risk-free rate return). With an index, a return from rebalancing the index's component weights—a **rebalance return**—would also be added. Using historical data (at the risk of it becoming outdated over time), one can demonstratively use the total return deconstruction to analyze commodities.

EXAMPLE 17   Total Returns for Futures Contracts (1)

A commodity futures market with pricing in backwardation will exhibit which of the following characteristics?

A. The roll return is usually negative.
B. Rolling an expiring futures contract forward will require buying more contracts in order to maintain the same dollar position in the futures markets.
C. Rolling an expiring futures contract forward will require buying fewer contracts in order to maintain the same dollar position in the futures markets.

Solution: B is correct. Commodity futures markets in backwardation exhibit price curves in which longer-dated futures prices are priced lower than near-dated contracts and the nearest-dated contract is priced lower than the current spot price. With a lower futures price on the futures curve, rolling contracts forward in backwardation would require purchasing more contracts to maintain the same dollar position. A is incorrect because the roll return is usually positive, not negative, in markets in backwardation. C is incorrect because an investor would need to purchase more, not fewer, contracts in markets in backwardation to maintain his or her total dollar position.

EXAMPLE 18   Total Returns for Futures Contracts (2)

An investor has realized a 5% price return on a commodity futures contract position and a 2.5% roll return after all her contracts were rolled forward. She had held this position for one year with collateral equal to 100% of the position at a risk-free rate of 2% per year. Her total return on this position (annualized excluding leverage) was:

A. 5.5%.
B. 7.3%.
C. 9.5%.

Solution: C is correct. Total return on a commodity futures position is expressed as

$$\text{Total return} = \text{Price return} + \text{Roll return} + \text{Collateral return.}$$

In this case, she held the contracts for one year, so the price return of 5% is an annualized figure. In addition, the roll return is also an annual 2.5%. Her collateral return equals 2% per year × 100% initial collateral investment = 2%.

So, her total return (annualized) is

$$\text{Total return} = 5\% + 2.5\% + 2\% = 9.5\%.$$

EXAMPLE 19   Total Returns for Futures Contracts (3)

An investor has a $10,000 position in long futures contracts (for a hypothetical commodity) that he wants to roll forward. The current contracts, which are close to expiration, are valued at $4.00 per contract, whereas the longer-term contract he wants to roll into is valued at $2.50 per contract. What are the transactions—in terms of buying and selling new contracts—he needs to execute in order to maintain his current exposure?

A. Close out (sell) 2,500 near-term contracts and initiate (buy) 4,000 of the longer-term contracts.
B. Close out (buy) 2,500 near-term contracts and initiate (sell) 4,000 of the longer-term contracts.
C. Let the 2,500 near-term contracts expire and use any proceeds to purchase an additional 2,500 of the longer-term contracts.

Solution: A is correct. To roll over the same level of total exposure ($10,000), he will need to do the following:

Sell

$$\$10,000/\$4.00 \text{ per contract} = 2,500 \text{ existing contracts.}$$

And replace this position by purchasing

$10,000/$2.50 per contract = 4,000 existing contracts.

9. CONTANGO, BACKWARDATION, AND THE ROLL RETURN

To reiterate, contango and backwardation—and the resulting roll return—fundamentally reflect underlying supply and demand expectations and are accounting mechanisms for the commodity term structure. We can gain a sense of these patterns by again examining the history of an index. Recall that from January 1970 to March 2019, the historical roll return of the S&P GSCI subtracted 1.3% from the average annual total return, with a standard deviation of 4.7%. That historical roll return varied over this time period, as depicted in Exhibit 13.

EXHIBIT 13   Historical One-Year S&P GSCI Price and Roll Return (Monthly Returns, January 1970–December 2019)

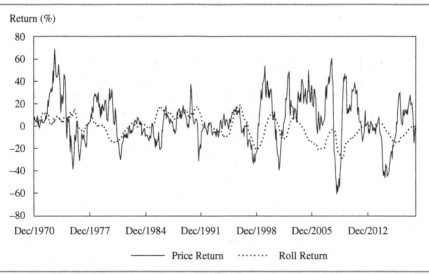

Note: The roll return is rolling monthly.

As the graph shows, periods of either backwardation or contango do not persist indefinitely. A simple review of the Exhibit 13 history demonstrates as much. Furthermore, with a correlation of 3%, roll return is not very indicative of price return, also contrary to popular belief. Positive price returns are associated with negative roll returns as well as positive roll returns. In some cases, certain sectors are indeed associated with contango, as can be seen in Exhibit 14.

EXHIBIT 14 Average Annual Sector Roll Return and Standard Deviation[a]

	S&P GSCI Total	Energy	Industrial Metals	Agriculture	Livestock	Precious Metals	Softs
Mean roll return (annual)[b]	−1.3%	−1.5%	−1.3%	−4.5%	−1.1%	−5.1%	−5.5%
Standard deviation of the mean (annual)[b]	0.4%	0.8%	0.5%	0.4%	0.5%	0.2%	0.6%
Maximum roll return (annual)[b]	18.9%	31.5%	45.9%	29.2%	35.5%	−0.4%	25.6%
Minimum roll return (annual)[b]	−29.6%	−39.5%	−16.6%	−18.6%	−31.2%	−15.4%	−24.9%

[a] The periods covered vary by sector:
• S&P GSCI total: December 1969–March 2019
• Energy: December 1982–March 2019
• Industrial metals: December 1976–March 2019
• Agriculture: December 1969–March 2019
• Livestock: December 1969–March 2019
• Precious metals: December 1972–March 2019
• Softs: December 1994–March 2019
[b] Calculated using rolling 12-month periods of monthly data.
Sources: Based on data from Bloomberg and Coloma Capital Futures.

Exhibit 14 highlights a few important factors. First, industrial metals, agriculture, livestock, precious metals, and softs have statistically strong negative mean roll returns. Only energy has a statistical possibility of a positive mean roll return, but that opportunity has diminished after 2010. Note from our comparison of the commodity sectors that industrial metals, agriculture, livestock, precious metals, and softs are stored for extended periods in warehouses, silos, and feedlots. In fact, precious metals historically have had negative roll returns because of gold's perpetual storage as an alternative currency. Historically, energy is consumed on a real-time basis apart from various strategic reserves, with the minimal storage buffer thus creating a lower or negative convenience yield. However, since 2010, the emergence of shale oil production in the United States has increased oil's convenience yield to the point that historical scarcity risk is much lower than before. Also, oil supply risk has shifted to China during this period as that country took over the United States' position as the lead oil importer. Finally, OPEC (with the inclusion of Russia and a few other non-OPEC members) regained some pricing power as the cartel achieved some success with supply restriction. Bringing it all together, one can conclude that indexes and long-only strategies that overweight agriculture, livestock, precious metals, and softs should expect to see negative roll returns (or roll yields). Energy commodities (apart from natural gas) have an opportunity for positive roll return, assuming producers successfully withhold supply from the market.

In conclusion, roll return can have an important impact on any single period return but overall has been relatively modest compared with price return. Furthermore, roll return is very sector dependent, which leads to a conclusion that sector diversification or concentration will have a profound impact on an investor's overall roll return based on a diversified portfolio of commodity futures.

EXAMPLE 20   Roll Return

When measuring its contribution to the total return of a commodity futures position, the roll return:

A. typically has a significant contribution to total return over both single and multiple periods.
B. typically has a modest contribution to total return in any single period but can be significant over multiple periods.
C. is always close to zero.

Solution: B is correct. Historically, the roll return has had a relatively modest impact on overall commodity futures return in the short term but can be meaningful over longer time periods. A is incorrect because the roll return is typically modest over shorter periods of time, as noted earlier. C is incorrect because futures contracts generate positive or negative roll returns, depending on the commodity and prevailing market conditions.

10. COMMODITY SWAPS

Instead of futures, some investors can gain market exposure to or hedge risk of commodities via swaps. A **commodity swap** is a legal contract involving the exchange of payments over multiple dates as determined by specified reference prices or indexes relating to commodities. In the world of commodities, a series of futures contracts often forms the basis of the reference prices. For example, an independent oil refiner may want to hedge its oil purchases over an extended period. The refiner may not want to manage a large number of futures contracts but maintain flexibility with regard to its oil supply source. By entering into a swap contract—particularly one that is cash settled instead of physically settled—the refiner can be protected from a price spike and yet maintain flexibility of delivery.

Based on this example, one can see why commercial participants use swaps: The instrument provides both risk management and risk transfer while eliminating the need to set up and manage multiple futures contracts. Swaps also provide a degree of customization not possible with standardized futures contracts. The refiner in the example may negotiate a swap for a specific quality of crude oil (e.g., Heavy Louisiana Sweet instead of West Texas Intermediate, or WTI) as its reference price or a blend of crudes that shifts throughout the year depending on the season. Customization through the use of a swap may also have value by changing the quantity of crude oil hedged over time, such as lowering the exposure during the planned shutdown and maintenance periods at the refinery.

On the other side of the transaction from the refiner (or other hedging or speculating entity) would be a swap dealer, typically a financial intermediary, such as a bank or trading company. The dealer, in turn, may hedge its price risk exposure assumed in the swap through the futures market or, alternatively, negotiate its own swap with another party or arrange an oil purchase contract with a crude oil producer. The dealer may also choose to keep the price risk exposure, seeking to profit from its market information. A diagram demonstrating this swap transaction is shown in Exhibit 15.

EXHIBIT 15   Swap Market Participant Structure

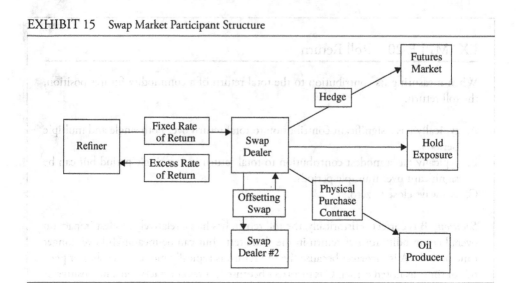

To further understand the diagram in Exhibit 15, assume we had the following scenario:

1. An oil refiner goes long a swap at the end of December that pays the amount exceeding $70 per barrel every month-end through September.
2. The oil refiner would pay a swap counterparty a premium (in this example, $25) for this privilege because it is effectively long a series of call options.

The flow of funds in the swap transaction would be as shown in Exhibit 16.

EXHIBIT 16   Flow of Funds for Swap Transaction Example

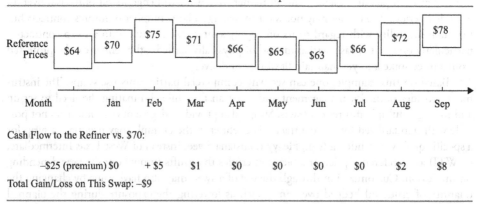

Total gain/loss on this swap to the refiner is −$9 (found by summing the cash flows and ignoring present value calculations or other considerations).

Although this example of a swap lost money and effectively increased the refiner's cost of a barrel of oil by $1 for this time period (given that the net loss on the swap was $9 over nine months), the swap protected the company against the risk of a cash squeeze during those months when an oil price spike could have impaired the liquidity of the company. The swap also defined the cost up front, giving a measure of cash flow predictability. Note that accounting standards and practices for swaps may also have an impact on the attractiveness of swaps. Given that oil prices are subject to many events beyond a company's control, a company looking to protect itself from financing risk may find that a swap can be a valuable tool.

There are many types of swaps available in the marketplace because they are not standard-ized, exchange-traded contracts like futures. The previous example of the refiner is an example of an "excess return swap." In an excess return swap, the payments to either party are driven primarily by the changes in price of each of the futures contracts that make up the index. The net change in the prices of the underlying futures contracts is defined as the "excess" return, and the excess return is multiplied by the contract's notional amount to determine the payments between buyer and seller.

10.1. Total Return Swap

Another common swap in commodities is a "total return swap." In a total return swap, the change in the level of the index will be equal to the returns generated by the change in price of each of the futures contracts that make up the index plus a return based on interest earned on any cash collateral posted on the purchase of the futures contracts that make up the index. If the level of the index increases, the swap buyer receives payment net of the fee paid to the seller; if the level of the index decreases between two valuation dates, the swap seller receives payment (plus the fee charged to the buyer). This type of swap is generally used by large institutional investors (e.g., pension plans) as opposed to commodity producers or buyers. With a total return swap, the investor seeks exposure to commodity returns, often because of the low return correlation of commodities with other asset classes (e.g., stocks or bonds) or as a reflection of the view that commodities provide a valuable inflation hedge for asset/liability matching (ALM). Therefore, such investors would engage in a total return swap that provides them with long exposure to the future returns from a commodity index that is used as the reference price. Again, accounting treatment with respect to futures often drives these decisions.

As an example of a total return swap, assume an investor who manages a defined benefit retirement plan desires commodity exposure for the reasons noted earlier. Given the size of the portfolio manager's plan assets (assume £2 billion), the manager is seeking approximately 5% exposure of plan assets to commodities. More specifically, the manager has decided that this £100 million exposure (5% of £2 billion) should be to the (hypothetical) China Futures Com-modity Index (CFCI) and should remain for five years. Based on this decision, the manager issues a request for proposals (RFP) and, after evaluating the various bidders, contracts with a Swiss bank for a total return swap that will provide the desired exposure.

If on the first day of the swap agreement the CFCI increased by 1%, then the swap dealer would owe the manager £1 million (£100 million × 1%). If on the second day the CFCI declined by 5%, then the manager would owe £5 million to the dealer. Commonly, the dealer will hedge its short index exposure with futures or the physical commodity investments. Because the manager would be seeking the risk–return exposure offered by commodities, the manager would not generally hedge its exposure.

10.2. Basis Swap

Another common commodity swap is a basis swap, in which periodic payments are exchanged based on the values of two related commodity reference prices that are not perfectly correlated. These swaps are often used to adjust for the difference (called the basis) between a highly liquid futures contract in a commodity and an illiquid but related material. For example, a swap may pay the difference between the average daily prices of Brent crude oil (very liquid) and heavy crude oil available for delivery in the Gulf of Mexico (less liquid). This can be a very valuable arrangement for, in this example, refineries on the US Gulf Coast that have heavily invested in processing cheaper heavy crudes that come from such countries as Mexico or Venezuela. Because prices of these crudes do not always move in tandem with more common crudes, such as Brent, they derive a price basis between the two. It should be noted that "basis" has other meanings as well, depending on the commodity in question. For example, in grains, the basis may refer to the difference between the soybean contract and physical soybeans available for delivery at the Mississippi River.

10.3. Variance Swaps and Volatility Swaps

Two final types of relatively common commodity swaps are variance swaps and volatility swaps. Variance swaps of commodities are similar in concept to variance swaps of equities in that there is a variance buyer and a variance seller. Two parties agree to periodically exchange payments based on the proportional difference between an observed/actual variance in the price levels of a commodity (over consecutive time periods), and some fixed amount of variance established at the outset of the contract. If this difference is positive, the variance swap buyer receives a payment; if it is negative, the variance swap seller receives payment. Often the variance differences (observed versus fixed) are capped to limit upside and losses.

Volatility commodity swaps are very similar to variance swaps, with the exception that the direction and amount of payments are determined relative to the observed versus expected volatility for a reference price commodity. In this arrangement, the two sides are not speculating on the level or direction of prices but instead on how volatile prices will be versus expectations. A volatility seller will profit if realized volatility is lower than expectations, whereas the counterparty volatility buyer anticipates higher than expected volatility.

EXAMPLE 21   Commodity Swaps (1)

A portfolio manager enters into a $100 million (notional) total return commodity swap to obtain a long position in commodity exposure. The position is reset monthly against a broad-based commodity index. At the end of the first month, the index is up 3%, and at the end of the second month, the index declines 2%. What are two payments that would occur between the portfolio manager and the swap dealer on the other side of the swap transaction?

A. No payments are exchanged because a net cash flow only occurs when the swap agreement expires.

B. $3 million would be paid by the swap dealer to the portfolio manager (after Month 1), and $2 million would be paid by the portfolio manager to the swap dealer (after Month 2).

C. $3 million would be paid by the portfolio manager to the swap dealer (after Month 1), and $2 million would be paid by the swap dealer to the portfolio manager (after Month 2).

Solution: B is correct. Because the portfolio manager has a long position in the total return commodity swap, he or she will receive payments when the commodity index rises and make payments when the commodity index declines. The payment calculations after the first two months are as follows:

$$\text{Month 1: } \$100 \text{ million} \times 3\% = \$3 \text{ million.}$$
$$\text{Month 2: } \$100 \text{ million} \times -2\% = -\$2 \text{ million.}$$

A is incorrect because swap payments are made periodically (in this case monthly) and not withheld to the end of the contract. C is incorrect because the payments would be in the opposite direction for each month.

EXAMPLE 22   Commodity Swaps (2)

In a commodity volatility swap, the direction and amount of payments are determined relative to the observed versus reference:

A. direction in the price of a commodity.
B. variance for the price of a commodity.
C. volatility for the price of a commodity.

Solution: C is correct. In a commodity volatility swap, the two sides of the transaction are speculating on expected volatility. A volatility seller will profit if realized volatility is lower than expectations, whereas the volatility buyer benefits from higher than expected volatility. A is incorrect because a volatility swap is based on price volatility, not direction. B is incorrect because a volatility swap is based on price volatility as opposed to price variance (price volatility squared).

---

11. COMMODITY INDEXES

As in other parts of the investment universe, indexes have been created to portray the aggregate movement of commodity prices, investment vehicles, and investing approaches. In fact, one could say that an asset class does not exist without the presence of at least one representative index.

Commodity indexes play three primary roles in commodity sector investments. First, an index can be used as a benchmark to evaluate broader moves in commodity pricing. Second, as a broad indicator, an index can be used for macroeconomic or forecasting purposes by examining statistically significant relationships between movements in the commodity index and other macroeconomic variables. Finally, an index can act as the basis for an investment vehicle or contract providing the information needed to record, monitor, and evaluate price changes that affect contract value.

Although there are a number of commodity indexes, the following are used most frequently for the purposes just mentioned: (1) the S&P GSCI; (2) the Bloomberg Commodity Index (BCOM), formerly known as the Dow Jones–UBS Commodity Index (DJ–UBS); (3) the Deutsche Bank Liquid Commodity Index (DBLCI); (4) the Thomson Reuters/CoreCommodity CRB Index (TR/CC CRB); and (5) the Rogers International Commodities Index (RICI). The following are key characteristics that differentiate each of these indexes:

- The *breadth* of coverage (number of commodities and sectors) included in each index, noting that some commodities have multiple reference contracts (e.g., for crude oil, the common contracts are for West Texas Intermediate in the United States and Brent crude for Europe).
- The relative *weightings* assigned to each component/commodity and the related methodology for how these weights are determined.
- The *rolling methodology* for determining how those contracts that are about to expire are rolled over into future months. This decision has a direct impact on the roll return (or yield) of the overall commodity. Recall that roll return is one of the three key components of overall commodity returns.
- The methodology and frequency for *rebalancing* the weights of the individual commodities, sectors, and contracts in the index to maintain the relative weightings assigned to each investment. As with stocks and bonds within a portfolio, the opportunity to earn positive rebalance returns for commodities depends on the correlation of the underlying components of the index and the propensity of underperforming components to revert back to the mean. For example, a drought may cause cotton prices to increase, but a strong crop the following year will cause prices to collapse. A rebalance sale of the overvalued cotton exposure into an undervalued exposure should "lock in" some of that gain. The rebalance return will likely vary depending on the methodology used by the index.
- The *governance* of indexes is important because it is the process by which all the aforementioned rules are implemented. For example, some indexes are rules-based, whereas others are selection-based. The rules-based indexes follow a quantitative methodology, whereas selection-based indexes are more qualitative in that an index committee picks the commodities. Also, governance oversees the independence of index providers so that, according to best practices of the Index Industry Association, the asset price should be independent from the index provider, which, in turn, should be independent from the product provider (e.g., the exchange-traded fund or swap provider).

For the index to be a viable and useful construct, it should be investable; that is, investors or their agents should be able to replicate the methodology outlined to translate the index concept into a representation of the asset class. For this reason, index providers and investors must be mindful of the venues (physical or electronic) for trading each commodity index, the liquidity and turnover of contracts based on each commodity index, and the term structure of each index (i.e., how far into the future the index extends and which months it covers). The weighting method for components in an index is key to diversification and—combined with rebalancing frequency—influences the opportunity to earn positive rebalance returns.

An index that requires investments in exchanges all over the world is more difficult and expensive for an investor to replicate. An emphasis on illiquid contracts has a negative impact on transaction costs. Contracts without a full yield curve may be a challenge to analyze and trade. In other words, seemingly small execution concerns are magnified when constructing a benchmark that represents an entire asset class, such as commodities. And indexes that choose (perhaps inadvertently) contracts that more commonly trade in backwardation may appear to improve forward-looking performance (because this generates a positive roll return), whereas those that more commonly trade in contango may hurt performance. Exhibit 17 summarizes the various elements of the main indexes discussed.

EXHIBIT 17   Overview of Major Commodity Indexes

	Index				
Element	S&P GSCI	BCOM	DBLCI	TR/CC CRB	RICI
Adoption date	1991	1998	2003	2005 (current version)	1998
Number of commodities	24	23	14	19	38
Weighting method	Production weighted	Production and liquidity weighted	Fixed weight	Fixed weight	Fixed weight
Rolling methodology	Nearby most liquid contract, monthly	Front month to next or second month	Optimized on roll return	Front month to next month	Front month to next month
Rebalancing frequency	Annually	Annually	Annually	Monthly	Monthly
Individual investor funds available?	Yes	Yes	Yes	Yes in some jurisdictions as well as an exchange-traded fund on a related index	Yes

Note: Information is as of 30 April 2019.

Sources: Information from respective sponsor websites, Bloomberg, and authors' research.

Exhibit 17 helps distinguish the key characteristics that differentiate these five commercially important commodity indexes. In terms of coverage (the number of commodities and sectors included in the index), all five of these indexes have broad sector coverage, including energy, grains, livestock, precious metals, industrial metals, and softs. The only exception is the DBLCI, which does not have any livestock exposure. At the other extreme, the RICI includes relatively exotic (and thus illiquid) commodities, such as lumber, oats, and rubber. As a further example of its unique nature, the RICI once included adzuki beans (the red beans found in many Asian cuisines) and palm oil.

11.1. S&P GSCI

The S&P GSCI is the second oldest of the selected commodity indexes. The index is based on 24 commodities and applies liquidity screens to include only those contracts with an established minimum level of trading volume and available historical pricing. It uses a world production value-weighting scheme that gives the largest weight to the most valuable commodity on the basis of physical trade value. It should be no surprise that crude oil has the highest single weight and energy has the highest sector weight (historically as high as 80%) in this index. This approach is most similar to a market-capitalization weighted index of nearly all major bond and stock market indexes. Like some market-capitalization indexes (particularly in emerging or frontier markets), the resulting weights of the S&P GSCI can be highly concentrated. The rolling methodology focuses on owning the front (i.e., near-term) contracts to address the highest liquidity and where supply and demand shocks are most likely to have an impact.

11.2. Bloomberg Commodity Index

The BCOM (formerly the DJ–UBS) is based on 23 commodities. It includes liquidity as both a weighting factor and a screening factor, although the index is selection-based, meaning a committee uses judgment to pick the included commodities. The rules of index construction also place caps on the size of the sectors (33% maximum) and floors on individual commodities (2% minimum). These differences mean that very different index composition and weights can occur. For example, the energy sector currently dominates the S&P GSCI (as high as 80% weight), whereas the BCOM's exposure is much lower (approximately 30%). However, exposure to natural gas as a single component of energy is higher in the BCOM (approximately 9%) than in the S&P GSCI (approximately 3%). Given that natural gas had an annualized roll cost of about 19% (often the highest roll cost of all the commodities), the higher weighting of natural gas in the BCOM implies that the index has to find other sources of return (e.g., price return and rebalance return) to overcome the drag that natural gas inventory storage creates through negative roll return. The rolling methodology focuses on owning the front (i.e., near-term) contracts.

11.3. Deutsche Bank Liquid Commodity Index

The DBLCI uses a fixed-weighting scheme to allocate exposure. The most notable/unique feature of this index is its rolling methodology. Instead of focusing on near-term contracts, it is optimized based on the time value of maximized backwardation/minimized contango for the contracts that fall within the next 12 calendar months. As an example, a June 2014 copper futures contract may be at 1% backwardation versus a May 2014 copper contract. But if the July 2014 copper contract is at a 3% backwardation (1.5% per month, or 3% divided by two months) versus the 1% backwardation per month on the June 2014 contract, then the DBLCI will roll to the July 2014 contract in preference to the June 2014 contract. Therefore, one could argue the DBLCI takes an active decision with regard to roll return positioning as compared with the other indexes.

11.4. Thomson Reuters/CoreCommodity CRB Index

The TR/CC CRB consists of 19 commodities and is a continuation of the first investable commodity index published by the Commodities Research Bureau in 1978 (although an earlier iteration started in 1957). It uses a fixed-weighting scheme to allocate exposure. An index management committee decides the weights based on a number of factors, including diversification, sector representation, liquidity, and economic importance. It also clusters the fixed weights into a number of tiers. As a result, constituents are moved from tier to tier. The rolling methodology focuses on owning the front (i.e., near-term) contracts that mechanically focus on the front month or second front month and do not require a particular calculation.

11.5. Rogers International Commodity Index

The RICI uses a fixed-weighting scheme to allocate exposure among 38 different commodities and was designed by investor Jim Rogers in the late 1990s. An index management committee decides the weights based on a number of factors, including diversification, sector representation, liquidity, and economic importance. Like the TR/CC CRB Index, it also clusters the fixed weights into a number of tiers. As a result, constituents are moved from tier to tier as they gain or lose relative importance as seen by the committee. Energy is the largest weight but is still a highly diversified basket. Some energy constituents are denominated in non-US dollar terms—such as rubber (traded in Japan in Japanese yen) and cocoa (traded in London in British pounds)—which potentially adds a foreign exchange exposure element to the index returns.

11.6. Rebalancing Frequency

Rebalancing frequency plays a role in index returns, especially for those indexes that rebalance more frequently, such as the TR/CC CRB and RICI. Theoretically, from portfolio management theory, rebalancing is more important if a market is frequently mean reverting because there are more peaks to sell and valleys to buy. However, frequent rebalancing can lead to underperformance in a trending market because the outperforming assets are sold but continue up in price, whereas the underperforming assets are purchased but still drift lower.

The relative performance of the monthly rebalanced indexes (TR/CC CRB and RICI) versus the annual rebalance of the other indexes will depend on the length of time of price trends. More frequent mean reversions should favor the former two indexes, but a longer-term trend will more likely favor the annually rebalancing indexes. If an index uses a floating weighting scheme, such as production value (fully or partially), then the higher (lower) futures prices usually coincide with higher (lower) physical prices. Therefore, with this kind of approach, the magnitude of rebalancing weights is generally lower than for a fixed-weight scheme because the post-rebalance weights will generally drift in line with the current portfolio weights. As a result, the S&P GSCI and BCOM indexes typically have lower rebalancing costs and—in a trending market—have an opportunity to outperform their fixed-weight index counterparts, particularly those that have a relatively frequent rebalance period.

11.7. Commodity Index Summary

There is no dominant index based on a particular methodology. Relative performance will occur based on the circumstances of the markets and the time period examined. Evaluating which index is superior for a *long-term* investment generates modest if any value. Per the authors' research, these indexes all have been highly correlated (well above 70%) with each other and have had low (roughly 0%) correlations with traditional asset classes (e.g., US large-cap stocks, US bonds, international stocks). As with equities, for which there are many different index providers, commodity indexes act in parallel even when their returns (and Sharpe ratios) frequently differ dramatically over time.

EXAMPLE 23   Commodity Indexes (1)

All else being equal, compared with an equally weighted commodity index, a production value-weighted index (such as the S&P GSCI) will be:

A. less sensitive to energy sector returns.
B. more sensitive to energy sector returns.
C. equally sensitive to energy sector returns.

Solution: B is correct. The energy sector will make up a sizable portion of a production value-weighted index and thus will be a meaningful driver of returns for such an index. A is incorrect because a production value-weighted index will be more, not less, sensitive to the energy sector. C is incorrect because a production value-weighted index will be more, not equally, sensitive to the energy sector.

EXAMPLE 24   Commodity Indexes (2)

Which of the following statements is *not* correct regarding commodity futures indexes?

A. Commodity sectors in backwardation typically improve index returns.
B. An index that invests in several futures exchanges provides a high degree of diversification.
C. Total returns of the major commodity indexes have low correlation with traditional asset classes, such as equities and bonds.

Solution: B is correct. Commodity futures exchanges throughout the world are highly correlated and thus provide little diversification benefits. A is incorrect because markets in backwardation typically have positive roll yields and thus will likely improve index returns (although the price return may still not be positive and thus the total return may still be negative). C is incorrect because commodity index returns do indeed have historically low correlation with equities and bonds.

SUMMARY

- Commodities are a diverse asset class comprising various sectors: energy, grains, industrial (base) metals, livestock, precious metals, and softs (cash crops). Each of these sectors has a number of characteristics that are important in determining the supply and demand for each commodity, including ease of storage, geopolitics, and weather.
- Fundamental analysis of commodities relies on analyzing supply and demand for each of the products as well as estimating the reaction to the inevitable shocks to their equilibrium or underlying direction.

- The life cycle of commodities varies considerably depending on the economic, technical, and structural (i.e., industry, value chain) profile of each commodity as well as the sector. A short life cycle allows for relatively rapid adjustment to outside events, whereas a long life cycle generally limits the ability of the market to react.
- The valuation of commodities relative to that of equities and bonds can be summarized by noting that equities and bonds represent financial assets whereas commodities are physical assets. The valuation of commodities is not based on the estimation of future profitability and cash flows but rather on a discounted forecast of future possible prices based on such factors as the supply and demand of the physical item.
- The commodity trading environment is similar to other asset classes, with three types of trading participants: (1) informed investors/hedgers, (2) speculators, and (3) arbitrageurs.
- Commodities have two general pricing forms: spot prices in the physical markets and futures prices for later delivery. The spot price is the current price to deliver or purchase a physical commodity at a specific location. A futures price is an exchange-based price agreed on to deliver or receive a defined quantity and often quality of a commodity at a future date.
- The difference between spot and futures prices is generally called the basis. When the spot price is higher than the futures price, it is called backwardation, and when it is lower, it is called contango. Backwardation and contango are also used to describe the relationship between two futures contracts of the same commodity.
- Commodity contracts can be settled by either cash or physical delivery.
- There are three primary theories of futures returns.
  - In insurance theory, commodity producers who are long the physical good are motived to sell the commodity for future delivery to hedge their production price risk exposure.
  - The hedging pressure hypothesis describes when producers along with consumers seek to protect themselves from commodity market price volatility by entering into price hedges to stabilize their projected profits and cash flow.
  - The theory of storage focuses on supply and demand dynamics of commodity inventories, including the concept of "convenience yield."
- The total return of a fully collateralized commodity futures contract can be quantified as the spot price return plus the roll return plus the collateral return (risk-free rate return).
- The roll return is effectively the weighted accounting difference (in percentage terms) between the near-term commodity futures contract price and the farther-term commodity futures contract price.
- A commodity swap is a legal contract between two parties calling for the exchange of payments over multiple dates as determined by several reference prices or indexes.
- The most relevant commodity swaps include excess return swaps, total return swaps, basis swaps, and variance/volatility swaps.
- The five primary commodity indexes based on assets are: (1) the S&P GSCI; (2) the Bloomberg Commodity Index, formerly the Dow Jones–UBS Commodity Index; (3) the Deutsche Bank Liquid Commodity Index; (4) the Thomson Reuters/CoreCommodity CRB Index; and (5) the Rogers International Commodities Index.
- The key differentiating characteristics of commodity indexes are:
  - the breadth and selection methodology of coverage (number of commodities and sectors) included in each index, noting that some commodities have multiple reference contracts,
  - the relative weightings assigned to each component/commodity and the related methodology for how these weights are determined,
  - the methodology and frequency for rolling the individual futures contracts,

- the methodology and frequency for rebalancing the weights of the individual commodities and sectors, and
- the governance that determines which commodities are selected.

REFERENCES

Cootner, Paul H. 1960. "Returns to Speculators: Telser versus Keynes." *Journal of Political Economy* 68 (4): 396–404. doi:10.1086/258347

De Roon, Frans A., Theo E. Nijman, and Chris Veld. 2000. "Hedging Pressure Effects in Futures Markets." *Journal of Finance* 55 (3): 1437–56. doi:10.1111/0022-1082.00253

Erb, Claude B., and Campbell R. Harvey. 2006. "The Strategic and Tactical Value of Commodity Futures." *Financial Analysts Journal* 62 (2): 69–97. doi:10.2469/faj.v62.n2.4084

Fama, Eugene F., and Kenneth R. French. 1987. "Commodity Futures Prices: Some Evidence on Forecast Power, Premiums and the Theory of Storage." *Journal of Business* 60 (1): 55–73. doi:10.1086/296385

Gorton, Gary, and K. Geert Rouwenhorst. 2006. "Facts and Fantasies about Commodity Futures." *Financial Analysts Journal* 62 (2): 47–68. doi:10.2469/faj.v62.n2.4083

Hicks, John R. 1939. Value and Capital: *An Inquiry into Some Fundamental Principles of Economic Theory.* London: Oxford University Press.

Ilmanen, Antti. 2011. *Expected Returns: An Investor's Guide to Harvesting Market Rewards.* Hoboken, NJ: John Wiley & Sons. doi:10.1002/9781118467190

Kaldor, Nicholas. 1939. "Speculation and Economic Stability." *Review of Economic Studies* 7 (1): 1–27. doi:10.2307/2967593

Keynes, John M. 1930. *The Applied Theory of Money.* vol. 2. A Treatise on Money. London: Macmillan.

Kolb, Robert W. 1992. "Is Normal Backwardation Normal?" *Journal of Futures Markets* 12 (1): 75–91. doi:10.1002/fut.3990120108

PROBLEMS

The following information relates to Questions 1–8.

Raffi Musicale is the portfolio manager for a defined benefit pension plan. He meets with Jenny Brown, market strategist with Menlo Bank, to discuss possible investment opportunities. The investment committee for the pension plan has recently approved expanding the plan's permitted asset mix to include alternative asset classes.

Brown proposes the Apex Commodity Fund (Apex Fund) offered by Menlo Bank as a potentially suitable investment for the pension plan. The Apex Fund attempts to produce trading profits by capitalizing on the mispricing between the spot and futures prices of commodities. The fund has access to storage facilities, allowing it to take delivery of commodities when necessary. The Apex Fund's current asset allocation is presented in Exhibit 1.

EXHIBIT 1   Apex Fund's Asset Allocation

Commodity Sector	Allocation (%)
Energy	31.9
Livestock	12.6
Softs	21.7
Precious metals	33.8

Brown explains that the Apex Fund has had historically low correlations with stocks and bonds, resulting in diversification benefits. Musicale asks Brown, "Can you identify a factor that affects the valuation of financial assets like stocks and bonds but does not affect the valuation of commodities?"

Brown shares selected futures contract data for three markets in which the Apex Fund invests. The futures data are presented in Exhibit 2.

EXHIBIT 2   Selected Commodity Futures Data*

Month	Gold Price	Coffee Price	Gasoline Price
July	1,301.2	0.9600	2.2701
September	1,301.2	0.9795	2.2076
December	1,301.2	1.0055	2.0307

* Gold: US$/troy ounce; coffee: US$/pound; gasoline: US$/gallon.

Menlo Bank recently released a report on the coffee market. Brown shares the key conclusion from the report with Musicale: "The coffee market had a global harvest that was greater than expected. Despite the large harvest, coffee futures trading activity is balanced between producers and consumers. This balanced condition is not expected to change over the next year."

Brown shows Musicale the total return of a recent trade executed by the Apex Fund. Brown explains that the Apex Fund took a fully collateralized long futures position in nearby soybean futures contracts at the quoted futures price of 865.0 (US cents/bushel). Three months later, the entire futures position was rolled when the near-term futures price was 877.0 and the farther-term futures price was 883.0. During the three-month period between the time that the initial long position was taken and the rolling of the contract, the collateral earned an annualized rate of 0.60%.

Brown tells Musicale that the pension fund could alternatively gain long exposure to commodities using the swap market. Brown and Musicale analyze the performance of a long position in an S&P GSCI total return swap having monthly resets and a notional amount of $25 million. Selected data on the S&P GSCI are presented in Exhibit 3.

EXHIBIT 3   Selected S&P GSCI Data

Reference Date	Index Level
April (swap initiation)	2,542.35
May	2,582.23
June	2,525.21

1. The Apex Fund is *most likely* to be characterized as:
   A. a hedger.
   B. a speculator.
   C. an arbitrageur.
2. Which factor would *most likely* affect the supply or demand of all four sectors of the Apex Fund?
   A. Weather
   B. Spoilage
   C. Government actions

3. The *most appropriate* response to Musicale's question regarding the valuation factor is:
   A. storage costs.
   B. transportation costs.
   C. expected future cash flows.
4. Which futures market in Exhibit 2 is in backwardation?
   A. Gold
   B. Coffee
   C. Gasoline
5. Based on the key conclusion from the Menlo Bank coffee market report, the shape of the coffee futures curve in Exhibit 2 is *most consistent* with the:
   A. insurance theory.
   B. theory of storage.
   C. hedging pressure hypothesis.
6. Based on Exhibit 2, which commodity's roll returns will *most likely* be positive?
   A. Gold
   B. Coffee
   C. Gasoline
7. The Apex Fund's three-month total return on the soybean futures trade is *closest* to:
   A. 0.85%.
   B. 1.30%.
   C. 2.22%.
8. Based on Exhibit 3, on the June settlement date, the party that is long the S&P GSCI total return swap will:
   A. owe a payment of $552,042.23.
   B. receive a payment of $1,502,621.33.
   C. receive a payment of $1,971,173.60.

The following information relates to Questions 9–15.

Jamal Nabli is a portfolio manager at NextWave Commodities (NWC), a commodity-based hedge fund located in the United States. NWC's strategy uses a fixed-weighting scheme to allocate exposure among 12 commodities, and it is benchmarked against the Thomson Reuters/CoreCommodity CRB Index (TR/CC CRB). Nabli manages the energy and livestock sectors with the help of Sota Yamata, a junior analyst.

Nabli and Yamata meet to discuss a variety of factors that affect commodity values in the two sectors they manage. Yamata tells Nabli the following:

Statement 1: Storage costs are negatively related to futures prices.
Statement 2: In contrast to stocks and bonds, most commodity investments are made by using derivatives.
Statement 3: Commodities generate future cash flows beyond what can be realized through their purchase and sale.

Nabli and Yamata then discuss potential new investments in the energy sector. They review Brent crude oil futures data, which are presented in Exhibit 4.

EXHIBIT 4   Selected Data on Brent Crude Oil Futures

Spot Price	Near-Term Futures Price	Longer-Term Futures Price
77.56	73.64	73.59

Yamata presents his research related to the energy sector, which has the following conclusions:

- Consumers have been more concerned about prices than producers have.
- Energy is consumed on a real-time basis and requires minimal storage.

After concluding the discussion of the energy sector, Nabli reviews the performance of NWC's long position in lean hog futures contracts. Nabli notes that the portfolio earned a −12% price return on the lean hog futures position last year and a −24% roll return after the contracts were rolled forward. The position was held with collateral equal to 100% of the position at a risk-free rate of 1.2% per year.

Yamata asks Nabli to clarify how the state of the futures market affects roll returns. Nabli responds as follows:

Statement 4: Roll returns are generally negative when a futures market is in contango.

Statement 5: Roll returns are generally positive when a futures market is in backwardation.

As part of their expansion into new markets, NWC is considering changing its benchmark index. Nabli investigates two indexes as a possible replacement. These indexes both use similar weighting and rebalancing schemes. Index A includes contracts of commodities typically in contango, whereas Index B includes contracts of commodities typically in backwardation. Nabli asks Yamata how the two indexes perform relative to each other in a market that is trending upward.

Because of a substantial decline in drilling activity in the North Sea, Nabli believes the price of Brent crude oil will increase more than that of heavy crude oil. The actual price volatility of Brent crude oil has been lower than its expected volatility, and Nabli expects this trend to continue. Nabli also expects the level of the ICE Brent Index to increase from its current level. Nabli and Yamata discuss how to use swaps to take advantage of Nabli's expectations. The possible positions are: (1) a basis swap long on Brent crude oil and short on heavy crude oil, (2) a long volatility swap on Brent crude oil, and (3) a short position in an excess return swap that is based on a fixed level (i.e., the current level) of the ICE Brent Index.

9. Which of Nabli's statements regarding the valuation and storage of commodities is correct?
   A. Statement 1
   B. Statement 2
   C. Statement 3
10. Based on Exhibit 1, Yamata should conclude that the:
    A. calendar spread for Brent crude oil is $3.97.
    B. Brent crude oil futures market is in backwardation.
    C. basis for the near-term Brent crude oil futures contract is $0.05 per barrel.
11. Based on Exhibit 4 and Yamata's research on the energy sector, the shape of the futures price curve for Brent crude oil is most consistent with the:
    A. insurance theory.
    B. theory of storage.
    C. hedging pressure hypothesis.
12. The total return (annualized excluding leverage) on the lean hog futures contract is:
    A. −37.2%.
    B. −36.0%.
    C. −34.8%.

13. Which of Nabli's statements about roll returns is correct?
    A. Only Statement 4
    B. Only Statement 5
    C. Both Statement 4 and Statement 5

14. The *best* response to Nabli's question about the relative performance of the two indexes is that Index B is *most likely* to exhibit returns that are:
    A. lower than those of Index A.
    B. the same as those of Index A.
    C. higher than those of index A.

15. Given Nabli's expectations for crude oil, the *most appropriate* swap position is the:
    A. basis swap.
    B. volatility swap.
    C. excess return swap.

The following information relates to Questions 16–22.

Mary McNeil is the corporate treasurer at Farmhouse, which owns and operates several farms and ethanol production plants in the United States. McNeil's primary responsibility is risk management. Katrina Falk, a recently hired junior analyst at Farmhouse, works for McNeil in managing the risk of the firm's commodity price exposures. Farmhouse's risk management policy requires the use of futures to protect revenue from price volatility, regardless of forecasts of future prices, and prohibits risk managers from taking speculative positions.

McNeil meets with Falk to discuss recent developments in two of Farmhouse's commodity markets, grains and livestock. McNeil asks Falk about key characteristics of the two markets that affect revenues and costs. Falk tells McNeil the following:

Statement 1: The life cycle for livestock depends on the product and varies widely by product.

Statement 2: Grains have uniform, well-defined seasons and growth cycles specific to geographic regions.

A material portion of Farmhouse's revenue comes from livestock exports, and a major input cost is the cost of grains imported from outside the United States. Falk and McNeil next discuss three conclusions that Falk reached in an analysis of the grains and livestock markets:

Conclusion 1: Assuming demand for grains remains constant, extreme heat in the regions from which we import our grains will result in a benefit to us in the form of lower grain prices.

Conclusion 2: New tariffs on cattle introduced in our primary export markets will likely result in higher prices for our livestock products in our local market.

Conclusion 3: Major improvements in freezing technology allowing for longer storage will let us better manage the volatility in the prices of our livestock products.

McNeil asks Falk to gather spot and futures price data on live cattle, wheat, and soybeans, which are presented in Exhibit 5. Additionally, she observes that: (1) the convenience yield of soybeans exceeds the costs of its direct storage and (2) commodity producers as a group are less interested in hedging in the forward market than commodity consumers are.

EXHIBIT 5   Selected Commodity Price Data*

Market	Live Cattle Price	Wheat Price	Soybeans Price
Spot	109	407	846
Futures	108	407	850

* Live cattle: US cents per pound; wheat and soybeans: US cents per bushel.

A key input cost for Farmhouse in producing ethanol is natural gas. McNeil uses positions in natural gas (NG) futures contracts to manage the risk of natural gas price volatility. Three months ago, she entered into a long position in natural gas futures at a futures price of $2.93 per million British thermal units (MMBtu). The current price of the same contract is $2.99. Exhibit 6 presents additional data about the three-month futures position.

EXHIBIT 6   Selected Information—Natural Gas Futures Three-Month Position*

Commodity	Total Current $ Exposure	Position	Near-Term Futures (Current Price)	Farther-Term Futures
Natural Gas (NG)	5,860,000	Long	2.99	3.03

*NG: $ per MMBtu; 1 contract = 10,000 MMBtu.

The futures position is fully collateralized earning a 3% rate. McNeil decides to roll forward her current exposure in the natural gas position.

Each month, McNeil reports the performance of the energy futures positions, including details on price returns, roll returns, and collateral returns, to the firm's executive committee. A new committee member is concerned about the negative roll returns on some of the positions. In a memo to McNeil, the committee member asks her to explain why she is not avoiding positions with negative roll returns.

16. With respect to its risk management policy, Farmhouse can be *best* described as:
    A. a trader.
    B. a hedger.
    C. an arbitrageur.
17. Which of Falk's statements regarding the characteristics of the grains and livestock markets is correct?
    A. Only Statement 1
    B. Only Statement 2
    C. Both Statement 1 and Statement 2
18. Which of Falk's conclusions regarding commodity markets is correct?
    A. Conclusion 1
    B. Conclusion 2
    C. Conclusion 3

19. Which commodity market in Exhibit 5 is currently in a state of contango?
    A. Wheat
    B. Soybeans
    C. Live cattle

20. Based on Exhibit 5 and McNeil's two observations, the futures price of soybeans is *most* consistent with the:
    A. insurance theory.
    B. theory of storage.
    C. hedging pressure hypothesis.

21. Based on Exhibit 6, the total return from the long position in natural gas futures is *closest* to:
    A. 1.46%.
    B. 3.71%.
    C. 4.14%.

22. The *most appropriate* response to the new committee member's question is that:
    A. roll returns are negatively correlated with price returns.
    B. such roll returns are the result of futures markets in backwardation.
    C. such positions may outperform other positions that have positive roll returns.

CHAPTER 6

HEDGE FUND STRATEGIES

Barclay T. Leib, CFE, CAIA, Kathryn M. Kaminski, PhD, CAIA, Mila
Getmansky Sherman, PhD

LEARNING OUTCOMES

The candidate should be able to:

- discuss how hedge fund strategies may be classified;
- discuss investment characteristics, strategy implementation, and role in a portfolio of *equity-related* hedge fund strategies;
- discuss investment characteristics, strategy implementation, and role in a portfolio of *event-driven* hedge fund strategies;
- discuss investment characteristics, strategy implementation, and role in a portfolio of *relative value* hedge fund strategies;
- discuss investment characteristics, strategy implementation, and role in a portfolio of *opportunistic* hedge fund strategies;
- discuss investment characteristics, strategy implementation, and role in a portfolio of *specialist* hedge fund strategies;
- discuss investment characteristics, strategy implementation, and role in a portfolio of *multi-manager* hedge fund strategies;
- describe how factor models may be used to understand hedge fund risk exposures;
- evaluate the impact of an allocation to a hedge fund strategy in a traditional investment portfolio.

1. INTRODUCTION AND CLASSIFICATION OF HEDGE FUND STRATEGIES

Hedge funds form an important subset of the alternative investments opportunity set, but they come with many pros and cons in their use and application across different asset classes and investment approaches. The basic tradeoff is whether the added fees typically involved with hedge fund investing result in sufficient additional alpha and portfolio diversification benefits to justify the high fee levels. This is an ongoing industry debate.

Some argue that investing in hedge funds is a key way to access the very best investment talent—those individuals who can adroitly navigate investment opportunities across a potentially wider universe of markets. Others argue that hedge funds are important because the alpha that may be produced in down markets is hard to source elsewhere.

The arguments against hedge funds are also non-trivial. In addition to the high fee levels, the complex offering memorandum documentation needs to be understood by investors (i.e., the limited partners). Other issues include lack of full underlying investment transparency/attribution, higher cost allocations associated with the establishment and maintenance of the fund investment structures, and generally longer–lived investment commitment periods with limited redemption availability.

In addition, each hedge fund strategy area tends to introduce different types of added portfolio risks. For example, to achieve meaningful return objectives, arbitrage-oriented hedge fund strategies tend to utilize significant leverage that can be dangerous to limited partner investors, especially during periods of market stress. Long/short equity and event-driven strategies may have less beta exposure than simple, long-only beta allocations, but the higher hedge fund fees effectively result in a particularly expensive form of embedded beta. Such strategies as managed futures or global macro investing may introduce natural benefits of asset class and investment approach diversification, but they come with naturally higher volatility in the return profiles typically delivered. Extreme tail risk in portfolios may be managed with the inclusion of relative value volatility or long volatility strategies, but it comes at the cost of a return drag during more normal market periods. In other words, some hedge fund strategies may have higher portfolio diversification benefits, while others may simply be return enhancers rather than true portfolio diversifiers.

Also, the hedge fund industry continues to evolve in its overall structure. Over the past decade, traditional limited partnership formats have been supplemented by offerings of liquid alternatives (liquid alts)—which are mutual fund, closed-end fund, and ETF-type vehicles that invest in various hedge fund-like strategies. Liquid alts are meant to provide daily liquidity, transparency, and lower fees while opening hedge fund investing to a wider range of investors. However, empirical evidence shows that liquid alts significantly underperform similar strategy hedge funds, which suggests that traditional hedge funds may be benefiting from an illiquidity premium phenomenon that cannot be easily transported into a mutual fund format.

Investors must understand the various subtleties involved with investing in hedge funds. Although secular bull market trends have arguably made "hedged" strategies less critical for inclusion in portfolio allocations than they were during the mid-to-late 2000s, the overall popularity of hedge funds tends to be somewhat cyclical. Notably, as demonstrated by the endowment model of investing, placing hedge funds as a core allocation can increase net returns and reduce risk.

This chapter presents the investment characteristics and implementation for the major categories of hedge fund strategies. It also provides a framework for classifying and evaluating these strategies based on their risk profiles. Section 1 summarizes some distinctive regulatory and investment characteristics of hedge funds and discusses ways to classify hedge fund strategies. Sections 2 through 12 present investment characteristics and strategy implementation for each of the following hedge fund strategy categories: equity-related; event-driven; relative value; opportunistic; specialist; and multi-manager strategies. Section 13 introduces a conditional factor model as a unifying framework for understanding and analyzing the risk exposures of these strategies. Section 16 evaluates the contributions of each hedge fund strategy to the return and risk profile of a traditional portfolio of stocks and bonds. The chapter concludes with a summary.

1.1. Classification of Hedge Funds and Strategies

The most important characteristics of hedge funds are summarized as follows:

1. **Legal/Regulatory Overview:** Different countries have varying requirements for investor eligibility to access hedge fund investments. These regulations are typically intended to limit access to traditional hedge funds to sophisticated investors with a minimum income or net-worth requirement, and they allow hedge fund managers to accept only a limited number of investment subscriptions. Most traditional hedge funds in the United States are offered effectively as private placement offerings. Whether the underlying fund manager must register with regulatory authorities depends on assets under management (AUM); however, regardless of AUM, all US hedge funds are subject to regulatory oversight against fraudulent conduct. Hedge funds offered in other jurisdictions—attractive, tax-neutral locales like the Cayman Islands, the British Virgin Islands, or Bermuda—are typically presented to investors as stand-alone corporate entities subject to the rules and regulations of the particular locality.

   From a regulatory perspective, the advent of liquid alts has likely caused the greatest shift in the industry over the past decade. Some of the more liquid hedge fund strategies that meet certain liquidity and diversification requirements (generally long/short equity and managed futures strategies) are offered by many fund sponsors in mutual fund-type structures in the United States and in the undertakings for collective investment in transferable securities (UCITs) format in Europe and Asia. By law, these liquid alts vehicles can be more widely marketed to retail investors. Whereas traditional hedge funds typically offer only limited periodic liquidity, liquid alts funds may be redeemed by investors on a daily basis. Also, traditional hedge funds typically involve both a management fee and an incentive fee; however, liquid alts in most countries are prohibited from charging an incentive fee.

   Finally, the overall regulatory constraints for hedge funds are far less than those for regulated investment vehicles—except for the liquid alts versions, which have much higher constraints to provide liquidity to investors.

2. **Flexible Mandates—Few Investment Constraints:** Given the relatively low legal and regulatory constraints faced by hedge funds, their mandates are flexible; thus, they are relatively unhindered in their trading and investment activities in terms of investable asset classes and securities, risk exposures, and collateral. The fund prospectus (i.e., offering memorandum) will specify the hedge fund's mandate and objectives and will include constraints, if any, on investment in certain asset classes as well as in the use of leverage, shorting, and derivatives.

3. **Large Investment Universe:** Lower regulatory constraints and flexible mandates give hedge funds access to a wide range of assets outside the normal set of traditional investments. Examples include private securities, non-investment-grade debt, distressed securities, derivatives, and more-esoteric contracts, such as life insurance contracts and even music or film royalties.

4. **Aggressive Investment Styles:** Hedge funds may use their typically flexible investment mandates to undertake strategies deemed too risky for traditional investment funds. These strategies may involve significant shorting and/or concentrated positions in domestic and foreign securities that offer exposure to credit, volatility, and liquidity risk premiums.

5. **Relatively Liberal Use of Leverage:** Hedge funds generally use leverage more extensively than regulated investment funds. Their leveraged positions are implemented either by borrowing securities from a prime broker or by using implied leverage via derivatives. In many instances, such leverage is necessary to make the return profile of the strategy meaningful. In other instances, derivatives may be used to hedge away unwanted risks (e.g., interest rate or credit risk) that may create high "notional leverage" but result in a less risky portfolio. Within long/short equity trading, leverage is most often applied to quantitative approaches in which small statistical valuation aberrations—typically over short windows of time—are identified by a manager or an algorithm. Such quant managers will typically endeavor to be market neutral but will apply high leverage levels to make the opportunities they identify meaningful from a return perspective.

6. **Hedge Fund Liquidity Constraints:** Limited partnership-format hedge funds involve initial lock-up periods, liquidity gates, and exit windows. These provide hedge fund managers with a greater ability to take and maintain positions than vehicles that allow investors to withdraw their investment essentially at will. It is thus not surprising that empirical evidence shows that such privately-placed hedge funds significantly outperform similar-strategy liquid alts products by approximately 100 bps–200 bps, on average, per year.

7. **Relatively High Fee Structures:** Hedge funds have traditionally imposed relatively high investment fees on investors, including both management fees and incentive fees. These have historically been 1% or more of AUM for management fees and 10%–20% of annual returns for incentive fees. The incentive fee structure is meant to align the interests of the hedge fund manager with those of the fund's investors.

With this background, we now address how hedge funds are classified. One distinction is between single manager hedge funds and multi-manager hedge funds. A **single-manager fund** is a fund in which one portfolio manager or team of portfolio managers invests in one strategy or style. A **multi-manager fund** can be of two types. One type is a **multi-strategy fund**, in which teams of portfolio managers trade and invest in multiple different strategies within the same fund. The second type, a fund-of-hedge funds, often simply called a **fund-of-funds** (FoF), is a fund in which the fund-of-funds manager allocates capital to separate, underlying hedge funds (e.g., single manager and/or multi-manager funds) that themselves run a range of different strategies.

At the single manager and single strategy level, hedge fund strategies can be classified in various ways. The taxonomy is often based on some combination of:

1. the instruments in which the managers invest (e.g., equities, commodities, foreign exchange, convertible bonds);
2. the trading philosophy followed by the managers (e.g., systematic, discretionary); and
3. the types of risk the managers assume (e.g., directional, event driven, relative value).

Most prominent hedge fund data vendors use a combination of these criteria to classify hedge fund strategies. For example, Hedge Fund Research, Inc. (HFR) reports manager performance statistics on more than 30 strategies and divides funds into six single strategy groupings that are widely used in the hedge fund industry. HFR's six main single strategy groupings are: 1) equity hedge; 2) event driven; 3) fund-of-funds; 4) macro; 5) relative value; and 6) risk parity.

Lipper TASS, another well-known data vendor, classifies funds into the following ten categories: 1) dedicated short bias; 2) equity market neutral; 3) long/short equity hedge; 4) event driven; 5) convertible arbitrage; 6) fixed-income arbitrage; 7) global macro; 8) managed futures; 9) fund-of-funds; and 10) multi-strategy.

Morningstar CISDM goes even further and separates hedge funds in its database into finer categories, like merger arbitrage and systematic futures, among others. In addition, the Morningstar CISDM Database separates fund-of-funds strategies into several different sub-categories, such as debt, equity, event driven, macro/systematic, multi-strategy, and relative value.

Eurekahedge, an important index provider with its roots in Asia, has grown to include many smaller hedge fund managers globally. Its main strategy indexes include nine categories: 1) arbitrage; 2) commodity trading adviser (CTA)/managed futures; 3) distressed debt; 4) event driven; 5) fixed income; 6) long/short equities; 7) macro; 8) multi-strategy; and 9) relative value.

A final example of a prominent hedge fund data vendor is Credit Suisse. Its Credit Suisse Hedge Fund Index is an asset-weighted index that monitors approximately 9,000 funds and consists of funds with a minimum of US$50 million AUM, a 12-month track record, and audited financial statements. The index is calculated and rebalanced monthly, and it reflects performance net of all performance fees and expenses. Credit Suisse also subdivides managers into nine main sub-indexes for strategy areas: 1) convertible arbitrage; 2) emerging markets; 3) equity market neutral; 4) event driven; 5) fixed income; 6) global macro; 7) long/short equity; 8) managed futures; and 9) multi-strategy.

These different data providers use different methodologies for index calculation. HFR produces both the HFRX Index of equally weighted hedge funds, which includes those that are open or closed to new investment, and its HFRI index series, which tracks only hedge funds open to new investment. Because managers who have closed their funds to new investment are typically superior managers who are limited in their capacity to manage additional funds, the HFRX series regularly outperforms the HFRI series. However, the mix of managers represented by the HFRX Index would obviously not be replicable in real-time by an investor, thus limiting its usefulness. Meanwhile, the Credit Suisse Hedge Fund Index is weighted by fund size (i.e., AUM), so its overall performance is more reflective of the performance of the larger hedge funds, such as the multi-strategy managers.

Notably, less overlap exists in manager reporting to the different index providers than one might expect or is likely optimal. In fact, less than 1% of hedge fund managers self-report to all the index service providers mentioned. Clearly, no single index is all-encompassing.

Generally consistent with the above data vendor groupings and with a practice-based risk factor perspective, this chapter groups single hedge fund strategies into the following six categories: 1) equity; 2) event-driven; 3) relative value; 4) opportunistic; 5) specialist; and 6) multi-manager.

- **Equity-related hedge fund strategies** focus primarily on the equity markets, and the majority of their risk profiles involve equity-oriented risk. Within this equity-related bucket, long/short equity, dedicated short bias, and equity market neutral are the main strategies that will be discussed further.
- **Event-driven hedge fund strategies** focus on corporate events, such as governance events, mergers and acquisitions, bankruptcy, and other key events for corporations. The primary

risk for these strategies is event risk, the possibility that an unexpected event will negatively affect a company or security. Unexpected events include unforeseen corporate reorganization, a failed merger, credit rating downgrades, or company bankruptcy. The most common event-driven hedge fund strategies, merger arbitrage and distressed securities, will be discussed in detail.

- **Relative value hedge fund strategies** focus on the relative valuation between two or more securities. These strategies are often exposed to credit and liquidity risks because the valuation differences from which these strategies seek to benefit often are due to differences in credit quality and/or liquidity across different securities. The two common relative value hedge fund strategies to be covered further are fixed-income arbitrage and convertible bond arbitrage.
- **Opportunistic hedge fund strategies** take a top-down approach, focusing on a multi-asset (often macro-oriented) opportunity set. The risks for opportunistic hedge fund strategies depend on the opportunity set involved and can vary across time and asset classes. The two common opportunistic hedge fund strategies that are discussed in further detail are global macro and managed futures.
- **Specialist hedge fund strategies** focus on special or niche opportunities that often require a specialized skill or knowledge of a specific market. These strategies can be exposed to unique risks that stem from particular market sectors, niche securities, and/or esoteric instruments. We will explore two specialist strategies in further detail: volatility strategies involving options and reinsurance strategies.
- **Multi-manager hedge fund strategies** focus on building a portfolio of diversified hedge fund strategies. Managers in this strategy bucket use their skills to combine diverse strategies and dynamically re-allocate among them over time. The two most common types of multi-manager hedge funds are multi-strategy funds and fund-of-funds, which we will discuss in further detail.

Exhibit 1 shows the five single strategy hedge fund buckets that will be covered individually. Multi-strategy funds and fund-of funds—two types of multi-manager strategies—will also be covered. A discussion of each strategy's contributions to portfolio risk and return will follow.

EXHIBIT 1   Hedge Fund Strategies by Category

Equity	Event-Driven	Relative Value	Opportunistic	Specialist	Multi-Manager
• Long/Short Equity • Dedicated Short Bias • Equity Market Neutral	• Merger Arbitrage • Distressed Securitites	• Fixed Income Arbitrage • Convertible Bond Arbitrage	• Global Macro • Managed Futures	• Volatility Strategies • Reinsurance Strategies	• Multi-strategy • Fund-of-Funds

2. EQUITY STRATEGIES: LONG/SHORT EQUITY

Equity hedge fund strategies invest primarily in equity and equity-related instruments. As mentioned previously, the alpha related to equity strategies tends to derive from the wide variety of equity investments available globally combined with astute long and short stock picking.

The size and sign of equity market exposure often dictate the classification of equity hedge fund strategies. As the name suggests, long-only equity hedge fund strategies focus on holding only long positions in equities, and they sometimes use leverage. Long/short equity hedge fund strategies hold both long and short positions in equities that typically result in more-hedged, less-volatile overall portfolios. Short-biased strategies focus on strategic short selling of companies that are expected to lose value in the future (sometimes with an activist inclination, sometimes with long positions in other securities as an offset). Equity market-neutral strategies hold balanced long and short equity exposures to maintain zero (or close to zero) net exposure to the equity market and such factors as sector and size (i.e., market cap). They then focus on, for example, pairs of long and short securities whose prices are out of historical alignment and are expected to experience mean reversion. The following sections discuss long/short equity, dedicated short bias, and equity market-neutral hedge fund strategies.

2.1. Long/Short Equity

Long/short (L/S) equity managers buy equities of companies they expect will rise in value (i.e., they take long positions in undervalued companies) and sell short equities of companies they think will fall in value (i.e., they take short positions in overvalued companies). The objective of long/short equity strategies is to be flexible in finding attractive opportunities on both the long and short sides of the market and to size them within a portfolio. Depending on their specific mandates, long/short equity strategies can shift between industry sectors (e.g., from technology to consumer goods), factors (e.g., from value to growth), and geographic regions (e.g., from Europe to Asia). In practice, however, managers tend to maintain their philosophical biases and areas of focus, typically with a heavy emphasis on fundamental research.

Although market timing using "beta tilts" can play a factor in manager performance, studies have shown that most fundamental long/short equity managers offer little added alpha from such adjustments. They are typically either too net long at market highs or not net long enough at market lows. Most L/S equity managers are not known for their portfolio-level market-timing abilities, but those with such market-timing skills may be particularly valuable from a portfolio allocation perspective.

L/S equity managers also are typically able to take concentrated positions in high conviction buys or sells and can readily apply leverage to increase these positions (although higher levels of leverage are used mostly by quantitatively-oriented managers, not fundamental managers). As a result, stock selection defines manager skill for most L/S equity managers—with market-timing ability being an additive, but generally secondary, consideration. L/S equity is one of the most prevalent hedge fund strategies. It accounts for about 30% of all hedge funds.

2.1.1. Investment Characteristics

Because manager skill derives mainly from stock selection, it is not surprising that individual long/short equity managers tend to have a focus based on their own unique skill sets. As a result, many long/short equity managers specialize in either a specific geographic region, sector, or investment style. However, several key characteristics define long/short equity managers: their strategy focus, their flexibility in holding long and short positions over time, and their use of leverage. Given the specific mandate for a long/short equity manager, his/her exposures to various equity factors can be very different from other long/short equity managers. For example, a manager focusing on small-cap growth stocks would have a positive exposure to the size factor and a negative exposure to the value factor. Conversely, a manager with a focus on large-cap value stocks would have a negative exposure to the size factor and a positive exposure to the value factor.

Given that equity markets tend to rise over the long run, most long/short equity managers typically hold net long equity positions. Some managers maintain their short positions as a hedge against unexpected market downturns. Other managers are more opportunistic; they tend to take on more short positions after uncovering negative issues with a company's management, strategies, and/or financial statements or whenever their valuation models suggest selling opportunities in certain stocks or sectors. As a result, performance during market crisis periods is important for differentiating between hedge fund managers. Given that hedge funds typically carry high fees, it is important to avoid paying such added fees just for embedded beta exposure that could be achieved more cheaply by investing in traditional long-only strategies. The goal in long/short equity investing is generally to find more sources of idiosyncratic alpha (primarily via stock picking and secondarily by market timing) rather than embedded systematic beta. Exhibit 2 presents some key aspects of this important strategy area.

EXHIBIT 2   Long/Short Equity—Risk, Liquidity, Leverage, and Benchmarking

Risk Profile and Liquidity

- Diverse opportunities globally create a wide universe from which to create alpha through astute stock picking.
- Diverse investment styles include value/growth, large cap/small cap, discretionary/quantitative, and industry specialized.
- They typically have average exposures of 40%–60% net long, composed of gross exposures of 70%–90% long, vs. 20%–50% short, but they can vary widely. Return profiles are typically aimed to achieve average annual returns roughly equivalent to a long-only approach but with a standard deviation 50% lower than a long-only approach.
- Some managers use index-based short hedges to reduce market risk, but most search for single-name shorts for portfolio alpha and added absolute return.
- Some managers are able to add alpha via market timing of portfolio beta tilt, but evidence suggests that most L/S managers do this poorly.
- This strategy can typically be handled by both limited partner and mutual fund-type vehicles.
- Attractiveness: Liquid, diverse, with mark-to-market pricing driven by public market quotes; added short-side exposure typically reduces beta risk and provides an additional source of potential alpha and reduced portfolio volatility.

Leverage Usage

- Variable: The more market-neutral or quantitative the strategy approach, the more levered the strategy application tends to be to achieve a meaningful return profile.

Benchmarking

- L/S equity benchmarks include HFRX and HFRI Equity Hedge Indices; Lipper TASS L/S Equity Hedge; Morningstar/CISDM Equity L/S Index; and Credit Suisse L/S Equity Index.

2.1.2. Strategy Implementation

When long and short stock positions are placed together into a portfolio, the market exposure is the net of the beta-adjusted long and short exposures. For example, with many strong sells and a relatively large short position, the strategy could be net short for brief periods of time. Typically, most long/short equity managers end up with modest net long exposures averaging between 40%–60% net long. Many long/short equity managers are naturally sector-specific, often designing their funds around their industry specialization. Such specialist L/S fund managers analyze fundamental situations that they know well from both a top-down and bottom-up analytical perspective. Natural areas of specialization include potentially more complex sectors, such as telecom/media/technology (TMT), financial, consumer, health care, and biotechnology sectors. Conversely, generalist L/S managers search further afield, thus having flexibility to invest across multiple industry groups. Typically, these generalists avoid complex sectors; for example, they may avoid biotechnology because corporate outcomes may be deemed too binary depending on the success or failure of drug trials. Although generalist managers do take a more balanced and flexible approach, they may miss detailed industry subtleties that are increasingly important to understand in a world where news flows 24/7 and is increasingly nuanced.

Overall, long/short equity investing in most instances is a mix of extracting alpha on the long and short sides from single-name stock selection combined with some naturally net long embedded beta.

EXAMPLE 1   Long/Short Equity Investing Dilemma

The Larson family office views L/S equity investing as a significant portion of the hedge fund universe and would like to access managers talented not only at long investing but also at short selling. However, it does not want to pay high hedge fund fees just for long-biased beta because it has access to long-biased beta at lower fees elsewhere in its portfolio. But, Larson will pay hedge fund fees for strategies that can produce strong risk-adjusted performance in a unique and differentiated fashion.

1. Discuss some potential hedge fund strategies the Larson family office should consider adding to its existing portfolio.
2. Discuss some of the problems and risks that it may encounter.

Solution to 1: The Larson family office should consider managers focused on an L/S equity strategy with a sector-specialization as opposed to a generalist fundamental L/S strategy. Generalist L/S managers can benefit from the flexibility to scan a wide universe of stocks to find investments, but they may not be able to develop a sufficient information edge in their analysis to dependably deliver sufficient alpha relative to their fees and natural long beta positioning. However, managers running specialist L/S equity strategies—especially in such complex sectors as technology, finance, and biotechnology/health care—are more likely to have the specialized capabilities to perform the "deep-dive" differentiated analysis required to develop more original views and stronger portfolio performance.

Solution to 2: A key problem with selecting sector-specialist L/S equity hedge funds is that they are more difficult to analyze and assess. There are also fewer to choose from

compared to generalist L/S hedge funds. Sectors can fall out of favor, risking an allocation to a good fund but in the wrong area given dynamic macroeconomic and financial
market conditions. Moreover, generalist L/S strategies, by definition, can readily reallocate capital more efficiently as opportunities emerge in different sectors. Put another
way, the Larson family office could potentially find itself with too much single sector,
short-sided, or idiosyncratic exposure at the wrong time if it chooses a sector-specialist
L/S equity fund.

3. EQUITY STRATEGIES: DEDICATED SHORT SELLING AND SHORT-BIASED

Dedicated short-selling hedge fund managers take short-only positions in equities deemed
to be expensively priced versus their deteriorating fundamental situations. Such managers may
vary their short exposures only in terms of portfolio sizing by, at times, holding higher levels
of cash. **Short-biased** hedge fund managers use a less extreme version of this approach. They
also search for opportunities to sell expensively priced equities, but they may balance short
exposure with some modest value-oriented, or possibly index-oriented, long exposure. This
latter approach can potentially help short-biased hedge funds cope with long bull market periods in equities. Both types of short sellers actively aim to create an uncorrelated or negatively
correlated source of return by seeking out failing business models, fraudulent accounting,
corporate mismanagement, or other factors that may sour the market's perception of a given
equity. Because of the overall secular up-trend in global equity markets, especially across the
past several decades, it has been very difficult to be a successful short seller. As a result, fewer
such managers are in existence today than in the 1990s.

One exception is the emergence of **activist short selling**, whereby managers take a short
position in a given security and then publicly present their research backing the short thesis.
Typically, if the hedge fund manager has a solid reputation from its past activist short-selling
forays, the release of such research causes a significant stock price plunge into which the activist
short seller might cover a portion of its short position. In the United States, this practice has
not been deemed to be market manipulation by securities' regulators as long as the activist
short seller is not publishing erroneous information, is not charging for such information
(which might create potential conflicts of interest between subscribers and investors), and is
acting only in the best interests of its limited partner investors.

3.1. Investment Characteristics

Short-selling managers focus on situations involving overvalued equities of companies facing
deteriorating fundamentals that typically have not yet been perceived by the market. They also
attempt to maximize returns during periods of market declines. If these short-selling managers
can achieve success with their approaches, they can provide a unique and useful source of negatively correlated returns compared to many other strategy areas.

Short selling involves borrowing securities, selling them "high," and then after prices have
declined, buying the same securities back "low" and returning them to the lender. To borrow
the securities to short sell, the manager must post collateral with the securities lender to cover
potential losses. The manager must also pay interest on the securities loan, which can be high

if the securities are difficult for the lender to locate. One key risk is that the lender may want the securities back at an inopportune time—such as before the expected price decline has materialized, which could be disadvantageous for the hedge fund manager.

Short selling in general is a difficult investment practice to master in terms of risk management because of the natural phenomenon that positions will grow if prices advance against the short seller but will shrink if prices decline. This is the opposite of what occurs with long-only investing, and it is more difficult to manage. Additionally, access to company management for research purposes can be blocked for fund managers who become known as active short sellers.

From a regulatory perspective, many countries limit or impose stringent rules on short selling. In the United States, the "uptick rule" states that when a stock decreases by 10% or more from its prior closing price, a short sale order can be executed only at a price higher than the current best (i.e., highest) bid. This means the stock's price must be rising to execute the short sale. Although many emerging markets have allowed short selling, particularly to enhance market liquidity (e.g., the Saudi Stock Exchange allowed short sales beginning in 2016), there is always concern that limits could be placed on short selling during extreme market environments or that regulations could change. For example, for a brief period during the global financial crisis of 2007–2009, new short sales on a designated list of financial stocks were banned by the US SEC to lessen systematic market stress.

Given the difficult operational aspects of short selling, and because equity markets tend to secularly rise over time, successful short-selling managers typically have something of a short-term "attack and retreat" style. The return profile for a successful short-biased manager might best be characterized by increasingly positive returns as the market declines and the risk-free return when the market rises. In some idealized short-selling world, this would entail being short the market during down periods and investing in low-risk government debt when the market is not declining. But, the actual goal of a short seller is to pick short-sale stocks that can still generate positive returns even when the general market trend is up. Skillful, dedicated short-biased managers look for possible short-selling targets among companies that are overvalued, that are experiencing declining revenues and/or earnings, or that have internal management conflicts, weak corporate governance, or even potential accounting frauds. Other possible short-sale candidates are companies that may have single products under development that the short seller believes will ultimately either be unsuccessful or non-repeatable. Exhibit 3 shows some important aspects of this strategy area.

EXHIBIT 3   Dedicated Short Sellers and Short-Biased—Risk, Liquidity, Leverage, and Benchmarking

---

Risk Profile and Liquidity

- Dedicated short sellers: They only trade with short-side exposure, although they may moderate short beta by also holding cash.
- Short-biased managers: They are focused on good short-side stock picking, but they may moderate short beta with some value-oriented long exposure or index-oriented long exposure as well as cash.
- Dedicated short sellers tend to be 60%–120% short at all times. Short-biased managers are typically around 30%–60% net short. The focus in both cases tends to be on single equity stock picking as opposed to index shorting.
- Return goals are typically less than those for most other hedge fund strategies but with a negative correlation benefit. They are more volatile than a typical L/S equity hedge fund given short beta exposure.

- Managers have some ability to add alpha via market timing of portfolio beta tilt, but it is difficult to do with consistency or added alpha.
- This strategy is typically handled best in a limited partnership because of difficult operational aspects of short selling.
- Attractiveness: Liquid, negatively correlated alpha to that of most other strategies, with mark-to-market pricing from public prices. Historic returns have been lumpy and generally disappointing.

Leverage Usage

- Low: There is typically sufficient natural volatility that short-selling managers do not need to add much leverage.

Benchmarking

- Short-biased indexes include Eurekahedge Equity Short Bias Hedge Fund Index and Lipper TASS Dedicated Short-Bias Index. Some investors also compare short-biased funds' returns to the inverse of returns on related stock indexes.

Note: Each index has different methodologies for fund inclusion. Because there are fewer short-selling managers, the construction of an acceptably diverse index is particularly difficult. The Lipper TASS Dedicated Short-Bias Index, for example, includes just four managers.

3.2. Strategy Implementation

Because finding strategic selling opportunities is key to dedicated short-biased strategies, stock selection is an important part of the investment process. Short-selling managers typically take a bottom-up approach by scanning the universe of potential sell targets to uncover and sell short those companies whose shares are most likely to substantially decline in value over the relevant time horizon. Managers search for, among other factors, inherently flawed business models, unsustainable levels of corporate leverage, and indications of poor corporate governance and/or accounting gimmickry. Tools that may be helpful to dedicated short-biased managers in finding potential sell candidates include monitoring single name credit default swap spreads, corporate bond yield spreads, and/or implied volatility of exchange-traded put options. Traditional technical analysis and/or pattern recognition techniques may assist the manager in the market timing of short sales. Various accounting ratios and measures, such as the Altman *Z*-score for judging a company's bankruptcy potential and the Beneish *M*-score for identifying potentially fraudulent financial statements, may also be useful. Because of the inherent difficulty and dangers of short selling, most successful short sellers do significant "deep-dive" forensic work on their short-portfolio candidates. As such, short sellers serve as a valuable resource in creating more overall pricing efficiency in the market.

EXAMPLE 2   Candidate for Short-Biased Hedge Fund Strategy

Kit Stone, a short-biased hedge fund manager, is researching Generic Inc. (GI) for possible addition to his portfolio. GI was once a drug industry leader, but for the past 10 years its R&D budgets have declined. Its drug patents have all expired, so it now operates in the competitive generic drug business. GI has staked its future on a new treatment for gastro-intestinal disease. R&D was financed by debt, so GI's leverage ratio is twice the industry average. Early clinical trials were inconclusive. Final clinical trial results for GI's new drug are to be revealed within one month. Although the market is constructive, many medical experts remain doubtful of the new drug's efficacy. Without any further insights into the trial results, Stone reviews the following information.

Generic Inc. (GI)			Industry Average		
PE (X)	PB (X)	T12M EPS Growth	PE (X)	PB (X)	T12M EPS Growth
30	3.5	3%	20	2.5	18%

Additionally, Stone notes that GI shares are very thinly traded, with a high short-interest ratio of 60%. Stone's broker has informed him that it is expensive to borrow GI shares for shorting; they are on "special" (i.e., difficult to borrow), with a high borrowing cost of 20% per year. Moreover, there is an active market for exchange-traded options on GI's shares. Prices of one-month GI options appear to reflect a positive view of the company.

1. Discuss whether Stone should add GI shares to his short-biased portfolio.
2. Discuss how Stone might instead take advantage of the situation using GI options.

Solution to 1: Generic Inc. appears to be substantially overvalued. Its main business relies on the competitive generic drug market; it has taken on substantial debt to fund R&D; and skepticism surrounds its new drug. GI's P/Es and P/Bs are higher than industry averages by 50% and 40%, respectively, and its trailing 12-month EPS growth is meager (3% vs. 18% industry average). However, although Stone would normally decide to add GI to his short-biased portfolio, the stock's high short-interest ratio and high cost to borrow (for shorting) are very concerning. Both factors suggest significant potential that a dangerous short-squeeze situation could develop if clinical results really do show efficacy of GI's new drug. So, based on the negative demand/supply dynamics for the stock, Stone decides not to add GI to his portfolio.

Solution to 2: Stone might instead consider expressing his negative view on GI by simply purchasing put options. Alternatively, Stone could purchase a long put calendar spread, where he would buy a put with expiry beyond and sell a put with expiry before the expected release date of the clinical trial results. In that case, the premium received from writing the shorter tenor put would finance, in part, the cost of buying the longer tenor put. As a third possibility, Stone might even consider buying GI shares and then lending them at the attractive 20% rate. In that case, he would need to hedge this long stock position with the purchase of out-of-the-money puts, thereby creating a protective put position. As a final possibility, if out-of-the-money calls are deemed to be expensive because of positive sentiment, Stone could sell such calls to finance the purchase of out-of-the-money puts, creating a short risk reversal that provides synthetic short exposure.

4. EQUITY STRATEGIES: EQUITY MARKET NEUTRAL

Equity market-neutral (EMN) hedge fund strategies take opposite (i.e., long and short) positions in similar or related equities that have divergent valuations, and they also attempt to maintain a near net zero portfolio exposure to the market. EMN managers neutralize market risk by constructing their portfolios such that the expected portfolio beta is approximately equal to zero. Moreover, managers often choose to set the betas for sectors or industries as well as for such common risk factors as market size, price-to-earnings ratio, or book-to-market ratio, which are also equal to zero. Because these portfolios do not take beta risk but do attempt to neutralize so many other factor risks, they typically must apply leverage to the long and short positions to achieve a meaningful expected return from their individual stock selections. Approaches vary, but equity market-neutral portfolios are often constructed using highly quantitative methodologies; the portfolios end up being more diverse in their holdings; and the portfolios are typically modified and adjusted over shorter time horizons. The condition of zero market beta can also be achieved with the use of derivatives, including stock index futures and options. Whichever way they are constructed, the overall goal of equity market-neutral portfolios is to capture alpha while minimizing portfolio beta exposure.

Although **pairs trading** is just one subset of equity market-neutral investing, it is an intuitively easy example to consider. With this strategy, pairs are identified of similar under- and overvalued equities, divergently valued shares of a holding company and its subsidiaries, or different share classes of the same company (multi-class stocks typically having different voting rights) in which their prices are out of alignment.

In whatever manner they are created, the pairs are monitored for their typical trading patterns relative to each other—conceptually, the degree of co-integration of the two securities' prices. Positions are established when unusually divergent spread pricing between the two paired securities is observed. Underpinning such a strategy is the expectation that the differential valuations or trading relationships will revert to their long-term mean values or their fundamentally-correct trading relationships, with the long position rising and the short position declining in value. Situations will obviously vary, but strictly quantitative EMN pairs trading, while attempting to minimize overall beta exposure, may still have effective short volatility "tail risk" exposure to abnormal market situations of extreme stress. This is less the case if a fundamental pricing discrepancy is being exploited in anticipation of a possible event that would cause that discrepancy to correct.

Another type of EMN trading is **stub trading**, which entails buying and selling stock of a parent company and its subsidiaries, typically weighted by the percentage ownership of the parent company in the subsidiaries. Assume parent company A owns 90% and 75% of subsidiaries B and C, respectively, and shares of A are determined to be overvalued while shares of B and C are deemed undervalued, all relative to their historical mean valuations. Then, for each share of A sold short, the EMN fund would buy 0.90 and 0.75 shares of B and C, respectively.

Yet another type of EMN approach may involve **multi-class trading**, which involves buying and selling different classes of shares of the same company, such as voting and non-voting shares. As with pairs trading, the degree of co-integration of returns and the valuation metrics for the multi-class shares are determined. If/when prices move outside of their normal ranges, the overvalued shares are sold short while the undervalued shares are purchased. The goal is to gain on the change in relative pricing on the two securities as market pricing reverts to more normal ranges.

Fundamental trade setups—although not per se "equity market neutral" but still designed to be market neutral—may be created that are long or short equity hedged against offsetting bond exposures if relative pricing between the stocks and bonds is deemed to be out of alignment. Such pairs trading is referred to as capital structure arbitrage and will be discussed in the event-driven strategies section. In these situations, attractive expected outcomes are often created from relative security mispricings designed to exploit potential event situations (e.g., a potential merger or bankruptcy) that would have an impact on relative pricing. Moreover, when two bonds are positioned relative to each other (e.g., to exploit a misunderstood difference in bond covenants or a potential differential asset recovery), a market-neutral strategy can also be employed.

When building market-neutral portfolios, sometimes large numbers of securities are traded and positions are adjusted on a daily or even an hourly basis using algorithm-based models. Managers following this approach are referred to as **quantitative market-neutral** managers. The frequent adjustments implemented by such managers are driven by the fact that market prices change faster than company fundamental factors. This price movement triggers a rebalancing of the EMN portfolio back to a market neutrality. When the time horizon of EMN trading shrinks to even shorter intervals and mean reversion and relative momentum characteristics of market behavior are emphasized, quantitative market-neutral trading becomes what is known as statistical arbitrage trading. With EMN and statistical arbitrage trading, a natural push/pull occurs between maintaining an optimal beta-neutral portfolio and the market impacts and brokerage costs of nearly continuous adjusting of the portfolio. So, many EMN managers use trading-cost hurdle models to determine if and when they should rebalance a portfolio.

Overall, the main source of skill for an EMN manager is in security selection, with market timing being of secondary importance. Sector exposure also tends to be constrained, although this can vary by the individual manager's approach. Managers that are overall beta neutral and specialize in sector rotation exposure as their source of alpha are known as market-neutral tactical asset allocators or macro-oriented market-neutral managers.

4.1. Investment Characteristics

Equity market-neutral fund managers seek to insulate their portfolios from movements in the overall market, and they can take advantage of divergent valuations by trading specific securities. As discussed, this is often a quantitatively driven process that uses a substantial amount of leverage to generate meaningful return objectives. However, many discretionary EMN managers implement their positions with significantly less leverage.

Overall, EMN managers generally are more useful for portfolio allocation during periods of non-trending or declining markets because they typically deliver returns that are steadier and less volatile than those of many other hedge strategy areas. Over time, their conservative and constrained approach typically results in less-volatile overall returns than those of managers who accept beta exposure. The exception to this norm is when the use of significant leverage may cause forced portfolio downsizing. By using portfolio margining techniques offered by prime brokers, market-neutral managers may run portfolios with up to 300% long versus 300% short exposures. Prime broker portfolio margining rules generally allow managers to maintain such levered positioning until a portfolio loss of a specified magnitude (i.e., excess drawdown) is incurred. At the time of such excess drawdown, the prime broker can force the manager to downsize his/her overall portfolio exposure. This is a key strategy risk, particularly for quantitative market-neutral managers.

Despite the use of substantial leverage and because of their more standard and overall steady risk/return profiles, equity market-neutral managers are often considered as preferred replacements for (or at least a complement to) fixed-income managers during periods when fixed-income returns are unattractively low/and or the yield curve is flat. EMN managers are, of course, sourcing a very different type of alpha with very different risks than in fixed-income investing. EMN managers must deal with leverage risk, including the issues of availability of leverage and at what cost, and tail risk, particularly the performance of levered portfolios during periods of market stress. Exhibit 4 presents important aspects of this strategy area.

EXHIBIT 4   Equity Market Neutral—Risk, Liquidity, Leverage, and Benchmarking

Risk Profile and Liquidity

- They have relatively modest return profiles, with portfolios aimed to be market neutral, and differing constraints to other factors and sector exposures are allowed.
- They generally have high levels of diversification and liquidity and lower standard deviation of returns than many other strategies across normal market conditions.
- Many different types of EMN managers exist, but many are purely quantitative managers (vs. discretionary managers).
- Time horizons vary, but EMN strategies are typically oriented toward mean reversion, with shorter horizons than other strategies and more active trading.
- Because of often high leverage, EMN strategies typically do not meet regulatory leverage limits for mutual fund vehicles. So, limited partnerships are the preferred vehicle.
- Attractiveness: EMN strategies typically take advantage of idiosyncratic short-term mispricing between securities whose prices should otherwise be co-integrated. Their sources of return and alpha, unlike those of many other strategies, do not require accepting beta risk. So, EMN strategies are especially attractive during periods of market vulnerability and weakness.

Leverage Usage

- High: As many beta risks (e.g., market, sector) are hedged away, it is generally deemed acceptable for EMN managers to apply higher levels of leverage while striving for meaningful return targets.

Benchmarking

- Market-neutral indexes include HFRX and HFRI Equity Market Neutral Indices; Lipper TASS Equity Market Neutral Index; Morningstar/CISDM Equity Market Neutral Index; and Credit Suisse Equity Market Neutral Index.

4.2. Strategy Implementation

Equity market-neutral portfolios are constructed in four main steps. First, the investment universe is evaluated to include only tradable securities with sufficient liquidity and adequate short-selling potential. Second, securities are analyzed for buy and sell opportunities using fundamental models (which use company, industry, and economic data as inputs for valuation) and/or statistical and momentum-based models. Third, a portfolio is constructed with constraints to maintain market risk neutrality, whereby the portfolio's market value-weighted beta is approximately zero and there is often dollar (i.e., money), sector, or other factor risk neutrality. Fourth, the availability and cost of leverage are considered in terms of desired return profile and acceptable potential portfolio drawdown risk. The execution costs of the strategy rebalancing are also introduced as a filter for decision making as to how often the portfolio should be rebalanced. Markets are dynamic because volatility and leverage are always changing; therefore, the exposure to the market is always changing. Consequently, EMN managers must actively manage their funds' exposures to remain neutral over time. However, costs are incurred every time the portfolio is rebalanced. So, EMN managers must be very careful to not allow such costs to overwhelm the security-selection alpha that they are attempting to capture.

Note that the following is a simplified example. In reality, most EMN managers would likely not hedge beta on a stock-by-stock basis but rather would hedge beta on an overall portfolio basis. They would also likely consider other security factor attributes.

EXAMPLE 3 Equity Market-Neutral Pairs Trading:

Ling Chang, a Hong Kong–based EMN manager, has been monitoring PepsiCo Inc. (PEP) and Coca-Cola Co. (KO), two global beverage industry giants. After examining the Asia marketing strategy for a new PEP drink, Chang feels the marketing campaign is too controversial and the overall market is too narrow. Although PEP has relatively weak earnings prospects compared to KO, 3-month valuation metrics show PEP shares are substantially overvalued versus KO shares (relative valuations have moved beyond their historical ranges). As part of a larger portfolio, Chang wants to allocate $1 million to the PEP versus KO trade and notes the historical betas and S&P 500 Index weights, as shown in the following table.

Stock	Beta	S&P 500 Index Weight
PEP	0.65	0.663
KO	0.55	0.718

Discuss how Chang might implement an EMN pairs trading strategy.

Solution: Chang should take a short position in PEP and a long position in KO with equal beta-weighted exposures. Given Chang wants to allocate $1 million to the trade, she would take on a long KO position of $1 million. Assuming realized betas will be similar to historical betas, to achieve an equal beta-weighted exposure for the short PEP position, Chang needs to short $846,154 worth of PEP shares [= –$1,000,000 / (0.65/0.55)]. Only the overall difference in performance between PEP and KO shares would affect the performance of the strategy because it will be insulated from the effect of market fluctuations. If over the next 3 months the valuations of PEP and KO revert to within normal ranges, then this pairs trading EMN strategy should reap profits.

Note: The S&P 500 Index weights are not needed to answer this question.

5. EVENT-DRIVEN STRATEGIES: MERGER ARBITRAGE

Event-driven (ED) hedge fund strategies take positions in corporate securities and derivatives that are attempting to profit from the outcome of mergers and acquisitions, bankruptcies, share issuances, buybacks, capital restructurings, re-organizations, accounting changes, and similar events. ED hedge fund managers analyze companies' financial statements and regulatory filings and closely examine corporate governance issues (e.g., management structure, board composition, issues for shareholder consideration, proxy voting) as well as firms' strategic objectives, competitive position, and other firm-specific issues. Investments can be made either proactively in anticipation of an event that has yet to occur (i.e., a **soft-catalyst event-driven approach**), or investments can be made in reaction to an already announced corporate event in which security prices related to the event have yet to fully converge (i.e., a **hard-catalyst event-driven approach**). The hard approach is generally less volatile and less risky than soft-catalyst investing. Merger arbitrage and distressed securities are among the most common ED strategies.

5.1. Merger Arbitrage

Mergers and acquisitions can be classified by the method of purchase: cash-for-stock or stock-for-stock. In a cash-for-stock acquisition, the acquiring company (A) offers the target company (T) a cash price per share to acquire T. For example, assume T's share price is $30 and A decides to purchase T for $40 per share (i.e., A is offering a 33% premium to purchase T's shares). In a stock-for-stock acquisition, A offers a specific number of its shares in exchange for 1 T share. So, if A's share price is $20 and it offers 2 of its shares in exchange for 1 T share, then T's shareholders would receive a value of $40 per T share, assuming A's share price is constant until the merger is completed. Although merger deals are structured in different ways for many reasons (e.g., tax implications, corporate structure, or provisions to dissuade a merger, such as a "poison pill"[1]), acquiring companies are generally more likely to offer cash for their target companies when cash surpluses are high. However, if the stock prices are high and acquiring companies' shares are considered richly valued by management, then stock-for-stock acquisitions can take advantage of potentially overvalued shares as a "currency" to acquire target companies.

5.1.1. Investment Characteristics

In a cash-for-stock acquisition, the merger-arb manager may choose to buy just the target company (T), expecting it to increase in value once the acquisition is completed. In a stock-for-stock deal, the fund manager typically buys T and sells the acquiring company (A) in the same ratio as the offer, hoping to earn the spread on successful deal completion. If the acquisition is unsuccessful, the manager faces losses if the price of T (A) has already risen (fallen) in anticipation of the acquisition. Less often, managers take the view that the acquisition will fail—usually due to anti-competition or other regulatory concerns. In this case, he/she would sell T and buy A.

---

[1]A poison pill is a pre-offer takeover defense mechanism that gives target company bondholders the right to sell their bonds back to the target at a pre-specified redemption price, typically at or above par; this defense increases the acquirer's need for cash and raises the cost of the acquisition.

For most acquisitions, the initial announcement of a deal will cause the target company's stock price to rise toward the acquisition price and the acquirer's stock price to fall (either because of the potential dilution of its outstanding shares or the use of cash for purposes other than a dividend payment). The considerable lag time between deal announcement and closing means that proposed merger deals can always fail for any variety of reasons, including lack of financing, regulatory hurdles, and not passing financial due diligence. Hostile takeover bids, where the target company's management has not already agreed to the terms of a merger, are typically less likely to be successfully completed than friendly takeovers, where the target's management has already agreed to merger terms.

Approximately 70%–90% of announced mergers in the United States eventually close successfully. Given the probability that some mergers will not close for whatever reason as well as the costs of establishing a merger arbitrage position (e.g., borrowing the acquiring stock, commissions) and the risk that merger terms might be changed because of market conditions (especially in stressed market environments), merger arbitrage typically offers a 3%–7% return spread depending on the deal-specific risks. Of course, a particularly risky deal might carry an even larger spread. If the average time for merger deal completion is 3-4 months—with managers recycling capital into new deals several times a year and typically applying some leverage to their portfolio positions—then attractive return/risk profiles can be created, earning net annualized returns in the range of 7%–12%, with little correlation to non-deal-specific factors. Diversifying across a variety of mergers, deals, and industries can further help hedge the risk of any one deal failing. So overall, this strategy can be a good uncorrelated source of alpha.

When merger deals do fail, the initial price rise (fall) of the target (acquirer) company is typically reversed. Arbitrageurs who jumped into the merger situation after its initial announcement stand to incur substantial losses on their long (short) position in the target (acquirer)—often as large as negative 20% to 40%. So, the strategy thus does have left-tail risk associated with it.

Corporate events are typically binary: An acquisition either succeeds or fails. The merger arbitrage strategy can be viewed as selling insurance on the acquisition. If the acquisition succeeds (no adverse event occurs), then the hedge fund manager collects the spread (like the premium an insurance company receives for selling insurance) for taking on event risk. If the acquisition fails (an adverse event occurs), then he/she faces the losses on the long and short positions (similar to an insurance company paying out a policy benefit after an insured event has occurred). Thus, the payoff profile of the merger arbitrage strategy resembles that of a riskless bond and a short put option. The merger arbitrage investor also can be viewed as owning an additional call option that becomes valuable if/when another interested acquirer (i.e., white knight) makes a higher bid for the target company before the initial merger proposal is completed. Exhibit 5 shows risk and return attributes of merger arbitrage investing.

EXHIBIT 5   Event-Driven Merger Arbitrage—Risk, Liquidity, Leverage, and Benchmarking

Risk Profile and Liquidity

- Merger arbitrage is a relatively liquid strategy—with defined gains from idiosyncratic single security takeover situations but occasional downside shocks when merger deals unexpectedly fail.
- To the extent that deals are more likely to fail in market stress periods, this strategy has market sensitivity and left-tail risk attributes. Its return profile is insurance-like plus a short put option.

- Because cross-border merger and acquisition (M&A) usually involves two sets of governmental approvals and M&A deals involving vertical integration often face anti-trust scrutiny, these situations carry higher risks and offer wider merger spread returns.
- Some merger arbitrage managers invest only in friendly deals trading at relatively tight spreads, while others embrace riskier hostile takeovers trading at wider spreads. In the latter case, there may be expectations of a higher bid from a white knight.
- The preferred vehicle is limited partnership because of merger arbitrage's use of significant leverage, but some low-leverage, low-volatility liquid alts merger arbitrage funds do exist.
- Attractiveness: Relatively high Sharpe ratios with typically low double-digit returns and mid–single digit standard deviation (depending on specific levels of leverage applied), but left-tail risk is associated with an otherwise steady return profile.

Leverage Usage

- Moderate to high: Managers typically apply 3 to 5 times leverage to this strategy to generate meaningful target return levels.

Benchmarking

- Sub-indexes include HFRX or HFRI Merger Arbitrage Index; CISDM Hedge Fund Merger Arbitrage Index; and Credit Suisse Merger Arbitrage Index.

5.1.2. Strategy Implementation

Merger arbitrage strategies are typically established using common equities; however, a range of other corporate securities, including preferred stock, senior and junior debt, convertible securities, options, and other derivatives, may also be used for positioning and hedging purposes. Often for a cash-for-stock acquisition, a hedge fund manager may choose to use leverage to buy the target firm. For a stock-for-stock acquisition, leverage may also often be used, but short selling the acquiring firm may be difficult due to liquidity issues or short-selling constraints, especially in emerging markets. Merger arbitrage strategies can utilize derivatives to overcome some short-sale constraints or to manage risks if the deal were to fail. For example, the manager could buy out-of-the money (O-T-M) puts on T and/or buy O-T-M call options on A (to cover the short position).

Convertible securities also provide exposure with asymmetrical payoffs. For example, the convertible bonds of T would also rise in value as T's shares rise because of the acquisition; the convertibles' bond value would provide a cushion if the deal fails and T's shares fall. When the acquiring company's credit is superior to the target company's credit, trades may be implemented using credit default swaps (CDS). In this case, protection would be sold (i.e., shorting the CDS) on the target company to benefit from its improved credit quality (and decline in price of protection and the CDS) once a merger is completed. If the pricing is sufficiently cheap, buying protection (i.e., going long the CDS) on the target may also be used as a partial hedge against a merger deal failing. Overall market risk (that could potentially disrupt a merger's consummation) might also be hedged by using added short equity index ETFs/futures or long equity index put positions.

In sum, the true source of return alpha for a merger arbitrage hedge fund manager is in the initial decision as to which deals to embrace and which to avoid. However, once involved with a given merger situation, there may be multiple ways to implement a position depending on the manager's deal-specific perspectives.

EXAMPLE 4   Merger Arbitrage Strategy Payoffs

An acquiring firm (A) is trading at $45/share and has offered to buy target firm (T) in a stock-for-stock deal. The offer ratio is 1 share of A in exchange for 2 shares of T. Target firm T was trading at $15 per share just prior to the announcement of the offer. Shortly thereafter, T's share price jumps up to $19 while A's share price falls to $42 in anticipation of the merger receiving required approvals and the deal closing successfully. A hedge fund manager is confident this deal will be completed, so he buys 20,000 shares of T and sells short 10,000 shares of A.

What are the payoffs of the merger arbitrage strategy if the deal is successfully completed or if the merger fails?

Solution: At current prices it costs $380,000 to buy 20,000 shares of T, and $420,000 would be received for short selling 10,000 shares of A. This provides a net spread of $40,000 to the hedge fund manager if the merger is successfully completed. If the merger fails, then prices should revert to their pre-merger announcement levels. The manager would need to buy back 10,000 shares of A at $45 (costing $450,000) to close the short position, while the long position in 20,000 shares of T would fall to $15 per share (value at $300,000). This would cause a total loss of $110,000 [= (A: +$420,000 − $450,000) + (T: −$380,000 + $300,000)]. In sum, this merger strategy is equivalent to holding a riskless bond with a face value of $40,000 (the payoff for a successful deal) and a short binary put option, which expires worthless if the merger succeeds but pays out $110,000 if the merger fails.

---

6. EVENT-DRIVEN STRATEGIES: DISTRESSED SECURITIES

Distressed securities strategies focus on firms that either are in bankruptcy, facing potential bankruptcy, or under financial stress. Firms face these circumstances for a wide variety of reasons, including waning competitiveness, excessive leverage, poor governance, accounting irregularities, or outright fraud. Often the securities of such companies have been sold out of long-only portfolios and may be trading at a significant discount to their eventual work-out value under proper stewardship and guidance. Because hedge funds are not constrained by institutional requirements on minimum credit quality, hedge fund managers are often natural candidates to take positions in such situations. Hedge funds, generally, also provide their investors only periodic liquidity (typically quarterly or sometimes only annually), making the illiquid nature of such securities less problematic than if such positions were held within a mutual fund. Hedge fund managers may find inefficiently priced securities before, during, or after the bankruptcy process, but typically they will be looking to realize their returns somewhat faster than the longer-term orientation of private equity firms. However, this is not always the case; for example, managers that invest in some distressed sovereign debt (e.g., Puerto Rico, Venezuela) often must face long time horizons to collect their payouts.

At times, distressed hedge fund managers may seek to own the majority or all of a certain class of securities within the capital structure, which enables them to exert creditor control in the corporate bankruptcy or reorganization process. Such securities will vary by country depending on individual bankruptcy laws and procedures. Some managers are active in their distressed investing by building concentrated positions and placing representatives on the boards of the companies they are seeking to turn around. Other distressed managers may be more "passive" in their orientation, relying on others to bear the often substantial legal costs of a corporate capital structure reorganization that may at times involve expensive proxy contests.

By nature, distressed debt and other illiquid assets may take several years to resolve, and they are generally difficult to value. Therefore, hedge fund managers running portfolios of distressed securities typically require relatively long initial lock-up periods (e.g., no redemptions allowed for the first two years) from their investors. Distressed investment managers may also impose fund-level or investor-level redemption gates that are meant to limit the amount of money that investors (i.e., limited partners) may withdraw from a partnership during any given quarter. As for valuing distressed securities, external valuation specialists may be needed to provide an independent estimate of fair value. Valuations of distressed securities with little or no liquidity (e.g., those deemed Level 3 assets for US accounting purposes) are subject to the smoothing effect of "mark-to-model" price determination.

The bankruptcy process typically results in one or two outcomes: liquidation or firm reorganization. In a liquidation, the firm's assets are sold off over some time period; then, based on the priority of their claim, debt- and equity-holders are paid off sequentially. In this case, claimants on the firm's assets are paid in order of priority from senior secured debt, junior secured debt, unsecured debt, convertible debt, preferred stock, and finally common stock. In a re-organization, a firm's capital structure is re-organized and the terms for current claims are negotiated and revised. Current debtholders may agree to extend the maturity of their debt contracts or even to exchange their debt for new equity shares. In this case, existing equity would be canceled (so existing shareholders would be left with nothing) and new equity issued, which would also be sold to new investors to raise funds to improve the firm's financial condition.

6.1. Investment Characteristics

Distressed securities present new sets of risks and opportunities and thus require special skills and increased monitoring. As previously mentioned, many institutional investors, like banks and insurance companies, by their mandates cannot hold non-investment-grade securities in their portfolios. As a result, many such investors must sell off investments in firms facing financial distress. This situation may result in illiquidity and significant price discounting when trades do occur, but it also creates potentially attractive opportunities for hedge funds. Moreover, the movement from financial distress to bankruptcy can unfold over long periods and because of the complexities of legal proceedings, informational inefficiencies cause securities to be improperly valued.

To successfully invest in distressed securities, hedge fund managers require specific skills for analyzing complicated legal proceedings, bankruptcy processes, creditor committee discussions, and re-organization scenarios. They also must be able to anticipate market reactions to these actions. At times, and depending on relative pricing, managers may establish "capital structure arbitrage" positions: For the same distressed entity, they may be long securities where they expect to receive acceptable recoveries but short other securities (including equity) where the value-recovery prospects are dim.

Current market conditions also affect the success of distressed securities strategies. In liquidation, assets may need to be sold quickly, and discounted selling prices will lower the total recovery rate. When illiquid assets must be sold quickly, forced sales and liquidity spirals may lead to fire-sale prices. For re-organizations, current market conditions partly determine whether (and how much) a firm can raise capital from asset sales and/or from the issuance of new equity. Exhibit 6 provides some key attributes of distressed securities investing.

EXHIBIT 6   Distressed Securities—Risk, Liquidity, Leverage, and Benchmarking

Risk Profile and Liquidity

- The return profile for distressed securities investing is typically at the higher end of event-driven strategies but with more variability.
- Outright shorts or hedged positions are possible, but distressed securities investing is usually long-biased. It is subject to security-specific outcomes but still impacted by the health of the macro-economy.
- Distressed securities investing typically entails relatively high levels of illiquidity, especially if using a concentrated activist approach. Pricing may involve "mark-to-model" with return smoothing. Ultimate results are generally binary: either very good or very bad.
- Attractiveness: Returns tend to be "lumpy" and somewhat cyclical. Distressed investing is particularly attractive in the early stages of an economic recovery after a period of market dislocation.

Leverage Usage

- Moderate to low: Because of the inherent volatility and long-biased nature of distressed securities investing, hedge fund managers utilize modest levels of leverage, typically with 1.2 to 1.7 times NAV invested, and with some of the nominal leverage from derivatives hedging.

Benchmarking

- Hedge fund sub-indexes include HFRX and HFRI Distressed Indices; CISDM Distressed Securities Index; Lipper TASS Event-Driven Index; and Credit Suisse Event Driven Distressed Hedge Fund Index.

Note: Alpha produced by distressed securities managers tends to be idiosyncratic. Also, the strategy capitalizes on information inefficiencies and structural inabilities of traditional managers to hold such securities.

6.2. Strategy Implementation

Hedge fund managers take several approaches when investing in distressed securities. In a liquidation situation, the focus is on determining the recovery value for different classes of claimants. If the fund manager's estimate of recovery value is higher than market expectations, perhaps due to illiquidity issues, then he/she can buy the undervalued debt securities in hopes of realizing the higher recovery rate. For example, assume bankrupt company X's senior secured debt is priced at 50% of par. By conducting research on the quality of the collateral and by estimating potential cash flows (and their timing) in liquidation, the hedge fund manager estimates a recovery rate of 75%. He/she can buy the senior secured debt and expect to realize the positive difference in recovery rates. However, even assuming the manager is correct, if the liquidation process drags on and/or market conditions deteriorate, then this premium may be only partly realized, if at all.

In a reorganization situation, the hedge fund manager's focus is on how the firm's finances will be restructured and on assessing the value of the business enterprise and the future value of different classes of claims. There are various avenues for investing in a re-organization. The manager will evaluate the different securities of the company in question and purchase those deemed to be undervalued given the likely re-organization outcome. The selection of security will also depend on whether the manager seeks a control position or not. If so, he/she will be active in the negotiating process and will seek to identify fulcrum securities that provide leverage (or even liquidation) in the reorganization. **Fulcrum securities** are partially-in-the-money claims (not expected to be repaid in full) whose holders end up owning the reorganized company. Assuming the re-organization is caused by excessive financial leverage but the company's operating prospects are still good, a financial restructuring may be implemented whereby senior unsecured debt purchased by the hedge fund manager is swapped for new shares (existing debt and equity are cancelled) and new equity investors inject fresh capital into the company. As financial distress passes and the intrinsic value of the reorganized company rises, an initial public offering (IPO) would likely be undertaken. The hedge fund manager could then exit and earn the difference between what was paid for the undervalued senior unsecured debt and the proceeds received from selling the new shares of the revitalized company in the IPO.

EXAMPLE 5   Capital Structure Arbitrage in the Energy Crisis of 2015–2016

With a sudden structural increase in US energy reserves caused by modern fracking techniques, oil prices tumbled dramatically from more than \$60/barrel in mid-2015 to less than \$30/barrel in early 2016. Debt investors suddenly became concerned about the very survivability of the smaller, highly levered exploration and production (E&P) companies if such low energy prices were to persist. Prices of many energy-related, junior, unsecured, non-investment-grade debt securities fell dramatically. However, retail equity investors generally reacted more benignly. As a result, the shares of several such E&P companies still carried significant implied enterprise value while their debt securities traded as if bankruptcy was imminent.

1. Discuss why such a divergence in the valuation of the debt and equity securities of these E&P companies might have occurred.
2. Discuss how a hedge fund manager specializing in distressed securities might take advantage of this situation.

Solution to 1: This divergence in valuation occurred because of structural differences between the natural holders of debt and equity securities. Institutional holders of the debt likely felt more compelled, or in some cases were required by investment policy, to sell these securities as credit ratings on these bonds were slashed. Retail equity investors were likely less informed as to the potential seriousness of the impact of such a sharp energy price decline on corporate survivability. With equity markets overall still moving broadly higher, retail equityholders may have been expressing a "buy the dip" mentality. Such cross-asset arbitrage situations represent a significant opportunity for nimble and flexible hedge fund managers that are unrestrained by a single asset class perspective or other institutional constraints.

Solution to 2: An astute hedge fund manager would have realized three key points: 1) the junior unsecured debt securities were temporarily undervalued; 2) although bankruptcy in certain specific companies was indeed possible (depending on how long energy prices stayed low), detailed research could uncover those E&P companies for which bankruptcy was less likely; and 3) the unsecured debt securities could be purchased with some safety by shorting the still overvalued equities (or buying put options on those equities) as a hedge.

If energy prices subsequently remained low for too long and bankruptcy was indeed encountered, the equities would become worthless. However, the unsecured debt might still have some recovery value from corporate asset sales, or these securities might become the fulcrum securities that would be converted in a bankruptcy reorganization into new equity in an ongoing enterprise. Alternatively, if oil prices were to recover (as indeed transpired; oil prices closed 2017 at more than $60/barrel), the unsecured debt securities of many of these companies would rebound far more substantially than their equity shares would rise.

In sum, a distressed securities hedge fund arbitrageur willing to take a position in the unsecured debt hedged against short equity (or long puts on the equity) could make money under a variety of possible outcomes.

7. RELATIVE VALUE STRATEGIES: FIXED INCOME ARBITRAGE

We have previously described equity market-neutral investing as one specific equity-oriented relative value hedge fund approach, but other types of relative value strategies are common for hedge funds involving fixed-income securities and hybrid convertible debt. Like equity market-neutral trading, many of these strategies involve the significant use of leverage. Changes in credit quality, liquidity, and implied volatility (for securities with embedded options) are some of the causes of relative valuation differences. During normal market conditions, successful relative value strategies can earn credit, liquidity, or volatility premiums over time. But, in crisis periods—when excessive leverage, deteriorating credit quality, illiquidity, and volatility spikes come to the fore—relative value strategies can result in losses. Fixed-income arbitrage and convertible bond arbitrage are among the most common relative value strategies.

7.1. Fixed-Income Arbitrage

Fixed-income arbitrage strategies attempt to exploit pricing inefficiencies by taking long and short positions across a range of debt securities, including sovereign and corporate bonds, bank loans, and consumer debt (e.g., credit card loans, student loans, mortgage-backed securities). Arbitrage opportunities between fixed-income instruments may develop because of variations in duration, credit quality, liquidity, and optionality.

7.1.1. Investment Characteristics
In its simplest form, fixed-income arbitrage involves buying the relatively undervalued securities and short selling the relatively overvalued securities with the expectation that the mispricing will resolve itself (reversion back to normal valuations) within the specified investment horizon.

Valuation differences beyond normal historical ranges can result from differences in credit quality (investment-grade versus non-investment-grade securities), differences in liquidity (on-the-run versus off-the-run securities), differences in volatility expectations (especially for securities with embedded options), and even differences in issue sizes. More generally, fixed-income arbitrage can be characterized as exploiting price differences relative to expected future price relationships, with mean reversion being one important aspect. In many instances, realizing a net positive relative carry over time may also be the goal of the relative security positioning, which may involve exploiting kinks in a yield curve or an expected shift in the shape of a yield curve.

Where positioning may involve the acceptance of certain relative credit risks across different security issuers, fixed-income arbitrage morphs into what is more broadly referred to as L/S credit trading. This version of trading tends to be naturally more volatile than the exploitation of small pricing differences within sovereign debt alone.

Unless trading a price discrepancy directly involves establishing a desired yield curve exposure, fixed-income arbitrageurs will typically immunize their strategies, which involve both long and short positions, from interest rate risk by taking duration-neutral positions. However, duration neutrality provides a hedge against only small shifts in the yield curve. To hedge against large yield changes and/or non-parallel yield curve movements (i.e., steepening or flattening), the manager might employ a range of fixed-income derivatives, including futures, forwards, swaps, and swaptions (i.e., options on a swap). Moreover, fixed-income securities also vary in their complexity. For example, in addition to interest rate risk, straight government debt is exposed to sovereign risk (and potentially currency risk), which can be substantial in many countries, while asset-backed and mortgaged-backed securities are subject to credit risk and pre-payment risk. Derivatives are also useful for hedging such risks.

Fixed-income security pricing inefficiencies are often quite small, especially in the more-efficient developed capital markets, but the correlation aspects across different securities is typically quite high. Consequently, it may be necessary and acceptable to utilize substantial amounts of leverage to exploit these inefficiencies. Typical leverage ratios in fixed-income arbitrage strategies can be 4 to 5 times (assets to equity). In the case of some market-neutral multi-strategy funds, where fixed-income arbitrage may form just a portion of total risk, fixed-income arbitrage leverage levels can sometimes be as high as 12 to 15 times assets to equity. Of course, leverage will magnify the myriad risks to which fixed-income strategies are exposed, especially during stressed market conditions.

Another factor that has compounded the risks of fixed-income arbitrage strategies has been the inclination of financial engineers to create tranched, structured products around certain fixed-income cash flows—particularly involving residential mortgages—to isolate certain aspects of credit risk and prepayment risk. For example, within a pool of mortgages, cash flows may be divided such that some credit tranche holders have seniority over others or so that interest-only income payments flow to one set of holders and principal-only payoffs flow to another set of holders. The risks of relative value strategies involving mortgage-related securities, which are especially relevant during periods of market stress, include negative convexity aspects of many mortgage-backed securities and some of the structured products built around them; underlying default rates potentially exceeding expectations and resulting in a high-volatility environment; balance sheet leverage of hedge funds; and hedge fund investor redemption pressures.

Globally, fixed-income markets are substantially larger in total issuance size and scale than equity markets and come in a myriad of different securities types. Away from on-the-run government securities and other sovereign-backed debt securities, which in most developed financial markets are generally very liquid, the liquidity aspects of many fixed-income securities are typically poor. This creates relative value arbitrage opportunities for hedge fund managers, but it also entails positioning and liquidity risks in portfolio management. Natural price opaqueness must often be overcome—particularly for "off-the-run" securities that may trade only occasionally. Liquidity in certain municipal bond markets and corporate debt markets, for example, can be particularly thin. Some key points of fixed-income arbitrage appear in Exhibit 7.

EXHIBIT 7   Fixed-Income Arbitrage—Risk, Liquidity, Leverage, and Benchmarking

Risk Profile and Liquidity

- The risk/return profile of fixed-income arbitrage trading derives from the high correlations found across different securities, the yield spread pick-up to be captured, and the sheer number of different types of debt securities across different markets with different credit quality and convexity aspects in their pricing. Structured products built around debt securities introduce added complexity that may result in mispricing opportunities.
- Yield curve and carry trades within the US government universe tend to be very liquid but typically have the fewest mispricing opportunities. Liquidity for relative value positions generally decreases in other sovereign markets, mortgage-related markets, and especially across corporate debt markets.
- Attractiveness: A function of correlations between different securities, the yield spread available, and the high number and wide diversity of debt securities across different markets.

Leverage Usage

- High: This strategy has high leverage usage, but leverage availability typically diminishes with product complexity. To achieve the desired leverage, prime brokers offer collateralized repurchase agreements with associated leverage "haircuts" depending on the types of securities being traded. The haircut is the prime broker's cushion against market volatility and illiquidity if posted collateral ever needs to be liquidated.

Benchmarking

- This is a broad category that encompasses the following sub-indexes: HFRX and HFRI Fixed Income Relative Value Indices; Lipper TASS Fixed Income Arbitrage Index; CISDM Debt Arbitrage Index; and Credit Suisse Fixed Income Arbitrage Index.

Note: HFRX and HFRI also offer more granular hedge fund fixed-income, relative value indexes related to sovereign bonds trading, credit trading, and asset-backed trading.

7.1.2. Strategy Implementation

The most common types of fixed-income arbitrage strategies include yield curve trades and carry trades. Considering yield curve trades, the prevalent calendar spread strategy involves taking long and short positions at different points on the yield curve where the relative mispricing of securities offers the best opportunities, such as in a curve flattening or steepening, to profit. Perceptions and forecasts of macroeconomic conditions are the backdrop for these types of trades. The positions can be in fixed-income securities of the same issuer; in that case, most credit and liquidity risks would likely be hedged, making interest rate risk the main concern. Alternatively, longs and shorts can be taken in the securities of different issuers—but typically ones operating in the same industry or sector. In this case, differences in credit quality, liquidity, volatility, and issue-specific characteristics would likely drive the relative mispricing. In either case, the hedge fund manager aims to profit as the mispricing reverses (mean reversion occurs) and the longs rise and shorts fall in value within the targeted time frame.

Carry trades involve going long a higher yielding security and shorting a lower yielding security with the expectation of receiving the positive carry and of profiting on long and short sides of the trade when the temporary relative mispricing reverts to normal. A classic example of a fixed-income arbitrage trade involves buying lower liquidity, off-the-run government securities and selling higher liquidity, duration matched, on-the-run government securities. Interest rate and credit risks are hedged because long and short positions have the same duration and credit exposure. So, the key concern is liquidity risk. Under normal conditions, as time passes the more (less) expensive on- (off-) the-run securities will decrease (increase) in price as the current on-the-runs are replaced by a more liquid issue of new on-the-run bonds that then become off-the-run bonds.

The payoff profile of this fixed-income arbitrage strategy resembles a short put option. If the strategy unfolds as expected, it returns a positive carry plus a profit from spread narrowing. But, if the spread unexpectedly widens, then the payoff becomes negative. Mispricing of government securities is generally small, so substantial leverage would typically be used to magnify potential profits. But, with highly levered positions, even a temporary negative price shock can be sufficient to set off a wave of margin calls that force fund managers to sell at significant losses. Such a scenario in the wake of the 1997 Asian Financial Crisis and the 1998 Russian Ruble Crisis led to the collapse and subsequent US Federal Reserve-supervised bailout of legendary hedge fund Long-Term Capital Management. It is important to note that there are far more complex relative value fixed-income strategies beyond just yield curve trades, carry trades, or relative credit trades.

EXAMPLE 6   Fixed-Income Arbitrage: Treasuries versus Inflation Swap + TIPS

Guernsey Shore Hedge Fund closely monitors government bond markets and looks for valuation discrepancies among the different issues.

Portfolio manager Nick Landers knows that Treasury Inflation-Protected Securities (TIPS) pay a coupon (i.e., real yield) while accruing inflation into the principal, which is paid at maturity. This insulates the TIPS owner from inflation risk.

Landers also understands that because the US government issues both TIPS and Treasuries that have the same maturity, they should trade at similar yields after adjusting for inflation. Landers knows that by using OTC inflation swaps, the inflation-linked components of TIPS can be locked in, thereby fixing all payments to be similar to those of a Treasury bond.

After accounting for expected inflation in normal periods, global investors often prefer Treasuries to inflation-indexed bonds. This may be because market participants do not fully trust the way inflation may be measured over time. As such, inflation-hedged TIPS (as a package with the associated offsetting inflation swap) have typically yielded about 25 bps to 35 bps more than similar maturity Treasuries.

During a period of extreme market distress, in November 2XXX, Landers keenly observed that TIPS were particularly mispriced. Their yields, adjusted for inflation, were substantially higher than straight Treasuries, while inflation swaps were priced as if outright deflation was imminent. Landers notes the information on the relative pricing of these different products and considers whether to implement the follow trade:

November 2XXX	Fixed Rate	Inflation Rate	Cost
Buy 5-year TIPS	Receive 3.74%	Receive inflation	–1,000,000
Short 5-year Treasuries	Pay 2.56%	—	+1,000,000
Inflation swap: receive fixed rate and pay inflation index	Receive 1.36%	Pay inflation	0
Net of three trades	Receive 2.54%	—	0

Discuss whether Landers has uncovered a risk-free arbitrage, and if so, discuss some of the risks he may still face with its execution.

Solution: The situation observed by Landers occurred during a period of extreme market stress. In such turbulent times, instances of very attractive, near risk-free arbitrage can occur, as in this case. Often these periods are characterized by a fear of deflation, so straight Treasury bonds are in high demand for flight-to-quality reasons. But there would be some operational hurdles to overcome. For Landers to short the expensive Treasuries and buy the more attractive TIPS, Guernsey Shore would need access as a counterparty to the interbank repurchase market to borrow the Treasury bonds. Bank credit approval (via an International Swaps and Derivatives Association [ISDA] relationship) would also be required for accessing the inflation swap market for yield enhancement and to lock in the inflation hedge. Unfortunately, during periods of extreme market distress, credit lines to hedge funds typically shrink (or are withdrawn), not expanded. Moreover, there is potential for "losing the borrow" on the short Treasuries (i.e., the lender demanding return of his/her Treasuries), which makes the trade potentially difficult to maintain. Assuming Guernsey Shore met these operational requirements, Landers would need to act quickly to capture the fixed-income arbitrage profit of 2.54%. Such extreme levels of arbitrage rarely persist for very long.

8. RELATIVE VALUE STRATEGIES: CONVERTIBLE BOND ARBITRAGE

Convertible bonds are hybrid securities that can be viewed as a combination of straight debt plus a long equity call option with an exercise price equal to the strike price times the conversion ratio. The conversion ratio is the number of shares for which the bond can be exchanged. The bond's conversion value is the current stock price times the conversion ratio. The conversion price is the current convertible bond price divided by the conversion ratio. If the current conversion value is significantly below the convertible bond price (or equivalently, the current share price is significantly below the conversion price), the call is out-of-the-money and the convertible bond will behave more like a straight bond. Conversely, if the conversion value is significantly above the convertible bond price (or equivalently, the current share price is significantly above the conversion price), the call is in-the-money and the convertible bond will behave more like the underlying equity.

8.1. Investment Characteristics

Convertible securities are naturally complex and thus generally not well understood. They are impacted by numerous factors, including overall interest rate levels, corporate credit spreads, bond coupon and principal cash flows, and the value of the embedded stock option (which itself is influenced by dividend payments, stock price movements, and equity volatility). Convertibles are often issued sporadically by companies in relatively small sizes compared to straight debt issuances, and thus they are typically thinly-traded securities. Moreover, most convertibles are non-rated and typically have fewer covenants than straight bonds. Because the equity option value is embedded within such thinly-traded, complex securities, the embedded options within convertibles tend to trade at relatively low implied volatility levels compared to the historical volatility level of the underlying equity. Convertibles also trade cyclically relative to the amount of new issuance of such securities in the overall market. The higher the new convertible issuance that the market must absorb, the cheaper their pricing and the more attractive the arbitrage opportunities for a hedge fund manager.

The key problem for the convertible arbitrage manager is that to access and extract the relatively cheap embedded optionality of the convertible, he/she must accept or hedge away other risks that are embedded in the convertible security. These include interest rate risk, credit risk of the corporate issuer, and market risk (i.e., the risk that the stock price will decline and thus render the embedded call option less valuable). Should the convertible manager desire, all these risks can be hedged using a combination of interest rate derivatives, credit default swaps, and short sales of an appropriate delta-adjusted amount of the underlying stock. The purchase of put options can also be a stock-sale substitute. The use of any such hedging tools may also erode the very attractiveness of the targeted convertible holding.

Convertible managers who are more willing to accept credit risk may choose to not hedge the credit default risk of the corporate issuer; instead, they will take on the convertible position more from a credit risk perspective. Such managers are known as credit-oriented convertible managers. Other managers may hedge the credit risk but will take a more long-biased, directional view of the underlying stock and then underhedge the convertible's equity exposure. Yet other managers may overhedge the equity risk to create a bearish tilt with respect to the underlying stock, thus providing a more focused exposure to increased volatility. These managers are referred to as volatility-oriented convertible managers. In sum, several different ways and styles can be utilized to set up convertible arbitrage exposures. Exhibit 8 presents some key aspects of convertible bond arbitrage.

EXHIBIT 8   Convertible Bond Arbitrage—Risk, Liquidity, Leverage, and Benchmarking

Risk Profile and Liquidity

- Convertible arbitrage managers strive to extract and benefit from this structurally cheap source of implied volatility by delta hedging and gamma trading short equity hedges against their long convertible holdings.
- Liquidity issues surface for convertible arbitrage strategies in two ways: 1) naturally less-liquid securities because of their relatively small issue sizes and inherent complexities; 2) availability and cost to borrow underlying equity for short selling.

- Attractiveness: Convertible arbitrage works best during periods of high convertible issuance, moderate volatility, and reasonable market liquidity. It fares less well in periods of acute credit weakness and general illiquidity, when the pricing of convertible securities is unduly impacted by supply/demand imbalances.

Leverage Usage

- High: Because of many legs needed to implement convertible arbitrage trades (e.g., short sale, CDS transaction, interest rate hedge), relatively high levels of leverage are used to extract a modest ultimate gain from delta hedging. Managers typically run convertible portfolios at 300% long versus 200% short, the lower short exposure being a function of the delta-adjusted equity exposure needed from short sales to balance the long convertible.

Benchmarking

- Sub-indexes include HFRX and HFRI FI-Convertible Arbitrage Indices; Lipper TASS Convertible Arbitrage Index; CISDM Convertible Arbitrage Index; and Credit Suisse Convertible Arbitrage Index.

Note: Convertible bond arbitrage is a core hedge fund strategy area that is run within many multi-strategy hedge funds together with L/S equity, merger arbitrage, and other event-driven distressed strategies.

8.2. Strategy Implementation

A classic convertible bond arbitrage strategy is to buy the relatively undervalued convertible bond and take a short position in the relatively overvalued underlying stock. The number of shares to sell short to achieve a delta neutral overall position is determined by the delta of the convertible bond. For convertible bonds with low conversion prices relative to the current stock price (i.e., the long call is I-T-M), the delta will be close to 1. For convertibles with high conversion prices relative to the current stock price (i.e., the long call is O-T-M), the delta will be closer to 0. The combination of a long convertible and short equity delta exposure would create a situation where for small changes in the equity price, the portfolio will remain essentially balanced. As the underlying stock price moves further, however, the delta hedge of the convertible will change because the convertible is an instrument with the natural positive convexity attributes of positive gamma. Because stock gamma is always zero, the convertible arbitrage strategy will leave the convertible arbitrageur "synthetically" longer in total equity exposure as the underlying security price rises and synthetically less long as the equity price falls. This added gamma-driven exposure can then be hedged at favorable levels with appropriate sizing adjustments of the underlying short stock hedge—selling more stock at higher levels and buying more stock at lower levels. The convertible arbitrage strategy will be profitable given sufficiently large stock price swings and proper periodic rebalancing (assuming all else equal). If realized equity volatility exceeds the implied volatility of the convertible's embedded option (net of hedging costs), an overall gain is achieved by the arbitrageur.

Several circumstances can create concerns for a convertible arbitrage strategy. First, when short selling, shares must be located and borrowed; as a result, the stock owner may subsequently want his/her shares returned at a potentially inopportune time, such as during stock price run-ups or more generally when supply for the stock is low or demand for the stock is high.

This situation, particularly a short squeeze, can lead to substantial losses and a suddenly unbalanced exposure if borrowing the underlying equity shares becomes too difficult or too costly for the arbitrageur (of course, initially locking in a "borrow" over a "term period" can help the arbitrageur avoid short squeezes, but this may be costly to execute). Second, credit issues may complicate valuation given that bonds have exposure to credit risk; so when credit spreads widen or narrow, there would be a mismatch in the values of the stock and convertible bond positions that the convertible manager may or may not have attempted to hedge away. Third, the strategy can lose money because of time decay of the convertible bond's embedded call option during periods of reduced realized equity volatility and/or from a general compression of market implied volatility levels.

Convertible arbitrage strategies have performed best when convertible issuance is high (implying a wider choice among convertible securities and generally cheaper prices), general market volatility levels are moderate, and the liquidity to trade and adjust positions is ample. On the other hand, extreme market volatility also typically implies heightened credit risks; given that convertibles are naturally less-liquid securities, convertible managers generally do not fare well during such periods. The fact that hedge funds have become the natural market makers for convertibles and they typically face significant redemption pressures from investors during crises implies further unattractive left-tail risk attributes to the strategy during periods of market stress.

EXAMPLE 7   Convertible Arbitrage Strategy

Cleopatra Partners is a Dubai-based hedge fund engaging in convertible bond arbitrage. Portfolio manager Shamsa Khan is considering a trade involving the euro-denominated convertible bonds and stock of QXR Corporation. She has assembled the following information:

QXR Convertible Bond		
Price (% of par)	120	—
Coupon (%)	5.0	—
Remaining maturity (years)	1.0	—
Conversion ratio	50	—
S&P Rating	BBB	—

QXR Inc.		Industry Average
Price (per share)	30	--
P/E (x)	30	20
P/BV (x)	2.25	1.5
P/CF (x)	15	10

Additional Information:
- It costs €2 to borrow each QXR share (paid to the stock lender) to carry the short position for a year.
- The stock pays a €1 dividend.

1. Discuss (using only the information in the table) the basic trade setup that Khan should implement.
2. Demonstrate (without using the additional information) that potential profits earned are the same whether QXR's share price falls to €24, rises to €36, or remains flat at €30.
3. Discuss (using also the additional information) how the results of the trade will change.

Solution to 1: QXR's convertible bond price is €1,200 [= €1,000 × (120/100)], and its conversion ratio is 50; so, the conversion price is €24 (€1,200/50). This compares with QXR's current share price of €30. QXR's share valuation metrics are all 50% higher than its industry's averages. It can be concluded that in relative terms, QXR's shares are overvalued and its convertible bonds are undervalued. Thus, Khan should buy the convertibles and short sell the shares.

Solution to 2: By implementing this trade and buying the bond at €1,200, exercising the bond's conversion option, and selling her shares at the current market price, Khan can lock in a profit of €6 per share under any of the scenarios mentioned, as shown in the following table:

QXR Share Price	Profit on:		
	Long Stock via Convertible Bond	Short Stock	Total Profit
24	0	6	6
36	12	–6	6
30	6	0	6

Solution to 3: The €2 per share borrowing costs and the €1 dividend payable to the lender together represent a €3 per share outflow that Khan must pay. But, the convertible bond pays a 5% coupon or €50, which equates to an inflow of €1 per share equivalent (€50 coupon/50 shares per bond). Therefore, the total profit outcomes, as indicated in the table, would each be reduced by €2. In sum, Khan would realize a total profit of €4 per each QXR share.

9. OPPORTUNISTIC STRATEGIES: GLOBAL MACRO STRATEGIES

Opportunistic hedge fund strategies seek to profit from investment opportunities across a wide range of markets and securities using a variety of techniques. They invest primarily in asset classes, sectors, regions, and across macro themes and multi-asset relationships on a global basis (as opposed to focusing on the individual security level). So, broad themes, global relationships, market trends, and cycles affect their returns.

Although opportunistic hedge funds can sometimes be difficult to categorize and may use a variety of techniques, they can generally be divided by: 1) the type of analysis and approach that drives the trading strategy (technical or fundamental), 2) how trading decisions are implemented (discretionary or systematic), and 3) the types of instruments and/markets in which they trade. Fundamental-based strategies use economic data as inputs and focus on fair valuation of securities, sectors, markets, and intra-market relationships. Technical analysis utilizes statistical methods to predict relative price movements based on past price trends.

Discretionary implementation relies on manager skills to interpret new information and make investment decisions, and it may be subject to such behavioral biases as overconfidence and loss aversion. Systematic implementation is rules-based and executed by computer algorithms with little or no human intervention; however, it may encounter difficulty coping with new, complex situations (not seen historically). As the absolute size of systematic trend-following funds has increased in significance, so too has the issue of negative execution slippage caused by the simultaneous reversal of multiple trend-following models that sometimes create a "herding effect." Such effects can temporarily overwhelm normal market liquidity and at times temporarily distort fundamental market pricing of assets (i.e., trend-following "overshoots" caused by momentum-signal triggers). We now discuss the two most common hedge fund strategies: global macro and managed futures.

9.1. Global Macro Strategies

Global macro strategies focus on global relationships across a wide range of asset classes and investment instruments, including derivative contracts (e.g., futures, forwards, swaps, and options) on commodities, currencies, precious and base metals, and fixed-income and equity indexes—as well as on sovereign debt securities, corporate bonds, and individual stocks. Given the wide range of possibilities to express a global macro view, these strategies tend to focus on certain themes (e.g., trading undervalued emerging market currencies versus overvalued US dollar using OTC currency swaps), regions (e.g., trading stock index futures on Italy's FTSE MIB versus Germany's DAX to capitalize on differences in eurozone equity valuations), or styles (e.g., systematic versus discretionary spread trading in energy futures). Global macro managers typically hold views on the relative economic health and central bank policies of different countries, global yield curve relationships, trends in inflation and relative purchasing power parity, and capital trade flow aspects of different countries (typically expressed through relative currency or rate-curve positioning).

It is important to note that because global macro managers tend to be anticipatory and sometimes contrarian in setting their strategies. Some macro managers may try to extract carry gains or ride momentum waves, but most have a tendency to be early in their positioning and then benefit when some rationality eventually returns to relative market pricing. This can make an allocation to global macro strategies particularly useful when a sudden potential reversal in markets is feared. For example, many global macro managers sensed the developing sub-prime mortgage crisis in the United States as early as 2006. They took on long positions in credit default swaps (CDS) (i.e., they purchased protection) on mortgage bonds, on tranches of mortgage structured products, or simply on broader credit indexes that they deemed particularly vulnerable to weakening credit conditions. Although they had to wait until 2007–2008 for these CDS positions to pay off, some global macro managers performed spectacularly well as market conditions morphed into the global financial crisis. Including global macro managers with significant subprime mortgage-focused CDS positions within a larger portfolio turned out to be a very valuable allocation.

It is important to note that because global macro managers trade a wide variety of instruments and markets and typically do so by different methods, these managers are fairly heterogeneous as a group. Thus, global macro funds are not as consistently dependable as a source of short alpha when compared to pure systematic, trend-following managed futures funds that typically attempt to capture any significant market trend. But, as noted earlier, global macro managers tend to be more anticipatory (compared to managed futures managers), which can be a useful attribute.

9.1.1. Investment Characteristics

Global macro managers use fundamental and technical analysis to value markets, and they use discretionary and systematic modes of implementation. The view taken by global macro portfolio managers can be directional (e.g., buy bonds of banks expected to benefit from "normalization" of US interest rates) or thematic (e.g., buy the "winning" companies and short sell the "losing" companies from Brexit). Because of their heterogeneity, added due diligence and close attention to the current portfolio of a macro manager may be required by an allocator to correctly anticipate the factor risks that a given global macro manager will deliver.

Despite their heterogeneity, a common feature among most global macro managers is the use of leverage, often obtained through the use of derivatives, to magnify potential profits. A margin-to-equity ratio typically of 15% to 25% posted against futures or forward positions allows a manager to control face amounts of assets up to 6 to 7 times a fund's assets. The use of such embedded leverage naturally allows the global macro manager ease and flexibility in relative value and directional positioning.

Generally, the key source of returns in global macro strategies revolves around correctly discerning and capitalizing on trends in global markets. As such, mean-reverting low volatility markets are the natural bane of this strategy area. Conversely, steep equity market sell-offs, interest rate regime changes, currency devaluations, volatility spikes, and geopolitical shocks caused by such events as trade wars and terrorism are examples of global macro risks; however, they can also provide some of the opportunities that global macro managers often attempt to exploit. Of course, the exposures selected in any global macro strategy may not react to the global risks as expected because of either unforeseen contrary factors or global risks that simply do not materialize. Thus, macro managers tend to produce somewhat lumpier and uneven return streams than other hedge fund strategies, and generally higher levels of volatility are associated with their returns.

Notably, the prevalence of quantitative easing since the global financial crisis of 2007–2009 resulted in generally benign market conditions for most of the subsequent decade, which was an especially imperfect environment for global macro managers. Although equity and fixed-income markets generally trended higher during this period, overall volatility levels across these and many other markets, such as currencies and commodities, were relatively low. In some cases, central bankers intervened to curtail undesirable market outcomes, thereby preventing certain global macro trends from fully materializing. Because such intervention substantially moderates the trendiness and the volatility of markets, which are the lifeblood of global macro strategies, some hedge fund allocators began avoiding these strategies. This may be short-sighted, however, because such opportunistic strategies as global macro can be very useful over a full market cycle in terms of portfolio diversification and alpha generation.

9.1.2. Strategy Implementation

Global macro strategies are typically top-down and employ a range of macroeconomic and fundamental models to express a view regarding the direction or relative value of an asset or asset class. Positions may comprise a mix of individual securities, baskets of securities, index futures, foreign exchange futures/forwards, precious or base metals futures, agricultural futures, fixed-income products or futures, and derivatives or options on any of these. If the hedge fund manager is making a directional bet, then directional models will use fundamental data regarding a specific market or asset to determine if it is undervalued or overvalued relative to history and the expected macro trend. Conversely, if the manager's proclivity is toward relative value positioning, then that manager will consider which assets are under- or overvalued relative to each other given historical and expected macro conditions.

For example, if currencies of the major ASEAN block countries (i.e., Indonesia, Malaysia, Philippines, Singapore, and Thailand) are depreciating against the US dollar, a directional model might conclude that the shares of their key exporting companies are undervalued and thus should be purchased. However, further investigation might signal that the public bonds of these exporters are cheap relative to their shares, so the bonds should be bought and the shares sold short. This situation might occur in the likely scenario that the share prices react quickly to the currency depreciation and bond prices take longer to react to the trend.

Successful global macro trading requires the manager to have both a correct fundamental view of the selected market(s) and the proper methodology and timing to express tactical views. Managers who repeatedly implement a position too early/unwind one too late or who choose an inappropriate method for implementation will likely face redemptions from their investors. Given the natural leverage used in global macro strategies, managers may be tempted to carry many (possibly too many) positions simultaneously; however, the diversification benefits of doing so are typically less than those derived from more idiosyncratic long/short equity strategies. This is because of the nature of "risk-on" or "risk-off" market conditions (often caused by central bank policies) that impact a variety of asset classes in a correlated manner.

EXAMPLE 8　Global Macro Strategy

Consider the following (hypothetical) macroeconomic scenario: Emerging market (EM) countries have been growing rapidly (in fact, overheating) and accumulating both historically large government budget deficits and trade deficits as expanding populations demand more public services and foreign goods. EM central banks have been intervening to support their currencies for some time, and electoral support for candidates promoting exorbitant business taxes and vast social welfare schemes in many EM countries has risen dramatically. These trends are expected to continue.

Melvin Chu, portfolio manager at Bermuda-based Global Macro Advisers (GMA), has been considering how to position his global macro hedge fund. After meeting with a senior central banker of a leading EM country, GMA's research director informs Chu that it appears this central bank may run out of foreign exchange reserves soon and thus may be unable to continue its supportive currency intervention.

Discuss a global macro strategy Chu might implement to profit from these trends by using options.

Solution: Assuming this key EM country runs out of foreign currency reserves, then it is likely its currency will need to be devalued. This initial devaluation might reasonably be expected to trigger a wave of devaluations and economic and financial market turbulence in other EM countries in similar circumstances. So, Chu should consider trades based on anticipated EM currency depreciation (maybe even devaluation) as well as trades benefitting from rising interest rates, downward pressure on equities, and spikes in volatility in the EM space.

A reasonable way for Chu to proceed would be to buy put options. If his expectations fail to materialize, his losses would then be capped at the total of the premiums paid for the options. Chu should consider buying puts on the following: a variety of EM currencies, EM government bond futures, and EM equity market indexes. He should buy in-the-money puts to implement his high conviction trades and out-of-the money puts for trades where he has a lower degree of confidence. Moreover, to take advantage of a possible flight-to-safety, Chu should consider buying call options on developed market (DM) reserve currencies as well as call options on bond futures for highly-rated DM government issuers.

10. OPPORTUNISTIC STRATEGIES: MANAGED FUTURES

Managed futures, which gained its first major academic backing in a classic paper by John Lintner in 1983, is a hedge fund strategy that focuses on investments using futures, options on futures, and sometimes forwards and swaps (primarily on stock and fixed-income indexes) and commodities and currencies. As futures markets have evolved over time and in different countries—gaining in size (i.e., open interest) and liquidity—some managers have also engaged in trading sector and industry index futures as well as more exotic contracts, such as futures on weather (e.g., temperature, rainfall) and derivatives contracts on carbon emissions.

10.1. Investment Characteristics

The uncorrelated nature of managed futures with stocks and bonds generally makes them a potentially attractive addition to traditional portfolios for improved risk-adjusted return profiles (i.e., improved efficient frontiers in a mean–variance framework). The value added from managed futures has typically been demonstrated during periods of market stress; for example, in 2007–2009 managers using this strategy benefitted from short positions in equity futures and long positions in fixed-income futures at a time when equity indexes were falling and fixed-income indexes were rising. Put another way, managed futures demonstrated natural positive skewness that has been useful in balancing negatively-skewed strategies.

The return profile of managed futures tends to be very cyclical. Between 2011 and 2018, the trendiness (i.e., directionality) of foreign exchange and fixed-income markets deteriorated, volatility levels in many markets dissipated, and periods of acute market stress temporarily disappeared. Except for equity markets in some developed countries, many markets became range-bound or mean-reverting, which hurt managed futures performance. The diversification benefit of trend following strong equity markets is also (by definition) less diversifying to traditional portfolios than if such trends existed in other non-equity markets.

In a world where sovereign bonds have approached the zero-yield boundary, the correlation benefit of managed futures has also changed. The past practice of trend following the fixed-income markets as they get higher may likely not be as repeatable going forward. Assuming managed futures managers begin to trend follow fixed-income markets as they get lower (i.e., as developed market interest rates "normalize"), then positive returns may still be realized—although with a very different type of correlation behavior to equity markets (i.e., not as valuable).

Also, given the upward sloping nature of most global yield curves, less natural fixed-income "carry" contribution may occur from trend following the fixed-income markets to the downside (i.e., higher interest rates and lower prices).

Managed futures strategies are typically characterized as highly liquid, active across a wide range of asset classes, and able to go long or short with relative ease. High liquidity results from futures markets being among the most actively traded markets in the world. For example, the E-mini S&P 500 futures contract on the Chicago Mercantile Exchange has 3 to 4 times the daily dollar volume of the SPDR S&P 500 ETF (SPY), the world's most actively traded equity index fund. Futures contracts also provide highly liquid exposures to a wide range of asset classes that can be traded across the globe 24 hours a day. Because futures contracts require relatively little collateral to take positions as a result of the exchanges' central clearinghouse management of margin and risk, it is easier to take long and short positions with higher leverage than traditional instruments.

For example, futures contracts require margin from 0.1% to 10% of notional value for both long and short positions, as compared to standard equity market margin levels in the United States of 50%. Thus, the capital efficiency of futures contracts makes it easier for managed futures managers to be dynamic in both their long and short exposures. A traditional long-only portfolio is levered by borrowing funds to purchase additional assets. Futures portfolios do not own assets; they acquire asset exposures based on the notional value of the futures contracts held. The majority (typically 85% to 90%) of capital in a managed futures account is invested in short-term government debt (or other highly liquid collateral acceptable to the futures clearing house). The remainder (10% to 15%) is used to collateralize long and short futures contracts.

10.2. Strategy Implementation

Highly liquid contracts allow managed futures funds the flexibility to incorporate a wide range of investment strategies. Most managed futures strategies involve some "pattern recognition" trigger that is either momentum/trend driven or based on a volatility signal. Managers trade these signals across different time horizons, often with short-term mean reversion filters imposed on top of their core longer-term models. For example, a manager might have traded using a long-term horizon model that suggested gold prices would trend lower; as a result, the manager established a short position in gold futures some time ago. A short-term moving average of gold prices crossing below a longer-term moving average could have triggered this view. But later, that manager might also trade using a second, shorter time horizon model, which suggests that the downside momentum in gold prices has temporarily subsided and a mean-reverting bounce is likely. The results of these two models would be weighted and combined into an adjusted net position, typically with the longer-term model weighted more heavily than the shorter-term filter.

Such fundamental factors as carry relationships or volatility factors are often added to the core momentum and breakout signal methodologies, and they can be particularly useful regarding position sizing. Many managed futures managers implement their portfolios' relative position sizing by assessing both the volatility of each underlying futures position as well as the correlation of their return behaviors against one another. Generally, the greater the volatility of an asset, the smaller its portfolio sizing; and the greater its correlation to other futures being positioned, the smaller its portfolio sizing. Being attentive to correlation aspects between different futures contracts would then become a second step of analysis for most managed futures traders as a portfolio sizing risk constraint.

Besides core position sizing and sizing adjustments for volatility and correlation, managed futures managers will have either a price target exit methodology, a momentum reversal exit methodology, a time-based exit methodology, a trailing stop-loss exit methodology, or some combination thereof. A key to successful managed futures strategies is to have a consistent approach and to avoid overfitting of a model when backtesting performance across different markets and time periods. The goal is to have a model that performs well in a future "out of sample" period. Of course, trading models have a natural tendency to degrade in effectiveness over time as more and more managers use similar signals and the market opportunity being exploited consequently diminishes. Managed futures traders are thus constantly searching for new and differentiated trading signals. In today's world, many new signals are increasingly being developed using nontraditional, unstructured data and other types of "big data" analysis.

Apart from this accelerating search for more unique nonprice signals, the most common type of managed futures approach is typically referred to as **time-series momentum** (TSM) trend following. Momentum trading strategies are driven by the past returns of the individual assets. Simply put, managers go long assets that are rising in price and go short assets that are falling in price. TSM strategies are traded on an absolute basis, meaning the manager can be net long or net short depending on the current price trend of an asset. Such TSM strategies work best when an asset's (or market's) own past returns are a good predictor of its future returns.

A second, less common approach is using **cross-sectional momentum** (CSM) strategies, which are implemented with a cross-section of assets (generally within an asset class) by going long those that are rising in price the most and by shorting those that are falling the most. Such CSM strategies generally result in holding a net zero or market-neutral position. CSM strategies work well when a market's out- or underperformance relative to other markets is a reliable predictor of its future performance. However, CSM may be constrained by limited futures contracts available for a cross section of assets at the asset class level.

Global macro strategies and managed futures strategies often involve trading the same subset of markets but in different ways. It is important to understand the respective attributes of these two strategies. Exhibit 9 provides such a comparison.

EXHIBIT 9   Managed Futures and Global Macro Strategies—Comparison of Risk, Liquidity, Leverage, and Benchmarking

Risk Profile and Liquidity

- Both global macro and managed futures strategies are highly liquid but with some crowding aspects and execution slippage in managed futures as AUM have grown rapidly. Being more heterogeneous in approaches used, global macro strategies face less significant execution crowding effects.
- Typically, managed futures managers tend to take a more systematic approach to implementation than global macro managers, who are generally more discretionary in their application of models and tools.
- Returns of managed futures strategies typically exhibit positive right-tail skewness in periods of market stress, which is very useful for portfolio diversification. Global macro strategies have delivered similar diversification in such stress periods but with more heterogeneous outcomes.
- Despite positive skewness, managed futures and global macro managers are somewhat cyclical and at the more volatile end of the spectrum of hedge fund strategies (with volatility

positively related to the strategy's time horizon). In addition, macro managers can also be early and overly anticipatory in their positioning.

Leverage Usage

- High: High leverage is embedded in futures contracts. Notional amounts up to 6 to 7 times fund assets can be controlled with initial margin-to-equity of just 10% – 20% (with individual futures margin levels being a function of the volatility of the underlying assets). Active use of options by many global macro managers adds natural elements of leverage and positive convexity.

Benchmarking

- Managed futures are best tracked by such sub-indexes as HFRX and HFRI Macro Systematic Indices; CISDM CTA Equal-Weighted Index; Lipper TASS Managed Futures Index; and Credit Suisse Managed Futures Index.
- Global macro strategies are best tracked by HFRX and HFRI Macro Discretionary Indices; CISDM Hedge Fund Global Macro Index; Lipper TASS Global Macro Index; and Credit Suisse Global Macro Index.

EXAMPLE 9   Cross-Sectional and Time-Series Momentum

An institutional investor is considering adding an allocation to a managed futures strategy that focuses on medium-term momentum trading involving precious metals. This investor is evaluating two different managed futures funds that both trade precious metals futures, including gold, silver, platinum, and palladium futures. Of the two funds being considered, one is run using a cross-sectional momentum (CSM) strategy, and the other is managed using a time-series momentum (TSM) strategy. Both funds use trailing 6-month returns for developing their buy/sell signals, and they both volatility-weight their futures positions to have equal impact on their overall portfolios.

Explain how the CSM and TSM strategies would work and compare their risk profiles.

Solution: For the CSM strategy, each day the manager will examine the returns for the four metals in question and then take a long position in the two metals futures with the best performance (i.e., the top 50%) in terms of trailing 6-month risk-adjusted returns and a short position in the two metals contracts with the worst performance (i.e., the bottom 50%) of returns. According to this strategy, the top (bottom) 50% will continue their relative value out- (under-) performance. Note that it is possible for metals contracts (or markets more generally) in the top (bottom) 50% to have negative (positive) absolute returns—for example, during bear (bull) markets. The CSM strategy is very much a relative momentum strategy, with the established positions acting as a quasi-hedge relative to each other in terms of total sector exposure. This CSM-run fund would likely deliver an overall return profile with somewhat less volatility than the TSM strategy.

For the TSM strategy, each day the manager will take a long position in the precious metals futures with positive trailing 6-month returns and sell short those metals contracts with negative trailing 6-month returns. According to this TSM strategy, the metals futures (or markets, more generally) with positive (negative) returns will continue to rise (fall) in absolute value, resulting in an expected profit on both long and short positions. However, by utilizing a TSM strategy, the fund might potentially end up with long positions in all four metals contracts or short positions in all these precious metals futures at the same time.

Consequently, the CSM strategy typically results in a net zero market exposure during normal periods, while the TSM strategy can be net long or net short depending on how many metal (or markets, generally) have positive and negative absolute returns. The return profile of the TSM managed fund is thus likely to be more volatile than that of the CSM managed fund and also far more sensitive to periods when the precious metals sector is experiencing strong trends (i.e., directionality).

11. SPECIALIST STRATEGIES

Specialist hedge fund strategies require highly specialized skill sets for trading in niche markets. Two such typical specialist strategies are volatility trading and reinsurance/life settlements.

11.1. Volatility Trading

Over the past several decades, volatility trading has become an asset class unto itself. Niche hedge fund managers specialize in trading relative volatility strategies globally across different geographies and asset classes. For example, given the plethora of structured product offerings in Asia with inexpensive embedded options that can be stripped out and resold (usually by investment banks), volatility pricing in Asia is often relatively cheap compared to the more expensive implied volatility of options traded in North American and European markets. In these latter markets, there is a proclivity to buy out-of-the-money options as a protective hedge (i.e., insurance). The goal of **relative value volatility arbitrage** strategies is to source and buy cheap volatility and sell more expensive volatility while netting out the time decay aspects normally associated with options portfolios. Depending on the instruments used (e.g., puts and calls or variance swaps), these strategies may also attempt to extract value from active gamma trading adjustments when markets move.

11.1.1. Investment Characteristics and Strategy Implementation

The easiest way to understand relative value volatility trading is through a few examples. Throughout the 1980s and 1990s, options on the Japanese yen consistently traded at lower volatility levels within Asian time zones than similar options were traded in London, New York, or Chicago (i.e., IMM futures market). Capturing the volatility spread between these options is a type of relative value volatility trading known as time-zone arbitrage—in this case of a single underlying fungible global asset, the Japanese yen. As a second arbitrage example, managers in today's markets may periodically source Nikkei 225 implied volatility in Asia at cheaper levels than S&P 500 implied volatility is being traded in New York, even though the Nikkei 225 typically has realized volatility higher than that of the S&P 500. This type of relative value volatility trading is known as cross-asset volatility trading, which may often involve idiosyncratic, macro-oriented risks.

Of course, another simpler type of volatility trading involves outright long volatility traders who may trade against consistent volatility sellers. Equity volatility is approximately 80% *negatively* correlated with equity market returns. Otherwise stated, volatility levels tend to go up when equity markets fall, with options pricing skew reflecting such a tendency. Clearly, this makes the long volatility strategy a useful potential diversifier for long equity investments, albeit at the cost to the option premium paid by the volatility buyer. Selling volatility provides a volatility risk premium or compensation for taking on the risk of providing insurance against crises for holders of equities and other securities.

In the United States, the most liquid volatility contracts are short-term VIX Index futures contracts, which track the 30-day implied volatility of S&P 500 Index options as traded on the Chicago Board Options Exchange (CBOE). Because volatility is non-constant but high levels of volatility are difficult to perpetuate over long periods of time (markets eventually calm down after sudden jump shifts), VIX futures are often prone to mean reversion. Given this fact and the fact that VIX futures prices typically slide down a positively sloped implied volatility curve as expiration approaches, many practitioners prefer trading simple exchange-traded options, over-the-counter (OTC) options, variance swaps, and volatility swaps. The general mean-reverting nature of volatility still impacts these products, but it does so in a less explicit fashion than with the futures.

Multiple paths can be taken to implement a volatility trading strategy. If a trader uses simple exchange-traded options, then the maturity of such options typically extends out to no more than approximately two years. In terms of expiry, the longer-dated options will have more absolute exposure to volatility levels (i.e., vega exposure) than shorter-dated options, but the shorter-dated options will exhibit more delta sensitivity to price changes (i.e., gamma exposure). Traders need to monitor the following: the term structure of volatility, which is typically upward sloping but can invert during periods of crisis; the volatility smile across different strike prices, whereby out-of-the-money options will typically trade at higher implied volatility levels than at-the-money options; and the volatility skew, whereby out-of-the-money puts may trade at higher volatility levels than out-of-the-money calls. Volatility traders strive to capture relative timing and strike pricing opportunities using various types of option spreads, such as bull and bear spreads, straddles, and calendar spreads.

To extract an outright long volatility view, options are purchased and delta hedging of the gamma exposure is required. How the embedded gamma of the long options position is managed is also important. For example, one could have a positive view of a volatility expansion but then fail to capture gains in a volatility spike during an adverse market move by poorly managing gamma exposure. Conversely, some managers may use options to extract a more intermediate-term, directional insurance protection-type view of both price and volatility and not engage in active delta hedging.

A second, similar path might be to implement the volatility trading strategy using OTC options. Then the tenor and strike prices of the options can be customized, and the tenor of expiry dates can be extended beyond what is available with exchange-traded options. However, by utilizing OTC options, the strategy is subject to counterparty credit risk as well as added illiquidity risk.

Migrating to the use of VIX Index futures (or options on VIX futures) can more explicitly express a pure volatility view without the need for constant delta hedging of an equity put or call for isolating the volatility exposure. However, as just mentioned, volatility pricing tends to be notoriously mean reverting. Also, an abundant supply of traders and investors typically are looking to sell volatility to capture the volatility premium and the volatility roll down payoff. Roll down refers to the fact that the term structure of volatility tends to be positively sloped, so the passage of time causes added option price decay. In other words, the theta of a long option position is always negative, and if shorter-dated options have a lower implied volatility, then the passage of time increases the rate of natural theta decay.

A fourth path for implementing a volatility trading strategy would be to purchase an OTC volatility swap or a variance swap from a creditworthy counterparty. A volatility swap is a forward contract on future realized price volatility. Similarly, a variance swap is a forward contract on future realized price variance, where variance is the square of volatility. In both cases, at inception of the trade the strike is typically chosen such that the fair value of the swap is zero. This strike is then referred to as fair volatility or fair variance, respectively. At expiry of the swaps, the receiver of the floating leg pays the difference between the realized volatility (or variance) and the agreed-on strike times some prespecified notional amount that is not initially exchanged. Both volatility and variance swaps provide "pure" exposure to volatility alone—unlike standardized options in which the volatility exposure depends on the price of the underlying asset and must be isolated and extracted via delta hedging. These swaps can thus be used to take a view on future realized volatility, to trade the spread between realized and implied volatility, or to hedge the volatility exposure of other positions. These OTC products also offer the advantage of longer-dated, tailored maturities and strikes.

A long volatility strategy utilizing OTC volatility or variance swaps, options, or swaptions requires finding undervalued instruments. This is accomplished by being in frequent contact with options dealers around the world in a variety of asset classes. Once implemented, positions are held until they are either exercised, sold during a volatility event, actively delta hedged (in the case of a long options position), or expire. A long volatility strategy is a convex strategy because the movement of volatility pricing is typically asymmetric and skewed to the right. Also, strike prices of options may be set such that the cost of the options is small, but their potential payoffs are often many multiples of the premiums paid for the options.

Long volatility strategies are potentially attractive but also come with key challenges and risks for implementation. Given that OTC options, as well as volatility and variance swaps, are not exchange-traded, they must be negotiated. These contracts are typically structured under ISDA documentation; they are subject to bilateral margin agreements (as negotiated within an ISDA Credit Support Annex document), but they still carry more counterparty risk and liquidity risk to both establish and liquidate than instruments traded on an exchange. Also, smaller hedge funds may not even be able to access ISDA-backed OTC derivatives with banking counterparts until surpassing a minimum AUM threshold, generally $100 million. Above all, although the purchase of volatility assets provides positively convex outcomes, it almost always involves some volatility curve roll down risk and premium expense. Key aspects of volatility trading are presented in Exhibit 10.

EXHIBIT 10   Volatility Trading Strategies—Risk, Liquidity, Leverage, and Benchmarking

Risk Profile and Liquidity

- Long volatility positioning exhibits positive convexity, which can be particularly useful for hedging purposes. On the short side, option premium sellers generally extract steadier returns in normal market environments.
- Relative value volatility trading may be a useful source of portfolio return alpha across different geographies and asset classes.

- Liquidity varies across the different instruments used for implementation. VIX Index futures and options are very liquid; exchange-traded index options are generally liquid, but with the longest tenors of about two years (with liquidity decreasing as tenor increases); OTC contracts can be customized with longer maturities but are less liquid and less fungible between different counterparties.

Leverage Usage

- The natural convexity of volatility instruments typically means that outsized gains may be earned at times with very little up-front risk. Although notional values appear nominally levered, the asymmetric nature of long optionality is an attractive aspect of this strategy.

Benchmarking

- Volatility trading is a niche strategy that is difficult to benchmark.
- CBOE Eurekahedge has the following indexes:

Long (and Short) Volatility Index, composed of 11 managers with a generally long (short) volatility stance; Relative Value Volatility Index (composed of 35 managers); and Tail Risk Index (composed of 8 managers), designed to perform best during periods of market stress.

EXAMPLE 10   Long Volatility Strategy Payoff

Consider the following scenario: Economic growth has been good, equity markets have been rising, and interest rates have been low. However, consumer debt (e.g., subprime mortgages, credit card debt, personal loans) has been rising rapidly, surpassing historic levels. In mid-January, Serena Ortiz, a long volatility hedge fund manager, purchased a basket of long-dated (one-year), 10% out-of-the money put options on a major stock index for $100 per contract at an implied volatility level of 12%.

As of mid-April, consumer debt is still at seemingly dangerous levels and financial markets appear ripe for a major correction. However, the stock index has risen another 20% above its mid-January levels, and volatility is low. So, Ortiz's options are priced even more cheaply than before, at $50 per contract.

Now jump forward in time by another three months to mid-July, when a crisis—unexpected by many participants—has finally occurred. Volatility has spiked, and the stock index has fallen to 25% below its April level and 10% below its starting January level. Ortiz's put options are now trading at an implied volatility pricing of 30%.

1. Discuss the time, volatility, and price impact on Ortiz's long volatility exposure in put options as of mid-July.
2. Discuss what happens if the market subsequently moves broadly sideways between July and the January of the next year.

Solution to 1: Despite an initial 50% mark-to-market loss on her put exposure as of mid-April, Ortiz likely has substantial unrealized profits by mid-July. As six months passed (other things being equal), Ortiz would have suffered some time decay loss in her long put position, but her options have also gone from being 10% out-of-the-money to now being at-the-money. Implied volatility has increased 2.5 times (from 12% to 30%), which on a six-month, at-the-money put will have a significant positive impact on the option's pricing (the closer an option is to being at-the-money, the greater the impact that changes in implied volatility will have on its price). So, as of mid-July, Ortiz will likely have a significant mark-to-market gain.

Solution to 2: If the market subsequently moves broadly sideways until January of the next year, Ortiz's at-the-money option premium will slowly erode because of time decay. Assuming the puts remain at-the-money, their volatility value will eventually dissipate; Ortiz will ultimately lose all of her original $100 investment per contract unless she has nimbly traded against the position with active delta hedging of the underlying stock index futures. This would entail buying and selling the index futures over time to capture small profitable movements to offset the time decay and volatility erosion in the puts.

11.2. Reinsurance/Life Settlements

Although still somewhat nascent, hedge funds have also entered the world of insurance, reinsurance, life settlements, and catastrophe reinsurance. Underlying insurance contracts provide a payout to the policyholder (or their beneficiaries) on the occurrence of a specific insured event in exchange for a stream of cash flows (periodic premiums) paid by the policyholder. Common types of insurance contracts sold by insurance providers include vehicle and home insurance, life insurance, and catastrophe insurance, which covers damage from such events as floods, hurricanes, or earthquakes. The insurance market encompasses a wide range of often highly specific and detailed contracts that are less standardized than other financial contracts. As a result, insurance contracts are generally not liquid and are difficult to sell or purchase after contract initiation.

Although the primary market for insurance has existed for centuries, the secondary market for insurance has grown substantially in the last several decades. Individuals who purchased whole or universal life policies and who no longer want or need the insurance can surrender their policies to the original insurance issuer. However, such policyholders are increasingly finding that higher cash values (i.e., significantly above surrender value) are being paid for their policies by third-party brokers, who, in turn, offer these policies as investments to hedge funds. Hedge funds may formulate a differentiated view of individual or group life expectancy; if correct, investment in such life policies can provide attractive uncorrelated returns.

Reinsurance of catastrophe risk has also increasingly attracted hedge fund capital. These new secondary markets have improved liquidity and enhanced the value of existing insurance contracts. For insurance companies, the reinsurance market allows for risk transfer, capital management, and solvency management. For hedge funds, the reinsurance market offers a source of uncorrelated return alpha.

11.2.1. Investment Characteristics and Strategy Implementation

Life insurance protects the policyholder's dependents in the case of his/her death. The secondary market for life insurance involves the sale of a life insurance contract to a third party—a **life**

settlement. The valuation of a life settlement typically requires detailed biometric analysis of the individual policyholder and an understanding of actuarial analysis. So, a hedge fund manager specialized in investing in life settlements would require such expert knowledge and skills or would need to source such knowledge from a trusted partner/actuarial adviser.

A hedge fund strategy focusing on life settlements involves analyzing pools of life insurance contracts being offered for sale, typically being sold by a third-party broker who purchased the insurance contracts from the original policyholders. The hedge fund would look for the following policy characteristics: 1) the surrender value being offered to an insured individual is relatively low; 2) the ongoing premium payments to keep the policy active are also relatively low; and, yet, 3) the probability is relatively high that the designated insured person is indeed likely to die within a certain period of time (i.e., earlier than predicted by standard actuarial methods).

On finding the appropriate policy (or, more typically, a pool of policies), the hedge fund manager pays a lump sum (via a broker) to the policyholder(s), who transfers the right to the eventual policy benefit to the hedge fund. The hedge fund is then responsible for making ongoing premium payments on the policy in return for receiving the future death benefit. This strategy is successful when the present value of the future benefit payment received by the hedge fund exceeds the present value of intervening payments made by the hedge fund. The two key inputs in the hedge fund manager's analysis are the expected policy cash flows (i.e., up-front, lump-sum payment to buy the policy; ongoing premium payments to the insurance company; and the eventual death benefit to be received) and the time to mortality. Neither of these factors has anything to do with the overall behavior of financial markets. Thus, this strategy area is unrelated and uncorrelated with other hedge fund strategies.

Catastrophe insurance protects the policyholder in case of such events as floods, hurricanes, and earthquakes, which are highly idiosyncratic and also unrelated and uncorrelated with financial market behavior. Insurance companies effectively reinsure portions of their exposure (typically above a given threshold and for a limited amount) with reinsurance companies, who, in turn, deal with hedge funds as a source of capital. An attractive and uncorrelated return profile may be achieved if by making such reinsurance investments a hedge fund can do the following: 1) obtain sufficient policy diversity in terms of geographic exposure and type of insurance being offered; 2) receive a sufficient buffer in terms of loan loss reserves from the insurance company; and 3) receive enough premium income.

Valuation methods for catastrophe insurance may require the hedge fund manager to consider global weather patterns and make forecasts using sophisticated prediction models that involve a wide range of geophysical inputs. But, more generally, assumptions are made as to typical weather patterns; the worst-case loss potentials are made from different reinsurance structures. These assumptions are then weighed against the reinsurance income to be received. If a catastrophic event does occur, then hedge fund managers hope to have enough geographic diversity that they are not financially harmed by a single event, thereby continuing to benefit when insurance premiums are inevitably increased to cover future catastrophic events.

Organized markets for catastrophe bonds and catastrophe risk futures continue to develop. These bonds and financial futures can be used to take long positions or to hedge catastrophe risk in a portfolio of insurance contracts. Their issuance and performance tend to be seasonal. Many such catastrophe bonds are issued before the annual North American hurricane season begins (May/June) and may perform particularly well if a given hurricane season is benign.

EXAMPLE 11   Investing in Life Settlements

Mikki Tan runs specialty hedge fund SingStar Pte. Ltd. (SingStar), based in Singapore, that focuses on life settlements. SingStar is staffed with biometric and actuarial science experts who perform valuation analysis on pools of life insurance policies offered for sale by insurance broker firms. These intermediaries buy the policies from individuals who no longer need the insurance and who want an up-front cash payment that is higher than the surrender value offered by their insurance companies.

Tan knows that Warwick Direct has been buying many individuals' life insurance policies that were underwritten by NextLife, an insurance company with a reputation in industry circles for relatively weak underwriting procedures (i.e., charging low premiums for insuring its many relatively unhealthy policyholders) and for paying low surrender values. Tan is notified that Warwick Direct is selling a pool of life settlements heavily weighted with policies that were originated by NextLife. Parties wishing to bid will be provided with data covering a random sample of the life insurance policies in the pool.

Tan asks SingStar's experts to analyze the data, and they report that many of the policies in the pool were written on individuals who have now developed early-onset Alzheimer's and other debilitating diseases and thus required the up-front cash for assisted living facilities and other special care. Moreover, the analysts indicate that early-onset Alzheimer's patients have a life expectancy, on average, that is 10 years shorter than persons without the disease.

Discuss how Tan and SingStar's team might proceed given this potential investment.

Solution: SingStar's financial, biometric, and actuarial experts need to work together to forecast expected cash flows from this potential investment and then value it using an appropriate risk-adjusted discount rate. The cash flows would include the following:

- The ongoing premium payments that SingStar would need to make to the originating insurance companies (in this case, mainly to NextLife) to keep the policies active. The low premiums NextLife is known to charge as well as the shorter average life expectancy of many individuals represented in the pool are important factors to consider in making this forecast.
- The timing of future benefit payments to be received by SingStar on the demise of the individuals (the formerly insured). The prevalence of early-onset Alzheimer's disease and other debilitating diseases as well as the shorter average life expectancy of many individuals in the pool are key factors to consider in formulating this forecast.

Once an appropriate discount rate is decided on—one that compensates for the risks of the investment—then its present value can be determined. The difference between the PV and any minimum bid price set by Warwick Direct, as well as Tan's perceptions of the competition in bidding, will determine Tan's proposed purchase price. If SingStar ultimately buys the pool of life settlement policies and the forecasts (e.g., biometric, actuarial, and financial) of Tan's team are met or exceeded, then this investment should yield attractive returns to SingStar that are uncorrelated to other financial markets.

12. MULTI-MANAGER STRATEGIES

The previous sections examined individual hedge fund strategies. In practice, most investors invest in a range of hedge fund strategies. Three main approaches are used to combine individual hedge fund strategies into a portfolio: 1) *creating one's own mix of managers* by investing directly into individual hedge funds running different strategies; 2) *fund-of-funds*, which involves investing in a single fund-of-funds manager who then allocates across a set of individual hedge fund managers running different strategies; and 3) *multi-strategy funds*, which entails investing in a single fund that includes multiple internal management teams running different strategies under the same roof. Of course, approaches (1) and (2) are not specific to combinations of strategies; they apply to individual strategies too.

12.1. Fund-of-Funds

Fund-of-funds (FoF) managers aggregate investors' capital and allocate it to a portfolio of separate, individual hedge funds following different, less correlated strategies. The main roles of the FoF manager are to provide diversification across hedge fund strategies; to make occasional tactical, sector-based reallocation decisions; to engage in underlying manager selection and due diligence; and to perform ongoing portfolio management, risk assessment, and consolidated reporting. FoF managers can provide investors with access to certain closed hedge funds, economies of scale for monitoring, currency hedging capabilities, the ability to obtain and manage leverage at the portfolio level, and such other practical advantages as better liquidity terms than would be offered by an individual hedge fund manager.

Disadvantages of the FoF approach include a double layer of fees the investor must pay; a lack of transparency into individual hedge fund manager processes and returns; the inability to net performance fees on individual managers; and an additional principal–agent relationship. Regarding fees, in addition to management and incentive fees charged by the individual hedge funds (with historical norms of 1%–2% and 10%–20%, respectively) in which the FoF invests, investors in a fund-of-funds historically paid an additional 1% management fee and 10% incentive fee (again, historical norms) on the performance of the total FoF portfolio. As the performance of funds of funds has generally waned, fees have become more negotiable; management fees of 50 bps and incentive fees of 5% (or simply just a 1% flat total management fee) are becoming increasingly prevalent.

Occasionally, liquidity management of FoF can result in liquidity squeezes for FoF managers. Most FoFs require an initial one-year lock-up period, and then they offer investors monthly or quarterly liquidity thereafter, typically with a 30- to 60-day redemption notice also being required. However, the underlying investments made by the FoF may not fit well with such liquidity needs. Some underlying managers or newer underlying investments may have their own lock-up provisions or liquidity (i.e., redemption) gates. So, the FoF manager must stagger his/her underlying portfolio investments to create a conservative liquidity profile while carefully assessing the probability and potential magnitude of any FoF-level redemptions that he/she might face. FoFs may also arrange a reserve line of credit as an added liquidity backstop to deal with the potential mismatch between cash flows available from underlying investments and cash flows required to meet redemptions.

12.1.1. Investment Characteristics
FoFs are important hedge fund "access vehicles" for smaller high-net-worth investors and smaller institutions. Most hedge funds require minimum initial investments that range from

$500,000 to $5,000,000 (with $1,000,000 being the most typical threshold). To create a reasonably diversified portfolio of 15–20 managers, $15–20 million would be required, which is a large amount even for most wealthy families and many small institutions. Selecting the 15–20 different hedge fund managers would itself require substantial time and resources that most such investors may lack. In addition, investors may potentially face substantial tax reporting requirements for each separate hedge fund investment owned. By comparison, a high-net-worth investor or small institution can typically start FoF investments with just $100,000, effectively achieving a portfolio that includes a diversified mix of talented hedge fund managers. Through their network of relationships and their large scale, FoFs may also provide access to successful managers whose funds are otherwise closed to new investment. Overall, FoFs may thus be considered convenient for access, diversification, liquidity, and operational tax reporting reasons.

But FoFs are also designed to provide other attractive features, even for such institutional investors as endowments, foundations, and pension plans. Such institutional clients may initially turn to FoFs as their preferred path to navigate their way into the hedge fund space. FoFs offer expertise not only in individual manager selection and due diligence but also in strategic allocation, tactical allocation, and style allocation into individual hedge fund strategies. The FoF strategic allocation is the long-term allocation to different hedge fund styles. For example, a FoF may have a strategic allocation of 20% to long/short equity strategies, 30% to event-driven strategies, 30% to relative value strategies, and 20% to global macro strategies. Tactical allocations include periodically overweighting and underweighting different hedge fund styles across different market environments depending on the level of conviction of the FoF manager. The overall capital or risk exposure can also be geared up or down to reflect the opportunity set in different market conditions.

Through their prime brokerage services, commercial banks provide levered capital to FoFs. Such leverage is typically collateralized by the existing hedge fund assets held in custody by these banks. Because hedge funds often deliver full funds back to redeeming investors with some substantial time lag (a 10% holdback of the total redemption amount until audit completion is typical), access to leverage can often be useful from a bridge loan point of view. In this way, capital not yet returned can be efficiently redeployed for the benefit of remaining investors.

Another attractive aspect of larger FoFs is that by pooling smaller investor assets into a larger single investment commitment, the FoF may be able to extract certain fee breaks, improved liquidity terms, future capacity rights, and/or added transparency provisions from an underlying hedge fund. The FoF may also be able to secure a commitment from the underlying fund to receive the best terms that might subsequently be offered to any future investor. These can all be valuable concessions that a smaller investor would most likely be unable to obtain by investing directly. Some FoFs have argued that these concessions made at the underlying fund manager level can be worth more than the added layering of fees by the FoF.

Overall, by combining different and ideally less correlated strategies, a FoF portfolio should provide more diversification, less extreme risk exposures, lower realized volatility, and generally less single manager tail risk than direct investing in individual hedge fund strategies. FoFs may also achieve economies of scale, manager access, research expertise, potential liquidity efficiencies, useful portfolio leverage opportunities, and potentially valuable concessions from the underlying funds.

12.1.2. Strategy Implementation

Implementing a FoF portfolio is typically a multi-step process that transpires over several months. First, FoF managers will become acquainted with different hedge fund managers via the use of various databases and introductions at prime broker-sponsored capital introduction events, where hedge fund managers present their perceived opportunity sets and qualifications to potential investors. Then, the FoF manager must decide the desired strategic allocation of the portfolio across the different hedge fund strategy groupings.

Next, with both quantitative and qualitative top-down and bottom-up approaches, the formal manager selection process is initiated. For each strategy grouping, the FoF manager screens the available universe of hedge funds with the goal to formulate a select "peer group" of potential investment candidates. This is followed by direct interviews of each hedge fund manager as well as a review of their relevant materials, such as presentation booklets, Alternative Investment Management Association Due Diligence Questionnaires (AIMA DDQs), recent quarterly letters and risk reports, as well as past audits. Typically, FoF managers will meet with prospective hedge fund managers on several different occasions (with at least one onsite visit at their offices). FoF managers will have an increasingly granular focus not only on the hedge fund managers' investment philosophy and portfolio construction but also on the firms' personnel, operational, and risk management processes.

Once an individual hedge fund is deemed a true candidate for investment, the fund's Offering Memorandum and Limited Partnership Agreement will be fully reviewed. The fund's service providers (e.g., auditor, legal adviser, custodian bank, prime broker) will be verified and other background checks and references obtained. At some larger FoF firms, these more operational aspects of the due diligence process will be performed by a dedicated team of specialists who validate the original FoF team's investment conclusions or cite concerns that may need to be addressed prior to an allocation. At this point, the FoF manager may endeavor to obtain certain concessions, agreed to in "side letters," from the hedge fund manager entitling the FoF to reduced fees, added transparency provisions, capacity rights to build an investment in the future, and/or improved redemption liquidity provisions. The larger the potential investment, the greater the FoF's negotiation advantage.

After a hedge fund is approved and the strategy is included in the FoF portfolio, then the process moves into the ongoing monitoring and review phases. The main concerns are monitoring for performance consistency with investment objectives and for any style drift, personnel changes, regulatory issues, or other correlation/return shifts that may transpire when compared to other managers both within the portfolio and when compared to similar hedge fund peers.

12.2. Multi-Strategy Hedge Funds

Multi-strategy hedge funds combine multiple hedge fund strategies under the same hedge fund structure. Teams of managers dedicated to running different hedge fund strategies share operational and risk management systems under the same roof.

12.2.1. Investment Characteristics

A key advantage to this approach is that the multi-strategy manager can reallocate capital into different strategy areas more quickly and efficiently than would be possible by the FoF manager. The multi-strategy manager has full transparency and a better picture of the interactions of the different teams' portfolio risks than would ever be possible for the FoF manager to achieve. Consequently, the multi-strategy manager can react faster to different real-time market impacts—for example, by rapidly increasing or decreasing leverage within different strategies depending on the perceived riskiness of available opportunities. Teams within a multi-strategy manager also can be fully focused on their respective portfolios because the business, operational, and regulatory aspects of running the hedge fund are handled by other administrative professionals. Many talented portfolio managers decide to join a multi-strategy firm for this reason.

The fees paid by investors in a multi-strategy fund can be structured in many ways, some of which can be very attractive when compared to the FoF added fee layering and netting risk attributes. Conceptually, the FoF investor always faces netting risk, whereby he/she is responsible for paying performance (i.e., incentive) fees due to winning underlying funds while suffering return drag from the performance of losing underlying funds. Even if the FoF's overall performance (aggregated across all funds) is flat or down, FoF investors must still pay incentive fees due to the managers of the winning underlying funds.

The fee structure is more investor-friendly at multi-strategy hedge funds where the general partner absorbs the netting risk arising from the divergent performances of his/her fund's different strategy teams. This is an attractive outcome for the multi-strategy fund investor because: 1) the GP is responsible for netting risk; and 2) the only investor-level incentive fees paid are those due on the total fund performance after netting the positive and negative performances of the various strategy teams. Although beneficial to investors, this structure can at times cause discord within a multi-strategy fund. Because the GP is responsible for netting risk, the multi-strategy fund's overall bonus pool may shrink; thus, high-performing strategy teams will be disaffected if they do not receive their full incentive amounts, which ultimately results in personnel losses.

However, some multi-strategy hedge fund firms operate with a pass-through fee model. Using this model, they may charge no management fee but instead pass through the costs of paying individual teams (inclusive of salary and incentive fees earned by each team) before an added manager level incentive fee is charged to the investor on total fund performance. In this instance, the investor does implicitly pay for a portion of netting risk between the different teams (in place of a management fee), while the multi-strategy fund's GP bears a portion of that netting risk (via the risk that the total fund-level incentive fee may not cover contractual obligations that the GP is required to pay individual teams).

The main risk of multi-strategy funds is that they are generally quite levered: Position transparency is closely monitored in-house, and fee structures are typically tilted toward performance (due to high costs of the infrastructure requirements). Leverage applied to tight risk management is usually benign, but in market stress periods, risk management miscalibrations can certainly matter. The left-tail, risk-induced implosions of prominent multi-strategy funds, such as Ritchie Capital (2005) and Amaranth Advisors (2006), are somewhat legendary. Moreover, the operational risks of a multi-strategy firm, by definition, are not well diversified because all operational processes are performed under the same fund structure. Finally, multi-strategy funds can be somewhat limited in the scope of strategies offered because they are constrained by the available pool of in-house manager talent and skills (and are often staffed by managers with similar investment styles and philosophies).

12.2.2. Strategy Implementation

Multi-strategy funds invest in a range of individual hedge fund strategies. As mentioned, the breadth of strategies they can access is a function of the portfolio management skills available within the particular multi-strategy fund. Similar to a FoF manager, a multi-strategy fund will engage in both strategic and tactical allocations to individual hedge fund strategies. Given that multi-strategy fund teams manage each strategy directly and operate under the same fund roof, compared FoF managers, they are more likely to be well informed about when to tactically reallocate to a particular strategy and more capable of shifting capital between strategies quickly. Conversely, multi-strategy funds may also be less willing to exit strategies in which core expertise is in-house. Common risk management systems and processes are also more likely to reveal interactions and correlations between the different strategies run by the various portfolio management teams. Such nuanced aspects of risk might be far harder to detect within a FoF structure.

Exhibit 11 compares some key attributes of fund-of-funds and multi-strategy funds that investors must consider when deciding which of these two multi-manager types best fits their needs.

EXHIBIT 11   Fund-of-Funds and Multi-Strategy Funds—Comparison of Risk, Liquidity, Leverage, and Benchmarking

Risk Profile and Liquidity

- FoF and multi-strategy funds are designed to offer steady, low-volatility returns via their strategy diversification. Multi-strategy funds have generally outperformed FoFs but with more variance and occasional large losses often related to their higher leverage.
- Multi-strategy funds offer potentially faster tactical asset allocation and improved fee structure (netting risk handled at strategy level) but with higher manager-specific operational risks. FoFs offer a potentially more diverse strategy mix but with less transparency and slower tactical reaction time.
- Both groups typically have similar initial lock-up and redemption periods, but multi-strategy funds also often impose investor-level or fund-level gates on maximum redemptions allowed per quarter.

Leverage Usage

- Multi-strategy funds tend to use significantly more leverage than most FoFs, which gravitate to modest leverage usage. Thus, multi-strategy funds are somewhat more prone to left-tail blow-up risk in stress periods. Still, better strategy transparency and shorter tactical reaction time make multi-strategy funds overall more resilient than FoFs in preserving capital.

Benchmarking

- FoFs can be tracked using such sub-indexes as HFRX and HFRI Fund of Funds Composite Indices; Lipper/TASS Fund-of-Funds Index; CISDM Fund-of-Funds Multi-Strategy Index; and the broad Credit Suisse Hedge Fund Index as a general proxy for a diversified pool of managers.
- Multi-strategy managers can be tracked via HFRX and HFRI Multi-Strategy Indices; Lipper/TASS Multi-Strategy Index; CISDM Multi-Strategy Index; and CS Multi-Strategy Hedge Fund Index.

Note: The FoF business model has been under significant pressure since 2008 because of fee compression and increased investor interest in passive, long-only investing and the advent of liquid alternatives for retail investors. Conversely, multi-strategy funds have grown as many institutional investors prefer to invest directly in such funds and avoid FoF fee layering.

EXAMPLE 12   Fund-of-Funds: Net-of-Fee Returns

Squaw Valley Fund of Funds (SVFOF) charges a 1% management fee and 10% incentive fee and invests an equal amount of its assets into two individual hedge funds: Pyrenees Fund (PF) and Ural Fund (UF), each charging a 2% management fee and a 20% incentive fee. For simplicity in answering the following questions, please ignore fee compounding and assume that all fees are paid at year-end.

1. If the managers of both PF and UF generate 20% gross annual returns, what is the net-of-fee return for an investor in SVFOF?
2. If PF's manager earns a gross return of 20% but UF's manager loses 5%, what is the net-of-fee return for an investor in SVFOF?

Solution to 1: Incentive fees are deducted only from gross gains net of management fees and expenses. Thus, the answer becomes:

Net of Fees Return for PF and UF Investor = (20% − 2% − 3.6%) = 14.4%, where 3.6% = 20% × (20% − 2%);
Net of Fees Return for SVFOF Investor = (14.4% − 1% − 1.34%) = **12.06%**, where 1.34% = 10% × (14.4% − 1%).

Solution to 2:

Net of Fees Return for PF Investor = (20% − 2% − 3.6%) = 14.4%;
Net of Fees Return for UF Investor = (−5% − 2% − 0%) = −7.0%;
Gross Return for SVFOF Investor = (0.5 × 14.4% + 0.5 × − 7.0%) = 3.7%;
Net of Fees Return for SVFOF Investor = (3.7% − 1% − 0.27%) = **2.43%**, where 0.27% = 10% × (3.7% − 1%).

In conclusion, if both PF and UF managers generate gross returns of 20%, then the net-of-fee return for SVFOF's investor is 12.06%, with fees taking up 39.7% of the total gross investment return [(2% + 3.6% + 1% + 1.34%)/20% = 39.7%] and the remainder going to the SVFOF investor.

But, if PF's manager earns a 20% gross return and UF's manager loses 5%, then the net-of-fee return for the SVFOF investor is a meager 2.43%. In this case, most (67.6%) of the original gross return of 7.5% [= 20% x 0.50 + (−5% x 0.50)] goes to PF, UF, and SVFOF managers as fees. Note that {[0.50 x (2% + 3.6% + 2% + 0%)] + (1% + 0.27%)}/7.5% equals 67.6%. This is an example of fee netting risk that comes with investing in FoFs.

EXAMPLE 13   Fund-of-Funds or Multi-Strategy Funds—Which to Choose?

The Leonardo family office in Milan manages the €435 million fortune of the Da Vinci family. Mona, the family's matriarch, trained as an economist and worked at Banca d'Italia for many years. She is now retired but still monitors global financial markets. The portfolio that Leonardo manages for the Da Vinci family consists of traditional long-only stocks and bonds, real estate, private equity, and single manager hedge funds following distressed securities and merger arbitrage strategies.

Mona believes global financial markets are about to enter a prolonged period of heightened volatility, so she asks Leonardo's senior portfolio manager to sell some long-only stocks and the merger arbitrage hedge fund and then buy a multi-manager hedge fund. Mona's objectives are to increase the portfolio's diversification, flexibility, and transparency while maximizing net-of-fees returns during the volatile period ahead.

Discuss advantages and disadvantages that Leonardo's portfolio manager should consider in choosing between a FoF and a multi-strategy fund.

Solution: Leonardo's portfolio manager understands that both multi-strategy funds and FoFs are designed to offer steady, low-volatility returns via their strategy diversification.

However, digging deeper he sees that multi-strategy funds have generally outperformed FoFs. This may be because of such key advantages as their enhanced flexibility and the fast pace of tactical asset allocation (important in dynamic, volatile markets) given that the different strategies are executed within the same fund structure. Another advantage of this set-up of multi-strategy funds is increased transparency regarding overall positions and exposures being carried. Moreover, many multi-strategy funds have an investor-friendly fee structure, in which fee netting risk is handled at the strategy level and absorbed (or partially absorbed) by the general partner of the multi-strategy fund. As for disadvantages, Leonardo's portfolio manager should consider that multi-strategy funds entail higher manager-specific operational risks, so detailed due diligence is important; moreover, they tend to use relatively high leverage, which may increase the variance of returns.

The main advantages of FoFs are that they offer a potentially more diverse strategy mix with lower leverage (and somewhat less return variance), and they have less operational risk (i.e., each separate underlying hedge fund is responsible for its own risk management). Leonardo's portfolio manager realizes that FoFs also entail reduced transparency into the portfolio decisions made at the underlying hedge funds as well as a slower tactical reaction time. Another key disadvantage is that FoFs require a double layer of fees to be paid, with netting risk borne by the investor, which imposes a substantial drag on net-of-fees returns.

13. ANALYSIS OF HEDGE FUND STRATEGIES USING A CONDITIONAL FACTOR RISK MODEL

From the foregoing discussion, it is reasonable to conclude the following: L/S equity and event-driven managers tend to be exposed to some natural equity market beta risk; arbitrage managers often are exposed to credit spread risk and market volatility tail risk; opportunistic managers tend to have risk exposures to the trendiness (or directionality) of markets; and relative value managers do not expect trendiness but are typically counting on mean reversion. Each strategy has unique sources of factor exposures and resulting vulnerabilities. Moreover, risk factor exposures in many strategies arise from simply holding financial instruments whose prices are directly impacted by those risk factors. That is, long and short exposures to a given risk factor in different securities are not equal, thereby giving rise to a non-zero *net* exposure. Following a practice-based risk factor perspective, this chapter uses a conditional linear factor model to uncover and analyze hedge fund strategy risk exposures. While this is just one way to go about explaining hedge fund strategies' risks and returns, it is representative of the widely used risk factor approach.

One may ask why it is necessary to use such a model to investigate hedge fund strategies. It is because a linear factor model can provide insights into the intrinsic characteristics and risks in a hedge fund investment. Moreover, given the dynamic nature of hedge fund strategies, a conditional model allows for the analysis in a specific market environment to determine, for example, whether hedge fund strategies are exposed to certain risks under abnormal market conditions. A conditional model can show whether hedge fund risk exposures (e.g., to credit or volatility) that are insignificant during calm market periods may become significant during turbulent market periods. The importance of using a conditional factor model is underscored by the fact that the hedge fund industry is dynamic; for example, it experienced a huge decline in AUM during the global financial crisis. Specifically, after recording more than a 25% compound annual growth rate (CAGR) in assets between 2000 and 2007, the global hedge fund industry's aggregate AUM declined by 17% CAGR between 2007 and 2009 (the period of the global financial crisis) from a high of more than $2.6 trillion. Moreover, global AUM did not surpass the 2007 high until 2014. In short, thousands of hedge funds were shuttered during this time as performance plunged when many managers were caught off guard by their funds' actual risk exposures during the crisis period and in its aftermath.

13.1. Conditional Factor Risk Model

A simple conditional linear factor model applied to a hedge fund strategy's returns can be represented as:

$$(\text{Return on HF}_i)_t = \alpha_i + \beta_{i,1}(\text{Factor 1})_t + \beta_{i,2}(\text{Factor 2})_t + \ldots + \beta_{i,K}(\text{Factor } K)_t + D_t\beta_{i,1}(\text{Factor 1})_t$$
$$+ D_t\beta_{i,2}(\text{Factor 2})_t + \ldots + D_t\beta_{i,K}(\text{Factor } K)_t + (\text{error})_{i,t},$$

where

- $(\text{Return on HF}_i)_t$ is the return of hedge fund i in period t;
- $\beta_{i,1}(\text{Factor 1})_t$ represents the exposure to risk factor 1 (up to risk factor K) for hedge fund i in period t during normal times;
- $D_t\beta_{i,1}(\text{Factor 1})_t$ represents the *incremental* exposure to risk factor 1 (up to risk factor K) for hedge fund i in period t during financial crisis periods, where D_t is a dummy variable that equals 1 during financial crisis periods (i.e., June 2007 to February 2009) and 0 otherwise;
- α_i is the intercept for hedge fund i; and
- $(\text{error})_{i,t}$ is random error with zero mean and standard deviation of σ_i.

Each factor beta represents the expected change in hedge fund returns for a one-unit increase in the specific risk factor, holding all other factors (independent variables) constant.

The portion of hedge fund returns not explained by the risk factors is attributable to three sources: 1) alpha, the hedge fund manager's unique investment skills; 2) omitted factors; and 3) random errors. The starting point for building this model is the identification of a comprehensive set of asset class and macro-oriented, market-based risks, including the behavior of stocks, bonds, currencies, commodities, credit spreads, and volatility. Following Hasanhodzic and Lo (2007) and practice, the model starts with the following six factors:

- **Equity risk (SNP500):** monthly total return of the S&P 500 Index, including dividends.
- **Interest rate risk (BOND):** monthly return of the Bloomberg Barclays Corporate AA Intermediate Bond Index.
- **Currency risk (USD):** monthly return of the US Dollar Index.
- **Commodity risk (CMDTY):** monthly total return of the Goldman Sachs Commodity Index (GSCI).
- **Credit risk (CREDIT):** difference between monthly seasoned Baa and Aaa corporate bond yields provided by Moody's.
- **Volatility risk (VIX):** first-difference of the end-of-month value of the CBOE Volatility Index (VIX).

Once these potentially relevant macro risk factors were identified for analysis, the next consideration was the appropriateness of using them together in the model. To address the issue of highly correlated risk factors and to avoid potential multi-collinearity problems, a four-step "stepwise regression" process was used to build a conditional linear factor model that is less likely to include highly correlated risk factors. This process is described briefly in the accompanying sidebar.

Practical Steps for Building Hedge Fund Risk Factor Models

The following four-step procedure describes a stepwise regression process that can help build linear conditional factor models that are less likely to include highly correlated risk factors, thereby avoiding multi-collinearity issues.

Step 1: Identify potentially important risk factors.

Step 2: Calculate pairwise correlations across all risk factors. If two-state conditional models are used, calculate correlations across all risk factors for both states—for example, during normal market conditions (state 1) and during market crisis conditions (state 2). For illustration purposes, risk factors A and B can be assumed to be highly correlated if the correlation coefficient between them exceeds 60%.

Step 3: For highly correlated risk factors A and B, regress the return series of interest (e.g., hedge fund returns) on all risk factors excluding factor A. Then, regress the same returns on the all risk factors, but this time exclude factor B. Given the adjusted R^2 for regressions without A and without B, keep the risk factor that results in the highest adjusted R^2.

Step 4: Repeat step 3 for all other highly correlated factor pairs, with the aim of eliminating the least useful (in terms of explanatory power) factors and thereby avoiding multi-collinearity issues.

To address the multi-collinearity problem, the stepwise regression procedure was implemented using two of the hedge fund databases mentioned previously: Lipper TASS (TASS) and Morningstar Hedge/CISDM (CISDM). The accompanying sidebar provides useful background for practitioners on these two important sources of hedge fund information.

Hedge Fund Databases

The analysis in this chapter uses two well-known hedge fund databases to evaluate hedge fund strategies: Lipper TASS (TASS) and Morningstar Hedge/CISDM (CISDM) databases. These databases are among the ones most widely used for hedge fund research.

The analysis covers the period of 2000–2016. Each database is separated into "live" (operating/open), "defunct" (non-operating/shut down or operating/closed to new investment or operating/delisted and relisted with another database), and "all" funds (live + defunct) groups. Hedge fund return data are filtered to exclude funds that: 1) do not report net-of-fee returns; 2) report returns in currencies other than US dollar; 3) report returns less frequently than monthly; 4) do not provide AUM or estimates; and 5) have less than 36 months of return data. TASS and CISDM databases have a total of 6,352 and 7,756 funds, respectively. Importantly, 82% (18%) and 80% (20%) of all TASS and CISDM funds, respectively, are defunct (live). This is consistent with the relatively high attrition rate of hedge funds and the relatively short life of a typical hedge fund.

Databases that include defunct funds can be highly useful for asset allocators because the historical track record of managers that may be starting new funds might be found to include defunct funds. Then, further analysis could be conducted to determine if such funds became defunct because of the managers' poor performance and/or excessive redemptions, so they were shut down, or because of the managers' initial success, such that an overabundance of inflows caused subsequent investment capacity issues. From a data analysis point of view, including defunct funds also helps to appropriately adjust for database survivorship bias that might otherwise yield incorrect analytical conclusions.

Live, Defunct, and All Funds in TASS Database from 2000–2016

Grouping	TASS Primary Categories	Number of Live Funds	Number of Defunct Funds	Total Number of Funds
Equity	Dedicated short bias	4	38	42
Equity	Equity market neutral	38	270	308
Equity	Long/short equity hedge	350	1,705	2,055
Event driven	Event driven	87	465	552
Relative value	Convertible arbitrage	17	162	179
Relative value	Fixed income arbitrage	42	167	209
Opportunistic	Global macro	59	266	325
Opportunistic	Managed futures	1	2	3
Multi-manager	Fund of funds	454	1,711	2,165
Multi-manager	Multi-strategy	100	414	514
Total		1,152	5,200	6,352

Live, Defunct, and All Funds in CISDM Database from 2000–2016

Grouping	CISDM Categories	Number of Live Funds	Number of Defunct Funds	Total Number of Funds
Equity	Asia/Pacific long/short equity	31	203	234
Equity	Bear market equity	2	36	38
Equity	Equity market neutral	40	272	312
Equity	Europe long/short equity	47	161	208
Equity	Global long/short equity	86	406	492
Equity	US long/short equity	218	849	1,067
Equity	US small-cap long/short equity	67	171	238
Event driven	Merger arbitrage	22	16	38
Event driven	Distressed securities	46	159	205
Event driven	Event driven	63	228	291
Relative value	Convertible arbitrage	25	125	150
Relative value	Debt arbitrage	32	141	173
Opportunistic	Global macro	84	380	464
Opportunistic	Systematic futures	182	518	700
Multi-manager	Fund of funds – debt	20	97	117
Multi-manager	Fund of funds – equity	104	592	696
Multi-manager	Fund of funds – event	10	124	134
Multi-manager	Fund of funds – macro/systematic	30	163	193
Multi-manager	Fund of funds – multi-strategy	164	789	953
Multi-manager	Fund of funds – relative value	12	83	95
Multi-manager	Multi-strategy	111	395	506
Specialist	Volatility	28	30	58
Specialist	Long/short debt	115	279	394
Total		1,539	6,217	7,756

Using TASS and CISDM datasets, the stepwise regression procedure resulted in both BOND and CMDTY factors being dropped from the final conditional linear risk model because of multi-collinearity issues. This is because retaining CREDIT and SNP500 factors produced higher adjusted R^2s compared to retaining BOND and CMDTY factors.

Exhibit 12 provides useful information for interpreting the effects of the factor exposures included in the conditional risk model on hedge fund strategy returns. For both normal and crisis periods, it shows the four risk factors, the typical market trend during these periods, the hedge fund manager's desired position (long or short), and the desired factor exposure for benefitting from a particular market trend.

EXHIBIT 12   Interpretation of Conditional Risk Factor Exposures

Period/ Risk Factor	Typical Market Trend	Desired Position	Desired Factor Exposure	Comments
Normal				
SNP500	Equities Rising	Long	Positive	Aims to add risk, increase return
CREDIT	Spreads Flat/Narrowing	Long	Positive	Aims to add risk, increase return
USD	USD Flat/Depreciating	Short	Negative	Sells USD to boost returns
VIX	Volatility Falling	Short	Negative	Sells volatility to boost returns
Crisis				
DSNP500	Equities Falling Sharply	Short	Negative	Aims to reduce risk
DCREDIT	Spreads Widening	Short	Negative	Aims to reduce risk
DUSD	USD Appreciating	Long	Positive	USD is haven in crisis periods
DVIX	Volatility Rising	Long	Positive	Negative correlation with equities

14. EVALUATING EQUITY HEDGE FUND STRATEGIES: APPLICATION

Using data from the CISDM and TASS databases from 2000 to 2016, this section discusses key return and risk characteristics for hedge funds pursuing equity-related strategies. More specifically, the conditional factor model is used to assess average risk exposures (during both normal and crisis market periods) for all "live" funds in each of the equity-related categories in these databases. Finally, the heterogeneity among funds, which is masked in the average exposures, is then revealed in an analysis showing the percentage of all hedge funds in each category that have significant factor exposures (positive and negative) during normal and crisis periods.

Note that the results of such a risk factor analysis may vary somewhat based on the hedge fund database used, the time period examined, and the specification of the factor model. However, the key takeaway is that such an analysis can uncover unintended adverse risk exposures to a hedge fund—stemming from the strategy it pursues—that may assert themselves only during turbulent market periods. As mentioned previously, unintended adverse risk exposures that revealed themselves during the global financial crisis resulted in the demise of literally thousands of hedge funds worldwide. Thus, understanding how to interpret the results of such a risk factor analysis is a key practical competency for any practitioner involved in advising on the strategies followed by hedge funds or in managing or owning the hedge funds themselves. First, we describe how the factor model can be used to understand risk exposures of equity-related hedge fund strategies. Then, we turn to understanding risks of multi-manager strategies.

The key return characteristics are shown for equity-related hedge fund strategies by category in Exhibit 13. In addition to the Sharpe ratio, we calculate the Sortino ratio.[2] The Sortino

---

[2]In addition to Sharpe and Sortino ratios, other performance measures can be used, such as the Treynor ratio, information ratio, return on VaR, Jensen's alpha, M^2, maximum drawdown, and gain-to-loss ratio.

ratio replaces standard deviation in the Sharpe ratio with downside deviation, so it concentrates on returns below a specified threshold. For example, if the threshold return is zero, then the Sortino ratio uses downside deviation based on losses. Because hedge funds potentially invest in illiquid securities (which artificially smooth returns, thus lowering the measured standard deviation), besides measuring risk and return one should also investigate the autocorrelation of returns. Rho is a measure of first order serial autocorrelation, the correlation between a fund's return and its own lagged returns. High Rho signals smoothed returns and thus is an indicator of potential liquidity issues (specifically, illiquidity and infrequent trading) in the underlying securities.

Exhibit 13 shows that L/S Equity Hedge (TASS) has the highest mean return (11.30%) but also the highest standard deviation (22.86%). Among categories with more than four funds, EMN (TASS) has the highest Sharpe ratio; notably, despite having the highest standard deviation, L/S Equity Hedge (TASS) also has the highest Sortino ratio; and Global L/S Equity (CISDM) shows the largest Rho. Overall, these results indicate that by accepting some beta and illiquidity exposure, L/S equity managers generally outperform equity market-neutral managers in terms of total returns delivered. Returns of L/S equity managers, however, are also more volatile than those of EMN managers and so produce lower Sharpe ratios. Intuitively, these results are in line with expectations.

EXHIBIT 13   Key Return Characteristics for Equity Hedge Fund Strategies (2000–2016)

Database	Category	Sample Size	Annualized Mean (%)		Annualized Sharpe Ratio		Annualized Sortino Ratio		Rho (%)	
			Mean	SD	Mean	SD	Mean	SD	Mean	SD
TASS	Dedicated short bias	4	2.91	14.75	2.27	4.36	1.35	1.07	20.0	45.7
CISDM	Bear market equity	2	2.04	7.37	0.29	1.18	0.70	1.47	9.15	1.79
TASS	Equity market neutral	38	7.81	10.20	0.83	0.56	0.80	0.53	9.3	15.8
CISDM	Equity market neutral	40	7.48	8.82	0.79	0.81	0.65	0.92	16.29	8.88
TASS	Long/short equity hedge	350	11.30	22.86	0.62	0.64	1.33	1.04	11.0	13.5
CISDM	Global long/short equity	86	8.83	16.93	0.44	0.57	0.76	1.09	17.43	15.63
CISDM	Asia/Pacific long/short equity	31	8.87	20.27	0.45	0.36	0.73	0.57	16.72	10.49
CISDM	Europe long/short equity	47	7.05	11.59	0.56	0.37	0.69	1.08	13.92	10.53
CISDM	US long/short equity	218	9.41	17.50	0.62	0.46	0.60	0.55	12.76	8.98
CISDM	US small cap long/short equity	67	9.88	19.60	0.65	0.48	1.14	0.86	11.71	7.44

Taking a more granular view of factor risks, Exhibit 14 presents average risk exposures (equity, credit, currency, and volatility) for equity-related hedge fund strategies using the conditional risk factor model from 2000 to 2016. The crisis period is from June 2007 to February 2009, and crisis period factors are preceded by the letter D (e.g., the crisis period equity factor is DSNP500). Light (dark) shaded coefficients have *t*-statistics greater than 1.96 (1.67) and are significant at the 5% (10%) level.

EXHIBIT 14   Risk Exposures for Equity Hedge Funds Using the Conditional Risk Factor Model (2000–2016)

Strategy	Dedicated Short Bias	Bear Market Equity	Equity Market Neutral	Equity Market Neutral	Asia/ Pacific Long/ Short Equity	Europe Long/ Short Equity	Global Long/ Short Equity	US Long/ Short Equity	US Small Cap Long/ Short Equity	Long/ Short Equity Hedge
Database	TASS	CISDM	TASS	CISDM	CISDM	CISDM	CISDM	CISDM	CISDM	TASS
Sample Size	4	2	38	40	31	47	86	218	67	350
Normal Times Exposures										
Intercept	−0.02	0.00	0.01	0.01	0.01	0.01	0.02	−0.01	0.01	0.01
SNP500	−0.28	−0.46	0.11	0.09	0.42	0.24	0.52	0.58	0.58	0.41
USD	−0.13	−0.07	−0.02	0.00	−0.02	0.06	−0.01	−0.03	−0.01	−0.04
CREDIT	1.24	0.22	−0.12	−0.07	−0.26	−0.23	−0.77	0.63	−0.09	−0.20
VIX	0.04	−0.05	0.01	0.00	−0.01	0.02	−0.01	−0.03	0.03	0.07
Crisis Times Exposures (Incremental)										
DSNP500	0.04	0.11	0.04	0.05	−0.02	−0.14	−0.04	0.03	−0.02	−0.03
DUSD	−0.08	−0.06	−0.17	−0.02	0.15	−0.42	−0.07	−0.07	−0.09	−0.17
DCREDIT	0.02	0.05	0.06	0.10	−0.01	0.07	0.16	0.03	−0.20	0.07
DVIX	0.00	−0.02	−0.06	−0.04	−0.04	−0.09	−0.04	0.02	−0.02	−0.02

On average, funds following EMN strategies maintain low exposure to equity market risk (0.11, significant at 10%) as well as a neutral exposure to the other risk factors in the model in both normal and crisis periods. L/S equity strategies maintain significant (at the 5% level) average beta loadings to equity risk during normal periods. The equity risk betas range from 0.24 for Europe L/S Equity to 0.58 for both US and US Small Cap L/S Equity strategies. Although there are no significant incremental (i.e., additional) exposures to equity risk (DSNP500) during crisis periods, total exposures during crisis periods (normal + crisis) are positive and significant for all L/S equity strategies. For example, the total equity exposure in crisis times for US L/S Equity is 0.61 (= 0.58 + 0.03). Because they show average exposures across all live funds in the given strategy category, these results mask significant heterogeneity between funds in their exposures to the four risk factors.

Exhibit 15 highlights this heterogeneity by presenting the percentage of funds experiencing significant (at the 10% level or better) factor exposures within each strategy category. The (T) indicates funds from the TASS database, and all other funds are from CISDM; gray (white) bars signify positive (negative) factor exposures. The y-axis indicates the percentage of funds within each strategy category that experienced the significant risk exposures.

EXHIBIT 15   Significant Positive and Negative Factor Exposures for Funds by Equity Hedge Strategy During Normal and Crisis Periods (2000–2016)

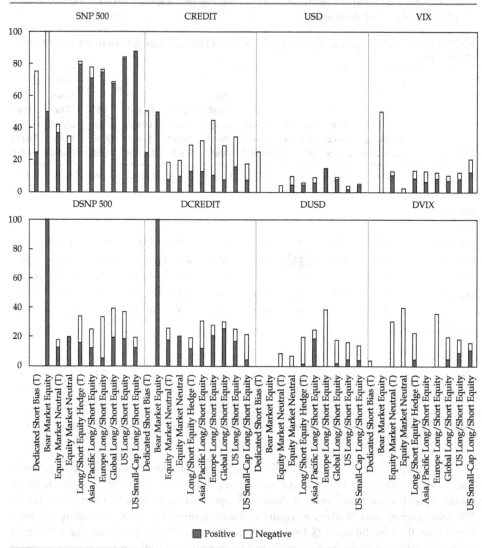

For example, with the exception of dedicated short-biased funds, most equity-related hedge funds have significant positive exposure to equity risk during normal market periods (30%+ for EMN funds and 70%+ for L/S equity funds). However, during crisis periods, less than 40% of L/S equity funds have any significant incremental equity exposure; for those that do, their added exposure is mixed (negative and positive). This suggests that managers were able to decrease adverse crisis period effects on their returns—likely by deleveraging, outright selling of stock (short sales, too) and equity index futures, and/or by buying index put options. This also indicates that although they did not reduce long beta tilting by much, on average L/S equity managers did not make things worse by trying to aggressively "bottom pick" the market. Finally, these results are consistent with the average incremental equity exposure during crisis periods of approximately zero, as seen in the previous exhibit.

As one might intuitively expect, most L/S equity managers do not have significant exposure to CREDIT. Only about one-third of L/S equity funds have significant exposure to CREDIT—mainly negative exposure, indicating that they are unlikely to benefit from moderating credit risk (spreads narrowing, credit upgrades). Interestingly, for the 25% of funds with significant incremental crisis period CREDIT exposure, these exposures become more positive, which would tend to hurt returns as spreads widen and credit downgrades accelerate during market sell-offs. Similarly, exposures to USD and VIX for L/S equity funds are marginal during normal times, with few funds having any significant exposures. However, in most cases during crisis periods, any significant additional exposures are mainly negative. For example, about 40% of Europe L/S Equity funds show significant negative exposure to USD—perhaps expecting a crisis-induced flight to quality into the euro or Japanese yen as opposed to USD. Again, nearly 40% of these funds show negative added VIX exposure (i.e., short volatility) during crisis times. Returns of some high-profile hedge funds have been hurt by being unexpectedly short volatility during crisis periods, which underscores why understanding the heterogeneity of factor exposures is important to understanding risk profiles of hedge funds.

EXAMPLE 14   Dedicated Short-Biased Hedge Fund

Bearish Asset Management (BAM) manages a short-biased hedge fund that varies its portfolio's short tilt depending on perceived opportunities. Using the fund's monthly returns for the past 10 years, which include periods of financial market crisis, a conditional risk factor model was estimated. The following table provides factor beta estimates with corresponding *t*-statistics [dark (light) shaded are significant at the 5% (10%) level].

Interpret the factor loadings. Also, what can you infer about BAM's overall risk exposure during crisis periods?

Coefficient	Estimate	*t*-Statistic
Normal Times Exposures		
Intercept	0.005	1.10
USD	0.072	0.72
CREDIT	−0.017	−0.07
SNP500	−0.572	−9.65
VIX	−0.164	−2.19
Crisis Times Exposures (Incremental)		
DUSD	0.456	1.31
DCREDIT	−0.099	−0.40
DSNP500	0.236	1.74
DVIX	0.105	1.03

Solution: BAM's fund has highly significant negative loadings on equity risk (SNP500) and volatility risk (VIX). The negative equity risk exposure is as expected for a short-biased strategy. But the negative VIX loading is consistent with short volatility exposure. This suggests that BAM's manager may be selling puts against some of its short exposures, thereby attempting to also capture a volatility premium. During crisis periods, the equity beta rises from -0.572 to -0.336 ($= -0.572 + 0.236 = -0.336$). This negative exposure is still significant and suggests that despite being a short-biased fund, BAM had less negative equity risk exposure during crisis periods. In this case, the manager may be purposefully harvesting some of its short exposure into market weakness.

15. EVALUATING MULTI-MANAGER HEDGE FUND STRATEGIES: APPLICATION

It is important to understand the risks of multi-manager hedge fund strategies. Exhibit 16 shows that multi-strategy hedge funds outperform funds-of-funds: They have higher mean returns (7.85%/TASS and 8.52%/CISDM) and among the highest Sharpe ratios and Sortino ratios. Multi-strategy funds have higher Rho (more than 20%) compared to FoF, indicating relatively high serial autocorrelation. This is reasonable because multi-strategy funds may be simultaneously running strategies using less liquid instruments, such as convertible arbitrage, fixed-income arbitrage, and other relative value strategies. That is why, unlike FoFs, they often impose investor-level or fund-level gates on maximum quarterly redemptions.

EXHIBIT 16   Key Return Characteristics for Multi-Manager Hedge Fund Strategies (2000–2016)

Database	Category	Sample Size	Annualized Mean (%)		Annualized Sharpe Ratio		Annualized Sortino Ratio		Rho (%)	
			Mean	SD	Mean	SD	Mean	SD	Mean	SD
CISDM	Fund of funds – debt	20	6.52	7.94	0.89	0.66	0.68	1.17	13.89	4.24
CISDM	Fund of funds – equity	104	4.69	9.15	0.41	0.28	0.44	0.91	12.27	10.61
CISDM	Fund of funds – event	10	4.59	4.99	0.75	0.51	0.56	1.19	13.76	6.71
CISDM	Fund of funds – macro/ systematic	30	5.09	10.16	0.39	0.39	0.57	0.60	8.15	3.52
CISDM	Fund of funds – multi-strategy	164	4.47	7.18	0.54	1.84	1.34	1.43	12.43	9.31
CISDM	Fund of funds – relative value	12	5.31	8.58	0.70	0.42	1.31	0.63	15.86	13.77
TASS	Fund of funds	454	5.73	10.03	0.38	0.71	0.52	0.62	19.9	18.1
CISDM	Multi-strategy	111	8.52	11.01	0.89	1.36	1.32	1.58	20.09	16.24
TASS	Multi-strategy	100	7.85	11.51	0.86	1.40	1.00	1.05	22.7	24.3

Exhibit 17 presents average risk exposures for multi-manager hedge fund strategies using the conditional risk factor model. The crisis period is from June 2007 to February 2009, and light (dark) shaded betas have *t*-statistics of more than 1.96 (1.67).

EXHIBIT 17 Risk Exposures for Multi-Manager Hedge Funds Using the Conditional Risk Factor Model (2000–2016)

Strategy	Fund of Funds – Debt	Fund of Funds – Equity	Fund of Funds – Event	Fund of Funds – Macro/ Systematic	Fund of Funds – Multi- Strategy	Fund of Funds – Relative Value	Fund of Funds	Multi- Strategy	Multi- Strategy
Database	CISDM	CISDM	CISDM	CISDM	CISDM	CISDM	TASS	CISDM	TASS
Sample Size	20	104	10	30	163	12	454	111	100
Normal Times Exposures									
Intercept	0.01	0.01	0.01	0.01	0.01	0.01	0.01	0.10	0.01
SNP500	0.16	0.33	0.14	−0.02	0.21	0.12	0.24	−0.14	0.22
USD	−0.01	0.01	0.01	−0.07	0.00	0.01	0.01	−0.41	−0.01
CREDIT	−0.36	−0.43	−0.22	−0.10	−0.28	−0.14	−0.45	−5.71	−0.03
VIX	0.00	0.03	0.00	0.04	0.01	0.02	0.01	−0.03	0.01
Crisis Times Exposures (Incremental)									
DSNP500	−0.02	0.02	−0.01	−0.01	0.00	0.02	0.00	0.05	0.06
DUSD	0.03	−0.09	−0.19	−0.21	−0.20	−0.27	−0.05	−0.05	−0.05
DCREDIT	−0.10	0.09	−0.13	0.01	0.03	−0.10	0.09	0.07	−0.05
DVIX	0.03	−0.09	−0.03	−0.05	−0.07	−0.06	−0.05	−0.02	−0.05

Results show that all FoF strategies (except macro/systematic) have significant positive exposure to equity risk (ranging from 0.14 to 0.33) for the full period. The finding for macro/systematic is consistent with results presented earlier for opportunistic hedge funds, which show they tend not to be exposed to equity risks in aggregate. Interestingly, multi-strategy funds have significant equity exposure but differing signs—negative (positive) for CISDM (TASS)—which highlights the heterogeneity between the two databases.

Multi-manager funds as a group do not appear to provide significant hedging benefits (via diversification) in crisis times. If they did, then significant negative exposures to DSNP500 would be observed. This is consistent with the research findings that in the 2007–2009 global financial crisis, diversification across hedge fund strategies did not decrease total portfolio risk. These researchers conclude that during crises, simple diversification is insufficient; rather, it is important to focus on such other risks as liquidity, volatility, and credit—particularly because these risks may be magnified by the application of leverage.

Exhibit 18 tells a different story when individual funds are studied. The majority of multi-manager funds have significant positive exposure to the equity factor, but around 30% of funds show a mix of negative and positive incremental exposures (DSNP 500) to equities during the crisis period. This suggests that at least some funds (ones with negative loadings) were able to shield their investors from substantial market declines by either deleveraging, selling equity pre-crisis, and/or short selling. About 40% of all multi-manager funds have significant, mostly negative, exposure to CREDIT, indicating that they generally were not positioned to benefit from improving credit spreads. In crisis times, they took on additional (mostly negative) CREDIT exposure. For example, about 50% of FoF-Debt and FoF-Relative Value funds experienced incremental negative CREDIT exposure during turbulent periods, which hedged them from deteriorating credit conditions.

EXHIBIT 18 Significant Positive and Negative Factor Exposures for Multi-Manager Hedge Funds During Normal and Crisis Periods (2000–2016)

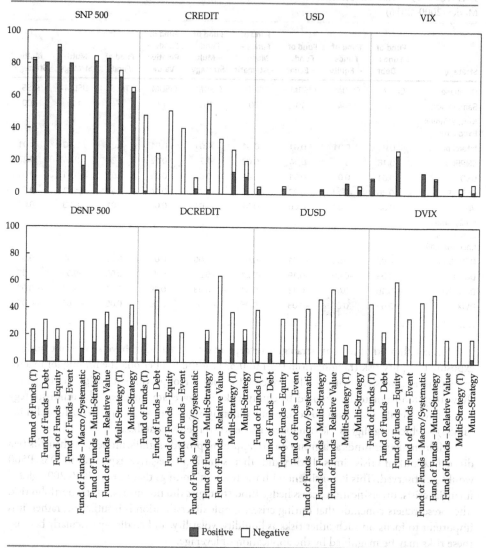

For the full period, multi-manager funds have minimal exposures to USD and VIX. Notably, these exposures increase dramatically, becoming significantly negative during financial crises. For example, only 2% of FoF-Equity have negative exposure to VIX overall. But, 60% of these funds show additional significant negative VIX exposure in crisis times. A similar pattern is revealed for USD exposure. Such negative exposures would seem undesirable during times when volatility is spiking and the USD is likely appreciating. Natural embedded leverage may be a partial explanation for these seemingly undesirable exposures during crisis times. In sum, as crisis periods generate potentially unexpected exposures to systematic risks, it is essential to use conditional factor models to understand risks of hedge fund strategies.

16. PORTFOLIO CONTRIBUTION OF HEDGE FUND STRATEGIES

This section examines the return and risk contributions of the hedge fund strategies previously covered when added to a traditional 60% stock/40% bond investment portfolio.

16.1. Performance Contribution to a 60/40 Portfolio

For each hedge fund strategy category that has been discussed, we now consider an equal-weighted portfolio of the individual funds in that category. We examine the impact of a 20% allocation to such a hedge fund strategy portfolio when combined with a traditional investment portfolio consisting of 60% stocks and 40% bonds. The S&P500 Total Return Index and the Bloomberg Barclays Corporate AA Intermediate Bond Index are used to proxy the 60%/40% portfolio. When the hedge fund strategy portfolio is added to the traditional portfolio, the resulting allocations for the combined portfolio are 48% stocks, 32% bonds, and 20% in the particular hedge fund strategy portfolio. Please note this exercise is for illustrating the portfolio performance contribution of hedge fund strategies; practically speaking, it is unlikely an investor would hold an allocation (here 20%) that included an equal weighting of all live funds in one particular hedge fund strategy category.

Exhibit 19 provides performance and risk metrics for the combined portfolios from 2000 to 2016. It shows that when added to a traditional 60%/40% portfolio (with a mean return of 6.96%), a 20% allocation to the US Small Cap L/S Equity strategy generates the highest mean return (7.53%) of all the combined portfolios—an improvement of 57 bps. Adding a 20% allocation of an equal-weighted portfolio of funds in any of the following hedge fund categories to the traditional portfolio produces average annual returns of more than 7.30%: fixed-income arbitrage, distressed securities, or systematic futures. Adding a 20% allocation of any of the hedge fund strategies shown in Exhibit 19 to the traditional portfolio almost always decreases total portfolio standard deviation while increasing Sharpe and Sortino ratios (and also decreasing maximum drawdown in about one-third of the combined portfolios). These results demonstrate that hedge funds act as both risk-adjusted return enhancers and diversifiers for the traditional stock/bond portfolio.

EXHIBIT 19   Performance and Risk of 48/32/20 Portfolio, Where 20% Allocation Is to an Equal-Weighted Portfolio for Each Hedge Fund Strategy Category (2000–2016)

Category	Type	Database	Mean Return (%)	SD (%)	Sharpe Ratio	Sortino Ratio	Maximum Drawdown (%)
60% Stocks/40% Bonds	*Traditional Portfolio*	—	*6.96*	*8.66*	*0.62*	*1.13*	*14.42*
Long/Short Equity Hedge	Equity	TASS	7.22	8.29	0.68	1.45	21.34
Global Long/Short Equity	Equity	CISDM	7.06	8.17	0.67	1.22	22.51
U.S. Long/Short Equity	Equity	CISDM	7.17	8.22	0.68	1.24	16.77
U.S. Small Cap Long/Short Equity	Equity	CISDM	7.53	8.75	0.68	1.23	27.02

Asia/Pacific Long/ Short Equity	Equity	CISDM	6.44	8.12	0.60	1.07	21.74
Europe Long/ Short Equity	Equity	CISDM	6.79	7.69	0.67	1.24	15.20
Dedicated Short Bias	Equity	TASS	6.02	5.59	0.79	1.02	16.06
Bear Market Equity	Equity	CISDM	5.97	5.68	0.77	1.43	16.62
Equity Market Neutral	Equity	TASS	6.81	7.17	0.73	1.80	10.72
Equity Market Neutral	Equity	CISDM	6.79	7.13	0.73	1.36	4.99
Event Driven	Event Driven	TASS	7.13	7.76	0.71	1.44	20.96
Event Driven	Event Driven	CISDM	7.19	7.83	0.71	1.31	20.57
Distressed Securities	Event Driven	CISDM	7.40	7.67	0.75	1.38	20.00
Merger Arbitrage	Event Driven	CISDM	6.85	7.22	0.73	1.35	5.60
Convertible Arbitrage	Relative Value	TASS	6.76	7.75	0.66	1.27	31.81
Fixed-Income Arbitrage	Relative Value	TASS	7.50	7.82	0.75	1.39	12.68
Convertible Arbitrage	Relative Value	CISDM	6.91	7.68	0.69	1.25	27.91
Global Macro	Opportunistic	TASS	6.96	7.36	0.73	1.29	5.14
Global Macro	Opportunistic	CISDM	6.97	7.29	0.74	1.38	5.19
Systematic Futures	Opportunistic	CISDM	7.34	6.94	0.83	1.68	8.04
Fund of Funds	Multi-manager	TASS	6.43	7.53	0.64	1.23	18.92
Multi-strategy	Multi-manager	TASS	6.98	7.57	0.71	1.13	17.35
Fund of Funds – Debt	Multi-manager	CISDM	6.56	7.40	0.67	1.22	17.77
Fund of Funds – Equity	Multi-manager	CISDM	6.39	7.76	0.62	1.11	21.63
Fund of Funds – Event	Multi-manager	CISDM	6.35	7.48	0.63	1.15	21.37
Fund of Funds - Macro/Systematic	Multi-manager	CISDM	6.47	7.05	0.69	1.31	10.65
Fund of Funds – Multi-strategy	Multi-manager	CISDM	6.36	7.41	0.64	1.17	18.17
Fund of Funds - Relative Value	Multi-manager	CISDM	6.46	7.22	0.67	1.23	17.16
Multi-strategy	Multi-manager	CISDM	7.00	7.47	0.72	1.34	13.83

The Sharpe ratio measures risk-adjusted performance, where risk is defined as standard deviation, so it penalizes both upside and downside variability. The Sortino ratio measures risk-adjusted performance, where risk is defined as downside deviation, so it penalizes only downside variability below a minimum target return. For hedge fund strategies with large negative events, the Sortino ratio is considered a better performance measure. The combined portfolio with the highest Sharpe ratio (0.83) includes a 20% allocation to systematic futures hedge funds. High Sharpe ratios are also achieved from allocations to distressed securities, fixed-income arbitrage, and global macro or equity market-neutral strategies. Adding allocations of 20% consisting of hedge funds from equity market-neutral (TASS), systematic futures, L/S equity hedge, or event-driven (TASS) categories to the traditional portfolio produces combined portfolios with by far the best Sortino ratios.

Exhibit 20 plots the Sharpe and Sortino ratios for 48/32/20 portfolios, where the 20% allocation is to an equal-weighted portfolio of the funds in each hedge fund strategy category. As a point of reference, the Sharpe and Sortino ratios for the 60/40 portfolio are 0.62 and 1.13, respectively. This graphic visually demonstrates that adding allocations of systematic futures, equity market-neutral, global macro, or event-driven hedge fund strategies, among others, to the traditional portfolio is effective in generating superior risk-adjusted performance—as evidenced by their relatively high Sharpe and Sortino ratios. Moreover, the implication is that despite the flexibility to invest in a wide range of strategies, fund-of-funds and multi-manager funds do not enhance risk-adjusted performance very much.

EXHIBIT 20   Sharpe and Sortino Ratios for 48/32/20 Portfolios, Where 20% Allocation Is to an Equal-Weighted Portfolio for Each Hedge Fund Strategy Category

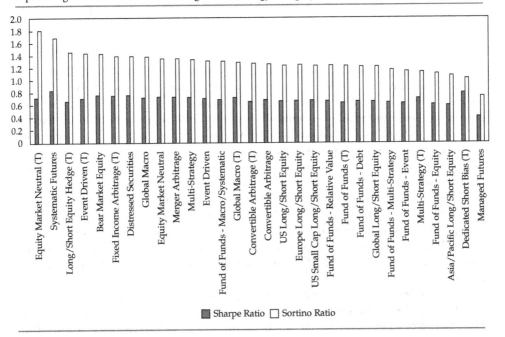

16.2. Risk Metrics

Considering the different risk exposures and investments that hedge fund strategies entail, many investors consider these strategies for portfolio risk reduction or risk mitigation. Exhibit 21 illustrates which strategies may be most effective in reducing risk in a traditional portfolio (with standard deviation of 8.66%). The exhibit presents the standard deviation of returns for 48/32/20 portfolios, where the 20% allocation is to an equal-weighted portfolio for each hedge fund strategy category.

EXHIBIT 21   Standard Deviations for 48/32/20 Portfolios, Where 20% Allocation Is to an Equal-Weighted Portfolio for Each Hedge Fund Strategy Category

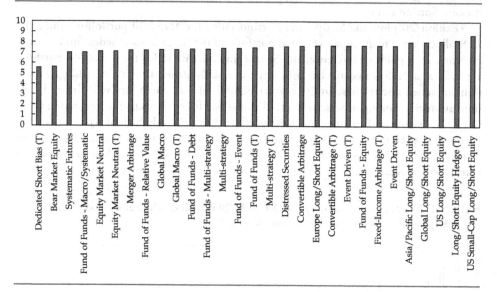

Besides dedicated short-biased and bear market-neutral strategies—for which there are only 6 live funds in total—it can be seen that among the hedge fund strategies that produce the lowest standard deviations of returns in the combined portfolios are systematic futures (6.94%) and FoF-macro/systematic and equity market neutral (a little more than 7.0%). These strategies appear to provide significant risk-reducing diversification benefits; and as discussed previously, they are also the same categories of hedge funds that enhance risk-adjusted returns when added to the traditional 60/40 portfolio. It is evident that standard deviations are relatively high for combined portfolios with event-driven/distressed securities and relative value/convertible arbitrage strategies, indicating they provide little in the way of risk-reduction benefits. This may be attributed to the binary, long-biased nature of most event-driven/distressed securities investing and the typical leverage downsizing/liquidity issues of relative value/convertible arbitrage during periods of market stress.

A drawdown is the difference between a portfolios' highest value (i.e., high-water mark) for a period and any subsequent low point until a new high-water mark is reached. Maximum drawdown is the *largest* difference between a high-water mark and a subsequent low point. The results for maximum drawdown for the 48/32/20 portfolios are shown in Exhibit 22.

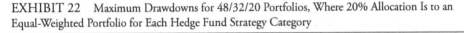

EXHIBIT 22   Maximum Drawdowns for 48/32/20 Portfolios, Where 20% Allocation Is to an
Equal-Weighted Portfolio for Each Hedge Fund Strategy Category

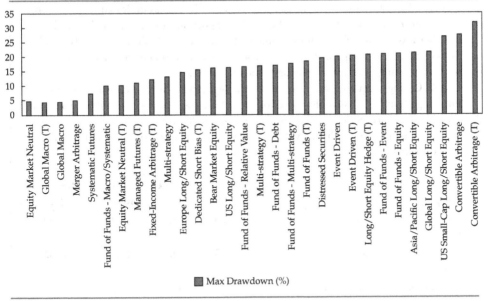

The graphic shows that when combined with the traditional stock and bond portfolio
(with a maximum drawdown of 14.42%), the hedge fund strategy portfolios that generate the
smallest maximum drawdowns are the opportunistic strategies—specifically, global macro and
systematic futures as well as merger arbitrage and equity market-neutral strategies. Notably, the
conditional risk model showed that these strategies did not have much exposure to high equity
or credit risk during crisis periods. In addition, they also tend to be the strategies with the lowest serial autocorrelation, signaling good liquidity. This suggests that these types of strategies
provide risk mitigation for traditional assets because they are not exposed to the same risks, are
relatively opportunistic, and are liquid even during periods of market stress. On the other side
of the spectrum, L/S equity strategies, event-driven/distressed securities strategies, and relative
value/convertible arbitrage strategies show high maximum drawdowns when combined with
the traditional portfolio. This is unsurprising because the conditional risk model showed that
these event-driven and relative value strategies tended to hold equity risk and that their credit
risk also became significant during crisis periods.

EXAMPLE 15   Combining a Hedge Fund Strategy with a Traditional Portfolio

DIY Investment Advisors is a "CIO in a box." Its clients are mainly small institutions
and local college endowments. Evergreen Tech, a private 4-year college, is a client with a
$150 million endowment and an enrollment of 3,000 students. The endowment's port-
folio, which supports 5% of Evergreen's current annual spending needs, has a traditional
asset allocation of 60% stocks/40% bonds. Evergreen plans to dramatically increase
enrollment to 4,000 students over the next 5 years.

Patricia Chong, principal of DIY, wants to recommend to Evergreen's investment committee (IC) that it add alternative investments to the endowment's portfolio, specifically a 20% allocation to a hedge fund strategy. The IC has indicated to Chong that Evergreen's main considerations for the combined portfolio are that any hedge fund strategy allocation should a) maximize risk-adjusted returns; b) limit downside risk; and c) not impair portfolio liquidity. The IC is also sensitive to fees and considers it important to avoid layering of fees for any hedge fund allocation.

At Chong's request, DIY's hedge fund analysts perform due diligence on numerous hedge funds and assemble the following information on several short-listed funds, showing their past performance contribution to a 48% stocks/32% bonds/20% hedge fund strategy portfolio. Finally, Chong believes historical returns are good proxies for future returns.

Category	Type	Mean Return (%)	SD (%)	Sharpe Ratio	Sortino Ratio	Maximum Drawdown (%)
60% Stocks/40% Bonds	Traditional Portfolio	6.96	8.66	0.62	1.13	14.42
US small-cap long/short equity	Equity	7.53	8.75	0.68	1.23	27.02
Event driven	Event driven	7.19	7.83	0.71	1.31	20.57
Sovereign debt fixed-income arbitrage	Relative value	7.50	7.82	0.75	1.39	12.68
Fund-of-funds – equity	Multi-manager	6.39	7.76	0.62	1.11	21.63

Use the information provided to answer the following questions.

1. Discuss which hedge fund strategy Chong should view as *least* suitable for meeting the considerations expressed by Evergreen's IC.
2. Discuss which hedge fund strategy Chong should view as *most* suitable for meeting the considerations expressed by Evergreen's IC.

Solution to 1: Based on the IC's considerations, Chong should view a 20% allocation to the fund-of-funds equity hedge fund strategy as least suitable for Evergreen's endowment portfolio. Such an allocation offers no improvements in the combined portfolio's Sharpe and Sortino ratios (to 0.62 and 1.11, respectively). The substantially higher maximum drawdown (50% higher at 21.63%) indicates much more downside risk would be in the combined portfolio. Portfolio liquidity may also be impaired due to two levels of redemption lock-ups and liquidity gates. Finally, given the FoF structure for this strategy allocation, Evergreen would need to pay two layers of fees and would also likely face fee netting risk.

Solution to 2: Based on the IC's considerations, Chong should view a 20% allocation to the sovereign debt fixed-income arbitrage hedge fund strategy as most suitable for Evergreen's endowment portfolio. Such an allocation would result in significant increases in the combined portfolio's Sharpe and Sortino ratios (to 0.75 and 1.39, respectively), the highest such ratios among the strategies presented. Besides the improvement in Sortino ratio, the lower maximum drawdown (12.68%) indicates less downside risk in the combined portfolio than with any of the other strategy choices. Portfolio liquidity would also likely not be impaired as this strategy focuses on sovereign debt, which typically has good liquidity for most developed market issuers. Finally, similar to the other non-FoF strategies shown, Evergreen would pay only one layer of fees and would also not face any fee netting risk.

SUMMARY

- Hedge funds are an important subset of the alternative investments space. Key characteristics distinguishing hedge funds and their strategies from traditional investments include the following: 1) lower legal and regulatory constraints; 2) flexible mandates permitting use of shorting and derivatives; 3) a larger investment universe on which to focus; 4) aggressive investment styles that allow concentrated positions in securities offering exposure to credit, volatility, and liquidity risk premiums; 5) relatively liberal use of leverage; 6) liquidity constraints that include lock-ups and liquidity gates; and 7) relatively high fee structures involving management and incentive fees.
- Hedge fund strategies are classified by a combination of the instruments in which they are invested, the trading philosophy followed, and the types of risks assumed. Some leading hedge fund strategy index providers are Hedge Fund Research; Lipper TASS; Morningstar Hedge/CISDM; Eurekahedge; and Credit Suisse. There is much heterogeneity in the classification and indexes they provide, so no one index group is all-encompassing.
- This chapter classifies hedge fund strategies by the following categories: equity-related strategies; event-driven strategies; relative value strategies; opportunistic strategies; specialist strategies; and multi-manager strategies.
- Equity L/S strategies take advantage of diverse opportunities globally to create alpha via managers' skillful stock picking. Diverse investment styles include value/growth, large cap/small cap, discretionary/quantitative, and industry specialization. Some equity L/S strategies may use index-based short hedges to reduce market risk, but most involve single name shorts for portfolio alpha and added absolute return.
- Equity L/S strategies are typically liquid and generally net long, with gross exposures at 70%–90% long vs. 20%–50% short (but they can vary).
- Equity L/S return profiles are typically aimed to achieve average annual returns roughly equivalent to a long-only approach but with standard deviations that are 50% lower. The more market-neutral or quantitative the strategy approach, the more levered the strategy application to achieve a meaningful return profile.
- Dedicated short sellers only trade with short-side exposure, but they may moderate short beta by also holding cash. Short-biased managers are focused on short-side stock picking, but they typically moderate short beta with some value-oriented long exposure and cash.
- Dedicated short strategies tend to be 60%–120% short at all times, while short-biased strategies are typically around 30%–60% net short. The focus in both cases is usually on single equity stock picking, as opposed to index shorting, and using little if any leverage.

- Dedicated short-selling and short-biased strategies have return goals that are typically less than most other hedge fund strategies but with a negative correlation benefit. Returns are more volatile than a typical L/S equity hedge fund given short beta exposure.
- Equity market-neutral (EMN) strategies take advantage of idiosyncratic short-term mispricing between securities. Their sources of return and alpha do not require accepting beta risk, so EMN strategies are especially attractive in periods of market vulnerability/weakness. There are many types of EMN managers, but most are purely quantitative managers (vs. discretionary managers).
- As many beta risks (e.g., market, sector) are hedged away, EMN strategies generally apply relatively high levels of leverage in striving for meaningful return targets.
- Equity market-neutral strategies exhibit relatively modest return profiles. Portfolios are aimed at market neutrality and with differing constraints to other factor/sector exposures. Generally high levels of diversification and liquidity with lower standard deviation of returns are typical due to an orientation toward mean reversion.
- Merger arbitrage is a relatively liquid strategy. Defined gains come from idiosyncratic, single security takeover situations, but occasional downside shocks can occur when merger deals unexpectedly fail.
- Cross-border M&A usually involves two sets of governmental approvals. M&A deals involving vertical integration often face antitrust scrutiny and thus carry higher risks and offer wider merger spread returns.
- Merger arbitrage strategies have return profiles that are insurance-like, plus a short put option, with relatively high Sharpe ratios; however, left-tail risk is associated with otherwise steady returns. Merger arbitrage managers typically apply moderate to high leverage to generate meaningful target return levels.
- Distressed securities strategies focus on firms in bankruptcy, facing potential bankruptcy, or under financial stress. Hedge fund managers seek inefficiently priced securities before, during, or after the bankruptcy process, which results in either liquidation or reorganization.
- In liquidation, the firm's assets are sold off and securities holders are paid sequentially based on priority of their claims—from senior secured debt, junior secured debt, unsecured debt, convertible debt, preferred stock, and finally common stock.
- In re-organization, a firm's capital structure is re-organized and terms for current claims are negotiated and revised. Debtholders either may agree to maturity extensions or to exchanging their debt for new equity shares (existing shares are canceled) that are sold to new investors to improve the firm's financial condition.
- Outright shorts or hedged positions are possible, but distressed securities investing is usually long-biased, entails relatively high levels of illiquidity, and has moderate to low leverage. The return profile is typically at the higher end of event-driven strategies, but it is more discrete and cyclical.
- For fixed-income arbitrage, the attractiveness of returns is a function of the correlations between different securities, the yield spread pick-up available, and the high number and wide diversity of debt securities across different markets, each having different credit quality and convexity aspects in their pricing.
- Yield curve and carry trades within the US government space are very liquid but have the fewest mispricing opportunities. Liquidity for relative value positions generally decreases in other sovereign markets, mortgage-related markets, and across corporate debt markets.
- Fixed-income arbitrage involves high leverage usage, but leverage availability diminishes with trade and underlying instrument complexity.

- Convertible arbitrage strategies strive to extract "underpriced" implied volatility from long convertible bond holdings. To do this, managers will delta hedge and gamma trade short equity positions against their convertible positions. Convertible arbitrage works best in periods of high convertible issuance, moderate volatility, and reasonable market liquidity.
- Liquidity issues may arise from convertible bonds being naturally less-liquid securities due to their relatively small issue sizes and inherent complexities as well as the availability and cost to borrow underlying equity for short selling.
- Convertible arbitrage managers typically run convertible portfolios at 300% long vs. 200% short. The lower short exposure is a function of the delta-adjusted exposure needed from short sales to balance the long convertibles.
- Global macro strategies focus on correctly discerning and capitalizing on trends in global financial markets using a wide range of instruments. Managed futures strategies have a similar aim but focus on investments using mainly futures and options on futures, on stock and fixed-income indexes, as well as on commodities and currencies.
- Managed futures strategies typically are implemented via more systematic approaches, while global macro strategies tend to use more discretionary approaches. Both strategies are highly liquid and use high leverage.
- Returns of managed futures strategies typically exhibit positive right-tail skewness during market stress. Global macro strategies generally deliver similar diversification in stress periods but with more heterogeneous outcomes.
- Specialist hedge fund strategies require highly specialized skill sets for trading in niche markets. Two such typical specialist strategies—which are aimed at generating uncorrelated, attractive risk-adjusted returns—are volatility trading and reinsurance/life settlements.
- Volatility traders strive to capture relative timing and strike pricing opportunities due to changes in the term structure of volatility. They try to capture volatility smile and skew by using various types of option spreads, such as bull and bear spreads, straddles, and calendar spreads. In addition to using exchange-listed and OTC options, VIX futures, volatility swaps, and variance swaps can be used to implement volatility trading strategies.
- Life settlements strategies involve analyzing pools of life insurance contracts offered by third-party brokers, where the hedge fund purchases the pool and effectively becomes the beneficiary. The hedge fund manager looks for policies with the following traits: 1) The surrender value being offered to the insured individual is relatively low; 2) the ongoing premium payments are also relatively low; and 3) the probability is relatively high that the insured person will die sooner than predicted by standard actuarial methods.
- Funds-of-funds and multi-strategy funds typically offer steady, low-volatility returns via their strategy diversification. Multi-strategy funds have generally outperformed FoFs, but they have more variance due to using relatively high leverage.
- Multi-strategy funds offer potentially faster tactical asset allocation and generally improved fee structure (netting risk between strategies is often at least partially absorbed by the general partner), but they have higher manager-specific operational risks. FoFs offer a potentially more diverse strategy mix, but they have less transparency, slower tactical reaction time, and contribute netting risk to the FoF investor.
- Conditional linear factor models can be useful for uncovering and analyzing hedge fund strategy risk exposures. This chapter uses such a model that incorporates four factors for assessing risk exposures in both normal periods and market stress/crisis periods: equity risk, credit risk, currency risk, and volatility risk.
- Adding a 20% allocation of a hedge fund strategy group to a traditional 60%/40% portfolio (for a 48% stocks/32% bonds/20% hedge funds portfolio) typically decreases total portfolio standard deviation while it increases Sharpe and Sortino ratios (and also often

decreases maximum drawdown) in the combined portfolios. This demonstrates that hedge funds act as both risk-adjusted return enhancers and diversifiers for the traditional stock/bond portfolio.

REFERENCES

Hasanhodzic, Jasmina, and Andrew Lo. 2007. "Can Hedge-Fund Returns Be Replicated?: The Linear Case." *Journal of Investment Management* 5 (2): 5–45.

Lintner, John. 1983. "The Potential Role of Managed Commodity-Financial Futures Accounts (and/or Funds) in Portfolios of Stocks and Bonds." Working paper, Division of Research, Graduate School of Business Administration, Harvard University.

PROBLEMS

1. Bern Zang is the chief investment officer of the Janson University Endowment Investment Office. The Janson University Endowment Fund (the "Fund") is based in the United States and has current assets under management of $10 billion, with minimal exposure to alternative investments. Zang currently seeks to increase the Fund's allocation to hedge funds and considers four strategies: dedicated short bias, merger arbitrage, convertible bond arbitrage, and global macro.

    At a meeting with the Fund's board of directors, the board mandates Zang to invest only in event-driven and relative value hedge fund strategies.

    Determine, among the four strategies under consideration by Zang, the two that are permitted given the board's mandate. **Justify** your response.

    i.   Dedicated short bias
    ii. Merger arbitrage
    iii. Convertible bond arbitrage
    iv. Global macro

Determine, among the four strategies under consideration by Zang, the two that are permitted given the board's mandate. (circle two)	**Justify** your response.
Dedicated short bias	
Merger arbitrage	
Convertible bond arbitrage	
Global macro strategies	

The following information relates to Questions 2 and 3.

Jane Shaindy is the chief investment officer of a large pension fund. The pension fund is based in the United States and currently has minimal exposure to hedge funds. The pension fund's board has recently approved an additional investment in a long/short equity strategy. As part of Shaindy's due diligence on a hedge fund that implements a long/short equity strategy, she uses a conditional linear factor model to uncover and analyze the hedge fund's risk exposures. She is interested in analyzing several risk factors, but she is specifically concerned about whether the hedge fund's long (positive) exposure to equities increases during turbulent market periods.

2. **Describe** how the conditional linear factor model can be used to address Shaindy's concern.

   During a monthly board meeting, Shaindy discusses her updated market forecast for equity markets. Due to a recent large increase in interest rates and geopolitical tensions, her forecast has changed from one of modestly rising equities to several periods of non-trending markets. Given this new market view, Shaindy concludes that a long/short strategy will not be optimal at this time and seeks another equity-related strategy. The Fund has the capacity to use a substantial amount of leverage.

3. **Determine** the *most appropriate* equity-related hedge fund strategy that Shaindy should employ. **Justify** your response.

4. Gunnar Patel is an event-driven hedge fund manager for Senson Fund, which focuses on merger arbitrage strategies. Patel has been monitoring the potential acquisition of Meura Inc. by Sellshom, Inc. Sellshom is currently trading at $60 per share and has offered to buy Meura in a stock-for-stock deal. Meura was trading at $18 per share just prior to the announcement of the acquisition.

   The offer ratio is 1 share of Sellshom in exchange for 2 shares of Meura. Soon after the announcement, Meura's share price jumps to $22 while Sellshom's falls to $55 in anticipation of the merger receiving required approvals and the deal closing successfully.

   At the current share prices of $55 for Sellshom and $22 for Meura, Patel attempts to profit from the merger announcement. He buys 40,000 shares of Meura and sells short 20,000 shares of Sellshom.

   Calculate the payoffs of the merger arbitrage under the following two scenarios:
   i. The merger is successfully completed.
   ii. The merger fails.

5. John Puten is the chief investment officer of the Markus University Endowment Investment Office. Puten seeks to increase the diversification of the endowment by investing in hedge funds. He recently met with several hedge fund managers that employ different investment strategies. In selecting a hedge fund manager, Puten prefers to hire a manager that uses the following:
   - Fundamental and technical analysis to value markets
   - Discretionary and systematic modes of implementation
   - Top-down strategies
   - A range of macroeconomic and fundamental models to express a view regarding the direction or relative value of a particular asset

     Puten's staff prepares a brief summary of two potential hedge fund investments:

     Hedge Fund 1: A relative value strategy fund focusing only on convertible arbitrage.

     Hedge Fund 2: An opportunistic strategy fund focusing only on global macro strategies.

Determine which hedge fund would be *most appropriate* for Puten.
Justify your response.

6. Yankel Stein is the chief investment officer of a large charitable foundation based in the United States. Although the foundation has significant exposure to alternative investments and hedge funds, Stein proposes to increase the foundation's exposure to relative value hedge fund strategies. As part of Stein's due diligence on a hedge fund engaging in convertible bond arbitrage, Stein asks his investment analyst to summarize different risks associated with the strategy.

Describe how each of the following circumstances can create concerns for Stein's proposed hedge fund strategy:
i.   Short selling
ii. Credit issues
iii. Time decay of call option
iv. Extreme market volatility

	Describe how each of the following circumstances can create concerns for Stein's proposed hedge fund strategy:
Short selling	
Credit issues	
Time decay of call option	
Extreme market volatility	

The following information relates to Questions 7 and 8.

Sushil Wallace is the chief investment officer of a large pension fund. Wallace wants to increase the pension fund's allocation to hedge funds and recently met with three hedge fund managers. These hedge funds focus on the following strategies:

Hedge Fund A: Specialist—Follows relative value volatility arbitrage
Hedge Fund B: Multi-manager—Multi-strategy fund
Hedge Fund C: Multi-manager—Fund-of-funds

7. **Describe** three paths for implementing the strategy of Hedge Fund A.

After a significant amount of internal discussion, Wallace concludes that the pension fund should invest in either Hedge Fund B or C for the diversification benefits from the different strategies employed. However, after final due diligence is completed, Wallace recommends investing only in Hedge Fund B, noting its many advantages over Hedge Fund C.

8. **Discuss** *two* advantages of Hedge Fund B relative to Hedge Fund C with respect to investment characteristics.

9. Kloss Investments is an investment adviser whose clients are small institutional investors. Muskogh Charitable Foundation (the "Foundation") is a client with $70 million of assets under management. The Foundation has a traditional asset allocation of 65% stocks/35% bonds. Risk and return characteristics for the Foundation's current portfolio are presented in Panel A of Exhibit 1.

   Kloss' CIO, Christine Singh, recommends to Muskogh's investment committee that it should add a 10% allocation to hedge funds. The investment committee indicates to Singh that Muskogh's primary considerations for the Foundation's portfolio are that any hedge fund strategy allocation should: a) limit volatility, b) maximize risk-adjusted returns, and c) limit downside risk.

   Singh's associate prepares expected risk and return characteristics for three portfolios that have allocations of 60% stocks, 30% bonds, and 10% hedge funds, where the 10% hedge fund allocation follows either an equity market-neutral, global macro, or convertible arbitrage strategy. The risk and return characteristics of the three portfolios are presented in Panel B of Exhibit 1.

EXHIBIT 1

Hedge Fund Strategy	SD (%)	Sharpe Ratio	Sortino Ratio	Maximum Drawdown (%)
Panel A: Current Portfolio				
N/A	8.75	0.82	1.25	16.2
Panel B: Three Potential Portfolios with a 10% Hedge Fund Allocation				
Equity market neutral	8.72	0.80	1.21	15.1
Global macro	8.55	0.95	1.35	15.0
Convertible arbitrage	8.98	0.83	1.27	20.2

Discuss which hedge fund strategy Singh should view as most suitable for meeting the considerations expressed by Muskogh's investment committee.

The following information relates to Questions 10–17.

Snohomish Mukilteo is a portfolio analyst for the Puyallup-Wenatchee Pension Fund (PWPF). PWPF's investment committee (IC) asks Mukilteo to research adding hedge funds to the PWPF portfolio.

A member of the IC meets with Mukilteo to discuss hedge fund strategies. During the meeting, the IC member admits that her knowledge of hedge fund strategies is fairly limited but tells Mukilteo she believes the following:

Statement 1: Equity market-neutral strategies use a relative value approach.
Statement 2: Event-driven strategies are not exposed to equity market beta risk.
Statement 3: Opportunistic strategies have risk exposure to market directionality.

The IC member also informs Mukilteo that for equity-related strategies, the IC considers low volatility to be more important than negative correlation.

Mukilteo researches various hedge fund strategies. First, Mukilteo analyzes an event-driven strategy involving two companies, Algona Applications (AA) and Tukwila Technologies (TT). AA's management, believing that its own shares are overvalued, uses its shares to acquire TT. The IC has expressed concern about this type of strategy because of the potential for loss if the acquisition unexpectedly fails. Mukilteo's research reveals a way to use derivatives to protect against this loss, and he believes that such protection will satisfy the IC's concern.

Next, while researching relative value strategies, Mukilteo considers a government bond strategy that involves buying lower-liquidity, off-the-run bonds and selling higher-liquidity, duration-matched, on-the-run bonds.

Mukilteo examines an opportunistic strategy implemented by one of the hedge funds under consideration. The hedge fund manager selects 12 AAA rated corporate bonds with actively traded futures contracts and approximately equal durations. For each corporate bond, the manager calculates the 30-day change in the yield spread over a constant risk-free rate. He then ranks the bonds according to this spread change. For the bonds that show the greatest spread narrowing (widening), the hedge fund will take long (short) positions in their futures contracts. The net holding for this strategy is market neutral.

Mukilteo also plans to recommend a specialist hedge fund strategy that would allow PWPF to maintain a high Sharpe ratio even during a financial crisis when equity markets fall.

The IC has been considering the benefits of allocating to a fund of funds (FoF) or to a multi-strategy fund (MSF). Mukilteo receives the following email from a member of the IC:

> From my perspective, an FoF is superior even though it entails higher manager-specific operational risk and will require us to pay a double layer of fees without being able to net performance fees on individual managers. I especially like the tactical allocation advantage of FoFs—that they are more likely to be well informed about when to tactically reallocate to a particular strategy and more capable of shifting capital between strategies quickly.

Finally, Mukilteo creates a model to simulate adding selected individual hedge fund strategies to the current portfolio with a 20% allocation. The IC's primary considerations for a combined portfolio are: (1) that the variance of the combined portfolio must be less than 90% of that of the current portfolio and (2) that the combined portfolio maximize the risk-adjusted return with the expectation of large negative events. Exhibit 2 provides historical performance and risk metrics for three simulated portfolios.

EXHIBIT 2   Performance of Various Combined Portfolios

Hedge Fund Strategy	Standard Deviation(%)	Sharpe Ratio	Sortino Ratio	Maximum Drawdown (%)
Current Portfolio				
NA	7.95	0.58	1.24	14.18
Three Potential Portfolios with a 20% Hedge Fund Allocation				
Merger arbitrage	7.22	0.73	1.35	5.60
Systematic futures	6.94	0.83	1.68	8.04
Equity market neutral	7.17	0.73	1.80	10.72

10. Which of the IC member's statements regarding hedge fund strategies is *incorrect*?
   A. Statement 1
   B. Statement 2
   C. Statement 3
11. Based on what the IC considers important for equity-related strategies, which strategy should Mukilteo *most likely* avoid?
   A. Long/short equity
   B. Equity market neutral
   C. Dedicated short selling and short biased
12. Which of the following set of derivative positions will *most likely* satisfy the IC's concern about the event-driven strategy involving AA and TT?
   A. Long out-of-the-money puts on AA shares and long out-of-the-money calls on TT shares
   B. Long out-of-the-money calls on AA shares and long out-of-the-money puts on TT shares
   C. Long risk-free bonds, short out-of-the-money puts on AA shares, and long out-of-the-money calls on TT shares
13. The government bond strategy that Mukilteo considers is *best* described as a:
   A. carry trade.
   B. yield curve trade.
   C. long/short credit trade.
14. The opportunistic strategy that Mukilteo considers is *most likely* to be described as a:
   A. global macro strategy.
   B. time-series momentum strategy.
   C. cross-sectional momentum strategy.
15. The specialist hedge fund strategy that Mukilteo plans to recommend is *most likely*:
   A. cross-asset volatility trading between the US and Japanese markets.
   B. selling equity volatility and collecting the volatility risk premium.
   C. buying longer-dated out-of-the-money options on VIX index futures.
16. Based on the email that Mukilteo received, the IC member's perspective is correct with regard to:
   A. layering and netting of fees.
   B. tactical allocation capabilities.
   C. manager-specific operational risks.
17. Based on the IC's primary considerations for a combined portfolio, which simulated hedge fund strategy portfolio in Exhibit 2 creates the *most suitable* combined portfolio?
   A. Merger arbitrage
   B. Systematic futures
   C. Equity market neutral

The following information relates to Questions 18–23.

Lynet Xu is the chief investment officer for the North University Endowment Fund (the Fund), which is based in Europe. The Fund's investment committee recently made the decision to add hedge funds to the Fund's portfolio to increase diversification. Xu meets with Yolanda Anderson, a junior analyst, to discuss various hedge fund strategies that might be suitable for the Fund. Anderson tells Xu the following:

Statement 1: Relative value strategies tend to use minimal leverage.

Statement 2: Long/short equity strategies are typically not exposed to equity market beta risk.

Statement 3: Global macro strategies come with naturally higher volatility in the return profiles typically delivered.

Xu tells Anderson that while she is open to using all hedge fund strategies, she is particularly interested in opportunistic hedge fund strategies. Xu states that she prefers opportunistic hedge fund strategies that use high leverage, have high liquidity, and exhibit right-tail skewness.

Xu asks Anderson to research an event-driven strategy involving a potential merger between Aqua Company and Taurus, Inc. Aqua has offered to buy Taurus in a stock-for-stock deal: The offer ratio is two shares of Aqua for three shares of Taurus. Aqua was trading at €50 per share prior to the merger announcement, and it fell to €45 per share after the merger announcement. Taurus was trading at €15 per share prior to the announcement, and it rose to €20 per share in anticipation of the merger deal receiving required approvals and closing successfully. Xu decides to enter into a merger arbitrage trade: She buys 22,500 shares of Taurus at €20 per share and sells short 15,000 shares of Aqua at €45 per share.

Xu and Anderson discuss an equity strategy involving two large European car companies, ZMD and Tarreras. Anderson recently attended a trade show where she inspected ZMD's newest model car. Based on information from the trade show and other analysis conducted by Anderson, Xu concludes that ZMD will not meet its revenue expectations. Current valuation metrics indicate that ZMD shares are overvalued relative to shares of Tarreras. Xu decides to take a short position in ZMD and a long position in Tarreras with equal beta-weighted exposure.

Xu next reviews a convertible arbitrage strategy and analyzes a trade involving the euro-denominated stock and convertible bonds of AVC Corporation, a European utility company. Anderson gathers selected data for AVC Corporation, which is presented in Exhibit 3.

EXHIBIT 3   Selected Data for AVC Corporation

AVC Convertible Bond		AVC Stock	
Price (% of par)	115	Current price (per share)	€28
Coupon (%)	6	P/E	25
Remaining maturity (years)	2	P/BV	2.25
Conversion ratio	50	P/CF	15

Based on comparisons with industry ratios, Xu believes that AVC's shares are overvalued in relative terms and the convertible bonds are undervalued. Anderson analyzes the potential profit outcomes of a long position in the convertible bond combined with a short stock position, assuming small changes in the share price and ignoring dividends and borrowing costs. She offers the following conclusion to Xu: "The profit earned on the convertible arbitrage trade will be the same regardless of whether the share price of AVC decreases or increases."

Finally, Xu and Anderson consider a hedge fund that specializes in reinsurance and life settlements. Xu tells Anderson about three characteristics that hedge fund managers look for when investing in life settlements:

Characteristic 1:   The surrender value offered to the insured individual is relatively high.

Characteristic 2:   The ongoing premium payments to keep the policy active are relatively low.

Characteristic 3:   There is a high probability that the designated insured person is likely to die within the period predicted by standard actuarial methods.

18. Which of Anderson's three statements regarding hedge fund strategies is correct?
    A. Statement 1
    B. Statement 2
    C. Statement 3

19. Which opportunistic hedge fund strategy meets Xu's preferences?
    A. Only global macro
    B. Only managed futures
    C. Both global macro and managed futures

20. Assuming the merger between Aqua and Taurus successfully closes, the payoff on Xu's merger arbitrage trade will be:
    A. –€187,500.
    B. €225,000.
    C. €412,500.

21. Which equity hedge fund strategy *best* describes the ZMD and Tarreras positions taken by Xu?
    A. Short bias
    B. Long/short equity
    C. Equity market neutral

22. Anderson's conclusion about the profitability of the AVC convertible arbitrage trade is:
    A. correct.
    B. incorrect, because the profit will be higher if the share price decreases.
    C. incorrect, because the profit will be higher if the share price increases.

23. Which of the three characteristics of life settlements noted by Anderson is correct?
    A. Characteristic 1
    B. Characteristic 2
    C. Characteristic 3

CHAPTER 7

CAPITAL MARKET EXPECTATIONS: FORECASTING ASSET CLASS RETURNS

Christopher D. Piros, PhD, CFA

LEARNING OUTCOMES

The candidate should be able to:

- discuss approaches to setting expectations for fixed-income returns;
- discuss risks faced by investors in emerging market fixed-income securities and the country risk analysis techniques used to evaluate emerging market economies;
- discuss approaches to setting expectations for equity investment market returns;
- discuss risks faced by investors in emerging market equity securities;
- explain how economic and competitive factors can affect expectations for real estate investment markets and sector returns;
- discuss major approaches to forecasting exchange rates;
- discuss methods of forecasting volatility;
- recommend and justify changes in the component weights of a global investment portfolio based on trends and expected changes in macroeconomic factors.

1. INTRODUCTION

This chapter focuses on capital market expectations. A central theme is that a disciplined approach to setting expectations will be rewarded. This chapter builds on that foundation and examines setting expectations for specific asset classes—fixed income, equities, real estate, and currencies. Estimation of variance–covariance matrices is covered as well.

The chapter begins with an overview of the techniques frequently used to develop capital market expectations. The discussion of specific asset classes begins with fixed income in Sections 3 and 4, followed by equities, real estate, and currencies in Sections 5–7. Estimation of variance–covariance structures is addressed in Section 8. Section 9 illustrates the use of macroeconomic analysis to develop and justify adjustments to a global portfolio.

2. OVERVIEW OF TOOLS AND APPROACHES

This section provides a brief overview of the main concepts, approaches, and tools used in professional forecasting of capital market returns. Whereas subsequent sections focus on specific asset classes, the emphasis here is on the commonality of techniques.

2.1. The Nature of the Problem

Few investment practitioners are likely to question the notion that investment opportunities change in systematic, but imperfectly predictable, ways over time. Yet the ramifications of that fact are often not explicitly recognized. Forecasting returns is not simply a matter of estimating constant, but unknown, parameters—for example, expected returns, variances, and correlations. Time horizons matter. There are two aspects of this issue: the need to ensure intertemporal consistency and the relative usefulness of specific information (e.g., the business cycle) over short, intermediate, and long horizons. The choice among forecasting techniques is effectively a choice of the information on which forecasts will be based (in statistical terms, the information on which the forecast is "conditioned") and how that information will be incorporated into the forecasts. The fact that opportunities change over time should, at least in principle, affect strategic investment decisions and how positions respond to changing forecasts.[1]

Although investment opportunities are not constant, virtually all forecasting techniques rely on notions of central tendency, toward which opportunities tend to revert over time. This fact means that although asset prices, risk premiums, volatilities, valuation ratios, and other metrics may exhibit momentum, persistence, and clustering in the short run, over sufficiently long horizons, they tend to converge to levels consistent with economic and financial fundamentals.

What are we trying to forecast? In principle, we are interested in the whole probability distribution of future returns. In practice, however, forecasting expected return is by far the most important consideration, both because it is the dominant driver of most investment decisions and because it is generally more difficult to forecast within practical tolerances than such risk metrics as volatility. Hence, the primary focus here is on expected return. In terms of risk metrics, we limit our attention to variances and covariances.

2.2. Approaches to Forecasting

At a very high level, there are essentially three approaches to forecasting: (1) formal tools, (2) surveys, and (3) judgment. Formal tools are established research methods amenable to precise

---

[1] For example, in general, it is not optimal to choose a portfolio on the mean–variance-efficient frontier based on forecasts for the coming period. In addition, the distinction between "strategic" and "tactical" asset allocation is less clear cut since, in general, the optimal allocation evolves with the investor's remaining investment horizon. See Piros (2015) for a non-technical exposition of these issues.

definition and independent replication of results. Surveys involve asking a group of experts for their opinions. Judgment can be described as a qualitative synthesis of information derived from various sources and filtered through the lens of experience.

Surveys are probably most useful as a way to gauge consensus views, which can serve as inputs into formal tools and the analyst's own judgment. Judgment is always important. There is ample scope for applying judgment—in particular, economic and psychological insight—to improve forecasts and numbers, including those produced by elaborate quantitative models. In using survey results and applying their own judgment, analysts must be wary of the psychological traps discussed in the Capital Market Expectations Part 1 reading in the CFA curriculum. Beyond these brief observations, however, there is not much new to be said about surveys and judgment.

The formal forecasting tools most commonly used in forecasting capital market returns fall into three broad categories: statistical methods, discounted cash flow models, and risk premium models. The distinctions among these methods will become clear as they are discussed and applied throughout the chapter.

2.2.1. Statistical Methods

All the formal tools involve data and statistical analysis to some degree. Methods that are primarily, if not exclusively, statistical impose relatively little structure on the data. As a result, the forecasts inherit the statistical properties of the data with limited, if any, regard for economic or financial reasoning. Three types of statistical methods will be covered in this chapter. The first approach is to use well-known sample statistics, such as sample means, variances, and correlations, to describe the distribution of future returns. This is undoubtedly the clearest example of simply taking the data at face value. Unfortunately, sampling error makes some of these statistics—in particular, the sample mean—very imprecise. The second approach, **shrinkage estimation**, involves taking a weighted average of two estimates of the same parameter—one based on historical sample data and the other based on some other source or information, such as the analyst's "prior" knowledge. This "two-estimates-are-better-than-one" approach has the desirable property of reducing forecast errors relative to simple sample statistics. The third method, **time-series estimation**, involves forecasting a variable on the basis of lagged values of the variable being forecast and often lagged values of other selected variables. These models have the benefit of explicitly incorporating dynamics into the forecasting process. However, since they are reduced-form models, they may summarize the historical data well without providing much insight into the underlying drivers of the forecasts.

2.2.2. Discounted Cash Flow

Discounted cash flow (DCF) models express the idea that an asset's value is the present value of its expected cash flows. They are a basic method for establishing the intrinsic value of an asset on the basis of fundamentals and its fair required rate of return. Conversely, they are used to estimate the required rate of return implied by the asset's current price.

2.2.3. Risk Premium Models

The risk premium approach expresses the expected return on a risky asset as the sum of the risk-free rate of interest and one or more risk premiums that compensate investors for the asset's exposure to sources of *priced risk* (risk for which investors demand compensation).

There are three main methods for modeling risk premiums: (1) an equilibrium model, such as the CAPM, (2) a factor model, and (3) building blocks. Equilibrium models and factor models both impose a structure on how returns are assumed to be generated. Hence, they can be used to generate estimates of: (1) expected returns and (2) variances and covariances.

3. FORECASTING FIXED INCOME RETURNS

There are three main ways to approach forecasting fixed-income returns. The first is discounted cash flow. This method is really the only one that is precise enough to use in support of trades involving individual fixed-income securities. This type of "micro" analysis will not be discussed in detail here since it is covered extensively elsewhere in CFA Program curriculum readings that focus on fixed income. DCF concepts are also useful in forecasting the more aggregated performance needed to support asset allocation decisions. The second approach is the risk premium approach, which is often applied to fixed income, in part because fixed-income premiums are among the building blocks used to estimate expected returns on riskier asset classes, such as equities. The third approach is to include fixed-income asset classes in an equilibrium model. Doing so has the advantage of imposing consistency across asset classes and is especially useful as a first step in applying the Black–Litterman framework.

3.1. Applying DCF to Fixed Income

Fixed income is really all about discounted cash flow. This stems from the facts that almost all fixed-income securities have finite maturities and that the (promised) cash flows are known, governed by explicit rules, or can be modeled with a reasonably high degree of accuracy (e.g., mortgage-backed security prepayments). Using modern arbitrage-free models, we can value virtually any fixed-income instrument. The most straightforward and, undoubtedly, most precise way to forecast fixed-income returns is to explicitly value the securities on the basis of the assumed evolution of the critical inputs to the valuation model—for example, the spot yield curve, the term structure of volatilities, and prepayment speeds. A whole distribution of returns can be generated by doing this for a variety of scenarios. As noted previously, this is essentially the only option if we need the "micro" precision of accounting for rolling down the yield curve, changes in the shape of the yield curve, changes in rate volatilities, or changes in the sensitivity of contingent cash flows. But for many purposes—for example, asset allocation—we usually do not need such granularity.

Yield to maturity (YTM)—the single discount rate that equates the present value of a bond's cash flows to its market price—is by far the most commonly quoted metric of valuation and, implicitly, of expected return for bonds. For bond portfolios, the YTM is usually calculated as if it were simply an average of the individual bonds' YTM, which is not exactly accurate but is a reasonable approximation.[2] Forecasting bond returns would be very easy if we

---

[2] Bear in mind that yield to maturity does not account for optionality. However, various yield measures derived from option-adjusted valuation can be viewed as conveying similar information. To keep the present discussion as simple as possible, we ignore the distinction here. If optionality is critical to the forecast, it may be necessary to apply a granular DCF framework.

could simply equate yield to maturity with expected return. It is not that simple, but YTM does provide a reasonable and readily available first approximation.

Assuming cash flows are received in full and on time, there are two main reasons why realized return may not equal the initial yield to maturity. First, if the investment horizon is shorter than the amount of time until the bond's maturity, any change in interest rate (i.e., the bond's YTM) will generate a capital gain or loss at the horizon. Second, the cash flows may be reinvested at rates above or below the initial YTM. The longer the horizon, the more sensitive the realized return will be to reinvestment rates. These two issues work in opposite directions: Rising (falling) rates induce capital losses (gains) but increase (decrease) reinvestment income. If the investment horizon equals the (Macaulay) duration of the bond or portfolio, the capital gain/loss and reinvestment effects will roughly offset, leaving the realized return close to the original YTM. This relationship is exact if: (a) the yield curve is flat and (b) the change in rates occurs immediately in a single step. In practice, the relationship is only an approximation. Nonetheless, it provides an important insight: *Over horizons shorter than the duration, the capital gain/loss impact will tend to dominate such that rising (declining) rates imply lower (higher) return, whereas over horizons longer than the duration, the reinvestment impact will tend to dominate such that rising (declining) rates imply higher (lower) return.*

Note that the timing of rate changes matters. It will not have much effect, if any, on the capital gain/loss component because that ultimately depends on the beginning and ending values of the bond or portfolio. But it does affect the reinvestment return. The longer the horizon, the more it matters. Hence, for long-term forecasts, we should break the forecast horizon into subperiods corresponding to when we expect the largest rate changes to occur.

EXAMPLE 1   Forecasting Return Based on Yield to Maturity

Jesper Bloch works for Discrete Asset Management (DAM) in Zurich. Many of the firm's more risk-averse clients invest in a currency-hedged global government bond strategy that uses cash flows to purchase new issues and seasoned bonds all along the yield curve to maintain a roughly constant maturity and duration profile. The yield to maturity of the portfolio is 3.25% (compounded annually), and the modified duration is 4.84. DAM's chief investment officer believes global government yields are likely to rise by 200 bps over the next two years as central banks remove extraordinarily accommodative policies and inflation surges. Bloch has been asked to project approximate returns for this strategy over horizons of two, five, and seven years. What conclusions is Bloch likely to draw?

Solution: If yields were not expected to change, the return would be very close to the yield to maturity (3.25%) over each horizon. The Macaulay duration is 5.0 (= 4.84 × 1.0325), so if the yield change occurred immediately, the capital gain/loss and reinvestment impacts on return would roughly balance over five years. Ignoring convexity (which is not given), the capital loss at the end of two years will be approximately 9.68% (= 4.84 × 2%). Assuming yields rise linearly over the initial two-year period, the higher reinvestment rates will boost the cumulative return by approximately 1.0% over two years, so the annual return over two years will be approximately −1.09% [= 3.25 + (−9.68 + 1.0)/2]. Reinvesting for three more years at the 2.0% higher rate adds another 6.0% to the cumulative return, so the five-year annual return would be approximately 2.71% [= 3.25 + (−9.68 + 1.0 + 6.0)/5]. With an additional two years of reinvestment income, the seven-year annual return would be about 3.44% [= 3.25 + (−9.68 + 1.0 + 6.0 + 4.0)/7]. As expected, the capital loss dominated the return over two years, and higher reinvestment rates dominated over seven years. The gradual nature of the yield increase extended the horizon over which the capital gain/loss and reinvestment effects would balance beyond the initial five-year Macaulay duration.

We have extended the DCF approach beyond simply finding the discount rates implied by current market prices (e.g., YTMs), which might be considered the "pure" DCF approach. For other asset classes (e.g., equities), the connection between discount rates and valuations/returns is vague because there is so much uncertainty with respect to the cash flows. For these asset classes, discounted cash flow is essentially a conceptual framework rather than a precise valuation model. In contrast, in fixed income there is a tight connection between discount rates, valuations, and returns. We are, therefore, able to refine the "pure" DCF forecast by incorporating projections of how rates will evolve over the investment horizon. Doing so is particularly useful in formulating short-term forecasts.

3.2. The Building Block Approach to Fixed-Income Returns

The building block approach forms an estimate of expected return in terms of required compensation for specific types of risk. The required return for fixed-income asset classes has four components: the short-term default-free rate, the term premium, the credit premium, and the liquidity premium. As the names indicate, the premiums reflect compensation for interest rate risk, duration risk, credit risk, and illiquidity, respectively. Only one of the four components—the short-term default-free rate—is (potentially) observable. For example, the term premium and the credit premium are implicitly embedded in yield spreads, but they are not *equal* to observed yield spreads. Next, we will consider each of these components and summarize applicable empirical regularities.

3.2.1. The Short-term Default-free Rate

In principle, the short-term default-free rate is the rate on the highest-quality, most liquid instrument with a maturity that matches the forecast horizon. In practice, it is usually taken to be a government zero-coupon bill at a maturity that is issued frequently—say, every three months. This rate is virtually always tied closely to the central bank's policy rate and, therefore, mirrors the cyclical dynamics of monetary policy. Secular movements are closely tied to expected inflation levels.

Under normal circumstances, the observed rate is a reasonable base on which to build expected returns for risky assets. In extreme circumstances, however, it may be necessary to adopt a normalized rate. For example, when policy rates or short-term government rates are negative, using the observed rate without adjustment may unduly reduce the required/expected return estimate for risky instruments. An alternative to normalizing the short rate in this circumstance would be to raise the estimate of one or more of the risk premiums on the basis of the notion that the observed negative short rate reflects an elevated willingness to pay for safety or, conversely, elevated required compensation for risk.

Forecast horizons substantially longer than the maturity of the standard short-term instrument call for a different type of adjustment. There are essentially two approaches. The first is to use the yield on a longer zero-coupon bond with a maturity that matches the horizon. In theory, that is the right thing to do. It does, however, call into question the role of the term premium since the longer-term rate will already incorporate the term premium. The second approach is to replace today's observed short-term rate with an estimate of the return that would be generated by rolling the short-term instrument over the forecast horizon; that is, take account of the likely path of short-term rates. This approach does not change the interpretation of the term premium. In addition to helping establish the baseline return to which risk premiums will be added, explicitly projecting the path of short-term rates may help in estimating the term premium.

In many markets, there are futures contracts for short-term instruments. The rates implied by these contracts are frequently interpreted as the market's expected path of short-term rates. As such, they provide an excellent starting point for analysts in formulating their own projections. Some central banks—for example, the US Federal Reserve Board—publish projections of future policy rates that can also serve as a guide for analysts. Quantitative models, such as the Taylor rule, provide another tool.[3]

3.2.2. The Term Premium

The default-free spot rate curve reflects the expected path of short-term rates and the required term premiums for each maturity. It is tempting to think that given a projected path of short-term rates, we can easily deduce the term premiums from the spot curve. We can, of course, derive a set of forward rates in the usual way and subtract the projected short-term rate for each future period. Doing so would give an implied sequence of period-by-period premiums. This may be a useful exercise, but it will not give us what we really want—the expected returns for bonds of different maturities over our forecast horizon. The implication is that although the yield curve contains the information we want and may be useful in forecasting returns, we cannot derive the term premium directly from the curve itself.

A vast amount of academic research has been devoted over many decades to addressing three fundamental questions: Do term premiums exist? If so, are they constant? And if they exist, how are they related to maturity? The evidence indicates that term premiums are positive and increase with maturity, are roughly proportional to duration, and vary over time. The first of these properties implies that term premiums are important. The second allows the analyst to be pragmatic, focusing on a single term premium, which is then scaled by duration. The third property implies that basing estimates on current information is essential.

Ilmanen (2012) argued that there are four main drivers of the term premium for nominal bonds.

---

[3] See the "Capital Market Expectations Part 1" reading in the CFA Program curriculum for discussion of the Taylor rule.

- *Level-dependent inflation uncertainty:* Inflation is arguably the main driver of long-run variation in both nominal yields and the term premium. Higher (lower) levels of inflation tend to coincide with greater (less) inflation uncertainty. Hence, nominal yields rise (fall) with inflation because of changes in both expected inflation and the inflation risk component of the term premium.
- *Ability to hedge recession risk:* In theory, assets earn a low (or negative) risk premium if they tend to perform well when the economy is weak. When growth and inflation are primarily driven by aggregate demand, nominal bond returns tend to be negatively correlated with growth and a relatively low term premium is warranted. Conversely, when growth and inflation are primarily driven by aggregate supply, nominal bond returns tend to be positively correlated with growth, necessitating a higher term premium.
- *Supply and demand:* The relative outstanding supply of short-maturity and long-maturity default-free bonds influences the slope of the yield curve.[4] This phenomenon is largely attributable to the term premium since the maturity structure of outstanding debt should have little impact on the expected future path of short-term rates.[5]
- *Cyclical effects:* The slope of the yield curve varies substantially over the business cycle. It is steep around the trough of the cycle and flat or even inverted around the peak. Much of this movement reflects changes in the expected path of short-term rates. However, it also reflects countercyclical changes in the term premium.

Although the slope of the yield curve is useful information on which to base forecasts of the term premium, other indicators work as well or better. Exhibit 1 shows correlations with subsequent excess bond returns (7- to 10-year Treasury bond return minus 3-month Treasury bill return) over 1-quarter, 1-year, and 5-year horizons for eight indicators. The indicators are listed in descending order of the (absolute value of the) correlation with one-year returns. The first four are derived from the bond market. The *ex ante* real yield has the strongest relationship over each horizon. Next on the list are the two most complex indicators. The Cochrane and Piazzesi curve factor is a composite measure capturing both the slope and the curvature of the yield curve.[6] The Kim and Wright premium is derived from a three-factor term structure model.[7] The slope of the yield curve is next on the list. Note that it has the weakest relationship over the five-year horizon. The supply indicator—the share of debt with maturity greater than 10 years—has a particularly strong relationship over the longest horizon. Since this variable tends to change gradually over time, it is not surprising that it is more closely related to long-run average returns than it is to shorter-term returns. The three cyclical proxies—the corporate profit-to-GDP ratio, business confidence, and the unemployment rate—are at the bottom of the list since they had the weakest correlation with return over the next year.

---

[4] As discussed in the CFA Program curriculum reading "Capital Market Expectations Part 1", temporary changes in the relative *flow* of bonds to the market may not have a lasting impact on the curve unless they result in a significant, permanent change in the amounts outstanding.

[5] Supply/demand effects will be more pronounced if there are reasons for certain investors to prefer or require bonds of specific maturities. This is most likely to occur at the very long end of the curve because the supply of very long-term bonds is typically limited and some institutions must fund very long-term liabilities. As an example, the long end of the UK curve was severely squeezed in the 1990s.

[6] See Cochrane and Piazzesi (2005).

[7] See Kim and Wright (2005). The three factors in the theoretical model do not correspond directly with observable variables but may be thought of as proxies for the level, slope, and curvature of the term structure.

EXHIBIT 1   Correlations with Future Excess Bond Returns, 1962–2009

	Return Horizon		
Current Indicator	**1 Quarter**	**1 Year**	**5 Years**
Ex ante real yield	0.28	0.48	0.69
Cochrane and Piazzesi curve factor	0.24	0.44	0.32
Kim and Wright model premium*	0.25	0.43	0.34
Yield curve slope (10 year − 3 month)	0.21	0.34	0.06
Share of debt > 10 years	0.13	0.28	0.66
Corporate profit/GDP	−0.13	−0.25	−0.52
ISM business confidence	−0.10	−0.20	−0.30
Unemployment rate	0.11	0.18	0.24

* Kim and Wright model results are for 1990–2009.

Source: Ilmanen (2012, Exhibit 3.14).

3.2.3. The Credit Premium

The credit premium is the additional expected return demanded for bearing the risk of default losses—importantly, in addition to compensation for the *expected* level of losses. Both expected default losses and the credit premium are embedded in credit spreads. They cannot be recovered from those spreads unless we impose some structure (i.e., a model) on default-free rates, default probabilities, and recovery rates. The two main types of models—structural credit models and reduced-form credit models—are described in detail in other chapter.[8] In the following discussion, we will focus on the empirical behavior of the credit premium.

An analysis of 150 years of defaults among US non-financial corporate bonds showed that the severity of default losses accounted for only about half of the 1.53% average yield spread.[9] Hence, holders of corporate bonds did, on average, earn a credit premium to bear the risk of default. However, the pattern of actual defaults suggests the premium was earned very unevenly over time. In particular, high and low default rates tended to persist, causing clusters of high and low annual default rates and resultant losses. The study found that the previous year's default rate, stock market return, stock market volatility, and GDP growth rate were predictive of the subsequent year's default rate. However, the aggregate credit spread was not predictive of subsequent defaults. Contemporaneous financial market variables—stock returns, stock volatility, and the riskless rate—were significant in explaining the credit spread, but neither GDP growth nor changes in the default rate helped explain the credit spread. This finding suggests that credit spreads were driven primarily by the credit risk premium and financial market conditions and only secondarily by fundamental changes in the expected level of default losses. Thus, credit spreads do contain information relevant to predicting the credit premium.

Ilmanen (2012) hypothesized that credit spreads and the credit premiums embedded in them are driven by different factors, depending on credit quality. Default rates on top-quality

---

[8] See the CFA Program curriculum reading "Credit Analysis Models." More in-depth coverage can be found in Jarrow and van Deventer (2015).
[9] See Giesecke, Longstaff, Schaefer, and Strebulaev (2011). Default rates were measured as a fraction of the par value of outstanding bonds. The authors did not document actual recovery rates, instead assuming 50% recovery. Hence, the true level of losses could have been somewhat higher or lower.

(AAA and AA) bonds are extremely low, so very little of the spread/premium is due to the likelihood of actual default in the absence of a change in credit quality. Instead, the main driver is "downgrade bias"—the fact that a deterioration in credit quality (resulting in a rating downgrade) is much more likely than an improvement in credit quality (leading to an upgrade) and that downgrades induce larger spread changes than upgrades do.[10] Bonds rated A and BBB have moderate default rates. They still do not have a high likelihood of actual default losses, but their prospects are more sensitive to cyclical forces and their spreads/premiums vary more (countercyclically) over the cycle. Default losses are of utmost concern for below-investment-grade bonds. Defaults tend to cluster in times when the economy is in recession. In addition, the default rate and the severity of losses in default tend to rise and fall together. These characteristics imply big losses at the worst times, necessitating substantial compensation for this risk. Not too surprisingly, high-yield spreads/premiums tend to rise ahead of realized default rates.

Exhibit 2 shows three variables that have tended to predict excess returns (over T-bills) for an index of US investment-grade corporate bonds over the next quarter and the next year. Not surprisingly, a high corporate option-adjusted spread is bullish for corporate bond performance because it indicates a large cushion against credit losses—that is, a higher credit premium. A steep Treasury curve is also bullish because, as mentioned earlier, it tends to correspond to the trough of the business cycle when default rates begin to decline. Combining these insights with those from Exhibit 1, the implication is that a steep yield curve predicts both a high term premium and a high credit premium. Higher implied volatility in the equity market was also bullish for corporates, most likely reflecting risk-averse pricing—that is, high risk premiums—across all markets.

EXHIBIT 2   Correlations with US Investment-Grade Corporate Excess Returns, 1990–2009

Current Indicator	Return Horizon	
	1 Quarter	1 Year
Corporate option-adjusted spread	0.25	0.46
VIX implied equity volatility	0.28	0.39
Yield curve slope (10 year – 2 year)	0.20	0.27

Source: Ilmanen (2012, Exhibit 4.15).

How are credit premiums related to maturity? Aside from situations of imminent default, there is greater risk of default losses the longer one must wait for payment. We might, therefore, expect that longer-maturity corporate bonds would offer higher credit risk premiums. The historical evidence suggests that this has not been the case. Credit premiums tend to be especially generous at the short end of the curve. This may be due to "event risk," in the sense that a default, no matter how unlikely, could still cause a huge proportional loss but there is no way that the bond will pay more than the issuer promised. It may also be due, in part, to illiquidity since many short-maturity bonds are old issues that rarely trade as they gradually approach maturity. As a result, many portfolio managers use a strategy known as a "credit barbell" in which they concentrate credit exposure at short maturities and take interest rate/duration risk via long-maturity government bonds.

---

[10] Liquidity relative to government bonds is also an important contributor to yield spreads on very high-quality private sector bonds. By definition, of course, this is really the liquidity premium, rather than part of the credit premium.

3.2.4. The Liquidity Premium

Relatively few bond issues trade actively for more than a few weeks after issuance. Secondary market trading occurs primarily in the most recently issued sovereign bonds, current coupon mortgage-backed securities, and a few of the largest high-quality corporate bonds. The liquidity of other bonds largely depends on the willingness of dealers to hold them in inventory long enough to find a buyer. In general, liquidity tends to be better for bonds that are: (a) priced near par/reflective of current market levels, (b) relatively new, (c) from a relatively large issue, (d) from a well-known/frequent issuer, (e) standard/simple in structure, and (f) high quality. These factors tend to reduce the dealer's risk in holding the bond and increase the likelihood of finding a buyer quickly.

As a baseline estimate of the "pure" liquidity premium in a particular market, the analyst can look to the yield spread between fixed-rate, option-free bonds from the highest-quality issuer (virtually always the sovereign) and the next highest-quality large issuer of similar bonds (often a government agency or quasi-agency). Adjustments should then be made for the factors listed previously. In general, the impact of each factor is likely to increase disproportionately as one moves away from baseline attributes. For example, each step lower in credit quality is likely to have a bigger impact on liquidity than that of the preceding step.

EXAMPLE 2   Fixed-Income Building Blocks

Salimah Rahman works for SMECo, a Middle Eastern sovereign wealth fund. Each year, the fund's staff updates its projected returns for the following year on the basis of developments in the preceding year. The fund uses the building block approach in making its fixed-income projections. Rahman has been assigned the task of revising the key building block components for a major European bond market. The following table shows last year's values:

	Description	Value
Risk-free rate	3-month government bill	3.50%
Term premium	5-year duration	0.50%
Credit premium	Baa/BBB corporate	0.90%
Liquidity premium	Government-guaranteed agency	0.15%

Although inflation rose modestly, the central bank cut its policy rate by 50 bps in response to weakening growth. Aggregate corporate profits have remained solid, and after a modest correction, the stock market finished higher for the year. However, defaults on leveraged loans were unexpectedly high this year, and confidence surveys weakened again recently. Equity option volatility spiked mid-year but ended the year somewhat lower. The interest rate futures curve has flattened but remains upward sloping. The 10-year government yield declined only a few basis points, while the yield on comparable government agency bonds remained unchanged and corporate spreads—both nominal and option adjusted—widened.

Indicate the developments that are likely to cause Rahman to increase/decrease each of the key building blocks relative to last year.

Guideline answer: Based on the reduction in policy rates and the flattening of the interest rate futures curve, Rahman is virtually certain to reduce the short-term rate component. Steepening of the yield curve (10-year yield barely responded to the 50 bp rate cut) indicates an increase in both the term premium and the credit premium. Declining confidence also suggests a higher term premium. Widening of credit spreads is also indicative of a higher credit premium. However, the increase in loan defaults suggests that credit losses are likely to be higher next year as well, since defaults tend to cluster. All else the same, this reduces the expected return on corporate bonds/loans. Hence, the credit premium should increase less than would otherwise be implied by the steeper yield curve and wider credit spreads. Modest widening of the government agency spread indicates an increase in the liquidity premium. The resilience of the equity market and the decline in equity option volatility suggest that investors are not demanding a general increase in risk premiums.

4. RISKS IN EMERGING MARKET BONDS

Emerging market debt was once nearly synonymous with crisis. The Latin American debt crisis of the 1980s involved bank loans but essentially triggered development of a market for emerging market bonds. In the early 1990s, the Mexican crisis occurred. In the late 1990s, there was the Asian crisis, followed by the Russian crisis, which contributed to the turmoil that sank the giant hedge fund Long-Term Capital Management. There have been other, more isolated, events, such as Argentina's forced restructuring of its debt, but the emerging market bond market has grown, deepened, and matured. What started with only a few government issuers borrowing in hard currencies (from their perspective foreign, but widely used, currencies) has grown into a market in which corporations as well as governments issue in their local currencies and in hard currencies. The discussion here applies not just to emerging markets but also to what are known as "frontier" markets (when they are treated separately or as a subset of emerging markets).

Investing in emerging market debt involves all the same risks as investing in developed country debt, such as interest rate movements, currency movements, and potential defaults. In addition, it poses risks that are, although not entirely absent, less significant in developed markets. These risks fall roughly into two categories: (1) economic and (2) political and legal. A slightly different breakdown would be "ability to pay" and "willingness to pay."

Before discussing these country risks, note that some countries that are labeled as emerging markets may in fact be healthy, prosperous economies with strong fundamentals. Likewise, the political and legal issues discussed in this section may or may not apply to any particular country. Furthermore, these risks will, in general, apply in varying degrees across countries. Emerging markets are widely recognized as a very heterogeneous group. It is up to the analyst to assess which considerations are relevant to a particular investment decision.

4.1. Economic Risks/Ability to Pay

Emerging market economies as a whole have characteristics that make them potentially more vulnerable to distress and hence less likely to be able to pay their debts on time or in full, such as the following:

- Greater concentration of wealth and income; less diverse tax base
- Greater dependence on specific industries, especially cyclical industries, such as commodities and agriculture; low potential for pricing power in world markets
- Restrictions on trade, capital flows, and currency conversion
- Poor fiscal controls and monetary discipline
- Less educated and less skilled work force; poor or limited physical infrastructure; lower level of industrialization and technological sophistication
- Reliance on foreign borrowing, often in hard currencies not their own
- Small/less sophisticated financial markets and institutions
- Susceptibility to capital flight; perceived vulnerability contributing to actual vulnerability

Although history is at best an imperfect guide to the future, the analyst should examine a country's track record on critical issues. Have there been crises in the past? If so, how were they handled/resolved? Has the sovereign defaulted? Is there restructured debt? How have authorities responded to fiscal challenges? Is there inflation or currency instability?

The analyst should, of course, examine the health of the macroeconomy in some detail. A few indicative guidelines can be helpful. If there is one ratio that is most closely watched, it is the ratio of the fiscal deficit to GDP. Most emerging countries have deficits and perpetually struggle to reduce them. A persistent ratio above 40% is likely a cause for concern. A debt-to-GDP ratio exceeding 70%–80%, perhaps of only mild concern for a developed market, is a sign of vulnerability for an emerging market. A persistent annual real growth rate less than 4% suggests that an emerging market is catching up with more advanced economies only slowly, if at all, and per capita income might even be falling—a potential source of political stress. Persistent current account deficits greater than 4% of GDP probably indicate lack of competitiveness. Foreign debt greater than 50% of GDP or greater than 200% of current account receipts is also a sign of danger. Finally, foreign exchange reserves less than 100% of short-term debt is risky, whereas a ratio greater than 200% is ample. It must be emphasized that the numbers given here are merely suggestive of levels that may indicate a need for further scrutiny.

When all else fails, a country may need to call on external support mechanisms. Hence, the analyst should consider whether the country has access to support from the International Monetary Fund (IMF), the World Bank, or other international agencies.

4.2. Political and Legal Risks/Willingness to Pay

Investors in emerging market debt may be unable to enforce their claims or recover their investments. Weak property rights laws and weak enforcement of contract laws are clearly of concern in this regard. Inability to enforce seniority structures within private sector claims is one important example. The principle of sovereign immunity makes it very difficult to force a sovereign borrower to pay its debts. Confiscation of property, nationalization of companies, and corruption are also relevant hazards. Coalition governments may also pose political instability problems. Meanwhile, the imposition of capital controls or restrictions on currency conversion may make it difficult, or even impossible, to repatriate capital.

As with economic risks, history may provide some guidance with respect to the severity of political and legal risks. The following are some pertinent questions: Is there a history of nationalization, expropriation, or other violations of property rights? How have international disputes been resolved and under which legal jurisdiction? Has the integrity of the judicial system and process been questioned? Are political institutions stable? Are they recognized as legitimate and subject to reasonable checks and balances? Has the transfer of power been peaceful, orderly, and lawful? Does the political process give rise to fragile coalitions that collapse whenever events strain the initial compromises with respect to policy?

EXAMPLE 3 Emerging Market Bonds

Belvia has big aspirations. Although still a poor country, it has been growing rapidly, averaging 6% real and 10% nominal growth for the last five years. At the beginning of this period of growth, a centrist coalition gained a narrow majority over the authoritarian, fiscally irresponsible, anti-investor, anti-business party that had been in power for decades. The government has removed the old barriers to trade, including the signing of a regional free-trade agreement, and removed capital controls. Much of its growth has been fueled by investment in its dominant industry—natural resources—financed by debt and foreign direct investment flows. These policies have been popular with the business community, as has the relaxation of regulations affecting key constituencies. Meanwhile, to ensure that prosperity flows rapidly to the people, the government has allowed redistributive social payments to grow even faster than GDP, resulting in a large and rising fiscal deficit (5% of GDP this year, projected to be 7% in two years). The current account deficit is 8% of GDP. Despite the large current account deficit, the local currency has appreciated significantly since it was allowed to float two years ago. The government has just announced that it will issue a large 10-year local currency bond under Belvian law—the first issue of its kind in many years.

Despite a very strong relationship with the bank marketing the bond, Peter Valt has decided not to invest in it. When pressed for his reasoning, what risks is he likely to identify?

Solution: There are several significant risks and warning signs. Coalition governments are often unstable, and the most likely alternative would appear to be a return to the previously dominant party that lacks fiscal discipline. That regime is likely to undo the recent pro-growth policies and might even disavow the debt, including this new bond. The bond will be governed by Belvian law, which, combined with the principle of sovereign immunity, will make it very difficult for foreigners to enforce their claims. In addition, the relaxation of regulations affecting key constituencies hints strongly at corruption and possibly at payoffs within the current regime. With respect to the economy, fiscal discipline remains poor, there is heavy reliance on a single industry, and the current account deficit is almost certainly unsustainable (e.g., over the 10-year life of this bond). In addition, the currency is very likely to be overvalued, which will both make it very difficult to broaden global competitiveness beyond natural resources and increase the investor's risk of substantial currency losses.

---

5. FORECASTING EQUITY RETURNS

The task of forecasting equity market returns is often the central focus of setting capital market expectations. In this section, we discuss applying each of the major methodologies to equities.

5.1. Historical Statistics Approach to Equity Returns

The *Credit Suisse Global Investment Returns Yearbook 2018*[11] updated the seminal work of Dimson, Marsh, and Staunton (2002) to include asset returns in 21 countries for the 118-year period of 1900–2017. Exhibit 3 shows the mean real return for each market portfolio centered within a 95% confidence interval. Results are also shown for a world portfolio, a world ex-US portfolio, and Europe. The portfolios are ordered from left to right on the basis of the mean return.

The means range from a low of 5.0% for Austria to a high of 9.4% in South Africa. Note that both of these values lie within the confidence interval for every country. From a statistical perspective, there is really no difference among these markets in terms of mean real return. This illustrates the fact that sample averages, even derived from seemingly long histories, are very imprecise estimates unless the volatility of the data is small relative to the mean. Clearly that is not the case for equity returns. Nonetheless, sample means are frequently cited without regard to the quality of information they convey.

EXHIBIT 3   Historical Mean Returns with Confidence Intervals by Country, 1900–2017

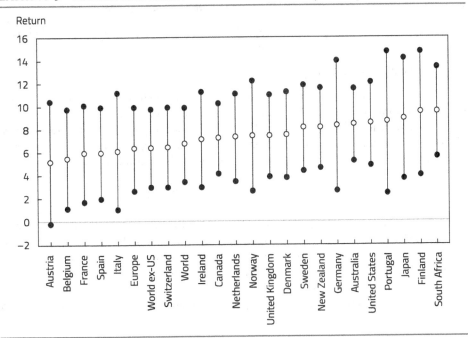

Source: Dimson, Marsh, and Staunton (2018, Chapter 1, Table 1. Real, local currency percent returns).

As indicated in Section 2, shrinkage estimators can often provide more reliable estimates by combining the sample mean with a second estimate of the mean return. However, the application of a common shrinkage estimator confirms that there is no basis for believing that the true expected returns for the countries in Exhibit 3 are different.

---

[11]Dimson, Marsh, and Staunton (2018).

5.2. DCF Approach to Equity Returns

Analysts have frequently used the Gordon (constant) growth model form of the dividend discount model, solved for the required rate of return, to formulate the long-term expected return of equity markets. Although this model is quite simple, it has a big advantage over using historical stock returns to project future returns. The vast majority of the "noise" in historical stock returns comes from fluctuations in the price-to-earnings ratio (P/E) and the ratio of earnings to GDP. Since the amount of earnings appears in the numerator of one ratio and the denominator of the other, the impact of these ratios tends to cancel out over time, leaving the relationship between equity market appreciation and GDP growth much more stable. And GDP growth itself, especially the real growth component, is much less volatile and hence relatively predictable.[12] As an illustration, Exhibit 4 shows historical volatilities (defined as the standard deviation of percentage changes) for the S&P 500 Index return, P/E, the earnings-to-GDP ratio, real US GDP growth, and inflation for 1946–2016. The Gordon growth model allows us to take advantage of this relative stability by linking long-term equity appreciation to a more stable foundation—economic growth.

EXHIBIT 4   Historical Comparison of Standard Deviations in the United States, 1946–2016

S&P 500	P/E	Earnings/GDP	Real GDP Growth	Inflation
16.1	28.5	28.9	3.0	3.2

Note: Standard deviation of % changes

In the United States and other major markets, share repurchases have become an important way for companies to distribute cash to shareholders. Grinold and Kroner (2002) provided a restatement of the Gordon growth model that takes explicit account of repurchases. Their model also provides a means for analysts to incorporate expectations of valuation levels through the familiar price-to-earnings ratio. The **Grinold–Kroner model**[13] is

$$E(R_e) \approx \frac{D}{P} + (\%\Delta E - \%\Delta S) + \%\Delta P/E, \qquad (7.1)$$

where $E(R_e)$ is the expected equity return, D/P is the dividend yield, $\%\Delta E$ is the expected percentage change in total earnings, $\%\Delta S$ is the expected percentage change in shares outstanding, and $\%\Delta P/E$ is the expected percentage change in the price-to-earnings ratio. The term in parentheses, $(\%\Delta E - \%\Delta S)$, is the growth rate of earnings per share. Net share repurchases ($\%\Delta S < 0$) imply that earnings per share grows faster than total earnings.

With a minor rearrangement of the equation, the expected return can be divided into three components:

- Expected cash flow ("income") return: $D/P - \%\Delta S$
- Expected nominal earnings growth return: $\%\Delta E$
- Expected repricing return: $\%\Delta P/E$

The expected nominal earnings growth return and the expected repricing return constitute the expected capital gains.

---

[12] See the previous reading "Capital Market Expectations: Part I" for a discussion of projecting trend growth.
[13] See Grinold and Kroner (2002) for a derivation. The model is shown here in a slightly modified form.

In principle, the Grinold–Kroner model assumes an infinite horizon. In practice, the analyst typically needs to make projections for finite horizons, perhaps several horizons. In applying the model, the analyst needs to be aware of the implications of constant growth rate assumptions over different horizons. Failure to tailor growth rates to the horizon can easily lead to implausible results. As an example, suppose the P/E is currently 16.0 and the analyst believes that it will revert to a level of 20 and be stable thereafter. The P/E growth rates for various horizons that are consistent with this view are 4.56% for 5 years, 2.26% for 10 years, 0.75% for 30 years, and an arbitrarily small positive number for a truly long-term horizon. Treating, say, the 2.26% 10-year number as if it is appropriate for the "long run" would imply an ever-rising P/E rather than convergence to a plausible long-run valuation. The only very long-run assumptions that are consistent with economically plausible relationships are $\%\Delta E$ = Nominal GDP growth, $\%\Delta S = 0$, and $\%\Delta P/E = 0$. The longer the (finite) horizon, the less the analyst's projection should deviate from these values.

EXAMPLE 4   Forecasting the Equity Return Using the Grinold–Kroner Model

Cynthia Casey uses the Grinold–Kroner model in forecasting developed market equity returns. Casey makes the following forecasts:

- a 2.25% dividend yield on Canadian equities, based on the S&P/TSE Composite Index;
- a 1% rate of net share repurchases for Canadian equities;
- a long-term corporate earnings growth rate of 6% per year, based on a 1 percentage point (pp) premium for corporate earnings growth over her expected Canadian (nominal) GDP growth rate of 5%; and
- an expansion rate for P/E multiples of 0.25% per year.

1. Based on the information given, what expected rate of return on Canadian equities is implied by Casey's assumptions?
2. Are Casey's assumptions plausible for the long run and for a 10-year horizon?

Solution to 1: The expected rate of return on Canadian equities based on Casey's assumptions would be 9.5%, calculated as

$$E(R_e) \approx 2.25\% + [6.0\% - (-1.0\%)] + 0.25\% = 9.5\%.$$

Solution to 2: Casey's assumptions are not plausible for the very long run. The assumption that earnings will grow 1% faster than GDP implies one of two things: either an ever-rising ratio of economy-wide earnings to GDP or the earnings accruing to businesses not included in the index (e.g., private firms) continually shrinking relative to GDP. Neither is likely to persist indefinitely. Similarly, perpetual share repurchases would eventually eliminate all shares, whereas a perpetually rising P/E would lead to an arbitrarily high price per Canadian dollar of earnings per share. Based on Casey's economic growth forecast, a more reasonable long-run expected return would be 7.25% = 2.25% + 5.0%.

> Casey's assumptions are plausible for a 10-year horizon. Over 10 years, the ratio of earnings to GDP would rise by roughly $10.5\% = (1.01)^{10} - 1$, shares outstanding would shrink by roughly $9.6\% = 1 - (0.99)^{10}$, and the P/E would rise by about $2.5\% = (1.0025)^{10} - 1$.

Most of the inputs to the Grinold–Kroner model are fairly readily available. Economic growth forecasts can easily be found in investment research publications, reports from such agencies as the IMF, the World Bank, and the OECD, and likely from the analyst firm's own economists. Data on the rate of share repurchases are less straightforward but are likely to be tracked by sell-side firms and occasionally mentioned in research publications. The big question is how to gauge valuation of the market in order to project changes in the P/E.

The fundamental valuation metrics used in practice typically take the form of a ratio of price to some fundamental flow variable—such as earnings, cash flow, or sales—with seemingly endless variations in how the measures are defined and calculated. Whatever the metric, the implicit assumption is that it has a well-defined long-run mean value to which it will revert. In statistical terms, it is a stationary random variable. Extensive empirical evidence indicates that these valuation measures are poor predictors of short-term performance. Over multi-year horizons, however, there is a reasonably strong tendency for extreme values to be corrected. Thus, these metrics do provide guidance for projecting intermediate-term movements in valuation.

Gauging what is or is not an extreme value is complicated by the fact that all the fundamental flow variables as well as stock prices are heavily influenced by the business cycle. One method of dealing with this issue is to "cyclically adjust" the valuation measure. The most widely known metric is the cyclically adjusted P/E (CAPE). For this measure, the current price level is divided by the average level of earnings for the last 10 years (adjusted for inflation), rather than by the most current earnings. The idea is to average away cyclical variation in earnings and provide a more reliable base against which to assess the current market price.

5.3. Risk Premium Approaches to Equity Returns

The Grinold–Kroner model and similar models are sometimes said to reflect the "supply" of equity returns since they outline the sources of return. In contrast, risk premiums reflect "demand" for returns.

5.3.1. Defining and Forecasting the Equity Premium

The term "equity premium" is most frequently used to describe the amount by which the expected return on equities exceeds the riskless rate ("equity versus bills"). However, the same term is sometimes used to refer to the amount by which the expected return on equities exceeds the expected return on default-free bonds ("equity versus bonds"). From the discussion of fixed-income building blocks in Sections 3 and 4, we know that the difference between these two definitions is the term premium built into the expected return on default-free bonds. The equity-versus-bonds premium reflects an incremental/building block approach to developing expected equity returns, whereas the equity-versus-bills premium reflects a single composite premium for the risk of equity investment.

Exhibit 5 shows historical averages for both of these equity premium concepts by country for the period 1900–2017.[14] For each country, the bottom portion of the column is the realized term premium (i.e., bonds minus bills) and the top segment is the realized equity-versus-bonds premium. The whole column represents the equity-versus-bills premium. The equity-versus-bills premiums range from 3.0% to 6.3%, the equity-versus-bonds premiums range from 1.8% to 5.2%, and the term premiums range from −0.6% to 2.9%.

EXHIBIT 5   Historical Equity Premiums by Country, 1900–2017

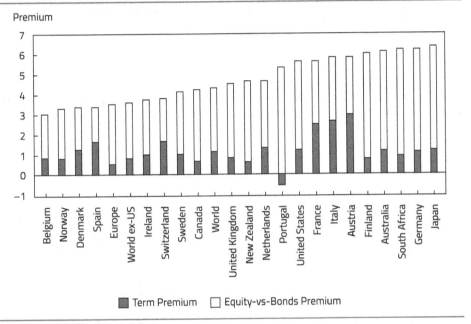

Notes: Germany excludes 1922–1923. Austria excludes 1921–1922. Returns are shown in percentages.
Source: Dimson et al. (2018, Chapter 2, Tables 8 and 9).

As with the mean equity returns in Exhibit 3, these historical premiums are subject to substantial estimation error. Statistically, there is no meaningful difference among them. Thus, the long-run cross section of returns/premiums provides virtually no reliable information with which to differentiate among countries.

Since equity returns are much more volatile than returns on either bills or bonds, forecasting either definition of the equity premium is just as difficult as projecting the absolute level of equity returns. That is, simply shifting to focus on risk premiums provides little, if any, specific insight with which to improve forecasts. The analyst must, therefore, use the other modes of analysis discussed here to forecast equity returns/premiums.

---

[14] These premiums reflect geometric returns. Therefore, the equity versus bills premium is the sum of the term premium and the equity versus bonds premium. Premiums using arithmetic returns are systematically higher and are not additive.

5.3.2. An Equilibrium Approach

There are various global/international extensions of the familiar capital asset pricing model (CAPM). We will discuss a version proposed by Singer and Terhaar (1997) that is intended to capture the impact of incomplete integration of global markets.

The Singer–Terhaar model is actually a combination of two underlying CAPM models. The first assumes that all global markets and asset classes are fully integrated. The full integration assumption allows the use of a single global market portfolio to determine equity-versus-bills risk premiums for all assets. The second underlying CAPM assumes complete segmentation of markets such that each asset class in each country is priced without regard to any other country/asset class. For example, the markets for German equities and German bonds are completely segmented. Clearly, this is a very extreme assumption.

Recall the basic CAPM pricing relationship:

$$RP_i = \beta_{i,M} RP_M,$$ (7.2)

where $RP_i = [E(R_i) - R_F]$ is the risk premium on the ith asset, RP_M is the risk premium on the market portfolio, R_F is the risk-free rate, and $\beta_{i,M}$—asset i's sensitivity to the market portfolio—is given by

$$\beta_{i,M} = \frac{\text{Cov}(R_i, R_M)}{\text{Var}(R_M)} = \rho_{i,M}\left(\frac{\sigma_i}{\sigma_M}\right).$$ (7.3)

Standard deviations are denoted by σ, and ρ denotes correlation.

Under the assumption of full integration, every asset is priced relative to the global capitalization-weighted market portfolio. Using Equations 7.2 and 7.3 and denoting the global market portfolio by "GM," the first component of the Singer–Terhaar model is

$$RP_i^G = \beta_{i,GM} RP_{GM} = \rho_{i,GM}\sigma_i\left(\frac{RP_{GM}}{\sigma_{GM}}\right).$$ (7.4)

A superscript G has been added on the asset's risk premium to indicate that it reflects the global equilibrium. The term in parentheses on the far right is the Sharpe ratio for the global market portfolio, the risk premium per unit of global market risk.

Now consider the case of completely segmented markets. In this case, the risk premium for each asset will be determined in isolation without regard to other markets or opportunities for diversification. The risk premium will be whatever is required to induce investors with access to that market/asset to hold the existing supply. In terms of the CAPM framework, this implies treating each asset as its own "market portfolio." Formally, we can simply set β equal to 1 and ρ equal to 1 in the previous equations since each asset is perfectly correlated with itself. Using a superscript S to denote the segmented market equilibrium and replacing the global market portfolio with asset i itself in Equation 7.4, the segmented market equilibrium risk premium for asset i is

$$RP_i^S = 1 \times RP_i^S = 1 \times \sigma_i\left(\frac{RP_i^S}{\sigma_i}\right).$$ (7.5)

This is the second component of the Singer–Terhaar model. Note that the first equality in Equation 7.5 is an identity; it conveys no information. It reflects the fact that in a completely segmented market, the required risk premium could take any value. The second equality is more useful because it breaks the risk premium into two parts: the risk of the asset (σ_i) and the Sharpe ratio (i.e., compensation per unit of risk) in the segmented market.[15]

The final Singer–Terhaar risk premium estimate for asset i is a weighted average of the two component estimates

$$RP_i = \varphi RP_i^G + (1 - \varphi)RP_i^S. \tag{7.6}$$

To implement the model, the analyst must supply values for the Sharpe ratios in the globally integrated market and the asset's segmented market; the degree to which the asset is globally integrated, denoted by φ; the asset's volatility; and the asset's β with respect to the global market portfolio. A pragmatic approach to specifying the Sharpe ratios for each asset under complete segmentation is to assume that compensation for non-diversifiable risk (i.e., "market risk") is the same in every market. That is, assume all the Sharpe ratios equal the global Sharpe ratio.

In practice, the analyst must make a judgment about the degree of integration/segmentation—that is, the value of φ in the Singer–Terhaar model. With that in mind, some representative values that can serve as starting points for refinement can be helpful. Developed market equities and bonds are highly integrated, so a range of 0.75–0.90 would be reasonable for φ. Emerging markets are noticeably less integrated, especially during stressful periods, and there are likely to be greater differences among these markets, so a range of 0.50–0.75 would be reasonable for emerging market equities and bonds. Real estate market integration is increasing but remains far behind developed market financial assets, perhaps on par with emerging market stocks and bonds overall. In general, relative real estate market integration is likely to reflect the relative integration of the associated financial markets. Commodities for which there are actively traded, high-volume futures contracts should be on the higher end of the integration scale.

To illustrate the Singer–Terhaar model, suppose that an investor has developed the following projections for German shares and bonds.

	German Shares	German Bonds
Volatility (σ_i)	17.0%	7.0%
Correlation with global market ($\rho_{i,M}$)	0.70	0.50
Degree of integration (φ)	0.85	0.85
Segmented market Sharpe ratio (RP_i^S/σ_i)	0.35	0.25

The risk-free rate is 3.0%, and the investor's estimate of the global Sharpe ratio is 0.30. Note that the investor expects compensation for undiversifiable risk to be higher in the German stock market and lower in the German bond market under full segmentation. The following are the fully integrated risk premiums for each of the assets (from Equation 7.4):

Equities: $0.70 \times 17.0\% \times 0.30 = 3.57\%$.
Bonds: $0.50 \times 7.0\% \times 0.30 = 1.05\%$.

---

[15] A somewhat more complex model would allow for integration of asset classes within each country. Doing so would entail incorporating local market portfolios and allowing assets to be less than perfectly correlated with those portfolios. Equation (7.5) would then look exactly like Equation (7.4) with the local segmented market portfolio replacing the global market portfolio (GM).

The following are the fully segmented risk premiums (from Equation 7.5):

Equities: $17.0\% \times 0.35 = 5.95\%.$
Bonds: $7.0\% \times 0.25 = 1.75\%.$

Based on 85% integration ($\varphi = 0.85$), the final risk estimates (from Equation 7.6) would be as follows:

Equities: $(0.85 \times 3.57\%) + (1 - 0.85) \times 5.95\% = 3.93\%.$
Bonds: $(0.85 \times 1.05\%) + (1 - 0.85) \times 1.75\% = 1.16\%.$

Adding in the risk-free rate, the expected returns for German shares and bonds would be 6.93% and 4.16%, respectively.

Virtually all equilibrium models implicitly assume perfectly liquid markets. Thus, the analyst should assess the actual liquidity of each asset class and add appropriate liquidity premiums. Although market segmentation and market liquidity are conceptually distinct, in practice they are likely to be related. Highly integrated markets are likely to be relatively liquid, and illiquidity is one reason that a market may remain segmented.

EXAMPLE 5   Using the Singer–Terhaar Model

Stacy Adkins believes the equity market in one of the emerging markets that she models has become more fully integrated with the global market. As a result, she expects it to be more highly correlated with the global market. However, she thinks its overall volatility will decline. Her old and new estimates are as follows:

	Previous Data	New Data
Volatility (σ_i)	22.0%	18.0%
Correlation with global market ($\rho_{i,M}$)	0.50	0.70
Degree of integration (φ)	0.55	0.75
Sharpe ratio (global and segmented markets)	0.30	0.30

If she uses the Singer–Terhaar model, what will the net impact of these changes be on her risk premium estimate for this market?

Solution: The segmented market risk premium will decline from 6.6% (calculated as $22.0\% \times 0.30 = 6.6\%$) to 5.4% (= $18\% \times 0.30$). The fully integrated risk premium will increase from 3.30% (= $0.50 \times 22.0\% \times 0.30$) to 3.78% (= $0.70 \times 18.0\% \times 0.30$). The weighted average premium will decline from 4.79% [= $(0.55 \times 3.30\%) + (0.45 \times 6.60\%)$] to 4.19% [= $(0.75 \times 3.78\%) + (0.25 \times 5.40\%)$], so the net effect is a decline of 60 bps.

5.4. Risks in Emerging Market Equities

Most of the issues underlying the risks of emerging market (and "frontier market" if they are classified as such) bonds also present risks for emerging market equities: more fragile economies, less stable political and policy frameworks, and weaker legal protections. However, the risks take somewhat different forms because of the different nature of equity and debt claims. Again, note that emerging markets are a very heterogeneous group. The political, legal, and economic issues that are often associated with emerging markets may not, in fact, apply to a particular market or country being analyzed.

There has been a debate about the relative importance of "country" versus "industry" risk factors in global equity markets for over 40 years. The empirical evidence has been summarized quite accurately as "vast and contradictory."[16] Both matter, but on the whole, country effects still tend to be more important than (global) industry effects. This is particularly true for emerging markets. Emerging markets are generally less fully integrated into the global economy and the global markets. Hence, local economic and market factors exert greater influence on risk and return in these markets than in developed markets.

Political, legal, and regulatory weaknesses—in the form of weak standards and/or weak enforcement—affect emerging market equity investors in various ways. The standards of corporate governance may allow interested parties to manipulate the capital structure of companies and to misuse business assets. Accounting standards may allow management and other insiders to hide or misstate important information. Weak disclosure rules may also impede transparency and favor insiders. Inadequate property rights laws, lack of enforcement, and weak checks and balances on governmental actions may permit seizure of property, nationalization of companies, and prejudicial and unpredictable regulatory actions.

Whereas the emerging market debt investor needs to focus on ability and willingness to pay specific obligations, emerging market equity investors need to focus on the many ways that the value of their ownership claims might be expropriated by the government, corporate insiders, or dominant shareholders.

EXAMPLE 6 Emerging Market Equity Risks

Bill Dwight has been discussing investment opportunities in Belvia with his colleague, Peter Valt (see Example 3). He is aware that Valt declined to buy the recently issued government bond, but he believes the country's equities may be attractive. He notes the rapid growth, substantial investment spending, free trade agreement, deregulation, and strong capital inflows as factors favoring a strong equity market. In addition, solid global growth has been boosting demand for Belvia's natural resources. Roughly half of the public equity market is represented by companies in the natural resources sector. The other half is a reasonably diversified mix of other industries. Many of these firms remain closely held, having floated a minority stake on the local exchange in the last few years. Listed firms are required to have published two years of financial statements conforming to standards set by the Belvia Public Accounting Board, which is made up of the heads of the three largest domestic accounting firms. With the help of a local broker, Dwight has identified a diversified basket of stocks that he intends to buy.

---

[16] Marcelo, Quirós, and Martins (2013).

Discuss the risks Dwight might be overlooking.

Guideline answer: Dwight might be overlooking several risks. He is almost certainly underestimating the vulnerability of the local economy and the vulnerability of the equity market to local developments. The economy's rapid growth is being driven by a large and growing fiscal deficit, in particular, rapidly rising redistributive social payments, and investment spending financed by foreign capital. Appreciation of the currency has made industries other than natural resources less competitive, so the free trade agreement provides little support for the economy. When the government is forced to tighten fiscal policy or capital flows shrink, the domestic economy is likely to be hit hard. Political risk is also a concern. A return to the prior regime is likely to result in a less pro-growth, less business-friendly environment, which would most likely result in attempts by foreign investors to repatriate their capital. Dwight should also have serious concerns about corporate governance, given that most listed companies are closely held, with dominant shareholders posing expropriation risk. He should also be concerned about transparency (e.g., limited history available) and accounting standards (local standards set by the auditing firms themselves).

6. FORECASTING REAL ESTATE RETURNS

Real estate is inherently quite different from equities, bonds, and cash. It is a physical asset rather than a financial asset. It is heterogeneous, indivisible, and immobile. It is a factor of production, like capital equipment and labor, and as such, it directly produces a return in the form of services. Its services can be sold but can be used/consumed only in one location. Owning and operating real estate involves operating and maintenance costs. All these factors contribute to making real estate illiquid and costly to transfer. The characteristics just described apply to direct investment in real estate (raw land, which does not produce income, is an exception). We will address the investment characteristics of equity REITs versus direct real estate, but unless otherwise stated, the focus is on directly held, unlevered, income-producing real estate.

6.1. Historical Real Estate Returns

The heterogeneity, indivisibility, immobility, and illiquidity of real estate pose a severe problem for historical analysis. Properties trade infrequently, so there is virtually no chance of getting a sequence of simultaneous, periodic (say, quarterly) transaction prices for a cross section of properties. Real estate owners/investors must rely heavily on appraisals, rather than transactions, in valuing properties. Owing to infrequent transactions and the heterogeneity of properties, these appraisals tend to reflect slowly moving averages of past market conditions. As a result, returns calculated from appraisals represent weighted averages of (unobservable) "true" returns—returns that would have been observed if there had been transaction prices—in previous periods. This averaging does not, in general, bias the mean return. It does, however, significantly distort estimates of volatility and correlations. The published return series is too smooth; that is, the usual sample volatility substantially understates the true volatility of returns. Meanwhile, by disguising the timing of response to market information, the smoothing tends to understate the strength of contemporaneous correlation with other market variables and spuriously induce a lead/lag structure of correlations.

In order to undertake any meaningful analysis of real estate as an asset class, the analyst must first deal with this data issue. It has become standard to "unsmooth" appraisal-based returns using a time-series model. Such techniques, which also apply to private equity funds, private debt funds, and hedge funds, are briefly described in a later section.

6.2. Real Estate Cycles

Real estate is subject to cycles that both drive and are driven by the business cycle. Real estate is a major factor of production in the economy. Virtually every business requires it. Every household consumes "housing services." Demand for the services provided by real estate rises and falls with the pace of economic activity. The supply of real estate is vast but essentially fixed at any point in time.[17] As a result, there is a strong cyclical pattern to property values, rents, and occupancy rates. The extent to which this pattern is observable depends on the type of real estate. As emphasized previously, changes in property values are obscured by the appraisal process, although indications can be gleaned from transactions as they occur. The extent to which actual rents and occupancy rates fully reflect the balance of supply and demand depends primarily on the type of property and the quality of the property. High-quality properties with long leases will tend to have little turnover, so fluctuations in actual rents and occupancy rates are likely to be relatively small. In contrast, demand for low-quality properties is likely to be more sensitive to the economy, leading to more substantial swings in occupancy and possibly rents as well. Properties with short leases will see rents adjust more completely to current supply/demand imbalances. Room rates and occupancy at low-quality hotels will tend to be the most volatile.

Fluctuations in the balance of supply and demand set up a classic boom–bust cycle in real estate. First, the boom: Perceptions of rising demand, property values, lease rates, and occupancy induce development of new properties. This investment spending helps drive and/or sustain economic activity, which, in turn, reinforces the perceived profitability of building new capacity. Then, the bust: Inevitably, optimistic projections lead to overbuilding and declining property values, lease rates, and occupancy. Since property has a very long life and is immobile, leases are typically for multiple years and staggered across tenants. In addition, since moving is costly for tenants, it may take many months or years for the excess supply to be absorbed.

A study by Clayton, Fabozzi, Gilberto, Gordon, Hudson-Wilson, Hughes, Liang, MacKinnon, and Mansour (2011) suggested that the US commercial real estate crash following the global financial crisis was the first to have been driven by the capital markets rather than by a boom–bust cycle in real estate fundamentals.[18] The catalyst was not overbuilding, Clayton et al. argued, but rather excess leverage and investment in more speculative types of properties. Consistent with that hypothesis, both the collapse in property prices and the subsequent recovery were unusually rapid. The authors attributed the accelerated response to underlying conditions to appraisers responding more vigorously to signals from the REIT and commercial mortgage-backed security markets. It remains to be seen whether this phenomenon will persist in less extreme circumstances.

---

[17] Yau, Schneeweis, Szado, Robinson, and Weiss (2018) found that real estate represents from one-third to as much as two-thirds of global wealth.
[18] Data from the Investment Property Databank indicate that commercial property values dropped by 21.8% globally and US property values decreased by 33.2% in 2008–2009. Other countries suffered steep losses as well, notably Ireland (55.5%) and Spain (20.1%).

6.3. Capitalization Rates

The capitalization (cap) rate, defined as net operating income (NOI) in the current period divided by the property value, is the standard valuation metric for commercial real estate. It is analogous to the earnings yield (E/P) for equities. It is not, strictly speaking, a cash flow yield because a portion of operating income may be reinvested in the property.[19] As with equities, an estimate of the long-run expected/required rate of return can be derived from this ratio by assuming a constant growth rate for NOI—that is, by applying the Gordon growth model.

$$E(R_{re}) = \text{Cap rate} + \text{NOI growth rate.} \qquad (7.7)$$

The long-run, steady-state NOI growth rate for commercial real estate as a whole should be reasonably close to the growth rate of GDP. The observation that over a 30-year period UK nominal rental income grew about 6.5% per annum, roughly 2.5% in real terms,[20] is consistent with this relationship.

Over finite horizons, it is appropriate to adjust this equation to reflect the anticipated rate of change in the cap rate.

$$E(R_{re}) = \text{Cap rate} + \text{NOI growth rate} - \%\Delta\text{Cap rate.} \qquad (7.8)$$

This equation is analogous to the Grinold–Kroner model for equities, except there is no term for share buybacks. The growth rate of NOI could, of course, be split into a real component and inflation.

Exhibit 6 shows private market cap rates as of March 2018 for US commercial properties differentiated by type, location, and quality. The rates range from 4.7% for offices in gateway cities, such as New York City, to 9.5% for skilled nursing (i.e., 24-hour old-age care) properties. There is a clear pattern of high cap rates for riskier property types (hotels versus apartments, skilled nursing facilities versus medical offices), lower-quality properties (low-productivity versus high-productivity malls), and less attractive locations (offices in secondary versus gateway cities).

EXHIBIT 6   Cap Rates (%) as of March 2018

Property Type	Average	Higher Risk	Lower Risk
Hotels	7.2	Limited Service 7.7	Full Service 7.1
Health Care	6.6	Skilled Nursing 9.5	Medical Office 5.7
Retail Malls	5.6	Low Productivity 8.8	High Productivity 5.0
Industrial	5.4		
Office	5.2	Secondary Cities 6.6	Gateway Cities 4.7
Apartments	4.8		

Source: CenterSquare Investment Management (2018). Gateway cities include Boston, Chicago, Los Angeles, New York City, San Francisco, and Washington, DC.

---

[19] Ilmanen (2012) indicated that the difference between cap rates and cash flow yields may be on the order of 3 percentage points. Although significant reinvestment of NOI reduces the cash flow yield, it should increase the growth rate of NOI if the investment is productive.

[20] Based on data from Investment Property Databank Limited.

Retail properties provide a good example of the impact of competition on real estate. Brick-and-mortar stores have been under increasing competitive pressure from online retailers, such as Amazon. The pressure is especially intense for lower-productivity (less profitable) locations. As a result, cap rates for high- and low-productivity malls began to diverge even before the global financial crisis. In 2006, the difference in cap rates was 1.2 percentage points; by 2018, it was 3.2 percentage points.[21]

Cap rates reflect long-term discount rates. As such, we should expect them to rise and fall with the general level of long-term interest rates, which tends to make them pro-cyclical. However, they are also sensitive to credit spreads and the availability of credit. Peyton (2009) found that the spread between cap rates and the 10-year Treasury yield is positively related to the option-adjusted spread on three- to five-year B-rated corporate bonds and negatively related to ratios of household and non-financial-sector debt to GDP. The countercyclical nature of credit spreads mitigates the cyclicality of cap rates. The debt ratios are effectively proxies for the availability of debt financing for leveraged investment in real estate. Since real estate transactions typically involve substantial leverage, greater availability of debt financing is likely to translate into a lower required liquidity premium component of expected real estate returns. Not surprisingly, higher vacancy rates induce higher cap rates.

6.4. The Risk Premium Perspective on Real Estate Expected Return

As a very long-lived asset, real estate is quite sensitive to the level of long-term rates; that is, it has a high effective duration. Indeed, this is often the one and only characteristic mentioned in broad assessments of the likely performance of real estate as an asset class. Hence, real estate must earn a significant term premium. Income-earning properties are exposed to the credit risk of the tenants. In essence, a fixed-term lease with a stable stream of payments is like a corporate bond issued by the tenant secured with physical assets. The landlord must, therefore, demand a credit premium commensurate with what his or her average tenant would have to pay to issue such debt. Real estate must also earn a significant equity risk premium (relative to corporate debt) since the owner bears the full brunt of fluctuations in property values as well as uncertainty with respect to rent growth, lease rollover/termination, and vacancies. The most volatile component of return arises, of course, from changes in property values. As noted previously, these values are strongly pro-cyclical, which implies the need for a significant equity risk premium. Combining the bond-like components (term premium plus credit premium) with a stock-like component implies a risk premium somewhere between those of corporate bonds and equities.

Liquidity is an especially important risk for direct real estate ownership. There are two main ways to view illiquidity. For publicly traded equities and bonds, the question is not whether one can sell the security quickly but, rather, at what price. For real estate, however, it may be better to think of illiquidity as a total inability to sell the asset except at randomly spaced points in time. From this perspective, the degree of liquidity depends on the average frequency of these trading opportunities. By adopting this perspective, one can ask how large the liquidity premium must be to induce investors to hold an asset with a given level of liquidity. Ang, Papanikolaou, and Westerfield (2014) analyzed this question. Their results suggest liquidity premiums on the order of 0.60% for quarterly average liquidity, 0.90% for annual

---

[21] CenterSquare Investment Management (2018). These are cap rates implied by REIT pricing, which is why the 2018 differential does not exactly match the private market figures given in Exhibit 6.

liquidity, and 2%, 4%, and 6% for liquidity on average every 2, 5, and 10 years, respectively.[22] All things considered, a liquidity premium of 2%–4% would seem reasonable for commercial real estate.

6.5. Real Estate in Equilibrium

Real estate can be incorporated into an equilibrium framework (such as the Singer–Terhaar model). Indeed, doing so might be deemed a necessity given the importance of real estate in global wealth. There are, however, a few important considerations. First, the impact of smoothing must have been removed from the risk/return data and metrics used for real estate. Otherwise, inclusion of real estate will distort the results for all asset classes. Second, it is important to recognize the implicit assumption of fully liquid assets in equilibrium models. Adjusting the equilibrium for illiquidity—that is, adding a liquidity premium—is especially important for real estate and other private assets. Third, although real estate investors increasingly venture outside their home markets, real estate is still location specific and may, therefore, be more closely related to local, as opposed to global, economic/market factors than are financial claims.

6.6. Public versus Private Real Estate

Many institutional investors and some ultra-wealthy individuals are able to assemble diversified portfolios of direct real estate holdings. Investors with smaller portfolios must typically choose between limited, undiversified direct real estate holdings or obtaining real estate exposure through financial instruments, such as REIT shares. Assessing whether these alternatives— direct real estate and REITs—have similar investment characteristics is difficult because of return smoothing, heterogeneity of properties, and variations in leverage.

A careful analysis of this issue requires: (1) transaction-based returns for unlevered direct real estate holdings, (2) firm-by-firm deleveraging of REIT returns based on their individual balance sheets over time, and (3) carefully constructing direct real estate and REIT portfolios with matching property characteristics. Exhibit 7 shows the results of such an analysis.

EXHIBIT 7   Direct Real Estate versus REITs: Four Property Types, 1994–2012

	Mean Return (%)			Standard Deviation (%)		
	Direct Real Estate	REITs		Direct Real Estate	REITs	
		Unlevered	Levered		Unlevered	Levered
Aggregate	8.80	9.29		11.09	9.71	
Apartment	9.49	9.08	11.77	11.42	9.50	20.69
Office	8.43	9.37	10.49	10.97	10.58	23.78
Industrial	9.00	9.02	9.57	11.14	11.65	23.46
Retail	8.96	9.90	12.04	11.54	10.03	23.73

Source: Ling and Naranjo (2015, Table 1).

---

[22] See Table 3 in Ang et al. (2014). The numbers cited here reflect an assumption of zero correlation between the investor's liquid and illiquid assets.

Deleveraging the REITs substantially reduces both their mean returns and their volatilities. The volatilities are roughly cut in half. Clearly, the deleveraged REIT returns are much more similar to the direct real estate returns than are the levered REIT returns. In the aggregate, REITs outperformed direct real estate by 49 bps per year with lower volatility. Looking at specific property types, REITs had higher returns and lower volatility in two categories—office and retail. Industrial REITs had essentially the same return as directly owned industrial properties but with higher volatility. Apartment REITs lagged the direct market but with significantly lower volatility.

Exhibit 7 certainly shows some interesting differences. The pattern of unlevered REIT returns by property type is not the same as for direct real estate. Retail REITs had the highest return, and industrial REITs had the lowest. Among directly owned properties, apartments had the highest return and offices the lowest. A similar mismatch appears with respect to volatilities.

Overall, this study tends to support the general conclusion reached by most comparisons: Public and private commercial real estate are different. The extent of the difference is less clear. It does appear that once we account for differences in leverage, REIT investors are not sacrificing performance to obtain the liquidity afforded by publicly traded shares. Perhaps REIT investors are able to capture a significant portion of the liquidity risk premium garnered by direct investors (because the REIT is a direct investor) as well as benefit from professional management.

What about the diversification benefits of real estate as an asset class? REITs are traded securities, and that fact shows up in their much higher short-term correlation with equities. In contrast, direct real estate is often touted as a good diversifier based on the notion that it is not very highly correlated with equities. As noted previously, the smoothed nature of most published real estate returns is a major contributor to the appearance of low correlation with financial assets, including with REITs. Once that is corrected, however, the correlation is higher, even over reasonably short horizons, such as a quarter or a year. Importantly, REITs are more highly correlated with direct real estate and less highly correlated with equities over multi-year horizons.[23] Thus, although REITs tend to act like stocks in the short run, they act like real estate in the longer run. From a strategic asset allocation perspective, REITs and direct real estate are more comparable than conventional metrics suggest.

6.7. Long-Term Housing Returns

Savills World Research (2016) estimated that residential real estate accounts for 75% of the total value of developed properties globally. Most individuals' homes are their primary, perhaps only, real estate investment. A relatively new database provides a global perspective on the long-term performance of residential real estate (housing), equities, and bonds.[24] The database covers 145 years (1870–2015) and 16 countries.

Jordà, Knoll, Kuvshinov, Schularick, and Taylor (2017) found that residential real estate was the best performing asset class over the entire sample period, with a higher real return and much lower volatility than equities. However, performance characteristics differed before and after World War II:

---

[23] Stefek and Suryanarayanan (2012).

[24] The database was developed for and is described in Jordà, Knoll, Kuvshinov, Schularick, and Taylor (2017).

- Residential real estate had a higher (lower) real return than equities before (after) World War II.
- Residential real estate had a higher real return than equities in every country except Switzerland, the United Kingdom, and the United States over 1950–1980 but a lower return than equities in every country for 1980–2015.
- Residential real estate and equities had similar patterns—that is, a strong correlation—prior to the war but a low correlation after the war.
- Equity returns became increasingly correlated across countries after the war, but residential real estate returns are essentially uncorrelated across countries.

Exhibit 8 shows the real returns for equities and residential real estate in each country since 1950.

EXHIBIT 8   Real Equity and Housing Returns by Country, 1950–2015

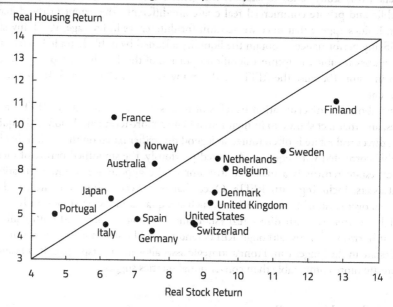

Note: Annual percentage returns are shown.
Source: Jordà et al. (2017).

EXAMPLE 7   Assessing Real Estate Investments

Tammi Sinclair, an analyst at a large retirement fund, recently attended investor presentations by three private real estate firms looking to fund new projects. Office Growth Partners specializes in building and owning low-cost, standardized office space for firms seeking to place sales representatives in the most rapidly growing small population areas across the region. Mega-Box Properties builds and owns large, custom-designed distribution facilities for multinational makers of brand-name products. The facilities are strategically located near major global transportation hubs. Exclusive Elegance Inc.

develops and then manages some of the world's most luxurious, sought-after residential buildings in prime locations. It never breaks ground on a new property until at least 85% of the units have been sold and, to date, has never failed to sell out before construction is complete.

Identify important characteristics of each business that Sinclair will need to consider in establishing a required rate of return for each potential investment.

Guideline answer: Office Growth Partners (OGP) is likely to be a very high-risk investment. It essentially chases hot markets, it builds generic office space, and its typical tenants (opportunistic sales forces) are apt to opt out as soon as the market cools. All these aspects suggest that its business is very exposed to a boom-and-bust cycle. It is likely to end up owning properties with persistently high vacancy rates and high turnover. Hence, Sinclair will likely require a rather high expected return on an investment in OGP.

Mega-Box's business should be fairly stable. The distribution centers are strategically located and designed to meet the needs of the tenant, which suggests long-term leases and low turnover will benefit both Mega-Box and the tenant firms. The average credit quality of the tenants—multinational makers of brand-name products—is likely to be solid and disciplined by the public bond and loan markets. All things considered, Sinclair should probably require a significantly lower expected return on an investment in Mega-Box than in OGP.

Exclusive Elegance appears to be even lower risk. First, it deals only in the very highest-quality, most sought-after properties in prime locations. These should be relatively immune to cyclical fluctuations. Second, it does not retain ownership of the properties, so it does not bear the equity/ownership risks. Third, it is fairly conservative in the riskiest portion of its business—developing new properties. However, Sinclair will need to investigate its record with respect to completing development projects within budget, maintaining properties, and delivering top-quality service to residents.

7. FORECASTING EXCHANGE RATES

Forecasting exchange rates is generally acknowledged to be especially difficult—so difficult that many asset managers either passively accept the impact of currency movements on their portfolio returns or routinely hedge out the currency exposure even if doing so is costly.

To get a sense for why exchange rates are so difficult to forecast, it is useful to distinguish between "money" and the currency in which it is denominated. Like equities and bonds, money is an asset denominated in a currency. Currencies are the units of account in which the prices of everything else—goods, services, real assets, financial assets, liabilities, flows, and balances—are quoted. An exchange rate movement changes the values of everything denominated in one currency relative to everything denominated in every other currency. That is a very powerful force. It works in the other direction as well. Anything that affects quantities, prices, or values within one currency relative to those in another will exert some degree of pressure on exchange rates. Perhaps even more importantly, anything that changes *expectations* of prices, quantities, or values within any currency can change expectations about the future path of currencies, causing an immediate reaction in exchange rates as people adjust their exposures.

Of course, currencies are not abstract accounting ledgers. They are inherently tied to governments, financial systems, legal systems, and geographies. The laws, regulations, customs, and conventions within and between these systems also influence exchange rates, especially when exchange rates are used as instruments or targets of policy. The consequence of all these aspects is that there is very little firm ground on which to stand for analysts trying to forecast exchange rates. The best we can hope to do is to identify the forces that are likely to be exerting the most powerful influences and assess their relative strength. On a related note, it is not possible to identify mutually exclusive approaches to exchange rate forecasting that are each complete enough to stand alone. Hence, the perspectives discussed in this section should be viewed as complementary rather than as alternatives.

7.1. Focus on Goods and Services, Trade, and the Current Account

There are three primary ways in which trade in goods and services can influence the exchange rate. The first is directly through flows. The second is through quasi-arbitrage of prices. The third is through competitiveness and sustainability.

7.1.1. Trade Flows

Trade flows do not, in general, exert a significant impact on contemporaneous exchange rate movements, provided they can be financed. Although gross trade flows may be large, net flows (exports minus imports) are typically much smaller relative to the economy and relative to actual and potential financial flows. If trade-related flows through the foreign exchange market become large relative to financing/investment flows, it is likely that a crisis is emerging.

7.1.2. Purchasing Power Parity

Purchasing power parity (PPP) is based on the notion that the prices of goods and services should change at the same rate regardless of currency denomination.[25] Thus, *the expected percentage change in the exchange rate should be equal to the difference in expected inflation rates*. If we define the *real exchange rate* as the ratio of price levels converted to a common currency, then PPP says that *the expected change in the real exchange rate should be zero*.

The mechanism underlying PPP is a quasi-arbitrage. Free and competitive trade should force alignment of the prices of similar products after conversion to a common currency. This is a very powerful force. It works, but it is slow and incomplete. As a result, the evidence indicates that PPP is a poor predictor of exchange rates over short to intermediate horizons but is a better guide to currency movements over progressively longer multi-year horizons.[26]

There are numerous reasons for deviations from PPP. The starting point matters. Relative PPP implicitly assumes that prices and exchange rates are already well aligned. If not, it will take time before the PPP relationship re-emerges. Not all goods are traded, and virtually every country imposes some trade barriers. PPP completely ignores the impact of capital flows, which often exert much more acute pressure on exchange rates over significant periods of time.

---

[25] This version of PPP is usually referred to as "relative PPP" to distinguish it from a stricter notion called "absolute PPP." Absolute PPP is an important concept but is not useful for practical forecasting. See previous CFA Program currency readings for a broader discussion of PPP concepts.

[26] See, for example, Abuaf and Jorion (1990); Exhibit 2 in "Currency Exchange Rates: Understanding Equilibrium Value" provides a useful visual illustration of PPP over different horizons.

Finally, economic developments may necessitate changes in the country's terms of trade; that is, contrary to PPP, the real exchange rate may need to change over time.

The impact of relative purchasing power on exchange rates tends to be most evident when inflation differentials are large, persistent, and driven primarily by monetary conditions. Under these conditions, PPP may describe exchange rate movements reasonably well over all but the shortest horizons. Indeed, the well-known "monetary approach" to exchange rates essentially boils down to two assumptions: (1) PPP holds, and (2) inflation is determined by the money supply.

7.1.3. Competitiveness and Sustainability of the Current Account

It is axiomatic that in the absence of capital flows prices, quantities, and exchange rates would have to adjust so that trade is always balanced. Since the prices of goods and services, production levels, and spending decisions tend to adjust only gradually, the onus of adjustment would fall primarily on exchange rates. Allowing for capital flows mitigates this pressure on exchange rates. The fact remains, however, that imposition of restrictions on capital flows will increase the sensitivity of exchange rates to the trade balance or, more generally, the current account balance.[27] This is not usually a major consideration for large, developed economies with sophisticated financial markets but can be important in small or developing economies.

Aside from the issue of restrictions on capital mobility, the extent to which the current account balance influences the exchange rate depends primarily on whether it is likely to be persistent and, if so, whether it can be sustained. These issues, in turn, depend mainly on the size of the imbalance and its source. Small current account balances—say, less than 2% of GDP—are likely to be sustainable for many years and hence would exert little influence on exchange rates. Similarly, larger imbalances that are expected to be transitory may not generate a significant, lasting impact on currencies.

The current account balance equals the difference between national saving and investment.[28] A current account surplus indicates that household saving plus business profits and the government surplus/deficit exceeds domestic investment spending. A current account deficit reflects the opposite. A current account deficit that reflects strong, profitable investment spending is more likely to be sustainable than a deficit reflecting high household spending (low saving), low business profits, or substantial government deficits because it is likely to attract the required capital inflow for as long as attractive investment opportunities persist. A large current account surplus may not be very sustainable either because it poses a sustainability problem for deficit countries or because the surplus country becomes unwilling to maintain such a high level of aggregate saving.

Whether an imbalance is likely to persist in the absence of terms-of-trade adjustments largely depends on whether the imbalance is structural. Structural imbalances arise from: (1) persistent fiscal imbalances; (2) preferences, demographics, and institutional characteristics affecting saving decisions; (3) abundance or lack of important resources; (4) availability/absence of profitable investment opportunities associated with growth, capital deepening, and innovation; and, of course, (5) the prevailing terms of trade. Temporary imbalances mainly arise from business cycles (at home and abroad) and associated policy actions.

---

[27] The Mundell–Fleming model of monetary and fiscal policy effects on the exchange rate with high/low capital mobility provides an important illustration of this point. See the CFA Program reading "Currency Exchange Rates: Understanding Equilibrium Value."

[28] See Chapter 4 of Piros and Pinto (2013) for discussion of balance of payments accounting.

If a change in the (nominal) exchange rate is to bring about a necessary change in the current account balance, it will have to induce changes in spending patterns, consumption/saving decisions, and production/investment decisions. These adjustments typically occur slowly and are often resisted by decision makers who hope they can be avoided. Rapid adjustment of the exchange rate may also be resisted because people only gradually adjust their expectations of its ultimate level. Hence, both the exchange rate and current account adjustments are likely to be gradual.

7.2. Focus on Capital Flows

Since the current account and the capital account must always balance and the drivers of the current account tend to adjust only gradually, virtually all of the short-term adjustment and much of the intermediate-term adjustment must occur in the capital account. Asset prices, interest rates, and exchange rates are all part of the equilibrating mechanism. Since a change in the exchange rate simultaneously affects the relative values of all assets denominated in different currencies, we should expect significant pressure to be exerted on the exchange rate whenever an adjustment of capital flows is required.

7.2.1. Implications of Capital Mobility
Capital seeks the highest risk-adjusted expected return. The investments available in each currency can be viewed as a portfolio. Designating one as domestic (d) and one as foreign (f), in a world of perfect capital mobility the exchange rate (expressed as domestic currency per foreign currency unit) will be driven to the point at which the expected percentage change in the exchange rate equals the "excess" risk-adjusted expected return on the domestic portfolio over the foreign portfolio. This idea can be expressed concretely using a building block approach to expected returns.

$$E(\%\Delta S_{d/f}) = (r^d - r^f) + (\text{Term}^d - \text{Term}^f) + (\text{Credit}^d - \text{Credit}^f) + (\text{Equity}^d - \text{Equity}^f) + (\text{Liquid}^d - \text{Liquid}^f). \tag{7.9}$$

The expected change in the exchange rate ($\%\Delta S_{d/f}$) will reflect the differences in the nominal short-term interest rates (r), term premiums (Term), credit premiums (Credit), equity premiums (Equity), and liquidity premiums (Liquid) in the two markets. The components of this equation can be associated with the expected return on various segments of the portfolio: the money market (first term), government bonds (first and second), corporate bonds (first–third), publicly traded equities (first–fourth), and private assets (all terms), including direct investment in plant and equipment.

As an example, suppose the domestic market has a 1% higher short-term rate, a 0.25% lower term premium, a 0.50% higher credit premium, and the same equity and liquidity premiums as the foreign market. Equation 7.9 implies that the domestic currency must be expected to depreciate by 1.25% (= 1% − 0.25% + 0.5%)—that is, $E(\%\Delta S_{d/f}) = 1.25\%$—to equalize risk-adjusted expected returns.

It may seem counterintuitive that the domestic currency should be expected to depreciate if its portfolio offers a higher risk-adjusted expected return. The puzzle is resolved by the key phrase "driven to the point . . ." in this subsection's opening paragraph. In theory, the exchange rate will instantly move ("jump") to a level where the currency with higher (lower) risk-adjusted expected return will be so strong (weak) that it will be expected to depreciate (appreciate) going forward. This is known as the *overshooting* mechanism, introduced by Dornbusch (1976). In reality, the move will not be instantaneous, but it may occur very quickly if there is a consensus about the relative attractiveness of assets denominated in each currency. Of course, asset prices will also be adjusting.

The overshooting mechanism suggests that there are likely to be three phases in response to relative improvement in investment opportunities. First, the exchange rate will appreciate ($S_{d/f}$ will decline) as capital flows toward the more attractive market. The more vigorous the flow, the faster and greater the appreciation of the domestic currency and the more the flow will also drive up asset prices in that market. Second, in the intermediate term, there will be a period of consolidation as investors begin to question the extended level of the exchange rate and to form expectations of a reversal. Third, in the longer run, there will be a retracement of some or all of the exchange rate move depending on the extent to which underlying opportunities have been equalized by asset price adjustments. This is the phase that is reflected in Equation 7.9.

Importantly, these three phases imply that the relationship between currency appreciation/depreciation and apparent investment incentives will not always be in the same direction. This fact is especially important with respect to interest rate differentials since they are directly observable. At some times, higher–interest rate currencies appreciate; at other times, they depreciate.

7.2.2. Uncovered Interest Rate Parity and Hot Money Flows

Uncovered interest rate parity (UIP) asserts that the expected percentage change in the exchange rate should be equal to the nominal interest rate differential. That is, only the first term in Equation 7.9 matters. The implicit assumption is that the response to short-term interest rate differentials will be so strong that it overwhelms all other considerations.

Contrary to UIP, the empirical evidence consistently shows that *carry trades*—borrowing in low-rate currencies and lending in high-rate currencies—earn meaningful profits on average. For example, Burnside, Eichenbaum, Kleshchelski, and Rebelo (2011) found that from February 1976 to July 2009, a strategy of rolling carry trades involving portfolios of high- and low-rate currencies returned 4.31% per annum after transaction costs versus the US dollar and 2.88% per annum versus the British pound.

The profitability of carry trades is usually ascribed to a risk premium, which is clearly consistent with the idea that the risk premiums in Equation 7.9 matter. The empirical results may also be capturing primarily the overshooting phase of the response to interest rate differentials. In any case, carry trades tend to be profitable on average, and UIP does not hold up well as a predictor of exchange rates.

Vigorous flows of capital in response to interest rate differentials are often referred to as *hot money flows*. Hot money flows are problematic for central banks. First, they limit the central bank's ability to run an effective monetary policy. This is the key message of the Mundell–Fleming model with respect to monetary policy in economies characterized by the free flow of capital. Second, a flood of readily available short-term financing may encourage firms to fund longer-term needs with short-term money, setting the stage for a crisis when the financing dries up. Third, the nearly inevitable overshooting of the exchange rate is likely to disrupt non-financial businesses. These issues are generally most acute for emerging markets since their economies and financial markets tend to be more fragile. Central banks often try to combat hot money flows by intervening in the currency market to offset the exchange rate impact of the flows. They may also attempt to *sterilize* the impact on domestic liquidity by selling government securities to limit the growth of bank reserves or maintain a target level of interest rates. If the hot money is flowing *out* rather than *in*, the central bank would do the opposite: sell foreign currency (thereby draining domestic liquidity) to limit/avoid depreciation of the domestic currency and buy government securities (thereby providing liquidity) to sterilize the impact on bank reserves and interest rates. In either case, if intervention is not effective or sufficient, capital controls may be imposed.

7.2.3. Portfolio Balance, Portfolio Composition, and Sustainability Issues

The earlier discussion on the implications of capital mobility implicitly introduced a portfolio balance perspective. Each country/currency has a unique portfolio of assets that makes up part of the global "market portfolio." Exchange rates provide an across-the-board mechanism for adjusting the relative sizes of these portfolios to match investors' desire to hold them. We will look at this from three angles: tactical allocations, strategic/secular allocations, and the implications of wealth transfer.

The relative sizes of different currency portfolios within the global market portfolio do not, in general, change significantly over short to intermediate horizons. Hence, investors do not need to be induced to make changes in their long-term allocations. However, they are likely to want to make tactical allocation changes in response to evolving opportunities—notably, those related to the relative strength of various economies and related policy measures. Overall, capital is likely to flow into the currencies of countries in the strongest phases of the business cycle. The attraction should be especially strong if the economic expansion is led by robust investment in real, productive assets (e.g., plant and equipment) since that can be expected to generate a new stream of long-run profits.

In the long run, the relative size of each currency portfolio depends primarily on relative trend growth rates and current account balances. Rapid economic growth is almost certain to be accompanied by an expanding share of the global market portfolio being denominated in the associated currency. Thus, investors will have to be induced to increase their strategic allocations to assets in that country/currency. All else the same, this would tend to weaken that currency—partially offsetting the increase in the currency's share of the global portfolio—and upward pressure on risk premiums in that market. However, there are several mitigating factors.

- *With growth comes wealth accumulation:* The share of global wealth owned by domestic investors will be rising along with the supply of assets denominated in their currency. Since investors generally exhibit a strong *home country bias* for domestic assets, domestic investors are likely to willingly absorb a large portion of the newly created assets.
- *Productivity-driven growth:* If high growth reflects strong productivity gains, both foreign and domestic investors are likely to willingly fund it with both financial flows and foreign direct investment.
- *Small initial weight in global portfolios:* Countries with exceptionally high trend growth rates are typically relatively small, have previously restricted foreign access to their local-currency financial markets, and/or have previously funded external deficits in major currencies (not their own). Almost by definition, these are emerging and frontier markets. Any of these factors would suggest greater capacity to increase the share of local-currency-denominated assets in global portfolios without undermining the currency.

Large, persistent current account deficits funded in local currency will also put downward pressure on the exchange rate over time as investors are required to shift strategic allocations toward that currency. Again, there are mitigating considerations.

- *The source of the deficit matters:* As discussed previously, current account deficits arising from strong investment spending are relatively easy to finance as long as they are expected to be sufficiently profitable. Deficits due to a low saving rate or weak fiscal discipline are much more problematic.
- *Special status of reserve currencies:* A few currencies—notably, the US dollar—have a special status because the bulk of official reserves are held in these currencies, the associated sovereign debt issuer is viewed as a safe haven, major commodities (e.g., oil) are priced in these currencies, and international trade transactions are often settled in them. A small current account deficit in a reserve-currency country is welcome because it helps provide liquidity to the global financial system. Historically, however, reserve currency status has not proven to be permanent.

Current account surpluses/deficits reflect a transfer of wealth from the deficit country to the surplus country. In an ideal world of fully integrated markets, perfect capital mobility, homogeneous expectations, and identical preferences,[29] a transfer of wealth would have virtually no impact on asset prices or exchange rates because everyone would be happy with the same portfolio composition. This is not the case in practice. To pick just one example, as long as investors have a home country bias, the transfer of wealth will increase the demand for the current-account-surplus country's assets and currency and decrease demand for those of the deficit country.

Does the composition of a particular currency's portfolio matter? A look back at Equation 7.9 suggests that it should matter to some degree. For the most part, however, we would expect asset price adjustments (changes in interest rates and risk premiums) to eliminate most of the pressure that might otherwise be exerted on the exchange rate. Nonetheless, some types of flows and holdings are often considered to be more or less supportive of the currency. Foreign direct investment flows are generally considered to be the most favorable because they indicate a long-term commitment and they contribute directly to the productivity/profitability of the economy. Similarly, investments in private real estate and private equity represent long-term capital committed to the market, although they may or may not represent the creation of new real assets. Public equity would likely be considered the next most supportive of the currency. Although it is less permanent than private investments, it is still a residual claim on the profitability of the economy that does not have to be repaid. Debt has to be serviced and must either be repaid or refinanced, potentially triggering a crisis. Hence, a high and rising ratio of debt to GDP gives rise to *debt sustainability* concerns with respect to the economy. This issue could apply to private sector debt. But it is usually associated with fiscal deficits because the government is typically the largest single borrower; typically borrows to fund consumption and transfers, rather than productive investment; and may be borrowing in excess of what can be serviced without a significant increase in taxes. Finally, as noted previously with respect to hot money flows, large or rapid accumulation of short-term borrowing is usually viewed as a clear warning sign for the currency.

---

[29] Note that these are essentially the assumptions underlying the standard CAPM.

EXAMPLE 8   Currency Forecasts

After many years of running moderately high current account deficits (2%–4% of GDP) but doing little infrastructure investment, Atlandia plans to increase the yearly government deficit by 3% of GDP and maintain that level of deficit for the next 10 years, devoting the increase to infrastructure spending. The deficits will be financed with local-currency government debt. Pete Stevens, CFA, is faced with the task of assessing the impact of this announcement on the Atlandian currency. After talking with members of the economics department at his firm, he has established the following baseline assumptions:

- All else the same, current account deficits will persistently exceed 6% of GDP while the program is in place. Setting aside any lasting impact of the policy/spending, the current account deficit will then fall back to 3% of GDP provided the economy has remained competitive.
- Pressure on wages will boost inflation to 1.5% above the global inflation rate. Because of limitations on factor substitutability, costs in the traded good sector will rise disproportionately.
- Expectations of faster growth will raise the equity premium.
- The central bank will likely tighten policy—that is, raise rates.

Questions:
1. What would purchasing power parity imply about the exchange rate?
2. What are the implications for competitiveness for the currency?
3. What is the likely short-term impact of capital flows on the exchange rate?
4. What does the overshooting mechanism imply about the path of the exchange rate over time? How does this fit with the answers to Questions 1–3?
5. What does a sustainability perspective imply?

Solutions:
1. Purchasing power parity would imply that the Atlandian currency will depreciate by 1.5% per year. The exchange rate, quoted in domestic (Atlandian) units per foreign unit as in Equation 7.9, will rise by a factor of $1.015^{10} = 1.1605$, corresponding to a 13.83% (= $1 - 1/1.1605$) decline in the value of the domestic currency.[30]
2. Since costs in the traded sector will rise faster than inflation, the exchange rate would need to depreciate faster than PPP implies in order to maintain competitiveness. Thus, to remain competitive and re-establish a 3% current account deficit after 10 years, the *real* exchange rate needs to depreciate.
3. Both the increase in short-term rates and the increase in the equity premium are likely to induce strong short-term capital inflows even before the current account deficit actually increases. This should put significant pressure on the Atlandian

---

[30] Note that a slightly different number is obtained if the 1.5% rate is applied directly to the foreign currency value of the Atlandian currency (i.e., the exchange rate expressed as foreign units per domestic unit). That calculation would give a cumulative depreciation of 14.03% (= $1 - 0.985^{10}$). The difference arises because (1/1.015) is not exactly equal to 0.985.

currency to appreciate (i.e., the $S_{d/f}$ exchange rate will decline if the Atlandian currency is defined as the domestic currency). The initial impact may be offset to some extent by flows out of government bonds as investors push yields up in anticipation of increasing supply, but as bonds are repriced to offer a higher expected return (a higher term premium), it will reinforce the upward pressure on the exchange rate.

4. The overshooting mechanism would imply that the initial appreciation of the Atlandian currency discussed previously will extend to a level from which the currency is then expected to depreciate at a pace that equalizes risk-adjusted expected returns across markets and maintains equality between the current and capital accounts. The initial appreciation of the currency in this scenario is clearly inconsistent with PPP, but the subsequent longer-term depreciation phase (from a stronger level) is likely to bring the exchange rate into reasonable alignment with PPP and competitiveness considerations in the long run.

5. It is highly unlikely that a current account deficit in excess of 6% of GDP is sustainable for 10 years. It would entail an increase in net foreign liabilities equaling 60% (= 6% × 10) of GDP. Servicing that additional obligation would add, say, 2%–3% of GDP to the current account deficit forever. Adding that to the baseline projection of 3% would mean that the current account deficit would remain in the 5%–6% range even after the infrastructure spending ended, so net foreign liabilities would still be accumulating rapidly. Closing that gap will require a very large increase in net national saving: 5%–6% of annual GDP *in addition to* the 3% reduction in infrastructure spending when the program ends. Standard macroeconomic analysis implies that such an adjustment would require some combination of a very deep recession and a very large depreciation in the real value of the Atlandian currency (i.e., the real $S_{d/f}$ exchange rate must increase sharply). As soon as investors recognize this, a crisis is almost certain to occur. Bond yields would increase sharply, and equity prices and the currency will fall substantially.

8. FORECASTING VOLATILITY

In some applications, the analyst is concerned with forecasting the variance for only a single asset. More often, however, the analyst needs to forecast the variance–covariance matrix for several, perhaps many, assets in order to analyze the risk of portfolios. Estimating a single variance that is believed to be constant is straightforward: The familiar sample variance is unbiased and its precision can be enhanced by using higher-frequency data. The analyst's task becomes more complicated if the variance is not believed to be constant or the analyst needs to forecast a variance–covariance (VCV) matrix. These issues are addressed in this section. In addition, we elaborate on de-smoothing real estate and other returns.

8.1. Estimating a Constant VCV Matrix with Sample Statistics

The simplest and most heavily used method for estimating constant variances and covariances is to use the corresponding sample statistic—variance or covariance—computed from historical return data. These elements are then assembled into a VCV matrix. There are two main problems with this method, both related to sample size. First, given the short to intermediate sample periods typical in finance, the method cannot be used to estimate the VCV matrix for large numbers of assets. If the number of assets exceeds the number of historical observations, then some portfolios will erroneously appear to be riskless. Second, given typical sample sizes, this method is subject to substantial sampling error. A useful rule of thumb that addresses both of these issues is that the number of observations should be at least 10 times the number of assets in order for the sample VCV matrix to be deemed reliable. In addition, since each element is estimated without regard to any of the others, this method does not address the issue of imposing cross-sectional consistency.

8.2. VCV Matrices from Multi-Factor Models

Factor models have become the standard method of imposing structure on the VCV matrix of asset returns. From this perspective, their main advantage is that the number of assets can be very large relative to the number of observations. The key to making this work is that the covariances are fully determined by exposures to a small number of common factors whereas each variance includes an asset-specific component.

In a model with K common factors, the return on the ith asset is given by

$$r_i = \alpha_i + \sum_{k=1}^{K} \beta_{ik} F_k + \varepsilon_i, \tag{7.10}$$

where α_i is a constant intercept, β_{ik} is the asset's sensitivity to the kth factor, F_k is the kth common factor return, and ε_i is a stochastic term with a mean of zero that is unique to the ith asset. In general, the factors will be correlated. Given the model, the variance of the ith asset is

$$\sigma_i^2 = \sum_{m=1}^{K} \sum_{n=1}^{K} \beta_{im} \beta_{in} \rho_{mn} + v_i^2 \tag{7.11}$$

where ρ_{mn} is the covariance between the mth and nth factors and v_i^2 is the variance of the unique component of the ith asset's return. The covariance between the ith and jth assets is

$$\sigma_{ij} = \sum_{m=1}^{K} \sum_{n=1}^{K} \beta_{im} \beta_{jn} \rho_{mn} \tag{7.12}$$

As long as none of the factors are redundant and none of the asset returns are completely determined by the factors (so $v_i^2 \neq 0$), there will not be any portfolios that erroneously appear to be riskless. That is, we will not encounter the first problem mentioned in Section 8, with respect to using sample statistics.

Imposing structure with a factor model makes the VCV matrix much simpler. With N assets, there are $[N(N-1)/2]$ distinct covariance elements in the VCV matrix. For example, if $N = 100$, there are 4,950 distinct covariances to be estimated. The factor model reduces this problem to estimating $[N \times K]$ factor sensitivities plus $[K(K+1)/2]$ elements of the factor VCV matrix, Ω. With $N = 100$ and $K = 5$, this would mean "only" 500 sensitivities and 15 elements of the factor VCV matrix—almost a 90% reduction in items to estimate. (Of course, we also need to estimate the asset-specific variance terms, v_i^2, in order to get the N variances, σ_i^2.) If the factors are chosen well, the factor-based VCV matrix will contain substantially less estimation error than the sample VCV matrix does.

A well-specified factor model can also improve cross-sectional consistency. To illustrate, suppose we somehow know that the true covariance of any asset i with any asset j is proportional to asset i's covariance with any third asset, k, so

$$\frac{\sigma_{ij}}{\sigma_{ik}} = \text{Constant} \tag{7.13}$$

for any assets i, j, and k. We would want our estimates to come as close as possible to satisfying this relationship. Sample covariances computed from any given sample of returns will not, in general, do so. However, using Equation 7.12 with only one factor (i.e., $K = 1$) shows that the covariances from a single-factor model will satisfy

$$\frac{\sigma_{ij}}{\sigma_{ik}} = \frac{\beta_j}{\beta_k} \tag{7.14}$$

for all assets i, j, and k. Thus, in this simple example, a single-factor model imposes exactly the right cross-sectional structure.

The benefits obtained by imposing a factor structure—handling large numbers of assets, a reduced number of parameters to be estimated, imposition of cross-sectional structure, and a potentially substantial reduction of estimation error—come at a cost. In contrast to the simple example just discussed, in general, the factor model will almost certainly be mis-specified. The structure it imposes will not be exactly right. As a result, the factor-based VCV matrix is *biased*; that is, the expected value is not equal to the true (unobservable) VCV matrix of the returns. To put it differently, the matrix is not correct even "on average." The matrix is also *inconsistent*; that is, it does not converge to the true matrix as the sample size gets arbitrarily large. In contrast, the sample VCV matrix is unbiased and consistent. Thus, when we use a factor-based matrix instead of the sample VCV matrix, we are choosing to estimate something that is "not quite right" with relative precision rather than the "right thing" with a lot of noise. The point is that although factor models are very useful, they are not a panacea.

8.3. Shrinkage Estimation of VCV Matrices

As with shrinkage estimation in general, the idea here is to combine the information in the sample data, the sample VCV matrix, with an alternative estimate, the target VCV matrix—which reflects assumed "prior" knowledge of the structure of the true VCV matrix—and thereby mitigate the impact of estimation error on the final matrix. Each element (variance or covariance) of the final shrinkage estimate of the VCV matrix is simply a weighted average of the corresponding elements of the sample VCV matrix and the target VCV matrix. The same weights are used for all elements of the matrix. The analyst must determine how much weight to put on the target matrix (the "prior" knowledge) and how much weight to put on the sample data (the sample VCV matrix).

Aside from a technical condition that rules out the appearance of riskless portfolios, virtually any choice of target VCV matrix will increase (or at least not decrease) the efficiency of the estimates versus the sample VCV matrix. "Efficiency" in this context means a smaller mean-squared error (MSE), which is equal to an estimator's variance plus the square of its bias. Although the shrinkage estimator is biased, its MSE will in general be smaller than the MSE of the (unbiased) sample VCV matrix. The more plausible (and presumably less biased) the selected target matrix, the greater the improvement will be. A factor-model-based VCV matrix would be a reasonable candidate for the target.

EXAMPLE 9   Estimating the VCV Matrix

Isa Berkitz is an analyst at Barnsby & Culp (B&C), a recently formed multi-family office. Berkitz has been asked to propose the method for estimating the variance–covariance matrix to be used in B&C's asset allocation process for all clients. After examining the existing client portfolios and talking with the clients and portfolio managers, Berkitz concludes that in order to support B&C's strategic and tactical allocation needs, the VCV matrix will need to include 25 asset classes. For many of these classes, she will be able to obtain less than 10 years of monthly return data. Berkitz has decided to incorporate both the sample statistics and factor-model approaches using shrinkage estimation.

    Explain the strengths and weaknesses of the two basic approaches and why Berkitz would choose to combine them using the shrinkage framework.

Solution: The VCV matrix based on sample statistics is correct on average (it is unbiased) and convergences to the true VCV matrix as the sample size gets arbitrarily large (it is "consistent"). The sample VCV method cannot be used if the number of assets exceeds the number of observations, which is not an issue in this case. However, it is subject to large sampling errors unless the number of observations is large relative to the number of assets. A 10-to-1 rule of thumb would suggest that Berkitz needs more than 250 observations (20+ years of monthly data) in order for the sample VCV matrix to give her reliable estimates, but she has at most 120 observations. In addition, the sample VCV matrix does not impose any cross-sectional consistency on the estimates. A factor-model-based VCV matrix can be used even if the number of assets exceeds the number of observations. It can substantially reduce the number of unique parameters to be estimated, it imposes cross-sectional structure, and it can substantially reduce estimation errors. However, unless the structure imposed by the factor model is exactly correct, the VCV matrix will not be correct on average (it will be biased). Shrinkage estimation—a weighted average of the sample VCV and factor-based VCV matrices—will increase (or at least not decrease) the efficiency of the estimates. In effect, the shrinkage estimator captures the benefits of each underlying methodology and mitigates their respective limitations.

8.4. Estimating Volatility from Smoothed Returns

The available return data for such asset classes as private real estate, private equity, and hedge funds generally reflect smoothing of unobservable underlying "true" returns. The smoothing dampens the volatility of the observed data and distorts correlations with other assets. Thus, the raw data tend to understate the risk and overstate the diversification benefits of these asset classes. Failure to adjust for the impact of smoothing will almost certainly lead to distorted portfolio analysis and hence poor asset allocation decisions.

    The basic idea is that the observed returns are a weighted average of current and past true, unobservable returns. One of the simplest and most widely used models implies that the current observed return, R_t, is a weighted average of the current true return, r_t, and the previous observed return:

$$R_t = (1 - \lambda)\, r_t + \lambda R_{t-1}, \tag{7.15}$$

where $0 < \lambda < 1$. From this equation, it can be shown that

$$\text{var}(r) = \left(\frac{1+\lambda}{1-\lambda}\right)\text{var}(R) > \text{var}(R). \tag{7.16}$$

As an example, if $\lambda = 0.8$, then the true variance, $\text{var}(r)$, of the asset is 9 times the variance of the observed data. Equivalently, the standard deviation is 3 times larger.

This model cannot be estimated directly because the true return, r_t, is not observable. To get around this problem, the analyst assumes a relationship between the unobservable return and one or more observable variables. For private real estate, a natural choice might be a REIT index, whereas for private equity, an index of similar publicly traded equities could be used.

EXAMPLE 10   Estimating Volatility from Smoothed Data

While developing the VCV matrix for B&C, Isa Berkitz noted that the volatilities for several asset classes—notably, real estate and private equity categories—calculated directly from available return data appear to be very low. The data are from reputable sources, but Berkitz is skeptical because similar publicly traded classes—for example, REITs and small-cap equities—exhibit much higher volatilities. What is the likely cause of the issue?

Guideline answer: The very low volatilities are very likely due to smoothing within the reported private asset returns. That is, the observed data reflect a weighted average of current and past true returns. For real estate, this smoothing arises primarily because the underlying property values used to calculate "current" returns are based primarily on backward-looking appraisals rather than concurrent transactions.

8.5. Time-Varying Volatility: ARCH Models

The discussion up to this point has focused on estimating variances and covariances under the assumption that their true values do not change over time. It is well known, however, that financial asset returns tend to exhibit **volatility clustering**, evidenced by periods of high and low volatility. A class of models known collectively as autoregressive conditional heteroskedasticity (ARCH) models has been developed to address these time-varying volatilities.[31]

One of the simplest and most heavily used forms of this broad class of models specifies that the variance in period t is given by

$$\begin{aligned}
\sigma_t^2 &= \gamma + \alpha\,\sigma_{t-1}^2 + \beta\,\eta_t^2 \\
&= \gamma + (\alpha + \beta)\,\sigma_{t-1}^2 + \beta\left(\eta_t^2 - \sigma_{t-1}^2\right),
\end{aligned} \tag{7.17}$$

where α, β, and γ are non-negative parameters such that $(\alpha + \beta) < 1$. The term η_t is the unexpected component of return in period t; that is, it is a random variable with a mean of zero

---

[31] Chapter 12 of Campbell, Lo, and MacKinlay (1997) provides an excellent, detailed explanation of these models. The present discussion draws on that book.

conditional on information at time $(t - 1)$. Rearranging the equation as in the second line shows that $(\eta_t^2 - \sigma_{t-1}^2)$ can be interpreted as the "shock" to the variance in period t. Thus, the variance in period t depends on the variance in period $(t - 1)$ plus a shock. The parameter β controls how much of the current "shock" feeds into the variance. In the extreme, if $\beta = 0$, then variance would be deterministic. The quantity $(\alpha + \beta)$ determines the extent to which the variance in future periods is influenced by the current level of volatility. The higher $(\alpha + \beta)$ is, the more the variance "remembers" what happened in the past and the more it "clusters" at high or low levels. The unconditional expected value of the variance is $[\gamma/(1 - \alpha - \beta)]$.

As an example, assume that $\gamma = 0.000002$, $\alpha = 0.9$, and $\beta = 0.08$ and that we are esti-mating daily equity volatility. Given these parameters, the unconditional expected value of the variance is 0.0001, implying that the daily standard deviation is 1% (0.01). Suppose the esti-mated variance at time $(t - 1)$ was 0.0004 (= 0.02^2) and the return in period t was 3% above expectations ($\eta_t = 0.03$). Then the variance in period t would be

$$\sigma_t^2 = 0.000002 + (0.9 \times 0.0004) + (0.08 \times 0.03^2) = 0.000434,$$

which is equivalent to a standard deviation of 2.0833%. Without the shock to the variance (i.e., with $\eta_t^2 = \sigma_{t-1}^2 = 0.0004$), the standard deviation would have been 1.9849%. Even without the shock, the volatility would have remained well above its long-run mean of 1.0%. Including the shock, the volatility actually increased. Note that the impact on volatility would have been the same if the return had been 3% *below* expectations rather than above expectations.

The ARCH methodology can be extended to multiple assets—that is, to estimation of a VCV matrix. The most straightforward extensions tend to be limited to only a few assets since the number of parameters rises very rapidly. However, Engle (2002) developed a class of models with the potential to handle large matrices with relatively few parameters.

EXAMPLE 11   ARCH

Sam Akai has noticed that daily returns for a variety of asset classes tend to exhibit peri-ods of high and low volatility but the volatility does seem to revert toward a fairly stable average level over time. Many market participants capture this tendency by estimat-ing volatilities using a 60-day moving window. Akai notes that this method implicitly assumes volatility is constant within each 60-day window but somehow not constant from one day to the next. He has heard that ARCH models can explicitly incorporate time variation and capture the observed clustering pattern.

Explain the models to him.

Guideline answer: The key idea is to model variance as a linear time-series process in which the current volatility depends on its own recent history or recent shocks. The shocks to volatility arise from unexpectedly large or small returns. In one of the sim-plest ARCH models, the current variance depends only on the variance in the previous period and the unexpected component of the current return (squared). Provided the coefficients are positive and not "too large," the variance will exhibit the properties Akai has observed: periods of time at high/low levels relative to a well-defined average level.

9. ADJUSTING A GLOBAL PORTFOLIO

The coverage of capital market expectations has provided an intensive examination of topics with which analysts need to be familiar in order to establish capital market expectations for client portfolios. This section brings some of this material together to illustrate how analysts can develop and justify recommendations for adjusting a portfolio. The discussion that follows is selective in the range of assets and scenarios it considers. It focuses on connecting expectations to the portfolio and is about "direction of change" rather than the details of specific forecasts.

9.1. Macro-Based Recommendations

Suppose we start with a fairly generic portfolio of global equities and bonds (we assume no other asset classes are included or considered) and we are asked to recommend changes based primarily on macroeconomic considerations. Further assume that the portfolio reflects a reasonable strategic allocation for our clients. Hence, we do not need to make any wholesale changes and can focus on incremental improvements based on assessment of current opportunities. To be specific, we limit our potential recommendations to the following:

- Change the overall allocations to equities and bonds.
- Reallocate equities/bonds between countries.
- Adjust the average credit quality of our bond portfolios.
- Adjust duration and positioning on the yield curves.
- Adjust our exposures to currencies.

To approach the task systematically, we begin with a checklist of questions.

1. Have there been significant changes in the drivers of trend growth, globally or in particular countries?
2. Are any of the markets becoming more/less globally integrated?
3. Where does each country stand within its business cycle? Are they synchronized?
4. Are monetary and fiscal policies consistent with long-term stability and the phases of the business cycle?
5. Are current account balances trending and sustainable?
6. Are any currencies under pressure to adjust or trending? Have capital flows driven any currencies to extended levels? Have any of the economies become uncompetitive/supercompetitive because of currency movements?

There are certainly many more questions we could ask. In practice, the analyst will need to look into the details. But these questions suffice for our illustration. We will examine each in turn. It must be noted, however, that they are inherently interrelated.

9.1.1. Trend Growth

All else the same, an increase in trend growth favors equities because it implies more rapid long-run earnings growth. Faster growth due to productivity is especially beneficial. In contrast, higher trend growth generally results in somewhat higher real interest rates, a negative for currently outstanding bonds. Identifiable changes in trend growth that have not already been fully factored into asset prices are most likely to have arisen from a shock (e.g., new technology). A global change would provide a basis for adjusting the overall equity/bond allocation. Country-specific or regional changes provide a basis for reallocation within equities toward the markets experiencing enhanced growth prospects that have not already been reflected in market prices.

9.1.2. Global Integration

All else the same, the Singer–Terhaar model implies that when a market becomes more globally integrated, its required return should decline. As prices adjust to a lower required return, the market should deliver an even higher return than was previously expected or required by the market. Therefore, expected increases in integration provide a rationale for adjusting allocations toward those markets and reductions in markets that are already highly integrated. Doing so will typically entail a shift from developed markets to emerging markets.

9.1.3. Phases of the Business Cycle

The best time to buy equities is generally when the economy is approaching the trough of the business cycle. Valuation multiples and expected earnings growth rates are low and set to rise. The Grinold–Kroner model could be used to formalize a recommendation to buy equities. At this stage of the cycle, the term premium is high (the yield curve is steep) and the credit premium is high (credit spreads are wide). However, (short-term) interest rates are likely to start rising soon and the yield curve can be expected to flatten again as the economy gains strength. All else the same, the overall allocation to bonds will need to be reduced to facilitate the increased allocation to equities. Within the bond portfolio, overall duration should be reduced, positions with intermediate maturities should be reduced in favor of shorter maturities (and perhaps a small amount of longer maturities) to establish a "barbell" posture with the desired duration, and exposure to credit should be increased (a "down in quality" trade). The opposite recommendations would apply when the analyst judges that the economy is at or near the peak of the cycle.

To the extent that business cycles are synchronized across markets, this same prescription would apply to the overall portfolio. It is likely, however, that some markets will be out of phase—leading or lagging other markets—by enough to warrant reallocations between markets. In this case, the recommendation would be to reallocate equities from (to) markets nearest the peak (trough) of their respective cycles and to do the opposite within the bond portfolio with corresponding adjustments to duration, yield curve positioning, and credit exposure within each market.

9.1.4. Monetary and Fiscal Policies

Investors devote substantial energy dissecting every nuance of monetary and fiscal policy. If policymakers are doing what we would expect them to be doing at any particular stage of the business cycle—for example, moderate countercyclical actions and attending to longer-term objectives, such as controlling inflation and maintaining fiscal discipline—their activities may already be reflected in asset prices. In addition, the analyst should have factored expected policy actions into the assessment of trend growth and business cycles.

Significant opportunities to add value by reallocating the portfolio are more likely to arise from structural policy changes (e.g., a shift from interest rate targeting to money growth targeting, quantitative easing, and restructuring of the tax code) or evidence that the response to policy measures is not within the range of outcomes that policymakers would have expected (e.g., if massive quantitative easing induced little inflation response). Structural policy changes are clearly intentional and the impact on the economy and the markets is likely to be consistent with standard macroeconomic analysis, so the investment recommendations will follow from the implications for growth trends and business cycles. Almost by definition, standard modes of analysis may be ineffective if policy measures have not induced the expected responses. In this case, the analyst's challenge is to determine what, why, and how underlying linkages have changed and identify the value-added opportunities.

9.1.5. Current Account Balances

Current account balances ultimately reflect national saving and investment decisions, including the fiscal budget. Current accounts must, of course, net out across countries. In the short run, this is brought about in large measure by the fact that household saving and corporate profits (business saving) are effectively residuals whereas consumption and capital expenditures are more explicitly planned. Hence, purely cyclical fluctuations in the current account are just part of the business cycle. Longer-term trends in the current account require adjustments to induce deliberate changes in saving/investment decisions. A rising current account deficit will tend to put upward pressure on real required returns (downward pressure on asset prices) in order to induce a higher saving rate in the deficit country (to mitigate the widening deficit) and to attract the increased flow of capital from abroad required to fund the deficit. An expanding current account surplus will, in general, require the opposite in order to reduce "excess" saving. This suggests that the analyst should consider reallocation of portfolio assets from countries with secularly rising current account deficits to those with secularly rising current account surpluses (or narrowing deficits).

9.1.6. Capital Accounts and Currencies

Setting aside very high inflation situations in which purchasing power parity may be important even in the short term, currencies are primarily influenced by capital flows. When investors perceive that the portfolio of assets denominated in a particular currency offers a higher risk-adjusted expected return than is available in other currencies, the initial surge of capital tends to drive the exchange rate higher, often to a level from which it is more likely to depreciate rather than continue to appreciate. At that point, the underlying assets may remain attractive in their native currency but not in conjunction with the currency exposure. An analyst recommending reallocation of a portfolio toward assets denominated in a particular currency must, therefore, assess whether the attractiveness of the assets has already caused an "overshoot" in the currency or whether a case can be made that there is meaningful appreciation yet to come. In the former case, the analyst needs to consider whether the assets remain attractive after taking account of the cost of currency hedging.

There is one final question that needs to be addressed for all asset classes and currencies. The previous discussion alluded to it, but it is important enough to be asked directly: *What is already reflected in asset prices?* There is no avoiding the fact that valuations matter.

9.2. Quantifying the Views

Although the analyst may not be required to quantify the views underlying his or her recommendations, we can very briefly sketch a process that may be used for doing so using some of the tools discussed in earlier sections.

Step 1:   Use appropriate techniques to estimate the VCV matrix for all asset classes.

Step 2:   Use the Singer–Terhaar model and the estimated VCV matrix to determine equilibrium expected returns for all asset classes.

Step 3:   Use the Grinold–Kroner model to estimate returns for equity markets based on assessments of economic growth, earnings growth, valuation multiples, dividends, and net share repurchases.

Step 4:   Use the building block approach to estimate expected returns for bond classes based primarily on cyclical and policy considerations.

Step 5:   Establish directional views on currencies relative to the portfolio's base currency based on the perceived attractiveness of assets and the likelihood of having overshot sustainable levels. Set modest rates of expected appreciation/depreciation.

Step 6:   Incorporate a currency component into expected returns for equities and bonds.

Step 7:   Use the Black–Litterman framework to combine equilibrium expected returns from Step 2 with the expected returns determined in Steps 3–6.

SUMMARY

The following are the main points covered in the reading.

- The choice among forecasting techniques is effectively a choice of the information on which forecasts will be conditioned and how that information will be incorporated into the forecasts.
- The formal forecasting tools most commonly used in forecasting capital market returns fall into three broad categories: statistical methods, discounted cash flow models, and risk premium models.
- Sample statistics, especially the sample mean, are subject to substantial estimation error.
- Shrinkage estimation combines two estimates (or sets of estimates) into a more precise estimate.
- Time-series estimators, which explicitly incorporate dynamics, may summarize historical data well without providing insight into the underlying drivers of forecasts.
- Discounted cash flow models are used to estimate the required return implied by an asset's current price.
- The risk premium approach expresses expected return as the sum of the risk-free rate of interest and one or more risk premiums.
- There are three methods for modeling risk premiums: equilibrium models, such as the CAPM; factor models; and building blocks.
- The DCF method is the only one that is precise enough to use in support of trades involving individual fixed-income securities.
- There are three main methods for developing expected returns for fixed-income asset classes: DCF, building blocks, and inclusion in an equilibrium model.
- As a forecast of bond return, YTM, the most commonly quoted metric, can be improved by incorporating the impact of yield changes on reinvestment of cash flows and valuation at the investment horizon.
- The building blocks for fixed-income expected returns are the short-term default-free rate, the term premium, the credit premium, and the liquidity premium.

- Term premiums are roughly proportional to duration, whereas credit premiums tend to be larger at the short end of the curve.
- Both term premiums and credit premiums are positively related to the slope of the yield curve.
- Credit spreads reflect both the credit premium (i.e., additional expected return) and expected losses due to default.
- A baseline estimate of the liquidity premium can be based on the yield spread between the highest-quality issuer in a market (usually the sovereign) and the next highest-quality large issuer (often a government agency).
- Emerging market debt exposes investors to heightened risk with respect to both ability to pay and willingness to pay, which can be associated with the economy and political/legal weaknesses, respectively.
- The Grinold–Kroner model decomposes the expected return on equities into three components: (1) expected cash flow return, composed of the dividend yield minus the rate of change in shares outstanding, (2) expected return due to nominal earnings growth, and (3) expected repricing return, reflecting the rate of change in the P/E.
- Forecasting the equity premium directly is just as difficult as projecting the absolute level of equity returns, so the building block approach provides little, if any, specific insight with which to improve equity return forecasts.
- The Singer–Terhaar version of the international capital asset pricing model combines a global CAPM equilibrium that assumes full market integration with expected returns for each asset class based on complete segmentation.
- Emerging market equities expose investors to the same underlying risks as emerging market debt does: more fragile economies, less stable political and policy frameworks, and weaker legal protections.
- Emerging market investors need to pay particular attention to the ways in which the value of their ownership claims might be expropriated. Among the areas of concern are standards of corporate governance, accounting and disclosure standards, property rights laws, and checks and balances on governmental actions.
- Historical return data for real estate is subject to substantial smoothing, which biases standard volatility estimates downward and distorts correlations with other asset classes. Meaningful analysis of real estate as an asset class requires explicit handling of this data issue.
- Real estate is subject to boom–bust cycles that both drive and are driven by the business cycle.
- The cap rate, defined as net operating income in the current period divided by the property value, is the standard valuation metric for commercial real estate.
- A model similar to the Grinold–Kroner model can be applied to estimate the expected return on real estate:

$$E(R_{re}) = \text{Cap rate} + \text{NOI growth rate} - \%\Delta\text{Cap rate}.$$

- There is a clear pattern of higher cap rates for riskier property types, lower-quality properties, and less attractive locations.
- Real estate expected returns contain all the standard building block risk premiums:

  - Term premium: As a very long-lived asset with relatively stable cash flows, income-producing real estate has a high duration.
  - Credit premium: A fixed-term lease is like a corporate bond issued by the leaseholder and secured by the property.

- Equity premium: Owners bear the risk of property value fluctuations, as well as risk associated with rent growth, lease renewal, and vacancies.
  - Liquidity premium: Real estate trades infrequently and is costly to transact.

- Currency exchange rates are especially difficult to forecast because they are tied to governments, financial systems, legal systems, and geographies. Forecasting exchange rates requires identification and assessment of the forces that are likely to exert the most influence.
- Provided they can be financed, trade flows do not usually exert a significant impact on exchange rates. International capital flows are typically larger and more volatile than trade-financing flows.
- PPP is a poor predictor of exchange rate movements over short to intermediate horizons but is a better guide to currency movements over progressively longer multi-year horizons.
- The extent to which the current account balance influences the exchange rate depends primarily on whether it is likely to be persistent and, if so, whether it can be sustained.
- Capital seeks the highest risk-adjusted expected return. In a world of perfect capital mobility, in the long run, the exchange rate will be driven to the point at which the expected percentage change equals the "excess" risk-adjusted expected return on the portfolio of assets denominated in the domestic currency over that of the portfolio of assets denominated in the foreign currency. However, in the short run, there can be an exchange rate overshoot in the opposite direction as hot money chases higher returns.
- Carry trades are profitable on average, which is contrary to the predictions of uncovered interest rate parity.
- Each country/currency has a unique portfolio of assets that makes up part of the global "market portfolio." Exchange rates provide an across-the-board mechanism for adjusting the relative sizes of these portfolios to match investors' desire to hold them.
- The portfolio balance perspective implies that exchange rates adjust in response to changes in the relative sizes and compositions of the aggregate portfolios denominated in each currency.
- The sample variance–covariance matrix is an unbiased estimate of the true VCV structure; that is, it will be correct on average.
- There are two main problems with using the sample VCV matrix as an estimate/forecast of the true VCV matrix: It cannot be used for large numbers of asset classes, and it is subject to substantial sampling error.
- Linear factor models impose structure on the VCV matrix that allows them to handle very large numbers of asset classes. The drawback is that the VCV matrix is biased and inconsistent unless the assumed structure is true.
- Shrinkage estimation of the VCV matrix is a weighted average of the sample VCV matrix and a target VCV matrix that reflects assumed "prior" knowledge of the true VCV structure.
- Failure to adjust for the impact of smoothing in observed return data for real estate and other private assets will almost certainly lead to distorted portfolio analysis and hence poor asset allocation decisions.
- Financial asset returns exhibit volatility clustering, evidenced by periods of high and low volatilities. ARCH models were developed to address these time-varying volatilities.
- One of the simplest and most used ARCH models represents today's variance as a linear combination of yesterday's variance and a new "shock" to volatility. With appropriate parameter values, the model exhibits the volatility clustering characteristic of financial asset returns.

REFERENCES

Abuaf, Niso, and Philippe Jorion. 1990. "Purchasing Power Parity in the Long Run." *Journal of Finance* (March): 157–74. doi:10.1111/j.1540-6261.1990.tb05085.x

Ang, Andrew, Dimitris Papanikolaou, and Mark M. Westerfield. 2014. "Portfolio Choice with Illiquid Assets." *Management Science* 6 (11). doi:10.1287/mnsc.2014.1986

Burnside, Craig, Martin Eichenbaum, Isaac Kleshchelski, and Sergio Rebelo. 2011. "Do Peso Problems Explain the Returns to the Carry Trade?" *Review of Financial Studies* 24 (3): 853–91. doi:10.1093/rfs/hhq138

Campbell, John Y., Andrew W. Lo, and A. Craig MacKinlay. 1997. *The Econometrics of Financial Markets*. Princeton, NJ: Princeton University Press.

CenterSquare Investment Management Plc. 2018. "The REIT Cap Rate Perspective" (March). www .centersquare.com/documents/20182/32181/March+2018_CenterSquare+REIT+Cap+Rate+Pers pective/0f802c79-00bd-4e18-8655-98ca90a87e63. Accessed January 2019.

Clayton, Jim, Frank J. Fabozzi, S. Michael Gilberto, Jacques N. Gordon, Susan Hudson-Wilson, William Hughes, Youguo Liang, Greg MacKinnon, and Asieh Mansour. 2011. "The Changing Face of Real Estate Investment Management." Special Real Estate Issue *Journal of Portfolio Management*:12–23.

Cochrane, John H., and Monika Piazzesi. 2005. "Bond Risk Premia." *American Economic Review* (March): 138–60. doi:10.1257/0002828053828581

Dimson, Elroy, Paul Marsh, and Mike Staunton. 2002. *Triumph of the Optimists*. Princeton, NJ: Princeton University Press. doi:10.1515/9781400829477

Dimson, Elroy, Paul Marsh, and Mike Staunton. 2018. *Credit Suisse Global Investment Returns Yearbook 2018*. Zurich: Credit Suisse Research Institute.

Dornbusch, R. Dec 1976. "Expectations and Exchange Rate Dynamics." *Journal of Political Economy* 84 (6): 1161–76. doi:10.1086/260506

Engle, Robert. 2002. "Dynamic Conditional Correlation: A Simple Class of Multivariate Generalized Autoregressive Conditional Heteroskedasticity Models." *Journal of Business & Economic Statistics* (July): 339–50. doi:10.1198/073500102288618487

Giesecke, Kay, Francis A. Longstaff, Stephen Schaefer, and Ilya Strebulaev. 2011. "Corporate Bond Default Risk: A 150-Year Perspective." *Journal of Financial Economics* 102 (2): 233–50. doi:10.1016/j .jfineco.2011.01.011

Grinold, Richard, and Ken Kroner. 2002. "The Equity Risk Premium: Analyzing the Long-Run Prospects for the Stock Market." *InvestmentInsights* 5 (3).

Ilmanen, Antti. 2012. *Expected Returns on Major Asset Classes*. Charlottesville, VA: Research Foundation of CFA Institute.

Jarrow, Robert A., and Donald R. van Deventer. 2015. "Credit Analysis Models." In *Fixed Income Analysis*, 3rd ed. CFA Institute Investment Series/Wiley.

Jordà, Òscar, Katharina Knoll, Dmitry Kuvshinov, Moritz Schularick, and Alan M. Taylor. 2017. "The Rate of Return on Everything, 1870–2015." NBER Working Paper No. 24112 (December). doi:10.3386/w24112

Kim, Don H., and Jonathan H. Wright. 2005. "An Arbitrage-Free Three-Factor Term Structure Model and the Recent Behavior of Long-Term Yields and Distant-Horizon Forward Rates." Federal Reserve Board Working Paper 2005-33 (August). doi:10.2139/ssrn.813267

Ling, David C., and Andy Naranjo. 2015. "Returns and Information Transmission Dynamics in Public and Private Real Estate Markets." *Real Estate Economics* 43 (1): 163–208. doi:10.1111/1540-6229.12069

Marcelo, José Luis Miralles, Luis Miralles Quirós José, and José Luís Martins. 2013. "The Role of Country and Industry Factors during Volatile Times." *Journal of International Financial Markets, Institutions and Money* 26 (October): 273–90. doi:10.1016/j.intfin.2013.06.005

Peyton, Martha S. 2009. "Capital Markets Impact on Commercial Real Estate Cap Rates: A Practitioner's View." Special Real Estate Issue *Journal of Portfolio Management* 38–49. doi:10.3905/JPM.2009.35.5.038

Piros, Christopher D. 2015. "Strategic Asset Allocation: Plus ça change, plus c'est la meme chose." *Investments & Wealth Monitor* (March/April): 5–8.

Piros, Christopher D., and Jerald E. Pinto. 2013. *Economics for Investment Decision Makers Workbook: Micro, Macro, and International Economics.* Hoboken, NJ: John Wiley & Sons, Inc.

Savills World Research. 2016. *Around the World in Dollars and Cents.* London: Savills.

Singer, Brian D., and Kevin Terhaar. 1997. *Economic Foundations of Capital Market Returns.* Charlottesville, VA: Research Foundation of the Institute of Chartered Financial Analysts.

Stefek, Daniel, and Raghu Suryanarayanan. 2012. "Private and Public Real Estate: What Is the Link?" *Journal of Alternative Investments* (Winter): 66–75.

Yau, Jot K., Thomas Schneeweis, Edward A. Szado, Thomas R. Robinson, and Lisa R. Weiss. 2018. "Alternative Investments Portfolio Management." CFA Program Level III Curriculum Reading 26.

PROBLEMS

1. An investor is considering adding three new securities to her internationally focused fixed income portfolio. She considers the following non-callable securities:
   - 1-year government bond
   - 10-year government bond
   - 10-year BBB rated corporate bond

   She plans to invest equally in all three securities being analyzed or will invest in none of them at this time. She will only make the added investment provided that the expected spread/premium of the equally weighted investment is at least 1.5 percent (150bp) over the 1-year government bond. She has gathered the following information:

Risk free interest rate (1-year, incorporating 2.6% inflation expectation)	3.8%
Term premium (10-year vs. 1-year government bond)	1%
10-year BBB credit premium (over 10-year government bond)	75bp
Estimated liquidity premium on 10-year corporate bonds	55bp

   Using only the information given, address the following problems using the risk premium approach:

   A. Calculate the expected return that an equal-weighted investment in the three securities could provide.
   B. Calculate the expected total risk premium of the three securities and determine the investor's probable course of action.

2. Jo Akumba's portfolio is invested in a range of developed markets fixed income securities. She asks her adviser about the possibility of diversifying her investments to include emerging and frontier markets government and corporate fixed income securities. Her adviser makes the following comment regarding risk:

   All emerging and frontier market fixed income securities pose economic, political and legal risk. Economic risks arise from the fact that emerging market countries have poor fiscal discipline, rely on foreign borrowing, have less diverse tax base and significant dependence on specific industries. They are susceptible to capital flight. Their ability to pay is limited. In addition, weak property rights, weak enforcement of contract laws and political instability pose hazard for emerging markets debt investors.

Discuss the statement made.

3. An Australian investor currently holds a A$240 million equity portfolio. He is considering rebalancing the portfolio based on an assessment of the risk and return prospects facing the Australian economy. Information relating to the Australian investment markets and the economy has been collected in the following table:

10-Year Historical	Current	Capital Market Expectations
Average government bond yield: 2.8%	10-year government bond yield: 2.3%	
Average annual equity return: 4.6%	Year-over-year equity return: −9.4%	
Average annual inflation rate: 2.3%	Year-over-year inflation rate: 2.1%	Expected annual inflation: 2.3%
Equity market P/E (beginning of period): 15×	Current equity market P/E: 14.5×	Expected equity market P/E: 14.0×
Average annual dividend income return: 2.6%		Expected annual income return: 2.4%
Average annual real earnings growth: 6.0%		Expected annual real earnings growth: 5.0%

Using the information in the table, address the following problems:

A. Calculate the historical Australian equity risk premium using the "equity versus bonds" premium method.
B. Calculate the expected annual equity return using the Grinold–Kroner model (assume no change in the number of shares outstanding).
C. Using your answer to Part B, calculate the expected annual equity risk premium.

4. An analyst is reviewing various asset alternatives and is presented with the following information relating to the broad equity market of Switzerland and various industries within the Swiss market that are of particular investment interest.

Expected risk premium for overall global investable market (GIM) portfolio	3.5%
Expected standard deviation for the GIM portfolio	8.5%
Expected standard deviation for Swiss Healthcare Industry equity investments	12.0%
Expected standard deviation for Swiss Watch Industry equity investments	6.0%
Expected standard deviation for Swiss Consumer Products Industry equity investments	7.5%

Assume that the Swiss market is perfectly integrated with the world markets. Swiss Healthcare has a correlation of 0.7 with the GIM portfolio.

Swiss Watch has a correlation of 0.8 with the GIM portfolio.
Swiss Consumer Products has a correlation of 0.8 with the GIM portfolio.

A. Basing your answers only upon the data presented in the table above and using the international capital asset pricing model—in particular, the Singer–Terhaar approach—estimate the expected risk premium for the following:
   i) Swiss Health Care Industry
   ii) Swiss Watch Industry
   iii) Swiss Consumer Products Industry
B. Judge which industry is most attractive from a valuation perspective.

5. Identify risks faced by investors in emerging market equities over and above those that are faced by fixed income investors in such markets.

6. Describe the main issues that arise when conducting historical analysis of real estate returns.

7. An analyst at a real estate investment management firm seeks to establish expectations for rate of return for properties in the industrial sector over the next year. She has obtained the following information:

Current industrial sector capitalization rate ("cap" rate)	5.7%
Expected cap rate at the end of the period	5.5%
NOI growth rate (real)	1%
Inflation expectation	1.5%

Estimate the expected return from the industrial sector properties based on the data provided.

8. A client has asked his adviser to explain the key considerations in forecasting exchange rates. The adviser's firm uses two broad complementary approaches when setting expectations for exchange rate movements, namely focus on trade in goods and services and, secondly, focus on capital flows. Identify the main considerations that the adviser should explain to the client under the two approaches.

9. Looking independently at each of the economic observations below, indicate the country where an analyst would expect to see a strengthening currency for each observation.

	Country X	Country Y
Expected inflation over next year	2.0%	3.0%
Short-term (1-month) government rate	Decrease	Increase
Expected (forward-looking) GDP growth over next year	2.0%	3.3%
New national laws have been passed that enable foreign direct investment in real estate/financial companies	Yes	No
Current account surplus (deficit)	8%	−1%

10. Fap is a small country whose currency is the Fip. Three years ago, the exchange rate was considered to be reflecting purchasing power parity (PPP). Since then, the country's inflation has exceeded inflation in the other countries by about 5% per annum. The Fip exchange rate, however, remained broadly unchanged.

> *What would you have expected the Fip exchange rate to show if PPP prevailed?*
> *Are Fips over or undervalued, according to PPP?*

The following information relates to Questions 11–18.

Richard Martin is chief investment officer for the Trunch Foundation (the foundation), which has a large, globally diversified investment portfolio. Martin meets with the foundation's fixed-income and real estate portfolio managers to review expected return forecasts and potential investments, as well as to consider short-term modifications to asset weights within the total fund strategic asset allocation.

Martin asks the real estate portfolio manager to discuss the performance characteristics of real estate. The real estate portfolio manager makes the following statements:

Statement 1:   Adding traded REIT securities to an equity portfolio should substantially improve the portfolio's diversification over the next year.

Statement 2:   Traded REIT securities are more highly correlated with direct real estate and less highly correlated with equities over multi-year horizons.

Martin looks over the long-run valuation metrics the manager is using for commercial real estate, shown in Exhibit 1.

EXHIBIT 1   Commercial Real Estate Valuation Metrics

Cap Rate	GDP Growth Rate
4.70%	4.60%

The real estate team uses an in-house model for private real estate to estimate the true volatility of returns over time. The model assumes that the current observed return equals the weighted average of the current true return and the previous observed return. Because the true return is not observable, the model assumes a relationship between true returns and observable REIT index returns; therefore, it uses REIT index returns as proxies for both the unobservable current true return and the previous observed return.

Martin asks the fixed-income portfolio manager to review the foundation's bond portfolios. The existing aggregate bond portfolio is broadly diversified in domestic and international developed markets. The first segment of the portfolio to be reviewed is the domestic sovereign portfolio. The bond manager notes that there is a market consensus that the domestic yield curve will likely experience a single 20 bp increase in the near term as a result of monetary tightening and then remain relatively flat and stable for the next three years. Martin then reviews duration and yield measures for the short-term domestic sovereign bond portfolio in Exhibit 2.

EXHIBIT 2   Short-Term Domestic Sovereign Bond Portfolio

Macaulay Duration	Modified Duration	Yield to Maturity
3.00	2.94	2.00%

The discussion turns to the international developed fixed-income market. The foundation invested in bonds issued by Country XYZ, a foreign developed country. XYZ's sovereign yield curve is currently upward sloping, and the yield spread between 2-year and 10-year XYZ bonds is 100 bps.

The fixed-income portfolio manager tells Martin that he is interested in a domestic market corporate bond issued by Zeus Manufacturing Corporation (ZMC). ZMC has just been downgraded two steps by a major credit rating agency. In addition to expected monetary actions that will raise short-term rates, the yield spread between three-year sovereign bonds and the next highest-quality government agency bond widened by 10 bps.

Although the foundation's fixed-income portfolios have focused primarily on developed markets, the portfolio manager presents data in Exhibit 3 on two emerging markets for Martin to consider. Both economies increased exports of their mineral resources over the last decade.

EXHIBIT 3   Emerging Market Data

Factor	Emerging Republic A	Emerging Republic B
Fiscal deficit/GDP	6.50%	8.20%
Debt/GDP	90.10%	104.20%
Current account deficit	5.20% of GDP	7.10% of GDP
Foreign exchange reserves	90.30% of short-term debt	70.10% of short-term debt

The fixed-income portfolio manager also presents information on a new investment opportunity in an international developed market. The team is considering the bonds of Xdelp, a large energy exploration and production company. Both the domestic and international markets are experiencing synchronized growth in GDP midway between the trough and the peak of the business cycle. The foreign country's government has displayed a disciplined approach to maintaining stable monetary and fiscal policies and has experienced a rising current account surplus and an appreciating currency. It is expected that with the improvements in free cash flow and earnings, the credit rating of the Xdelp bonds will be upgraded. Martin refers to the foundation's asset allocation policy in Exhibit 4 before making any changes to either the fixed-income or real estate portfolios.

EXHIBIT 4   Trunch Foundation Strategic Asset Allocation—Select Data

Asset Class	Minimum Weight	Maximum Weight	Actual Weight
Fixed income—Domestic	40.00%	80.00%	43.22%
Fixed income—International	5.00%	10.00%	6.17%
Fixed income—Emerging markets	0.00%	2.00%	0.00%
Alternatives—Real estate	2.00%	6.00%	3.34%

11. Which of the real estate portfolio manager's statements is correct?
    A. Only Statement 1
    B. Only Statement 2
    C. Both Statement 1 and Statement 2
12. Based only on Exhibit 1, the long-run expected return for commercial real estate:
    A. is approximately double the cap rate.
    B. incorporates a cap rate greater than the discount rate.
    C. needs to include the cap rate's anticipated rate of change.
13. Based on the private real estate model developed to estimate return volatility, the true variance is *most likely*:
    A. lower than the variance of the observed data.

    B. approximately equal to the variance of the observed data.

    C. greater than the variance of the observed data.

14. Based on Exhibit 2 and the anticipated effects of the monetary policy change, the expected annual return over a three-year investment horizon will *most likely* be:

    A. lower than 2.00%.

    B. approximately equal to 2.00%.

    C. greater than 2.00%.

15. Based on the building block approach to fixed-income returns, the dominant source of the yield spread for Country XYZ is *most likely* the:

    A. term premium.

    B. credit premium.

    C. liquidity premium.

16. Using the building block approach, the required rate of return for the ZMC bond will *most likely*:

    A. increase based on the change in the credit premium.

    B. decrease based on the change in the default-free rate.

    C. decrease based on the change in the liquidity premium.

17. Based only on Exhibit 3, the foundation would *most likely* consider buying bonds issued by:

    A. only Emerging Republic A.

    B. only Emerging Republic B.

    C. neither Emerging Republic A nor Emerging Republic B.

18. Based only on Exhibits 3 and 4 and the information provided by the portfolio managers, the action *most likely* to enhance returns is to:

    A. decrease existing investments in real estate by 2.00%.

    B. initiate a commitment to emerging market debt of 1.00%.

    C. increase the investments in international market bonds by 1.00%.

The following information relates to Questions 19–26.

Judith Bader is a senior analyst for a company that specializes in managing international developed and emerging markets equities. Next week, Bader must present proposed changes to client portfolios to the Investment Committee, and she is preparing a presentation to support the views underlying her recommendations.

    Bader begins by analyzing portfolio risk. She decides to forecast a variance–covariance matrix (VCV) for 20 asset classes, using 10 years of monthly returns and incorporating both the sample statistics and the factor-model methods. To mitigate the impact of estimation error, Bader is considering combining the results of the two methods in an alternative target VCV matrix, using shrinkage estimation.

    Bader asks her research assistant to comment on the two approaches and the benefits of applying shrinkage estimation. The assistant makes the following statements:

    Statement 1: Shrinkage estimation of VCV matrices will decrease the efficiency of the estimates versus the sample VCV matrix.

    Statement 2: Your proposed approach for estimating the VCV matrix will not be reliable because a sample VCV matrix is biased and inconsistent.

    Statement 3: A factor-based VCV matrix approach may result in some portfolios that erroneously appear to be riskless if any asset returns can be completely determined by the common factors or some of the factors are redundant.

Bader then uses the Singer–Terhaar model and the final shrinkage-estimated VCV matrix to determine the equilibrium expected equity returns for all international asset classes by country. Three of the markets under consideration are located in Country A (developed market), Country B (emerging market), and Country C (emerging market). Bader projects that in relation to the global market, the equity market in Country A will remain highly integrated, the equity market in Country B will become more segmented, and the equity market in Country C will become more fully integrated.

Next, Bader applies the Grinold–Kroner model to estimate the expected equity returns for the various markets under consideration. For Country A, Bader assumes a very long-term corporate earnings growth rate of 4% per year (equal to the expected nominal GDP growth rate), a 2% rate of net share repurchases for Country A's equities, and an expansion rate for P/E multiples of 0.5% per year.

In reviewing Countries B and C, Bader's research assistant comments that emerging markets are especially risky owing to issues related to politics, competition, and accounting standards. As an example, Bader and her assistant discuss the risk implications of the following information related to Country B:

- Experiencing declining per capita income
- Expected to continue its persistent current account deficit below 2% of GDP
- Transitioning to International Financial Reporting Standards, with full convergence scheduled to be completed within two years

Bader shifts her focus to currency expectations relative to clients' base currency and summarizes her assumptions in Exhibit 5.

EXHIBIT 5   Baseline Assumptions for Currency Forecasts

	Country A	Country B	Country C
Historical current account	Persistent current account deficit of 5% of GDP	Persistent current account deficit of 2% of GDP	Persistent current account surplus of 2% of GDP
Expectation for secular trend in current account	Rising current account deficit	Narrowing current account deficit	Rising current account surplus
Long-term inflation expectation relative to global inflation	Expected to rise	Expected to keep pace	Expected to fall
Capital flows	Steady inflows	Hot money flowing out	Hot money flowing in

During a conversation about Exhibit 5, Bader and her research assistant discuss the composition of each country's currency portfolio and the potential for triggering a crisis. Bader notes that some flows and holdings are more or less supportive of the currency, stating that investments in private equity make up the majority of Country A's currency portfolio, investments in public equity make up the majority of Country B's currency portfolio, and investments in public debt make up the majority of Country C's currency portfolio.

19. Which of the following statements made by Bader's research assistant is correct?
    A. Statement 1
    B. Statement 2
    C. Statement 3

20. Based on expectations for changes in integration with the global market, all else being equal, the Singer–Terhaar model implies that Bader should shift capital from Country A to:
    A. only Country B.
    B. only Country C.
    C. both Countries B and C.

21. Using the Grinold–Kroner model, which of the following assumptions for forecasting Country A's expected equity returns is plausible for the very long run?
    A. Rate of net share repurchases
    B. Corporate earnings growth rate
    C. Expansion rate for P/E multiples

22. Based only on the emerging markets discussion, developments in which of the following areas *most likely* signal increasing risk for Country B's equity market?
    A. Politics
    B. Competitiveness
    C. Accounting standards

23. Based on Bader's expectations for current account secular trends as shown in Exhibit 5, Bader should reallocate capital, all else being equal, from:
    A. Country A to Country C.
    B. Country B to Country A.
    C. Country C to Country A.

24. Based on Bader's inflation expectations as shown in Exhibit 5, purchasing power parity implies that which of the following countries' currencies should depreciate, all else being equal?
    A. Country A
    B. Country B
    C. Country C

25. Based on Exhibit 5, which country's central bank is *most likely* to buy domestic bonds near term to sterilize the impact of money flows on domestic liquidity?
    A. Country A
    B. Country B
    C. Country C

26. Based on the composition of each country's currency portfolio, which country is most vulnerable to a potential crisis?
    A. Country A
    B. Country B
    C. Country C

CHAPTER 8

ASSET ALLOCATION TO ALTERNATIVE INVESTMENTS

Adam Kobor, PhD, CFA, and Mark D. Guinney, CFA

LEARNING OUTCOMES

The candidate should be able to:

- explain the roles that alternative investments play in multi-asset portfolios;
- compare alternative investments and bonds as risk mitigators in relation to a long equity position;
- compare traditional and risk-based approaches to defining the investment opportunity set, including alternative investments;
- discuss investment considerations that are important in allocating to different types of alternative investments;
- discuss suitability considerations in allocating to alternative investments;
- discuss approaches to asset allocation to alternative investments;
- discuss the importance of liquidity planning in allocating to alternative investments;
- discuss considerations in monitoring alternative investment programs.

1. INTRODUCTION AND THE ROLE OF ALTERNATIVE INVESTMENTS IN A MULTI-ASSET PORTFOLIO

Asset allocation is a critical decision in the investment process. The mathematical and analytical processes inherent in contemporary asset allocation techniques are complicated by the idiosyncrasies of alternative investments. Approaches to incorporating alternative assets into the strategic asset allocation have developed rapidly as allocations to assets other than stocks and bonds have accelerated in the aftermath of the 2008 global financial crisis. The term "alternative" understates the prominence of alternative investment allocations in many investment programs, because institutional and private clients have been increasingly turning to these investments not just to supplement traditional long-only stocks and bonds but also sometimes to replace them altogether. For example, the Yale Endowment and the Canada Pension Plan Investment Board both have close to 50% of their assets allocated to alternatives.[1] Although these two funds are admittedly outliers, between 2008 and 2017 most of the pension funds around the world substantially expanded their allocations to alternative asset classes. On average, pension funds in developed markets increased their allocation from 7.2% to 11.8% of assets under management (AUM) in 2017, a 63% increase.[2]

"Alternative" investment has no universally accepted definition. For the purposes of this reading, alternative investments include private equity, hedge funds, real assets (including energy and commodity investments), commercial real estate, and private credit.

The reading begins with a discussion of the role alternative assets play in a multi-asset portfolio and explores how alternatives may serve to mitigate long-only equity risk, a role traditionally held by bonds. We then consider different ways investors may define the opportunity set—through the traditional asset class lens or, more recently, using a risk- or factor-based lens. An allocation to alternatives is not for all investors, so the reading describes issues that should be addressed when considering an allocation to alternatives. We then discuss approaches to asset allocation when incorporating alternatives in the opportunity set and the need for liquidity planning in private investment alternatives. Finally, the reading discusses the unique monitoring requirements for an alternatives portfolio.

1.1. The Role of Alternative Investments in a Multi-asset Portfolio

Allocations to alternatives are playing an increasing role in investor portfolios largely driven by the belief that these investments increase the risk-adjusted return expectations for their programs. Some allocations are driven by expectations of higher returns, while others are driven by the expected diversification (risk-reduction) benefits. In the aggregate, the portfolio's *risk-adjusted* return is expected to improve. Exhibit 1 provides a framework for how the common alternative strategies are generally perceived to affect the risk/return profile of a "typical" 60/40 portfolio of public stocks and bonds.

EXHIBIT 1   Alternative Investments in the Risk/Reward Continuum

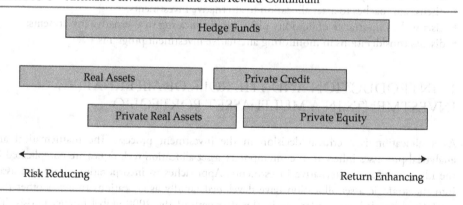

[1]Boston Consulting Group (BCG), "The Rise of Alternative Assets and Long-Term Investing" (March 2017).
[2]See Ivashina and Lerner 2018.

Although we present a simplified view, real assets are generally believed to mitigate the risks to the portfolio arising from unexpected inflation. At the other end of the spectrum, venture capital investments (private equity) are expected to provide a sufficient return premium over public equities to compensate for their illiquidity risk and heightened operational complexity. Hedge funds, the least homogenous of strategies, span the spectrum from "risk reducing" or diversifying (many arbitrage strategies) to "return enhancing" (e.g., an activist fund that takes significant positions in public companies with the goal of improving performance through management changes, capital allocation policies, and/or company strategy).

Risk reduction can mean different things to different investors. Institutions may choose to add non-correlated strategies to their portfolios to reduce the volatility of the overall investment program. Private clients are frequently concerned with reducing only downside volatility—the "left tail" risk associated with significant public equity market drawdowns. An insurance pool whose liabilities are sensitive to inflation might benefit from real assets that could reduce its asset–liability mismatch. Exhibit 2 provides some guidance as to how an allocator might view alternative assets vis-à-vis traditional asset classes.

In the context of asset allocation, investors may categorize an asset class based on the role it is expected to play in the overall portfolio. The roles and their relative importance will vary among investors, but it is common to identify the following functional roles:

- *Capital growth*: This role may be a top priority for portfolios with a long-term time horizon and relatively high-return target. Usually, public and private equity investments would be the most obvious choices for this role.
- *Income generation*: Certain asset classes, like fixed income or real estate, are capable of generating reasonably steady cash flow stream for investors.
- *Risk diversification*: In the case of an equity-oriented portfolio, investors may seek assets that diversify the dominant equity risk. Real assets and several hedge fund strategies may fit here. Similarly, fixed-income investors may be interested in diversifying pure yield curve risk via private credit.
- *Safety*: Certain asset classes may play the role of safe haven when most of the risky asset classes suffer. Government bonds or gold may potentially play such roles in a well-diversified portfolio.

EXHIBIT 2 Illustrative Capital Market Assumptions

	Traditional Assets				Alternative Assets					
	Public Equities	Cash	Govt Bonds	Broad Fixed Income	Private Credit	Hedge Funds	Commodities	Public Real Estate	Private Real Estate	Private Equity
Expected Return (Geometric Average)	6.5%	2.0%	2.3%	2.8%	6.5%	5.0%	4.5%	6.0%	5.5%	8.5%
Volatility	17.0%	1.1%	4.9%	3.4%	10.0%	8.1%	25.2%	20.4%	13.8%	15.7%
Correlation with Equities	1.00	−0.12	−0.60	−0.41	0.70	0.83	0.21	0.60	0.37	0.81
Equity Beta	1.00	−0.01	−0.17	−0.08	0.40	0.40	0.31	0.72	0.30	0.74

Source: Authors' own data.

Exhibit 3 illustrates how each of the alternative assets is generally perceived to fulfill these functional roles.

EXHIBIT 3   The Role of Asset Classes in a Multi-Asset Portfolio

Asset Class		Capital Growth	Income	Diversifying Public Equities	Safety
Fixed Income and Credit	Governments		M	H	H
	Inflation-Linked		M	H	H/M
	Inv.-Grade Credit		M	H	M
	High-Yield Credit		H	M	
	Private Credit		H	M	
Equities	Public Equity	H	M		
	Private Equity	H	M	M	
Real Estate	Public Real Estate	M	H	M	
	Private Real Estate	M	H	M	
Real Assets	Public Real Assets (Energy, Metal, etc.)			H	
	Private Real Assets (Timber, etc.)	H	H	H	
Hedge Funds	Absolute Return		M	H	
	Equity Long/Short			M	

Notes: H = high/strong potential to fulfill the indicated role; M = moderate potential to fulfill the indicated role.

Exhibit 4 illustrates the potential contributions the various alternative strategies might make to a portfolio dominated by equity risk. Note that the graph illustrates the *average* investment characteristics of each asset class over some extended period of time. Some assets—gold, for example—may not consistently exhibit attractive *aggregate* characteristics compared to other strategies but may serve the portfolio well during many major market shocks.

1.1.1. The Role of Private Equity in a Multi-Asset Portfolio

Private equity investments are generally viewed as a return enhancer in a portfolio of traditional assets. The expectation for a return premium over public equities stems from the illiquidity risk that comes with most forms of private equity investment. Because of the strong link between the fundamentals of private and public companies, there are limited diversification benefits when added to a portfolio that otherwise contains significant public equity exposure. Private equity volatility is not directly observable because holdings are not publicly traded. Assets tend to be

EXHIBIT 4   Diversification Potential of Various Alternative Asset Classes

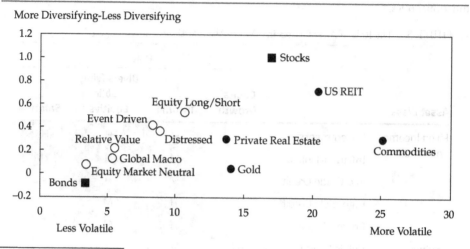

More Diversifying-Less Diversifying

Sources: Bloomberg and authors' own data and calculations.

valued at the lower of cost or the value at which the company raises additional capital or when ownership changes hands (e.g., through an initial public offering or a sale to a strategic buyer or to another private equity sponsor). Consequently, private equity indexes do not provide a true picture of the strategy's risk. For asset allocation exercises, volatility is often estimated using a public equity proxy with an adjustment to better represent the nature of the private equity program. For example, a proxy for early stage venture capital might be microcap technology companies. A proxy for buyout funds might start with the volatility of a geographically relevant large-cap equity index (e.g., S&P 500, Nikkei), which is then adjusted for relative financial leverage.

1.1.2. The Role of Hedge Funds in a Multi-Asset Portfolio
As illustrated in Exhibit 1, hedge funds span the spectrum from being risk reducers to return enhancers. Generally speaking, long/short equity strategies are believed to deliver equity-like returns with less than full exposure to the equity premium but with an additional source of return that might come from the manager's shorting of individual stocks. Short-biased equity strategies are expected to lower a portfolio's overall equity beta while producing some measure of alpha. Arbitrage and event-driven strategies, executed properly, look to exploit small inefficiencies in the public markets while exhibiting low to no correlation with traditional asset classes. However, most hedge fund arbitrage strategies involve some degree of "short volatility" risk. Because of this "short volatility" risk, the volatility in an arbitrage strategy is non-symmetrical; the aggregate volatility may look muted if the period from which the data are drawn does not include a market stress period. "Opportunistic" strategies (e.g., global macro and managed futures), although very volatile as stand-alone strategies, provide exposures not otherwise readily accessible in traditional stock and bond strategies.

1.1.3. The Role of Real Assets in a Multi-asset Portfolio
This category includes timber, commodities, farmland, energy, and infrastructure assets. The common thread for these investments is that the underlying investment is a physical asset with a relatively high degree of correlation with inflation broadly or with a sub-component

of inflation, such as oil (energy funds), agricultural products (farmland), or pulp and wood products (timber).

Timber investments provide both growth and inflation-hedging properties in a multi-asset portfolio. Growth is provided through the biological growth of the tree itself as well as through the appreciation in the underlying land value. Timber's inflation-hedging characteristics are derived from the unique nature in which the value of the asset is realized: If the market for timber products is weak, the owner of the asset can leave it "on the stump" waiting for prices to rise. While waiting, the volume of the asset increases—the tree continues to grow—and there is ultimately more of the asset to sell when prices recover. At the same time, the volatility of the timber asset rises; the market for more mature timber is more volatile, and the potential loss from pests and natural disasters rises.

Commodities investments (i.e., tradable commodities) fall into the following four categories:

1. Metals (gold, silver, platinum, copper)
2. Energy (crude oil, natural gas, heating oil, gasoline)
3. Livestock and Meat (hogs, pork bellies, live cattle)
4. Agricultural (corn, soybeans, wheat, rice, cocoa, coffee, cotton, sugar)

Although it is possible to own the commodity asset directly (e.g., corn, wheat, barrel of oil), most investors will invest in commodity derivatives (i.e., futures contracts) whose price is directly related to the price of the physical commodity. Investors generally own commodities as a hedge against a core constituent of inflation measures as well as a differentiated source of alpha. Gold and other precious metals are frequently owned directly because they are thought to be a good store of value in the face of a depreciating currency. Storage and insurance costs come with owning commodities directly.

Farmland investing involves two primary approaches. The higher return/risk strategy involves owning the farmland while providing the farmer a salary for tending and selling the crops. The investor retains the commodity risk and the execution risk. This approach requires a long time horizon and has high sensitivity to natural disasters and regulatory risk, such as trade disputes. In the other main approach, the investor owns the farmland but leases the property to the farmer. The farmer retains the risk for execution and commodity prices. If an investor pursues this second strategy, farmland is more like core commercial real estate investing than a real asset (commodity) strategy.

Energy investments consist of strategies that focus on the exploration, development, transportation, and delivery of energy (primarily oil and natural gas-based energy sources but also increasingly wind, hydroelectric, and solar) as well as all the ancillary services that facilitate energy production. Investors usually do not own the land that holds the minerals. Most energy investments are executed through call-down, private equity-style funds and are usually long-dated, illiquid holdings. Energy assets are generally considered real assets because the investor owns the mineral rights to certain commodities (e.g., natural gas, oil, methane) that can be correlated with certain inflationary factors. Master limited partnerships (MLPs) are another frequently used vehicle for energy investments. MLPs generally construct and own the pipelines that carry oil or natural gas from the wellhead to the storage facility. MLPs rarely take ownership of the energy assets. The companies charge a fee based on the volume of oil/natural gas they transport. This fee is often pegged to the Producer Price Index.

Infrastructure is a strategy that typically involves the construction and maintenance of public-use projects, such as building bridges, toll roads, or airports. Because of the illiquid nature of these assets, the holding period associated with these funds can be even longer than the typical illiquid strategy, with some lasting 20 years or longer. These assets tend to generate stable or modestly growing income, and the asset itself often requires minimal upkeep or capital expenditures once built. The revenue generated by the assets tends to have high correlation with overall inflation, though it is often subject to regulatory risks because governmental agencies may be involved in price setting with certain jurisdictions and assets.

1.1.4. The Role of Commercial Real Estate in a Multi-asset Portfolio

Real estate investing involves the development, acquisition, management, and disposition of commercial properties, including retail, office, industrial, housing (including apartments), and hotels. Strategies range from *core,* the ownership of fully occupied properties and collecting rents, to *opportunistic,* ground-up property development (land acquisition, construction, and sale) and/or the purchase of distressed assets with the intent to rehabilitate them.

Real estate investments are believed to provide protection against unanticipated increases in inflation. Two fundamental attributes of real estate investment contribute to this inflation protection. Well-positioned properties frequently have the ability to increase rents in response to inflationary pressures, and the value of the physical buildings may increase with inflation (properties are often valued as a function of replacement cost). In this way, real estate contributes both income and capital gain potential to a portfolio. Building a diversified private commercial real estate program can be challenging for all but the largest and most sophisticated allocators. The public real estate market is a fraction of the size of the private real estate market, but it may be easier and cheaper to build a diversified real estate investment program in some geographies (e.g., United States, Europe) via the public markets. However, private real estate can offer exposures that are difficult if not impossible to achieve through publicly-traded real estate securities. Investing directly (or in a private fund) offers customization by geography, property type, and strategy (e.g., distressed, core, development).

1.1.5. The Role of Private Credit in a Multi-asset Portfolio

Private credit includes distressed investment and direct lending. Although both strategies involve the ownership of fixed-income assets, their roles in an investment program are quite different. Direct-lending assets are income-producing, and the asset owner assumes any default or recovery risks. Direct-lending assets generally behave like their public market counterparts with similar credit profiles (i.e., high-quality, direct-lending assets behave like investment-grade bonds, and low-quality, direct-lending assets behave like high-yield bonds). Distressed debt assets have a more equity-like profile. The expected return is derived from the value of a company's assets relative to its debt. Illiquidity risks are high with both strategies. Direct-lending assets have no secondary market.

Direct-lending funds provide capital to individuals and small businesses that generally cannot access more traditional lending channels. Some loans are unsecured while others might be backed by an asset, such as a house or car. Direct lending is one of the least liquid debt strategies because there is typically no secondary market for these instruments. Investors in direct-lending strategies gain access to a high-yielding but riskier segment of the debt market that is not available via the traditional public markets.

Distressed funds typically purchase the securities of an entity that is under stress and where the stress is relieved through legal restructuring or bankruptcy. The investment can take the form of debt or equity, and in many strategies, the manager often takes an active role throughout the restructuring or bankruptcy. Because many investors are precluded from owning companies or entities that are in bankruptcy or default, managers of distressed funds are often able to purchase assets (usually the debt) at a significant discount. Experience with the bankruptcy process frequently distinguishes these managers from others. Although the asset is usually a bond, distressed investments typically have low sensitivity to traditional bond risks (i.e., interest rate changes or changes in spreads) because the idiosyncratic risk of the company itself dominates all other risks.

2. DIVERSIFYING EQUITY RISK

In this section, we examine the claim that alternative assets may be better risk mitigators than government bonds. To address this question, we must agree on *which* risks alternatives are said to mitigate and on *what* time horizon is relevant. If your investment horizon is short term, volatility may be the most important risk measure. If you are a long-term investor, not achieving the long-horizon return objective may be the most relevant concern.

2.1. Volatility Reduction over the Short Time Horizon

Let's look first at the short horizon investor and consider how alternative asset classes compare to bonds as a volatility reducer in an equity-dominated portfolio. Advocates of alternative investments as risk reducers sometimes argue that alternative investments' volatilities calculated based on reported returns are significantly lower than the volatility of public equities. An immediate technical challenge is that reported returns of many alternative asset classes need an adjustment called **unsmoothing** for proper risk estimation. (Various approaches have been developed to unsmooth a return series that demonstrates serial correlation. The specifics of those approaches are beyond the scope of this reading.) In the case of private investments, reported returns are calculated from appraisal-based valuations that may result in volatility and correlation estimates that are too low. (The underlying assumptions in most appraisal models tend to lead to gradual and incremental changes in appraised value that may not accurately capture the asset's true price realized in an actual transaction. The low volatility of the return stream may also dampen the reported correlation between the appraisal-based asset and the more volatile market-based asset.) Other factors may also contribute to underestimated risk across alternatives. For example, **survivorship bias** and **back-fill bias** (reporting returns to a database only after they are known to be good returns) in hedge fund databases can potentially lead to an understatement of downside risk. Additionally, a hedge fund "index" includes many managers whose returns exhibit low correlation; in the same way that combining stocks and bonds in a portfolio can be expected to lower overall portfolio volatility, so too does combining several hedge funds into an "index."

As an example, we build a hypothetical, equally-weighted index of long/short equity hedge funds with volatilities ranging from 6% to 11%. As shown in Exhibit 5, given the less-than-perfect correlation among the constituents of our index, the index volatility is only 4.9%:

EXHIBIT 5   Volatility Is Less Than the Sum of Its Parts

	Fund 1	Fund 2	Fund 3	Fund 4	Fund 5	Combined
Volatility	10.9%	6.5%	8.5%	9.7%	8.1%	**4.9%**
Correlation						
Fund 1		−0.02	0.14	0.00	0.15	
Fund 2			0.27	0.39	0.29	
Fund 3				0.25	−0.03	
Fund 4					0.14	

Exhibit 6 shows the correlations of fixed-income and alternative asset classes to public equities based on observed market data over 1997–2017. We also show each asset class's estimated equity beta. To estimate correlations and betas, we used unsmoothed return data for alternative asset classes. We discuss unsmoothing of returns in more detail in a later section.

EXHIBIT 6   Fixed-Income's and Alternative's Equity Beta and Correlation with Equities

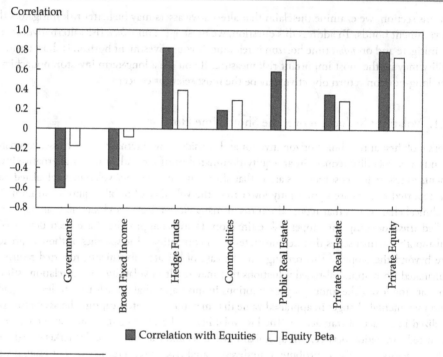

Sources: Bloomberg and authors' own data and calculations.

Most of the alternative investment categories had positive, but less than perfect, correlation with equities. Although certain alternatives (e.g., commodities, particularly gold) may rally during a public equity market downturn, other alternative investments—like hedge funds, private credit, or private equities—also experience drawdowns at the same time the equity market falls. Hedge funds and private equities have a correlation co-efficient with equities over +0.8, and this indicates a fairly strong positive relationship between public equities and these alternative investments.

Government bonds, however, have a −0.6 estimated correlation with equities, which indicates a negative relationship of moderate strength. This is consistent with the tendency for government bonds to serve as a risk haven during "risk-off" or "flight to quality" episodes.

Although correlation and beta have the same sign and are statistically interrelated, we have to remember that they quantify two different things. The correlation coefficient quantifies the strength of a linear relationship between two variables, thus playing a crucial role in portfolio diversification: The lower the correlation, the stronger the asset's diversification power. Beta, however, measures the response of an asset to a unit change in a reference index; for example, equity beta measures how various assets would respond to a 1% rise of public equities. Hedge funds' beta is estimated at around 0.4; thus, we would expect a 0.4% return (excluding manager alpha) from hedge funds if equities rose by 1%. Hedge funds' relatively low beta (0.4) and high correlation (+0.8) means that hedge funds' rise or fall is milder than those of public equities in magnitude, but this directional relationship is fairly strong in a statistical sense. Commodities also have an equity beta of similar positive magnitude (0.3), but their correlation with equities is much weaker (+0.2); so, we can expect that a much bigger portion of commodity price changes would be driven by factors unrelated to the equity markets.

In Exhibit 7, we compare the total return volatility of public equities (black bar) with volatilities of portfolios comprised of 70% equity and 30% other asset classes. Using 20 years of data, the volatility of public equities is estimated at approximately 17%. A portfolio allocated 70% to equity and 30% to cash would imply a portfolio volatility of 11.9% (70% × 17%). Portfolios of 70% equities and 30% any of the alternative asset classes also reduces portfolio volatility relative to an all-equity portfolio, but the lowest volatility of 11.1% could be achieved by combining equities with government bonds because of the negative correlation between these two asset classes.

EXHIBIT 7   Volatility of Portfolios Comprised of 70% Equities and 30% Other Asset Class

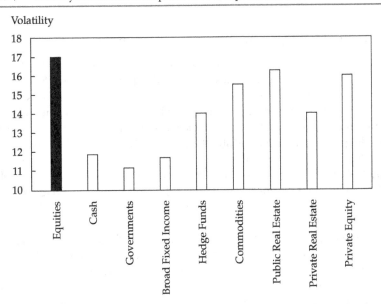

Sources: Bloomberg and authors' own data and calculations.

Bear in mind, however, that this analysis is based on 20 years of returns ending in 2017, a period that was characterized by a persistent negative equity–bond correlation. Because there was limited inflation in developed markets over this period, economic growth prospects were the dominant influence on asset prices. Positive growth surprises are good for equities (better earnings outlook) and negative for bonds (potential central bank rate increases). If inflation becomes a threat, bonds' risk mitigation power could erode. Exhibit 8 looks at the US equity–bond correlation since the 1950s. As the chart suggests, the correlation between US equities and government bonds was, in fact, positive in the 1970s through the 1990s when inflation was also more elevated.

EXHIBIT 8   Long-Term Historical Equity–Bond Correlation and Inflation

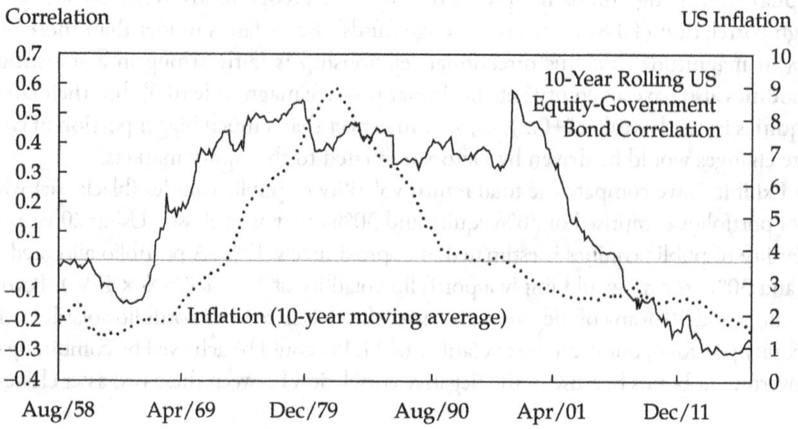

Sources: Bloomberg and the authors' own data and calculations.

2.2. Risk of Not Meeting the Investment Goals over the Long Time Horizon

Volatility is not always the most relevant risk measure. An endowment portfolio is often focused on generating a total return equal to at least the spending rate, say 5%, plus inflation to preserve real value of capital over a long time horizon. When bond yields are very low, the likelihood of meeting the investment objective would be reduced given a heavy allocation to bonds, simply because the portfolio's value would likely grow more slowly than the rate implied by the spending rate and inflation. Exhibit 9 illustrates this point: We show the probability of achieving a 5% real (7.1% nominal[3]) return over various horizons up to 10-years for three 70% equity/30% other asset class portfolios. We used quarterly rebalancing. Although allocating the 30% "other" to government bonds would lead to the greatest reduction in portfolio volatility, government bonds also have lower expected return compared to hedge funds and private equity (see Exhibit 2).

The 70% public equities/30% government bond portfolio has an expected return of 5.7%[4], below the nominal return target of 7.1%. The 70% public equities/30% private equities portfolio has an expected geometric return of 7.2%, slightly over the return target. Both portfolios' expected returns are 50th percentile returns; there is a 50% probability that this is the return that would be realized over time. Thus, the 70% public equities/30% private equities portfolio, with a nominal expected return of 7.2%, has slightly better than a 50% probability of meeting the 7.1% nominal return target. The 70% public equities/30% government

---

[3]By using the Fisher equation to combine the 5% real return and 2% inflation: (1 + 5%) * (1 + 2%) −1 = 7.1%.

[4]Note that geometric expected return is approximated as the expected arithmetic return minus half of the investment's variance. Thus, portfolio expected geometric return is not simply the weighted average of the asset classes' expected geometric returns because portfolio variance benefits from diversification.

EXHIBIT 9   The Probability of Achieving Investment Objectives over the Longer Time Horizon

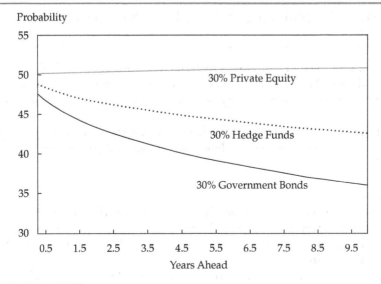

Note: Portfolios comprised of 70% equities and 30% other asset classes.

Source: Authors' calculations.

bond portfolio, with an expected return less than the nominal return target, therefore has less than a 50% probability of meeting the required return. Why does the 70% public equities/30% private equities portfolio maintain its 50%+ probability of meeting the return target over time while the probability that the 70% public equities/30% government bond portfolio meets the return target declines over time? As the time horizon lengthens, return accumulation (compounding) becomes more and more important. In a simplified way, return accumulates proportionally with time, whereas volatility scales with the square root of time. Thus, as we lengthen the time horizon, the gap between the cumulative return target and the expected return accumulation widens faster than the range of possible portfolio return outcomes. As a result, the likelihood of a low-returning portfolio catching up to the target return declines over time.

To summarize, bonds have been a more effective volatility mitigator than alternatives over shorter time horizons, but over long horizons, a heavy allocation to bonds would reduce the probability of achieving the investment goal. It is important to emphasize that volatility and the probability of achieving the target return are two very different dimensions of risk. Volatility addresses interim fluctuations in portfolio return, whereas achieving a return target takes on increasing importance as we expand the time horizon over multiple years. Both risks are important, especially for a program that is distributing 7% of assets per year as in this example. Although the 30% allocation to private equity increases the chance of meeting the expected return, a severe and sustained short-term drawdown in the public equity markets could significantly handicap the fund's ability to achieve its long-term return objectives. This is why drawdowns (related to volatility) need to be considered and managed.

EXAMPLE 1   Mitigating Equity Risk by Allocating to Hedge Funds or Bonds

The investment committee of a major foundation is concerned about high equity valuations and would like to increase the allocation either to hedge funds or to high-grade, fixed-income assets to diversify equity risk. As the risk manager of this foundation:

1. Discuss the justifications and the limitations of using bonds to mitigate equity risk.
2. Discuss the justifications and the limitations of using hedge funds to mitigate equity risk.

Solution to 1:
- Supporting argument: Bonds have exhibited negative correlation and beta to equities in a low inflation environment, so as long as inflation stays at or below average historical levels, this negative equity–bond correlation should lead to the highest reduction in portfolio volatility.
- Limitations: The negative stock/bond correlation may be temporary, and amid high inflation the stock/bond correlation could turn positive. Furthermore, if bonds' expected return is low, a heavy allocation to bonds may reduce the probability of achieving the foundation's long-term return objectives.

Solution to 2:
- Supporting argument: With an equity beta of around 0.4 (see Exhibit 2), hedge funds would reduce an equity-dominated portfolio's overall beta. With higher expected returns than bonds, an allocation to hedge funds would make achieving the long-term return target more feasible.
- Limitations: Although a well-constructed hedge fund portfolio may reduce portfolio volatility and beta, hedge funds are often highly actively managed, levered investment strategies, and individual hedge funds may suffer significant and permanent losses during turbulent times.

3. TRADITIONAL APPROACHES TO ASSET CLASSIFICATION

In this section, we consider how traditional approaches to asset allocation can be adapted to include alternative investments and how investors can apply risk-based approaches to incorporate alternatives in their asset allocation. This reading extends the asset allocation framework introduced in earlier readings on asset allocation. Although the ultimate goal of meeting the investment objectives subject to the relevant constraints remains the same, investors often face several analytical and operational challenges when introducing alternative asset classes.

3.1. Traditional Approaches to Asset Classification

When defining asset classes for the traditional approaches to asset allocation, investors may group and classify alternative assets along several dimensions. Two common approaches (in addition to the growth–income–diversification–safety roles described earlier) are with respect to the liquidity of the asset class and with respect to asset behavior under various economic conditions.

3.1.1. A Liquidity-Based Approach to Defining the Opportunity Set

Certain alternative investments, like REITs or commodity futures, are highly liquid and can be easily traded in public markets. Private investments, however, are highly illiquid and usually require long-term commitments (more than 10 years) from the investors. Of course, there are differences among various private asset classes in this respect as well. Private equity investments may require longer than a 10-year commitment, while the term of a private credit fund can be shorter, say 5 to 8 years. Although public equity and private equity may be similar asset classes from the fundamental economic point of view, they differ significantly in their liquidity characteristics.

The long investment horizon and the lack of liquidity in many of the alternative asset classes make it difficult to accurately characterize their risk characteristics for purposes of the asset allocation exercise. One approach to dealing with this issue is to make the initial asset allocation decision using only the broad, liquid asset classes in which the underlying data that drive risk, return, and correlation assumptions are robust (e.g., stocks, bonds, and real estate). A second iteration of the asset allocation exercise would break the equity/fixed-income/real estate asset allocation down further by using the asset groupings as shown in Exhibit 10, which illustrates a possible categorization of asset classes that incorporates their broad liquidity profile.

EXHIBIT 10   Major Asset Class Categories

	Equity & Equity-Like	Fixed Income & Fixed Income-Like	Real Estate
Marketable/Liquid	Public Equity	Fixed Income	Public Real Estate
	Long/Short Equity Hedge Funds	Cash	Commodities
Private/Illiquid	Private Equity	Private Credit	Private Real Estate Private Real Assets

3.1.2. An Approach Based on Expected Performance under Distinct Macroeconomic Regimes

Investors may also categorize asset classes based on how they are expected to behave under different macroeconomic environments, and investors may assign roles to them in a broad macroeconomic context:

- *Capital growth assets* would be expected to benefit from healthy economic growth. Public and private equities would belong to this category.
- *Inflation-hedging assets*—so-called "real assets" such as real estate, commodities, and natural resources but also inflation-linked bonds—would be expected to outperform other asset classes when inflation expectations rise or actual inflation exceeds expectations.
- *Deflation-hedging assets* (e.g., nominal government bonds) would be expected to outperform most of the other asset classes when the economy slows and inflation becomes very low or negative.

In Exhibit 11, we illustrate how investors may think about the expected performance of various asset classes in a broad macroeconomic context. Each asset class is positioned along the continuum to illustrate the macroeconomic environment in which we would expect it to generate strong performance. Such mapping is usually based on both historical experience and qualitative judgment. Considering the fundamental economic drivers of asset classes could help investors construct portfolios that are better diversified and more robust under various economic conditions and scenarios.

EXHIBIT 11　Asset Classes Grouped by the Macroeconomic Environment under Which They Would Be Expected to Generate Strong Performance

		Inflation Environment		
		Deflation	Moderate Inflation	High Inflation
Economic Environment	High Growth		Public Equity Private Equity High-Yield Bonds Private Credit	Real Estate Commodities
	Low Growth/ Recession	Government Bonds		Inflation-Linked Bonds Gold

Source: Authors' data.

Exhibit 12 illustrates the average quarterly total return of various asset classes and alternative strategies under stronger and weaker economic growth environments between 1997 and 2017, a period of low to moderate inflation in developed markets.

EXHIBIT 12　Historical Asset Class Performance under Stronger and Weaker Economic Growth Periods (1997–2017)

Average Quarterly Return (%)

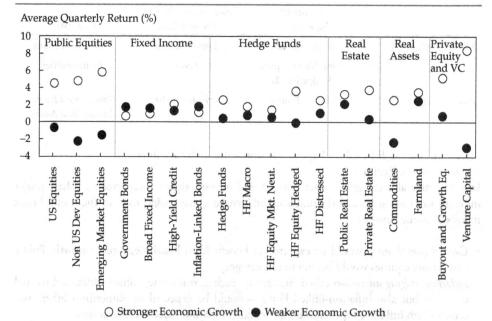

○ Stronger Economic Growth　● Weaker Economic Growth

Notes: Strong and weak economic periods were determined using quarterly GDP data. Strong growth periods were those quarters when GDP growth exceeded the average GDP growth through the full historical sample.

Sources: The exhibit is based on the authors' calculations. Index data is based on the following. US Equities: Russell 3000; Non-US Developed Market Equities: MSCI EAFE USD Net unhedged; Emerging Market Equities: MSCI Emerging Markets Net USD unhedged; Governments: Bloomberg Barclays US Treasury Index; Broad Fixed Income: Bloomberg Barclays US Aggregate; High Yield: Bloomberg Barclays US Corporate High Yield; Inflation-Linked Bonds: Bloomberg Barclays US Government Inflation-Linked Bonds Index; Hedge Funds: HFRI; Public Real Estate: Dow Jones Equity REIT Index; Private Real Estate: NCREIF Property Index; Commodities: S&P GSCI Total Return Index; Farmland: NCREIF Farmland Index; Buyout and Growth Equities: Cambridge Associates US Private Equity Index; Venture Capital: Cambridge Associates US Venture Capital Index.

Public and private equities, hedge funds, and commodities posted strong returns amid strong economic growth conditions and weaker returns amid weaker economic conditions. Commodities exhibit a bigger disparity between returns in periods of stronger and weaker growth than does the hedge fund category.

Within fixed income, government bonds posted higher returns during periods of weaker economic growth—when investors likely reallocated from risky assets to safer assets. On the other hand, high-yield bonds (and potentially private credit, if we assume a behavior pattern similar to that of high-yield bonds) performed well during periods of stronger economic growth but posted lower returns during weaker economic periods, likely because of concerns about weakening credit quality.

Understanding how various asset classes behave under distinct macroeconomic regimes enables investors to tailor the asset allocation to align with their fundamental goals or to mitigate their fundamental risks. If the investment portfolio has a specific goal, such as hedging inflation risk, then it would be logical to build a portfolio that is dominated by asset classes that are expected to perform best amid rising inflation. Even if the portfolio's goal is to generate high return over the long run, combining "growth" asset classes with "inflation-hedging" or "deflation-hedging" asset classes could make the asset allocation more resilient to changing economic and market conditions. This approach can be extended to macroeconomic scenario analysis and stress testing when the analyst evaluates how various asset allocation options would perform under conditions of high or low economic growth and/or inflation, and it can identify which economic conditions would hurt the investment portfolio the most.

4. RISK-BASED APPROACHES TO ASSET CLASSIFICATION AND COMPARING RISK-BASED AND TRADITIONAL APPROACHES

When we assign traditional and alternative asset classes to certain functional roles in the portfolio, or when we assess how different asset classes would perform under distinct macroeconomic regimes, we can also easily realize that many traditional and alternative asset classes share similar characteristics that can result in high correlations. We may put public equities in the same functional bucket as private equity, and we may expect elevated default rates from high-yield bonds and private credit during recessionary environments.

Exhibit 13 compares the betas of various traditional and alternative asset classes to global equities. The chart clearly shows that private equity and venture capital asset classes have global equity betas similar to public equites. On the other hand, betas of various hedge fund strategies differ significantly. Hedge fund returns, in aggregate, had a beta of 0.4. However, global macro or equity market-neutral strategies had betas as low as 0.1. The long/short "equity hedged" strategy's beta is estimated to be much higher, around 0.5, which is consistent with its long equity bias.

Many investors have begun to view asset allocation through a risk factor lens to capture these similarities. In this section, we extend the risk factor asset allocation framework introduced in earlier readings to alternative investments using the following risk factors:

- *Equity market return*: representative of the general direction of global equity markets, and investors may also refer to this as the best market proxy for "growth."
- *Size*: excess return of small-cap equities over large-cap equities.
- *Value*: excess return of value versus growth stocks (*negative* factor sensitivity = *growth* bias.

EXHIBIT 13   Global Equity Beta of Various Asset Classes, 1997–2017

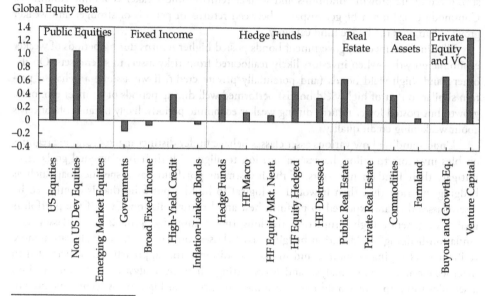

Note: Betas were estimated as a regression slope of representative index returns relative to the global equity return stream over the time period 1997–2017.

Sources: Authors' calculations; index data sources are the same as those in Exhibit 12.

- *Liquidity*: the Pastor–Stambaugh liquidity factor[5]—a market-wide liquidity measure based on the excess returns of stocks with large sensitivity to changes in aggregate liquidity (less-liquid stocks) versus stocks with less sensitivity to changing liquidity (more-liquid stocks).
- *Duration*: sensitivity to 10-year government yield changes.
- *Inflation*: sensitivity to 10-year breakeven inflation changes obtained from the inflation-linked bond markets.
- *Credit spread*: sensitivity to changes in high-yield spread.
- *Currency*: sensitivity to changes in the domestic currency versus a basket of foreign currencies.

This framework can easily be extended further to other risk factors, like momentum or volatility.

Exhibit 14 illustrates risk factor sensitivities of various traditional and alternative investment strategies using a construct as discussed by Naik, Devarajan, Nowobilski, Page, and Pedersen (2016). The parameters in the table are regression coefficients based on 20 years of historical data. Quarterly index returns representing each asset class were regressed on the risk factors listed previously. Note that for conventional reasons we changed the signs of the nominal duration and credit spread sensitivities. The 4.2 duration of broad fixed income, for example, means that this asset class would experience an approximate 4.2% decline in response to a 100 bps increase in the nominal interest rates.

---

[5] For more details on Pastor–Stambaugh liquidity factors, see Naik et al. (2016).

EXHIBIT 14 Factor Sensitivity Estimates across Various Asset Classes

Asset Classes	Equity	Size	Value	Liquidity	Nominal Duration	Inflation	Credit Spread	Currency	R-squared
US Equities	1.0								1.00
Non-US Dev Equities	0.9							0.7	0.86
Emerging Mkt Equities	1.1	0.5						0.5	0.66
Government Bonds					4.8				0.96
Broad Fixed Income					4.2		0.6		0.89
High-Yield Credit					4.1		4.2		0.95
Inflation-Linked Bonds					6.6	7.0			0.82
Hedge Funds	0.3	0.1					0.6		0.74
HF Macro	0.2	0.2			1.9	3.1	−0.9	0.1	0.28
HF Equity Mkt. Neut.	0.1								0.14
HF Equity Hedged	0.5								0.72
HF Distressed	0.1	0.2					1.8		0.72
Commodities						18.0		0.8	0.36
Public Real Estate	0.9				4.6	0.9			0.38
Private Real Estate	0.2			0.1		2.4			0.20
Buyout & Growth Equities	0.6	0.2	−0.3	0.1					0.70
Venture Capital	0.8	0.6	−1.8	0.2					0.38

Note: Only statistically significant slopes are displayed in the exhibit. Sources are the same as those for Exhibit 12.

In a risk factor–based asset allocation framework, the factors represent the systematic risks embedded in the selected asset classes and investment strategies. The primary systematic risk factors would fully, or almost fully, explain the behavior of broad, passive traditional public asset classes. There should be a relatively larger portion of unexplained risk in the alternative asset classes. This arises from such issues as the appraisal-based valuation in real estate, the idiosyncratic risks in the portfolio companies of private equity funds, or the idiosyncratic risks in hedge funds resulting from active management. (This last one is logically intuitive if you subscribe to the belief that returns generated by hedge fund strategies should be primarily driven by *alpha* rather than systematic risk factors.)

The extension of the risk factor framework to alternative asset classes allows every asset class to be described using the same framework. Investors can therefore more clearly understand their sources of investment risk and identify the intended and unintended tilts and biases they have in the portfolio. Furthermore, a risk factor framework enables investors to more efficiently allocate capital and risk in a multi-dimensional framework (i.e., a framework that seeks to do more than simply achieve the highest return at a given level of volatility). If an investor, for example, would like to increase the portfolio's inflation risk-mitigating exposure, decomposing this specific risk factor from inflation-linked bonds, real estate, or commodity asset classes could help the investor to identify the asset classes and exposures that are most likely to facilitate that goal.

Risk factor–based approaches improve upon the traditional approaches in identifying the investment opportunity set but do have certain limitations. As mentioned earlier, a small set of systematic risk factors is insufficient to describe the historical return stream of alternative asset classes. Note that all non-zero-risk factor coefficients displayed in the table are statistically significant based on their *t*-statistics. Although our eight illustrative factors fit the total return history of traditional asset classes with *r*-squared statistics of 0.8–1.0, the *r*-squared ratios for alternative investments are lower, ranging between 0.3 and 0.7. Increasing the number of risk factors would certainly improve the goodness of fit, but too many factors could make the risk factor–based asset allocation framework difficult to handle and interpret. In addition, certain risk factor sensitivities can be quite volatile, making a "point in time" factor–based definition of an asset class a poor descriptor of the class's expected behavior. For example, the aggregate hedge fund inflation beta typically fluctuates in the range of 0.3 to 0.4, while the inflation beta of commodities fluctuates much more widely.[6]

EXAMPLE 2   Applying Risk Factors for Inflation Hedging

1. The CIO (chief investment officer) of the United Retired Workers Plan would like to reduce inflation risk in the portfolio. Based on the data displayed in Exhibit 14, which asset classes would you recommend as potential inflation-hedging tools?
2. The CIO is not only concerned about inflation but also rising interest rates. Which alternative asset classes would you recommend for consideration?

---

[6]For further detail on expanding asset allocation to risk allocation, we refer to Naik et al. (2016) and Cambridge Associates LLC (2013).

Solution to 1: Commodities and inflation-linked bonds have the highest factor sensitivity to inflation, so they are the most obvious candidates. Real estate (both public and private) also has some potential to protect against inflation. Based on the data presented, macro hedge fund strategies also exhibited a positive inflation beta, but given their active nature, further analysis may be needed before choosing them as inflation-hedging vehicles.

Solution to 2: Commodities and private real estate would be the likely asset classes to hedge against rising interest rates, given their zero-factor sensitivity to nominal duration. Some of the hedge fund strategies also show zero-factor sensitivity to duration, but the relationship may not hold true in the future given the actively managed nature of hedge funds. Although Exhibit 14 indicates equity strategies (both public and private) also show little to no sensitivity to rising interest rates (duration) bonds and equities have been more highly correlated in the past.

4.1. Illustration: Asset Allocation and Risk-Based Approaches

Let's look at an example of how a risk-based approach may enhance traditional asset allocation. In Exhibit 15, we show two investment portfolios, Portfolio A and Portfolio B, that have exactly the same high-level asset allocations. However, the underlying investments in the two portfolios are quite different. The fixed-income assets in Portfolio A are government bonds, while the fixed-income assets in Portfolio B are high-yield bonds. Hedge fund investments in Portfolio A are represented by very low equity beta market neutral strategies, while Portfolio B is invested in the higher beta long/short equity hedge funds. Similarly, Portfolio B's investments in real assets and private equity have higher risk than those in Portfolio A.

As a result of these major differences between nominally similar broad asset allocations, it is not surprising that Portfolio B has higher volatility, beta, and expected return compared to Portfolio A. Let's look more closely at the risk contribution of each of the following asset classes.

4.1.1. Portfolio A.

The majority of the risk in Portfolio A comes from public and private equity. Hedge funds contribute approximately 5% to the total risk, and fixed income actually reduces risk because government bonds had negative correlations with public equities in our historical data sample.

4.1.2. Portfolio B.

Private equity explains about half of the total portfolio risk of Portfolio B. (In this portfolio, the private equity allocation is represented by the higher risk venture capital.) Public equities, hedge funds, and real assets each contribute roughly the same to the total risk of the portfolio. This is consistent with the equity-like characteristics of the underlying assets in the portfolio. The long/short equity hedged strategy has an equity beta of around 0.5, and REITs have an equity beta of 0.9. In Portfolio B, fixed income contributes positively to total risk, consistent with high-yield bonds' positive correlation with equities over the time series.

EXHIBIT 15   Traditional Asset Allocation and Risk Contribution Comparison

	Asset Allocation		Underlying Investments		% Contribution to Risk	
Broad Asset Classes	Portfolio A	Portfolio B	Portfolio A	Portfolio B	Portfolio A	Portfolio B
Fixed Income	20%	20%	Government Bonds	High-Yield Bonds	−6.5%	7.6%
Public Equities	20%	20%	US Equities	Non-US Developed Equities	51.4%	18.2%
Hedge Funds	20%	20%	Equity Market Neutral	Long/Short Equity	5.4%	11.1%
Real Assets	20%	20%	Inflation-linked bonds	REITs	0.7%	13.2%
Private Equity	20%	20%	Buyout	Venture Capital	48.9%	49.8%
Total	**100%**	**100%**				
			Expected Return		**5.3%**	**8.8%**
			Volatility		**5.9%**	**16.5%**
			Equity Beta		**0.30**	**0.79**

Notes: The percentage contribution to risk is a result of three components: the asset allocation to a specific asset, its volatility, and its correlation with the other assets. For fixed income, the contribution to total risk is negative in the case of Portfolio A because government bonds have negative correlations with other asset classes; however, it is positive in the case of Portfolio B because high-yield bonds have positive correlations with the other asset classes.

Source: Authors' calculations.

Although the nominal asset allocations of the two portfolios are the same, the risk profile and the risk allocation among asset classes are significantly different. Let's go one step further and apply the risk factor sensitivities of Exhibit 14 to our hypothetical portfolios. Exhibit 16 shows the absolute contribution to total portfolio risk by risk factor. This approach moves beyond the borders of asset classes and aggregates the equity risk factor embedded in public equities, private equities, venture capital, and REITs into a single-factor contribution. Both portfolios are highly dominated by exposure to equity risk. Portfolio A's total risk is almost fully explained by the exposure to the equity factor, while about 70% of Portfolio B's total risk comes from the equity risk factor alone. Portfolio B also has exposure to the size and value factors, driven by the allocation to venture capital. Finally, we can also see that although Portfolio B is not directly investing in government bonds, some risk mitigation benefit still arises from the low "duration" component of high-yield bonds and REITs.

EXHIBIT 16   Absolute Contribution to Total Risk by Risk Factors

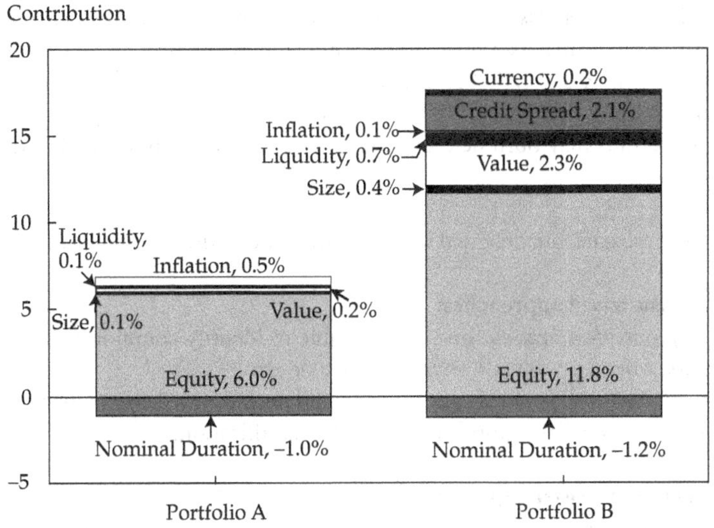

This is an extreme example (the two portfolios have vastly different expected returns), but it is useful to illustrate how factor sensitivities can be used to explore the underlying risk exposures in seemingly similar asset allocations.

4.2. Comparing Risk-Based and Traditional Approaches

Investors often employ multiple approaches in setting their asset allocation for a portfolio that includes alternative investments. When applying these various approaches, investors must consider their strengths and limitations.

Main strengths of traditional approaches:
* *Easy to communicate.* Listing the roles of various asset classes is intuitive and easy to explain to the decision makers, who often have familiarity with the traditional asset class-based approach. Scenario analyses based on historical or expected behavior of various

asset classes under different macroeconomic conditions can help to introduce quantitative aspects of the portfolio's expected performance and risk and substantiate the asset allocation proposal.
- *Relevance for liquidity management and operational considerations.* Public and private asset class mandates have vastly distinct liquidity profiles. Thus, although private and public equity would have a lot of commonality in their risk factor exposures, they would be positioned very differently from a liquidity management perspective. Similarly, investors must implement the target asset allocation by allocating to investment managers. The traditional categorization of asset classes may be necessary to identify the relevant mandates—what portion of the equity portfolio she would like to allocate to equity-oriented hedge funds rather than to long-only equity managers.

Main limitations of traditional approaches:
- *Over-estimation of portfolio diversification.* Without a proper analytical framework for assessing risk, investors may have a false sense of diversification. An allocation spread across a large number of different asset classes may appear to be very well diversified, when, in fact, the underlying investments may be subject to the same underlying risks.
- *Obscured primary drivers of risk.* Investments with very different risk characteristics may be commingled under the same asset class category. For example, government bonds and high-yield bonds may both be classified as "fixed income," but each has distinct risk characteristics.

Risk-based approaches are designed to overcome some of these limitations.

Key benefits of risk-based approaches:
- *Common risk factor identification.* Investors are able to identify common risk factors across all investments, whether public or private, passive or active.
- *Integrated risk framework.* Investors are able to build an integrated risk management framework, leading to more reliable portfolio-level risk quantification.

Key limitations of risk-based approaches:
- *Sensitivity to the historical look-back period.* Empirical risk factor exposure estimations may be sensitive to the historical sample. For example, the duration of a bond portfolio or the beta of a diversified equity portfolio could be reasonably stable, but the estimated inflation sensitivity of real assets can change rapidly over time. Thus, the analyst has to be cautious when interpreting some of the risk factor sensitivities, such as the "inflation beta" of commodities.
- *Implementation hurdles.* Establishing a strategic target to different risk factors is a very important high-level decision, but converting these risk factor targets to actual investment mandates requires additional considerations, including liquidity planning, time and effort for manager selection, and rebalancing policy.
- *Determining which risk factors should be used and how to measure them in different asset classes.* One drawback with risk-based approaches is the decision on which risk factors to use is somewhat subjective and how these factors are measured can also be subjective. For example, if using a liquidity factor, should it be measured by the Pastor-Stambaugh metric or by some other metric?

This issue is highlighted by noting that in the CFA Program's Level III reading "Hedge Fund Strategies," hedge fund returns are analyzed via a conditional factor model using just four risk factors: equities, credit, currencies, and volatility. These risk factors were selected as they are deemed to provide a reasonably broad cross-section of risk exposures for the typical hedge fund, and each of the factor returns can be realized through relatively liquid instruments.

In sum, a limitation of risk-based approaches is the potential subjectivity embedded in their implementation.

5. RISK CONSIDERATIONS, RETURN EXPECTATIONS AND INVESTMENT VEHICLE

In addition to the risk, return, and correlation characteristics relevant to the decision to invest in the alternative asset classes, many operational and practical complexities must be considered before finalizing a decision to invest. It is essential that the investor be fully aware of these complexities: Failure to grasp these differences between traditional and alternative investments can derail an investment program. The primary factors to consider include:

- properly defining risk characteristics;
- establishing return expectations;
- selection of the appropriate investment vehicle;
- operational liquidity issues;
- expense and fee considerations;
- tax considerations (applicable for taxable entities); and
- build vs. buy.

5.1. Risk Considerations

Mean–variance optimization (MVO), widely used in modeling asset allocation choices, cannot easily accommodate the characteristics of most alternative investments. MVO characterizes an asset's risk using standard deviation. Standard deviation is a one-dimensional view of risk and an especially poor representation of the risk characteristics of alternative investments—where assets suffer some degree of illiquidity, valuations may be subjective, and returns may be "chunky" and not normally distributed. The non-standard deviation risks are usually accommodated in an MVO framework by assigning a higher standard deviation than might be derived solely by looking at the historical returns of the asset class.

Most approaches to asset allocation assume that the portfolio's allocation to an asset class is always fully invested. Although this is not an assumption that is limited to alternatives, the problem is exaggerated with the private alternative strategies where it could take several years for capital to be invested and where capital is returned to the investor as investments are sold. Thus, it is rare that the *actual* asset allocation of a program with a significant exposure to alternatives will mirror the *modeled* asset allocation. This suggests that the investor must carefully (and continually) monitor the program's aggregate exposures to ensure that the risks are in line with the strategic asset allocation. A case in point: Some investors over-allocated to private equity, real-estate, and other call-down funds prior to 2008 in order to more quickly reach their asset allocation targets. Many of these investors then found themselves in a situation where they were receiving capital calls for these commitments during 2008 and 2009, a period where their public assets had lost considerable value and liquidity and cash were scarce. Some investors had to reduce distributions, sell illiquid investments in the secondary market at severely discounted prices, and/or walk away from their fund commitments, thereby forfeiting earlier investments.

Although every strategy (and, by extension, each individual fund) will have its own unique risk profile, we provide two examples of the complications that might be encountered when modelling an allocation to alternative investments.

5.1.1. Short-only Strategy

A short-biased fund can provide strong diversification benefits, lowering a portfolio's aggregate exposure to the equity risk factor; however, a short-only fund has a risk profile quite unlike a long-only equity fund. Most investors understand that a long-only equity fund has theoretically infinite upside potential and a downside loss bounded by zero (assuming no leverage). A short-biased or short-only fund has the opposite distribution. A short-selling strategy is capped on its upside but has unlimited downside risk.

5.1.2. Option Payouts

Some hedge fund strategies will structure their trades as call options either by owning call options outright or by synthetically replicating a call option (e.g., convertible bond arbitrage in which the manager goes long the convertible bond, short the equity for the same underlying, and hedges the interest rate risk). If executed properly, the fund would have limited downside but unlimited upside. It is difficult, if not impossible, to accurately model such a return profile by looking simply at a fund's historical standard deviation or other risk metrics, especially if the fund's track record does not encompass a full market cycle.

5.2. Return Expectations

Given the limited return history of alternative investments (relative to stocks and bonds) and the idiosyncratic nature of alternative investment returns, no single accepted approach to developing the return expectations required in an asset allocation exercise exists. One approach that can be applied with some consistency across asset classes is a "building blocks" approach: Begin with the risk-free rate, estimate the return associated with the factor exposures relevant to the asset class (e.g., credit spreads, level and shape of the yield curve, equity, leverage, liquidity), apply an assumption for manager alpha, and deduct appropriate fees (management and incentive) and taxes. Where the portfolio already contains an allocation to alternative investments, the underlying money managers can be helpful in estimating exposures and return potential. The portfolio's current positions can be characterized by their known exposures, rather than through a generic set of exposures that may not be truly representative of the program's objectives for the asset class exposure. Say, for example, that the investor's hedge fund program deliberately excludes long/short equity hedge funds because the investor chooses to take equity risk in the long-only portion of the portfolio. The return (and risk) characteristics of this hedge fund allocation would be very different from those of a broad-based allocation to hedge funds, which typically has a significant weight to long/short equity funds.

5.3. Investment Vehicle

Most alternative investments are implemented through a private (limited) partnership that is controlled by a general partner (GP), the organization and individuals that manage the investments. The asset owner becomes a limited partner (LP) in the private partnership. The main rationale for using the limited partnership format is that it limits the investor's liability to the amount of capital that she has contributed; she is not responsible for the actions of or the debts incurred by the GP. The investor may invest directly into a manager's fund or through a fund of funds, a private partnership that invests in multiple underlying partnerships. Larger investors may also consider making co-investments alongside a manager into a portfolio company, or they may make direct private equity investments on their own.

Private limited partnerships are the dominant investment vehicle for most alternative investments in private equity, real estate, private credit, and real assets. In the United States, hedge funds will tend to employ two structures: a limited partnership (typically Delaware-based) or an offshore corporation or feeder fund (possibly based in the Cayman Islands, Bermuda, or the British Virgin Islands) that usually feeds into an underlying limited partnership (i.e., feeder fund). European hedge funds tend to register their vehicles in Ireland or Luxembourg[7] as a public limited company, a partnership limited by shares, or a special limited partnership.

There are growing opportunities to invest in alternatives using mutual funds, undertakings for collective investment in transferable securities (UCITS), and/or separately managed accounts (SMAs), although the strategies implemented through these more-liquid vehicles are unlikely to have the same risk/return profile as their less-liquid counterparts. The requirements and demands of a broader investor base have made mutual funds, UCITS, and SMAs increasingly popular. We describe the structure, benefits, and drawbacks of each of these vehicles.

5.3.1. Direct Investment in a Limited Partnership

An investor with the necessary scale and expertise can purchase limited partnership interests directly from the GP. GPs have broad discretion to select and manage the underlying investments and will typically invest a portion of their capital in the fund alongside the limited partners. Because each limited partnership follows its own distinct investment strategy, the investor must often invest in multiple partnerships to diversify idiosyncratic risk. In order to maintain the limited liability shield afforded by the limited partnership structure, the investor must not become too involved in the operation of the fund itself.

5.3.2. Funds of Funds (FOFs)

Many investors lack the necessary scale and investment/operational expertise to access, evaluate, and develop a diversified alternative investment program. An FOF pools the capital of these investors, allowing them to achieve an allocation to an asset class that would otherwise be unobtainable. An FOF manager will typically specialize in a certain alternative strategy, such as Asian private equity funds, and may invest in either many or just a handful of underlying funds. The FOF manager is responsible for sourcing, conducting due diligence on, and monitoring the underlying managers. Using an FOF simplifies the investor's accounting and reporting: Capital calls from the underlying funds are frequently consolidated into a single capital call by the FOF, and investors receive a single report consolidating the accounting

---

[7] See Eurekahedge, "2016 Key Trends in Global Hedge Funds" (August 2016).

and investment results of all the underlying funds. The FOF manager does charge additional fees for these services. Investors in an FOF also lose a degree of flexibility to customize their exposures.

5.3.3. SMAs/Funds of One

As large institutions and family offices increased capital allocated to the alternative investment space, many of them demanded more-favorable investment terms and conditions than those offered to smaller investors. Some alternative investment managers, interested in accessing these large pools of capital, have agreed to offer investment management services to these clients through a highly customizable SMA. SMAs have very high minimum investments and pose greater operational challenges for both the manager and the investor. In instances where an SMA is impractical, fund managers have created a "fund of one"—a limited partnership with a single client. These funds have many of the same benefits as an SMA but can be easier to implement. (For example, an SMA requires that the *investor* must be approved by each of the counterparties to any derivatives contracts. In a fund of one, GPs must obtain and maintain these approvals, which is something that they do in the ordinary course of running their investment businesses.)

SMAs and funds of one cannot generally avail themselves of the alignment of interests that arises from the investment of GP capital alongside that of the LPs. When other clients are invested in the GP's primary investment vehicles at the GP's standard fees and to which the GP has committed some of its own capital, there is a risk that the GP favors these other funds in allocating capital-constrained investment opportunities.

5.3.4. Mutual Funds/UCITS/Publicly Traded Funds

A number of open-ended mutual funds and UCITS seek to replicate some alternative investment strategies, particularly hedge funds. Nominally, these allow smaller investors to access asset classes that would otherwise be unavailable to them. It should be noted, however, that these vehicles often operate with regulatory restrictions that limit the fund manager's ability to implement the investment strategy offered via their primary investment vehicle. Accordingly, the investor must be cautious in considering whether the track record achieved in the manager's primary investment vehicle is representative of what might be achieved in a mutual fund, UCIT, or other publicly-traded vehicle. For example, a mutual fund that offers daily liquidity is unlikely to be a suitable investment vehicle for a distressed or activist investment fund, where the time horizon to realize investment returns may be one to two years. This "liquid-alt" space grew significantly following the global financial crisis.

6. LIQUIDITY

Traditional assets are generally highly liquid, and the vehicles that are typically used by investors to access the asset class (e.g., separate accounts or daily valued commingled funds, such as mutual funds and UCITS) typically do not impose additional liquidity constraints. That is not the case with many alternative assets, where both the vehicle and the underlying instruments may expose the investor to some degree of liquidity risk. We address liquidity risks at the fund and security level separately.

6.1. Liquidity Risks Associated with the Investment Vehicle

The most common vehicle employed by alternative asset managers is the private limited partnership previously described. (Some investors will invest via an offshore corporate structure used for certain tax and regulatory reasons. This offshore corporation is typically a "feeder" fund—a vehicle that channels investors' assets to the master limited partnership.) The private placement memorandum (PPM) details the subscription and redemption features of the partnership. Liquidity provisions differ across asset classes but are substantially similar within asset classes. Exhibit 17 details the typical liquidity considerations associated with investing in a private limited partnership. SMA liquidity provisions may be negotiated directly with the manager.

EXHIBIT 17   Typical Liquidity Provisions for Alternative Investment Vehicles

	Subscription	Redemption	Lock-Up
Hedge Funds	• Typically accept capital on a monthly or quarterly basis.	• Quarterly or annual redemptions with 30 to 90 days' notice required. • May be subject to a gate limiting the amount of fund or investor assets that can be redeemed at any one redemption date. • 10% holdback of the redemption amount pending completion of the annual audit.	• Typically one year in the US; shorter in Europe. • Redemptions prior to the lock-up period may be permitted but are subject to a penalty, typically 10%.
Private Equity, Private Credit, Real Estate, and Real Asset Funds	• Funds typically have multiple "closes." The final close for new investors is usually one year after the first close. Committed capital is called for investment in stages over a 3-year investment period.	• No redemption provisions. Fund interests may be sold on the secondary market, subject to GP approval. • Distributions paid as investments are realized over the life of the fund. Unrealized assets may be distributed in kind to the LP at fund termination.	• Typical 10-year life, with GP option to extend fund term 1 to 2 years.

6.1.1. Secondary Markets
Although fund terms may prevent investors from redeeming early, a small but growing secondary market for many alternative funds exists. Some brokers will match sellers and buyers of limited partnership interests, and some secondary funds' main objective is to buy limited partnership interests from the original investor. These transactions typically occur at a significant discount to the net asset value (NAV) of the fund and usually require the GP to approve the transaction.

6.1.2. Understanding a Drawdown Structure
Private equity/credit, private real estate, and real asset funds typically call investors' capital in stages as fund investments are identified. This investment period is specified in the PPM and typically ranges from three to five years from the initial capital call. Thus, although an investor may have committed a specified percentage of the portfolio to an asset class, the allocation may not be fully funded until some point well into the future. We will illustrate the drawdown structure for a single fund using a hypothetical commitment to a real estate fund:

The Chan Family Partnership commits €5,000,000 to Uptown Real Estate LP. The fund has a three-year investment period. When fully invested, Uptown expects to hold 12 to 15 properties. The capital call schedule for Uptown may look something like this:

- Year 1: €1,500,000 of the €5,000,000 committed is called, covering three investments
- Year 2: €2,500,000 is called, covering six investments
- Year 3: €500,000 is called, covering two investments
- Year 6: €2,000,000 is distributed by Uptown Real Estate
- More distributions in subsequent years

Expanding on this example, Exhibit 18 shows how the cash flows for our hypothetical fund might operate throughout the fund's life.

EXHIBIT 18   Hypothetical Capital Call—Distribution Schedule

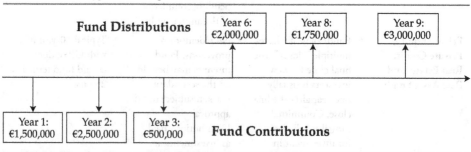

In reality, most funds will have several capital calls in a year. It is also possible that a fund may make a distribution before the final capital call occurs. Because of the highly uncertain liquidity profile of call down (or drawdown) funds (private equity/credit, real estate/real assets), it is incumbent on the investor to plan for multiple contingencies. Funds may end up calling significantly less capital than the investor assumed or may call capital at a faster pace than planned. Capital may be returned to the investor more quickly or more slowly than originally anticipated. Each of these scenarios could result in investors being under or over their target allocations. Critically, investors will want to verify that they have suitable liquidity, such that even under adverse conditions they are able to meet their capital calls. Investors who are unable to meet their capital calls may be required to forfeit their entire investment in the fund (or such other penalties as may be specified in the PPM).

The capital commitment/drawdown structure also presents potential opportunity costs for the investor. Returning to Exhibit 18, having committed €5,000,000 to Uptown Real Estate LP, the Chan Family Partnership is obligated to meet the GP's capital calls but must address the opportunity cost of having the committed capital invested in lower-returning liquid (cash) assets pending the capital call—or face the risk of having insufficient assets available to meet the capital call if the funds were invested in another asset class that has experienced a loss in the interim. Also note that only €4,500,000 of the €5,000,000 commitment was called before distributions began.

6.2. Liquidity Risks Associated with the Underlying Investments

The investor must be aware of any potential mismatch between the fund terms and the liquidity profile of the underlying instruments held by the fund. This is particularly important if the investor is negotiating fund terms or if other investors have terms that may be different from his own. Because the private market funds rarely offer interim liquidity, this problem most often arises in hedge funds. We provide a few examples of the issues an investor may encounter.

6.2.1. Equity-oriented Hedge Funds

The majority of assets in a typical equity-oriented hedge fund are liquid, marketable securities compatible with monthly or quarterly fund-level liquidity terms. Short positions may be notably less liquid than long positions, so funds that make greater use of short selling will have correspondingly lower overall liquidity. This should be taken into consideration when evaluating the potential for a liquidity mismatch between the fund's terms and the underlying holdings. Some otherwise liquid hedge fund strategies may own a portion of their holdings in illiquid or relatively illiquid securities. The GP may designate these securities as being held in a "side pocket." Such "side-pocketed" securities are not subject to the fund's general liquidity terms. The redeeming investor's pro rata share of the side pocket would remain in the fund and be distributed at such time as the fund manager liquidates these assets, which could take quarters or even years to accomplish. If the percentage of assets held in side pockets is large, this could render the fund's liquidity terms irrelevant. The investor must evaluate the illiquidity challenges inherent in the underlying holdings, including side pockets, in order to estimate a liquidity profile for the total portfolio.

6.2.2. Event-Driven Hedge Funds

Event-driven strategies, by their nature, tend to have longer investment horizons. The underlying investments in a merger arbitrage strategy, for example, are generally liquid, but the nature of the strategy is such that returns are realized in "chunks." It is in the manager's and the investor's interests to ensure that the liquidity terms provide the necessary flexibility to execute the investment thesis. A hedge fund focused on distressed investing is dealing with both the workout horizon (the time frame over which the negotiations between the creditors and the company are being conducted) and the lesser liquidity of the distressed assets. The fund terms for a distressed strategy are likely to be much longer than other hedge fund strategies. (In fact, many distressed funds choose to organize in a private equity fund structure.)

6.2.3. Relative Value Hedge Funds

Many relative value hedge funds will invest in various forms of credit, convertibles, derivatives, or equities that have limited or at least uncertain liquidity characteristics. Many funds will include provisions in the fund documents to restrict redemptions under certain scenarios so that they are not forced to sell illiquid securities at inopportune moments. Without such provisions, the fund manager may be forced to sell what securities they *can* (i.e., the more liquid holdings) rather than the securities that they *want*. This could have the unfortunate consequence of leaving remaining investors in the fund holding a sub-optimally illiquid portfolio. On the other hand, funds that deal in managed futures or similar instruments may have very flexible terms (daily or weekly liquidity, only a few days notification, etc.). This was a scenario many hedge fund managers faced during the global financial crisis as investors made significant redemption requests to meet their own cash needs. The liquid funds were disproportionately affected as investors sought to raise cash wherever they could find it.

6.2.4. Leverage

A fund's use of leverage and its agreements with counterparties providing the leverage can also affect the alignment between fund terms and the investment strategy. If a strategy is levered, lenders have a first claim on the assets. The lenders' claims are superior to those of the LPs, and the lenders have preferential liquidity terms; most lenders can make a margin call on stocks, bonds, or derivatives positions with just two days' notice. Given that margin calls are most likely to happen when the markets (and/or the fund) are stressed, the LPs' liquidity can evaporate as the most-liquid positions in the portfolio are sold to meet margin calls. The need to de-lever and sell assets to meet margin calls will typically result in a lower return when the market eventually recovers.

7. FEES AND EXPENSES, TAX CONSIDERATIONS, AND OTHER CONSIDERATIONS

In addition to management fees of 0.5% to 2.5% of assets and incentive fees of 10% to 20% of returns, investments in alternative assets often entail higher expenses passed through to or paid directly by the investor. These fees can result in a significant variation between the gross and net of fee returns. Consider a hedge fund that was earning a 3% gross quarterly return (12.6% annualized). After deducting a 2% management and a 20% incentive fee, accrued quarterly, the net return at year-end is just 8.2%.

Fees can have a larger impact on the difference between gross and net returns for such call-down-type fund structures as private equity funds, where the management fee is charged on *committed* capital, not invested capital. If the manager is slow to deploy capital, there can be a pronounced J-curve effect (negative IRRs in the early years) that can be difficult to overcome (the adage 'it takes a 100% return to recover from a 50% loss').

In addition, most alternative investment funds will pass through normal fund expenses, including legal, custodial, audit, administration, and accounting fees. For smaller funds, these additional costs can add up to another 0.5%. Larger funds can spread these same costs out over the larger asset base, and the pass-through to investors is likely to be in the range of 0.05% to 0.20% of assets. Some of these expenses have a limited life (e.g., the capitalized organizational expenses), so the impact can vary over time. Funds may also pass through to investors costs associated with acquiring an asset, including the due diligence costs and any brokerage commissions paid. A careful evaluation of the fund's offering documents is essential to understanding the all-in cost of an investment in alternatives.

7.1. Tax Considerations

For taxable investors, the tax implications associated with many alternatives can have a significant impact on their relative attractiveness. In many instances, a tax inefficient strategy, one that generates substantial short-term gains or taxable income, can significantly erode the anticipated return benefits. This arises frequently with many hedge fund strategies, especially those funds and fund companies where tax-exempt investors dominate the client base and the fund manager may be insensitive to tax efficiency. Vehicle selection becomes an important tool to mitigate potential tax consequences. For example, certain Asia-based investors may use European or other offshore vehicles that feed into US strategies in order to mitigate US tax withholding. Conversely, some funds benefit from preferential tax treatment that might add to its relative attractiveness.

Here are a few examples of these tax considerations:

- The US tax code has provisions that favor real estate, timber, and energy investments. Timber sales, for example, are taxed at lower capital gains rates rather than as ordinary income and may benefit from a depletion deduction. Commercial and residential building assets can be depreciated according to various schedules, with the depreciation offsetting income received on those assets. Some oil and natural gas royalty owners may benefit from a depletion deduction, offsetting income generated from the sale of the oil or gas.
- Some alternative investment strategies can generate unrelated business income tax (UBIT). UBIT arises when a US tax-exempt organization engages in activities that are not related to the tax-exempt purpose of that organization. Since most tax-exempt entities seek to mitigate (if not avoid) taxes, they will want to verify whether such a fund might generate UBIT and, if so, whether the fund manager has an offshore vehicle that may shield the investor from such income.
- The taxable investor faces additional costs and operational hurdles because of the more complex tax filings. Some taxable investors must estimate their expected annual income, including income that is derived from investments. Deriving an accurate estimate can be a challenge. Unfortunately, if the misestimation is large enough it might result in tax penalties.

Tax considerations, like fees, will affect the return assumptions used in the asset allocation exercise.

7.2. Other Considerations

Although smaller investors seeking to build a diversified alternative investment program are generally constrained to use an intermediary, such as a fund of funds, large investors have the opportunity to build a program in-house and must decide whether this approach is appropriate given their governance structure. Key questions to explore in evaluating the options include the following:

- What is the likelihood that the investor can identify and gain access to the top-tier managers in the investment strategy?

  Truly differentiated strategies and top-tier managers are notoriously capacity constrained, which tends to limit the amount of assets they can reasonably manage without negatively affecting investment returns. Fund managers who recognize this problem frequently limit the number of investors that they allow into their fund and may close their doors to new clients or capital. This can make it extremely difficult for investors to find and access top-tier managers. Investors who are subject to public disclosure requirements may be rejected by a manager who believes that success is based on a proprietary informational edge that could be eroded through these required public disclosures. Many studies on alternative assets have concluded that it may not be worth the costs and resources required to be successful in this space if investors do not have access to top-tier funds.

- What is the likelihood that the investor will be accorded the access needed to conduct effective due diligence on an investment strategy?

  It is not enough to know when or if to invest with a fund manager; it is equally, if not more, important to be able to determine when to terminate the relationship. Having poor to no access to the key decision makers within the organization could make it difficult to ascertain if the conditions have changed such that a redemption is warranted. The situation could be even worse if other clients have good (or preferential) access to the fund manager, which might result in their redeeming early, leaving other, less-informed investors subject to gates or other more-restrictive redemption terms that could be triggered.

- What skills and resources does the investor have in-house to evaluate and monitor an alternative investment program?

  This question is evaluated through a consideration of the cost tradeoffs, the investment expertise of in-house staff, the desire to tailor an investment program to investor-specific wants and needs, and the degree of control.

  - Cost is typically the overriding factor in the decision to build a program in-house or buy an existing off-the-shelf product. The all-in costs of compensation, benefits, rent, technology, reporting, travel, overhead, and other miscellaneous expenses associated with managing an alternative investments program can far exceed the costs associated with running a traditional asset portfolio. However, very large organizations may be able to justify the costs of building in-house teams.

  - Investors seeking to leverage a manager's expertise through co-investments and other direct investment opportunities must build an in-house team with the expertise to evaluate specific securities and deals and must provide the infrastructure needed to support those efforts.

  - Investors who require highly customized investment programs might be poorly served by consultants or FOFs who typically gain scale and margin by providing solutions that can be broadly applied to a large number of clients. For example, an endowment that wants their alternative investment program to consider environmental, social, and governance (ESG) factors (i.e., socially responsible investing) may have a difficult time finding an investment consultant who can deliver on the client's specific ESG requirements. Or, a family office that wants to emphasize tax-efficient angel investments might need to hire in-house resources in order to find and supervise these more specialized investments.

  - Those investors who desire a high degree of control and/or influence over the implementation of the investment program are more likely to have this need met through an in-house program.

EXAMPLE 3   Considerations in Allocating to Alternative Investments

The investment committee (IC) for a small endowment has decided to invest in private equity for the first time and has agreed upon a 10% strategic target. The internal investment team comprises the CIO (chief investment officer) and two analysts. The IC asks the CIO to recommend an implementation plan at the next meeting.

1. What are the options the CIO should include in her report as it relates to vehicles, and what factors might influence the recommendation?
2. The IC provided no guidance as to expectations for when the investment program should reach its 10% target weight. What additional information should the CIO gather before presenting her plan of action?

Solution to 1: The primary considerations for the CIO include the size of the private equity allocation, the team's expertise with private equity, and the available resources. Because this is a small endowment, it may be difficult to commit enough capital to achieve an adequate level of diversification. The size of the fund's investment team is also likely to be a concern. Unless there are financial resources to add a private equity specialist and/or employ an outside consultant, the fund-of-funds route would likely be the optimal vehicle(s) to implement a diversified private equity program.

Solution to 2: The CIO should factor in the cash flows and anticipated liquidity profile of the overall endowment in considering the speed with which they would commit to a significant PE program. If, for example, the foundation is embarking on a capital campaign and anticipated distributions are small over the next few years, then commitments may be accelerated after factoring in an appropriate vintage year diversification. (Because private investment returns are very sensitive to the fund's vintage year, it is common for investors to build up to a full allocation over a period of years, called vintage year diversification.) However, if the rest of the investment program is heavily exposed to illiquid investments (e.g., real estate, certain hedge fund strategies) and anticipated distributions to fund operating expenses are high, the CIO may want to commit at a slower pace.

EXAMPLE 4   Considerations in Allocating to Alternative Investments

A $100 million client of a family office firm has requested that all public securities investments meet certain ESG criteria. The ESG ratings will be provided by an independent third-party firm that provides a rating for most public equities and some fixed-income issuers. Moreover, the family would like to dedicate a percentage of assets to support an "environmental sustainability" impact theme.

1. Which alternative investment strategies may not be suitable for this client given the ESG requirements?
2. What additional information might the family office firm require from the client in order to meet the environmental sustainability threshold?

Solution to 1: Because the ESG criteria apply to all public securities, most hedge fund strategies would be precluded because they are typically owned in a commingled vehicle, such as a limited partnership or a mutual fund where transparency of holdings is limited and the investor has no influence over the composition of the underlying portfolio. Separate account strategies are available for certain large portfolios, but it is unlikely that a $100 million client would be eligible for a custom portfolio that would be allocating only a small asset base to any particular fund.

Solution to 2: The client and the manager would need to agree on a clear definition of environmental sustainability and the types of investments that might qualify for this theme. It is unlikely that most hedge funds, private credit, energy, or infrastructure strategies would be considered to positively impact environmental sustainability. The most likely candidates for consideration could be timber, sustainable farmland, and clean-tech funds under the venture capital category.

8. SUITABILITY CONSIDERATIONS

Alternative investments are not appropriate for all investors. We discuss briefly several *investor* characteristics that are important to a successful alternative investment program.

8.1. Investment Horizon

Investors with less than a 15-year investment horizon should generally avoid investments in private real estate, private real assets, and private equity funds. An alternative investment program in private markets may take 5 to 7 years to fully develop and another 10 to 12 years to unwind, assuming no new investments are made after the 7-year mark. Even a 10-year horizon may be too short to develop a robust private alternative investment program.

Other strategies can tolerate a shorter investment focus. Many hedge fund strategies that focus on public equities or managed futures have much shorter lock-ups (on the order of months or not at all). Some strategies can be entered and exited in shorter time frames, and the purchase or sale of limited partnership interests on the secondary market may be used to shorten the entry and exit phases of the process. However, the alternative investment program has a higher likelihood of success if the investor adopts a long-horizon approach coupled with an understanding of the underlying investment processes.

8.2. Expertise

A successful alternative investment program requires that the investor understand the risks entailed and the market environments that drive success or failure of each of the strategies. Understanding the breadth of the alternative investment opportunities and the complexity of strategies within each alternative class requires a relatively high level of investment expertise. Even if the investor is highly experienced, the risk of information asymmetry between the limited partner (LP) and the general partner (GP) is always there. A pension fund without full-time investment staff, or an individual without the resources to hire an adviser with a dedicated alternative investments team, is unlikely to have the investment expertise necessary to implement a successful alternative investment program.

Additionally, the investment philosophy of the asset owner (or its overseers) must be consistent with the principles of alternative investments. An investor whose investment philosophy is rooted in a belief that markets are fundamentally efficient may struggle to embrace an alternative investment program, where success is predicated on active management. A mismatch in philosophy could very well be a set up for failure when the alternative investments underperform traditional asset classes.

8.3. Governance

A robust investment governance framework ensures that an alternative investment program is structured to meet the needs of the investor. The following are hallmarks of a strong governance framework suitable to an alternative investment program:

- The long- and short-term objectives of the investment program are clearly articulated.
- Decision rights and responsibilities are allocated to those individuals with the knowledge, capacity, and time required to critically evaluate possible courses of action.
- A formal investment policy has been adopted to govern the day-to-day operations of the investment program.
- A reporting framework is in place to monitor the program's progress toward the agreed-on goals and objectives.

Investors without a strong governance program are less likely to develop a successful alternative investment program.

8.4. Transparency

Investors must be comfortable with less than 100% transparency into the underlying holdings of their alternative investment managers. In real estate, private equity, and real asset funds, the investor is typically buying into a "blind pool"—committing capital for investment in a portfolio of as-yet-unidentified assets. During the course of investment due diligence, the investor may have looked at the assets acquired in the manager's previous funds, but there is no assurance that the new fund will look anything like the prior funds. Hedge fund managers are generally reluctant to disclose the full portfolio to investors on an ongoing basis. Even if you were to have access to the full underlying portfolio, it is rarely apparent where the true risk exposures lie without a detailed understanding of the investment themes the manager is pursuing.

Reporting for alternative funds is often less transparent than investors are accustomed to seeing on their stock and bond portfolios. Generally, no legal requirements mandate the frequency, timing, and details of fund reporting for private investment partnerships. For many illiquid strategies (real estate/assets, private equity/credit), reporting is often received well past month- or quarter-end deadlines that investors are accustomed to with their traditional investments.

A typical hedge fund report, usually available on a quarterly basis, may detail performance, top 10 holdings, and some general commentary on the capital markets as well as some factors that influenced fund performance. The hedge fund manager may also provide a risk report that broadly outlines the major risk exposures of the fund. There is no commonality among the risk reports provided from fund to fund. This hampers an investor's efforts to develop a picture of aggregate risk exposure. Clients with separately managed accounts have access to portfolio holdings and may be able to produce their own risk reporting with a common set of risk metrics.

Private equity funds will provide more transparency into portfolio holdings, but the private equity fund report is unlikely to "slice-and-dice" the exposures by geography, sector, or industry. The investor must gather the additional information needed to develop a fuller exposure of the portfolio's risk exposures and progress toward meeting expectations. Private equity managers typically provide an abbreviated quarterly report with a more detailed annual report following the completion of the fund's annual audit.

This lack of transparency can shield questionable actions by GPs. In 2014, the US Securities and Exchange Commission found that more than 50% of private equity firms had collected or misallocated fees without proper disclosure to their clients.[8] This study and subsequent lawsuits have increased transparency within the industry, although the industry remains opaque at many levels.

Reporting for private real estate funds commonly consists of a quarterly report with details on the fund's size, progress in drawdowns, realizations to date, and valuations of unrealized investments as well as market commentary relevant to the fund's strategy. Reports typically include details on each investment such as the original acquisition cost(s), square footage, borrowing details (e.g., cost of debt, leverage ratios, and debt maturity dates), and fundamental metrics regarding the health of the properties (e.g., occupancy rates and, if appropriate, the estimated credit health of tenants). Often there is qualitative commentary on the health of the property's submarket, on anticipated next steps, and on the timing of realization(s). Reports are typically issued with a one-quarter lag to allow sufficient time to update property valuations. Annual reports, which frequently require updated third-party appraisals, may not be available until the second quarter following year end.

Investors should ensure that funds use independent administrators to calculate the fund and LPs' NAV. These administrators are also responsible for processing cash flows, including contributions, fee payments, and distributions that are consistent with the fund documents. The use of independent administrators is common practice among hedge funds. It is relatively uncommon for a fund investing in illiquid strategies (e.g., private equity/credit, real estate/natural resources) to use an independent administrator. Funds that do not use third-party administrators have wide discretion in valuing assets. In the midst of the Great Financial Crisis, it was not uncommon for two different private equity firms with ownership interests in the same company to provide very different estimates of the company's value.

The lack of transparency common with many alternative investments can challenge risk management and performance evaluation. High-quality alternative investment managers will engage an independent and respected accounting firm to perform an annual audit of the fund; the audit report should be available to the LPs.

Regulatory requirements for mutual funds and UCITS funds require such standardized information as costs, expected risks, and performance data. Additional information may also be available on a periodic basis. Information provided to one investor should be available to all shareholders. These rules have been interpreted by some mutual fund/UCITS managers to mean that they cannot provide more-detailed, non-standardized information given the complexity of sharing it with a broad audience. This can possibly restrict the level of transparency certain shareholders can obtain for these vehicles.

---

[8] Andrew Ceresney, "Keynote Address: Private Equity Enforcement," Securities Enforcement Forum West (12 May 2016).

EXAMPLE 5   Suitability Considerations in Allocating to Alternative Investments

---

The Christian family office is concerned with investor or manager fraud and so will invest only in separately managed accounts (SMAs).

1. What are the benefits and drawbacks to the use of SMAs?
2. The 75-year-old patriarch of the Christian family would like to consider a significant private equity allocation in a trust that he oversees on behalf of his youngest daughter. This would be the first alternative investment commitment made with any of the family's assets. The daughter is 40 years old. She will receive one-half of the assets outright upon his death. The remainder of the assets will be held in trust subject to the terms of the trust agreement. List some of the reasons why private equity may or may not be appropriate for this trust.

Solution to 1: Although an SMA allows for greater transparency and control of capital flows (the manager does not generally have the authority to distribute capital from the client account), it has several potential disadvantages: 1) SMAs are not available or appropriate for many alternative strategies; thus, the requirement to invest via an SMA may limit the ability to develop an optimal alternative investment program. 2) A manager cannot invest alongside the client in the client's SMA. This may reduce the alignment of interest between the manager and the client and may give rise to conflicts of interest as trades are allocated between the SMA and the manager's other funds.

Solution to 2:
- Successful private equity investment requires a long time horizon. Given the patriarch's age, it is likely that half of the trust's assets will be distributed before the private equity program has had time to mature. This may lead to an unintended doubling in the size of the private equity allocation.
- The patriarch has no experience investing in alternative assets. Unless he is willing to commit the time, money, and effort and engage an outside adviser with the relevant expertise and access to top-tier funds, the likelihood of a successful private equity investment program would be low.
- Because the beneficiary of the trust is relatively young, the time horizon of the investment likely matches the profile of the underlying investor. It may be appropriate for the trust to invest in long-dated private equity assets, provided the investment is sized appropriately and the necessary expertise has been retained.

9. ASSET ALLOCATION APPROACHES AND STATISTICAL PROPERTIES AND CHALLENGES OF ASSET RETURNS

We mentioned earlier that one approach to determining the desired allocation to the alternative asset classes is to make the initial asset allocation decision using only the broad, liquid asset classes and do a second iteration of the asset allocation exercise incorporating alternative assets.

After first addressing the challenges in developing risk and return assumptions for alternative asset classes, we then discuss three primary approaches that investors use to approach this second iteration.

1. *Monte Carlo simulation.* We discuss how Monte Carlo simulation may be used to generate return scenarios that relax the assumption of normally distributed returns. We illustrate how simulation can be applied to estimate the long-term risk profile and return potential of various asset allocation alternatives, and, in particular, we evaluate whether various asset allocation alternatives would satisfy the investor's ultimate investment objectives.
2. *Optimization techniques.* Mean–variance optimization (MVO) typically over-allocates to alternative asset classes, partly because risk is underestimated because of stale or infrequent pricing and the underlying assumption that returns are normally distributed. Practitioners usually address this bias towards alternatives by establishing limits on the allocations to alternatives. Optimization methods that incorporate downside risk (mean–CVaR optimization) or take into account skew may be used to enhance the asset allocation process.
3. *Risk factor–based approaches.* Risk factor–based approaches to alternative asset allocation can be applied to develop more robust asset allocation proposals.

These analytical techniques complement each other, and investors frequently rely on all of them rather than just using one or the other. Monte Carlo simulation can provide simulated non-normal (fat-tailed) data for a mean–CVaR optimization, but simulation can also be applied to analyze the long-term behavior of various asset allocation alternatives that are the results of portfolio optimization.

9.1. Statistical Properties and Challenges of Asset Returns

Alternative investments present the modeler with a number of analytical challenges. These two are particularly relevant in the asset allocation process:

1. Appraisal-based valuations used in private alternative investments often lead to stale and/ or artificially smoothed returns. Volatility and other risk measures estimated based on these smoothed time series would potentially understate the actual, fundamental risk.
2. Although even the public asset classes can exhibit non-normal return distributions, skewness and fat tails (excess kurtosis) are more pronounced with many of the alternative investment strategies. Leverage, sensitivity to the disappearance of liquidity, and even the asymmetric nature of performance fees all contribute to additional skewness and excess kurtosis among alternative investments. This option–payoff style quality can undermine a simplistic statistical approach.

Asset allocators use various analytical approaches to mitigate the impact of these challenges.

9.1.1. Stale Pricing and Unsmoothing

Appraisal-based valuation is common in private real estate and private equity. The valuation parameter assumptions in the appraisal process change quite slowly. This has a smoothing effect on reported returns and gives the illusion that illiquid assets' performance is much less volatile than that of public marketable assets with similar fundamental characteristics. This issue also affects hedge funds in which the manager invests in illiquid or less-liquid assets whose valuations are updated infrequently or are using models with static valuation assumptions. These artificially smoothed returns can be detected by testing the return stream for serial correlation. If serial correlation is detected and found statistically significant, the analyst needs to unsmooth the returns to get a more accurate representation of the risk and return characteristics of the asset class we are modelling.

To illustrate unsmoothing, we use a simple approach described by Ang (2014). Exhibit 19 illustrates the reported quarterly return history of the Cambridge Associates Private Equity Index, as well as the unsmoothed series.[9] The annualized volatility estimated using the reported quarterly return data and scaling using the square root of time convention is 9.5%.[10] The widely accepted rule of scaling by the square root of time, however, is based on the assumption of serially uncorrelated, normally-distributed returns. In our example, the serial correlation of the quarterly reported private equity returns is 0.38, which, given the number of observations, is significant with a *t*-statistic of 4.09. Because our returns are serially correlated, we want to unsmooth the returns to get a better estimate of volatility. The volatility calculated on the unsmoothed return series is 14.0%, significantly higher than the volatility estimated from the unsmoothed data.

EXHIBIT 19   C|A Private Equity Index Quarterly Returns

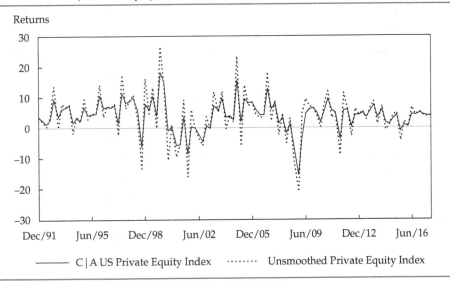

Exhibit 20 illustrates serial correlation and volatility estimates based on quarterly returns of a broad range of asset classes. Although the serial correlation of public marketable asset classes is generally low, private asset classes and some hedge fund strategies have higher serial

---

[9] We used the following formula to unsmooth the report total return time series:

$$r_{t,\text{unsmoothed}} = (r_{t,\text{reported}} - s \times r_{t-1,\text{reported}})/(1 - s),$$

where s denotes the estimated serial correlation of the time series.

[10] To scale volatility estimates to a longer (or shorter) time horizon, the volatility can be multiplied by the square root of time. For example, if we know the quarterly volatility and want an annual volatility estimate, we would multiply the quarterly volatility estimate by the square root of 4. (This scaling convention assumes price changes are independent and returns are not serially correlated over time.)

correlations that indicate stronger smoothing effects. The higher the serial correlation in the reported return series, the larger the difference between the volatility based on the unsmoothed and reported (smoothed) return data. The impact of smoothing is the highest in the case of private investments, as suggested by the serial correlation for private real estate (0.85) and private equity (0.38). The unsmoothed volatility of private real estate is, in fact, three times the volatility that we would estimate based on the reported returns. Given the serial correlation evident in private alternative strategies, it is not surprising that the distressed hedge fund strategy exhibits higher serial correlation (0.36) than other hedge fund strategies.

EXHIBIT 20   The Effect of Serial Correlation on Volatility

Quarterly Data Dec. 1997–Sept. 2017	Serial Correlation	Volatility (reported returns)	Volatility (unsmoothed)
US Equities	0.03	17.0%	17.7%
Non-US Developed Market Equities	0.08	19.2%	20.8%
Emerging Market Equities	0.17	26.2%	30.8%
Governments	−0.01	4.9%	4.9%
Broad Fixed Income	0.02	3.4%	3.5%
High-Yield Credit	0.34	10.0%	14.3%
Inflation-Linked Bonds	0.12	5.0%	5.7%
Hedge Funds—Aggregate	0.15	8.1%	9.5%
HF Macro	0.08	5.4%	5.9%
HF Equity Market Neutral	0.17	3.5%	4.1%
HF Equity Hedged	0.19	10.7%	13.1%
HF Distressed	0.36	8.9%	13.0%
Commodities	0.14	25.2%	28.8%
Public Real Estate	0.15	20.4%	24.0%
Private Real Estate	0.85	4.6%	13.8%
Private Equity	0.38	10.7%	15.7%

9.1.2. Skewness and Fat Tails

A common and convenient assumption behind asset pricing theory, as well as models applied for asset allocation and risk analytics, is that asset returns are normally distributed. Both academic researchers and practitioners are widely aware of the limitations of this assumption, but no standard quantitative method to replace this assumption of normality exists. Skewness and excess kurtosis, or so-called "fat tails," in the distributions of empirically observed asset returns may lead to underestimated downside risk measures in the case of both traditional and alternative asset classes. Non-normality of returns, however, can be more severe in private alternative asset class and certain hedge fund strategies than in most of the traditional asset classes.

In Exhibit 21, we show skewness and excess kurtosis parameters calculated based on 20 years of unsmoothed quarterly return data of various public and alternative asset classes. We also show 95% quarterly conditional value at risk (CVaR) estimates based on the assumption of normally distributed asset returns, as well as based on the observed (actual) distributions. Positive skewness indicates smaller downside risk potential, while negative skewness indicates greater downside risk potential. Excess kurtosis (i.e., a kurtosis parameter exceeding 3) similarly points toward greater downside risk than would be apparent from the numbers calculated using the assumption of normally-distributed returns. The observed (actual) CVaR estimates typically exceed the normal distribution-based CVaR figures when kurtosis is high and skewness is negative. Equity market-neutral hedge funds and private real estate have the biggest *relative* differences between the 95% normal distribution CVaR and the observed CVaR (columns C and D divided by column C). Both of these strategies have negative skewness and fairly high excess kurtosis. It's interesting to note that distressed hedge funds similarly have high kurtosis and negative skewness, but the difference in tail risk measures becomes mainly visible at the 99% confidence level, where the extreme but infrequent losses may occur.

EXHIBIT 21   Normal Distribution Assumption and Observed Downside Risk Measures

	(A)	(B)	(C)	(D)	(E)	(F)
Unsmoothed Quarterly Data Dec. 1997–Sept. 2017	Skewness	Excess Kurtosis	95% CVaR (Normal Distribution)	95% CVaR (Observed)	99% CVaR (Normal Distribution)	99% CVaR (Observed)
US Equities	−0.51	0.43	−15.3%	−17.7%	−20.3%	−23.9%
Non-US Dev Equities	−0.19	0.29	−18.9%	−19.8%	−24.8%	−20.7%
Emerging Mkt Equities	−0.23	−0.03	−28.2%	−25.4%	−37.0%	−27.7%
Governments	0.59	0.39	−3.5%	−3.2%	−4.9%	−4.0%
Broad Fixed Income	−0.05	−0.41	−2.1%	−2.4%	−3.1%	−3.1%
High-Yield Credit	0.18	6.14	−7.9%	−9.8%	−10.8%	−19.7%
Inflation-Linked Bonds	−0.32	1.08	−4.2%	−4.2%	−5.8%	−8.1%
Hedge Funds	−0.17	1.69	−7.6%	−8.6%	−10.3%	−9.7%
HF Macro	0.36	0.85	−4.3%	−4.1%	−6.0%	−5.1%
HF Equity Market Neutral	−1.17	3.55	−2.9%	−3.9%	−4.1%	−5.4%
HF Equity Hedged	0.08	2.24	−10.8%	−10.6%	−14.5%	−12.7%
HF Distressed	−1.25	3.52	−10.8%	−11.1%	−14.5%	−16.9%
Commodities	−0.71	1.62	−28.4%	−30.6%	−36.6%	−50.6%
Public Real Estate	−0.88	4.60	−20.9%	−24.5%	−27.7%	−40.2%
Private Real Estate	−2.80	9.62	−11.3%	−15.4%	−15.3%	−27.9%
Private Equity	−0.46	2.05	−12.2%	−15.7%	−16.7%	−22.6%

Source: Authors' calculations.

To further illustrate the impact of non-normality on the downside risk, in Exhibit 22 we compare the ratio of observed to normal CVaR measures with the skewness and excess kurtosis. Although the skewness or excess kurtosis alone doesn't fully explain the relative difference between observed and normal 95% CVaR (positive skewness may compensate high excess kurtosis or vice versa), we can see the evidence that higher kurtosis or more negative skewness usually increases the likely severity of any tail risk.

EXHIBIT 22   The Impact of Skewness and Kurtosis on Tail Risk

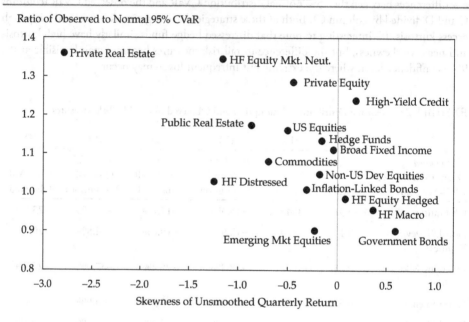

Source: Authors' calculations.

Analysts can choose to incorporate non-normality into their analyses in a few different ways. The most obvious and straightforward choice is to use empirically observed asset returns instead of working with the normal distribution. Still, in private investments where we typically have only quarterly return data, the analyses may be subject to serious limitations. Even with 20 years of quarterly return data, we have only 80 data points (and the industry has changed significantly over this time, further straining the validity of the data).

With sufficient data, analysts and researchers can capture the effects of fat tails by using advanced mathematical or statistical models:

• Time-varying volatility models (e.g., stochastic volatility), which assume that volatility is not constant over time but changes dynamically, can be used.
• Regime-switching models capture return, volatility, and correlation characteristics in different market environments (bull/bear or low volatility and moderate correlation vs. high volatility and elevated correlation). The combination of two or more normal distributions with different average returns, volatilities, and correlations could capture skewed and fat-tailed distributions.

- Extreme value theory and other fat-tailed distributions can be used when the analyst wants to focus on the behavior in the tails.

Although no single and uniformly accepted approach exists to address all of these quantitative challenges to the asset allocation exercise, a sound asset allocation process will do the following:

1. Adjust the observed asset class return data by unsmoothing the return series if the autocorrelation is significant.
2. Determine whether it is reasonable to accept an assumption of normal return distributions, in which case mean–variance optimization is appropriate to use.
3. Allow you to choose an optimization approach that takes the tail risk into account if the time series exhibits fat tails and skewness and if the potential downside risk would exceed the levels that would be observed with a normal distribution.

10. MONTE CARLO SIMULATION

Monte Carlo simulation can be a very useful tool in asset allocation to alternative investments. In this section, we discuss two applications of this modeling approach. First, we discuss how we can simulate risk factor or asset return scenarios that exhibit the skewness and kurtosis commonly seen in alternative investments. Second, we illustrate simulation-based risk and return analytics over a long time horizon in a broad asset allocation context.

At a very high level, we can summarize the model construction process in the following steps:

1. Identify those variables that we would like to randomly generate in our simulation. These variables may be asset class total returns directly, or risk factors, depending on the model.
2. Establish the quantitative framework to generate realistic random scenarios for the selected asset class returns or risk factors. Here, the analyst faces several choices, including the following:
   a. What kind of time-series model are we using? Will it be a random walk? Or will it incorporate serial correlations and mean-reversion-like characteristics?
   b. What kind of distribution should we assume for the shocks or innovations to the variables? Is normal distribution reasonable? Or, will we use some fat-tailed distribution model instead?
   c. Are volatilities and correlations stable over time? Or, do they vary across time?
3. If using a risk factor approach, convert the risk factors to asset or asset class returns using a factor-based model. In this reading, all our illustrations are based on linear factor models, but certain asset types with optionality need more-sophisticated models to incorporate non-linear characteristics as well.
4. Further translate realistic asset class return scenarios into meaningful indicators. We can simultaneously model, for example, the investment portfolio and the liability of a pension fund, enabling us to assess how the funding ratio is expected to evolve over time. Or, in the case of an endowment fund, we can assess whether certain asset allocation choices would improve the probability of meeting the spending rate target while preserving the purchasing power of the asset base.

10.1. Simulating Skewed and Fat-Tailed Financial Variables

A fairly intuitive way of incorporating non-normal returns into the analysis is to assume that there are two (or more) possible states of the world. Individually, each state can be described by using a normal distribution (*conditional normality*), but the combination of these two distributions will not be normally distributed.[11] Next, we show a fairly simplified application for the public equities and government bonds. Note that the same approach can be applied to more asset classes as well, or it can be applied to risk factor changes rather than asset class returns.

For this illustration, we assume that the capital markets can be described by two distinct regimes—a "quiet period" (Regime 1) and a high-volatility state (Regime 2). Exhibit 23 shows the quarterly return history of the US equities and government bonds as well as the model's more volatile regimes (the gray-shaded periods). It is easy to see that the global financial crisis—and such earlier crisis periods as the 1997 Asian currency contagion, the 1998 Russian ruble crisis and LTCM meltdown, and the 2002 tech bubble burst—all belong to the high-volatility regimes. The mean return and volatility statistics for the full period as well as each of the two regimes can be found in Exhibit 24. Equities outperformed government bonds over the full observation period, and it's interesting to see how dynamics changed between the quiet to the volatile periods. In the quiet period (Regime 1), equities outperformed bonds by around 4.6% quarterly, whereas in the volatile period (Regime 2), government bonds outperformed equities by more than 5%. The total return volatilities also jumped dramatically when the market switched from quiet to volatile periods. In addition, the correlation between equities and bonds was near zero during the quiet period but turned significantly negative (about −0.6) during the volatile period. Finally, we estimate that the low-volatility Regime 1 prevailed 62% of the time and the high-volatility Regime 2 prevailed 38% of the time.

EXHIBIT 23   US Equities and Government Bonds Return History and Identification of High-Volatility Regimes

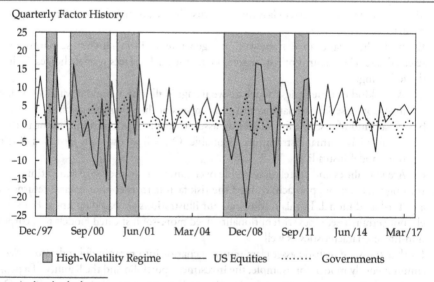

Source: Authors' calculations.

[11] The estimation process of such models is beyond the scope of this reading. Readers interested in additional details are referred to Hamilton (1989) and Kim and Nelson (1999).

EXHIBIT 24   Return Statistics (1997–2017)

	Equities	Government Bonds
Quarterly Average Return	2.1%	1.2%
Quarterly Return Volatility	8.5%	4.5%
Skewness	−0.5	0.6
Kurtosis	0.4	0.4
Average Return in Regime 1	5.1%	0.5%
Average Return in Regime 2	−3.1%	2.4%
Volatility in Regime 1	5.5%	1.9%
Volatility in Regime 2	13.7%	3.8%
Correlation in Regime 1		0.0
Correlation in Regime 2		−0.6

If we want to capture only skewness and fat tails in a simulation framework, we just need the normal distribution parameters of the distinct regimes and the overall state probabilities of either Regime 1 or Regime 2. Then, the analyst would generate normally distributed random scenarios based on the different means and covariances estimated under the two (or more) regimes with the appropriate frequency of the estimated probability of being the quiet or hectic regimes. This mixture of high- and low-volatility normal distributions would lead to an altogether skewed and fat-tailed distribution of asset class return or risk factor changes. In practice, some may build a more dynamic, multi-step simulation model for a longer time horizon, in which case it's also important to estimate the probability of switching from one regime to another.

Exhibit 25 shows histograms of equity returns, overlaid with the fitted normal distribution and the combined distributions from our regime-switching model. As the chart illustrates, the combination of two normal distributions improves the distribution fit and introduces some degree of skewness and fat-tail characteristics.

EXHIBIT 25   Normal and Fat-Tailed Distribution Fit for US Equity Quarterly Returns

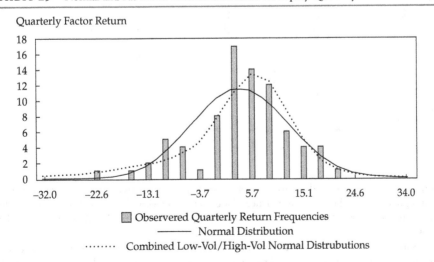

Source: Authors' calculations.

Several variations of regime-switching models are available. We have used a very basic set-up to illustrate the additional richness a regime-switching model can bring to the analysis. We could also apply a similar approach if we were to build asset classes using risk factors. We could overlay the non-normal distributions of the risk factors on the relevant asset class returns.[12]

10.2. Simulation for Long-Term Horizon Risk Assessment

We will now work through a practical application of Monte Carlo simulation in the context of asset allocation over a long time horizon. We simulate asset class returns in quarterly steps over a 10-year time horizon.[13] Such models exhibit some degree of mean-reversion and also capture dynamic interactions across risk factors or asset classes over multiple time periods.

The volatilities, correlations, and other parameters of the time series model are estimated based on the past 20 years of unsmoothed asset class return data. The expected returns for the selected asset classes (shown in Exhibit 26), however, are not based on historical average

EXHIBIT 26   Asset Class Expected Returns

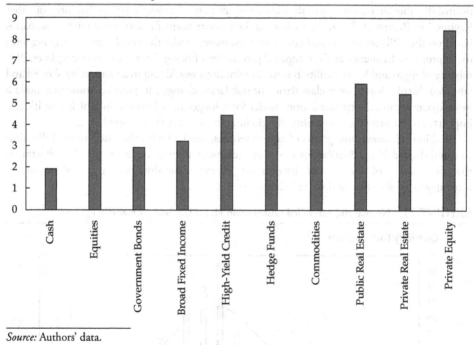

Source: Authors' data.

---

[12] In this reading, we assume that various asset classes have constant risk factor sensitivities over time, an assumption that can be relaxed in practice. For example, Berkelaar, Kobor, and Kouwenberg (2009) present time-varying risk factors for various hedge fund strategies in a similar Monte Carlo simulation framework.

[13] To ensure that we not only capture short-horizon risks but also properly assess long-term asset return behavior characteristics, we capture the linear interdependencies among multiple time series by working with a vector-autoregressive model.

returns but are illustrative, forward-looking estimates. Note that these return expectations mostly assume passive investments in the specific asset class and don't include the possible value-added from (or lost through) active management. Hedge funds are the exception, of course, because by definition hedge funds are actively managed investment strategies rather than a true stand-alone asset class. The expected returns are also generally assumed to be net of fees to make them comparable across asset classes.

Asset class–level expected returns are critically important to an asset allocation exercise. Return expectations should be reflective of the current market conditions—including valuations, levels of interest rates, and spreads. Setting return expectations requires a combination of objective facts (e.g., the current yield and spread levels) and judgment (how risk factors and valuation ratios might change from the current levels over the relevant time horizon).

In this example, we compare three possible portfolios:

- A portfolio 100% invested in government bonds
- A portfolio allocated 50% to global public equities and 50% to broad fixed income
- A diversified "endowment portfolio" allocated 40% to global public equities, 15% to fixed income, 20% to broad hedge funds, 15% to private equity, 5% to private real estate, and 5% to commodities

Exhibit 27 shows the risk and return statistics for the three portfolios. VaR and CVaR downside risk measures focus over the shorter, quarterly, and 1-year time horizons. The worst drawdown and the cumulative annualized total return ranges are expressed over a 10-year time horizon.

EXHIBIT 27   Portfolio Risk and Return Estimates

	Government Bond Portfolio	50/50 Portfolio	Endowment Portfolio
Expected Geometric Return over 10 Years	2.3%	5.6%	7.0%
Annual Total Return Volatility	4.2%	6.6%	11.2%
95% VaR over Q/Q (quarter over quarter)	−3.1%	−2.9%	−4.6%
95% VaR over 1 Year	−5.2%	−4.2%	−9.1%
95% CVaR over Q/Q	−4.0%	−3.9%	−6.4%
95% CVaR over 1 Year	−6.9%	−6.6%	−13.1%
99% VaR over Q/Q	−4.5%	−4.6%	−7.5%
99% VaR over 1 Year	−7.9%	−8.1%	−15.6%
99% CVaR over Q/Q	−5.2%	−5.5%	−8.7%
99% CVaR over 1 Year	−9.2%	−10.3%	−18.7%
Worst Drawdown over 10 Years	−19.8%	−22.5%	−36.9%

10-Year Return Distribution	Government Bond Portfolio	50/50 Portfolio	Endowment Portfolio
5% Low	0.0%	2.3%	1.9%
25% Low	1.2%	4.2%	4.8%
50% (Median)	2.3%	5.6%	7.0%
75% High	3.1%	7.0%	9.1%
95% High	4.5%	9.0%	12.2%

From Exhibit 27, we see that the multi-asset endowment portfolio generates a significantly higher return than the portfolio exclusively invested in government bonds, albeit at much higher downside risk as measured by VaR, CVaR, or worst drawdown. This table alone, however, is insufficient to determine which investment alternative a particular investor should choose.

Consider the case of a university endowment fund. Let's assume that the investment objective is to support a 5% annual spending rate as well as to preserve the purchasing power of the asset base over the 10-year time horizon. We use the same simulation engine to generate the analytics of Exhibit 28. Here, we plot the expected cumulative total return within a +/– 1 standard deviation range together with the cumulative spending rate, as well as the spending rate augmented with inflation on a cumulative basis. The latter two variables represent the

EXHIBIT 28   Cumulative Total Return Cones Simulated over a 10-Year Horizon

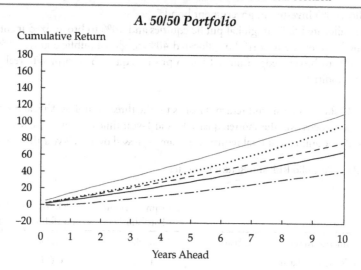

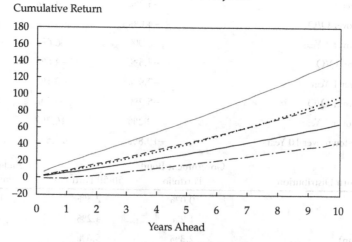

———— Cumulative Spending   ········ Cumulative Spending + Inflation

———— Exp. Cum. Return – 1 St. Dev.   – – – – Expected Cumulative Return

—·—·– Exp.Cum. Return + St. Dev

investment target, so we can meaningfully interpret the return potential of the two investment choices in the context of the investment objective. The 50% equities/50% government bond portfolio initially appeared to be a lower risk alternative in Exhibit 27, but Exhibit 28 shows that this choice is more likely to fall short of the return target, given that its median return of 5.6% is less than the nominal return target of approximately 7% (the 5% spending rate plus 2% inflation). At the same time, the endowment portfolio's 7% median return indicates that it would have a better chance of meeting the investment objective.

Exhibit 29 shows the probability of meeting the spending rate as well as the spending rate plus inflation at any point in time over the investment horizon. If risk is defined as the probability of falling short of meeting the return target (rather than the asset-only perspective of risk, volatility), the otherwise lower-risk 50% equities and 50% government bond portfolio becomes the higher-risk alternative.

EXHIBIT 29   Estimated Probability of Achieving the Investment Goal

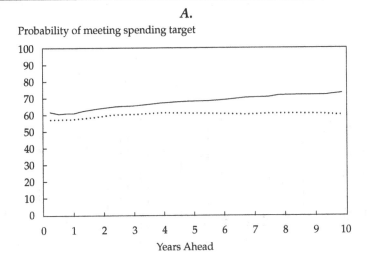

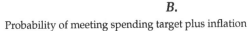

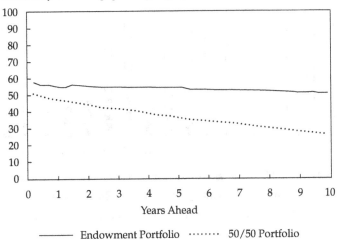

11. PORTFOLIO OPTIMIZATION

Portfolio optimization for asset allocation has been covered in great detail in earlier readings. Here we focus on some special considerations for optimization in the context of alternative investments.

11.1. Mean–Variance Optimization without and with Constraints

We mentioned earlier that mean–variance optimization would likely over-allocate to alternative, mainly illiquid, asset classes given their higher expected returns and potentially under-estimated risk. Some investors impose minimum and maximum constraints on various asset classes to compensate for this bias. Let's consider the ramifications of this approach.

Here, the input data for our optimization are comprised of the asset class expected returns depicted in Exhibit 26, while the covariance matrix is based on the unsmoothed asset class return history over the past 20 years. Exhibit 30 shows the optimized portfolio allocations

EXHIBIT 30 Unconstrained and Constrained Asset Allocations

A. Constrained Portfolios

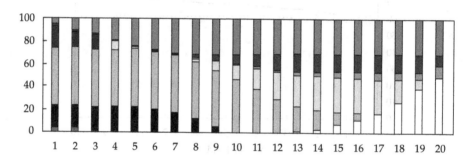

B. Unconstrained Portfolios

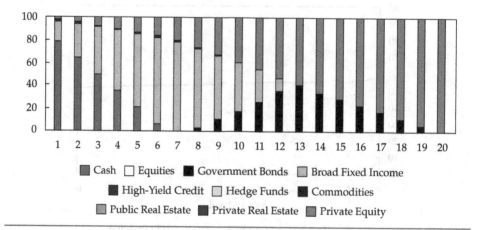

generated by the mean–variance optimization without and with constraints. Each column in these bar charts represents an optimized portfolio allocation subject to a return target. The exhibit progresses from low-return targets on the left to high-return targets on the right. In total, we show 20 possible portfolio allocations first without and then with constraints.

By reviewing Panel B of Exhibit 30, we can see that the unconstrained portfolio allocations are dominated by cash and fixed income at the lower end of the risk spectrum, and private equity becomes the dominant asset class for higher risk portfolios. Optimization is quite sensitive to the input parameters: It's quite common to see allocations concentrated in a small number of asset classes. Thus, investors shouldn't take the unconstrained output as the "best" allocation. Small changes in the input variables could lead to large changes in the asset allocations.

Because investors would potentially reject the raw, concentrated output of unconstrained mean–variance optimization, we also ran a constrained optimization where we capped private equity and hedge fund allocations at 30% each, private real estate at 15%, and major public asset classes at 50% each. The resulting constrained allocations, shown in the Panel A of Exhibit 30, are less concentrated and appear to be more diversified.

Exhibit 31 depicts the mean–variance efficient frontiers corresponding to the optimized portfolio allocations of Exhibit 30. Note that both frontiers contain 20 dots, each representing an optimized portfolio. The numbers under each bar in Exhibit 30 identify the allocation associated with each of the dots on the efficient frontiers in Exhibit 31 (e.g., the allocation associated with portfolio 20 on the efficient frontier in Exhibit 31 is the one shown at the rightmost edge of Exhibit 30).

Note that the constrained efficient frontier runs below its unconstrained peer (Exhibit 31). This is not unexpected, as we artificially prohibited the optimization from selecting the most efficient allocation it could get based on the available quantitative data.

EXHIBIT 31   Unconstrained and Constrained Mean–Variance Efficient Frontiers

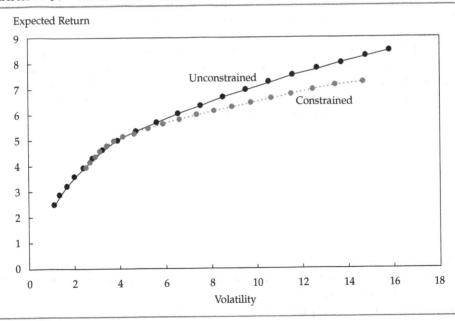

In practice, many investors are aware of the limits of the mean–variance framework—the possible underestimation of the true fundamental risks based on the reported returns of private investments—and they may also have in mind other constraints, such as capping illiquidity. Thus, introducing maximum and minimum constraints for certain asset classes may be a reasonable, although exogenous, adjustment to the quantitative optimization. However, not even constrained optimized allocations should be accepted without further scrutiny. In fact, similar volatility and expected return profiles can be achieved with a wide variety of asset allocations. So, although optimized portfolios may serve as analytical guidance, it's important to validate whether a change to an asset allocation policy results in a significant return increment and/or volatility reduction. Sometimes the results of a constrained optimization are largely driven by the constraints (especially if they are very tight). If that is the case, then the optimizer might not be able to perform its job due to the many (or very tight) constraints applied.

11.2. Mean–CVaR Optimization

Portfolio optimization can also improve the asset allocation decision through a risk management lens. An investor who is particularly concerned with the downside risk of a proposed asset allocation may choose to minimize the portfolio's CVaR rather than its volatility relative to a return target.[14] If the portfolio contains asset classes and investment strategies with negative skewness and long tails, the CVaR lens could materially alter the asset allocation decision. Minimizing CVaR subject to an expected return target is quantitatively much more complex than portfolio variance minimization. It requires a large number of historical or simulated return scenarios to properly incorporate potential tail risk into the optimization.[15]

Our first illustration is applied to three hedge fund strategies: macro, equity market neutral, and long/short equity hedged. Our expected returns for the three strategies are 3.6%, 3.6%, and 6.0%, respectively. The observed return distribution for macro strategy is fairly normal, while equity market neutral exhibits negative skew and the highest kurtosis of these three strategies (see Exhibit 21).

Panels A and B of Exhibit 32 compare 20 possible portfolio allocations generated by the mean–variance and mean–CVaR optimizations, varying from low to high risk/return profiles. The allocation to long/short equity hedged (the black bar) is similar under both the MVO and CVaR approaches. The macro strategy receives a much higher allocation using the CVaR approach than it does using the MVO approach.

---

[14]Because we are optimizing allocation to asset classes, the CVaR tail risk measure quantifies *systematic* asset class level risks. Individual asset managers or securities may impose additional idiosyncratic risk when the asset allocation is implemented in practice.

[15]Technical details are provided by Rockafellar and Uryasev (2000).

EXHIBIT 32   Hedge Fund Allocations

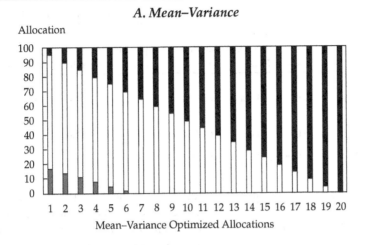

A. Mean–Variance

Allocation

Mean–Variance Optimized Allocations

B. Mean–CVaR

Allocation

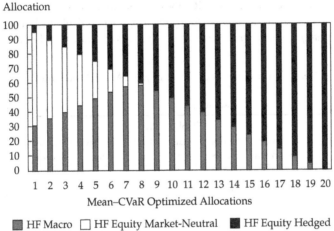

Mean–CVaR Optimized Allocations

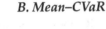
▨ HF Macro   ☐ HF Equity Market-Neutral   ■ HF Equity Hedged

Exhibit 33 compares portfolio #12 from the mean–variance efficient frontier to portfolio #12 from the mean–CVaR efficient frontier. Both portfolios allocated 60% to the long/short equity strategy. Under the CVaR-optimization approach, the remaining 40% of the portfolio is invested in global macro. Under the MVO approach, the remaining 40% of the portfolio is invested in equity market-neutral.

Let's compare the portfolio volatilities and downside risk measures. The mean–CVaR portfolio has higher volatility (7.8% vs 7.3%) but lower tail risk (−6.8% vs −7.7%). Exhibit 33 also shows a third portfolio, which evenly *splits* the 40% not allocated to equity-hedged between global macro and equity market neutral. The volatility of this portfolio lies between the two optimal portfolios. Although nominally more diversified than either of the #12 portfolios from the optimization, its CVaR is worse than that of the mean–CVaR optimized portfolio (but still better than that of the MVO portfolio). An investor may have qualitative considerations that warrant including this more-diversified portfolio among the options to be evaluated.

EXHIBIT 33   Mean–Variance and Mean–CVaR Efficient Hedge Fund Allocations

	Asset Allocation			Portfolio Characteristics			
	Macro	Equity Market Neutral	Long/Short Equity	Expected Return	Volatility	95% VaR	95% CVaR
Mean–Variance Optimal	0.0%	40.0%	60.0%	5.0%	7.3%	−3.7%	−7.7%
Mean–CVaR Optimal	40.0%	0.0%	60.0%	5.0%	7.8%	−4.1%	−6.8%
Combination	20.0%	20.0%	60.0%	5.0%	7.5%	−3.7%	−7.3%

Exhibit 34 compares the optimal allocations of a broad asset class portfolio through the mean–variance and mean–CVaR lenses. In this example, the optimal allocations were selected subject to a 6.8% expected return target. Both approaches allocated a significant portion of the portfolio to private equity and hedge funds (30% each). A notable difference, however, is in the allocation to public and private real estate. Where the MVO approach allocated 22% to the combined real estate categories, the CVaR approach allocated nothing at all to either real estate category. We can identify the reason for this by referring back to Exhibit 21: The public and private real estate categories are characterized by 99% CVaRs of −40.2% and −27.9%, respectively.

EXHIBIT 34   Mean–Variance and Mean–CVaR Efficient Multi-Asset Portfolios

	Asset Allocation						Portfolio Characteristics		
	Equities	Govt Bonds	Hedge Funds	Public Real Estate	Private Real Estate	Private Equity	Expected Return	Volatility	99% CVaR
Mean–Variance Optimal	18%	0%	30%	7%	15%	30%	6.8%	11.5%	−20.7%
Mean–CVaR Optimal	34%	6%	30%	0%	0%	30%	6.8%	12.1%	−15.6%

EXAMPLE 6   Asset Allocation Recommendation

The CIO (chief investment officer) of the International University Endowment Fund (the Fund) is preparing for the upcoming investment committee (IC) meeting. The Fund's annual asset allocation review is on the agenda, and the CIO plans to propose a new strategic asset allocation for the Fund. Subject to prudent risk-taking, the recommended asset allocation should offer

- the highest expected return and
- the highest probability of achieving the long-term 5% real return target.

The inflation assumption is 2%.

In addition, the risk in the Fund is one factor that is considered when lenders assign a risk rating to the university. The university's primary lender has proposed a loan covenant that would trigger a re-evaluation of the university's creditworthiness if the Fund incurs a loss greater than 20% over any 1-year period.

The investment staff produced the following tables to help the CIO prepare for the meeting.

Asset Allocation

Alternative	Cash	Public Equity	Govt	Credit	Hedge Fund	Real Estate	Private Equity
A	5.0%	60.0%	30.0%	5.0%	0.0%	0.0%	0.0%
B	4.0%	50.0%	16.0%	5.0%	10.0%	5.0%	10.0%
C	2.0%	40.0%	8.0%	5.0%	18.0%	7.0%	20.0%
D	1.0%	30.0%	5.0%	4.0%	20.0%	10.0%	30.0%
E	2.0%	40.0%	3.0%	3.0%	15.0%	7.0%	30.0%
F	2.0%	50.0%	3.0%	0.0%	10.0%	5.0%	30.0%
G	1.0%	56.0%	3.0%	0.0%	10.0%	0.0%	30.0%

Portfolio Characteristics

Alternative	Expected Return	Volatility	1-Year 99% VaR	1-Year 99% CVaR	10-Year Horizon: 5th Percentile Return	95th Percentile Return	Probability of Meeting 5% Real Return	Probability of Purchasing Power Impairment
A	6.0%	9.0%	−12.4%	−15.0%	1.6%	10.5%	37.0%	7.1%
B	6.7%	10.3%	−14.6%	−17.3%	2.0%	11.4%	46.1%	4.3%
C	7.1%	11.1%	−15.8%	−18.8%	2.2%	12.2%	52.1%	3.2%
D	7.4%	11.5%	−16.3%	−19.4%	2.4%	12.6%	56.1%	2.5%
E	7.7%	12.3%	−17.4%	−20.6%	2.4%	13.2%	58.8%	2.8%
F	7.8%	13.0%	−18.5%	−21.8%	2.2%	13.7%	60.8%	3.6%
G	7.9%	13.5%	−19.3%	−22.7%	2.1%	14.1%	61.0%	4.0%

Notes:

1-year horizon 99% VaR: the lowest return over any 1-year period at a 99% confidence level (i.e., only a 1% chance to experience a total return below this threshold).

1-year horizon 99% CVaR: the expected return if the return falls below the 99% VaR threshold.

5th and 95th percentile annualized returns over a 10-year time horizon: a 90% chance that the annualized 10-year total return will fall between these two figures

probability of purchasing power impairment[16]: as defined by the IC, the probability of losing 40% of the endowment's purchasing power over 10 years after taking gifts to the endowment, spending from the endowment, and total return into account.

---

[16] Similar measures of risk are proposed by Swensen (2009) in the context of endowment funds.

1. Which asset allocation is *most likely* to meet the committee's objective and constraints?

Solution to 1: Portfolio D. Portfolios E, F, and G have 1-year, 99% CVaRs, which, if realized, would trigger the loan covenant. Portfolio D has the next highest probability of meeting the 5% real return target and the lowest probability of purchasing power impairment. Portfolios A, B, and C have lower probabilities of meeting the return targets and higher probabilities of purchasing power impairment.

12. RISK FACTOR–BASED OPTIMIZATION

Increasingly, investors believe that viewing investment decisions through a risk factor lens (e.g., growth, inflation, credit risk) may improve the investment process. Separating fundamentally similar investments, like public and private equities, into distinct asset classes ignores the probability that both are exposed to the same risk factors. In this section, we will work through an asset allocation example using a risk factor lens.

Let's assume that an investor starts the asset allocation exercise by first allocating the overall risk budget across the main risk factors.[17] Instead of setting expectations for distinct asset classes, she may start thinking about the return expectations and correlation of the fundamental risk factors. Exhibit 35 shows her return expectations for the risk factors described in

EXHIBIT 35   Expected Factor Returns

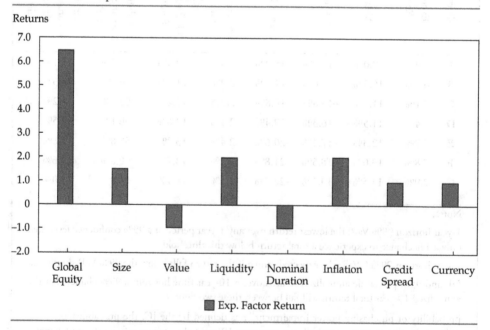

---

[17] Approaches to asset allocation and portfolio construction are expanding as the understanding of risk factors is increasing. A risk parity approach to asset allocation, for example, would allocate total risk in equal portion to the selected risk factors.

Exhibit 14. In this illustration, the global equity risk factor (a practical proxy for macroeconomic-oriented "growth") is expected to generate the highest return. She expects the duration and value factors to generate negative returns because stronger economic growth fueled by advances in technology would lead to rising rates and better returns for growth stocks. She is concerned about rising inflation, so she has assigned a positive expected return to the inflation factor.

Using these returns and the historical factor volatilities and correlations, we can optimize the risk factor exposure by minimizing factor-implied risk subject to a total return target of 6.5%. The black bars in Exhibit 36 show these optimal factor exposures. Note that the target exposures of the value and nominal duration factors are positive, although the associated expected factor returns are negative. The model allocates to these factors for their diversification potential because they are negatively correlated with other risk factors. Duration and equity factors have a correlation of −0.6, whereas value and equity factors have a correlation of −0.3 based on the data used for this illustration.

We have established optimal risk factor exposures, so now we must implement this target using actual investments. Some investors may have access to only public market investments, while other investors may also have access to private illiquid investments. The gray and white bars in Exhibit 36 illustrate the two possible implementations of the target factor exposures. Portfolio 1 assumes the investor is limited to public market investments. Portfolio 2 uses both public market investments and private, illiquid investments. The portfolio allocation details are displayed in Exhibit 37.

EXHIBIT 36   Optimal Risk Factor Allocations and Associated Asset Class Portfolios

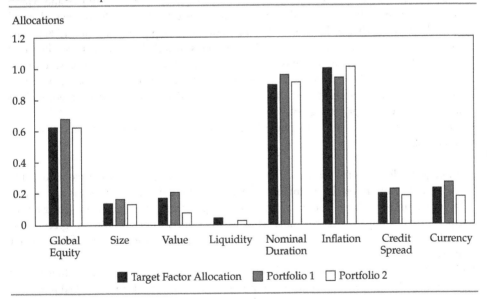

EXHIBIT 37   Asset Class Portfolios Designed Based on Optimal Risk Factor Allocations

	Portfolio 1	Portfolio 2
Domestic Equities; *Value Tilt*	21.0%	13.0%
Non-domestic Developed Market Equities; *Value Tilt*	21.0%	13.0%
Foreign Emerging Market Equities	21.0%	12.0%
Government Bonds	0.0%	5.0%
Broad Fixed Income	10.0%	0.0%
High-Yield Credit	2.0%	3.0%
Inflation-Linked Bonds	7.0%	0.0%
Hedge Funds	15.0%	10.0%
Commodities	3.0%	4.0%
Public Real Estate	0.0%	12.0%
Private Real Estate	0.0%	13.0%
Private Equity	0.0%	15.0%
Total	**100.0%**	**100.0%**
Expected Return	6.2%	6.9%
Volatility	13.5%	13.2%

Even though they have similar factor exposures, you can see some significant differences in the asset class allocations of the two portfolios. Portfolio 1 allocates 63% to public equities, whereas Portfolio 2 allocates 35% to public equities plus 15% to private equity for its higher return potential. Portfolio 1 allocates 18% to alternatives (15% in hedge funds and 3% in commodities, two of the most liquid alternative asset classes), while Portfolio 2 has allocated 54% to alternatives (10% hedge funds, 4% commodities, 12% public real estate, 13% private real estate, and 15% private equity). Portfolio 1 achieves its inflation sensitivity by allocating to inflation-linked bonds and commodities. Portfolio 2 achieves its desired exposure to the inflation factor through a combined allocation to real estate and commodities. The volatility of the two portfolios is similar, but Portfolio 2 is able to achieve a higher expected return given its ability to allocate to private equity.

Although a risk factor-driven approach is conceptually very elegant, we must mention a few caveats:

- While generally accepted asset class definitions provide a common language among the investment community, risk factors may be defined quite differently investor-to-investor. It's important to establish a common understanding of factor definitions and factor return expectations among the parties to an asset allocation exercise. This includes an agreement as to what financial instruments can be used to best match the factor exposures if they are not directly investable.
- Correlations among risk factors, just like correlations across asset classes, may dramatically shift under changing market conditions; thus, careful testing needs to be applied to understand how changing market conditions will affect the asset allocation.
- Some factor sensitivities are stable (like the nominal interest rate sensitivity of government bonds), while others are very unstable (like the inflation sensitivity of commodities). Factor sensitivities also need to be very carefully tested to validate whether the invested portfolio would truly deliver the desired factor exposures and not deliver unintended factor returns.

EXAMPLE 7   Selecting an Asset Allocation Approach

1. You have a new client who has unexpectedly inherited a substantial sum of money. The client is in his early 30s and newly married. He has no children and no other investible assets. What asset allocation approach is most suitable for this client?

2. Your client is a tax-exempt foundation that recently received a bequest doubling its assets to €200 million. There is an outside investment adviser but no dedicated investment staff; however, the six members of the investment committee (IC) are all wealthy, sophisticated investors in their own right. The IC conducts an asset allocation study every three years and reviews the asset allocation at its annual meeting. The current asset allocation is 30% equities, 20% fixed income, 25% private equity, and 25% real estate. Three percent of assets are paid out annually in grants; this expenditure is covered by an annuity purchased some years ago. The foundation's primary investment objective is to maximize returns subject to a maximum level of volatility. A secondary consideration is the desire to avoid a permanent loss of capital. What asset allocation approach is most suitable for this client?

Solution to 1: Mean–variance optimization with Monte Carlo simulation is most appropriate for this client. He has limited investment expertise, so your first responsibility is to educate him with respect to such basic investment concepts as risk, return, and diversification. A simple MVO approach supplemented with Monte Carlo simulation to illustrate potential upside and downside of an asset allocation choice is mostly likely to serve the asset allocation and investment education needs.

Solution to 2: Given the sophistication and investment objectives of the IC members, using a mean–CVaR optimization approach is appropriate to determine the asset allocation. This client has a more sophisticated understanding of risk and will appreciate the more nuanced view of risk offered by mean–CVaR optimization. Given the portfolio's exposure to alternative investments, the asset allocation decision will be enhanced by the more detailed picture of left-tail risk offered by CVaR optimization (the risk of permanent loss) relative to mean–variance optimization. The lack of permanent staff and a once-per-year meeting schedule suggest that a risk factor–based approach may not be appropriate.

---

13. LIQUIDITY PLANNING AND ACHIEVING AND MAINTAINING THE STRATEGIC ASSET ALLOCATION

Earlier, we addressed various aspects of liquidity associated with investing in alternative asset classes. In this section, we focus on multi-year horizon liquidity planning for private investments.

When managing portfolios that contain allocations to alternative investments, managing liquidity risk takes on critical importance. We need to ensure sufficient liquidity to meet interim obligations or goals, which might include:

- periodic payments to beneficiaries (e.g., a pension fund's retirement benefit payments or an endowment fund's distributions to support operating expenses);
- portfolio rebalancing or funding new asset manager mandates; or
- fulfilling a commitment made to a private investment fund when the general partner makes the capital call.

Alternative investments pose unique liquidity challenges that must be explicitly addressed before committing to an alternative investment program. Private investments—including private equity, private real estate, private real assets, and private credit—represent the most illiquid components of an investment portfolio. Private investments usually require a long-term commitment over an 8- to 15-year time horizon. An investor contributes capital over the first few years (the investment period) and receives distributions in the later years. Combined with the call down (or drawdown) structure of a private investment fund, this creates a need to model a hypothetical path to achieving and maintaining a diversified, fully-invested allocation to private investments. Here we will explore the challenges with private investment liquidity planning with three primary considerations:

1. How to achieve and maintain the desired allocation.
2. How to handle capital calls.
3. How to plan for the unexpected.

13.1. Achieving and Maintaining the Strategic Asset Allocation

Strategic planning is required to determine the necessary annual commitments an investor should make to reach and maintain the long-term target asset allocation. Large private investors often use a liquidity forecasting model for their private investment programs. Here, we illustrate one such model based on work published by Takahashi and Alexander (2001). We also discuss private investment commitment pacing as an application of this model. This model is only one possible way to forecast private investment cash flows; investors may develop their own model using their own assumptions and experience.

We will illustrate this model with a hypothetical capital commitment (CC) of £100 million to a fund with a contractual term (L) of 12 years.

We begin by modeling the capital contributions (C) to the fund. Certain assumptions must be made regarding the rate of contribution (RC). We'll assume that 25% is contributed in the first year and that 50% of the remaining commitments are contributed in each of the subsequent years:

Year 1: £100 million × 25% = £25 million
Year 2: (£100 million − £25 million) × 50% = £37.5 million
Year 3: (£100 million − £25 million − £37.5 million) × 50% = £18.75 million

and so on.

The capital contribution (C) in year t can be expressed with the following formula:

$$C_t = RC_t \times (CC - PIC_t) \tag{8.1}$$

where PIC denotes the already paid-in capital.

Alternatively, we can express this in words:

Capital Contribution = Rate of Contribution × (Capital Commitment − Paid-in-Capital)

In practice, the investment period is often limited to a defined number of years; also, not all of the committed capital may be called.

The next step is to estimate the periodic distribution paid to investors. Distributions (D) are a function of the net asset value (NAV). From one year to the next, the NAV rises as additional capital contributions are made and as underlying investments appreciate. NAV declines as distributions are made (or as assets are written down).

If the partnership investment develops as anticipated, then the fund's IRR would be equal to this rate.

To estimate the expected annual distribution payments, we need to make an assumption about the pattern of distributions. For example, an analyst may assume that the fund does not distribute any money in Year 1 or Year 2 but distributes 10% of the prevailing net asset value in Year 3, 20% in Year 4, 30% in Year 5, and 50% of the remaining balance in each of the remaining years. In the case of real estate funds, it is also possible that there is a pre-defined minimum annual distribution rate (called the "yield"). Once the annual rates of distribution are determined, the annual amount distributed is calculated by the following formula:

$$D_t = RD_t[NAV_{t-1} \times (1 + G)] \tag{8.2}$$

where

$$RD_t = (t/L)^B, \tag{8.3}$$
$$NAV_t = [NAV_{t-1} \times (1 + G)] + C_t - D_t \tag{8.4}$$

Again, in words:

Distributions at time t = Rate of Distribution at time t × [NAV at time t-1
× (1 + Growth Rate)], and
NAV at time t = prior NAV × (1 + Growth Rate) + Capital Contribution − Distributions

In Exhibit 38, we display the forecasted annual capital contributions, outstanding commitment forecast, distributions, NAV, and cumulative net cash flow for a private investment fund with a 12-year life. We assume that 25% of the committed capital is contributed in the first year and that 50% of the remaining commitments are contributed in each of the subsequent years. Using a bow (B) parameter of 2.5, we set the RD_t distribution rates such that the yearly distribution rates would increase fairly gradually. We assume a 13% growth rate from the investments in this fund.

EXHIBIT 38   Expected Annual Contribution, Outstanding Commitment, Rate of Distribution, Annual Distribution, NAV, and Net Cash Flow of a Hypothetical Private Investment Fund

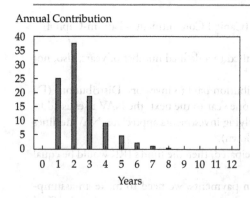

Annual Contribution

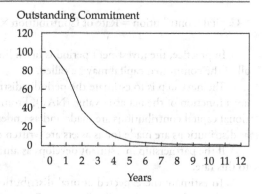

Outstanding Commitment

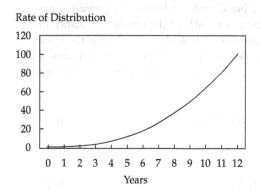

Rate of Distribution

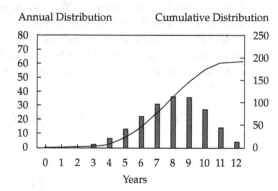

Annual Distribution   Cumulative Distribution

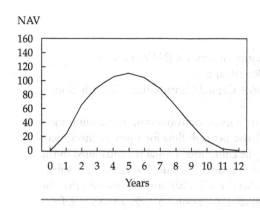

NAV

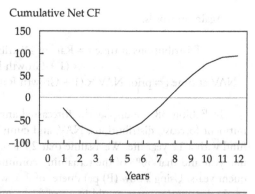

Cumulative Net CF

The corresponding annual RD$_t$ rates are displayed in Exhibit 39.

EXHIBIT 39   Assumed Annual Distribution Rates (RD$_t$)

Year	1	2	3	4	5	6	7	8	9	10	11	12
Rate of Distribution	0%	1%	3%	6%	11%	18%	26%	36%	49%	63%	80%	100%

How does the shape of the expected rate of distribution influence NAV and the annual distribution amounts? For illustration purposes we can change our assumption of RD by setting the bow parameter (B) to 5.0, such that early year distribution rates are very low and start increasing in the second half of the fund's life. The new distribution rates are shown in Exhibit 40, and Exhibit 41 shows how distributions and the NAV would react to this change.

EXHIBIT 40   Alternative Assumed Annual Distribution Rates (RD_t)

Year	1	2	3	4	5	6	7	8	9	10	11	12
Rate of Distribution	0%	0%	0%	0%	1%	3%	7%	13%	24%	40%	65%	100%

EXHIBIT 41   Rate of Distribution, Expected Annual Distribution, NAV, and Cumulative Net Cash Flow with Back-Loaded Distributions

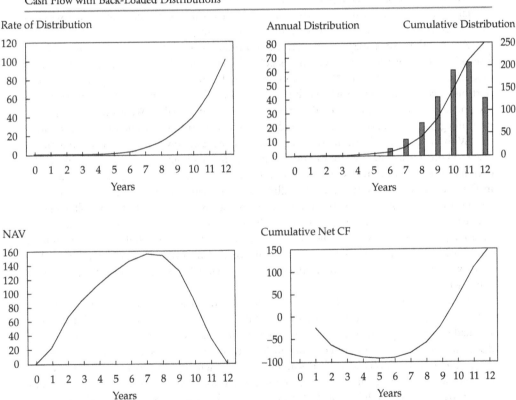

Although the annual capital contributions would not be affected, we can see that the lower distribution rate in the early years allows the NAV to grow higher. The cumulative net cash flow, however, would stay in the negative zone for a longer time.

EXAMPLE 8   Liquidity Planning for Private Investments

The NAV of an investor's share in a private renewable energy fund was €30 million at the end of 2020. All capital has been called. The investor expects a 20% distribution to be paid at the end of 2021. The expected growth rate is 12%. What is the expected NAV at year-end 2022?

Solution: The expected NAV at year-end 2022 is €30,105,600. The expected distribution at the end of 2021 is €6.72 million [(€30 million × 1.12) × 20%]. The NAV at year-end 2022 is therefore [(€30 million × 1.12) − 20%] × 1.12% = €30,105,600.

An important practical application of such models is to help determine the size of the annual commitment an investor needs to make to reach the target allocation of an asset class over the coming years (i.e., investment commitment pacing).

Assume that we manage an investment portfolio of £1 billion and that our strategic asset allocation target for private equities is 20%. We currently do not have any private equity investment in the portfolio. We also must project the growth of the aggregate investment portfolio, because we want to achieve the 20% allocation based on the expected *future* value of the portfolio and of the private equity investment, not today's value. We assume an aggregate portfolio growth rate of 6% per year, including both net contributions and investment returns.

With these assumptions, and the private investment cash flow and NAV forecasting model discussed previously, the investor can determine the annual commitments needed to reach the overall target allocation. By using the same cash flow forecasting parameters as for the analysis in Exhibit 38, we can see that a £100 million commitment would lead the NAV to peak at around £110 million five years from now. A rough approximation could be the following: In five years, the total portfolio size would be £1 billion × 1.06^5 ≈ £1.338 billion; so, at that point, the total private equity NAV should be approximately 20% × £1.338 billion = £268 million. Since we know that a £100 million commitment would lead to an NAV of £110 million in five years, we can extrapolate to arrive at the conclusion that a £243 million commitment today could achieve the goal.

However, this would result in a very concentrated private equity investment, with an NAV peaking in four to five years and then declining over the following years as distributions are made. A better practice is to spread commitments out over multiple years. A stable and disciplined multi-year commitment schedule leads to a more stable NAV size over time. It also achieves an important objective of diversifying exposure across vintage years. Thus, an investor can choose to commit a target amount of around £70 million per year over a period of four years (2017 through 2020) instead of concentrating the commitment in a single year. This schedule would bring the total private equity NAV to the target 20% level over five years. In Exhibit 42, we illustrate how the portfolio of private equity investments of different vintage years would build up over time. We also show how the total NAV would evolve beyond 2022 if no further capital commitment is made. As the chart suggests, the NAV would continue to grow through 2023 but would start to decline in later years as the 2017–2020 vintage private funds make distributions.

EXHIBIT 42   Commitment Pacing: Cumulative NAV of Private Equity Investments

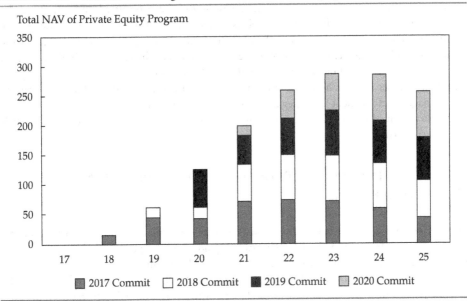

In Exhibit 43, we show how private equity investments would grow as a proportion of the overall investment portfolio. As in the previous chart, we extend the forecast beyond 2022 to show the proportion of private equity investments will start to decline without further capital commitments after 2020.

EXHIBIT 43   Commitment Pacing: Private Equity NAV as % of the Total Portfolio

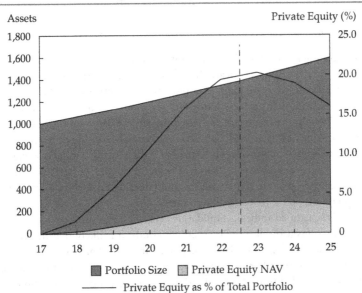

The investor must review her pacing model forecast periodically, updating it as needed based on the actual commitments and transactions that have occurred and refreshing the assumptions for the future. If the investor plans to maintain a 20% allocation to private equity investments over the long run, she will clearly have to make ongoing commitments in the future, although at a slower pace once private equity is an established asset class in the portfolio.

To summarize, cash flow and pacing models enable investors to better manage their portfolio liquidity, set realistic annual commitment targets to reach the desired asset allocation, and manage portfolio beta in aggregate. Investors need to validate their model assumptions and evaluate how different parameter settings and liquidity stress scenarios could impact their investment portfolios.

14. MANAGING THE CAPITAL CALLS AND PREPARING FOR THE UNEXPECTED

The investor makes an up-front commitment of a certain dollar amount to a private investment fund, and the funds will typically be called (paid in) over a period of three to four years. In many cases, the general partner (GP) will never call the full amount of the capital commitment. The limited partner (LP) is obligated to pay the capital call in accordance with the terms agreed to with the GP, often within 30 days of receiving the call notification. However, it is not practical to keep all the committed (but not yet called) capital in liquid reserves given the opportunity cost of being out of the markets during the investment phase. Investors must develop a strategy for maintaining the asset allocation while waiting for the fund to become fully invested. Capital pending investment in a private equity fund is often invested in public equities as a proxy for private equities. A similar approach may be followed in the case of other private asset classes: The investor may consider high yield as a placeholder for pending private credit investments, REITs as a placeholder for private real estate investments, and energy stocks or commodity futures as a proxy for private real asset investments.

14.1. Preparing for the Unexpected

The liquidity-planning model described here addresses the key components of cash inflows and outflows, but the model results are clearly heavily dependent on the assumptions. The model parameters can be based purely on judgment, but a better practice would be to verify estimates and forecasts with a sample of representative private funds' historical experience. Obviously, the realized cash flows in the future are likely to differ from what the model predicted based on the assumed parameters. Thus, it is advisable to run the analysis using different sets of assumptions and under different scenarios. In a bear market, GPs may call capital at a higher pace and/or make distributions at a slower pace than had been expected. This suggests that in addition to the base case scenario planning, the analyst should develop an additional set of assumptions with faster capital calls and lower distribution rates.

If the fund is scheduled to begin liquidation when the investor's public market portfolio is performing poorly (as it did in the 2007–2008 period), it is likely that the GP will exercise his option to extend the fund life. If this happens, investors may find themselves with an asset allocation significantly different from target or being unable to meet the capital calls that were intended to be funded from the distributions. These contingencies should be modeled as part of stress testing the asset allocation.

EXAMPLE 9   Private Investments, Asset Allocation, and Liquidity Planning

The Endowment Fund of the University of Guitan (the Fund) has $750 million in assets. The investment committee (IC) adopted the following strategic asset allocation four years ago. Private investments are at the lower end of the permitted range. To reach the target allocation among private investments, the investment team has made several new commitments recently, and they expect capital calls over the coming year equal to approximately about 20% of the current private asset net asset value.

	Strategic Asset Allocation Target	Permitted Range	Current Asset Allocation (%)	Current Asset Allocation ($mil)
Cash	2%	0 to 5%	3%	22.5
Public Equities (including long/short equity)	35%	30 to 40%	35%	262.5
Government Bonds	5%	4 to 10%	7%	52.5
High-Yield Credit	3%	2 to 5%	5%	37.5
Hedge Funds (excluding long/short equity)	20%	17 to 23%	23%	172.5
Private Real Estate	10%	7 to 13%	8%	60.0
Private Real Assets	5%	3 to 7%	4%	30.0
Private Equity	20%	15 to 22%	15%	112.5
Total				$750 mil
Expected Return	7.1%			
Expected Volatility	11.1%			
99% CVaR	−18.8%			
Assumed Inflation Rate	2%			

The strategic asset allocation has a 52% probability of meeting the 5% real return target (4% spend rate, 1% principal growth, and 2% inflation).

At its last meeting, the endowment committee of the board approved a temporary increase in the spending rate, raising it from 4% to 5% for the next five years to support the university's efforts to reposition itself in the face of declining enrollments. The spending rate is calculated as a percentage of the Fund's trailing 5-year average value.

The CIO (chief investment officer) has produced a capital market outlook that will guide the fund's tactical asset allocation strategy for the next several quarters. Key elements of the outlook are:

- accommodative central bank policies are ending;
- equity valuation metrics have recently set new highs;

- the economic cycle is at or near its peak (i.e., there is a meaningful probability of rising inflation and a weaker economic environment over the next several quarters); and
- returns will quite likely be lower than what has been experienced over the past five years.

She also developed the following stress scenario based on her capital market outlook:

Return Stress Scenario	
Cash	2%
Public Equities (including l/s equity)	−30%
Government Bonds	−3%
High-Yield Credit	−10%
Hedge Funds (excluding l/s equity)	−8%
Private Real Estate	0%
Private Real Assets	10%
Private Equity	−10%

1. Identify and discuss the liquidity factors that the CIO should consider as she develops her portfolio positioning strategy for the next 12 to 24 months.
2. Recommend and justify a tactical asset allocation strategy for the Fund.

Solution to 1: Given the market outlook, it is reasonable to assume cash flows into the fund from existing private investments will be negligible.

- The fund has next-12-month liabilities as follows:
  - Approximately $37.5 million to the university ($750 million × 5%). This is a high (conservative) estimate based on an assumption that the trailing 5-year average Fund value is less than the current $750 million.
  - Approximately $40.5 million in capital calls from private investment commitments (equally allocated across private real estate, private real assets, and private equity

$$[(\$60m + \$30m + \$112.5m) \times 20\%]$$

- Total liabilities next 12 months = $78 million
- Sources of immediate liquidity:
  - Cash = $22.5 million
  - Government bonds = $52.5 million
  - $75.0 million in total (less than the $78 million liability)
- Other liquidity:
  - Public equities are at the midpoint of the permitted range. The allocation could be reduced from 35% to 30% and remain within the permitted range. This would free up $37.5 million ($750 million × 5%) for reinvestment in more-defensive asset classes or to meet anticipated liquidity needs. However, if the return scenario

is realized (equities down 30%), then the equity allocation will fall below the 30% minimum and additional rebalancing will be required.

- High-yield credit is at the upper end of the allowed range. The allocation could be reduced from the current 5% to 2% or 3%, freeing up an additional $15 to $22.5 million. The limited liquidity in high-yield bond markets may make this challenging.
- The hedge fund allocation is at the upper end of the allowed range. The allocation could be reduced from the current 23% to something in the range of 17% to 20% (between the lower end of the band and the target allocation). However, given the required redemption notice (generally 60 to 90 days in advance of the redemption date), if the market weakens the hedge funds might invoke any gates allowed for in their documents.
- Longer term, a temporary increase in the spending rate reduces the probability that the fund will meet its real return target. This objective would be further threatened if the inflation rate does rise as the CIO fears. The liquidity profile of the Fund's investments should prepare for the possibility that, in a bad year, they may be called upon to dip into capital to fund the spending obligation.

Solution to 2:

- The Fund should target the upper end of the ranges for cash and government bonds in light of the current high equity valuations, weakening economic outlook, and threat of rising inflation. Given rising inflation and interest rate concerns, she may also consider shortening the duration of the government bond portfolio.
- The higher cash and bond allocation will also provide the liquidity buffer needed to meet the Fund's liabilities. Additional cash might be justified to fund the known payouts.
- A high allocation to real estate could also be considered a defensive positioning, but the current 8% allocation may rise toward its 13% maximum, even without additional allocations, given the expected decline in the balance of the portfolio. In addition, tactical tilts in private asset classes are difficult to implement because it would take an extended time period to make new commitments and invest the additional capital.
- The allocations to public equites and hedge funds could be reduced to fund the increases in cash and government bonds.

The following table summarizes the proposed allocation and looks at the likely end-of-year allocations if events unfold as forecast.

	Allowed Ranges		Current Allocation	Proposed Allocation		Expected Return Next 12 Months	Allocation 12 Months Forward	
	Lower Limit	Upper Limit	%	%	$ (mil)		%	$ (mil)
Cash	0%	5%	3%	10%	75	2%		0*
Public Equities	30%	40%	35%	30%	225	-30%	25%	157.50
Government Bonds	4%	10%	7%	10%	75	-3%	12%	72.75
High-Yield Credit	2%	5%	5%	5%	37.5	-10%	5%	33.75
Hedge Funds	17%	23%	23%	17%	127.5	-8%	19%	117.30
Private Real Estate	7%	13%	8%	8%	60	0%	12%	72.00
Private Real Assets	3%	7%	4%	5%	37.5	10%	8%	48.75
Private Equity	15%	22%	15%	15%	112.5	-10%	20%	123.75
Total				**100%**	**$750.0**		**100%**	**$625.80**

* Cash paid to fund liabilities ($37.5 million to the university and $40.5 million to fund private investment capital calls. Additional cash needs funded from government bond portfolio.

15. MONITORING THE INVESTMENT PROGRAM

The monitoring of an alternative investment program is time and labor intensive. Data are hard to come by and are not standardized among managers or asset classes. The analyst must spend a good amount of time gathering data and ensuring that the analysis is comparable across managers and asset classes. It is incumbent on the investor to both monitor the managers *and* the alternative investment program's progress toward the goals that were the basis for the investment in these assets.

15.1. Overall Investment Program Monitoring

When an investor makes a strategic decision to invest in alternative assets, specific goals are typically associated with the alternative investment program—return enhancement, income, risk reduction, safety, or a combination of the four. The goals may vary by asset class. A real estate program, for example, might be undertaken with the objective of replacing a portion of the fixed-income allocation—providing yield or income but also providing some measure of growth and/or inflation protection. The real estate program should be monitored relative to those goals, not simply relative to a benchmark.

We know that an alternative investment program is likely to take a number of years to reach fully-invested status. Is it reasonable to defer an assessment of the program until that point? Probably not. The investor must monitor developments in the relevant markets to ensure that the fundamental thesis underlying the decision to invest remains intact. Continuing with our real estate analogy, if real estate cap rates[18] fall to never-before-seen lows, what are the implications for the real estate's ability to continue to fulfill its intended role in the portfolio? Or if the managers hired within the real estate allocation allocate more to commercial office properties than was anticipated, what are the implications for the ability of real estate to fulfill the income-oriented goal? Only by monitoring the development of the portfolio(s) will the investor be able to adjust course and ensure that the allocation remains on track to achieve the goals established at the outset.

We also know that investor goals and objectives are subject to change. Perhaps a university experiences a persistent decline in enrollments and the endowment fund will be called upon to provide greater support to the university while it transitions to the new reality; what are the implications for a private equity program? Or what if the primary wage-earner in a two-parent household becomes critically ill; how might this affect the asset allocation? These types of events cannot be predicted, but it is important to continuously monitor the linkages between the asset allocation and the investor's goals, objectives, and circumstances. Particularly in the private markets—where changing course requires a long lead time and abruptly terminating an investment program can radically alter the risk and return profile of the portfolio—an early warning of an impending change can greatly improve the investor's ability to maintain the integrity of the investment program.

15.2. Performance Evaluation

Properly benchmarking an alternative investment strategy is a challenge that has important implications for judging the effectiveness of the alternative investment program. Many

---

[18]The ratio of net operating income (NOI) to property asset value (the inverse of price/earnings).

investors resort to custom index proxies (e.g., a static return premium over cash or equity index) or rely on peer group comparisons (e.g., Hedge Fund Research, Inc., Eurekahedge, Cambridge Private Equity Index). Both approaches have significant limitations.

Consider a private equity program benchmarked to the MSCI World Index plus 3%. This custom index may help frame the return expectation the investment committee holds with regard to its private equity assets, but it is unlikely to match the realized risk, return, and liquidity characteristics of the actual private equity program.

It is similarly challenging to develop a peer group representative of a manager's strategy given the high level of idiosyncratic risk inherent in most alternative investment funds. Existing providers follow vastly different rules in constructing these "benchmarks." They all have their own set of definitions (e.g., whether a fund is a credit fund or an event-driven fund), weighting methodology (asset weighted or equal weighted), method for dealing with potential survivorship bias, and other rules for inclusion (e.g., whether the fund is currently open or closed to new capital).

Exhibit 44 shows the returns from three different hedge fund index providers. An event driven fund that generated a 6% return over the relevant 5-year period might look attractive if evaluated relative to the Credit Suisse index, whereas it might look subpar if evaluated relative to the Eurekahedge index. Additionally, a manager's ranking within the peer group is affected as much by what *other* managers do as by his own actions. Clearly, peer group ranking is, at best, one small part of the overall benchmarking exercise.

EXHIBIT 44   The Trouble with Peer Groups

Strategy	Provider	3-Year Annualized Return (%)	5-Year Annualized Return (%)
		ending December 31, 2017	
Equity Hedge	HFRI	5.7	6.6
	Credit Suisse	4.3	7.1
	Eurekahedge	6.5	7.8
Event Driven	HFRI	3.8	5.9
	Credit Suisse	0.8	3.7
	Eurekahedge	6.8	7.2
Global Macro	HFRI	0.6	0.7
	Credit Suisse	2.0	2.7
	Eurekahedge	−0.1	1.2

The timing and nature of reported alternative investment returns also pose challenges to monitoring the performance of alternative investment managers. For call-down strategies such as private equity, private real estate, and real assets, tracking and calculating performance might require different systems and methodologies. Private equity, credit, and real estate returns are typically reported using internal rates of return (IRRs) rather than time-weighted returns (TWR) as is common in the liquid asset classes. IRRs are sensitive to the timing of cash flows into and out of the fund. Two managers may have similar portfolios but very different return profiles depending on their particular capital call and distribution schedule. Investors have to be wise to the ways in which a manager can bias their reported IRR. Alternative metrics, such as multiple on invested capital (MOIC) have been developed to provide an additional frame of reference. (MOIC is a private equity measure that divides the current value of the underlying companies plus any distributions received by the total invested capital.)

Pricing issues also complicate performance evaluation of most alternative strategies. Stale pricing common in many alternative strategies can distort reported returns and the associated risk metrics. Betas, correlations, Sharpe ratios, and other measures must be interpreted with a healthy degree of skepticism.

Although performance measurement has its challenges with all asset classes, relying exclusively on any single measure with alternative investments increases the likelihood of inaccurate or misleading conclusions. With respect to the more illiquid investment strategies, judgment as to whether a given fund is meeting its investment objectives should be reserved until most or even all of the investments have been monetized, and capital has been returned to the investor. If capital is returned quickly (thereby possibly producing extraordinarily high IRRs), the investor may want to put greater emphasis on the MOIC measure. Similarly, funds that return capital more slowly than expected might want to put greater weight on the IRR measure. Even a fund with both a weak MOIC and a weak IRR need the measures to be put into context. An appropriate peer group analysis can help ascertain whether the "poor" performance was common across all funds of similar vintage (perhaps suggesting a poor investment climate) or whether it was specific to that fund. Likewise, a fund that posts strong performance may simply have benefited from an ideal investment period.

Perhaps the best way to gain performance insight beyond the numbers is to develop a qualitative understanding of the underlying assets. What are the manager's expectations at the time of acquisition? How does the manager plan to add value to the investment over the holding period? What is the manager's exit strategy for the investment? The investor can monitor how the investment develops relative to the initial thesis. This type of qualitative assessment can lead to a better understanding of whether the manager did well for the right reasons, whether the manager was wrong but for the right reasons, or whether the manager was just wrong.

15.3. Monitoring the Firm and the Investment Process

In addition to monitoring the portfolio, monitoring of the investment process and the investment management firm itself are particularly important in alternative investment structures where the manager cannot be terminated easily, and the assets transferred to another manager in which the investor has more confidence. What follows is a non-exhaustive list of issues that the investor will want to monitor:

- *Key person risk*: Most alternative investment strategies depend to a large extent on the skill of a few key investment professionals. These are what are known as "key persons." Key persons are typically specified in the fund documents, with certain rights allocated to the limited partners in the event a key person leaves the firm. It is important to ensure that these investment professionals remain actively involved in the investment process. There are also other employees of the investment manager whose departure may negatively affect the operation of the business or signal an underlying problem. If, for example, the chief operating officer or chief compliance officer leaves the firm, it is important to understand why and what effect it may have on the business. Finally, it is important to note that for quantitatively oriented strategies, key person risk is often reduced because the quantitative investment process remains in place even if a key person leaves.

- *Alignment of interests*: Alignment of interest issues range from the complexity of the organization, structure of management fees, compensation of the investment professionals, growth in assets under management (AUM), and the amount of capital the key professionals have committed to the funds that they are managing. The investor will want to verify that the money manager's interests remain closely aligned with their own. Has the manager withdrawn a significant portion of her own capital that had been invested alongside the limited partners? If so, why? Is the manager raising a new fund? If so, what safeguards are in place to ensure that the investment professionals are not unduly distracted with fundraising, firm administration, or unfairly concentrated on managing other funds? Is the opportunity set deep enough to support the additional capital being raised? Will the funds have shared ownership interest in a given asset? If so, what conflicts of interest may arise (e.g., the manager may earn an incentive fee in one fund if the asset is sold, while it may be in the best interest of the second fund to sell the asset at a later date).
- *Style drift*: Fund documents often give managers wide latitude as to their investment options and parameters, but it is incumbent on the investor to understand where the fund manager has a competitive advantage and skill and confirm that the investments being made are consistent with the manager's edge.
- *Risk management*: The investor should understand the manager's risk management philosophy and processes and periodically confirm that the fund is abiding by them. Where a fund makes extensive use of leverage, a robust risk management framework is essential.
- *Client/asset turnover*: A critical part of the ongoing due diligence process should include a review of clients and assets. A significant gain or drop in either may be a sign of an underlying problem. An unusual gain in assets could make it difficult for the investment professionals to invest in suitably attractive investments, potentially handicapping future performance. Conversely, significant client redemptions may force the money manager to sell attractive assets as he looks to raise cash. If this occurs during periods of market turmoil when liquidity in the market itself may be low, the manager may be forced to sell what he can rather than what he should in order to optimize performance. This could hurt the returns of non-redeeming clients and/or leave the remaining clients with illiquid holdings that might make it difficult for them to redeem in the future.
- *Client profile*: Investors will want to gauge the profile of the fund manager's other clients. Are the fund's other clients considered long-term investors, or do they have a history of redeeming at the first sign of trouble? Are they new to the alternative investment space and perhaps don't understand the nuances of the fund's strategy and risks? You may have a strong conviction in a money manager's skills, but the actions of others may affect your ability to reap the benefits of those skills. If too many of her other clients elect to redeem, the manager may invoke the gates allowed by the fund's documents or, at the extreme, liquidate the fund at what might be the worst possible moment. This was a common occurrence during 2008–2009, when investors sought to raise cash by redeeming from their more liquid fund managers. Even if a money manager weathers massive outflows, profitability and the ability to retain key talent may be at risk.
- *Service providers:* Investors will want to ensure that the fund manager has engaged independent and reputable third-party service providers, including administrators, custodians, and auditors. Although an investor may have performed extensive checks prior to investing, it is good practice to periodically verify that these relationships are intact and working well. If the service provider changes, the investor will want to understand *why*. Has the fund's AUM grown to a level that cannot be handled adequately by the current provider? Perhaps the service provider has chosen to terminate the relationship because of actions taken by the fund manager. Exploring the motivation behind a change in a service provider can uncover early warning flags deserving of further investigation.

EXAMPLE 10 Monitoring Alternative Investment Programs

1. The O'Hara family office determined that the illiquidity risk inherent in private investments is a risk that the family is ill-suited to bear. As a result, they decided several years ago to unwind their private equity program. There are still a few remaining assets in the portfolio. The CIO (chief investment officer) notices that the private equity portfolio has delivered outstanding performance lately, especially relative to other asset classes. He presents the data to his research staff and wants to revisit their decision to stop making new private equity investments. Explain why the investment results that prompted the CIO's comments should not be relied upon.

2. The ZeeZaw family office has been invested in the Warriors Fund, a relatively small distressed debt strategy, which has performed very well for a number of years. In a recent conversation with the portfolio manager, the CIO for ZeeZaw discovered that the Warriors fund will be receiving a significant investment from a large institution within the next few weeks. What are some of the risks that might develop with the Warriors Fund as a result of this new client? What are some other issues that the CIO might want to probe with the Warriors Fund?

Solution to 1: With small, residual holdings, even a modest change in valuation can result in outsized returns; for example, a $2,000 investment that gets revalued to $3,000 would report a nominal return of 50%. The 50% return is not representative of private equity investment as a whole but is merely an artifact of the unwinding process. A more accurate picture of performance must consider the development of the fund IRR over time and consider other performance measures, such as the MOIC.

Solution to 2: The CIO should investigate whether the fund manager is able to appropriately deploy this new capital consistent with the investment process and types of investments that contributed to the Warriors Fund success. Because the fund was relatively small, a very large influx of capital might force the portfolio manager to make larger investments than is optimal or more investments than they did before. Either change without the appropriate resources could undermine future success. Finally, a large influx of cash could dilute near-term performance, especially if the funds remain undeployed for a significant period of time.

SUMMARY

- Allocations to alternatives are believed to increase a portfolio's risk-adjusted return. An investment in alternatives typically fulfills one or more of four roles in an investor's portfolio: capital growth, income generation, risk diversification, and/or safety.
- Private equity investments are generally viewed as return enhancers in a portfolio of traditional assets.
- Long/short equity strategies are generally believed to deliver equity-like returns with less than full exposure to the equity premium. Short-biased equity strategies are expected to

lower a portfolio's overall equity beta while producing some measure of alpha. Arbitrage and event-driven strategies are expected to provide equity-like returns with little to no correlation with traditional asset classes.

- Real assets (e.g., commodities, farmland, timber, energy, and infrastructure assets) are generally perceived to provide a hedge against inflation.
- Timber investments provide both growth and inflation-hedging properties.
- Commodities (e.g., metals, energy, livestock, and agricultural commodities) serve as a hedge against inflation and provide a differentiated source of alpha. Certain commodity investments serve as safe havens in times of crisis.
- Farmland investing may have a commodity-like profile or a commercial real-estate-like profile.
- Energy investments are generally considered a real asset as the investor owns the mineral rights to commodities that are correlated with inflation factors.
- Infrastructure investments tend to generate stable/modestly growing income and to have high correlation with overall inflation.
- Real estate strategies range from core to opportunistic and are believed to provide protection against unanticipated increases in inflation. Core real estate strategies are more income-oriented, while opportunistic strategies rely more heavily on capital appreciation.
- Bonds have been a more effective volatility mitigator than alternatives over shorter time horizons.
- The traditional approaches to defining asset classes are easy to communicate and implement. However, they tend to over-estimate portfolio diversification and obscure primary drivers of risk.
- Typical risk factors applied to alternative investments include equity, size, value, liquidity, duration, inflation, credit spread, and currency. A benefit of the risk factor approach is that every asset class can be described using the same framework.
- Risk factor–based approaches have certain limitations. A framework with too many factors is difficult to administer and interpret, but too small a set of risk factors may not accurately describe the characteristics of alternative asset classes. Risk factor sensitivities are highly sensitive to the historical look-back period.
- Investors with less than a 15-year investment horizon should generally avoid investments in private real estate, private real asset, and private equity funds.
- Investors must consider whether they have the necessary skills, expertise, and resources to build an alternative investment program internally. Investors without a strong governance program are less likely to develop a successful alternative investment program.
- Reporting for alternative funds is often less transparent than investors are accustomed to seeing on their stock and bond portfolios. For many illiquid strategies, reporting is often received well past typical monthly or quarter-end deadlines. Full, position-level transparency is rare in many alternative strategies.
- Three primary approaches are used to determine the desired allocation to the alternative asset classes:
  - Monte Carlo simulation may be used to generate return scenarios that relax the assumption of normally distributed returns.
  - Optimization techniques, which incorporate downside risk or take into account skew, may be used to enhance the asset allocation process.
  - Risk factor–based approaches to alternative asset allocation can be applied to develop more robust asset allocation proposals.

- Two key analytical challenges in modelling allocations to alternatives include stale and/or artificially smoothed returns and return distributions that exhibit significant skewness and fat tails (or excess kurtosis).
- Artificially smoothed returns can be detected by testing the return stream for serial correlation. The analyst needs to unsmooth the returns to get a more accurate representation of the risk and return characteristics of the asset class.
- Skewness and kurtosis can be dealt with by using empirically observed asset returns because they incorporate the actual distribution. Advanced mathematical or statistical models can also be used to capture the true behavior of alternative asset classes.
- Applications of Monte Carlo simulation in allocating to alternative investments include:
  1) simulating skewed and fat-tailed financial variables by estimating the behavior of factors and/or assets in low-volatility regimes and high-volatility regimes, then generating scenarios using the different means and covariances estimated under the different regimes; and
  2) simulating portfolio outcomes (+/− 1 standard deviation) to estimate the likelihood of falling short of the investment objectives.
- Unconstrained mean–variance optimization (MVO) often leads to portfolios dominated by cash and fixed income at the low-risk end of the spectrum and by private equity at the high-risk end of the spectrum. Some investors impose minimum and maximum constraints on asset classes. Slight changes in the input variables could lead to substantial changes in the asset allocations.
- Mean–CVaR optimization may be used to identify allocations that minimize downside risk rather than simply volatility.
- Investors may choose to optimize allocations to risk factors rather than asset classes. These allocations, however, must be implemented using asset classes. Portfolios with similar risk factor exposures can have vastly different asset allocations.
- Some caveats with respect to risk factor–based allocations are that investors may hold different definitions for a given risk factor, correlations among risk factors may shift under changing market conditions, and some factor sensitivities are very unstable.
- Cash flow and commitment-pacing models enable investors in private alternatives to better manage their portfolio liquidity and set realistic annual commitment targets to reach the desired asset allocation.
- An alternative investment program should be monitored relative to the goals established for the alternative investment program, not simply relative to a benchmark. The investor must monitor developments in the relevant markets to ensure that the fundamental thesis underlying the decision to invest remains intact.
- Two common benchmarking approaches to benchmarking alternative investments—custom index proxies and peer group comparisons—have significant limitations.
- IRRs are sensitive to the timing of cash flows into and out of the fund. Two managers may have similar portfolios but different return profiles depending on their capital call and distribution schedule.
- Pricing issues can distort reported returns and the associated risk metrics, such as betas, correlations, and Sharpe ratios.
- Monitoring of the firm and the investment process are particularly important in alternative investment structures where the manager cannot be terminated easily. Key elements to monitor include key person risk, alignment of interests, style drift, risk management, client/asset turnover, client profile, and service providers.

REFERENCES

Ang, A. 2011. "Illiquid Assets." *CFA Institute Conference Proceedings Quarterly* 28 (4). doi:10.2469/cp.v28.n4.5

Ang, A. 2014. *Asset Management: A Systematic Approach to Factor Investing.* New York: Oxford University Press. doi:10.1093/acprof:oso/9780199959327.001.0001

Berkelaar, A. B., A. Kobor, and R. R. P. Kouwenberg. 2009. "Asset Allocation for Hedge Fund Strategies: How to Better Manage Tail Risk." In *The VaR Modeling Handbook: Practical Applications in Alternative Investing, Banking, Insurance, and Portfolio Management*, ed. Greg N. Gregoriou. New York: McGraw-Hill.

Cambridge Associates LLC. 2013. "From Asset Allocation to Risk Allocation – The Risk Allocation Framework."

Getmansky, M., A. Lo, and I. Makarov. 2004. "An Econometric Model of Serial Correlation and Illiquidity in Hedge Fund Returns." *Journal of Financial Economics* 74 (3): 529–609. doi:10.1016/j.jfineco.2004.04.001

Hamilton, J. D. 1989. "A New Approach to the Economic Analysis of Nonstationary Time Series and the Business Cycle." *Econometrica* 57 (2): 357–84. doi:10.2307/1912559

Ivashina, Victoria, and Josh Lerner. 2018. "Looking for Alternatives: Pension Investments around the World, 2008 to 2017." Federal Reserve of Boston conference paper.

Kim, C., and C. R. Nelson. 1999. *State-Space Models with Regime Switching – Classical and Gibbs-Sampling Approaches and Applications.* Cambridge, MA: MIT Press.

Liu, Y., Sun, S., Huang, R., Tang, T. and Wu, X. Boston Consulting Group. March 2017. "The Rise of Alternative Assets and Long-Term Investing."

Lo, A. 2002. "The Statistics of Sharpe Ratios." *Financial Analysts Journal* 58 (4): 36–52. doi:10.2469/faj.v58.n4.2453

Naik, V., M. Devarajan, A. Nowobilski, S. Page, and N. Pedersen. 2016. *Factor Investing and Asset Allocation – A Business Cycle Perspective.* Charlottesville, VA: CFA Institute Research Foundation.

Rockafellar, R. T., and S. Uryasev. 2000. "Optimization of Conditional Value at Risk." *Journal of Risk* 2 (3): 21–42. doi:10.21314/JOR.2000.038

Rockafellar, R. T., and S. Uryasev. 2002. "Conditional Value at Risk for General Loss Distributions." *Journal of Banking & Finance* 26 (7): 1443–71. doi:10.1016/S0378-4266(02)00271-6

Swensen, D. F. 2009. *Pioneering Portfolio Management: An Unconventional Approach to Institutional Investment.* New York: Free Press.

Takahashi, D., and S. Alexander. 2001. "Illiquid Alternative Asset Fund Modeling." Yale School of Management (January).

PROBLEMS

The following information relates to Questions 1–8.

Kevin Kroll is the chair of the investment committee responsible for the governance of the Shire Manufacturing Corporation (SMC) defined benefit pension plan. The pension fund is currently fully funded and has followed an asset mix of 60% public equities and 40% bonds since Kroll has been chair. Kroll meets with Mary Park, an actuarial and pension consultant, to discuss issues raised at the last committee meeting.

Kroll notes that the investment committee would like to explore the benefits of adding alternative investments to the pension plan's strategic asset allocation. Kroll states:

Statement 1:   The committee would like to know which alternative asset would best mitigate the risks to the portfolio due to unexpected inflation and also have a relatively low correlation with public equities to provide diversification benefits.

The SMC pension plan has been able to fund the annual pension payments without any corporate contributions for a number of years. The committee is interested in potential changes to the asset mix that could increase the probability of achieving the long-term investment target return of 5.5% while maintaining the funded status of the plan. Park notes that fixed-income yields are expected to remain low for the foreseeable future. Kroll asks:

Statement 2:   If the public equity allocation remains at 60%, is there a single asset class that could be used for the balance of the portfolio to achieve the greatest probability of maintaining the pension funding status over a long time horizon? Under this hypothetical scenario, the balance of the portfolio can be allocated to either bonds, hedge funds, or private equities.

Park confirms with Kroll that the committee has historically used a traditional approach to define the opportunity set based on distinct macroeconomic regimes, and she proposes that a risk-based approach might be a better method. Although the traditional approach is relatively powerful for its ability to handle liquidity and manager selection issues compared to a risk-based approach, they both acknowledge that a number of limitations are associated with the existing approach.

Park presents a report (Exhibit 1) that proposes a new strategic asset allocation for the pension plan. Kroll states that one of the concerns that the investment committee will have regarding the new allocation is that the pension fund needs to be able to fund an upcoming early retirement incentive program (ERIP) that SMC will be offering to its employees within the next two years. Employees who have reached the age of 55 and whose age added to the number of years of company service sum to 75 or more can retire 10 years early and receive the defined benefit pension normally payable at age 65.

EXHIBIT 1   Proposed Asset Allocation of SMC Defined Benefit Pension Plan

Asset Class	Public Equities	Broad Fixed Income	Private Equities	Hedge Funds	Public Real Estate	Total
Target	45%	25%	10%	10%	10%	100%
Range	35%–55%	15%–35%	0%–12%	0%–12%	0%–12%	–

Kroll and Park then discuss suitability considerations related to the allocation in Exhibit 1. Kroll understands that one of the drawbacks of including the proposed alternative asset classes is that daily reporting will no longer be available. Investment reports for alternatives will likely be received after monthly or quarter-end deadlines used for the plan's traditional investments. Park emphasizes that in a typical private equity structure, the pension fund makes a commitment of capital to a blind pool as part of the private investment partnership.

In order to explain the new strategic asset allocation to the investment committee, Kroll asks Park why a risk factor–based approach should be used rather than a mean–variance-optimization technique. Park makes the following statements:

Statement 3:   Risk factor–based approaches to asset allocation produce more robust asset allocation proposals.

Statement 4:   A mean–variance optimization typically overallocates to the private alternative asset classes due to stale pricing.

Park notes that the current macroeconomic environment could lead to a bear market within a few years. Kroll asks Park to discuss the potential impact on liquidity planning associated with the actions of the fund's general partners in the forecasted environment.

Kroll concludes the meeting by reviewing the information in Exhibit 2 pertaining to three potential private equity funds analyzed by Park. Park discloses the following due diligence findings from a recent manager search. Fund A retains administrators, custodians, and auditors with impeccable reputations; Fund B has achieved its performance in a manner that appears to conflict with its reported investment philosophy; and Fund C has recently experienced the loss of three key persons.

EXHIBIT 2   Potential Private Equity Funds, Internal Rate of Return (IRR)

Private Equity Fund	Fund A	Fund B	Fund C
5-year IRR	12.9%	13.2%	13.1%

1. Based on Statement 1, Park should recommend:
   A. hedge funds.
   B. private equities.
   C. commodity futures.
2. In answering the question raised in Statement 2, Park would *most likely* recommend:
   A. bonds.
   B. hedge funds.
   C. private equities.
3. A limitation of the existing approach used by the committee to define the opportunity set is that it:
   A. is difficult to communicate.
   B. overestimates the portfolio diversification.
   C. is sensitive to the historical look-back period.
4. Based on Exhibit 1 and the proposed asset allocation, the greatest risk associated with the ERIP is:
   A. liability.
   B. leverage.
   C. liquidity.
5. The suitability concern discussed by Kroll and Park *most likely* deals with:
   A. governance.
   B. transparency.
   C. investment horizon.
6. Which of Park's statements regarding the asset allocation approaches is correct?
   A. Only Statement 3
   B. Only Statement 4
   C. Both Statement 3 and Statement 4

7. Based on the forecasted environment, liquidity planning should take into account that general partners may:
   A. call capital at a slower pace.
   B. make distributions at a faster pace.
   C. exercise an option to extend the life of the fund.
8. Based on Exhibit 2 and Park's due diligence, the pension committee should consider investing in:
   A. Fund A.
   B. Fund B.
   C. Fund C.

The following information relates to Questions 9–13.

Eileen Gension is a portfolio manager for Zen-Alt Investment Consultants (Zen-Alt), which assists institutional investors with investing in alternative investments. Charles Smittand is an analyst at Zen-Alt and reports to Gension. Gension and Smittand discuss a new client, the Benziger University Endowment Fund (the fund), as well as a prospective client, the Opeptaja Pension Plan (the plan).

The fund's current portfolio is invested primarily in public equities, with the remainder invested in fixed income. The fund's investment objective is to support a 6% annual spending rate and to preserve the purchasing power of the asset base over a 10-year time horizon. The fund also wants to invest in assets that provide the highest amount of diversification against its dominant equity risk. Gension considers potential alternative investment options that would best meet the fund's diversification strategy.

In preparation for the first meeting between Zen-Alt and the fund, Gension and Smittand discuss implementing a short-biased equity strategy within the fund. Smittand makes the following three statements regarding short-biased equity strategies:

Statement 1: Short-biased equity strategies generally provide alpha when used to diversify public equities.

Statement 2: Short-biased equity strategies are expected to provide a higher reduction in volatility than bonds over a long time horizon.

Statement 3: Short-biased equity strategies are expected to mitigate the risk of public equities by reducing the overall portfolio beta of the fund.

Gension directs Smittand to prepare asset allocation and portfolio characteristics data on three alternative portfolios. The fund's risk profile is one factor that potential lenders consider when assigning a risk rating to the university. A loan covenant with the university's primary lender states that a re-evaluation of the university's creditworthiness is triggered if the fund incurs a loss greater than 20% over any one-year period. Smittand states that the recommended asset allocation should achieve the following three goals, in order of priority and importance:

- Minimize the probability of triggering the primary lender's loan covenant.
- Minimize the probability of purchasing power impairment over a 10-year horizon.
- Maximize the probability of achieving a real return target of 6% over a 10-year horizon.

Smittand provides data for three alternative portfolios, which are presented in Exhibits 3 and 4.

EXHIBIT 3   Asset Allocation

Alternative Portfolio	Cash	Public Equity	Govt	Credit	Hedge Fund	Real Estate	Private Equity
A	4.0%	35.0%	6.0%	5.0%	20.0%	10.0%	20.0%
B	2.0%	40.0%	8.0%	3.0%	15.0%	7.0%	25.0%
C	1.0%	50.0%	3.0%	6.0%	10.0%	0.0%	30.0%

EXHIBIT 4   Portfolio Characteristics

Alternative Portfolio	1-Year 99% VaR	1-Year 99% CVaR	Probability of Meeting 6% Real Return (10-Year Horizon)	Probability of Purchasing Power Impairment (10-Year Horizon)
A	−16.3%	−19.4%	56.1%	2.5%
B	−17.4%	−20.6%	58.8%	2.8%
C	−19.3%	−22.7%	61.0%	4.0%

Notes:
• One-year horizon 99% VaR: the lowest return over any one-year period at a 99% confidence level
• One-year horizon 99% CVaR: the expected return if the return falls below the 99% VaR threshold
• Probability of purchasing power impairment: the probability of losing 40% of the fund's purchasing power over 10 years, after consideration of new gifts received by the fund, spending from the fund, and total returns

Gension next meets with the investment committee (IC) of the Opeptaja Pension Plan to discuss new opportunities in alternative investments. The plan is a $1 billion public pension fund that is required to provide detailed reports to the public and operates under specific government guidelines. The plan's IC adopted a formal investment policy that specifies an investment horizon of 20 years. The plan has a team of in-house analysts with significant experience in alternative investments.

During the meeting, the IC indicates that it is interested in investing in private real estate. Gension recommends a real estate investment managed by an experienced team with a proven track record. The investment will require multiple capital calls over the next few years. The IC proceeds to commit to the new real estate investment and seeks advice on liquidity planning related to the future capital calls.

9. Which asset class would *best* satisfy the Fund's diversification strategy?
   A. Private equity
   B. Private real estate
   C. Absolute return hedge fund
10. Which of Smittand's statements regarding short-biased equity strategies is *incorrect?*
   A. Statement 1
   B. Statement 2
   C. Statement 3

11. Based on Exhibit 4, which alternative portfolio should Gension recommend for the fund given Smittand's stated three goals?
    A. Portfolio A
    B. Portfolio B
    C. Portfolio C
12. Which of the following investor characteristics would *most likely* be a primary concern for the plan's IC with respect to investing in alternatives?
    A. Governance
    B. Transparency
    C. Investment horizon
13. With respect to liquidity planning relating to the plan's new real estate investment, Gension should recommend that the fund set aside appropriate funds and invest them in:
    A. 100% REITs.
    B. 100% cash equivalents.
    C. 80% cash equivalents and 20% REITs.

The following information relates to Questions 14–15.

Ingerðria Greslö is an adviser with an investment management company and focuses on asset allocation for the company's high-net-worth investors. She prepares for a meeting with Maarten Pua, a new client who recently inherited a $10 million portfolio solely comprising public equities.

Greslö meets with Pua and proposes that she create a multi-asset portfolio by selling a portion of his equity holdings and investing the proceeds in another asset class. Greslö advises Pua that his investment objective should be to select an asset class that has a high potential to fulfill two functional roles: risk diversification and capital growth. Greslö suggests the following three asset classes:

- Public real estate
- Private real assets (timber)
- Equity long/short hedge funds

14. **Determine** which asset class is *most likely* to meet Pua's investment objective. **Justify** your response.

Determine which asset class is *most likely* to meet Pua's investment objective. (Circle one.)	**Justify** your response.
Public Real Estate	
Private Real Assets (Timber)	
Equity Long/Short Hedge Funds	

Five years after his first meeting with Pua, Greslö monitors a private real estate investment that Pua has held for one year. Until recently, the investment had been managed by a local real estate specialist who had a competitive advantage in this market; the specialist's strategy was to purchase distressed local residential housing properties, make strategic property improvements, and then sell them. Pua is one of several clients who have invested in this opportunity.

Greslö learns that the specialist recently retired and the investment is now managed by a national real estate company. The company has told investors that it now plans to invest throughout the region in both distressed housing and commercial properties. The company also lengthened the holding period for each investment property from the date of the initial capital call because of the complexity of the property renovations, and it altered the interim profit distribution targets.

15. **Discuss** the qualitative risk issues that have *most likely* materialized over the past year.

The following information relates to Questions 16–18.

The Ælfheah Group is a US-based company with a relatively small pension plan. Ælfheah's investment committee (IC), whose members collectively have a relatively basic understanding of the investment process, has agreed that Ælfheah is willing to accept modest returns while the IC gains a better understanding of the process Two key investment considerations for the IC are maintaining low overhead costs and minimizing taxes in the portfolio. Ælfheah has not been willing to incur the costs of in-house investment resources.

Qauhtèmoc Ng is the investment adviser for Ælfheah. He discusses with the IC its goal of diversifying Ælfheah's portfolio to include alternative assets. Ng suggests considering the following potential investment vehicles:

- Publicly traded US REIT
- Relative value hedge fund
- Tax-efficient angel investment

Ng explains that for the relative value hedge fund alternative, Ælfheah would be investing alongside tax-exempt investors.

16. **Determine** which of the potential investment vehicles *best* meets the investment considerations for Ælfheah. **Justify** your response. **Explain** for *each* investment not selected why the investment considerations are not met.

Determine which of the potential investment vehicles *best* meets the investment considerations for Ælfheah. (Circle one.)	**Justify** your response.	**Explain** for *each* investment not selected why the investment considerations are not met.
Publicly traded US REIT		
Relative value hedge fund		
Tax-efficient angel investment		

Ng and the IC review the optimal approach to determine the asset allocation for Ælfheah, including the traditional and risk-based approaches to defining the investment opportunity set.

17. **Determine** which approach to determine the asset allocation is *most appropriate* for Ælfheah. **Justify** your response.

Determine which approach to determine the asset allocation is *most appropriate* for Ælfheah. (Circle one.)	**Justify** your response.
Traditional	
Risk based	

The following year, Ng and the IC review the portfolio's performance. The IC has gained a better understanding of the investment process. The portfolio is meeting Ælfheah's liquidity needs, and Ng suggests that Ælfheah would benefit from diversifying into an additional alternative asset class. After discussing suitable investment vehicles for the proposed alternative asset class, Ng proposes the following three investment vehicles for further review:

• Funds of funds (FOFs)
• Separately managed accounts (SMAs)
• Undertakings for collective investment in transferable securities (UCITS)

18. **Determine** the investment vehicle that would be *most appropriate* for Ælfheah's proposed alternative asset class. **Justify** your response.

Determine the investment vehicle that would be *most appropriate* for Ælfheah's proposed alternative asset class. (Circle one.)	**Justify** your response.
FOFs	
SMAs	
UCITS	

The following information relates to Questions 19–20.

Mbalenhle Calixto is a global institutional portfolio manager who prepares for an annual meeting with the investment committee (IC) of the Estevão University Endowment. The endowment has €450 million in assets, and the current asset allocation is 42% equities, 22% fixed income, 19% private equity, and 17% hedge funds.

The IC's primary investment objective is to maximize returns subject to a given level of volatility. A secondary objective is to avoid a permanent loss of capital, and the IC has indicated to Calixto its concern about left-tail risk. Calixto considers two asset allocation approaches for the endowment: mean–variance optimization (MVO) and mean–CVaR (conditional value at risk) optimization.

19. **Determine** the asset allocation approach that is *most suitable* for the Endowment. **Justify** your response.

Determine the asset allocation approach that is *most suitable* for the Endowment. (Circle one.)	**Justify** your response.
MVO	
Mean–CVaR optimization	

Calixto reviews the endowment's future liquidity requirements and analyzes one of its holdings in a private distressed debt fund. He notes the following about the fund:

- As of the most recent year end:
  - The NAV of the endowment's investment in the fund was €25,000,000.
  - All capital had been called.
- At the end of the current year, Calixto expects a distribution of 18% to be paid.
- Calixto estimates an expected growth rate of 11% for the fund.

20. **Calculate** the expected NAV of the fund at the end of the current year.

CHAPTER 9

INTEGRATED CASES IN RISK MANAGEMENT: INSTITUTIONAL

Steve Balaban, CFA, Arjan Berkelaar, PhD, CFA, Nasir Hasan, and Hardik Sanjay Shah, CFA

LEARNING OUTCOMES

The candidate should be able to:

- discuss financial risks associated with the portfolio strategy of an institutional investor;
- discuss environmental and social risks associated with the portfolio strategy of an institutional investor;
- analyze and evaluate the financial and non-financial risk exposures in the portfolio strategy of an institutional investor;
- discuss various methods to manage the risks that arise on long-term direct investments of an institutional investor;
- evaluate strengths and weaknesses of an enterprise risk management system and recommend improvements.

1. INTRODUCTION

The focus of this chapter is a fictional case study. The case itself will focus on the portfolio of a sovereign wealth fund (SWF) specifically looking at risk in terms of the SWF's long-term investments. There are three Learning Outcome Statements (LOS) within the case. Prior to the case, we provide two LOS outside the case. These LOS will provide some background information that will be helpful to the candidate in understanding the case.

2. FINANCIAL RISKS FACED BY INSTITUTIONAL INVESTORS

2.1. Long-Term Perspective

Institutional investors (also referred to as *asset owners*) such as pension funds, SWFs, endowments, and foundations are distinct from other institutional investors such as banks and insurance companies in terms of the time horizon over which they invest their assets. This long-term perspective allows these institutions to take on certain investment risks that other institutional investors simply cannot bear and to invest in in a broad range of alternative asset classes, including private equity, private real estate, natural resources, infrastructure, and hedge funds. This section will focus on the financial risks associated with the portfolio strategy of long-term institutional investors and in particular will focus on investments in illiquid asset classes. Banks and insurance companies are excluded from the discussion because they are typically much more asset/liability focused and face much tighter regulatory constraints to ensure capital adequacy.

This section will not cover the quantitative aspects of risk management or the mechanics behind various risk metrics, such as standard deviation and conditional value at risk, or risk management techniques, such as Monte Carlo simulation and factor modelling. Those topics are covered in other parts of the CFA Program curriculum. Instead, this chapter will cover key risk considerations faced by long-term institutional investors as they invest in a range of traditional and alternative asset classes, including private equity and infrastructure. An important distinguishing feature of long-term institutional investors is their ability to invest in illiquid asset classes. Since the late 1990s, such asset classes have become an ever more important part of the investment portfolios of pension funds, sovereign wealth funds, endowments, and foundations. In this chapter, we put particular emphasis on the financial risks that emanate from illiquid investments because these risks tend to be least well quantified but can pose an existential threat to long-term investors if not addressed and managed carefully. The focus is on how market and liquidity risk interact to create potential challenges at the overall portfolio level and affect the institutional investor's ability to meet its long-term objectives.

Section 2.2 briefly discusses the various lenses through which risk management can be viewed. Risk management is a very broad topic, and the goal is to simply provide the reader with a frame of reference. Section 2.3 focuses on the key financial risks that institutional investors face. The focus is on portfolio-level, top-down, long-term financial risk. Risk management for long-term institutional investors should primarily be concerned with events that may jeopardize the organization's ability to meet its long-term objectives. The interaction between market and liquidity risk plays a critical role. In Section 2.4 we discuss the challenges associated with investing in illiquid asset classes from a risk management perspective. We discuss two important aspects of illiquid asset classes: the uncertainty of cash flows and return-smoothing behavior in the return pattern. Section 2.5 describes how institutional investors address and manage liquidity risk at the overall portfolio level.

2.2. Dimensions of Financial Risk Management

The aim of risk management is to avoid an existential threat to the organization. In other words, risk management should focus on what types of events can jeopardize the organization's ability to meet its long-term objectives. Existential threats can arise from both financial risks (e.g., market losses and liquidity risk in the form of the inability to meet cash flows) and non-financial risks (e.g., reputational risks). In this chapter, we solely focus on financial risk. Financial risk needs to be viewed through multiple lenses. There is no simple template to financial risk management. It is not simply a matter of calculating, for example, the value at risk of a portfolio. There are several dimensions to sound financial risk management, and we cover them briefly in the following subsections. Our goal is to simply provide a frame of reference for the reader because risk management is a very broad topic.

2.2.1. Top-Down versus Bottom-Up Risk Analysis

Risk management requires both a top-down and a bottom-up perspective. From a top-down perspective, the board and chief investment officer (CIO) set overall risk guidelines for the portfolio that serve as guardrails within which the investment team is expected to operate. Risk management involves measuring, monitoring, and reporting portfolio results versus the guidelines. The investment team is tasked with implementing the overall investment strategy either through hiring external asset managers or by directly purchasing and managing securities and assets. The investment team takes a more bottom-up, sub-portfolio approach to managing the risks of each individual portfolio or asset class, while assessing and monitoring their interaction and impact on the risk level of the overall portfolio.

2.2.2. Portfolio-Level Risk versus Asset-Class-Specific Risk

Although risk management for an institutional investor is ultimately about controlling overall portfolio-level risk, risks also need to be managed and controlled at the asset-class or strategy level so that no particular asset class or strategy will have an undue adverse effect on the overall portfolio. Different asset classes require different risk management techniques. Some risk metrics and methods make sense for publicly traded asset classes, but they may not be meaningful when assessing the risk of, for example, illiquid asset classes or hedge fund investments. For some asset classes, such as public equities, detailed security-level information might be available, whereas for other asset classes, such as hedge funds, only monthly manager returns may be available. In the case of a public equity portfolio, risk analysis might be very granular and rely on sophisticated factor models, whereas risk analysis for hedge fund investments might simply involve calculating the historical volatility of observed returns. Because of differences in data transparency, data frequency, and risk methods used, it is difficult—if not impossible—to aggregate these results at the overall portfolio level. It is not uncommon for institutional investors to have an overall risk management system for portfolio-wide risk metrics in addition to asset-class-specific systems or approaches that provide a more in-depth risk view tailored to a particular asset class.

2.2.3. Return-Based versus Holdings-Based Risk Approaches

Financial risk management systems are typically described as being return based (risk estimation relies on the historical return streams of an external manager or a portfolio of securities) or holdings based (risk estimation relies on individual security holdings and the historical returns of those securities in the portfolio). Both approaches have their pros and cons, and they are not mutually exclusive. Return-based systems are relatively easy to implement but may produce risk estimates that are biased because they rely on past returns from a strategy that may be very different today compared with, for example, five years ago. Holdings-based risk systems, in contrast, tend to be more costly and time-consuming to implement. For many institutional investors that invest in hedge funds and illiquid asset classes, holdings-based risk systems for the entire portfolio are typically not feasible because of a lack of transparency on holdings and their related investment strategy (a multi-strategy fund may maintain a long position in a security within one strategy book and a short position in another strategy book), data being available with a one-month to three-month lag, and significant turnover in certain types of hedge fund investments.

2.2.4. Absolute versus Relative Risk

Investors are interested in both absolute risk and relative risk. Absolute risk concerns the potential for overall losses and typically relies on overall portfolio-level metrics, such as standard deviation, conditional value at risk, and maximum drawdown. Relative risk concerns underperformance versus policy benchmarks and relies on such metrics as tracking error (the standard deviation of returns relative to a benchmark).

2.2.5. Long-Term versus Short-Term Risk Metrics

Modern risk systems used by institutional investors typically focus on calculating volatility, value at risk, and conditional value at risk using sophisticated risk factor techniques. Given the heavy reliance on the current portfolio composition and the granular modeling of each component in the portfolio, these risk systems are most useful in providing an estimate for the potential for near-term losses. Institutional investors are also interested in calculating longer-term risks, such as the probability of losses, the probability of not being able to meet cash flows, and the probability of maintaining purchasing power or meeting a certain return target over longer time periods, such as 5 years, 10 years, 20 years, and so forth.

These long-term risk metrics are typically calculated using Monte Carlo simulation, where asset-class returns are simulated on the basis of a set of forward-looking capital market assumptions (typically expected returns, volatilities, and correlations) and total assets are calculated including cash flows, such as benefit payments and contributions in the case of pension funds and payouts (spending amounts) in case of endowments and foundations. These methods, although typically much less granular than a risk management system, are better able to incorporate future portfolio changes, different rebalancing methods, and cash flows.

2.2.6. Quantitative versus Qualitative Risks

At the end of the day, risk management is not simply a quantitative endeavor. Quantitative risk management techniques are backward looking by nature and typically parametric (i.e., they rely on historical data to estimate parameters). Although history can serve as a guide, it does not provide a prediction of the future. Risk management is about assessing the potential for future losses, and quantitative tools need to be complemented with qualitative assessments. However, with qualitative assessments, it is important for risk managers to be aware of their own biases because they are basing these assessments on their own past experience. Thus, it is important for risk managers to recognize and mitigate the backward-looking bias in both quantitative (explicit) and qualitative (implicit) risk analysis.

2.2.7. Pre- and Post-Investment Risk Assessment

Finally, although risk management efforts typically focus on measuring the risks of existing investments, a sound risk management philosophy ensures a proper assessment of financial risks prior to making investments. Institutional investors typically put a lot of effort into operational and investment due diligence prior to making investments. In addition to analyzing past investment performance, it is critical when hiring external managers to evaluate the character of the key decision makers, the business ethics of the firm, the investment experience of the team, the quality of operations (such as accounting and trade settlements), and the risk management practices of the external manager. As part of their investment due diligence, institutional investors also look at the quality of the non-executive directors of the fund, the integrity and independence of external auditors, fee structures, master fund and feeder fund structure, custodians, and safekeeping on assets. These considerations are even more important for illiquid investments because it is very difficult to exit from them (investors cannot easily change their mind). After investing, risk management might take on a more quantitative role, but continued due diligence and monitoring are of equal importance. In the case of external managers, this obligation resides with the team responsible for the hiring and firing of the managers. In the case of internal management, an in-house risk management team may be tasked with the ongoing due-diligence and monitoring responsibilities.

The various risk dimensions we have described should provide a sense of the wide-ranging nature of risk management as a discipline. For this reading, we focus exclusively on the key financial risks that long-term institutional investors face. We take a portfolio-level, top-down perspective and are primarily concerned with how illiquid asset classes and the interaction between market and liquidity risk affect an institutional investor's ability to meet its long-term objectives. This risk is unique to long-term institutional investors. The next section will provide a more in-depth description of this risk.

2.3. Risk Considerations for Long-Term Investors

Long-term institutional investors have the ability to invest a significant part of their portfolio in risky and illiquid assets because of their long-term investment horizon and relatively low liquidity needs. The past two decades have seen a steady increase in the allocation to illiquid asset classes, such private equity, private real estate, and infrastructure, by pension funds, sovereign wealth funds, endowments, and foundations. These asset classes create unique risk management challenges and can pose an existential threat if the risks are not addressed and managed carefully. As stated before, the ultimate objective of risk management is to ensure that the organization survives and can meet its long-term objectives.

We start with briefly describing and reviewing the main objectives of long-term institutional investors and their key risk considerations. Exhibit 1 provides an overview by institutional investor type. The ultimate risk consideration for each of these institutional investors is their ability to meet the payouts that they were set up to provide. This risk is largely affected by how the overall investment portfolio performs over time. On the one hand, a very low-risk portfolio that consists primarily of fixed-income investments is unlikely to cause a problem in providing the required payouts in the short run but will almost certainly jeopardize the organization's ability to provide the required payouts in the long run. On the other hand, a very risky and illiquid portfolio is expected to provide high expected returns in the long run but could cause significant pain in the short run during a significant market downturn or financial crisis. Long-term institutional investors aim to strike the right balance between these two extremes in designing their investment policy or strategic asset allocation.

EXHIBIT 1   Objectives and Risk Considerations by Institutional Investor Type

Institutional Investor	Main Objective	Key Risk Consideration
Pension funds	Provide retirement income to plan participants	Inability to meet pension payouts to beneficiaries
Sovereign wealth funds	Varies by type of SWF but most have been set up to provide some future financial support to the government	Inability to provide financial support to the government
Endowments and foundations	Provide financial support in perpetuity while maintaining intergenerational equity	Inability to provide financial support to the institution or to the mission

This process usually involves a Monte Carlo simulation exercise where asset-class returns are simulated on the basis of a set of forward-looking capital market assumptions and total assets are calculated including cash flows, such as benefit payments and contributions in the case of pension funds and payouts (spending amounts) in the case of endowments and foundations. Monte Carlo simulation allows institutional investors to calculate such metrics as the probability of maintaining purchasing power and the probability of a certain loss or drawdown (e.g., 25%) over a specific time period (e.g., 5 or 10 years) and to determine the appropriate trade-off between two such metrics. What is often ignored in this type of analysis, however, is the important interaction between potential market losses and liquidity. Pension funds, SWFs, endowments, and foundations are unique in that they can often tolerate significantly more market and liquidity risk than other investors. Their long-term investment horizon allows them to survive a significant market correction and even operate in a countercyclical way during a market crisis. As institutional investors invest more in such illiquid asset classes as private equity, private real estate, and infrastructure, however, their ability to tolerate market losses may diminish.

Institutional investors need liquidity to meet payouts (retirement payments in the case of pension plans, payouts to the university or foundation in the case of endowments and foundations, etc.), meet capital calls on their illiquid investments, and rebalance their portfolios. During a significant market downturn, these needs can become stretched and impact the institution's ability to meet cash flows, particularly if a large part of the portfolio is invested in illiquid asset classes, such as private equity, real estate, and infrastructure. Exhibit 2 shows the main liquidity needs and the main sources of liquidity for long-term institutional investors. Each of these liquidity needs and sources may be adversely affected during a financial crisis.

EXHIBIT 2   Liquidity Needs and Sources for Institutional Investors

Liquidity Needs	Liquidity Sources
Outflows (e.g., pension payouts to beneficiaries, university payouts, and financial support to the government)	Inflows (e.g., pension contributions, gifts, donations, government savings)
Capital calls for illiquid investments	Distributions from illiquid investments
Portfolio rebalancing	Investment income and proceeds from selling liquid asset classes (cash, fixed income, public equities)

We first start with discussing how liquidity needs may increase during a crisis. First, payouts might increase as the beneficiary requires additional financial support. For example, a university may need additional funds from its endowment to support its operations as other sources of income dry up, or a government might require additional financial support from the sovereign wealth fund to mitigate the crisis situation. Second, there might be an acceleration of capital calls as attractive investment opportunities present themselves during a crisis. Finally, rebalancing flows will be more significant during a crisis because of significant market movements. Good governance and best practice suggest that investors rebalance their portfolios at regular intervals. Sticking to rebalancing practices is particularly important during a financial crisis because failure to rebalance may prevent investors from fully participating in the rebound after the crisis.

Having discussed how the needs for liquidity may increase during a significant market downturn, we next turn to how sources of liquidity might dry up under those circumstances. First, inflows might decrease in a crisis. For example, donors might be struggling financially and donate less to their alma mater, or plan sponsors might be faced with budgetary challenges and, therefore, less inclined to contribute to the pension fund. Second, distributions from illiquid investments might be reduced because there are no attractive exit points due to depressed prices or lower profitability. Finally, investments that are otherwise liquid might become less liquid or simply undesirable to exit from. The main sources of liquidity during a financial crisis are typically cash and fixed-income investments. And most long-term institutional investors hold relatively low allocations to cash and fixed income in their portfolios.

Illiquid asset classes (such as private equity, real estate, and infrastructure) are not available to meet liquidity needs during a crisis. These asset classes cannot be rebalanced or redeemed because they are long term in nature and the assets can be locked up for 5–10 years or even longer. Semi-liquid asset classes, such as hedge fund investments, should not be expected to be liquid and available to meet liquidity needs during a financial crisis because many of these managers might impose redemption gates or have lockups in place or their investments might turn out to be less liquid than anticipated. Finally, although public equity investments are technically liquid, investors may be reluctant to sell part of their public equity portfolio to meet liquidity needs because the market value of these investments may have gone down significantly in a crisis. In addition, investors might not want to redeem from certain active external managers, even if the investments are liquid, because it may impact the future relationship with that manager (particularly for high-demand active managers with limited available capacity).

In conclusion, the main risk that long-term institutional investors face is having insufficient liquidity during a significant market downturn to meet their obligations and rebalance their portfolios. Liquidity needs tend to increase in a crisis while sources of liquidity dry up. This risk increases as institutional investors allocate more to illiquid asset classes. The combination of financial losses and not being able to meet cash flows or rebalance the portfolio because of insufficient liquidity can become a matter of survival. Managing this risk is, therefore, very important for long-term institutional investors. In the next section, we will discuss in more detail the risks associated with illiquid asset classes. In Section 2.5, we will discuss the various ways in which institutional managers manage liquidity risk.

2.4. Risks Associated with Illiquid Asset Classes

Illiquid asset classes, such as private equity, real estate, and infrastructure, offer the potential for returns in excess of those on publicly traded asset classes, such as public equity and fixed income. The higher expected return of these asset classes comes at a cost to investors in the form of illiquidity. Illiquid asset classes are typically subject to a drawdown structure where committed capital is called at an unknown schedule and investors receive profits at an unknown schedule. As a result, investors need to hold sufficient liquid assets to meet capital calls from their private fund managers. The uncertain pattern of cash flows poses both a liquidity and a risk management challenge for investors in illiquid asset classes.

In addition to the importance of adequately managing liquidity needs when investing in illiquid assets, these asset classes tend to be subject to stale pricing, appraisal-based valuations, and a lagged response to movements in public markets. As a result, illiquid asset classes exhibit returns that are smooth, understating the true volatility and correlation with publicly traded asset classes. For example, the standard deviation of observed returns for private equity is often smaller than that of public equity. Although this feature may be appealing for institutional investors, it causes traditional asset allocation models, such as mean–variance optimization, to over-allocate to private asset classes because the Sharpe ratios of observed returns are superior to those of publicly traded asset classes.

Finally, illiquid asset classes cannot be rebalanced easily and costlessly. Although investors could potentially, for example, sell their private equity stakes in the secondary market, this cannot be done instantaneously and investors may have to accept a significantly lower price compared with the true market value.

2.4.1. Cash Flow Modeling

Illiquid asset classes are subject to a drawdown structure. The investor (typically the limited partner, or LP, in the partnership agreement) commits capital, and this capital gets drawn down over time at the discretion of the general partner, or GP. Investors need to figure out both the commitment strategy (i.e., how much to commit each year) to reach a certain target allocation to illiquid assets and the liquidity needs to meet capital calls when required. Committing too much can pose severe liquidity risk because the percentage allocation to illiquid asset classes may soar due to the so-called denominator effect (total assets under management, or AUM, falls by a larger amount than the repricing of illiquid asset classes). Committing too little may prevent the investor from reaching the target allocation and may result in falling short of return expectations.

In managing liquidity needs and determining the appropriate commitment strategy to illiquid asset classes, investors need to be able to predict future cash flows.

2.4.2. Addressing Return-Smoothing Behavior of Illiquid Asset Classes

To calculate the true underlying economic risks of illiquid asset classes as part of their risk management efforts, institutional investors typically use one of two approaches: (1) Use public market proxies in place of private asset classes—for example, use small-cap public equities as a proxy for private equity—or (2) unsmooth observed returns of private asset classes. The objective of the latter is to remove the serial correlation structure of the original return series. The implicit assumption is that the serial correlations in reported returns are entirely due to the smoothing behavior funds engage in when reporting results. A common and simple technique to unsmooth the returns of illiquid asset classes and hedge funds is a method developed by Geltner (1993) to address appraisal-based valuations in real estate. The method proposed by Geltner removes only the first-order serial correlation in observed returns. Okunev and White (2003) extended the method of Geltner (1993) to include higher-order serial correlations. An alternative to the Geltner method is the GLM method proposed by Getmansky, Lo, and Makarov (2004). They assumed that observed returns for illiquid asset classes and hedge funds follow a moving-average process.

To show the effect of these different methods on the annualized volatility of various illiquid asset classes, we use quarterly historical returns for global buyouts, global venture capital, global private real estate, and global private natural resources for the period from Q1 1990 until Q4 2019. Exhibit 3 shows the annualized volatility of the observed returns and the volatility of adjusted returns using the three methods briefly discussed earlier. For the Okunev–White and GLM methods, we use up to four lags. Exhibit 4 shows the beta to global equity returns. For global equity returns, we use quarterly returns for the MSCI World Index from 1990 to 2019.

EXHIBIT 3   Impact of Unsmoothing on Annualized Volatility

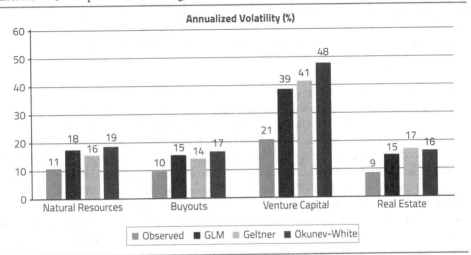

Source: Data is from Cambridge Associates.

EXHIBIT 4   Impact of Unsmoothing on Beta to Public Equities

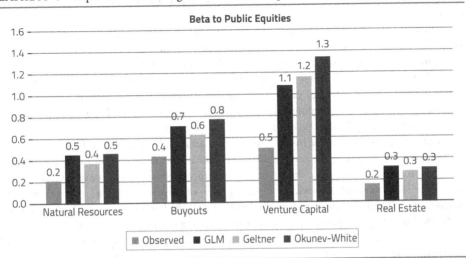

Source: Data is from Cambridge Associates.

As illustrated in Exhibits 3 and 4, after applying unsmoothing techniques, the resulting returns exhibit higher volatility and are typically more correlated with public equity markets. These unsmoothed return series can then be used along with returns on publicly traded asset classes to determine the covariance matrix to be used in a mean–variance optimization exercise when determining the appropriate allocation to illiquid asset classes and hedge funds. Mean–variance optimization, however, still falls short as an adequate asset allocation tool for institutional investors because it is not able to take into account the illiquid nature of some asset classes. Illiquid asset classes cannot be rebalanced easily without a potential significant price concession. Single-period optimization methods, such as mean–variance optimization, fail when illiquid asset classes are introduced, because such techniques implicitly assume that investors keep portfolio weights constant over time (i.e., portfolio weights are rebalanced perfectly) and they ignore the drawdown structure of illiquid asset classes and the uncertainty of cash flows. Currently, there are not any widely accepted alternatives. Most investors simply constrain the allocations to illiquid asset classes in the mean–variance optimization to achieve reasonable and practical portfolios.

2.4.3. Direct versus Fund Investments in Illiquid Asset Classes

In recent years, large pension funds and sovereign wealth funds have increasingly opted to invest directly in illiquid asset classes rather than through the more typical limited partner (LP)–general partner (GP) setup. Some large pension funds and SWFs have built up a large team of merchant banking professionals who are equally capable as a large private equity fund team. The main motivation behind such a move is to save on the high fees that institutional investors typically pay to GPs (2% base fee on committed capital and 20% fee on profits or over a certain hurdle rate). Being able to save on these fees should make the investments more profitable over the long term. Direct investments provide an institutional investor with control over each individual investment. This situation puts the investor in a better position to manage liquidity. In the case of direct investments, there are no unfunded commitments, making it easier to manage capital. The investor also has full discretion over the decision when to exit investments and will not have to be forced to sell in a down market. As a result, direct investments partially alleviate some of the liquidity challenges typically associated with private asset classes and resolve some of the principal–agent issues associated with fund investing.

There are also disadvantages to direct investments in private asset classes. Direct investments in private equity, real estate, or infrastructure require a dedicated and experienced in-house team. In some instances, rather than building out an in-house team for private investments, large pension funds and sovereign wealth funds acquire a general partner. For example, Ontario Teachers' Pension Plan purchased Cadillac Fairview, a large operating company for real estate. Managing and assembling an in-house team adds several challenges compared with the more nimble setup in the case of fund investing. The sourcing of deals may be constrained by the talent and network of the in-house team. As a result, it may be more difficult to diversify the portfolio across geography and industries. Direct investment portfolios may have higher concentration risk because direct investors opt for larger investments due to staffing issues and scalability. This risk could adversely affect the liquidity of these investments because they might be harder to sell and, therefore, potentially less liquid. If the investor relies on external managers for deal sourcing or a partnership agreement, there is a risk of adverse selection. Finally, the governance structure is not set up as well in the case of direct investing compared with fund investments. In contrast to fund managers, employees of a pension fund or sovereign wealth fund may not be able to sit on the board of a private company. Institutional investors may not be able to afford the liability issues associated with direct investing. For fund investments, the investor is a limited partner and has limited liability, whereas with direct investments, the investor may be considered a general partner, with additional liability risks. Finally, institutional investors may find it difficult to adequately compensate internal staff to ensure that they hire and retain talent. This is usually a problem for public pension funds because there is public pressure to keep compensation down.

2.5. Managing Liquidity Risk

In this section, we discuss some of the tools used by institutional investors to manage overall liquidity risk in their portfolios.

Liquidity management steps:

1. **Establish liquidity risk parameters.** Institutional investors typically create liquidity guidelines regarding what percentage of assets needs to be liquid and available on a daily or monthly basis. In addition, given the drawdown structure of illiquid asset classes, institutional investors need to keep track of uncalled commitments, not simply invested capital. It is typical for institutional investors to have internal guidelines or bands around the sum of invested capital and uncalled commitments as a percentage of total assets. In addition to such bands, they may have automatic or semiautomatic escalation triggers, such as reducing commitments to illiquid asset classes or even actively seeking to reduce investments through secondary sales once the sum of invested capital plus uncalled commitments reaches a certain level (expressed as a percentage of total assets). These liquidity risk parameters can either be internal or be included in an investment policy statement approved by the board.

2. **Assess the liquidity of the current portfolio and how it evolves over time.** The second step in managing liquidity risk at the overall portfolio level is to have a clear sense of the liquidity of the portfolio and measure liquidity parameters versus guidelines. Most institutional investors have an internal report that shows what percentage of the portfolio can be liquidated within a day, within a week, within a month, within a quarter, and within a year and what percentage of the portfolio takes more than a year to be liquidated. It is important not only to have a snapshot of that report at a given point in time but also to understand how it evolves over time as the portfolio changes. A good starting point for developing these statistics is to simply look at the legal terms that are in place with external managers. This is particularly relevant for active managers and hedge funds that have redemption notices and lockups included in the investment agreement. In the case of internal management, an even more granular assessment can be made depending on the types of securities being held and using market liquidity measures to gauge how much of these securities can be sold over different time frames during a financial crisis. As discussed in Section 2.3, investors may also want to take into account how redeeming from certain external managers during a crisis may impact the future relationship with that manager (in other words, they may not want to redeem even if the investments are liquid and instead include these investments in a less liquid category).

3. **Develop a cash flow model and project future expected cash flows.** The third step is to understand and model the various cash flows. As discussed in Section 2.3, institutional investors make payouts (retirement payments, foundation spending, etc.), they

receive inflows (gifts and donations for an endowment, pension contributions for a pension plan, etc.), they have to meet capital calls for illiquid asset classes and receive distributions, and they have to rebalance their portfolios. Most institutional investors model each of those cash flows and project future expected cash flows. Section 2.4 briefly discussed how capital calls and distributions are modeled for illiquid asset classes.

4. **Stress test liquidity needs and cash flow projections.** The standard cash flow modeling and projections assume business as usual, but it is important to stress test these cash flow projections and liquidity needs. As discussed in Section 2.4, cash flows are affected by market movements. For example, donations might be lower in a crisis and payouts might be higher. Institutional investors stress test their cash flow projections and liquidity needs. It is important to point out that this process is more of an art than a science and there is no universally accepted method for stress testing (as there are universally accepted methods for market risk calculations).

5. **Put in place an emergency plan.** Finally, institutional investors should put in place an emergency action plan. Such an action plan should include what to liquidate—and in what order—in a crisis to meet cash flows and how to rebalance the portfolio in a crisis. Having such a plan in place can help avoid the risk of panicking in a crisis. Sharing the emergency action plan with the board to get buy-in can also help when a crisis occurs and mitigate the risk of board members pressuring the investment team to make sub-optimal short-term decisions.

Exhibit 5 summarizes the five steps in developing a liquidity management plan.

EXHIBIT 5   Liquidity Management Steps

1. Establish liquidity risk parameters.
2. Assess the liquidity of current portfolio, and monitor the evolution over time.
3. Develop a cash flow model and project future cash flows.
4. Stress test liquidity needs and cash flow projections.
5. Develop an emergency action plan.

Long-term institutional investors are able take on certain investment risks that other institutional investors simply cannot bear. Since the late 1990s, they have increasingly invested in a broad range of alternative asset classes, including private equity, private real estate, natural resources, infrastructure, and hedge funds. In this reading, we focus on the financial risks that emanate from illiquid investments because these risks tend to be less well quantified but can pose an existential threat to long-term investors if not addressed and managed carefully. The focus has been on how market and liquidity risk interact to create potential challenges at the overall portfolio level and affect the institutional investor's ability to meet its long-term objectives. We propose several steps institutional investors can take to better manage liquidity at the overall portfolio level.

2.6. Enterprise Risk Management for Institutional Investors

Exhibit 6 provides a high-level view of a risk management framework in an enterprise context:

EXHIBIT 6   Risk Management Framework in an Enterprise Context

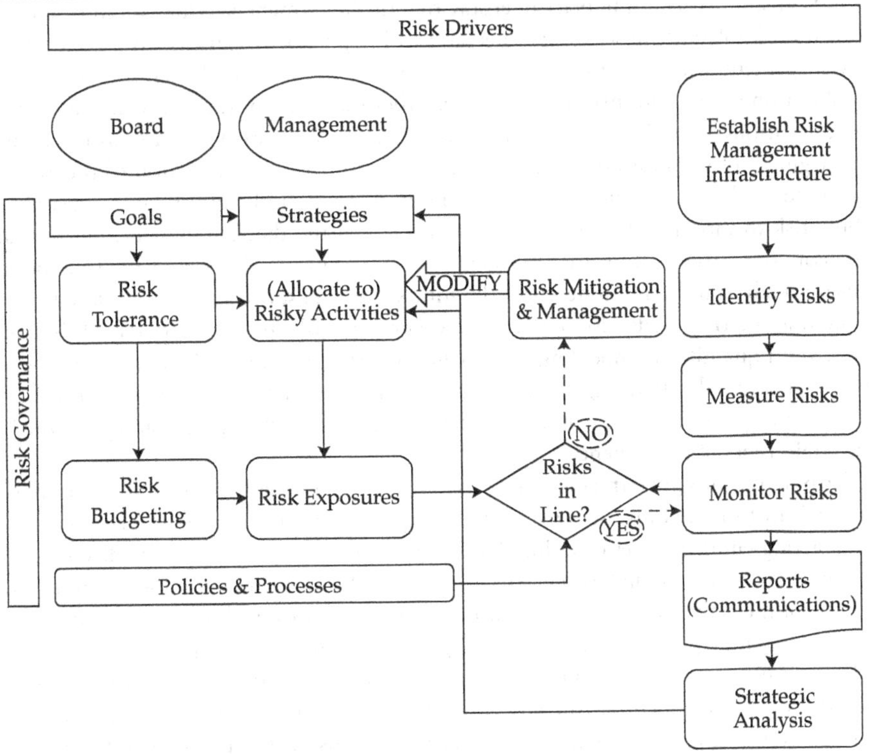

Source: "Risk Management: An Introduction," CFA Program Level I curriculum reading (2021).

We can apply this framework to the setting of an institutional investor in the following manner. The risk management process for an institutional investor starts with the board setting the overall risk tolerance for the organization that is consistent with its objectives and constraints. Risk tolerance should capture the amount of market risk that an institutional investor is willing and able to take in order to maximize expected returns, and it informs the most important investment decision that is made by the board—namely, the strategic asset allocation. Risk tolerance can be expressed in asset-only (for sovereign wealth funds, endowments, and foundations) or asset/liability terms (for pension funds and insurance companies). Typical risk measures used for setting the risk tolerance of institutional investors include volatility, maximum drawdown, and value at risk or conditional value at risk (sometimes referred to as *expected tail loss*, or *ETL*).

In addition to setting the overall risk tolerance (for market losses), the board usually approves additional risk parameters, limits, requirements, and guidelines (some quantitative and others procedural) that are codified in an investment policy statement (IPS). These may include liquidity risk parameters if the institutional investor has a significant allocation to illiquid asset classes, an active risk budget to limit and control the amount of active management pursued by investment staff, restrictions on leverage and the use of derivatives, ethical investment guidelines, and possibly credit risk parameters and constraints in the case of significant fixed-income investments (for example, for an insurance company). These additional guidelines and constraints are put in place to ensure that the investment activities are consistent with the board's risk tolerance and expectations (and with regulatory requirements if applicable).

Management (i.e., the investment team) is tasked with implementing the strategic asset allocation (SAA) and investing the assets either internally or through external managers across the various asset classes included in the SAA. The investment team is also responsible for managing and monitoring the risks associated with the implementation of the SAA and reporting to the board. The objective is not to minimize or eliminate risk but to measure and attribute risk to various risk exposures and factors to ensure that the investments adequately compensate the institution for the risks being taken. Institutional investors typically perform risk factor analysis to better understand the fund's risk exposures, such as exposure to equity risk, interest rate risk, credit risk, inflation risk, currency risk, and liquidity risk. This analysis includes both quantitative modeling and qualitative risk assessments. Quantitative tools may involve sophisticated risk management systems based on returns or holdings, scenario analysis, and stress testing. Other risks are more qualitative in nature, such as potential reputational risk from certain types of investments.

For public equity investments, active risk versus a benchmark needs to be measured and monitored. Institutional investors may have an explicit active risk budget in place. Part of the risk budgeting effort involves ensuring that the active risk budget accurately reflects the areas where most excess return can be expected. In addition, the investment team will want to ensure that most of the active risk in public equities comes from stock picking and not simply from loading on certain equity risk factors, such as growth, momentum, or quality.

For private equity investments, the board may want to understand whether the returns achieved on the investment adequately compensated the fund for giving up liquidity. One way to answer that question is by comparing the returns on the private equity investment with the return of public equities. Currency risk tends to sometimes be overlooked by institutional investors. This risk can have an outsized and unexpected impact on the overall return. Although currency risk can be hedged in some cases, doing so is typically costly or even impossible when investing in emerging and frontier markets. The risk of currency devaluation needs to be acknowledged and assessed prior to making investments. Another risk that gets overlooked is asset allocation drift. The investment portfolio should be rebalanced on a regular basis to bring it back in line with the strategic asset allocation that was approved by the board.

The risk management infrastructure of the institutional investor should be set up to identify and measure the aforementioned risks and monitor how they change over time and whether they are in line with the guidelines set up by the board in the IPS and with additional—more granular—internal guidelines set by the chief investment officer and risk team. The risk team is usually tasked with risk reporting to the various stakeholders, which may include an internal investment committee and the board to ensure adequate risk oversight. The investment team should recognize when risk exposures are not aligned with the overall risk tolerance and guidelines and take action to bring them back into alignment. These actions may involve hedging, rebalancing, and secondary sales or in the case of illiquid investments, reducing commitments.

3. ENVIRONMENTAL AND SOCIAL RISKS FACED BY INSTITUTIONAL INVESTORS

3.1. Universal Ownership, Externalities, and Responsible Investing

In this section, we define universal owners as large institutional investors that effectively own a slice of the whole economy and hence are generally managing their total market exposure, instead of focusing on a subset of issuers. Institutional investors such as sovereign wealth funds and public pension funds usually have large portfolios that are highly diversified and built with a long-term focus. Such portfolios are representative of global capital markets, thereby making such investors "universal owners."

Investing long term in widely diversified holdings inevitably exposes such portfolios to increasing costs related to negative environmental and social externalities. An externality is an impact that an individual's or a corporation's activities have on a third party. If everyone acts in their own self-interest, it could lead to an overall negative outcome for society. Examples of negative environmental externalities include plastic pollution in the ocean, poor air quality due to industrial and vehicular emissions, and water toxicity due to improper effluent management.

Universal owners find it challenging to effectively diversify risks arising from negative environmental and social externalities. Costs that are externalized by one portfolio company can negatively affect the profitability of another portfolio company, thereby adversely affecting the overall portfolio return. For example, a sovereign wealth fund invests in a plastic manufacturer that is saving waste treatment and disposal costs by directly releasing waste pellets and other chemical residues into a nearby river. Water toxicity arising as a result of these actions causes reduced productivity in the agriculture operations downstream, which the asset owner is also invested in. In addition, strengthening regulations related to environmental protection, for example, may lead to monetary fines and penalties, thereby leading to financial risks for a company causing such negative externalities.

According to the UN-backed Principles for Responsible Investment (PRI), environmental costs for universal owners are reflected in portfolio impacts via insurance premiums, taxes, inflated input prices, and the physical costs associated with weather-related disasters (PRI Association 2017). Also, the cost of remediating environmental damage is often significantly higher than the cost of preventing it. Given these facts, it is imperative for large institutional investors to internalize the price of such negative externalities by considering the impact of their investments on society and future generations.

Exhibit 7 provides a non-exhaustive list of environmental and social issues that we have introduced in Level I of the CFA Program curriculum.

EXHIBIT 7   Examples of Environmental and Social Factors

Environmental Issues	Social Issues
Climate change and carbon emissions	Customer satisfaction and product responsibility
Air and water pollution	Data security and privacy
Biodiversity	Gender and diversity
Deforestation	Occupational health and safety
Energy efficiency	Community relations and charitable activities
Waste management	Human rights
Water scarcity	Labor standards

In the next section, we share examples of how some of these environmental and social issues could impact the portfolio strategy for large institutional investors that have a long-term focus toward their investments.

Systemic risks have the potential to destabilize capital markets and lead to serious negative consequences for financial institutions and the broader economy. The unpredictable nature of such megatrends as climate change and their related impacts, both environmental and socioeconomic, pose clear systemic risks to global financial markets. A study carried out by researchers at the Grantham Research Institute on Climate Change and the Environment (2016) at the London School of Economics and Political Science and Vivid Economics projected that climate change could reduce the value of global financial assets by as much as $24 trillion—resulting in permanent damage that would far eclipse that from the 2007–09 financial crisis.

3.2. Material Environmental Issues for an Institutional Investor

For an institutional investor, such as a sovereign wealth fund, such megatrends as climate change and their related risks—both physical and transition risks—have the potential to cause significant harm to a portfolio's value over the medium to long term, particularly for investments in real assets (real estate, infrastructure) and private equity, neither of which are easily divestible. Next, we will discuss the impact of climate-related risks on an institutional investor's portfolio from the perspective of private equity and real asset investments.

3.2.1. Physical Climate Risks

As we have observed since the beginning of the current century, climate change has profoundly affected the physical world we live in. Annual average temperatures across the globe are continuously rising, and 19 of the 20 warmest years have occurred since 2001 (NASA 2019). Erratic weather patterns, such as heavy precipitation, droughts, and hurricanes, are both more frequent and of higher magnitude. Similarly, wildfires are causing more and more devastation every year. In addition, the chronic issue of sea-level rise is causing coastal flooding. As shown in Exhibit 8, an increase in extreme weather events has occurred.

EXHIBIT 8   Extreme Weather Events on the Rise

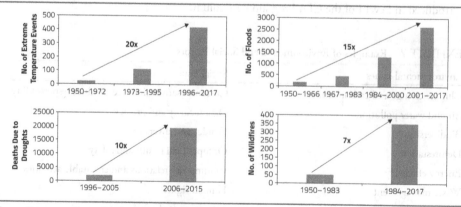

Source: Emergency Events Database (www.emdat.be).

With continued climate change, all these physical climate risks could become more severe in the future and, to a certain extent, become the new normal for the world. Depending on global responses to climate change in the coming decade, the degree of their impact on our economies and investments may be alleviated.

So, what does this mean for the portfolio strategy of large institutional investors with private equity and real asset investments?

3.2.2. Impact on Real Assets

Should these trends continue, the physical risks that we have discussed could create increased levels of stress on such assets as residential and commercial real estate and infrastructure, such as roads and railways. Rising sea levels that lead to flooding would impact both rents and property valuation for hitherto prime coastal properties. Prolonged exposure to extreme heat would negatively affect the useful life of roads and train tracks, which would lead to accelerated depreciation of such assets and, therefore, more frequent replacement costs for companies and governments (CFA Institute 2020).

Similarly, physical damage caused by frequent, large-scale weather-related events, such as hurricanes or even wildfires—once considered too irregular to insure against—could not only lead to large-scale drawdowns in the portfolio's asset value but also make it difficult or expensive to insure such assets. Most of the flooding-related losses around the world are uninsured, thereby causing additional stress on a country's economy and its people (see Exhibit 9).

EXHIBIT 9   Global Flood Losses and Insurance Levels

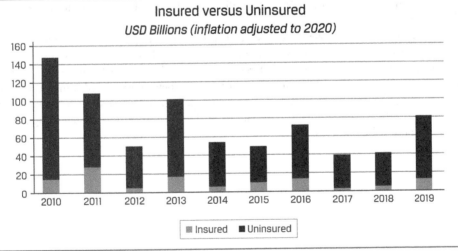

Source: Aon.

Because these physical climate-related risks continue to play out in a much larger and more frequent manner than previously anticipated, they will continue to bring down prices and rental yields of prime real estate, leading to permanent impairments of asset valuations.

For a large institutional investor that is looking to preserve capital and provide growth benefits to multiple generations, it is imperative that these risks be factored into the portfolio construction strategies.

3.2.3. Climate Transition Risks

In line with the 2015 Paris Climate Agreement, countries and companies around the world are already making efforts to dramatically reduce or eliminate their CO_2 emissions in order to limit the global temperature increase in this century to 2 degrees Celsius above preindustrial levels. To keep global warming less than 2°C, scientists project that energy-related CO_2 emissions need to fall 25% by 2030 and reach "net zero" by 2070 (Intergovernmental Panel on Climate Change 2018; IEA 2020).

One of the most ambitious efforts to incentivize decarbonization is the European Union's sustainable finance taxonomy, which helps investors understand whether an economic activity is environmentally sustainable. As of October 2020, looking at the scientific evidence about the current and potential impacts of climate change, it has become clear that the world needs to move toward a low-carbon future if we are to cap global warming at less than 2°C and prevent the negative effects that not doing so would bring to our climate, our ecosystems, and human life. What is currently unclear is the pace at which this decarbonization will happen.

Rapid decarbonization will lead to restrictions on carbon emissions, implementation of some form of carbon pricing, introduction of new technologies, and changes in the consumer behavior. All these effects can create massive disruptions in certain sectors, such as electricity generation (with the increasing cost competitiveness of renewable energy sources as compared with coal) and automobiles (with the impending widespread switch from internal combustion engines to electric vehicles. The International Energy Agency has forecast that in order to reach carbon neutrality by 2050, half of all cars in the world should be electric by 2030 (Lo 2020).

The PRI's Inevitable Policy Response (IPR) project aims to prepare financial markets for climate-related policy risks that are likely to emerge in the short to medium term. The IPR forecast a response by 2025 that will be forceful, abrupt, and disorderly because of the delayed action (see Exhibit 10). The PRI argues that markets have inefficiently priced climate transition risks, but its policy forecast is that a forceful policy response to climate change in the near term is a highly likely outcome, leaving portfolios of institutional investors exposed to significant risks that need to be mitigated.

EXHIBIT 10   IPR Key Policy Forecasts

Coal phase-outs	Sales ban on Internal Combustion Engines (ICE)	Carbon Pricing (Emission Allowances)	Zero carbon power
Early coal phase-out for first mover countries by 2030	Early sales ban for first mover countries by 2035	US$40–80/tCO$_2$ prices by 2030 for first movers	Significant ramp-up of renewable energy globally
Steady retirement of coal-fired power generation after 2030 in lagging countries	Other countries follow suit as automotive industry reaches tipping point	Global convergence accelerated by Border Carbon Adjustment (BCA) to >=$100/tCO$_2$ by 2050	Policy support of nuclear capacity increase in a small set of countries, nuclear phased out elsewhere

Carbon Capture and Storage (CCS) & industry decarbonisation	Energy efficiency	Green House Gas (GHG) removal (Land use-based)	Agriculture
Limited CCS support in power,	Increase in coverage and stringency of performance standards	Improved forestry and nature-based solutions	Technical support to improve agricultural yields
Policy incentives primarily for industrial and bioenergy CCS	Utility obligation programs	Stronger enforcement of zero deforestation	Increasing public investment in irrigation and AgTech
Public support for demonstration, and then deployment of hydrogen clusters	Financial and behavioral incentives	Controlled expansion of bioenergy crops	Incremental behavioural incentives away from beef

Source: PRI IPR (www.unpri.org/the-inevitable-policy-response-policy-forecasts/4849.article).

Given the uncertainty around the precise timing and magnitude of the impact of climate change, organizations are increasingly using climate-related scenario analysis to better understand how their businesses might perform under a variety of global warming scenarios—for example, in a world that is 2°C, 3°C, or 4°C warmer. The Task force on Climate-Related Financial Disclosures (TCFD) recommends organizations, including banks, asset managers, and asset owners, use scenario analysis to estimate the implications of such risks and opportunities for their businesses over time and also to inform their strategic thinking. The International Energy Agency and the Intergovernmental Panel on Climate Change both publicly offer a set of climate-related scenarios that are widely used. To learn more about climate-related scenario analysis, refer to the technical supplement issued by the TCFD.

3.2.4. Climate Opportunities

Although most of the investor focus in dealing with climate change has been on managing physical and transition risks, exciting investment opportunities are arising in companies focused on climate change mitigation and adaptation. These opportunities exist in secondary markets and, in some cases, investments in real assets and infrastructure projects, such as wind and solar farms and smart grids.

Because the levelized cost of energy for renewable energy generation technologies has considerably decreased since 2010, these have become cost competitive with some conventional generation technologies, such as coal-based power generation, as shown in Exhibit 11.

EXHIBIT 11   2019 Levelized Cost of Energy, Unsubsidized

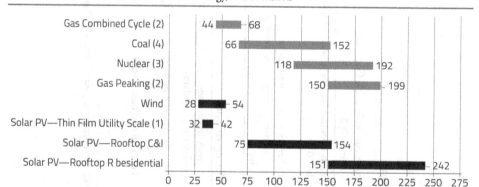

Note: Levelized cost of energy is a measure of the average net present cost of electricity generation for a power plant over its lifetime.

(1) Unless otherwise indicated herein, the low end represents a single-axis tracking system and the high end represents a fixed-tilt system.

(2) The fuel cost assumption for Lazard's global, unsubsidized analysis for gas-fired generation resources is $3.45/MMBTU.

(3) Unless otherwise indicated, the analysis herein does not reflect decommissioning costs, ongoing maintenance-related capital expenditures or the potential economic impacts of federal loan guarantees or other subsidies.

(4) High end incorporates 90% carbon capture and compression. Does not include cost of transportation and storage.

Sources: Data is from Lazard (www.lazard.com/perspective/lcoe2019).

This cost competitiveness, coupled with the urgency to decarbonize our economies to avoid the potentially catastrophic physical impacts of climate change, has created secular growth opportunity for such businesses and assets, thereby attracting increasingly large investor attention.

A summary of the business segments where such opportunities may lie follows.

3.2.4.1. Climate Mitigation   This category includes companies that are positioned to benefit, directly or indirectly, from efforts to curb or mitigate the long-term effects of global climate change, to address the environmental challenges presented by global climate change, or to improve the efficiency of resource consumption.

EXHIBIT 12   Climate Mitigation Opportunity Examples

Business Segment	Description
Clean energy	Companies in this segment are involved in the generation of clean energy from such sources as wind, solar, and small hydro. This segment also includes manufacturers of such equipment as windmills and solar panels, as well as related service providers.
Energy efficiency	This segment comprises businesses that provide products and services to improve the efficiency of energy consumption in a variety of processes. Examples include energy efficient transportation and building solution providers and recycling technology.
Batteries and storage	This segment includes companies that help improve battery storage capacity and efficiency. These improvements are critical, for instance, to sustainable growth and wider penetration of some of the previously mentioned technologies, such as clean energy generation and distribution and electric vehicles.
Smart grids	Smart grids are digitally enhanced versions of the conventional electricity grid, with a layer of communication network overlaying the traditional grid. They are a key enabler for energy security and reliability and integration of clean energy resources.
Materials	Such materials as copper and battery-grade lithium are key ingredients in the clean energy value chain because they are required in clean energy power generation, storage solutions, and electric vehicles, resulting in a projected demand rise as the world transitions toward a low-carbon future.

3.2.4.2. Climate Adaptation   This category includes companies that would help better adjust to actual or expected future change in climate with an aim to reduce vulnerability to the harmful effects of climate change, such as food insecurity, sea-level rise, and frequent extreme weather events.

EXHIBIT 13   Climate Adaptation Opportunity Examples

Business Segment	Description
Sustainable agriculture	Companies in this segment are involved in providing products that improve agriculture productivity and reduce the resource consumption in the entire process. Sustainable fish farming and timber production are other activities included here.
Water	This segment consists of businesses that provide products and services to improve the efficiency of water consumption in a variety of processes, including wastewater treatment and reuse.

Many institutional investors are increasing allocations to such sectors as part of their real-asset allocation or as a potential equity alpha opportunity with the expectation that companies in these sectors will outperform the broad equity market over a long period of time as the world transitions to a low carbon future. Evaluating and sufficiently managing both physical and transition climate risks in the portfolio and capturing some of the aforementioned secular growth opportunities could position large institutional investor portfolios to outperform and grow in value in the long term.

3.3. Material Social Issues for an Institutional Investor

Environmental issues, such as climate change and air pollution, are reasonably mature and quite well understood, making them easier to accommodate in discounted cash flow models. Social issues, such as community relation, occupational health and safety, privacy and data security, modern slavery and other human right violations in the supply chain, and inequality, however, are relatively challenging to quantify and integrate into financial models. Most social issues have largely qualitative data reported by companies, such as health and safety policies and initiatives, lists of product quality certifications, and human capital management policies, rather than metrics on which long-term performance can be judged. Nevertheless, these issues have the potential to cause reputational and financial damage to a company and its investors if not managed sufficiently well.

3.3.1. Managing Community Relations and the Social License to Operate

For large institutional investors, such as sovereign wealth funds and public pension funds, their investments may have positive social impacts, such as improving essential public infrastructure and services or providing better access to medicine and technology, or negative social impacts, via poor labor standards or forceful relocation and improper rehabilitation of communities by their portfolio companies. Good corporate behavior is usually well received by the community relations, leading to a sustainable and mutually beneficial long-term relationship. In many ways, these aspects are essential to keeping a company's social license to operate.

Let's take a hypothetical example of a sovereign wealth fund (SWF) that has invested in a dam-based hydroelectric power plant in an economically less developed part of its country. Although there will be a positive environmental impact of the project because it will generate electricity from a renewable source, the social impacts of the project could be mixed. On the positive side, rural electrification arising from this project will lead to economic development in the region, thereby improving the standard of living. Dam-based hydroelectric power plants require large-scale land acquisition, often leading to relocation and rehabilitation of indigenous communities. Some locals protest that they have not been sufficiently consulted by the government before issuing consent to establish this project. Moreover, there are allegations of acquisition of land for the project at unfair/poor valuations. In some instances, protesting locals were forcefully removed and relocated by local government authorities, leading to unrest. Eventually, the SWF decides to cease the project implementation owing to this wide variety of instances of pushback from the society.

This example highlights the importance of considering social risks when investing. Despite having the positive intent of supporting development of renewable power generation in a less economically developed part of the country, the SWF faced pushback and reputational damage for not holistically considering the interests of all the stakeholders involved, especially local communities that were the most affected by the project. Some of the best practices in community relation management include extensive stakeholder consultation meetings to better understand their needs and address their concerns, providing alternative employment opportunities to those affected, and ensuring fair land acquisition, rehabilitation, and resettlement practices.

3.3.2. Labor Issues in the Supply Chain

Another increasingly important social topic is the one related to poor labor practices, especially in the supply chain. Driven by globalization, a consumption boom across developed and emerging markets, and the availability of cheap labor in certain parts of the world, a large portion of the manufacturing and assembling activities across such key sectors as technology and garments has been outsourced to developing and frontier markets, such as India, Vietnam, and Malaysia. Although access to cheap, semi-skilled labor has led to better bottom lines for multinational companies, it has also come at the cost of exploitation of workers in such supply chains. Labor rights are being compromised in the form of heavy reliance on temporary workers, excessive or forced overtime, and low wages. Moreover, lax regulations in many countries allow legal prevention of unionization or any form of collective bargaining, thereby making such workers more vulnerable.

Large brands in the apparel industry, such as Nike and Gap, and in the technology space, such as Apple and Samsung, have all been accused of various levels of lapses in their supply chain related to the aforementioned labor management issues. Apart from suffering significant damage to their brands and reputations, which could lead to consumer boycotts, such companies may also face additional costs and/or fines related to product recalls and ad hoc shifting of supply chains.

For SWFs with equity exposure to some of the largest apparel brands and branded tech hardware companies, considering such issues while making investments is of paramount importance because lack of transparency in the supply chain and lapses in labor management may weigh heavily on the resilience of such supply chains amid global-scale disruptions, such as that caused by the COVID-19 pandemic. In addition to the financial risks, reputational risks may also arise because of a view that the SWF implicitly supports such improper and unethical business practices.

3.3.3. The "Just" Transition

Sustainable development involves meeting the needs of the present generation without compromising the ability of future generations to meet their own needs. Sustainable development includes economic, social, and environmental dimensions, all of which are interrelated. In the transition to environmentally sustainable economies and societies, several challenges may arise—for example, displacement of workers and job losses in certain industries, such as coal mining, fossil fuel extraction/production, and fossil fuel-based power generation. Similarly, increased energy costs due to carbon taxes and higher costs of commodities partly resulting from sustainable production practices may have adverse effects on the incomes of poor households. Therefore, a "just" transition is necessary to ensure that there are limited negative social impacts in our pursuit of positive environmental impacts via avoiding fossil fuels and implementing sustainable agriculture and business practices. Although there is no fixed set of guidelines, the just transition encourages a dialogue between workers, industry, and governments influenced by geographical, political, cultural, and social contexts in order to tackle some of the aforementioned challenges.

CASE STUDY

1. Case Study: Introduction

You are working as a Risk Analyst at a small sovereign wealth fund (SWF) and reporting to the Head of Risk. The SWF is considering making some new investments in direct private equity and direct infrastructure. You have been asked to review risk aspects of these investment opportunities, which will be discussed in an upcoming investment committee meeting. Assuming the investments will be made, you will also have the responsibility to monitor the risk of the investments as well as make recommended improvements to the SWF's risk management system. You are excited about these opportunities and look forward to putting your knowledge and skills learned from the CFA Program to work!

2. Case Study: Background

- Over 20 years ago, the "Republic of Ruritania" discovered an extremely large deposit of crucial rare earth metals that are key elements in the manufacturing of high-speed computers used in science and finance. The entire deposit was sold to various entities allowing Ruritania to secure its financial future. At the same time, the government of Ruritania "dollarized" the economy, moving from the domestic RRR currency to the USD.

- The government of Ruritania (R) decided to form a sovereign wealth fund, R-SWF, in order to grow the capital for future generations. This type of SWF is a "savings fund," intended to share wealth across generations by transforming non-renewable assets into diversified financial assets.

- R-SWF has built up a diversified portfolio of equities, fixed income, and alternative investments.

- In equities and fixed income, the SWF invests in developed markets, emerging markets, and frontier markets through both fund investing and direct investing.

- In alternatives, the SWF invests in private equity (PE), infrastructure, and real estate. Investment methods used include direct investing, making co-investments, and fund investing.

- The case study begins in Section 3 at an investment committee meeting to discuss two potential investments. The next scene, in Section 4, is set three years later, when the performance of the investments are discussed at another investment committee meeting. The final scene, in Section 5, is set five years later and provides additional information on investment performance.

3. R-SWF'S Investments: 1.0

Initial Case Facts (1.0)

Today, the investment committee of R-SWF is considering several new investments, including direct private equity and direct infrastructure investments. The investment committee will be discussing risk aspects of the investments, led by the Head of Risk and supported by *you*, a Risk Analyst.

- The investment committee meeting will open with an overview of asset allocation and a few basic discussions on the two proposed investments. However, the focus of the meeting is on the potential risks of the new investment proposals, not details on the investments

themselves. (An in-depth investment committee meeting on the new investments was held last month.)
- The meeting will then move on to a discussion of the potential risks of the two specific direct investments being considered.

    1. Direct infrastructure investment in an airport
    2. Direct PE investment in a beverage manufacturer

- The investment committee meeting will discuss key risks that R-SWF should consider as it decides whether to make new direct investments in PE and infrastructure.
- All investment committee participants (and CFA Program Level III candidates) are provided with a background memo with the following information:

    Memo A: Background on R-SWF's asset allocation and performance
    Memo B: Details on the proposed direct infrastructure investment
    Memo C: Details on the proposed direct private equity investment

---

Investment Committee Meeting Memo 1.0

To: R-SWF Investment Committee Members
From: R-SWF Chief Investment Officer

Re: Investment Committee Meeting Agenda

Distribution: Head of Risk, Head of PE, Head of Infrastructure, Head of Equities, and Level III Candidates in the CFA Program

An agenda for today's meeting is as follows:

Agenda
- Opening Remarks and Review of Asset Allocation: Chief Investment Officer
- Review of Infrastructure Investment Opportunity: Head of Infrastructure
- Review of Private Equity Investment Opportunity: Head of PE
- Discussion of Risk—Infrastructure Investment: Head of Risk + Everyone
- Discussion of Risk—PE Investment: Head of Risk + Everyone
- Closing Remarks: Chief Investment Officer

The investment committee meeting will discuss key risks that R-SWF should consider as it determines whether to make new direct investments in PE and infrastructure.

Memo 1A: Asset Allocation and Performance
- Since its inception, over a 25+ year period, R-SWF has built a diversified portfolio of investments. As of last month, the fund had AUM of $50 billion USD, with the fund outperforming its overall benchmark by 150 bps net of fees since inception. Of course, there have been short-term periods of underperformance as the fund pursued its long-term strategy.

- Asset allocation as of last month for the overall fund was as follows:

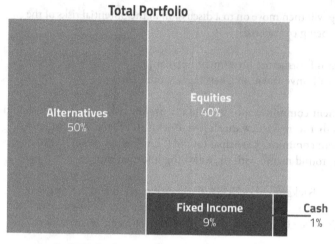

- As of last month, R-SWF had approximately 50% of assets invested in alternative investments, consistent with its long-term objectives.
- In today's investment committee meeting, R-SWF is considering two new investments in alternative investments—specifically, in direct private equity and direct infrastructure investments. *(Note: Funding for these two investments will come from a combination of cash, dividends, receivables, and fixed income. The mix will be determined by the Asset/Liability Committee, or ALCO).*
- Because today's investment committee meeting will focus on alternative investments, we will break the allocation of alternatives down further, as follows:

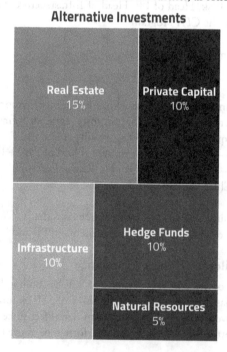

- As of last month, R-SWF had approximately 10% of assets invested in private capital and 10% of assets invested in Infrastructure.
- Next, we provide a breakdown of private capital and infrastructure:

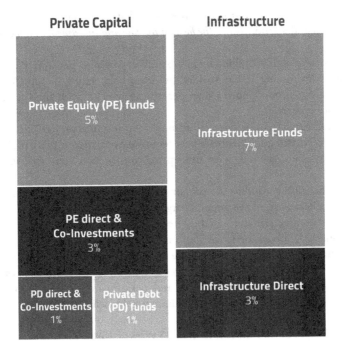

- As of last month, R-SWF had approximately 3% of assets invested in private equity direct and co-investment and 3% of assets invested in direct Infrastructure.
- The investment committee will be discussing risk aspects of the cases, led by the Head of Risk and supported by the Risk Analyst.
- Details on the proposed infrastructure investment are found in Memo 1B.
- Details on the proposed private equity investment are found in Memo 1C.

Memo 1B: Proposed Direct Infrastructure Investment

- The infrastructure direct investment opportunity is an investment in helping modernize an airport in the frontier market island nation of "Sunnyland."
- Sunnyland has beautiful beaches and several hotels, ranging from 3–star to 5–star. However, the Sunnyland Airport has only one small runway that can support airplanes of only up to 10 passengers.
- The Sunnyland government is keen on expanding the airport with a new terminal and new runway. Doing so will allow much larger aircraft to land (up to 150 passengers) and be a major boost to tourism.
- The airport is located about 2 km from the sea, providing scenic views on takeoff and landing. The new runway will be built 1 km from the sea, providing even nicer views.
- R-SWF has been approached by the Sunnyland Airport Authority (SAA) to consider a $100 million investment in a public–private partnership (PPP) on a build–operate–transfer (BOT) basis.

- For R-SWF (with assets of $50 billion), this is a small investment (0.2% of total assets). The investment will be about 2% of total infrastructure assets—$100 million/($100 million + $5,000 million)—which includes investments in funds and direct investments.
- Other facts about this infrastructure investment that are important for the investment committee to understand: *(Note: The focus of the case and investment committee discussion is risks.)*
- Total project cost of $500 million for new 5 million passenger per annum (pax) terminal
- $33 million investment to be provided by Airport Operating Group (AOG), which will operate the airport under a management agreement (with fixed fee plus/minus performance incentive)
- $300 million funding to be provided through non-recourse project finance debt (i.e., approx. 70/30 debt/equity) with 15–year tenor following 3-year grace period
- 2–year construction period, with fixed price construction contract awarded under tender
- 25–year concession (including 2–year construction period), with investor consortium entitled to collect all regulated airport charges (e.g., passenger departure charge, landing charges) and commercial revenue (duty free, retail, F&B, car parking), subject to payment of quarterly concession fee of 35% of all revenue to SAA
- Airport charges (70% of all revenue) are regulated by concession contract—that is, schedule of charges set and then subject to stated formula for future changes (e.g., CPI)
- Concession agreement includes quality and performance standards to be met for design/construction/development (including timely delivery of new terminal) and operations, respectively
- Expected IRR for full investment term of 25 years of 15%

Risk Discussion: Infrastructure Investment

The Head of Infrastructure believes the potential return on this project far outweighs the potential risk(s). However, she is happy to discuss potential risks with the investment committee.

Memo 1C: Proposed Direct Private Equity Investment

- The private equity direct investment opportunity is an investment in a local beverage company (Atsui Beverage Company Limited (ABC)) that manufactures and sells carbonated beverages. The investment will be used to modernize the plant.
- ABC is an unlisted beverage company located in the tropical, land-locked nation of "Atsui." Atsui has a developing economy and can be considered a frontier market.
- ABC is the only local manufacturer of carbonated beverages in Atsui. All other beverages are imported.
- ABC's factory is located near a river that allows for transport to the port. Also, the river is known for its unique biodiversity.
- R-SWF's Head of Private Equity has been on several vacations to Atsui and saw an investment opportunity.
- ABC is keen on modernizing its plant, but the founder is worried about giving up control. Thus, the founder is willing to sell only a minority stake of 35% in exchange for $25 million.

- For R-SWF (with assets of $50 billion), this is a small investment (0.05% of total assets). The investment will be about 0.4% of total PE assets—$25 million/($25 million + $6,000 million)—which includes investments in funds, co-investments, and direct investments.
- Other facts about this direct PE investment that are important for the investment committee to understand: *(Note: The focus of the case and investment committee discussion is risks.)*
  - R-SWF has been investing in PE for many years in funds. Over the years, R-SWF has developed direct investing capabilities through its co-investments and is now expanding its direct investing program.
  - Because of the increased direct investing capabilities of R-SWF and recent outperformance in returns, R-SWF is looking to increase its private equity allocation to direct investments over the next five years.
  - The government of Atsui has implemented tariffs on all soft drink imports. There is an upcoming election that could change this stance.
  - The cost to modernize the ABC plant is estimated to be $20 million.
  - Over the last 12 months, ABC had a revenue of $50 million. Revenue is expected to increase significantly over the next 10 years—with a modernized plant.
  - Over the last 12 months, ABC had an EBITDA of $7 million. This is an EBITDA margin of 14% and a 10× EBITDA multiple. The Head of PE feels that there is significant room for improvement.
  - With the new technology from the plant modernization, ABC will be able to expand into non-carbonated drinks, such as sports drinks and juices.
  - Once the plant is modernized, productivity will improve significantly, allowing ABC to reduce factory staff headcount by 40%, from 500 employees to 300 employees, which will drive a higher EBITDA margin in the future.
  - With a significant minority, R-SWF will be allowed to have two seats on the board of ABC. So, the board will expand from five members to seven members. R-SWF is planning to have the Head of PE join the board of ABC but hasn't decided on the other board seat.

Risk Discussion: Private Equity Investment
The Head of PE believes the potential return on this project far outweighs the potential risk(s). However, he is happy to discuss potential risks with the Investment Committee.

In-text Question

Please respond to the following question based on **Investment Committee Memo 1.0**.

- As R-SWF's Risk Analyst, do you anticipate liquidity risk will likely be highlighted as a significant financial risk in the upcoming risk discussions for either investment? Explain your thinking.

Guideline Answer:

- No. I do not anticipate the Head of Infrastructure or the Head of PE to highlight liquidity risk as a significant risk for either investment. Although liquidity risk is the main risk that long-term institutional investors face, particularly during a significant market decline, each of these investments represents a small portion of R-SWF's total assets. R-SWF does not have cash flow pressure, unlike many institutional investors that face pressure from the regular payment of liabilities. In addition, R-SWF has been growing over time and is making a concerted effort to expand its direct investment program.

Direct investments typically help mitigate some of the liquidity issues commonly experienced when investing in a fund because direct investment provides a greater amount of control and discretion over when to exit investments. Furthermore, as the direct investment program grows and the proportion of direct investments as part R-SWF's total assets increases, R-SWF's ability to manage capital should improve. I believe there are other financial risks that are more likely to be highlighted as a significant risk for each investment.

Investment Committee Meeting 1.0

Participants
Chief Investment Officer (CIO)
Head of Infrastructure
Head of PE
Head of Risk
Head of Equities
Analysts [no speaking role]

Chief Investment Officer: Good morning, everyone. Welcome to today's investment committee meeting of the sovereign wealth fund of the Republic of Ruritania. After running this money on behalf of our citizens and future generations since its inception, the fund has outperformed our benchmark by 150 basis points, net of fees, and we've grown AUM to $50 billion over 25 years. We are very blessed.

At last month's investment committee meeting, our **Head of Infrastructure** and our **Head of PE** got together to discuss the financials and particulars of two investment opportunities. As they both deserve our attention, today we are joined by our **Head of Risk**, along with our **Head of Equities**, to review them through the lens of risk. Our esteemed junior analysts are in the room with us to observe and provide additional analysis as required.

For now, as we consider our opportunities, I'm mostly here as a facilitator, to pave the way for a robust discussion of investment risk.

Memo A shows us our asset allocation as of mid-June, and we've got 50% in alternatives. We believe in alternatives because our liabilities are negligible and we take a long-term view of things. About 40% of our allocation is in listed equities, with a large portion of that in emerging markets, which we're also big believers in. If we do fund one or both of the two investments on the table, we'll do it with a mix of cash, dividends receivable, and fixed income, but that's not for this committee to decide; the ALCO will go over that at a later date.

In any event, our focus here is private capital, the private equity side. We've got about 3% of our investments in direct private equity and co-investments and about 3% in direct infrastructure.

Again, this meeting is primarily about risk. Let's go to Memo B and ask our **Head of Infrastructure** to talk us through the first investment. It's usually the depth of her infrastructure experience that gives R-SWF the comfort to proceed in the face of risk.

Infrastructure Investment Discussion

Head of Infrastructure: Thank you for the kind words, **CIO**. I'm glad everyone's here so we can apply the full breadth of the investment committee's expertise.

This is an airport BOT project, a PPP in the frontier island nation of Sunnyland, whose primary industry is tourism. The members of our hard-working analyst team who are new to infrastructure have been briefed on the build-operate-transfer models that private developers often adopt under private-public partnerships so they can operate the facilities they have designed and built for a number of years before handing them over to government agencies.

[**Head of Infrastructure** looks around the room to see a few polite nods from the assembled analysts.]

Funds are needed for an airport upgrade: A new terminal and a new, bigger runway will accommodate larger planes. Sunnyland needs to get rid of the passenger bottleneck to allow for an all-important boost in tourism. We're thinking $500 million and two years of construction time should be enough.

Ruritania is prepared to contribute $100 million, and we're insisting on bringing in AOG, a properly experienced airport operator, which will also be investing private equity—about $33 million. The rest of the capital will be no-recourse debt, about $300 million, and an equity injection from the government and other infrastructure investors for the remainder. The debt will be 15-year with a 3-year grace period.

With the BOT arrangements, of course, we take over the airport from the beginning under a 25-year concession agreement for all the cash flows from the terminal. So that's airport charges, like aircraft landing and passenger departure fees, as well as the commercial revenue from duty-free concessions, retail, and so forth, and we remit 35% of what we collect to the Sunnyland Airport Authority on a quarterly basis. If we want to charge more, any increases—say, for CPI adjustments—are worked out according to fixed formulas.

CIO has set the stage for this discussion of risk, and in that spirit, everyone should note the standards and conditions of our agreement with the government. You already know we've got a two-year development program—that's two years to see the revamped airport up and running—so if there are delays or shortfalls in quality, the concession agreement sets out the consequences.

Finally, our expected return for the full 25-year term given our fund's $100 million investment is a 15% IRR.

Chief Investment Officer: Thank you, **Head of Infrastructure**. That's a sufficient return, to be sure, but let's also understand that our involvement can help our friends down in Sunnyland. If we execute this project carefully, it means a boost to the wealth of all Sunnylanders.

You've been there recently, right?

Head of Infrastructure: I have. All indications are that it's an attractive tourist destination. Tourism is key to them now; they lack natural and other resources to diversify the economy. That's what they're depending on to build the economy.

Things are constrained because of the airport. The runway allows only for short, smaller aircraft, so just by increasing runway size and the associated facilities, you're paving a path for the whole nation to grow.

Chief Investment Officer: I ask the assembled team to consider for a minute the responsibilities we have to ourselves, to Ruritania; we all feel partly responsible for its success. When we invest in another sovereign country, such as Sunnyland, we may carry over a similar sense of responsibility, and we take that seriously. While our proposed $100 million investment is just 0.2% of our AUM, this single investment in transportation infrastructure will have an outsized impact on our investees.

With that in mind, let's move to the other proposal on the table. Our **Head of PE** has recently returned from Atsui, the site of the proposed private equity investment outlined in Memo C. Over to you, **Head of PE**.

Private Equity Investment Discussion

Head of PE: Yeah, I just got back. The company is called Atsui Beverage Company or ABC for short, and it was kind of "love at first sight"—or sip. I was on the beach, and a waiter brought me a drink and said it was called the "Mango Special." I thanked him but I was barely listening. You know how it is; my mind was elsewhere. But after the third sip, I was paying less attention to my leisure and more attention to just how good this drink was: refreshing, perfectly sweet, and unlike anything I'd tasted before. You know I'm always thinking about investments, ladies and gents, and I began to think I'd stumbled onto a winner.

I've been back to Atsui three times, and I introduced R-SWF to the team at the ABC plant that makes the Mango Special. I explained how sovereign wealth funds usually partner for the long term, and I built some trust while learning about their business. I know how small this is compared to the rest of our portfolio, but I'm still obsessed with this drink, so I figured out that we can invest $25 million for 35% of the business. They've got $50 million in revenue and $7 million in EBITDA. For those on the team who can't do math quickly like I can, that's a 14% EBITDA margin. And we're looking at a company valuation of roughly 10× EBITDA.

So, wait: Is this a good deal or not?

Well, let's think about it. ABC markets the only locally sourced carbonated beverage in Atsui, *and* tariffs are imposed on foreign competitors. That alone seems pretty great. And they'd use $20 million of our $25 million to modernize the plant. That way, they can turn out product way faster while also gearing up to make non-carbonated drinks like sports drinks and juices. We'd drive efficiency enough to cut headcount from 500 to 300, and that's even better for the EBITDA margin: new equipment, big changes.

I've got the most knowledge on the ground, so I could take a board seat along with someone else from our team. We've gotten pretty comfortable with co-investing, making some money, and developing our skills, and since we're expanding our direct investing effort anyway, this seems like a good fit. It's just $25 million out of our $50 billion pool, so it's a good way to learn, even if some of us think it's risky.

And, you know, sun, mango drinks, and the beach—I bet everyone wants to join the board!

Chief Investment Officer: So, the plant modernization allows for both a meaningful expansion of the product line *and* significant cost savings. But you said that a cut of 200 people underpins those savings?

Head of PE: Yeah.

Chief Investment Officer: OK. Any further questions for **Head of PE**?

Head of Risk: A question from me for **Head of PE**. You mentioned that these guys are the sole beverage manufacturer in Atsui and that there are entry barriers on foreign manufacturers coming in. You've been on the ground, so are local competitors raising their voices about giving ABC some competition?

Head of PE: I've done a lot of local research, and I'm not seeing anyone. When ABC thinks about threats, they think of the big international drink players, who are still scared off by the government's import tariffs.

Chief Investment Officer: A lot of senior officials are keen to grow the local industry. It's a small country, and there's a common emotional investment in ABC's success.

Head of Risk: These do seem like heavy tariffs. **CIO** mentioned they're as high as 100% if you try to buy Coke or Pepsi. The memo says there's an election coming up. Surely there's a risk those entry barriers fall away?

Head of PE: A mango drink is much better than cola, I promise!

Chief Investment Officer: I've done a little outreach myself to people in the know. Combining that with **Head of PE**'s research, I'd say a relaxing of tariffs after the election is a fair assumption.

Head of Equities: I have a question. Will this investment allow for ABC to start exports? Is that part of the expansion plan?

Head of PE: The markets nearby are also tropical, frontier nations. Business relations are decent, and the plant is next to a river that connects to a big port.

Chief Investment Officer: **Head of PE** has explained that the plant workers fish on the freshwater river during their lunch and during breaks, and the river does indeed connect to Atsui's major port. I see good potential for connecting to neighbouring buyers.

Head of Risk: But let's remember that this is a frontier market with a developing economy.

Chief Investment Officer: Quite right. Beverages are still somewhat of a luxury item. Nevertheless, there's plenty of growth potential for us and for them.

Head of Equities: Sure, that's encouraging on exports, but **Head of PE** said that ABC sees its competition as the big international drink players, who are still scared off by the government's tariffs. If the election brings in a government keen on foreign investment, that could completely overturn the advantage this particular business has.

   Let's apply a probability to a tariff reduction and to import markets opening up. Pepsi and Coca-Cola have much deeper pockets for waiting out a price war.

Head of PE: I hear you, but maybe I went too far by saying ABC sees them as competitors. Products like the Mango Special and their other drinks don't actually exist in the Coke and Pepsi product lines, and the Mango Special recipe is so proprietary that if we protect it, it's a real competitive advantage. The other ABC beverages use tropical fruit the multinationals don't have supply chains for, and we believe—I mean, *ABC* believes they have a way of mixing things that no one else can figure out. If that's the case, a path to exports is still there.

With investment, they still have time to get into other juices and diversify. And we're always talking to government officials and to people who could make up the government, and everyone's pretty aligned.

Chief Investment Officer: These risks are tied to the modernization program we're investing in, which means job cuts. In frontier markets, this is very sensitive: Unions may protest, and politicians may make it part of their election agenda, especially given that we're talking about one of the country's more popular companies. We're veering into reputational risk here.

Look, this is a rather small investment, of $25 million, but even a small investment can have an outsized negative impact on us if we don't manage the risk properly.

Thoughts?

Head of PE: We're not just investing and then forgetting things, folks. We're going to be proactive. Before modernization starts, we're going to do some research that shows us what issues are in the minds of all the people of Atsui, not just our workers, and we're going to design new community programs around that. We'll try to make a positive impact first.

We know that cutting employees is sensitive. But by helping many more people than we let go and by giving employees proper training so they have the skills for whatever they're doing next, we're going to be part of a sensible transition.

Head of Equities: That's going to be critical. Community relations is a key component of our social license to operate.

Chief Investment Officer: My dialogue with the **Head of PE** on the ground in Atsui has been ongoing, and he wants us to do right by the community. It's almost an impact investment in and of itself.

Any other questions on the PE investment?

Head of Risk: How comfortable are you with ABC's management? We'll only have a minority stake, and founders are sometimes not the best people to run a business.

So are these people reliable? Do they have the right skill set? The right education? Any worry about potential corruption?

Head of PE: Our due diligence is thorough, and we don't think corruption is an issue. We're new to direct investing, and so we'll be tracking progress extra carefully. And also we're the ones implementing a lot of the modernization, so there'll be more monitoring built in than ever before.

Do we keep management or not? You always have this question in private equity. With all the co-investing we've done, the directors of the funds we partner with find management teams and then keep them and then work *with* them to help them grow.

I see your point that we'd only hold 35% of ABC, but we'll also hold two board seats. I can't predict the future, but we've done a lot of due diligence and we've done a lot of interviews with management, customers, and suppliers. We've interviewed a lot of people who know the management.

We're paying $25 million, and $20 million goes to modernizing the plant. Management will take a little money off the table, and we'll structure it so that they are incentivized in alignment with growth and good oversight. After all, they'll still hold 65%.

We think they'll see that working with us will create success and that willful mismanagement or corruption or taking too much money out of the business works against them in the long run. We're coming to them with our track record through the co-investments we've made, our expertise, and our channels to other markets.

There's always risk, but that's my point of view.

Head of Equities: I support the PE investment. With management having this much skin in the game, their interests are aligned with ours.

Chief Investment Officer: This is a $25 million investment out of our $50 billion fund, and there are impact elements as well that make it more interesting.

Head of PE: Yeah, and to build our direct investment program, we must learn by doing. We've gotten really comfortable with co-investing, and that's great, but to me, it's the people who do this a lot on their own who tend to be really successful.

Yes, there's some risk with management and the government, but a lot of those are risks we're willing to take with one of our first direct investments, where we can get our hands dirty. It's a simple business, right? It's carbonated beverages, and then maybe we go into juices and non-carbonated stuff, right? We can really build the experience of working with management and the other skills that our direct program is going to need.

Hey, maybe our next committee meeting should be in Atsui!

General Discussion on Risk

Chief Investment Officer: I won't argue, but let me ask the committee about a risk that applies to both of these investments. We're an open forum, and so I ask the entire room: What bears more scrutiny?

Head of Risk: The first thing that comes to my mind when we're investing in frontier markets like these is, "How do we deal with the currency risk?" It's hard to hedge these currencies. Meanwhile, they can move wildly against the dollar, turning a really good investment into a really bad investment.

What's your read on this, **Head of PE**?

Head of PE: I'm not stressed about it. When it comes to me and most other visitors to Atsui, we're using US dollars.

Head of Infrastructure: I can speak to the currency risk in Sunnyland. When we're talking about the aviation industry and airports, a lot of revenues for infrastructure investors come in the form of regulated charges. Look at our own concession contract: 70% of the revenues are airport charges. It's typical with these arrangements to outsource the collection of these charges to international organizations like IATA. They collect the revenue from the airline, and almost all of that is paid in dollars, so we're comfortable there.

That leaves the 30% of our revenue coming from commercial sources—retail revenue in the terminal and past the gate and all that duty free and parking. In the big international airports, those transactions take place in the local currency, but we're in a locale that's expressly seeking international tourism. Pricing will be geared to international markets, so we'll have the freedom to price everything in dollars and benchmark the pricing against the affluent traveler.

Head of Risk:　I'm glad to hear that.

What about the borrowing side, though? To keep people happy and the logistics simple, I assume any borrowings will come from local banks that use their country's currency.

Head of Infrastructure:　It's a good thought, but no. The lenders are big international banks. The in-country banks may participate, but given the size of the loans and how long term these arrangements are—at least in Sunnyland—the local banks just don't have the capacity yet.

Whoever the lenders are, they'll be comfortable knowing the investors are getting their returns mostly in US dollars, which is what the $300 million of debt is denominated in.

Head of Risk:　Which brings me to defaults.

Head of Infrastructure:　Right, well, this is non-recourse financing, and the concession agreement outlines the terms of default and termination. These are matters that impinge on the direct arrangement between the government and the banks, so while it's something to be aware of, I don't see us getting dragged in.

Head of Risk:　Thanks.

Head of Equities:　I know the **Head of Risk** was coming to this, but the topic is coming up very often recently.

If you look at the World Economic Forum's "Global Risk Report" since 2017, climate risk and extreme weather feature in the top risks every time. Year over year, the weather gets more erratic. Sea-level rise may be gradual, but it doesn't stop. And while I understand the need to support Sunnyland's economy by expanding the airport, the memo says that the new runway is less than a kilometer from the sea.

Sure, you get a fantastic view when you take off and land, but the sea *is* rising, and the risk of flooding could become real even just during high tide. Running an airport in those conditions would not be possible.

It's a 25-year infrastructure investment. That's long enough for climate risks to materialize and impact operations. We've got to factor this in.

Head of Infrastructure

These points are well taken, but keep in mind that to even get as far as finding interested lenders for the airport, it means we've gone through the due diligence process. The big banks need environmental-impact statements before they jump on board, and even just in our role as equity investors, we had to satisfy ourselves that these kinds of issues were thought through.

Head of Risk:　Sure, and naming risks is necessary and commendable, but—

Head of Infrastructure:　—But that doesn't mean the risk goes away. Of course.

I'm obviously not an engineer or a contractor, but what I'd say to the committee is that the experts tells us, in the time frame we're looking at, environmental risks are unlikely to materialize, and even so, they're accounted for during the design process. The drainage systems are modified to handle increases in groundwater levels, and the engineers are building in once-in-50-years and once-in-100-years flood scenarios. Those are risks they're confident they can build for.

Chief Investment Officer: None of us are experts here, but my perspective is that we can take comfort from the fact that these kinds of challenges have been around for decades. Consider Kansai International Airport in Japan: People are always saying that it's sinking—and it *has* gone down a tiny bit—but it's been around for over 25 years and it's been fine.

It's important to be aware of it, and I'm glad you brought it up, but indications are that there's nothing really stopping us on this front.

Head of Infrastructure: That's right. We've come to rely on the reports from the technical adviser, and that's a fairly standard approach for us with these sorts of investments.

Head of PE: Agreed.

Head of Risk: What about previous foreign investment in Sunnyland? Did political risk come into play for other investments? What's the general feeling?

Head of PE: **Head of Infrastructure** called me from Sunnyland when I was on the beach in Atsui planning the ABC upgrades, and he asked me to look into it. Investment in Sunnyland has mostly been on the tourism side. There's a mixture of three- and five-star hotels, so major international hotel operators are around. And they're still arriving, but they feel the transportation bottleneck. Those who are there and the ones who are thinking about coming in are happy about the airport project.

Head of Infrastructure: And I haven't heard any horror stories about investors in Sunnyland getting burned because of unfair rule changes. Plus, relations are good. The Sunnyland authorities approached us as a fellow government institution, so we're comfortable on a sort of government-to-government basis.

Chief Investment Officer: One nice thing about an island nation is that it *is* an island. There's less political interference from the neighbours. From what **Head of Infrastructure** was telling me, we can feel positive that our investment in the airport will help the economy and stabilize the local political situation more than the contrary.

Head of Risk: Good to hear. Let's dig a little deeper on the modeling we've done for the airport investment. We expect a 15% IRR over 25 years. That is our base case. Have we done any stress tests to those baseline expectations? What if there are delays and we have to pay a penalty? What if construction costs overrun the budget? What if revenues fall short? Give us an idea of how bad the IRR could get if we don't achieve the base case.

Head of Infrastructure: Sure. I like how you've framed the question, because it covers some key risks.

From our perspective, the biggest risk is traffic—comparing the actual number of visitors and tourists coming in and out of the airport against our projections. We're not experts here, either, but we hired an established traffic consultant who looks at the global tourism numbers and the particulars of our development to make a determination.

The consultant produced a low case and a high case based on different traffic forecasts. The low case is also of interest to the banks, of course, which want confidence that they'll be paid.

Our analysis of the reasonable low case puts IRR down to around 10% or 11%. The high case pushes the return out into the high teens.

There are some sensitivities around CapEx, and we're looking to manage this risk through a fixed-price contract, the language of which says that whatever penalties we'd face for delayed or subpar construction will be passed down to the contractor. We've applied a ±10% sensitivity around that, and it does impinge on the IRR a little bit but not as much as the low-traffic case. If we run into real cost overruns or delays, we're looking at about a 13% IRR.

Head of PE: The airport's key source of revenue is tourist numbers, and we've got an exotic luxury destination on our hands, folks.

Head of Equities: Agreed. And therefore, we need to consider the risk of a prolonged global recession when discretionary vacations and spending take a nosedive. For a small island like Sunnyland, this is a big risk. Some scenario analysis that considers the impact of a downturn that lasts for two or three or even four years seems necessary.

Head of Infrastructure: We've done some work on those scenarios, and it's influenced by a specific responsibility of the government, which they have explicitly accepted, to aggressively promote tourism as soon as, if not before, a recession hits.

Think of the aviation industry, which has been through shocks again and again. With downtimes like the global financial crisis around 2009 and the few instances where travelers were spooked by crashes, the airlines came out with attractive deals and recovery was quick.

Sunnyland's government is used to adjusting and always reduces pricing to attract tourists when they need to. Our sense is that even a prolonged recession isn't a deal killer, because the authorities and the industry will react quickly.

Head of PE: I like your optimism.

Chief Investment Officer

Well, beyond optimism, we're starting from a low base; there's enormous room for growth in Sunnyland.

Head of Risk: If I may, **CIO**, just a follow-up question to the **Head of Equities**' point on the recession: We all experienced the coronavirus pandemic in 2020, and plenty of scientists have warned us that pandemics are going to be more likely—

Head of Equities: —Helped along by climate change!

Head of Risk: Yes, thank you, because of how we're damaging the environment, and again, this investment has a 25-year horizon. What if another pandemic causes rampant restrictions and people are simply not allowed to travel? Has that been factored into our scenario analysis?

Head of Infrastructure: To a limited extent, yes. We pass through 35% of whatever revenue we take on, so our payments to the government are handled that way in the concession agreement. That leaves the crucial aspect of defaults to lenders and what would trigger them.

The built-in debt-service reserve covers us for a period of time, and if travel is on hold for too much longer, then we turn to restructuring or rescheduling the financing.

But let's understand that the COVID-19 pandemic in 2020 was a game-changer, and the language and dynamics of certain contractual agreements were adjusted to avoid straight defaults in these cases. And the concern here is about short-term impact, whereas over 25 years, we expect things to gradually recover, so our concerns are more about keeping the project going and avoiding default during the problem period.

Voting on Infrastructure Investment

Chief Investment Officer: OK, I'm grateful for the expertise we have around this table. I think that's probably good for a committee vote. Let's start with our **Head of Infrastructure**: yes or no?

Head of Infrastructure: Yes.

Chief Investment Officer: How about our **Head of Risk**?

Head of Risk: I have my doubts, but because it is a $100 million investment on AUM of $50 billion, we'll give it a shot. I'll say "yes."

Chief Investment Officer: We have to take a little bit of risk, after all.
Head of PE, how about you?

Head of PE: Before we ultimately pull the trigger, we should take another look at our other investments and similar memos to see if they're related to tourism and it would mean too much correlation. Besides that, I'm a "yes."

Chief Investment Officer: OK. **Head of Equities**?

Head of Equities: Yes from me as well. Given the size of the investment, I think it's worth taking the risk.

Chief Investment Officer: And I vote "yes."
As a sovereign wealth fund, beyond our responsibility to manage risks and returns well, we want to give back, and where our participation helps nations develop, we feel a responsibility there as well.

Voting on Private Equity Investment

Chief Investment Officer: All right, very good. Let's move on to our direct private equity investment in ABC. **Head of PE**, what say you?

Head of PE: I'm in. Yes.

Chief Investment Officer: Very good. How about you, **Head of Equities**?

Head of Equities: I'm supportive of this. For one thing, it presents much less risk than the airport in Sunnyland. Yes.

Chief Investment Officer: OK. And our resident infrastructure expert, what say you?

Head of Infrastructure: Well, you might expect me to disagree with **Head of Equities** in terms of the risk—we have a minority position, for one thing. But the investment is small, so I'm fine. Yes.

Chief Investment Officer: OK. And finally, **Head of Risk?**

Head of Risk: **Head of PE** made some very good points. It *is* indeed a simple investment to understand and a chance to gain some experience in direct investment. Even if it doesn't work out financially, there's upside to building our experience and to having a positive impact on the wider community, to name but two areas of non-financial return. Yes from me.

Chief Investment Officer: OK, we have two investments that I'm excited to proceed with. I'd like **Head of Infrastructure** and **Head of PE** to run with those and keep us posted, and now it's time—

Head of PE: —To fight for the open board seat!

Head of Risk: Sounds fun, but actually, let's do this the old-fashioned way by filling the other board seat on the basis of experience?

Head of PE: One free Mango Special to our wise, risk-averse colleague!

Chief Investment Officer: And with that, we'll see everyone for the next investment committee meeting, in a month's time.

—The End—

In-text Questions

Please respond to the following questions based on **Investment Committee Meeting 1.0**.

1. The Head of Infrastructure identified a key risk to the Sunnyland airport investment. Explain what analysis could be shared with you to increase your confidence that the key risk is properly managed prior to making the investment in the Sunnyland airport.
2. Explain how the upcoming election most likely exposes the R-SWF's investment in ABC to financial risk. Discuss whether or not you believe the Head of PE's approach to managing this particular risk is sufficient.

Guideline Answers:

1. During the investment committee meeting, the Head of Infrastructure identified traffic as the key risk to the Sunnyland airport investment. The island might not draw an increased number of tourists simply because the airport can accommodate larger planes and more passengers. Although the Head of Infrastructure alluded to the fact that he has quantified the financial risk should the level of tourists not meet

expectations after the completion of the new airport, I would like to review his scenario analysis to feel comfortable with his assumptions. Scenario analysis would be the best way to manage this financial risk prior to making the investment in Sunnyland.

2. I do not think the Head of PE's approach to managing the financial risk due to the upcoming election is sufficient. My understanding is that the upcoming election will expose ABC to financial risk because the current government has imposed large tariffs on foreign competitors that would like to export their products to Atsui. In the event a different political party, specifically one that opposes such tariffs, wins the upcoming election in Atsui, it could have a significant effect on the profitability of ABC because the company would need to compete for local customers.

Of course, a change in government is not something that ABC can control. Although I believe the steps the Head of PE has taken to manage this particular risk are good, including building rapport with the current government, it is not clear to me that he has conducted a thorough analysis to illustrate the potential financial impact on ABC should the tariffs be reduced or eliminated after the upcoming election. This analysis should be done using scenario analysis. Despite this being a relatively small investment for R-SWF, the financial risk of a change in the tariff policy should be thoroughly modeled and assessed prior to making the investment.

4. R-SWF'S Investments: 2.0

Extension of Case Facts (2.0)
After Investment Committee Meeting 1.0, the investment committee of the sovereign wealth fund of Ruritania, R-SWF, added two new significant investments to its portfolio. These investments were direct infrastructure and direct private equity investments—the investments in the airport in Sunnyland and the beverage manufacturer in Atsui, respectively.

- Three years have passed, and the investment committee of R-SWF has decided to conduct an investment review of the two projects.
- Note: The focus of the meeting is on the risks (current and potential) of the new investment proposals, not details on the financial performance of the investments. (An in-depth meeting on the financial performance of the investments was held in the previous month).
- All investment committee participants (and Level III candidates in the CFA Program) are provided with a background memo with the following information:
  - Memo A: Update on R-SWF's asset allocation and performance
  - Memo B: Update on the direct infrastructure investment (airport expansion in Sunnyland) and a list of risks for discussion
  - Memo C: Provides details on the proposed direct private equity investment (investment in ABC) and a list of risks for discussion.

Investment Committee Meeting Memo 2.0

To: R-SWF Investment Committee Members
From: R-SWF Chief Investment Officer

Re: Investment Committee Meeting 2.0 Agenda

Distribution: Head of Risk, Head of PE, Head of Infrastructure, Head of Equities, and Junior Staff

Agenda

- Opening Remarks and Asset Allocation CIO—5 minutes
- Infrastructure Update CIO + Head of Infrastructure—5 minutes
- PE Update CIO + Head of PE—5 minutes
- Discussion of Risk—Infrastructure: Head of Infrastructure, Head of Risk, All—10 minutes
- Discussion of Risk—PE: Head of PE, Head of Risk, All—10 minutes
- Other Risks: Head of Equities + All—5–10 minutes
- Closing Remarks: CIO—5 minutes

Memo 2A: Asset Allocation and Performance

- Since its inception, R-SWF has built a diversified portfolio of investments. As of last month, the fund had AUM of $56 billion USD, with the fund outperforming its overall benchmark by 130 bps net of fees since inception. Of course, there have been short-term periods of underperformance as the fund pursued its long-term strategy.
- The asset allocation as of last month for the overall fund was as follows:

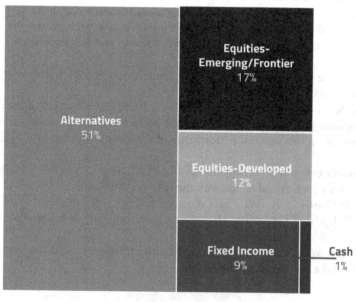

Total Portfolio

Alternatives 51%
Equities-Emerging/Frontier 17%
Equities-Developed 12%
Fixed Income 9%
Cash 1%

- R-SWF had approximately 51% of assets invested in alternative investments, consistent with its long-term objectives.
- Asset allocation was covered extensively in the prior month's investment committee meeting, so today's meeting will not provide any further breakdown.
- The investment committee will be discussing various points of view on risk aspects of the investments—including risk mitigation.
- The discussion will include "other risks" that were perhaps not covered well in the initial discussion. Discussion of environmental and social risks are challenging for long-term direct investing.
- Updates on the airport expansion in Sunnyland infrastructure investment are found in Memo 2B.
- Updates on the PE investment in ABC in Atsui are found in Memo 2C.

Memo 2B: Update on Infrastructure Investment in Sunnyland Airport

Investment Update

- Based on investment committee approval, the $100 million investment in Sunnyland has moved forward in accordance with agreed plans. This amount represents approximately 0.2% of total R-SWF assets.
- The Sunnyland government is happy with the progress of construction, which was completed recently. There was a delay in getting started, but that is Island life. Thankfully, there were no material cost overruns on the project.
- The new terminal is beautifully built and will be a great addition to the island nation as it further develops its tourism capabilities.
- We expect a grand opening of the new terminal in September, in time for the busy fall season. Tourist season is primarily from October through May, with the summer months being very hot (around 40°C) and humid.
- There are rumors that Airport Operating Group (AOG) is looking to renegotiate its contract for a higher fixed fee.
- One of the advantages of Sunnyland as a tourist attraction is its beautiful beaches with easy access to the airport, with the new runway, only 1 km from the sea, providing spectacular views.
- However, climate change has led to rising seas and more frequent storms. Storms are common in island nations; however, the rising seas are of concern.
- In addition, hotter temperatures are of additional concern. A few years ago, the tourist season was September through June, with only July and August being "too hot." However, in May this year, daytime highs were frequently 42°C or higher. There is a risk that the hotter temperatures lasting longer in the year will reduce tourism (and revenues for the airport project).
- Although this is a small investment in total, there are some risks we should focus on in today's discussion.

Risk Discussion: Infrastructure Investment

The following key risks are highlighted for discussion:

- Currency risk
- Expropriation risk by the Sunnyland government

- Risk that revenue from airport is less than expected
- Risk of project delays
- Risk of operating and maintenance costs being higher than projected
- Risk of default of AOG
- Risk that actual future (borrowing) interest rates will be higher than forecast
- Risk of underperformance regarding service quality—not meeting defined standards
- Other risks

Possible Mitigation of the Key Risks

- What should we do to mitigate the key risks?
- What should be our priorities? Action plan?

Memo 2C: Update on PE Investment in Atsui Beverage Company
Investment Update

- Based on investment committee approval, the $25 million investment in ABC has moved forward in accordance with agreed plans. This amount represents approximately 0.05% of total R-SWF assets.
- The modernization of the ABC plant went well, and the product expansion is starting to take shape. However, there several key updates that are unfortunately negative:
  - Atsui and surrounding nations went into a recession last year. Furthermore, a currency devaluation is anticipated. Beverages are considered a luxury item in Atsui.
  - A new government was elected in Atsui last year and took office in January. One of the first orders of business was to reduce tariffs on imported beverages from a 100% tariff to a 20% tariff. This change hurts our cost advantage over foreign brands. It is rumored that tariffs were reduced because Atsui wants to gain favor with foreign governments for potential loans.
  - Because the modern equipment will improve productivity, the original plan was to reduce headcount by 40%. In addition, due to slowing sales, management wanted to reduce staff by a total of 50%. However, labor laws are strict in Atsui. In order to terminate the employment of an Atsui citizen, significant notice (two years) is required. Plus, there is reputational risk for R-SWF for firing factory employees in a frontier market during a recession.
  - In order to make up for lower profits (due to the above reasons), plant management has started to cut corners to save on costs. Unfortunately, one way to do this was to dump waste into the nearby river rather than transport the waste for proper treatment. Although the waste is not toxic, it is starting to spoil the lovely fishing spot near the factory.
  - Another way ABC has tried to cut costs is by reducing employee breaks from one hour to 30 minutes and removing soap from the restrooms, requesting that employees bring their own.
- Although this is a small investment in total, there are some risks we should focus on in today's discussion.

Risk Discussion: Private Equity Investment

The following key risks are highlighted for discussion:

- Currency risk
- Expropriation risk by the Atsui government
- Quality control issues
- Challenges with local management (don't have a majority stake)
- Competitor pressure
- Growing trend of health foods that would result in avoidance of many carbonated beverages
- Elimination of tariffs protecting ABC from foreign-owned manufacturers
- Other risks

Possible Mitigation of the Key Risks

- What should we do to mitigate these risks?
- What should be our priorities? Action plan?

In-text Questions

Please respond to the following questions based on **Investment Committee Memo 2.0**.

4. The investment committee has identified several new risks that were not previously discussed (before Memos 2B and 2C). The CIO asks you to recommend how R-SWF can manage each of the following risks:
   a. Risk of actual future (borrowing) interest rates will be higher than forecast (Memo 2B)
   b. Growing trend of health foods that would result in avoidance of many carbonated beverages (Memo 2C)

Guideline Answers:

4a: R-SWF can manage the risk that actual future (borrowing) interest rates will be higher than forecast by hedging its interest rate exposure for the Sunnyland airport project.

4b: R-SWF can manage the risk of carbonated beverages falling out of favor due to an increasing preference for health foods by working to develop new healthy alternatives to carbonated, presumably sugar-filled drinks. As the production facility expands its ability to produce product, ABC could focus its new product development on healthy alternatives. The company can leverage its experience producing such beverages given the success of its natural mango drink in order to differentiate itself and increase market share.

Investment Committee Meeting 2.0

Participants
Chief Investment Officer (CIO)
Head of Infrastructure
Head of PE
Head of Risk
Head of Equities
Analysts [no speaking role]

Chief Investment Officer: Good morning, everyone, and welcome to today's investment committee meeting of the sovereign wealth fund of the Republic of Ruritania. We're grateful for the opportunity to serve our constituents.

During last month's committee meeting, we reviewed the financial statements of the two projects in question—the airport in Sunnyland and the beverage manufacturer in Atsui. Our **Head of PE** provided the Mango Specials, so thank you for that!

It's been three years—wow, time really flies—since we unanimously approved proceeding with both investments. We'll go through some updates, but today's focus is risks and sensible mitigation measures.

First, though, the bigger picture: In those three years, AUM have grown by $6 billion. We're still outperforming our overall benchmark, but our outperformance has been dulled by difficulties with some assets, primarily real estate, because commercial real estate has under-performed. So that's hurt us a little bit, but as ever, we are long-term investors, and we may reap the benefits of those investments yet.

As we discuss risk mitigation, let's consider environmental and social risks. The greater pressure we've put on ourselves to invest responsibly and sustainably is matched by increased scrutiny from outside observers.

Whether we've decided to make an exit on our own or because of outside pressure, our rather long-term horizon doesn't make it any easier for us to step away from an investment when the time comes. As a contrast, our **Head of Equities** was telling me before the meeting started that he wasn't too happy about how much one of his portfolio companies was polluting, and so he just went ahead and sold the position. It was a liquid investment in a public market, and he was done within the hour. That's a contrast we have to keep in mind.

Allow me to read this comment about ABC from the minutes of the last meeting, as a sort of touchstone for us today: "This is a rather small investment, of $25 million, but even a small investment can have an outsized negative impact on us if we don't manage the risk properly." But let's begin with Sunnyland airport. **Head of Infrastructure**, why don't you start us off?

Head of Infrastructure: Thanks, **CIO**.

The good news is that the new terminal is pretty much complete and in line with specifications. We received some good reviews, both from locals and the international trade press. The downside is delays: At the outset, we expected a two-year construction program, but we're now well into the third year, unfortunately. There were noticeable cost overruns, and those were borne by the contractor, according to the contract, but there are some delay penalties that have yet to be settled.

The government, the contractor, and ourselves and AOG as investors—we're in discussions about these penalties, and the contractors are pointing to variations they say arose from our side. What they're calling "variations" we see as necessary design thinking for optimizing the commerciality of the retail outlets. The "variations" were pretty minimal, so let's see where our discussions end up. And some further disagreements center around the offices of customs and immigration within the terminal, which the contractor is laying at the foot of the government.

We should also highlight that as we're nearing the startup of terminal operations, the operator, AOG, has started complaining that the costs of training local staff are higher than expected. They haven't said anything formally yet, but I imagine they'll want to renegotiate their fixed-fee contract—nothing too serious.

Meanwhile, the grand opening of the terminal is a month away, in late August. It should be a good, high-profile event, and we should make a good showing. At least four Ruritania representatives, I think.

And then always swirling around our work is the focus of the press on the environmental movement and climate change, so we need to think about the impact on tourism. The main tourist season is September through June, historically, but it's just getting too hot, and so really the prime window for visitors will narrow to October through May.

The debate in the local press is frequently about the impact of so many tourists flying to Sunnyland, and AOG is in dialogue with the airlines about it. We have yet to see how that plays out in terms of impact on the airport operations down the road, but at the grand opening, we'll be able to celebrate the start of the upcoming season in September; bookings are in line with optimistic projections for the first year with the new terminal and runway.

Chief Investment Officer: OK, thank you for that update.

And what can we say about ABC in Atsui?

Head of PE: So, there are positives and negatives. A big positive is that this has been a fantastic learning experience for our direct investment program. But there's been a currency devaluation, and you could argue it's going to get worse because of the recession—the recession that started last year and that you all know so well because we're in the middle of it.

Still, is that good or bad? We do sell to tourists who bring their own currency, and we've got a lot of flexibility to shift our pricing so we can keep prices where they should be relative to our costs, which is positive.

But following the recent election, the new administration is talking about dropping all sorts of import tariffs, including the ones on food and drink. They've basically said, "For sure, we're going to cut them from 100% to 20%."

Obviously, this hurts our cost advantage over foreign brands, and the challenge here is that the new government wants to win favor with foreign governments before asking them for big loans, so the issue is about more than just carbonated drinks.

Chief Investment Officer: There's a rumor that the new president likes Pepsi, so it's almost as if she doesn't want to pay double for a can, but 20% more is OK.

Head of PE: ABC's new modernized equipment is ready to go, but here's the problem: Management is now saying they want to reduce headcount by 50%, instead of just 40%, because of the slowing sales. But labor laws in Atsui are strict, and to let someone go, you usually have to give as much as two years' notice.

Head of Risk: Two years?

Head of PE: Yeah, and the other issue is that for us as a sovereign wealth fund, there's reputational risk. Flying in from world cities and firing factory employees in frontier markets mean bad publicity, especially in Atsui and especially during the recession.

And here's another thing: In order to make up for lower profits, management has started cutting corners. They're dumping waste in the nearby river rather than paying to transport it to the treatment site. Do you remember how the plant is right next to the river and the employees fish in it during lunch? It's spoiling the fishing spot. This is a problem. And it gets worse: Scientists are saying that the plant site and the river overlap with the range of a rare reptile that is found here and only one other place on earth. So our site has attracted the attention of people with no interest in soda or mangoes.

Head of Risk: This is a problem.

Head of PE: Now here's another thing: ABC has tried to cut costs by reducing employee breaks from an hour to 30 minutes and—this is probably a little granular for our meeting, but risks are risks, they have removed soap from the restrooms! Everyone has to bring their own soap now.

Now, I know we're a $50 billion sovereign wealth fund—

Chief Investment Officer: —$56 billion.

Head of PE: I know we're a $56 billion sovereign wealth fund, and here we are talking about removing soap from a few bathrooms in the tropics where we have a $25 million direct investment, but stuff like this can have a reputational impact.

Head of Risk: Agreed.

Chief Investment Officer: Our focus right now is risk, and we should be talking about this. We haven't really faced any of these health and safety or social issues before at the individual investment level, and it's a learning opportunity as we expand our direct investing program. **Head of PE**, when you went to the restroom and found out there was no soap, you had to borrow some from the plant manager. Is that right? Did he give it to you for free, or did he charge you?

Head of PE: He wanted to charge me, but I didn't need any soap because I had hand sanitizer with me. I got used to carrying hand sanitizer around with me everywhere back in the coronavirus days, so now I just do that when I'm in Atsui.

Chief Investment Officer: OK, then let's discuss infrastructure.

Three years ago when we approved this investment, we talked potential risks, including climate, and we were comfortable with the position that the threat of rising seas was well into the future. We may have to re-evaluate that position.

Head of Risk: Despite our comfort then, the fact is that storms have become more frequent and the sea level *has* risen measurably—in three short years.

Head of Infrastructure: The lenders have also raised this point, as has our in-country political adviser. I still don't see any impact in the immediate term. If you remember three years ago, much of our comfort came from the environmental-impact assessments, which were required and were factored into the design. What has been constructed can deal with it sufficiently.

The bigger worry is the force of an unanticipated and rare storm that compounds the impact of some already bad flooding. Originally, the engineers planned for a once-in-50-years or once-in-100-years scenario, and it may be that the risk of those events has increased.

There's a discussion to be had with the government about architectural solutions—maybe some proper flood barriers. As for the cost of them, if they'll even work, and whose responsibility that is—those issues are unclear. It's not in anybody's interest for the airport to shut down.

Head of Equities: My experience engaging with large public companies on climate risk tells me that a tiny island like Sunnyland can't have any meaningful impact on a global scale and hence they must focus on adaptation rather than worry too much about mitigation. **Head of Infrastructure** points to one of the more logical solutions: some sort of storm-surge barrier like the Netherlands has relied on for years.

As for who's going to pay for it, let's think beyond our own project for a minute. Rising seas aren't just going to have an impact on the airport; every five-star, beach-facing property will feel it too. The prime hotels feel it, and eventually the whole tourist ecosystem feels it, and with the country so dependent on tourism, my view is that this has to be a government-driven initiative. And a storm-surge barrier that successfully avoids damaging floods will be important enough to private interests, such as real estate and other infrastructure investors, that they'll form part of the funding circle.

Head of Infrastructure: I think that's right. It's a question for the whole economy and for the government. Serious talks are taking place in Sunnyland about a new tax to cover the costs, a sort of climate tax that would go to a host of worsening climate issues.

How the authorities end up structuring that tax will inform whether we can avoid it.

Chief Investment Officer: Understood, but as a sovereign institution, even if we could avoid such a tax to protect our investment value, from a reputational perspective, we should think twice.

Head of PE: **Head of Infrastructure** said that AOG might be asking for a higher fixed fee to operate the new terminal. I'm not sure if this is a question for this point in the meeting, but is there anything we can do to proactively protect ourselves against a higher contract fee in the event AOG gets its renegotiation?

Head of Infrastructure: We all signed a well-structured agreement, and that affords us some decent protection against any meddling in the fee structure, though there are break clauses if anything gets too out of line. Still, there are incentives built into the concession agreement to make sure everyone wins to a greater or lesser extent when traffic goes up.

Equally, we don't want a disgruntled operator. Happy employees, happy travelers, better experience, more traffic.

We haven't been formally approached about this, but let's not dismiss it out of hand just because we have a contract we can hide behind. AOG is a strong global operator. If they did activate a break clause in two or three years' time, that lands us with a responsibility we really don't want, which is finding a new operator. We're still satisfied with their cooperation. I recommend seeing how talks over the delays play out, and if we find that the government is liable for the delay, we'll request an extension to the concession and then sit down with AOG to positively collaborate on retooling the whole picture.

Chief Investment Officer: OK, we've covered the environmental and reputational risks, the climate risk, and the AOG item as well. Are there any other risks we should examine at this point?

Head of Risk: That covers the important ones. Currency risk and the risk of further delays are less of a concern. With climate change, we can't *solve* it; as **Head of Equities** insists, we have to adapt. It affects the entire nation, so hopefully the government will step in.

And I reinforce the idea of positive negotiations with AOG. We want a happy operator.

Chief Investment Officer: Right. OK, very good.

Head of Risk, it looks like something is still on your mind.

Head of Risk: Thanks for noticing. A little more scrutiny of ABC is warranted. I acknowledge its importance for boosting our direct investment know-how. It's been a great learning experience for **Head of PE** and his team, and it's a very small investment. Even if we lose money, it's not going to move the needle for our fund, but—and this is a substantial "but"—the reputational risk is a big concern.

We don't want to end up in the newspaper firing people during a recession, polluting the river, threatening endangered species, and being rather petty about soap.

Head of Infrastructure: True on all counts.

Head of Risk: Ladies and gentlemen, the writing is on the wall. I propose we exit this investment as soon as possible, if we can. Maybe we can't, and if that's the case, I would remain very concerned.

Head of PE: No, I'm happy you mentioned it, and it's good that it's all coming out in this room. Let me tell you how we see things.

Before we jumped into this as one of our first direct investments, we co-invested and participated in many private equity funds that invest in all kinds of things, including special situations and distressed investments, and we've always gone in with third-party experts or used our own experts. Just because things get a little dicey, it doesn't mean we exit.

When we started, ABC was a conventional, if small, investment. If that's changed and it now is a problem business, we've got a team whose job it is to make lemonade out of lemons, so let's think about passing ABC over to the distressed-asset team before it becomes properly distressed. I'm not saying we keep it or some other team takes it. I'm saying let's at least see if it's a better fit for someone else.

What if we keep going? We've got risks around firing employees, dumping waste in the river, and pettiness around soap. And we're shifting our mindset, and the challenge is less about the return and more about the reputational risk.

So we really need to figure out: Can we change how this business functions to manage that risk? We have a 35% interest, we know that management has skin in the game. But in what game? With management incentivized to improve the bottom line, we're motivating them to cut employees instead of keeping employees happy and avoiding resentment.

So we're asking ourselves a new question: How do we motivate management to keep people inside and outside the plant happy? We have two board seats, and investing more money in modernization seems to make less sense now.

And we've got employees now who don't have much to do, but they're collecting a salary, so why would they leave? And if we can't fire them, it's an issue. Maybe we pay them a percentage—say, half their regular salary—while offering them good training and assistance for eight months to find another job. At the same time, we'd convince management to shift to a less profit-driven focus.

I don't know if any of that will work. Maybe we should have divested earlier, but that's our thinking if we keep holding on.

Head of Equities: And what about the toxic stuff being released into the river?

Head of PE: It's actually not toxic, technically, but we don't even want to be talking about whether it's toxic or not toxic. Ending that practice is an important piece of our talks with management, and so is removing incentives to cut corners.

Can we fundamentally change the way things are going? If we can't, then maybe this is an investment for someone else. Or perhaps we sell our 35% stake back to management?

Chief Investment Officer: Thanks, **Head of PE.** We talked about this being a learning experience. We also talked about it displaying aspects of impact investment. Maybe part of the value is in education. In some less developed areas, they think it's maybe not a big deal to throw things into the river. Can we inform their thinking with the idea that wanting a beautiful river for fishing and enjoyment is a virtue and that it's not really that hard to dispose of waste properly? What can we intelligently say about impact?

Head of Equities: This line of thinking makes sense to me. Our experience in other developing nations as well as developed nations tells us that you'll save some costs in the short term with actions like dumping waste directly into water bodies, but in the long run, regulations catch up to you and the cost of pre-treatment or appropriate handling of waste is much lower than the penalties you get for taking such shortcuts.

If we decide to stay, we have to paint the picture for management that there's a fatal flaw in our approach at the moment. Public perception is one issue, but eventually regulations will be introduced with penalties and obligations to clean up the river.

If we do try to salvage the situation and continue with our investment, there's a path that involves the government. Our pitch should be that if there are legal roadblocks for cutting 50% of the jobs, you might be putting 100% of the jobs at risk because the company won't survive if tariffs are reduced to 20%. The government doesn't want the factory to shut down because of *its* rigid labor laws, so there may well be room for a more, let's say, negotiated conclusion.

It's worth exploring, again, in consultation with the local management.

Chief Investment Officer: Lobbying the government, reframing management's incentives—these are interesting ways to pivot. We should also consider as a committee the extent to which we want to maintain our direct investing/private equity approach or whether there is wisdom in recasting our work as more of an impact program. The committee's analysis has highlighted the difficulties faced by a sovereign wealth fund in cutting staff. It ends up being a headline risk.

The conventional private equity houses can more easily cut jobs for purely financial reasons. However, as a sovereign wealth fund, it is more complicated for us. Imagine the headline: "Government of Ruritania Cuts Jobs in XYZ during a Recession."

Head of Infrastructure: It's not a good look.

Chief Investment Officer: It's not a good look. Right.

Head of Risk: From my point of view, we've covered the main risks for ABC. I like the sequence: We engage with management to change the mindset, and we lobby government on how a two-year notice period and similar restrictions could jeopardize the whole business. We give it another year, and if we're not making progress, we look for an exit option, maybe handing things over to a team that is comfortable with these thorny issues.

Chief Investment Officer: Well summarized. I'm grateful for the focus we are putting on the risks here.
  And as for Sunnyland?

Head of Equities: I'd submit to the team that while the world's major governments have *started* taking action on climate change, we're not going to "fix" these problems easily so the planet can just go back to the way it was 30 years ago. The impact will intensify, and we have to adapt.
  In my mind, the focus should be on liaising with the government. They will have to drive things because of the scale of the investment required—

Chief Investment Officer: —And because of how long term the investment horizon is.
  Team, this is the sort of experienced scrutiny of risk we needed, so thank you very much. This was a highly worthwhile meeting, and let's keep a keen focus on the risks.

—The End—

In-text Questions

Please answer the following question based on **Investment Committee Meeting 2.0**.

1. In the template provided, state the primary environmental risk that has been identified by R-SWF's investment committee for each investment. Recommend how each risk can be managed in the future.

Investment	Primary Environmental Risk	Risk Management Recommendation
Sunnyland Airport		
Atsui Beverage Company		

2. Identify one significant social risk that both investments have in common and that was not originally identified by the investment committee. Discuss whether or not this risk is easily managed once recognized.

Guideline Answers

1. In the template provided, state the primary environmental risk that has been identified by R-SWF's investment committee for each investment. Recommend how each
   risk can be managed in the future.

Investment	Primary Environmental Risk	Risk Management Recommendation
Sunnyland Airport	Climate change due to rising sea levels	Given the uncertainty around the precise timing and magnitude of the impact of climate change and rising sea levels specifically, R-SWF should use climate-related scenario analysis to better understand how climate change will affect its investment in Sunnyland. In addition, since R-SWF cannot mitigate climate change, it must focus on adaptation strategies. In this case, a strategy to provide protection for the airport against a storm surge or higher sea levels is the most realistic option. An adaptation strategy is consistent with the development mandate of R-SWF's investment in Sunnyland.
Atsui Beverage Company	Waste management due to dumping waste into river	R-SWF must find a way to persuade the board and local management to stop dumping waste in the river in an effort to pursue sustainable development and a "just" transition. Although it might be a cost savings in the short run, in the long run, regulations will catch up. Cleanup of improperly disposed waste is far more costly than appropriately disposing of waste up front. One of the ways to encourage prioritization of protecting the river is to educate the local community about the importance of a healthy river. Community education, the pursuit of sustainable development, and a "just" transition are consistent with the impact investing element of this investment for R-SWF.

2. Reputational risk is very significant in the case of each investment and can have an
   outsized effect on the performance of the investments. Social issues, such as reputational risk, are generally quite difficult to manage even once identified and understood because they are relatively challenging to quantify and integrate into financial
   models. Furthermore, best practices include considering the interests of all the stakeholders involved, which is not easy.

   In Sunnyland, R-SWF must contribute to any effort to raise funds to implement
   protection against rising seas. This project will likely be expensive. However, it is not
   in R-SWF's best interest to appear to be avoiding contributing to the project to accommodate climate change. Doing so could significantly damage R-SWF's reputation in
   Sunnyland and beyond given the international attention paid to the construction of the
   new airport. In theory, reputational risk in this case is relatively simple to manage in
   that R-SWF simply needs to be a contributor to the project and overall community by
   supporting efforts to adapt to climate change so as to not destroy Sunnyland's tourism
   industry. However, execution of such a strategy to mitigate R-SWF's reputational risk in

Sunnyland will need to be closely monitored in order to effectively execute it. Managing this type of risk is not easy.

Reputational risk is also very significant in the case of ABC because of two major social issues: (1) occupational health and safety and (2) labor standards. Each of these issues could significantly damage R-SWF's reputation. Removing hand soap from the restrooms is an occupational health and safety issue that could cause reputational damage. Shortening employee breaks and firing people during a recession are social issues related to labor standards.

These types of choices indicate that local management is more concerned about profitability than reputational risk. In order to manage its reputational risk, R-SWF needs to persuade the board to adjust its incentive structure in order to encourage local management to reverse course on these short-sighted, destructive social issues, even if it is expensive. R-SWF does not want to be perceived as an investor that exploits its labor force. Soap should be provided for employees, breaks should be reasonable in length, and rather than firing employees, which can't be effectively executed because of the strict labor laws, ABC should focus on retraining employees for the future of the business. This is a complicated, multifaceted course especially as a minority owner. It isn't easily implemented but can be done. Any changes will need to be monitored to ensure they continue and have the desired outcome—a sustainable and mutually beneficial long-term relationship with the local community.

5. R-SWF'S Investments: 3.0

Second Extension of Case Facts (3.0)

You left R-SWF at the end of Year 3 and took a position as a Senior Risk Consultant at Kiken Consulting, a risk consulting firm.

In the summer of Year 5, you are reading the newspaper and notice some commentary on two of the R-SWF investments you had been involved with. You read the following excerpts with nostalgic interest.

Update on Infrastructure Investment

- The infrastructure investment continues to perform poorly because of a combination of the following:
  - lower revenue (fewer tourists) vs. forecast (50% lower than base case)
  - higher costs (mitigating flood damage) vs. forecast (50% higher than base case)
- The medium- and long-term forecast on this investment does not look promising.

Update on PE Investment

- The PE team was able to avoid a diplomatic crisis and reputational risk damage by finding a buyer for the 35% stake. They sold the full position at $27 million.
- The stake was sold to an international beverage company that had been exporting to Atsui. The company's sales had been adversely affected by a weaker Atsui currency. Thus, producing locally is advantageous because it provides a natural foreign exchange hedge.

You set the newspaper down and start thinking about Sunnyland and Atsui when your boss suddenly interrupts you with the following news:

> Kiken Consulting has a new client! R-SWF has hired the firm for a risk analysis project. Because you have prior knowledge on R-SWF's approach, your boss has assigned you to the project with a lead role. You are expected to evaluate the strengths and weaknesses of R-SWF's enterprise risk management system and to make recommendations for improvements.

In-text Question

Please respond to the following question.

1. Provide key facts/inputs from the R-SWF case, use them to evaluate the strengths and weaknesses of R-SWF's enterprise risk management processes, and make recommendations for improvements.

Guideline Answer

1. One of the main strengths of R-SWF's risk management process is that R-SWF dedicated an entire internal investment committee meeting to identifying and discussing the potential risks of two relatively small investment opportunities. Ample time was taken to allow senior management of R-SWF to express their concerns and discuss mitigation strategies to reduce potential risks. The investment committee was able to identify various potential risk factors, and senior management voted on both investment opportunities.

   One of the weaknesses of R-SWF's risk management process is that too little effort was made in trying to quantify the various risks and agreeing on specific actions that could be taken if some of those risk materialized. The team, with the help of the Head of Risk, could have done a better job at performing scenario analysis for both investments and presented a base case, an optimistic case, and a pessimistic case. Although the team identified and discussed several risk factors, they should have put together an action plan for risk mitigation and potential hedging tools prior to making the investments. This action plan would be conditional on certain bad outcomes materializing. Finally, since both investments were quite small in the overall scheme and had limited financial and liquidity risk implications for the fund, more consideration could have been given to identifying potential reputational risks and ESG.

REFERENCES

CFA Institute. 2020. "Climate Change Analysis in the Investment Process." CFA Institute (September). www.cfainstitute.org/en/research/industry-research/climate-change-analysis.

Geltner, D. 1993. "Estimating Market Values from Appraised Values without Assuming an Efficient Market." *Journal of Real Estate Research* 8:325–45.

Getmansky, M., A. W. Lo, and I. Makarov. 2004. "An Econometric Model of Serial Correlation and Illiquidity in Hedge Fund Returns." *Journal of Financial Economics* 74:529–609.

Grantham Research Institute on Climate Change and the Environment. "New Study Estimates Global Warming of 2.5 Centigrade Degrees by 2100 Would Put at Risk Trillions of Dollars of World's Financial Assets." Press release (4 April 2016). www.lse.ac.uk/GranthamInstitute/news/us2-5-trillion-of-the-worlds-financial-assets-would-be-at-risk-from-the-impacts-of-climate-change-if-global-mean-surface-temperature-rises-by-2-5c.

IEA. 2020. "World Energy Outlook 2020" (October). www.iea.org/reports/world-energy-outlook-2020.

Intergovernmental Panel on Climate Change. 2018. "Special Report: Global Warming of 1.5 ºC" (6 October). www.ipcc.ch/sr15/chapter/spm.

Lo, Joe. 2020. "IEA Outlines How World Can Reach Net Zero Emissions by 2050." *Climate Home News* (13 October). www.climatechangenews.com/2020/10/13/iea-outlines-world-can-reach-net-zero-emissions-2050.

NASA. 2019. "NASA Global Climate Change: Vital Signs of the Planet." https://climate.nasa.gov/vital-signs/global-temperature.

Okunev, J., and D. White. 2003. "Hedge Fund Risk Factors and Value at Risk of Credit Trading Strategies." Working paper, University of New South Wales.

PRI Association. "Macro Risks: Universal Ownership" (12 October 2017). www.unpri.org/sustainable-development-goals/the-sdgs-are-an-unavoidable-consideration-for-universal-owners/306.article.

GLOSSARY

Activist short selling A hedge fund strategy in which the manager takes a short position in a given security and then publicly presents his/her research backing the short thesis.

Adjusted funds from operations (AFFO) Funds from operations adjusted to remove any non-cash rent reported under straight-line rent accounting and to subtract maintenance-type capital expenditures and leasing costs, including leasing agents' commissions and tenants' improvement allowances.

Back-fill bias The distortion in index or peer group data which results when returns are reported to a database only after they are known to be good returns.

Backwardation A condition in futures markets in which the spot price exceeds the futures price; also, the condition in which the near-term (closer to expiration) futures contract price is higher than the longer-term futures contract price.

Basis The difference between the spot price and the futures price. As the maturity date of the futures contract nears, the basis converges toward zero.

Brownfield investment Investing in *existing* infrastructure assets.

Calmar ratio A comparison of the average annual compounded return to the maximum drawdown risk.

Cap rate A metric by which real estate managers are often judged; the annual rent actually earned (net of any vacancies) divided by the price originally paid for the property.

Capital loss ratio The percentage of capital in deals that have been realized below cost, net of any recovered proceeds, divided by total invested capital.

Capitalization rate The divisor in the expression for the value of perpetuity. In the context of real estate, it is the divisor in the direct capitalization method of estimating value. The cap rate equals net operating income divided by value.

Cash available for distribution See *adjusted funds from operations*.

Catch-up clause A clause in an agreement that favors the GP. For a GP who earns a 20% performance fee, a catch-up clause allows the GP to receive 100% of the distributions above the hurdle rate *until* she receives 20% of the profits generated, and then every excess dollar is split 80/20 between the LPs and GP.

Clawback A requirement that the general partner return any funds distributed as incentive fees until the limited partners have received back their initial investment and a percentage of the total profit.

Co-investing In co-investing, the investor invests in assets *indirectly* through the fund but also possesses rights (known as co-investment rights) to invest *directly* in the same assets. Through co-investing, an investor is able to make an investment *alongside* a fund when the fund identifies deals.

Collateral return The component of the total return on a commodity futures position attributable to the yield for the bonds or cash used to maintain the futures position. Also called *collateral yield*.

Collaterals Assets or financial guarantees underlying a debt obligation that are above and beyond the issuer's promise to pay.

Commercial real estate properties Income-producing real estate properties; properties purchased with the intent to let, lease, or rent (in other words, produce income).

Committed capital The amount that the limited partners have agreed to provide to the private equity fund.

Commodity swap A type of swap involving the exchange of payments over multiple dates as determined by specified reference prices or indexes relating to commodities.

Contango A condition in futures markets in which the spot price is lower than the futures price; also, the condition in which the near-term (closer to expiration) futures contract price is lower than the longer-term futures contract price.

Controlling shareholders A particular shareholder or block of shareholders holding a percentage of shares that gives them significant voting power.

Core real estate investment style Investing in high-quality, well-leased, core property types with low leverage (no more than 30% of asset value) in the largest markets with strong, diversified economies. It is a conservative strategy designed to avoid real estate–specific risks, including leasing, development, and speculation in favor of steady returns. Hotel properties are excluded from the core categories because of the higher cash flow volatility resulting from single-night leases and the greater importance of property operations, brand, and marketing.

Corporate governance The system of internal controls and procedures by which individual companies are managed.

Cost approach An approach that values a private company based on the values of the underlying assets of the entity less the value of any related liabilities. In the context of real estate, this approach estimates the value of a property based on what it would cost to buy the land and construct a new property on the site that has the same utility or functionality as the property being appraised.

Covenants The terms and conditions of lending agreements that the issuer must comply with; they specify the actions that an issuer is obligated to perform (affirmative covenant) or prohibited from performing (negative covenant).

Cross-sectional momentum A managed futures trend following strategy implemented with a cross-section of assets (within an asset class) by going long those that are rising in price the most and by shorting those that are falling the most. This approach generally results in holding a net zero (market-neutral) position and works well when a market's out- or underperformance is a reliable predictor of its future performance.

Cumulative voting A voting process whereby shareholders can accumulate and vote all their shares for a single candidate in an election, as opposed to having to allocate their voting rights evenly among all candidates.

Dedicated short-selling A hedge fund strategy in which the manager takes short-only positions in equities deemed to be expensively priced versus their deteriorating fundamental situations. Short exposures may vary only in terms of portfolio sizing by, at times, holding higher levels of cash.

Direct capitalization method In the context of real estate, this method estimates the value of an income-producing property based on the level and quality of its net operating income.

Direct investing Occurs when an investor makes a direct investment in an asset without the use of an intermediary.

Discounted cash flow method Income approach that values an asset based on estimates of future cash flows discounted to present value by using a discount rate reflective of the risks associated with the cash flows. In the context of real estate, this method estimates the value of an income-producing property based on discounting future projected cash flows.

Drawdown A percentage peak-to-trough reduction in net asset value.

Engagement/active ownership An ESG investment approach that uses shareholder power to influence corporate behavior through direct corporate engagement (i.e., communicating with senior management and/or boards of companies), filing or co-filing shareholder proposals, and proxy voting that is directed by ESG guidelines.

Equity REITs REITs that own, operate, and/or selectively develop income-producing real estate.

ESG integration An ESG investment approach that focuses on systematic consideration of material ESG factors in asset allocation, security selection, and portfolio construction decisions for the purpose of achieving the product's stated investment objectives. Used interchangeably with **ESG investing**.

ESG investing The consideration of environmental, social, and governance factors in the investment process. Used interchangeably with **ESG integration**.

ESG An acronym that encompasses environmental, social, and governance.

Fulcrum securities Partially-in-the-money claims (not expected to be repaid in full) whose holders end up owning the reorganized company in a corporate reorganization situation.

Fund investing In fund investing, the investor invests in assets indirectly by contributing capital to a fund as part of a group of investors. Fund investing is available for all major alternative investment types.

Fund-of-funds A fund of hedge funds in which the fund-of-funds manager allocates capital to separate, underlying hedge funds (e.g., single manager and/or multi-manager funds) that themselves run a range of different strategies.

Funds available for distribution (FAD) See *adjusted funds from operations.*

Funds from operations (FFO) Net income (computed in accordance with generally accepted accounting principles) *plus* (1) gains and losses from sales of properties and (2) depreciation and amortization.

Funds of hedge funds Funds that hold a portfolio of hedge funds, more commonly shortened to *funds of funds.*

Futures price The price at which the parties to a futures contract agree to exchange the underlying (or cash). In commodity markets, the price agreed on to deliver or receive a defined quantity (and often quality) of a commodity at a future date.

General partner (GP) The partner that runs the business and theoretically bears unlimited liability for the business's debts and obligations.

Green bonds Bonds used in green finance whereby the proceeds are earmarked toward environmental-related products.

Green finance A type of finance that addresses environmental concerns while achieving economic growth.

Green loans Any loan instruments made available exclusively to finance or re-finance, in whole or in part, new and/or existing eligible green projects. Green loans are commonly aligned in the market with the Green Loan Principles.

Greenfield investment Investing in infrastructure assets *that are to be constructed.*

Grinold–Kroner model An expression for the expected return on a share as the sum of an expected income return, an expected nominal earnings growth return, and an expected repricing return.

Gross lease A lease under which the tenant pays a gross rent to the landlord, who is responsible for all operating costs, utilities, maintenance expenses, and real estate taxes relating to the property.

Hard-catalyst event-driven approach An event-driven approach in which investments are made in reaction to an already announced corporate event (mergers and acquisitions, bankruptcies, share issuances, buybacks, capital restructurings, re-organizations, accounting changes) in which security prices related to the event have yet to fully converge.

Hedonic index Unlike a repeat-sales index, a hedonic index does not require repeat sales of the same property. It requires only one sale. The way it controls for the fact that different properties are selling each quarter is to include variables in the regression that control for differences in the characteristics of the property, such as size, age, quality of construction, and location.

Highest and best use The concept that the best use of a vacant site is the use that would result in the highest value for the land. Presumably, the developer that could earn the highest risk-adjusted profit based on time, effort, construction and development cost, leasing, and exit value would be the one to pay the highest price for the land.

High-water mark The highest value, net of fees, which a fund has reached in history. It reflects the highest cumulative return used to calculate an incentive fee.

Hostile takeover An attempt by one entity to acquire a company without the consent of the company's management.

Hurdle rate The minimum rate of return on investment that a fund must reach before a GP receives carried interest.

Impact investing Investments made with the intention to generate positive, measurable social and environmental impact alongside a financial return.

Income approach A valuation approach that values an asset as the present discounted value of the income expected from it. In the context of real estate, this approach estimates the value of a property based on an expected rate of return. The estimated value is the present value of the expected future income from the property, including proceeds from resale at the end of a typical investment holding period.

Indenture Legal contract that describes the form of a bond, the obligations of the issuer, and the rights of the bondholders. Also called the *trust deed*.

Leveraged buyout A transaction whereby the target company's management team converts the target to a privately held company by using heavy borrowing to finance the purchase of the target company's outstanding shares.

Life settlement The sale of a life insurance contract to a third party. The valuation of a life settlement typically requires detailed biometric analysis of the individual policyholder and an understanding of actuarial analysis.

Limited partners Partners with limited liability. Limited partnerships in hedge and private equity funds are typically restricted to investors who are expected to understand and to be able to assume the risks associated with the investments.

Limited partnership agreement (LPA) A legal document that outlines the rules of the partnership and establishes the framework that ultimately guides the fund's operations throughout its life.

Lockup period The minimum holding period before investors are allowed to make withdrawals or redeem shares from a fund.

Management buy-in Leveraged buyout in which the current management team is being replaced and the acquiring team will be involved in managing the company.

Management buyout A leveraged buyout event in which a group of investors consisting primarily of the company's existing management purchases at least controlling interest in its outstanding shares. At the extreme, they may purchase all shares and take the company private.

Management fee A fee based on assets under management or committed capital, as applicable—also called a *base fee*.

MAR ratio A variation of the Calmar ratio that uses a full investment history and the average drawdown.

Mark-to-market Refers to the current expected fair market value for which a given security would likely be available for purchase or sale if traded in current market conditions.

Minority shareholders Particular shareholders or a block of shareholders holding a small proportion of a company's outstanding shares, resulting in a limited ability to exercise control in voting activities.

Mortgages Loans with real estate serving as collateral for the loans.

Multi-class trading An equity market-neutral strategy that capitalizes on misalignment in prices and involves buying and selling different classes of shares of the same company, such as voting and non-voting shares.

Multi-manager fund Can be of two types—one is a multi-strategy fund in which teams of portfolio managers trade and invest in multiple different strategies within the same fund; the second type is a fund of hedge funds (or fund-of-funds) in which the manager allocates capital to separate, underlying hedge funds that themselves run a range of different strategies.

Multiple of invested capital (MOIC) A simplified calculation that measures the total value of all distributions and residual asset values relative to an initial total investment; also known as a *money multiple*.

Multi-strategy fund A fund in which teams of portfolio managers trade and invest in multiple different strategies within the same fund.

Negative screening An ESG investment style that focuses on the exclusion of certain sectors, companies, or practices in a fund or portfolio on the basis of specific ESG criteria.

Net asset value per share Net asset value divided by the number of shares outstanding.

Net asset value The difference between assets and liabilities, all taken at current market values instead of accounting book values.

Net lease A lease under which the tenant pays a net rent to the landlord and an additional amount based on the tenant's pro rata share of the operating costs, utilities, maintenance expenses, and real estate taxes relating to the property.

Net operating income   Gross rental revenue minus operating costs but before deducting depreciation, corporate overhead, and interest expense. In the context of real estate, a measure of the income from the property after deducting operating expenses for such items as property taxes, insurance, maintenance, utilities, repairs, and insurance but before deducting any costs associated with financing and before deducting federal income taxes. It is similar to EBITDA in a financial reporting context.

Non-cash rent   An amount equal to the difference between the average contractual rent over a lease term (the straight-line rent) and the cash rent actually paid during a period. This figure is one of the deductions made from FFO to calculate AFFO.

Non-residential properties   Commercial real estate properties other than multi-family properties, farmland, and timberland.

Notice period   The length of time (typically 30 to 90 days) in advance that investors may be required to notify a fund of their intent to redeem some or all of their investment.

Pairs trading   An equity market-neutral strategy that capitalizes on the misalignment in prices of pairs of similar under- and overvalued equities. The expectation is the differential valuations or trading relationships will revert to their long-term mean values or their fundamentally-correct trading relationships, with the long position rising and the short position declining in value.

Performance fee   Fees paid to the general partner from the limited partner(s) based on realized net profits.

Portfolio company   In private equity, the company in which the private equity fund is investing.

Positive screening   The process of including sectors or companies based on specific ESG criteria, typically ESG performance relative to industry peers

Prime brokers   Brokers that provide services that commonly include custody, administration, lending, short borrowing, and trading.

Principal–agent relationship   A relationship in which a principal hires an agent to perform a particular task or service; also known as an *agency relationship*.

Private equity funds   Funds that seek to invest in, optimize, and eventually exit portfolio companies to generate profits. See *venture capital funds*.

Proxy contest   Corporate takeover mechanism in which shareholders are persuaded to vote for a group seeking a controlling position on a company's board of directors.

Proxy voting   A process that enables shareholders who are unable to attend a meeting to authorize another individual to vote on their behalf.

Public–private partnership (PPP)   An agreement between the public sector and the private sector to finance, build, and operate public infrastructure, such as hospitals and toll roads.

Quantitative market-neutral   An approach to building market-neutral portfolios in which large numbers of securities are traded and positions are adjusted on a daily or even an hourly basis using algorithm-based models.

Real estate investment trusts   Tax-advantaged entities (companies or trusts) that own, operate, and—to a limited extent—develop income-producing real estate property.

Real estate operating companies   Regular taxable real estate ownership companies that operate in the real estate industry in countries that do not have a tax-advantaged REIT regime in place or that are engage in real estate activities of a kind and to an extent that do not fit in their country's REIT framework.

Rebalance return   A return from rebalancing the component weights of an index.

Redemptions   Withdrawals of funds by investors, as allowed by the notice period and other terms in the partnership agreement.

Relative value volatility arbitrage   A volatility trading strategy that aims to source and buy cheap volatility and sell more expensive volatility while netting out the time decay aspects normally associated with options portfolios.

Repeat sales index   As the name implies, this type of index relies on repeat sales of the same property. In general, the idea supporting this type of index is that because it is the same property that sold twice, the change in value between the two sale dates indicates how market conditions have changed over time.

Replacement cost   In the context of real estate, the value of a building assuming it was built today using current construction costs and standards.

Residential properties   Properties that provide housing for individuals or families. Single-family properties may be owner-occupied or rental properties, whereas multi-family properties are rental properties even if the owner or manager occupies one of the units.

Responsible investing   An overall (umbrella) term for several investment strategies—ESG investing, SRI investing, thematic investing, and impact investing—that incorporate ESG analysis in their investment processes.

Roll return   The component of the return on a commodity futures contract attributable to rolling long futures positions forward through time. Also called *roll yield*.

Sale-leaseback   A situation in which a company sells the building it owns and occupies to a real estate investor and the company then signs a long-term lease with the buyer to continue to occupy the building. At the end of the lease, use of the property reverts to the landlord.

Sales comparison approach   In the context of real estate, this approach estimates value based on what similar or comparable properties (comparables) transacted for in the current market.

Say on pay   A process whereby shareholders may vote on executive remuneration (compensation) matters.

Shareholder activism   Strategies used by shareholders to attempt to compel a company to act in a desired manner.

Shareholder engagement   The process whereby companies engage with their shareholders.

Short-biased   A hedge fund strategy in which the manager uses a less extreme version of dedicated short-selling. It involves searching for opportunities to sell expensively priced equities, but short exposure may be balanced with some modest value-oriented, or index-oriented, long exposure.

Shrinkage estimation   Estimation that involves taking a weighted average of a historical estimate of a parameter and some other parameter estimate, where the weights reflect the analyst's relative belief in the estimates.

Side letters   Side agreements created between the GP and specific LPs. These agreements exist *outside* the LPA. These agreements provide additional terms and conditions related to the investment agreement.

Single-manager fund   A fund in which one portfolio manager or team of portfolio managers invests in one strategy or style.

Socially responsible investing (SRI)   An investment approach that excludes investments in companies or industries that deviate from an organization's beliefs and sometimes includes investments with favorable environmental or social profiles.

Soft-catalyst event-driven approach   An event-driven approach in which investments are made proactively in anticipation of a corporate event (mergers and acquisitions, bankruptcies, share issuances, buybacks, capital restructurings, re-organizations, accounting changes) that has yet to occur.

Spot price   The current price of an asset or security. For commodities, the current price to deliver a physical commodity to a specific location or purchase and transport it away from a designated location.

Stabilized NOI   In the context of real estate, the expected NOI when a renovation is complete.

Staggered boards   Election process whereby directors are typically divided into multiple classes that are elected separately in consecutive years—that is, one class every year.

Stakeholder management   The identification, prioritization, and understanding of the interests of stakeholder groups and managing the company's relationships with these groups.

Straight voting   A shareholder voting process in which shareholders receive one vote for each share owned.

Straight-line rent adjustment   See *non-cash rent*.

Straight-line rent   The average annual rent under a multi-year lease agreement that contains contractual increases in rent during the life of the lease.

Stub trading   An equity market-neutral strategy that capitalizes on misalignment in prices and entails buying and selling stock of a parent company and its subsidiaries, typically weighted by the percentage ownership of the parent company in the subsidiaries.

Survivorship bias   Relates to the inclusion of only current investment funds in a database. As such, the returns of funds that are no longer available in the marketplace (have been liquidated) are excluded from the database. In addition, *backfill bias* is another problem, whereby certain surviving hedge funds may be added to databases and various hedge fund indexes only after they are initially successful and start to report their returns.

Sustainability linked loans   These are any types of loan instruments and/or contingent facilities (such as bonding lines, guarantee lines, or letters of credit) that incentivize the borrower's achievement of ambitious, pre-determined sustainability performance objectives.

Sustainable investing   A term used in a similar context to responsible investing, but its key focus is on factoring in sustainability issues while investing.

Taxable REIT subsidiaries   Subsidiaries that pay income taxes on earnings from non-REIT-qualifying activities like merchant development or third-party property management.

Tender offer   Corporate takeover mechanism that involves shareholders selling their interests directly to the group seeking to gain control.

Thematic investing   An ESG investment approach that focuses on investing in themes or assets specifically relating to ESG factors, such as clean energy, green technology, or sustainable agriculture.

Time-series estimation   Estimators that are based on lagged values of the variable being forecast; often consist of lagged values of other selected variables.

Time-series momentum   A managed futures trend following strategy in which managers go long assets that are rising in price and go short assets that are falling in price. The manager trades on an absolute basis, so be net long or net short depending on the current price trend of an asset. This approach works best when an asset's own past returns are a good predictor of its future returns.

Triple-net leases   Common leases in the United States and Canada that require each tenant to pay its share of the following three operating expenses common area maintenance and repair expenses; property taxes; and building insurance costs. Also known as *NNN leases*.

Unitranche debt   Consists of a hybrid or blended loan structure that combines different tranches of secured and unsecured debt into a single loan with a single, blended interest rate.

Universal owners   Long-term investors, such as pension funds, that have significant assets invested in globally diversified portfolios.

Unsmoothing   An adjustment to the reported return series if serial correlation is detected. Various approaches are available to unsmooth a return series.

Venture capital funds   Funds that seek to invest in, optimize, and eventually exit portfolio companies to generate profits. See *private equity funds*.

Venture capital   Investments that provide "seed" or startup capital, early-stage financing, or later-stage financing (including mezzanine-stage financing) to companies that are in early development stages and require additional capital for expansion or preparation for an initial public offering.

Volatility clustering   The tendency for large (small) swings in prices to be followed by large (small) swings of random direction.

Waterfall   Represents the distribution method that defines the order in which allocations are made to LPs and GPs. There are two major types of waterfall: *deal by deal* (or *American*) and *whole of fund* (or *European*).

ABOUT THE EDITORS
AND AUTHORS

Robert Brooks, PhD, CFA, is the Wallace D. Malone, Jr. endowed chair of Financial Management at The University of Alabama and president of Financial Risk Management, LLC, a financial risk management consulting firm focused on market risks. He has taught for over 30 years, primarily financial risk management classes, and is the author of over 75 articles appearing in the *Journal of Financial and Quantitative Analysis*, *Journal of Derivatives*, *Financial Analysts Journal*, and many others.

Brooks is the co-author of *An Introduction to Derivatives and Risk Management* (Seventh through Tenth Editions) with Don Chance and has authored several books including *Building Financial Risk Management Applications with C++*. He has testified in a subcommittee hearing of the US House of Representatives in Washington, D.C. as well as in a field hearing of the SEC in Birmingham, Alabama. He has consulted with major public utilities, energy companies, auditing firms, corporations, investment bankers, elected municipal officials, and commercial bankers regarding managing financial risks, derivatives valuation and software development. Further, he has testified in several court cases as well as conducting professional development seminars on various aspects of finance.

Don M. Chance, PhD, CFA, is the James C. Flores chair of MBA Studies and professor of Finance at Louisiana State University. He previously worked in banking and was a member of the finance faculty at Virginia Tech. He is the author or co-author of three books on derivatives and risk management and numerous academic and practitioner articles on a variety of finance topics. He has been a visiting scholar at universities in the United States, Australia, Scotland, Hong Kong, Singapore, and Korea. He has consulted and provided training for numerous companies and organizations, including CFA Institute, which honored him with the C. Stewart Shepard Award in 2015.

David M. Gentle, CFA, is principal of Omega Risk Consulting, which specializes in managing financial risk through the use of hedging and derivatives. Prior to this role, which commenced in 2010, Mr. Gentle was, from 1996, head of Structured Products at Australia's largest fund management firm, AMP Capital Investors, where he managed a range of large options and derivative-based investment products. Previous roles were as a quantitative analyst and researcher at Citibank, NatWest Markets, and Westpac Banking Corporation.

Prior to entering the finance industry, Mr. Gentle was an IT specialist and lecturer at Sydney University. He holds a BSc from the University of NSW, an MEc (Hons) from the University of Sydney, and a Graduate Diploma of Management from Macquarie University. He is a member of CFA Institute and CFA Society Melbourne.

Kenneth Grant is president and founder of General Risk Advisors, LLC. He began his career in the Chicago futures markets and, in the late 1980s, created the risk management group at the Chicago Mercantile Exchange. There, he led a project team responsible for the globalization of the SPAN Margin System—the first portfolio risk management system used on a global, institutional basis. In 1994, he moved to Société Generale as head of Risk Management for the North American Treasury/Capital Markets Group, eventually rising to the role of deputy director. Mr. Grant moved to the hedge fund industry in 1997, joining SAC Capital as its director of Risk Management and later serving as its chief investment strategist. Mr. Grant also spent two years as the head of Global Risk Management at the Tudor Investment Corporation, and 18 months in a similar role for Cheyne Capital. Mr. Grant formed Risk Resources LLC in late 2004 to provide customized, diagnostic risk management services to hedge funds, banks, broker-dealers, and other capital providers. The firm has worked with over 20 companies since its inception representing investment capital in excess of $50 billion. He is the author of *Trading Risk: Enhanced Profitability through Risk Control* (2004), and is principal author of the Managed Funds Association's *Sound Practices for Hedge Fund Managers* (MFA, 2000, 2003, 2005). He served on the MFA's board of directors from 2000 through 2004, was a member of its Executive Committee (2001–2003), and was a founding member of its Hedge Fund Advisory Committee. In 2011, he was awarded a patent for originating processes associated with the reverse engineering of risk management analytics. He is a lecturer in Risk Management in the School of Professional Studies at Columbia University.

John Marsland, CFA, is Chief Operating Officer, Investment at Schroder Investment Management in London and is responsible for global trading and investment operations. Mr. Marsland began his investment career in 1992 at UBS Philips & Drew as a UK economist, and subsequently moved into investment strategy, risk management, and quantitative fund management roles. Mr. Marsland read Economics at Downing College, University of Cambridge, and holds a MSc in Economics from Birkbeck College, University of London. He has been a CFA charterholder since 2000. He has served as a board member and vice-chair of CFA UK and as a member and chair of CFA Institute's Investment Foundations Investment Certificate Advisory Board.

Russell Rhoads, CFA, is director of Education for the CBOE Options Institute. His career before CBOE included positions at a variety of buyside firms including Highland Capital Management, Caldwell & Orkin Investment Counsel, Balyasny Asset Management, and Millennium Management. He is a financial author and editor having contributed to multiple magazines and edited several books for Wiley publishing. He is the author of six market related books including *Trading VIX Derivatives, Option Spread Trading, Trading Weekly Options*, and *Options Strategies for Advisors and Institutions*. He has also authored material for the CFA Program as well as for the CMT designation. He has been widely quoted in the financial press by publications such as *The Wall Street Journal* and *Forbes* and has appeared on several business television networks included Bloomberg TV.

In addition to his duties for the CBOE, Rhoads is an adjunct instructor at Loyola University and the University of Illinois—Chicago. He is a double graduate of the University of Memphis with a BBA and an MS in Finance and received a Master's Certificate in Financial Engineering from Illinois Tech in 2003. He is currently (2017) pursuing a PhD from Oklahoma State University.

Bob Strong, PhD, CFA is University Foundation professor emeritus of Investment Education at the University of Maine. The University of Maine Alumni Association selected him as the 2005 "Distinguished Maine Professor." The Carnegie Foundation named him the 2007 "Maine Professor of the Year." His three textbooks on investments, portfolio management, and derivatives have been used at over 100 universities.

Strong holds a bachelor of science in engineering from the United States Military Academy at West Point, a master of science in business administration from Boston University, and a PhD in finance from Penn State. He has also been a visiting professor of finance at Harvard University where he was deputy director of the Summer Economics Program from 1997 to 1999. Strong served for eight years as the University of Maine's Faculty Athletic Representative to the NCAA. He is past president of the Northeast Business and Economics Association, the Maine CFA Society, and the Bangor Rotary Club. He is an honorary captain in the Maine State Police and is chairman of the board of Bangor Savings Bank.

Barbara Valbuzzi, CFA, is equity strategist at Banca IMI and has over 20 years of experience in trading equity derivatives. Her career developed within the Intesa Sanpaolo group where she held positions as proprietary trader and senior equity derivatives trader. She now applies her trading and relative value experience on the Strategist team that she contributed to set up in 2015, developing trade recommendations and quantitative investment strategies. Early in her career, she served as portfolio manager at UBS Italia.

A graduate in Economics from Bocconi University, she also holds the Chartered Financial Analyst® designation. She is a member of CFA Institute and CFA Society Italy.

Wendy L. Pirie, PhD, CFA, is director of Curriculum Projects in the Education Division at CFA Institute. Prior to joining CFA Institute in 2008, Dr. Pirie taught for over 20 years at a broad range of institutions: large public universities; small, private, religiously affiliated colleges; and a military academy. She primarily taught finance courses but also taught accounting, taxation, business law, marketing, and statistics courses. Dr. Pirie's work has been published in the *Journal of Financial Research, Journal of Economics and Finance, Educational Innovation in Economics and Business*, and *Managerial Finance*.

Prior to entering academia, she was an auditor with Deloitte & Touche in Toronto, Canada. She is a Chartered Accountant (Ontario) and Certified Public Accountant (Virginia). She completed the ICAEW's Certificate in International Financial Reporting Standards. She holds a PhD in accounting and finance from Queen's University at Kingston, Ontario, and MBAs from the Universities of Toronto and Calgary. She is a member of CFA Institute, New York Society of Security Analysts, and CFA Society Chicago.

INDEX